Boats on the Nile with skysails.

Tourists returning from Karnak.

Tourists picnicking in a temple (c. 1900).

A gallery in the great hypostyle hall at Karnak
and sculptures in the Temple of Philae.

EVERYMAN GUIDES
PUBLISHED BY DAVID CAMPBELL PUBLISHERS LTD, LONDON

EGYPT – ISBN 1-85715-876-8

© 1995 David Campbell Publishers Ltd, London
© 1994 Editions Nouveaux-Loisirs, a subsidiary of Gallimard, Paris.

First published March 1995
Second edition August 1996

NUMEROUS SPECIALISTS AND ACADEMICS HAVE
CONTRIBUTED TO THIS GUIDE.

EGYPT:
EDITOR: Soraya Khalidy
PRACTICAL INFORMATION: Philippe Gallois, Veronika Vollmer
LAYOUT: Natacha Kotlarevsky, Michelle Bisganbiglia (Nature), François Chentrier (Practical information)
PICTURE RESEARCH: Marielle Blanc
COORDINATION: Eglal Errera, Christine Roussillon (Cairo)

NATURE: Philippe Dubois, Dominique Bénard (The Nile Valley), Peter Meininger (Climate, Sinai)
HISTORY (PHARAONIC): Alain Zivie
LIFE AND DEATH IN ANCIENT EGYPT: Guillemette Andreu Lanoë
HISTORY (POST-PHARAONIC): Robert Ilbert
LANGUAGE AND RELIGION: Robert Ilbert
ARTS & TRADITIONS: Eglal Errera, Mercédès Volait, Ghislaine Alleaume, Christian Gaubert, Nessim Henein (Boats)
PHARAONIC ARCHITECTURE: Nathalie Vaillant, Jean-Pierre Lange
HISTORY OF EXCAVATIONS: Nathalie Vaillant, Jean-Pierre Lange
COPTIC AND ISLAMIC ARCHITECTURE: Mercédès Volait
EGYPT AS SEEN BY WRITERS: Lucinda Gane

ITINERARIES:
ALEXANDRIA: Eglal Errera, Mercédès Volait
NILE DELTA: Ghislaine Alleaume, Jean-Luc Bovot, Nathalie Bosson
SINAI: Olivier Sanmartin
DESERTS: Nicole Levallois
MODERN CAIRO: Alain Roussillon, Mercédès Volait
ISLAMIC CAIRO: Sawsan Noweir, Hanaa Farid (Islamic Museum)

OLD CAIRO: Alain Roussillon (History), Sawsan Noweir, Hanaa Farid (Coptic Museum)
NECROPOLIS: Galila el-Kadi
MEMPHIS, GIZA AND SAQQARA: Alain Zivie
MEMPHIS TO THE FAIYUM: Jean-Luc Bovot
THE FAIYUM: Pierre Gazio
EL-MINIA TO THEBES: Vincent Rondot
THEBES: Jean-Pierre Golvin, Paul Geday (City Center)
THEBES TO ASWAN: Catherine Graindorge
ASWAN AND NUBIA: Catherine Graindorge
EGYPT IN THE MUSEUMS OF THE WORLD: Ester Coen
PRACTICAL INFORMATION: Jean-Luc Berger, Thierry Beaurepère, Paul Geday (movies)
ILLUSTRATIONS:
NATURE: François Desbordes, Gilbert Houbre, Bruce Pearson, Claire Felloni, Jean Chevalier, Anne Bodin
ARCHITECTURE: Philippe Biard, François Brosse, Philippe Cande, Claude Quiec, Jean-Claude Séné, Françoise Gastineau, Jean-Pierre Lange
ARTS & TRADITIONS: Maurice Pommier, Nathalie Fonteneau, Philippe Biard
ADVENTURE TRAILS: Jean-Benoît Héron, Jean-Pierre Lange, Philippe Biard, Gilbert Houbre, Jean-Claude Séné
PRACTICAL INFORMATION: Maurice Pommier
MAPS: Stéphane Girel
COLOR: Isabelle-Anne Chatelard
COMPUTER GRAPHICS: Paul Coulbois, Emmanuel Calamy, Patrick Alexandre, Kristof Chemineau
PHOTOGRAPHY: Wessam Amin, Patrick Godeau, Dylan Doyle.

WE WOULD ALSO LIKE TO THANK:
CEDEJ (Centre d'études documentaires et juridiques), The Press Office of the Egyptian Embassy, Christine Roussillon, Jacques Livet.

TRANSLATED BY WENDY ALLATSON.
EDITED AND TYPESET BY BOOK CREATION SERVICES, LONDON.
PRINTED IN ITALY BY EDITORIALE LIBRARIA.

EVERYMAN GUIDES
79 BERWICK STREET
LONDON W1V 3PF

EGYPT

EVERYMAN GUIDES

CONTENTS

ALEXANDRIA

DESERTS

CAIRO

THE FAIYUM

THEBES

THEBES TO ASWAN

▲ EGYPT

HOW TO USE THIS GUIDE

(Sample page shown from the guide to Venice)

The symbols at the top of each page refer to the different parts of the guide.

■ NATURAL ENVIRONMENT

● KEYS TO UNDERSTANDING

▲ ITINERARIES

◆ PRACTICAL INFORMATION

The itinerary map shows the main points of interest along the way and is intended to help you find your bearings.

The mini-map locates the particular itinerary within the wider area covered by the guide.

▲ CANNAREGIO

CHURCH OF SANTA MARIA DELLE PIETÀ
CHURCH OF SAN GEREMIA
PALAZZO LABIA
GHETTO
CHURCH OF SAN MARCUOLA
VENDRAMIN-CALERGI
CHURCH OF SAN MARZIALE
CHURCH OF SANTA MARIA DEI MIRACOLI
CA' D'ORO
FONDAMENTA DEL TINTORETTO
CHURCH OF MADONNA DELL'ORTO
PALAZZO CONTARINI DAL ZAFFO
OSPEDALETTO
CHURCH OF SANTA MARIA ASSUNTA
CHURCH OF SANTA MARIA DEI CROCIFERI
CHURCH OF SANTA MARIA DEI MIRACOLI

"The gateway to Venice, neither the sublime nor the Piazzale, nor the Grand Canal nor the imagined before us by propellers, turbulent as a great river."
Fernand Braudel, *Venice*

Santa Lucia Station.

Half a day

THE GATEWAY TO VENICE

PONTE DELLA LIBERTA. Built by the Austrians 50 years after the Treaty of Campo Formio in 1797 ● 34, to link Venice with Milan. The bridge ended the thousand-year separation from the mainland and shook the city's economy to its roots as Venice, already in the throes of the industrial revolution, saw its dependency on the mainland grow out of all recognition. **SANTA LUCIA STATION.** The present station dates from 1955, but still bears the name of the Renaissance church, finally demolished in 1861 to make way for it. Opposite is the green dome of the Church of San Simeone Piccolo.

BRIDGES TO VENICE
The Austrians conceived a project for a bridge between Mestre and Venice as early as the 1840s, but it was not until 1846 that construction of the Ponte della Liberta was begun. The span of this new viaduct was almost 11,500 feet, and it included 222 stone arches. On April 25, 1933, the Ponte della Liberta was opened. Built in less than two years by the engineer Umberto Fanucci, this bridge was intended for use by motor cars.

★ The star symbol signifies that a particular site has been singled out by the publishers for its special beauty, atmosphere or cultural interest.

● ▲ ■ ◆
The symbols alongside a title or within the text itself provide cross-references to a theme or place dealt with elsewhere in the guide.

At the beginning of each itinerary, the suggested means of transport to be used and the time it will take to cover the area are indicated:
▬ By boat
🚶 On foot
🚲 By bicycle
🕐 Duration

THE GATEWAY TO VENICE ★

PONTE DELLA LIBERTA. Built by the Austrians 50 years after the Treaty of Campo Formio in 1797 ● 34, to link Venice with Milan. The bridge ended the thousand-year separation from the mainland and shook the city's economy to its roots as Venice, already in the throes of the industrial revolution, saw

🚶 Half a day

BRIDGES TO VENICE

NATURE

The Nile is the longest river in the world, stretching for a distance of 4,163 miles. The Great – Egyptian – Nile is formed by the merging of the White Nile, which rises in the Ruwenzori range in Zaire, and the Blue Nile, which rises in the high plateaux of Ethiopia. It flows into the Mediterranean via a vast delta system. Alluvium deposited over the centuries has helped to create an extremely fertile strip of land (up to 12½ miles wide) which has given rise to a rich and diversified agriculture. This "linear oasis" has also favored the development of a very specific flora and fauna.

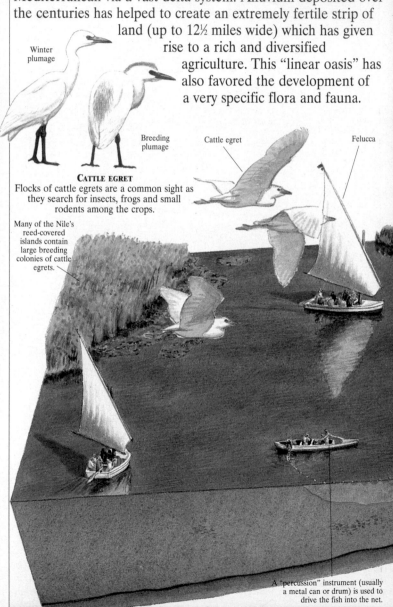

Winter plumage

Breeding plumage

CATTLE EGRET

Flocks of cattle egrets are a common sight as they search for insects, frogs and small rodents among the crops.

Cattle egret

Felucca

Many of the Nile's reed-covered islands contain large breeding colonies of cattle egrets.

A "percussion" instrument (usually a metal can or drum) is used to drive the fish into the net.

Hydraulic or diesel pumping station

Nile

Main canal

Cultivated land

Maximum level of water table.

Penetration limit of irrigation

Main drainage channel

IRRIGATION. In the Nile Valley, water is drawn from the river and channeled onto the land. It is raised in stages – using hydraulic machinery operated by men, animals or motors – and channeled to the highest plots of land via a network of canals and sluices. The *fellaheen* are past masters in the art of directing the water into their fields by making channels, intersected by primitive sluices, using an

House from the old village

Secondary canal

Tertiary canal

Main road running the length of the Nile Valley.

Underground canal which runs under the road and the drainage channel.

Saqia

Potato

Sunflower

Hibiscus flowers: used to prepare *karkadé*.

Guave

Okra

The main summer or *saïfi* (March to November) crops are usually corn, rice, sorghum, potatoes, sunflowers and cotton. Cotton is Egypt's main agricultural export.

Cotton

Corn

TIERED CROPS

Palm trees are perfectly adapted to hot, desert conditions. Their branches and leaves create a climate which favors the cultivation of crops growing beneath them.

Date palm

Mango

Orange tree

Corn

In winter *bersim* and vegetables are planted beneath the palm trees. In summer corn and cabbages are planted, as well as tomatoes and other food crops (oranges, lemons and mangos).

Cabbages

The black-winged kite is a common sight flying effortlessly above the crops and palm groves.

Eucalyptus

Main road which runs the entire length of the Nile Valley.

Young palms

Main drainage channel

Drying dates

The drainage channel removes excess water after irrigation, which would otherwise absorb salt (on contact with the water table), rise to the surface by capillary action and damage the crops.

Wheat: the straw is crushed and used for animal fodder.

type of clover
animal fodder –
ore than one
he cultivated
reas.

Bersim   Barley   Wheat   Sorghum Rice

WATER HYACINTH
This South American plant, favored by the changing conditions in the Nile, has colonized and obstructed 80% of its canals.

The *noria* or Persian wheel is a hydraulic device whose blades (or buckets) are activated by the waters of a canal.

PAPYRUS
Papyrus, the Pharaonic symbol of Lower Egypt, was widely cultivated for paper until the 10th century. It was believed to have died out by the beginning of the 19th century until a remaining site was found at Wadi Natrun ▲ *208*.

ACACIA
A common sight on the banks of the Nile, with its eye-catching balls of small, yellow flowers.

Secondary canal

Bersim

Saqia: an animal-operated, double wheel system.

Cabbages

Secondary canal

Flooded plot

Siphon beneath secondary drainage canal.

Underground cana

Bersim – used for covers r third of

Since the filling of the Aswan High Dam there are three annual seasons, apart from permanent crops (crops grown on trees, sugar cane). The main winter (October to April) crops are *bersim*, wheat, broad beans, barley, garlic and onions. Mealtimes in January are a monochrome study in various shades of green.

Onion

Fuul

Garlic

ancient tool known as the *selouka* (a broad-bladed hoe). Plots are divided into as many small, level basins as are required by the terrain, to ensure that the water is distributed equally.

Saqia

Tertiary canal

Brine

Chadouf

"CHADOUF"
The *chadouf* consists of a balance-bar with a counterweight at one end and a sort of water skin on the end of a rope at the other. Water can be raised to about 6½ feet.

The black kite – one of Egypt's sedentary birds – is a diurnal bird of prey which feeds mainly on animal carcasses and dead fish.

Modern agriculture: large plot.

Harvesting cotton

Pharaonic remains marking the limit of the Nile floods before the Aswan High Dam was built.

Aubergine

Strawberry

Chilli peppers

Zucchini

Sweet potato

Pepper

Mango

Orange

The season known as *nili* (July to October) corresponds to the former period of the Nile floods. It allows a third – interim – series of crops (usually fruit and vegetables) to be grown, depending on the timing of the previous series. Tomatos are by far the most widely grown vegetable.

Watermelon

Tomato

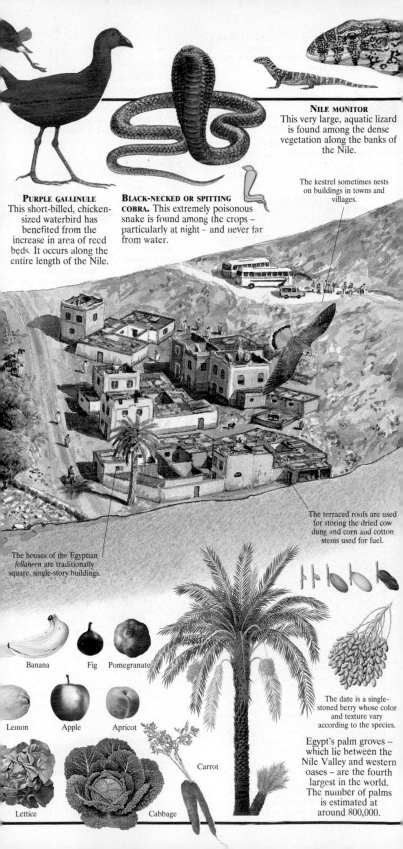

NILE MONITOR
This very large, aquatic lizard is found among the dense vegetation along the banks of the Nile.

The kestrel sometimes nests on buildings in towns and villages.

PURPLE GALLINULE
This short-billed, chicken-sized waterbird has benefited from the increase in area of reed beds. It occurs along the entire length of the Nile.

BLACK-NECKED OR SPITTING COBRA. This extremely poisonous snake is found among the crops – particularly at night – and never far from water.

The terraced roofs are used for storing the dried cow dung and corn and cotton stems used for fuel.

The houses of the Egyptian *fellaheen* are traditionally square, single-story buildings.

Banana

Fig

Pomegranate

Lemon

Apple

Apricot

Carrot

The date is a single-stoned berry whose color and texture vary according to the species.

Egypt's palm groves – which lie between the Nile Valley and western oases – are the fourth largest in the world. The number of palms is estimated at around 800,000.

Lettuce

Cabbage

FISHING

An adult rows upstream while a child unfurls a drift-net. The fisherman stops rowing and executes an encircling maneuver, letting the current carry the boat.

Fishing on the Nile is practiced by families who form their own particular society. They live and work on their large, half-decked rowing boats.

NILE PERCH. As the waters of the Nile have become less oxygenated and more polluted, the Nile perch – which has been fished for centuries – has decreased in number.

TILAPIA OR AFRICAN MOUTH-BROODER. Its numbers are increasing significantly, particularly in Lake Nasser where it is widely fished.

Agricultural work is done by hand as the plots are too small for the use of farm machinery. After they have been leveled, the plots are flooded every three weeks.

REEDS (PHRAGMITES COMMUN)

Following the permanent rise in the water level, reeds have colonized the shores of the Nile.

LOTUS

As a result of hydrological changes, the lotus grows only in the Faiyum and the Delta region.

Flooded plot

Washing clothes on the shores of the Nile.

Main canal fed by a pumping station situated upstream.

Water table saturated with brine: estimated at some 102.4 billion cubic feet.

F. Desbordes

Since the construction of the Aswan High Dam the waters of the Nile can be used for irrigation throughout the year, except for a three- to four-week period between mid-January and mid-February.

NILE CATFISH

This is one of the few fish that has proliferated in the Nile where it lives in the mud of the river bed

The Ancient Egyptians buried their dead in rock-cut tombs on the edge of the desert.

BLACK-WINGED KITE
For reasons as yet unclear, the numbers of this pretty little bird of prey have increased dramatically, especially in the Delta region.

REED WARBLER
Easily recognized by its grating cry in spring. This is another bird which has benefited from the extension of the reed beds.

PIED KINGFISHER
This large kingfisher captures its prey by hovering over and diving into the waters of canals and the Nile.

SWALLOW
The Egyptian race of the barn swallow is characterized by its brick-red breast and underbelly.

PYGMY SUNBIRD
This small bird, commonly found in Upper Egypt, is a reminder that the country is not far from the tropics.

Every part of the palm tree is used. The wood from its trunk is burned or transformed into roofing (**1**) or gutters (**2**). The branches are used for fuel, wind-breaks (**3**), or to make mats (**4**), furniture or baskets (**5**).

HOOPOE
In Egypt the hoopoe tends to be associated with the Nile as it is rarely seen beyond the Nile Valley.

COMMON BULBUL
The bulbul is found close to human habitation. Its bubbling calls are a common sound among crops and in oases.

■ CLIMATE

Although apparently uninhabited, the most arid desert regions harbor a flora and fauna well adapted to the harsh conditions.

Egypt has a total surface area of over 386,000 square miles and a predominately desert climate.
In fact 96 percent of the country is covered by desert and only the northern coastline has a Mediterranean climate. Although Egypt is part of Africa, the Sinai Peninsula encroaches upon Asia. The Egyptian part of the Nile covers a distance of 750 miles and marks the "border" between the Libyan Desert in the west and the Arabian Desert in the east. Rainfall is minimal and occurs mainly in winter in the Delta region where the northwest winds prevail.

Khamsin

Kharga Oasis

LAKE NASSER

ARABIAN DESERT

RED SEA

SINAI

"ACACIA RADDIANA"
Tolerant of the intense heat as well as the cold nights, this thorny shrub is well adapted to Egypt's arid, desert regions. It provides shelter and protection for a number of different species.

The silt once deposited in the Nile Delta is retained by the Aswan High Dam. The result is the erosion of the Mediterranean shores.

It rarely rains in the Arabian Desert. The regular mists which occur at high altitude are the main source of water for flora and fauna.

Wadis are seasonal desert rivers. After the rains, flowers and grasses bloom briefly on their banks. Only a few well-adapted plants survive during periods of drought.

Its position in the center of the desert and its altitude (70 feet below sea level) make Kharga Oasis ▲ *260* one of the hottest places on earth.

Male

BLACKBIRD   **COLLARED DOVE**
These two species are now found as far south as Israel due to the increasing number of artificial oases. This has meant they are beginning to be seen in Egypt.

LIBYAN DESERT

Farafra Oasis

Bahriya Oasis

THE FAIYUM

DELTA

MEDITERRANEAN SEA

In spring a dry, burning wind – the *khamsin* – blows from the south and causes sandstorms. The *khamsin* (which means "fifty" in Arabic) is so called because it can last for up to fifty days. Summer is the season of drought in Upper Egypt and of high humidity in the Nile Delta.

The high peaks of Sinai are the only place in Egypt where snow is found.

Isohyets (in mm) of average annual precipitation. Only the Mediterranean region has any degree of rainfall.

Average maximum temperature in °C (July).

Average maximum temperature in °C (January).

Aswan •
High dam
Lake Nasser
• Abu Simbel

Lake Nasser is an artificial lake which stretches for a distance of 312 miles and covers land once inhabited by thousands of Nubians. It was created by the construction of the Aswan High Dam, opened in 1971. The full extent of the dam's ecological impact is not yet known. Its positive effects include putting an end to the devastating Nile floods, more extensive cultivation as a result of irrigation, the production of electricity and improved navigation. However the fact that the silt is now retained by the dam may well lead to impoverished soil below the dam and the need to use chemical fertilizers. Also the river is no longer powerful enough to repel the inflow of salt water from the sea which is sterilizing the soil, while the banks of the Nile in the Delta region are becoming badly eroded.

Lake Nasser's many creeks (*khors*) represent almost 80% of the surface area when the lake is full. The shoreline covers an overall distance of 4,875 miles.

SOFT-SHELL TURTLE
This extremely rare, fish-eating turtle appears to be surviving in small numbers in the waters of Lake Nasser.

NILE CROCODILE
The Nile crocodile seems to have benefited from the creation of the lake and has become quite a regular feature of its shores. Some specimens reach lengths of up to 10 feet.

Summer

SPUR-WINGED PLOVER
The spur-winged plover, with its loud *peeyk peeyk peeyk* display calls, nests on the sandy shores of the lake.

OLIVACEOUS WARBLER
In the spring the indigenous population is joined by large numbers of migrating warblers.

REED WARBLER
These aquatic warblers tend to break their migratory journey in the clumps of tamarisk around Lake Nasser.

GULL-BILLED TERN
Lake Nasser lies on the terns' migratory route between Africa (where it overwinters) and the Black Sea.

Breeding plumage

TAMARISK
The tamarisk tolerates the variations in water level and is the lake's main shrub.

EGYPTIAN GOOSE
This goose has benefited from the creation of the lake and its numbers are increasing.

WHITE PELICAN
In spring and fall migrating pelicans are found in the area around Abu Simbel ▲ 464.

■ CORAL REEF

This colony of *Acropora* coral or *Stagshorn* coral has formed a clump which looks like a sunshade.

Egyptian coral reefs are found along the Red Sea coast and to the south and east of the Sinai Peninsula. This region of the world forms part of the Syro-African fault and is famed for the wealth and variety of its fish, corals and other invertebrates of Indo-Pacific origin. Coral reefs can only develop properly in warm, clear waters with a high salt content, little sediment and relatively little wave movement.

The scales of the emperor angelfish go through several stages before reaching the full beauty of adulthood.

Blue-speckled parrot fish

The masked puffer fish is a member of the puffer family, which can inflate themselves at the slightest hint of danger.

Soft coral *Dendronephtia*

Organ-pipe sponge

Red sponge

Sea slug *Chromodoris*

Sea urchin

Slingjaw wrass

Giant clam

Fan-worm *Sabella*

During the day the gray moray stays hidden in a crevice in the reef.

Sea anemone *Gyrostoma*

Banded *Amphiprion* or anemone-fish

Banded reef prawn

The biological diversity of coral reefs is truly remarkable. Corals, sponges, sea anemones, sea urchins, molluscs, and prawns live together in harmony or even – as in the case of sea anemones with the anemone-fish or *Amphiprion* – in symbiosis. Other species such as sponges act as filters.

The flying scorpion fish swims slowly through the semi-darkness of the reef in search of its prey.

"Fire" coral

The greatest variety of fish is found near the reef, which provides both food and shelter.

Barrier reef (terrace) Breakers

Sea level

Coastal rocks Lagoon Rim

Reef wall Fringing reef

Sandy slope

The three types of reef – terrace, fringing reef and bottom rock - are defined in terms of depth. The intermediate reef has the widest variety of fauna.

POLYPS
Polyps live in huge communities, growing on the calcareous skeletons of their predecessors. Over time, they form the coral reef.

Acropora Coral

The surgeon fish, endemic to the Red Sea, has a sharp spike at the end of its tail.

Butterfly fish – also known as "tobies" – live in shoals.

Blue tang, an endemic species, belongs to the "surgeon" family.

Anthias teaniatus

The red or tropical grouper – which rarely grows to more than 30 inches long – lives in the cracks and crevices of the reef.

Lyretail coralfish

Egypt's mangrove forests are typical of the coastal forests of tropical regions. They are found along the Red Sea coast and southeast coast of Sinai where they reach their most northerly latitude in the world (28° 13' N). This bushy, partly submerged forest – consisting mainly of salt-water mangroves (*Avicennia marina*) – is teeming with life. By retaining sediment its root system favors the development of a rich and abundant community of animals. It is a breeding ground and nursery for fish and many invertebrates, such as prawns, as well as a nesting site for several rare species of birds.

In 1989 the site of Ras Mohammed ▲ 248 was designated a national park to protect one of the most northerly growing mangrove forests in the world.

SALT-WATER MANGROVE
Avicennia marina is the most commonly found mangrove along the shores of the Red Sea. Mangroves have a specialized system of aerial roots which enables them to draw the nutrients they need from the soil.

DUGONG
The dugong has become extremely rare as a result of intensive hunting and pollution. Today the population is limited to a few sites along the south coast of the Red Sea.

Migrating shorebirds feed on the muddy foreshore of the mangrove forests.

Ghost crab

HAWKSBILL TURTLE
Every year this large marine turtle lays its eggs on the beaches along the eastern coast of Egypt.

GHOST CRAB
The best indication of the presence of these nocturnal crabs are the little mounds of sand formed at the entrance to their newly dug burrows.

OSPREY
This bird of prey feeds entirely on fish. On the Red Sea coast it has developed the habit of nesting on the ground, in low bushes or on uninhabited islands where it will be undisturbed. Elsewhere it nests high in the trees.

GOLDEN ACANTHODACTYL
This diurnal lizard is often found on sandy ground at the foot of mangroves.

The western reef heron builds its nest in the tallest mangroves.

Western reef heron (white form)

Western reef heron (dark form)

The green-backed heron is found in warmer areas worldwide, including the Americas.

The white spoonbill nests on the inaccessible islands of the Red Sea.

Breeding plumage

Winter plumage

Summer plumage

BLACK-BELLIED PLOVER
This shorebird from the Arctic tundra winters on the Red Sea coast. It has a black belly in breeding plumage.

WHITE-EYED GULL
A native of the Red Sea. Almost two thousand pairs nest on the islands off the coast of Hurghada ▲ *267*.

HERON
The – strictly coastal – western reef heron is a common sight in the mangrove forests.

LORANTHUS ACACIAE
This semi-parasitic plant lives on
acacias, the most predominant shrub
in the desert.

The Sinai Peninsula constitutes the only land "bridge" between Africa and Asia. The high mountain ranges in the south – which rise to a height of 8,650 feet with Mount Catherine (Jebel Katherina) and 7,497 feet with Mount Sinai (Jebel Musa or Mountain of Moses) – constitute some of the most spectacular scenery in Egypt. The Alpine topography produces exceptional variations in climate, flora and fauna. For example, the average minimum temperature at St Catherine's Monastery is 34°F while the maximum August temperature is 86°F. In the mountains above the monastery the annual precipitation – mainly in the form of snow – can be in excess of 11½ inches.

ST JOHN'S WORT
The remarkable flora of the Sinai Peninsula includes some ancient species which are only found in the Turco-Iranian region. St John's wort is one of the peninsula's twenty or so endemic species of plant.

Annual precipitation reaches 2½ inches.

Its toes are arranged like an elephant's.

ROCK HYRAX
The rock hyrax is about the size of a rabbit. It lives in colonies and feeds, mainly at night, on acacias. It can also be seen basking in the sun during the day.

IBEX
The ibex – a type of wild goat – lives on the steep, rocky slopes of high cliffs. It is frequently seen above St Catherine's Monastery.

EGYPTIAN SPINY-TAILED LIZARD
This large lizard, also known as a mastigure, is particularly active during the hottest part of the day.

FAN-TAILED RAVEN
The bird's short tail gives it a strange appearance in flight.

Male

SINAI ROSEFINCH
This attractive little bird is found only in Sinai, Israel and Jordan. It is sometimes seen inside St Catherine's Monastery.

Male

TRISTRAM'S GRACKLE
Characterized by its whistling calls and russet wings.

Thousands of steppe buzzards fly over Sinai in the summer (en route to Africa) and fall (en route to Russia).

SCARAB. The demi-god Khepri took the form or the head of a scarab. The ideogram represents the sound *hpr*.
BEE. Its ideogram represents the sound *bit*.

References to animals and plants were an important part of Ancient Egyptian civilization, whether on bas-reliefs, in the ideograms of hieroglyphs or through the sounds they represented. In addition to their linguistic and philosophical significance, they are also of great scientific interest since they are among the few pieces of historical evidence which provide detailed information on the composition of the flora and fauna which existed in the last few centuries BC.

EGYPTIAN VULTURE (PHARAOH'S CHICKEN)
The Egyptian vulture is a common sight in the desert regions. The vulture goddess Nekhbet (the symbol of Upper Egypt) and the cobra adorned the pharaoh's forehead. The ideogram represented the sound *tyw*.

LANNER FALCON
The god Horus was often represented as a falcon, as were Re, Montu and Sokar (mummified falcon) ● *60*. The ideogram represents the sound *hr(w)*.

GRIFFON VULTURE
The griffon vulture – once common in Egypt – no longer breeds there and is seen only occasionally during migration. The ideogram represents the sound *mwt*.

QUAIL
For some unknown reason the ideogram of the quail chick and not the adult is used to represent the sound *w*.

HORNED VIPER
The horned viper gave its name to the 12th nome of Upper Egypt. Today this nocturnal viper is found in desert regions.

EGYPTIAN COBRA (ASP)
The rearing cobra which adorns the pharaoh's forehead is an angry female cobra, the Delta goddess Wadjet, symbol of Lower Egypt.

HAMADRYAS BABOON. The baboon is not part of Egypt's indigenous fauna, due to the lack of forests and trees. Nevertheless, the Delta god Thoth ● *62* was sometimes depicted as a baboon. The ideogram represents the sounds *nd*, *ky* and *knd*.

HIPPOPOTAMUS. Now disappeared from the Nile Valley, it was considered to be a manifestation of negative forces because it devastated crops. It represented "heaviness", while the female symbolized fertility in the form of the hippopotamus goddess Taweret ● *60*.

White-fronted and red-breasted geese on a bas-relief in an Old Kingdom tomb at Meidum ▲ 357.

Male   Male

RED-BREASTED GOOSE
Breeding in small numbers in a few places in Siberia , this pretty little goose is today unknown in Egypt as it only winters as far south as the Black Sea. It appears that it used to overwinter in Egypt three thousand years ago.

PINTAIL AND TEAL
Bas-reliefs suggest that these ducks – still seen in Egypt today – were also found in Ancient Egypt, probably in winter.

Breeding plumage

GREATER FLAMINGO. In
the past large numbers of flamingos nested in Egypt whereas today they are simply passing visitors. The flamingo symbolizes the sound *dsr.*

SACRED IBIS. The sacred
ibis, which represented the god Thoth, is no longer found in Egypt. Although the rare hermit ibis – which symbolized the word "resplendent" – has also disappeared, the glossy ibis still exists.

GREAT CORMORANT
A common winter visitor, particularly on Lake Manzala ● 123. Its ideogram represents the sound *k*.

GOLDEN JACKAL
The incarnation of the funerary god Anubis, embalmer and guide of the dead ● 61. Jackals used to haunt the valleys in which the dead were buried. Its ideogram represents the sounds *zb* and *sb*.

WILD CAT
A variety of bob-tailed, wild cats lived in Egypt in Ancient times. The domestic cat appeared in 2100 BC. The cat goddess Bastet ● 62 symbolized femininity and love.

AFRICAN LION. Lions lived in
the desert and came to drink and hunt at the mouths of *wadis*, where the temples dedicated to the lion goddess Sekhmet ● 63 are usually found. The sphinx is derived from the lion, the epitome of the royal animal.

DOMESTIC COW
The milch cow, mother and wife of the Sun, was worshipped in the form of Hathor ● 63. She protected the world and suckled the pharaoh. The hieroglyph for the cow suckling her calf was the symbol of tenderness.

SPINY DESERT MOUSE
Although never far from human habitation, this nocturnal mouse is rarely seen.

Most pyramids and temples in Egypt are situated in a desert, and sometimes even a hostile, environment. A particular type of fauna has established itself on these sites which, abandoned by human beings, afford shelter from the heat and a daytime refuge for nocturnal species. The rugged cavities of the rock provide nesting places for certain types of birds, while rodents find enough to live on and in turn provide a source of food for their predators.

BROWN-NECKED RAVEN. Groups of these large birds are often seen wheeling and diving high above the pyramids and temples.

DESERT LARK
A native of hot deserts, this lark is well camouflaged by its dull-colored plumage.

WHITE-CROWNED BLACK WHEATEAR
This bird nests in the nooks and crevices of the stones of Abu Simbel ▲ *464*.

ROCK MARTIN
The pyramids and temples provide an alternative environment for this swallow, usually found near rocks and cliffs.

AGAMA OR GRAY LIZARD
Although this large lizard (up to 8½ inches long) is harmless to human beings, visitors are often alarmed by its size.

HISTORY

Cartouches of Snefru and Khufu (4th Dynasty).

Egyptology enjoys the paradoxical distinction of being a relatively recent historical science (barely two hundred years old) applied to a field which is as ancient as it is vast. It was first acknowledged as a science when Jean-François Champollion ▲ 216 provided the key to the wealth of texts and inscriptions by deciphering Egyptian hieroglyphs. From then on Egyptologists tried to define the history of Egypt within an exact chronological framework, in spite of the uncertainty which still surrounds the very early periods (up to and including 3000 BC). They grouped the dynasties (royal houses with a common geographical origin and possibly a common line of descent) into periods known as "kingdoms" and "intermediate periods". However, in so doing they in fact used the old dynastic divisions established by the Egyptian priest and historian, Manetho, who lived during the so-called "Greek period". His chronicles on Egypt (of which only fragments have survived) were based on sacerdotal sources which have long since disappeared. But although much more is now known about certain periods, it should not be forgotten that many centuries remain shrouded in mystery.

Pre-Dynastic knife from Jebel el-Arak.

PRE-PHARAONIC EGYPT

Cartouche of Khafre (4th Dynasty).

Vase and figurine of a woman from the Nagada I period.

CIRCA 7000–3100 BC. Egyptian history proper was preceded by a prehistoric period which lasted tens of thousands of years. Increasing numbers of field studies and research projects are constantly renewing and extending our knowledge of this period which had many connections – climatic, hydrological and ecological changes, population migration – with other developing African cultures. Although changes were slow they were continuous and had far-reaching effects. The main constituent traits of what was to become the Egyptian (also known as Pharaonic) civilization and culture – in the fields of politics, religion, technical progress and art – were formed during the period from 7000 to 4000 BC.

The Egyptian population – both coherent and heterogeneous as a result of racial intermixing – was also established within a framework which changed very little for several thousand years. It is possible to identify several major stages during this long pre-Dynastic period which tend to take their name from the sites with which they were particularly associated. The best known are the Badarian, Amratian and Gerzean (or Nagada) in the Nile Valley and Merimde and Omari in the Delta region. One of the outstanding characteristics of this pre-Dynastic period was the progressive organization of the country into principalities or "nomes" which were mostly gathered together into two kingdoms: the (culturally dominant) Lower (north) and Upper (south) Kingdoms. This was a period that was marked by numerous wars and challenges to unification before a truly unified, if not united, Egypt finally emerged.

Cartouches of Menkaure (4th Dynasty) and Unis (5th Dynasty).

CIRCA 3100–2700 BC: ARCHAIC OR THINITE PERIOD. Egypt was governed by a single pharaoh who was king of Upper and Lower Egypt. Its constituent elements were organized into a culture which, as a rule, transcended decentralizing and divergent influences. The birth of writing, after a long period of gestation, had far-reaching consequences. Egypt took its place in History. However, little is known of the first two Thinite Dynasties, so called because the first Thinite pharaohs came from the town of Thinis where they were either entombed or had their cenotaphs. But Memphis ▲ *332*, on the border of Upper and Lower Egypt, was soon to play a central role.

Limestone statue of Djoser from the king's funeral complex at Saqqara.

Cartouche of Djoser (3rd Dynasty).

OLD KINGDOM

CIRCA 2700–2600 BC: 3RD DYNASTY. The reign of Djoser saw the beginning of a period of power and success which was symbolized by the introduction of a spectacular and ambitious stone architecture, illustrated by the impressive complex of the Step Pyramid ▲ *346* at Saqqara. The architect of the complex, the writer and scholar Imhotep remains one of the first great names in history. This period marked the development of a strongly centralized monarchy which governed Egypt from Memphis, controlling the nomes via the nomarchs, or representatives of royal power.

CIRCA 2600–2450 BC: 4TH AND 5TH DYNASTIES. Judging by the magnificence of their pyramids, the reigns of Snefru, Khufu and Khafre (4th Dynasty) would appear to mark the apogee of this period. The construction of the pyramids of Dahshur ▲ *354*, Meidum ▲ *357* and Giza ▲ *334* suggests a flourishing and well-organized administration and economy. The 5th Dynasty witnessed the development of a "solar ideology" (Abusir and Abu Ghurob ● *82*) and the inscription of the famous Pyramid Texts on the walls of the Pyramid of Unis at Saqqara.

Stele of the Serpent-King (c. 3000 BC) from Abydos.

Cartouche of Tety (6th Dynasty).

CIRCA 2450–2200 BC: 6TH DYNASTY. Although the 6th Dynasty was powerful and well represented in the neighboring regions, and organized military and commercial expeditions to the southern tip of Africa, the increasing power of certain local nomarchs challenged the centralized power of Memphis and led to serious upheavals.

Cartouche of Pepy I (6th Dynasty).

39

Casket and cylindrical seals of King Mentuhotep.

First Intermediate Period

Cartouche of Mentuhotep (11th Dynasty).

Circa 2200–2050 bc. In less than two hundred years, Egypt experienced what has sometimes been defined as a social revolution, but very little is in fact known about it. Asiatic peoples appear to have controlled part of the Delta region while weak and sometimes overlapping dynasties continued to rule from Memphis, but particularly from Heracleopolis in Middle Egypt ▲ 360 and later from the small town of Thebes ▲ 394 in Upper Egypt. It would seem that, during this period, the monarchy was a victim of the deep-rooted, de-centralizing tendencies of Egyptian society and its "feudal lords" and suffered changes of fortune that had longlasting effects. The progressive development of the concept and practice of funeral rites, according to which the dead were identified with the god Osiris, is one possibility.

Middle Kingdom

Cartouche of Senwosret III (12th Dynasty).

Black granite statue (right) and cartouche of Amenemhet III (12th Dynasty).

Circa 2050–1990 bc: 11th Dynasty. With the reunification of Mentuhotep II in c. 2050 bc, the 11th-Dynasty Theban kings ruled over the whole of Egypt. Although this gave their town of origin an increasing prominence it did not detract from the importance of Memphis. In fact the Theban rulers traveled and, during the 12th Dynasty, readily built residences and new towns such as Ity-Tawy at the entrance to the Faiyum ▲ 362. This transfer of power toward the north, without abandoning Thebes, marked the return to strong, centralized government.

Circa 1990–1800 bc: 12th Dynasty. This corresponds to a period of power and stability which culminated with the reigns of Senwosret III and Amenemhet III in the second half of the 19th century bc. The military campaigns and mining expeditions to outlying provinces and neighboring countries (which made Egypt an international, dominant and almost imperial power), the development of the Faiyum and its economy, and achievements in its sculpture, architecture and literature made this a classic period (lasting almost two hundred years) whose writings became the authoritative texts of later centuries.

Second Intermediate Period

Statue of Senwosret III.

Circa 1800 bc: 13th Dynasty. The periods of balance and stability alternated, in Egypt as elsewhere, with periods of unrest. De-centralizing, provincial forces (combined with other factors that have, for the most part, defied historic analysis) helped to undermine the Theban rulers who succeeded their 12th-Dynasty counterparts. Egypt broke up into several kingdoms and principalities.

1730–1530 BC. According to later chronicles and Manetho a large part of Egypt came under the control of the Hyksos, an originally Asiatic people who had settled long before in the Delta region and become "Egyptianized". They had been joined by new arrivals following the population migrations which occurred in the Near East. From their eastern Delta capital of Avaris the Hyksos rulers proclaimed themselves fully-fledged pharaohs and extended their power to Middle Egypt, even trying to form an alliance with the Nubians in an attempt to weaken the power of the Theban rulers. This partly foreign domination provoked a reaction from Thebes and inspired a feeling of "national identity" among the Egyptians. The wars against the Hyksos (identified with the traditional and continually renewed struggle of the sun god against his enemies and the maintenance of order and their subsequent expulsion, which marked the end of the 17th Dynasty, constituted an event of considerable importance as well as the founding myth for the New Kingdom and beyond.

Scarab seals dating from the Hyksos period.

Cartouche of Thutmose I (18th Dynasty).

Cartouche of Thutmose II (18th Dynasty).

NEW KINGDOM

CIRCA 1550–1350 BC: IMPERIAL EGYPT.

The capture of Avaris by the Theban ruler Ahmose in c. 1530 BC marked the beginning of an extraordinary era of successive or concurrent periods of power, brilliance and crisis in Egypt. A very different Egypt emerged during the 18th Dynasty with the Ahmosids (Thutmose I–IV, Amenhotep I–III and the famous Hatshepsut ▲ 426), which reached the height of its splendor, as well as its breaking point, at the end of the long reign of Amenhotep III (c. 1390–50 BC). The expulsion of the Hyksos and a desire for maximum security soon put the new rulers on a war footing. But these were wars of expansion and acquisition which would guarantee an almost uninterrupted period of prosperity for Egypt lasting for several decades. This was achieved by a policy of direct domination or, more cooperatively, by vassal sovereigns positioned throughout the east as far as the Euphrates, and by expeditions and straightforward annexation in the south. Thebes (at the origin of this period of glory) and Memphis prospered. Trade expanded and acculturation was at its height. The army was extended, but improved living standards meant recruiting foreign mercenaries or levying a colonial force. Certain social groups became increasingly important, particularly the priests of Amun, the god of Thebes. The Temple of Karnak and its dependencies throughout Egypt became a power in their own right and an indispensable ally of the monarchy.

Cartouche and bust of Queen Hatshepsut (18th Dynasty).

The beginning of the New Kingdom heralded a period of exceptional brilliance with regard to civilization, culture and art, as well as the daily life of Egypt's ruling minority.

41

Cartouche of
Amenhotep IV (18th
Dynasty).

Akhenaten, Nefertiti
and their daughters
worshipping the Aten.

Cartouche of
Ramesses II (19th
Dynasty).

Painted wood coffin
of Ramesses II,
discovered in Thebes
in 1875.

Ramesses II fighting
the Hittites on the
shores of the
Orontes.

CIRCA 1350–30 BC: THE AMARNIAN PERIOD.

Beneath its apparent success lay the elements of a serious crisis, and the eastern Egyptian empire was under threat from the growing power of the Hittites. By his increasingly exclusive worship of the Aten, the physical manifestation of the sun god (which he reinforced by taking the name Akhenaton or Akhenaten), and by progressively distancing himself from Amun and Thebes, Amenhotep IV broke with tradition. This was further aggravated by his foundation of a new capital – Akhetaton (also Akhetaten) – in Middle Egypt ▲ 378 and from which his priests were excluded. During this period Egyptian domination in Syria and Palestine was showing signs of weakening. The reign of Akhenaten stands apart in the history of Egypt, with its theological and artistic innovations. But Akhenaten's successors did not pursue his ideology. The defenders of the old order prevailed, starting with the priests of Amun. The army decided the matter and their commander-in-chief, Horemheb, became pharaoh.

CIRCA 1300–1100 BC: THE RAMESSIDE DYNASTIES.

Ramesses I and Sety I, the rulers from the eastern Delta region who succeeded Horemheb, were also generals. The situation in Egypt had changed and the Hittites had become a force to be reckoned with. The long reign of Ramesses II (a large part of the 13th century BC) represented one of the last periods of Egyptian power. The pharaoh built monuments throughout the country and developed the northern capital of Piramesse (The Estate of Ramesses) near Avaris. During the reign of his son, Merneptah, the situation became even more precarious and external threats (from the Libyans and Sea Peoples) were only just repelled. The 19th Dynasty was overtaken by problems of succession.

Cartouches of Tutankhamun (18th Dynasty), Sety I (19th Dynasty) and Necho (26th Dynasty).

The 20th Dynasty (c. 1200–1100 BC) was dominated by a succession of Ramesses (ending with XI). The only exception in this period of political decline was the reign of Ramesses III. The repulsion of foreign invasions, an increasing number of mercenaries, economic problems, corruption, the increasing influence of the priests of Amun and struggles for succession all added to the weakening of political power.

Cartouche of Taharqa (25th Dynasty) and statue (Tanis).

THIRD INTERMEDIATE PERIOD

CIRCA 1100–750 BC. Although the high priest of Thebes was crowned sovereign, a strong, parallel power was established in Tanis ▲ 226, in the eastern Delta region, which set itself up as the northern equivalent of Thebes. Military commanders who had originally come from Libya also increased their influence and eventually ruled as pharaohs over a fragmented Egypt.

However, extensive architectural and artistic activity proved that political problems were not everything. In spite of a few more successes in the Near East, Egypt suffered the repercussions of the political and military upheavals of its neighbors and became a tempting prey for rival powers.

Statuette of Taharqa worshipping the falcon god, Horus.

CIRCA 750–600 BC: 25TH DYNASTY. The Kushites (inhabitants of Nubia and modern Sudan), steeped in Egyptian culture after centuries of domination and acculturation, finally conquered Egypt under Pi(ankh)y. These southern pharaohs (especially Taharqa) restored Egypt to its former unity and strength. Taharqa was finally defeated by the Assyrians in 664–3 BC.

"LATE" PERIOD

CIRCA 600–525 BC: 26TH DYNASTY. A new dynasty, which originated in the town of Sais ▲ 212, in the Delta region, seized power and gradually managed to free Egypt from Assyrian domination. Although Egypt was once again independent and ruled by indigenous sovereigns, the country was not out of danger and the age of power was over. However the reigns of Necho, Psamtik, Apries and Ahmose were far from marking the decline of Egyptian civilization. In some respects this period has even been referred to as the "Saite renaissance" and one only has to consider its remarkable statuary to understand why. Although no longer a great power, Egypt enjoyed considerable prestige, inspired envy and, like it or not, opened up to the winds of change sweeping the Mediterranean. Greek mercenaries, merchants or simply visitors came flocking to Egypt.

Painted limestone stele of the god Apis, dating from the Late period.

Cat wearing the cartouche of the pharaoh Psamtik I (26th Dynasty).

43

CIRCA 525–404 BC: 27TH DYNASTY.

The Persian empire exerted its conquering power, Egypt became a satrapy and the rulers of Susa became its new pharaohs.

CIRCA 380–43 BC: 30TH DYNASTY.

Renewed efforts for Egyptian independence culminated in the reigns of Nectanebo I and II. But the country continued to remain at the center of Greek and Persian rivalry and became a major strategic and economic asset.

THE GREEK PERIOD

Cleopatra VII (above) and Alexander the Great (right).

332–30 BC. The Persians regained control of Egypt but lost it less than ten years later when it was conquered, along with the rest of the Achemenid empire, by Alexander the Great and the Macedonians in 332 BC, and thus became part of the Greek empire. Alexander, who was legitimized by the oracle of Amun at Siwa ▲ 256, founded the town of Alexandria – destined for a glorious future – on the western coast of the Delta. Alexander's generals shared out his empire and the ancient Land of the Pharaohs fell to Ptolemy, son of Lagos, founder of the Ptolemaic dynasty which ruled Egypt (and occasionally part of the Near East) for three centuries until the last ruler in the Macedonian line, Cleopatra VII, was forced to surrender to Octavian (Augustus) and the Romans in 30 BC.

THE ROMAN PERIOD

30 BC–AD 313. The political change was abrupt. From this point on the seat of government lay beyond Egypt's borders, in Rome. However, for the sake of political expediency, the Roman emperors succeeded in establishing themselves as the successors of the pharaohs, even going as far as to have their names inscribed in a royal cartouche. In fact Egypt became a province which was directly answerable to the emperor. Its strategic and economic importance (among other things as the granary of the Roman empire) were considerable. But many things remained unchanged, particularly at administrative and cultural levels, and with regard to the use of Greek, the language of the ruling classes and elites. Alexandria continued to occupy a prominent position in all respects. Building was still carried on extensively throughout Egypt: sanctuaries and public buildings but also entire new towns which were important in the protection of the *limes* (the fortified frontier of the empire and its glacis). But the Roman empire developed and began to show signs of breaking up. Egypt was not indifferent to the process, particularly as it did not welcome an exploitation which was

Roman emperor represented as a pharaoh (1st century BC).

Statue of the god Osiris.

in many respects colonial. Rebellions were sporadic and often violent. The spiritual crisis represented, in particular, by the development of religions preaching salvation, also affected Egypt, whose ancient, indigenous forms of worship had long been established in a modified form in Rome. The theme of Osiris, the god who died and was resurrected, proved extremely successful and was complemented by the parallel theme of Isis, protectress and comforter, the divine mother of the god Horus. But it was emergent Christianity, initially rejected and eradicated and subsequently accepted and triumphant, that marked the end of the crisis and the break with the ancient world.

Roman mosaic with Nile scenes (1st century BC).

AD 313. Although the Emperor Constantine restored a certain unity within the Roman empire by ending the conflict with Christianity, theological (and political) quarrels were violent, especially with the heresy of Arius which enjoyed a degree of success in Egypt. Arianism finally lost the struggle under Theodosius, whose edict condemning paganism (AD 383) led to the temples being closed or converted into churches. This heralded the end of Ancient Egyptian culture, intrinsically associated with the Pharaonic monarchy (which had long since disappeared) and the temples of the gods which were now either burned or closed.

Title page of the (northern) Bohairic Coptic gospel-book.

THE BYZANTINE PERIOD

AD 395. Egypt became part of the eastern Roman empire. The Mono- versus Dyophysitic dispute (as to whether Christ had one or two natures) and its inherent religious and political implications led to uprisings and the ultimate defeat of Monophysitism. An edict issued by the emperor Justinian in AD 551 ordered the closure of the Temple of Philae ▲ 462 where the last defenders of the pagan faith, protected by the remoteness of Nubia, were still practicing the ancient cults, and the cult of Isis in particular. However, the Monophysites of Egypt joined forces and an indigenous, national church was established: the Coptic Church. Coptic also describes the final stage of the Ancient Egyptian language and the writing used to transcribe it which consisted of the Greek alphabet with seven additional symbols borrowed from the Egyptian demotic script ▲ 219.

The Roman emperor Justinian.

AD 619–40. The power of Byzantium declined and when the Persians invaded Egypt in AD 619 they encountered very little resistance. The process was repeated in AD 639 when Amr Ibn el-As, at the head of the army of the caliph Omar, took Babylon from Egypt ▲ 318. Alexandria fell in AD 640. Egypt became an Arab country and this marked the turning point in its history and the end of Ancient Egypt.

ABU SIMBEL

WADI ES-SEBUA

QASR IBRIM

MAHARRAQA

DAKKA

DENDUR

KALABSHA

KERTASSI

DABUD

ELEPHANTINE

PHILAE

ASWAN

DUSH

KHARGA

TEMP

DENDERA

MOUNTAIN
OF THEBES

ARMANT

DEIR EL-BAHRI

THEBES

DAKHLA

ABYDOS

E OF SETY I

ANTÆOPOLIS

TUNA EL-JEBEL

ANTINOE

MOUNT SINAI

ESNA

EDFU

KOM OMBO

JEBEL SILSILA
QUARRIES

BERENICE

LIFE AND DEATH IN ANCIENT EGYPT
FARMING, HUNTING AND FISHING

Everyday life in Ancient Egypt,
governed by the Nile floods
which irrigated crops and
perpetuated myths,
changed very little during
the three thousand years of
Pharaonic rule. The Egyptians respected their gods
and their laws, anxious to ensure an eternal life in the Hereafter
and pass on to their children the land and beliefs of their
ancestors. From the beginning of the 3rd millennium BC they
developed a complete system of written and figurative forms of
expression which today constitutes the wealth of information
that has enabled Egyptologists to reconstruct the life of these
ancient Nile-dwellers. The population, which consisted mainly
of peasants, lived under the double law of the Nile and the
pharaoh, the respective guarantors of fertility and order. The
Nile floods, coupled with the patient toil of the peasant-farmers,
brought prosperity to the land of Egypt, while the ebb and flow
of the great river determined not only the three four-month
seasons of the year but also the main events of the Egyptian
calendar.

The beginning of the Egyptian year coincided
with the heliacal rising of Sirius, about July 19,
and marked the beginning of *akhet* (the season
of floods) during which the Nile inundated the

land, covering it with fertile mud. The season of
peret followed *akhet* four months later, when the
waters receded and the land was visible once
again, ready for ploughing and sowing.

Fruit trees (figs, date palms, sycamores, acacias
and pomegranates) and a wide variety of
vegetables (onions, lentils, runner beans, broad
beans, chick peas, lettuce, cucumbers, cabbages

and horseradish) grew in abundance in
orchards and gardens. Crops shown in
ploughing scenes tend to be mainly flax and
cereals; men drive teams of oxen.

The Ancient Egyptians were fond of the meat of certain desert animals, which were tracked down in their dens by experienced hunters. Fishing was also an important activity for the inhabitants of the Nile shores and the marshlands of the Delta region. Nearly all the fish caught were edible, and a number of recipes have been found which prescribe a variety of methods for drying, salting and seasoning fish. The papyrus clumps and thickets favored by fishermen were also an ideal place to hunt the noisy flocks of wild ducks and other birds which circled above them.

This was a time of great activity in the fields. There was not a moment to lose. Crops had to be sown and the precious water saturating the land had to be stored.

By careful management of the floods, the Egyptian peasants could dedicate the third, dry season (*shemu*), lasting from mid-March to mid-July, to gathering and harvesting their crops.

Cattle and poultry breeding was also a part of traditional Egyptian iconography. Farmyards abounded with ducks, geese, pelicans and pigeons, which were plucked and roasted on smoking wood fires. Vines occupied pride of place on pergolas and were grown as much for the bunches of grapes as for the wine, which was drunk at family celebrations.

An Egyptian "marriage" was private, unmarked by any ceremony. It took the form of two young people deciding to live together as the concrete expression of their relationship. The house had to be provided by the man, who was responsible for the respectability of his household.

Houses are thought to have been about 95 square yards in area, made of sun-dried mudbrick. They consisted of four connecting rooms, a kitchen and a terrace.

The furniture of the Ancient Egyptians was simple, and consisted of stools, chairs, beds and storage chests, not forgetting the

Egyptian middle-class houses stood in an airy garden with a pool and consisted of reception rooms, bedrooms and bathrooms.

The Egyptian ideal of a large family not only ensured the social status of the parents but also guaranteed the funerary rites due to their ancestors' and that upon their death their own tombs would be observed. In spite of a high rate of infant mortality, the average family had between four and eight children.

uncomfortable but very common wood and stone head-rests which served as pillows.

Greeks who came to Egypt after the conquest of Alexander the Great were struck by the fact that Egyptian women enjoyed legally recognized, independent status. In the event of a "divorce", brought about by the breakdown of the relationship for reasons of infertility, adultery or "re-marriage" (for although polygamy was in fact legal, it was not widely practiced), the woman maintained her rights over her inheritance unless she had committed adultery.

18th-Dynasty make-up applicator (right).

WRITING. Papyrus sheets, made from the stem of the plant, were prepared using a papyrus-cutter and a smoothing tool. Reeds soaked in black ink, made with smoke-black, were used for writing. An ocher-based red ink was used for headings.

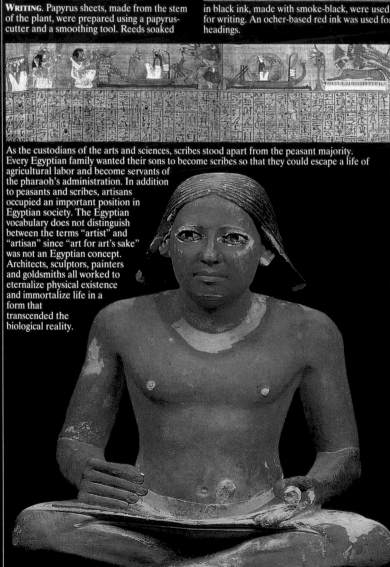

As the custodians of the arts and sciences, scribes stood apart from the peasant majority. Every Egyptian family wanted their sons to become scribes so that they could escape a life of agricultural labor and become servants of the pharaoh's administration. In addition to peasants and scribes, artisans occupied an important position in Egyptian society. The Egyptian vocabulary does not distinguish between the terms "artist" and "artisan" since "art for art's sake" was not an Egyptian concept. Architects, sculptors, painters and goldsmiths all worked to eternalize physical existence and immortalize life in a form that transcended the biological reality.

"Ostraca". *Ostraca* were limestone chips or terracotta shards used to make a sort of "rough draft".

Papyri and cloth scrolls were kept in wooden chests.

Artisans. The Egyptian middle class, created at the end of the Old Kingdom, included artisans whose highly esteemed skills were passed from father to son.

Although Egyptian society recognized the specialist skills of artisans, it did not acknowledge their independence. They were employed by the government, by temples or as part of wealthy households. They worked in workshops, in small groups, and formed corporations headed by high-ranking government officials.

Once a surface was smoothed and leveled for decoration, the designers drew a grid. An outline was sketched and corrected by the team leader. Then the sculptor carved out the relief with his bronze chisel. He was followed by the painter with his palette of colors,

BES
A strangely mutated dwarf, patron saint of childbirth.

TAWERET
Hippopotamus-goddess of mothers and children.

RE
Sun-god associated with Horus, who often assumed the form of a falcon.

RENENUTET
The serpent-goddess who presided over the harvest.

KHEPRI
Scarab-beetle demiurge representing the rising sun

ANUBIS. The embalmer of Osiris who became the patron of embalmers. This jackal-headed god introduced the dead into the other world and watched over their tombs.

SOBEK
The crocodile-god, symbol of fertility.

NUT. Nut, wife of the earth-god, Geb, was the embodiment of the celestial vault. She was the mother of the sun-god Re, swallowing the solar disk in the evening and giving birth to it each morning.

MUT
Goddess of Thebes and consort of Amun.

ASTRONOMICAL CALENDAR. The calendar divides the year into three four-month seasons. The figures below each month represent the stars and planets which appear in the sky at that time of year.

NEKHBET
Vulture-goddess, protectress of Upper Egypt. (Wadjet is the goddess of Lower Egypt.)

NEPHTHYS, ISIS AND OSIRIS
Nephthys, sister of Isis, took part in the ritual protection and resurrection of Osiris, murdered by his brother Seth.

BASTET
The cat-goddess Bastet is the embodiment of joy.

HAPI
The "spirit of the Nile" and the rising waters of the *nun*, the source of all life.

HORUS
The mythical first pharaoh of Egypt and the son of Isis and Osiris.

HATHOR
Wife of the sun-god Horus. In the form of the cow she was goddess of joy and music.

THOTH
God of wisdom and knowledge, patron of scribes and recorder of the Judgement of the Dead.

PTAH
God of Memphis, where he was believed to be the creator of all things.

ALLEGORY OF THE WORLD
The goddess Nut, symbolizing the celestial vault, is arched above the earth represented by the god Geb. The sun-god Re sails between them.

KHNUM
Ram-headed creator of life, who fashioned mankind on his potter's wheel.

MA'AT
Embodiment of universal order and harmony, depicted with a feather on her head.

SEKHMET
The lion-goddess who unleashes her anger on the last five days of the year.

MIN
God of fertility, represented with an erect phallus, his right arm bent and holding a whip.

AMUN
A Theban divinity worshipped during the New Kingdom, who became the supreme god.

FLIGHT OF THE "BA"
The *ba* (spiritual element) left the body of the deceased and was able to wander at will.

MUMMIFICATION
Mummification prevented the decomposition of the earthly remains, enabling the deceased's spiritual and physical elements to be reunited, intact, after death.

FAREWELL CEREMONY
Funeral processions accompanied the deceased to the tomb where they were buried, surrounded familiar objects likely to add to the comfort of their future life. Such preparations enabled the dea to enter the kingdom of Osiris, god of the Hereafter and symbol of resurrection and rebirth.

BANDAGING
Bandaging was carried out according to a strict ritual. Embalmers had to recite the appropriate sacred formulae at each stage of the process.

SARCOPHAGI
The sarcophagus was placed inside a casket. A door painted on the outer casing enabled the dead to observe the world of the living.

CANOPIC JARS
The stomach, intestines, liver and lungs were removed and preserved in the Canopic jars.

The sarcophagus was taken across the Nile by boat. Once on the far shore the procession went on to the necropolis, where priests performed the customary rites.

"BOOK OF THE DEAD"
This collection of texts (hymns and magic formulae), placed in the tomb, was believed to ensure the survival of the dead in the Hereafter.

JUDGEMENT
The deceased were led by Anubis into the presence of Osiris and his associated gods where they were "judged". First they had to declare themselves innocent of a series of wrong-doings against the gods and mankind. This was followed by the "weighing of the heart" which had to be as light as the feather of Ma'at, goddess of truth and justice. Ammit "the Devourer" waited to consume the deceased if their heart was too heavy. The results were recorded by Thoth.

Abbasid coins from
the time of Baybars.

EGYPT UNDER THE ARAB GOVERNORS

640–46
*Amr Ibn el-As
conquers Egypt.*

640
Foundation of Fustat.

642
Fall of Alexandria.

660–750
*Ommiad caliphate of
Damascus.*

706
*Arabic becomes the
official administrative
language.*

725
First Coptic rebellion.

750–868
*Abbasid caliphate of
Baghdad.*

868–905
*Egypt under Tulunid
control.*

When Amr Ibn el-As (580–664), who had been sent to Egypt
by the caliph Omar, seized the Byzantine fortress of Babylon,
he became master of the Nile Valley. The siege of Alexandria
(and the destruction of the Great Library) brought the Greek
chapter of Egypt's history to a close. Egypt became an Arabic
colony administered by governors nominated by the caliphs,
and although the first elected caliphate was
replaced by the Ommiad dynasty, neither
this, nor the subsequent accession of the
Abbasids of Baghdad, altered the post-
Arab-conquest status of Egypt: it remained
a province of the caliphate, mainly organized
by the Ommiads who were responsible for
imposing Arabic as the language of administration. The
introduction of the land tax known as the *kharadj* was
accompanied by the widespread Islamization of minor
officials. It was during this dynasty that the town of Fustat
▲ *324*, originally the encampment of the conquering Arab
tribes, became an important center. A new state was born in
Egypt, based (as the Copts discovered) on religion, in which
the only way to survive was to embrace the language and faith
of the new masters. Although the Copts initially enjoyed
greater freedom than they had under Byzantine rule, the
heavy taxation incurred by their protected status led to large-
scale conversions to Islam.

THE GREAT EGYPTIAN DYNASTIES

879
*Inauguration of the
Ibn Tulun Mosque.*

905–36
*Baghdad regains
direct control of Egypt.*

936–69
*Egypt under Ikshidid
control.*

969–1169
*Egypt under Fatimid
control.*

969
*Foundation of
El-Qahira.*

Salah ad-Din's
cavalcade (right and
below).

THE TULUNIDS. The political and artistic history of Muslim
Egypt really began with Ahmed Ibn Tulun (835–84) ▲ *312*,
who seized power in 868. For almost four centuries after this,
a series of dynasties,
including several of
foreign origin,
established
themselves
firmly in
Egypt. The
struggle with the
caliphate of Baghdad
brought about the
collapse of the Tulunids
(who were originally
only governors). But

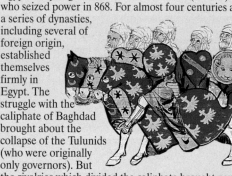

the rivalries which divided the caliphate brought new masters
to the country. These were the Turkman Mohammed Ibn
Tuglij, who was founder of the Ikshidid dynasty, the Fatimids,
who were the new masters in North Africa, and the
Ayyubids, whose empire extended as far as Syria. The
crises associated with the Crusades highlighted changing
alliances and the possibilities of autonomy. Fustat, which
was Egypt's key town, was later re-founded by the
Fatimids.

THE FATIMIDS. Royal palaces and mosques were built
to the north of Fustat, where the Fatimids founded El-Qahira
("the Triumphant One"). Egypt subsequently became one of the
centers of international trade. Warehouses, palaces and

Map of Egypt from the manuscript of El-Idrissi (12th century).

mosques provide evidence of the dynamic exchanges that took place in spite of the internal crises of the Fatimid regime and the despotic reign of the sultan El-Hakim (985–1021) ▲ 291 in particular. The Fatimids also made Cairo the capital of a Shi'ite caliphate, an occupation which led to a complete break with ancient traditions (although it did foster, for a while at least, remarkable intellectual activity). The subsequent return to power of the Sunni Muslims, who were led by Salah ad-Din el-Ayyubi, or Saladin (1138–93), did not destroy these achievements. Salah ad-Din built the imposing Citadel ▲ 304 which stands above Cairo on the boundary between the Tulunid and Fatimid cities. He also encouraged the development of the great medersa ● 112, which were religious colleges.

THE MAMELUKE EMPIRE IN EGYPT

Under the Mameluke sultans Egypt experienced another brutal revolution linked to the attacks of the Crusaders that the last of the Ayyubids were unable to repel. Baybars founded a regime which lasted for almost three centuries and presented some very distinctive characteristics: Turkish and Circassian soldiers who maintained a non-hereditary power until the end of the 14th century and who, in spite of their bloody power struggles and famed violence, created the only great modern Egyptian empire. In addition to stability of power the Mamelukes also ensured the prosperity and greatness of Egypt and Cairo, especially during the 14th century. As protectors of the Abbasid caliph and the two holy cities of Arabia, the Mamelukes, a vast foreign legion, became indissolubly linked to the history of Egypt, expressing their

influence through the magnificence of their palaces and mosques. Above and beyond their defeat by the Ottomans, they continued to be the true masters of Egypt until the accession of Mohammed Ali in the 19th century. The majority of the indigenous Egyptian population had been of the Muslim faith since the 13th century and eventually seemed more Arabian than their Bahrite and North African masters, who were soldiers from the Black Sea or the outlying parts of the Empire.

1167
Frankish support to prevent the Syrians conquering Egypt.

1169–1250
Ayyubid control.

1169
Restoration of Sunni Islam.

1193
Death of Saluh ad Din.

1249
Louis IX of France (St Louis) lands at Damietta (Seventh Crusade).

1251–1382
Bahrite Mamelukes.

1260
Baybars comes to power.

1279
Qala'un becomes sultan.

1291
St John of Acre is captured.

1366
Alexandria is plundered by Pierre de Lusignan.

1382–1517
Circassian Mamelukes.

1382
Sultan Barquq comes to power.

1467
Qaitbay becomes sultan.

1501
Sultanate of Qansu el-Ghuri.

Inauguration of the Suez Canal: arrival of the imperial yacht, *L'Aigle*, at Ismaïliya.

1517–1798: EGYPT, AN OTTOMAN PROVINCE

1517
Selim conquers Egypt.

1524
Egypt's new status: administered by a pasha.

1528
Renewal of the capitulations of 1507.

1569
Sinan Pasha's expedition to the Yemen.

1623
First overt rebellions against Istanbul.

Alexandria captured by Napoleon Bonaparte.

1707
Mameluke conflicts in Cairo.

1725
Rebellions and loss of pashas' authority.

1765–98
Mameluke opposition to the Ottomans.

1768
Ali Bey separates Egypt from the Ottoman empire.

When the Mameluke regime fell to the Ottomans Egypt once again became a province, a status which had never before been so clearly defined. The Ottomans mistrusted Egypt's autonomous aspirations and installed a *pasha*, an administrative governor, while the *aga*, or commander, of the Janissaries was responsible for the military. Egypt suffered crises or enjoyed long periods of prosperity according to the particular *pasha* appointed. In real terms the reins of power were held by the *beys* of Cairo, supported by an army that included a large body of Mamelukes who thus recovered much of their former power. During the 18th century the latter were the true masters of Egypt, at a time when Egypt was playing a less prominent role in the history of the eastern Mediterranean, although its continued economic prosperity

was borne out by its architecture as well as the account books of local merchants. Egypt's early commercial links with Europe served as a further indication of this sustained vitality. The accession of Ali Bey, however, in the second half of the 18th century, plunged Egypt into anarchy and left the country teetering on the brink of economic strangulation. The appearance of Bonaparte's fleet on July 1, 1798 came as a complete surprise, and the last Ottoman *pasha* barely had enough time to flee the country.

1798–1805: EUROPEAN INTERLUDE

1773
Death of Ali Bey.

1786
An Ottoman fleet is sent to Alexandria.

1788
The beys' return to power is followed by anarchy.

Mohammed Ali.

1798–1803
French occupation.

1803–5
Political vacuum. British presence.

The main advantage of the French presence was that it enabled Egypt to complete the break with Istanbul, even though it nominally remained an Ottoman province until 1914. It also facilitated the establishment of the initial elements of a centralized administration and an awareness of the importance of Egypt's past. The French occupation was too short-lived to make a lasting impression, however. It led, above all, to the installation of mercenaries sent from Istanbul to restore a basic level of order. They included Mehemet-Ali (Mohammed Ali) (1769–1849), the son of a tobacco merchant from Kavala, in Epirus, who seized power after the withdrawal of British troops. Mohammed Ali was the leader of an army of mercenaries who almost became emperor . . . but instead became viceroy.

1805–49: MOHAMMED ALI

After he had successfully managed to eliminate the last of the Mamelukes, Mohammed Ali played the part of the sultan's faithful servant. He went to Mecca to combat the Wahhabi "heretics", and he restored order in the rest of Egypt and conquered the Sudan. In 1819 he began to form a conquering army, officially to restore the sultan's authority in Greece and Syria, but clearly intended to be used to conquer the entire Ottoman empire. The fundamental reforms carried out in Egypt made the country a model of social and economic development. The Syrian campaign, however, finally provoked an international response. With the support of Great Britain the sultan managed to obtain Mohammed Ali's surrender, in return for which he was offered the hereditary viceroyalty of Egypt. Mohammed Ali's dynasty lasted until 1952.

1831
Syrian campaign.

1840–1922: BRITISH CONTROL

Mohammed Ali's successors were the prisoners of new international relations. Egypt's frontiers had been opened by a free-trade treaty and no longer protected the national economy. The construction of the Suez Canal ▲ 228 pushed the country into an economic dependency which was further aggravated by the cotton boom. Paradoxically the inauguration ceremonies of the Suez Canal in 1869 marked the end of an era and placed the finances of Egypt under Franco-British supervision. The national reaction precipitated the British bombardment of Alexandria and occupation of Cairo. Although Egypt's political and administrative structures remained officially intact, the country was effectively placed under the direct control of Europe. British control assumed two (successive) forms. Until 1914 Egypt remained an Ottoman province, governed by a virtually independent viceroy but under British supervision. In 1914 all links with Istanbul were finally severed but, although Egypt became a monarchy, British control became official and Egypt was declared a protectorate. At the same time this control brought about an unusual political calm. Egypt became a veritable Mediterranean retreat and entered a period of great prosperity and

1862
Cotton boom.

1875
Franco-British financial control.

1881
Orabi Pasha's nationalist movement.

1882
British occupation.

Battle of Tell el-Kebir.

1902
First Aswan Dam.

1907–8
The first Egyptian nationalist parties are founded.

1914
British protectorate.

1919
Saad Zaghlul's national revolution.

Banner used in a demonstration by Egyptian women at the opening of the first Parliament in December 1924.

INSTRUISEZ VOS FILLES RESPEC
TEZ LES DROITS DE VOS FEMMES
PAR LA FEMME ON JUGE DE LA
CIVILISATION D'UN PEUPLE

Egyptian ministers in December 1924 and Saad Zaghlul.

modernization. The Egyptian social elite grew rich and became aware of their need for independence. In 1907 they formed multicultural, liberal nationalist parties whose members were united in their rejection of the British presence. World War One was scarcely over when their leader, Saad Zaghlul ▲ 281, declared his intention of demanding full independence for Egypt. The British refusal to receive his delegation (*wafd*) provoked a series of disturbances and strikes. After three years of delays and excuses Great Britain finally decided to declare the end of the protectorate, but the British occupation and control of Egypt continued.

1922–52: LIBERAL EGYPT

The years that followed were known as Egypt's "liberal" era. The Wafd Party made repeated efforts to renegotiate and find an area of common ground with the British, finally succeeding in 1936. The multicultural Egyptian society of the 19th century was gradually disappearing and local elites were clearly Egyptian. However an increasingly corrupt regime condemned the ideology of the liberal model. The voice of Islam was raised in protest and the Muslim brotherhoods were born. Those in power sought legitimacy via the struggle with Israel and the creation of the Arab League, but the contradictions were too obvious and the defeat of 1949 too bitter. Individual acts of violence were followed by riots and, in 1952, the Cairo fire emphasized the powerlessness of the government. Within six months, a few young officers had taken over, abolishing the monarchy before taking up the reins of power. For the first time in its history, the future of Egypt was in the hands of the "sons of Nile *fellaheen*".

1922
End of the protectorate. Fuad I becomes king.

1928
Muslim brotherhoods founded.

1936
Anglo-Egyptian treaty.

1949
Defeat in the war against Israel.

1952–70: THE NASSER YEARS

The movement away from "liberal" Egypt took place gradually. After offering power to Mohammed Nejib (1901–84), Colonel Gamal Abd el-Nasser (1918–70) assumed total power in 1954 and became the representative of the Third-World countries in Bandung. He declared independence for the Sudan and obtained the departure of the last of the British troops before announcing the nationalization of the Suez Canal, his response to the American refusal to finance the

The 1973 Arab-Israeli War.

1952
The Cairo fire and the Free Officers' coup d'état.

1956
Suez Crisis.

NOUS SOMMES PRETS !

construction of the Aswan High Dam ▲ *460*. Continued tension led to the military operation of October 1956 which ended with the withdrawal of the combined Israeli, French and British forces and the radicalization of the Egyptian regime, expressed internally by nationalization and the execution of the Muslim brotherhoods, and externally by expulsions and projects for Arab unions. Nasser became the mouthpiece of the Arab world and, in this capacity, prioritized the war with Israel. The Six-Day War in June 1967 ▲ *234* dealt the final blow. Nasser was maintained in power by popular demand but died just as a truce had finally been agreed. However, Arab socialism also brought radical economic changes: there were more big industrial projects, and large towns destroyed the agricultural balance of the Nile Valley. In 1970, in spite of Soviet counsel, Egypt was unable to meet its accumulated deficits and imbalances.

Gamal Abd el-Nasser.

1960
Nationalization.

1961
Agricultural reform.

1967
Six-Day War.

1970
Nasser dies.

1971
Inauguration of the Aswan High Dam.

1972
Expulsion of Soviet advisors.

1973
Fourth Arab-Israeli (October) War.

1974
"Open door" policy.

Camp David Agreements.

1971–81: U-TURNS

This series of difficulties led Egypt to turn to the West and the new Gulf States. Anwar el-Sadat (1918–81) began to open up the economy to the West (*infitah*). By liberalizing the markets he risked destabilizing the middle classes on whose support Nasser had depended, but he intended to counter this weakness with rapid economic growth. Peace with Israel was a vital part of the process and the fourth Arab-Israeli War in October 1973 ▲ *235*, in which neither side managed to procure victory, provided an opportunity for the necessary negotiations which ended with the Camp David Agreements and the return of Sinai to Egypt. An economic upturn, however, was not forthcoming; or at least not for everyone. Inequalities became more pronounced and gave rise to violent social tensions. The Islamic movements re-emerged and Sadat paid with his life.

AT THE CROSSROADS. From this point onward Egypt has tried to overcome its contradictions. The peace with Israel did not prevent its reintegration into the Arab-Muslim camp. Its neighbors are intent on avoiding a destabilization which could plunge the region into uncontrollable chaos. Meanwhile the number of Western loans is increasing, accompanied by a policy of liberalization and control. But growing social unrest is matched by the mounting strength of the Islamic groups which represent the only form of structured opposition. Although briefly tempted by reconciliation, the government of Hosni Mubarak has been forced to adopt a confrontational stance since 1990. Today Egypt stands at a crossroads.

1978
Camp David.

1981
President Sadat is assassinated.

1981
The Sharia becomes the primary source of judicial law.

1991
Confrontations between Copts and Muslims.

1992
Demonstration over the cost of living.

FROM COPTIC TO ARABIC

Bilingual Coptic prayer book. The text written in the right-hand column is in Arabic, while the left-hand column is in Coptic.

The Arab conquest represents a fundamental break in the history of Egypt which is reflected in its language. During the next thousand years Arabic spread throughout Egypt, not only keeping pace with conversions to Islam but also explaining them. In 706 Arabic became the language of official documents. Whereas the early conquerors had Coptic prayers translated to ensure that they were not offensive to Islam, the lessons of the Scriptures, which, during services, were read in Greek and explained in Coptic, were soon read in Coptic and explained in Arabic. Coptic became a devotional language, which saved it from oblivion but did not prevent its irreversible decline. It was only kept alive by the monastic tradition. Place names are the only surviving evidence of the Coptic revenge on the Greeks during the Arab conquest: Akhmim ▲ 383 and Ashmunein, for example, both take their origin from their original Coptic names. The Jewish community was also Arabized, since from the 19th century onward commercial texts were written in Judeo-Arabic, which is Arabic that has been transcribed into Hebrew characters.

Covers of novels written in Arabic by Naguib Mahfouz ● 160. Although he makes extensive use of the Cairene dialect, his novels are read throughout the Arab world.

CLASSICAL AND DIALECTICAL ARABIC

As a result, Egypt became one of the main centers of Arabic culture, as evidenced not only by an extremely active academy of the Arabic language but also by the screening of Egyptian films in cinemas throughout the world. The growing importance of the Nile Valley, bordered by Arab countries, has finally relegated the traditional division between classical and dialectical Arabic to a position of secondary importance. But as well as being understood well beyond Egypt's natural borders (a phenomenon largely due to the media), this Arabic dialect also has a written form. The work of Naguib Mahfouz, winner of the Nobel Prize for Literature, is a famous example: his extremely "classical" approach is interspersed with many so-called "Egyptianisms". Opposition to this predominance of dialect is either ideological or political. For example, the language of the Koran must be jealously protected because it alone can strengthen the union of all Arabs, be they Muslim or non-Muslim. It should be pointed out, however, that the debate on the "levels of language" is, generally speaking, inappropriate. On the one hand modern classical Arabic is significantly different from the language of the Koran and, on the other, the dialects have borrowed from the terms and structures of modern Arabic. Apart from that, all that remains are the phonetic and semantic differences which make it possible to distinguish between the dialects of Upper and Lower Egypt, and the relative poverty or richness of vocabulary according to social class and background.

A MULTILINGUAL SOCIETY

In spite of the absolute dominance of Arabic, several European languages are strongly represented. Most well-to-do Egyptian families are bi- or even tri-lingual. The education system and the legacy of liberal Egypt are mainly responsible. In the 19th century French enjoyed second-language status in Egypt and was used in mixed courts and all administration. It was only between 1936 and 1949 that all references to French, English and Italian were excluded from official documents. However, the future of these multilingual skills, which constitute one of the riches of Egyptian culture, is guaranteed by religious teaching establishments and language schools.

THE TWENTY-EIGHT LETTERS OF THE ALPHABET.
From top to bottom, starting on the left: alif, ba, ta, tha, jim, ha, kha, dal, zal, ra, za, sin, shin, sad, daad, ta, za, aïn, ghaïn, fa, qaf, kaf, lam, mim, nun, ha, waw, ya.

● RELIGION

A few traces of Egypt's ancient religious traditions have survived. Although the "Night of the Tear" has disappeared with the Nile floods, the Festival of Spring is still celebrated throughout Egypt, and in Luxor the Nile boatmen still carry the barque of their saint just as the Ancient Egyptians carried the sacred barque of Amun ▲ 408. But these surviving remnants are few and far between.
Saint Mark preaching in Alexandria (above).

THE COPTIC CHURCH

Since the 12th and 13th centuries Egypt has been a predominately Muslim country. As the number of Arab garrisons increased the Coptic Christians gradually converted to Islam, often to escape the financial penalties and social restrictions imposed on non-Muslims. Initially the Coptic Church welcomed the Arabs, who were seen as liberators.

The adoption of the Monophysite doctrine was probably, and primarily, a means of opposing the Byzantines who, by way of reprisal, gradually closed the Coptic churches and monasteries. By marginalizing Alexandria's Hellenized (Jewish and Greek) elite and maintaining local administration, the Arabs enabled the exiled bishops to return to their sees, allowing freedom of worship and authorizing synods. The burden of financial penalties and the increasingly clear affirmation of Muslim sovereignty ruined many monasteries and led to rebellions and conversions. Christians had to wear a distinguishing mark, and the rebuilding of ruined churches was forbidden. There were several mass conversions (in particular in 725, 832 and 1171), which continued throughout the following centuries, with another significant conversion in Upper Egypt in 1750. Since the 13th century the Copts have tended to congregate in Middle and Upper Egypt.

The Coptic abbot Shenute officiating at a Christmas mass in a Coptic church.

ISLAM IN EGYPT

The Sunni branch of Islam was subsequently imposed throughout Egypt. In spite of two centuries of Shi'ite domination (969–1169) by the Fatimids, Egyptian Islam was an orthodox form whose principal rite was that of the Shafi'ite school. The only remaining Shi'ites were the Persian traders in Cairo. The El-Azhar ▲ 294 Mosque perpetuated this

At prayer in the mosque (right) and a prayer mat embroidered with the one hundred names of Allah (below).

THE MAINSTAYS OF ISLAM

Islam was the religion taught in Mecca by the prophet Mohammed (born c. 570–580, died 632). On July 16, 622 Mohammed and his companions left Mecca for Medina, the date which marks the beginning of the "Hegira" (exile) or Muslim era. Islam preaches obedience to the only God, Allah, his prophet, Mohammed, and the book revealed to him, the Koran. The five religious duties of all Muslims are the *shahada* (profession of faith, that Allah is the only God and that Mohammed is His prophet), *salat* (prayer five times a day), *zakat* (charity), *sawm* (the fast of Ramadan) and, at least once during their life, *hajj* (the pilgrimage to Mecca).

orthodox form of Islam by educating most of the doctors of Islamic law (*ulama*) destined to become prayer leaders in Egypt. From the Mameluke period onward, the major issues that had troubled Islam in its early stages were resolved. Religious teaching decided on its line of approach and mystical theology was included in the technical and moral teaching disseminated by the intermediaries of the *ulama* class. The Jewish and Christian minorities enjoyed a clearly defined protected status.

FRACTURES AND DIVISIONS

This balance was maintained until the 19th century, which saw the abolition of protected status for Armenian orthodox minorities by Mohammed Ali in an attempt to guarantee their support, and the sudden arrival of the European powers in Egypt, who introduced a number of new and competitive religious communities.

"El-Azhar was gradually waking up, roused from its torpor by the sound of the sheikhs' voices as they taught their lessons, punctuated by the discussions that arose, often acrimoniously, between them and their pupils. The students crowded round, voices were raised, sounds became merged and

The Egyptian Copts were caught up in the process and classified as Catholic or orthodox Copts, of the Latin or Oriental rite, either independent or assimilated. In 1900 there was a total of nineteen different Christian and Jewish institutional rites. The Muslims attempted to respond to this new upsurge of minority groups by calling for a reinterpretation of the religious texts

the sheikhs were obliged to raise their voices even higher in order to make themselves heard. They were sometimes even forced to adopt stentorian tones to pronounce the phrase 'God is all-knowing', which brought the lesson to a close."**

Taha Hussein

and the modernization of the Islamic doctrine. Two main fracture lines were appearing around the constitution of the national movement, however: on the one hand, opposition between Egyptians (Copts and Muslims) and foreigners and, on the other, the less apparent opposition between Muslims and other groups. There seemed to be an initial movement away from a liberal Egypt toward Nasser's Egypt. Religious matters were relegated to a position of secondary importance as successive regimes became increasingly secular in outlook, in spite of a very strong Islamic representation.

DEMANDS OF ISLAM. With the creation of the Muslim brotherhoods in 1928, the religious demands of Islam were very much in evidence, reaching a climax in the early 1980's when Islamic law was declared the primary source of judicial law. A parallel Coptic movement was established, while the expulsions of the Nasser regime considerably reduced the status of other communities. In 1956 the disappearance of the ancient Jewish community, the direct descendant of Alexandrian gnosis, was closely linked to the development of the Coptic Church. Against this background the future of the Coptic Church in Egypt and its four million worshippers became the symbol of Islamic-Christian cohabitation. It encountered increasingly bitter antagonism from the Islamic groups, who favored a return to the original hierarchy that recognized the protected status but not the equality of other religious groups. It should, however, be remembered that this exclusive form of Islam is in the minority, while the brotherhoods (*turuq*) and traditional structures of Azharist Islam continue to be the mainstays of religion in Egypt.

FRIDAY PRAYERS AT THE EL-HUSSEIN MOSQUE
Friday is a public holiday in Egypt and the day when Muslims gather at the mosque for their weekly prayer meeting.

ARCHITECTURE

The earliest Egyptian constructions, which dated from the end of the Neolithic age, appear to have been made of branches and wattle daubed with clay. There is evidence to suggest that brick was used to build houses in c. 4000 BC. The desire to create "mansions of eternity" for their dead led the Egyptians to replace mudbrick with stone in the funerary architecture of the Thinite period, a process which culminated in the construction of the funerary complex of Djoser at Saqqara in c. 2700 BC. From then on stone was used in all funerary architecture, while brick continued to be used for more utilitarian structures. Egyptian technology in the field of architecture was thus established during the Old Kingdom and lasted until the Roman period.

BRICK
During the annual floods the Nile carried and deposited the silt used to make bricks, thus providing a simple and inexpensive material for domestic architecture. The Egyptians used different types of bonding, such as that based on regular curves (above). Two types of roof were used in mudbrick architecture: the flat roof and the soffitless vault.

Today it is possible to date excavated remains more accurately using the cartouches found on the bricks.

MAKING MUDBRICK
The coarse impurities were removed from the clay soil, which was mixed with water to form a paste. Straw or grass was added to the paste to limit shrinkage and prevent cracking during drying. The mixture was kneaded, molded and dried in the sun.

SOFFITLESS VAULT
By using bricks added in successive, sloping layers it was possible to construct a soffitless vault. The arched vault was not transposed into stone architecture.

FLAT ROOFS
Flat roofs were made from reeds placed across beams and covered with clay.

STONE QUARRIES

Stone was extracted from two types of quarries, which were often a long way from the building site. Hard rock (sandstone and granite) was extracted from open quarries and soft rock (limestone and tufa) from closed quarries. The quarriers chipped out a groove along the line of the blocks to be extracted. Wooden wedges were then inserted and kept well soaked so that they swelled and shattered the stone, separating it from the rock face. The blocks were then rough hewn and taken to the point of embarkation.

Well-soaked wooden wedges were used to shatter the stone.

TRANSPORTING OBELISKS

According to an account by Pliny – and contrary to the symbolic representation (below) – the Nile floods were used to transport obelisks, which were carried submerged between two boats. This reduced their weight by one third.

On sandy or stony ground the sled was pulled over wooden rollers.

On clay soil the ground was soaked to make it slide more easily.

WATER LEVEL
The Egyptians used water and the principle of communicating vessels to ensure that foundations were horizontal.

FOUNDATIONS
Once the horizontal was established, it was a matter of leveling the rock or building low, parallel brick walls and filling the space between them with sand to the required level.

LEVELING
A channel, which was either built of clay or hewn out of the rock, was dug around the perimeter of the site and filled with water to determine the overall horizontal level.

Secondary channels were also built to create a second point of reference. A cord and two stakes made it possible to apply this horizontal to any point on the site.

BONDING
The Egyptians used a regular, isodomous type of bonding with (mortarless) open butt joints (1). Where economy was a priority, due to the need to transport the stone, irregular bonding was used (2). For wide walls (pylons) a dry-stone infill was used between two facings (3).

ERECTING AN OBELISK
The obelisk was hoisted horizontally, by means of a continuous series of balanced levers, onto a purpose-built platform which incorporated a sand-filled groove. The block was raised to its vertical position by draining away the sand on which it rested. Under the effect of its own weight, the obelisk gradually righted itself and slid into place. The most delicate operation involved removing the sled which separated it from its pedestal. This was done by using sacks of sand which were gradually emptied.

TOOLS

Most of the tools used for cutting and hewing stone were made of copper or diorite (a very resistant stone). A wooden level square, a vertical level, diorite chisels, a mallet, a brace, a wedge and a cord, which was used for marking out and measuring (above).

LIGHTING

To create enclosed spaces the Egyptians used light from the roof rather than the façade. The light filtered in through gaps or stone tracery.

CEILINGS

Ceilings were made of flagstones. The span of the flags was no greater than the size of the stones used (13–16 feet). A system for draining away water was introduced during the Late period.

CONSTRUCTION

The Egyptians had a limited number of lifting mechanisms at their disposal. The simplest way of raising stone blocks was by means of a ramp which was built using successive layers of sand infill.

Each layer of sand corresponded to a layer of blocks and the height of the ramp increased with each new layer. The last two layers consisted of lintels and flagstones together, which formed the ceiling.

FINISHINGS

The building was gradually cleared so that the finishing of the columns and decoration of the walls could be carried out from the ceiling downward. The fragile bas-reliefs, reserved for the interior walls, were rough-hewn with an adz, carved with copper, wood and stone tools and finally polished with an abrasive paste.

● RELIGIOUS ARCHITECTURE IN PHARAONIC EGYPT

The temple was both the house of a particular god and a symbolic representation of the universe. The columns with their plant-inspired decorations symbolized the terrestrial world which supported the cosmic world, represented by starred ceilings. The focal point of the edifice evoked the place where the universe was created and where the divinity resided. The sacred precinct was isolated by an enclosure wall. There were two main types of temple: the open, solar temples of the Old Kingdom (which have mostly disappeared) and the so-called "classic" temples, with enclosed sacred areas, which are typical of the New Kingdom and subsequent periods.

Archaic chapels, the predecessors of the naos.

Alabaster altar, situated in the center of the court in front of the obelisk, at Abu Ghurob. The four offering tables faced the four points of the compass.

TEMPLE OF ABU GHUROB (1st Dynasty) The temple, built by Niuserre on the edge of the desert, consists of an obelisk (115 feet) standing on a truncated, pyramidal base (65 feet). The complex is surrounded by an enclosure wall (360 feet x 262 feet) and is reached via a triple-porticoed access temple and an ascending causeway. About 30 yards to the south is a painted brick replica of a barque.

TEMPLE OF MENTUHOTEP AT DEIR EL-BAHRI (11th Dynasty)

The sepulcher of Mentuhotep introduced a new dimension to funerary architecture. An access ramp leads to the two terraces supported by square-columned porticos. It is thought that the complex was once surmounted by a pyramid. To the west was a temple reserved for private worship which consisted of a sanctuary and a hypostyle hall as well as a porticoed court.

TEMPLE OF QASR ES-SAGHAH
(Middle Kingdom) This incomplete sanctuary to the north of the Faiyum ▲ *361* has retained its archaic appearance: its limestone bonding consists of alternate header and front blocks. Inside the seven adjacent chapels are flanked by pillars.

TEMPLE OF MEDINET MADI (12th Dynasty)

This small temple, built to the south of the Faiyum ▲ *361* by Amenemhet III and Amenemhet IV, is the only Middle-Kingdom temple that can be dated with any certainty. It is less than 33 feet wide. It was dedicated to Sobek, god of the Faiyum, and Renenutet, goddess of the harvest ● *60*. A portico with two papyrus columns and closed capitals precedes the sanctuary hall where three niches contain statues of the divinities.

KIOSK OF SENWOSRET I AT KARNAK
(12th Dynasty) The kiosk or barque shrine was discovered by Henri Chevrier inside one of the pylons of the Great Temple of Amun-Re ▲ *404*. This beautifully proportioned edifice, with grooved cornices and square pillars, was designed to act as a "way station" during processions. The sacred barque was carried up the slipway situated in the center of the steps. With its four rows of sixteen pillars decorated with religious scenes, the kiosk foreshadowed the temples of later periods.

With the establishment of a colonial empire
(New Kingdom), the religious domain became
increasingly wealthy. Amun, divine protector of
Thebes, became the imperial divinity of Egypt,
and his priests of Amun enjoyed significant
political power. Mudbrick buildings and annexes
(warehouses, silos, stables, schools and
accommodation) were added to the temples. The
religious complex became an economic, cultural
and political center which played an important
part in everyday life. The Temple of Khonsu in
Karnak provided the
archetype for temples
which prevailed until
the Byzantine period.

The naos of Horus at
Edfu. From the Late
period onward, naos
were constructed from
stone and monoliths.

TEMPLE OF KHONSU AT KARNAK ▲ *412*
The sandstone structure (246 x 98 feet) was
built toward the end of the reign of
Ramesses III, on the site of a temple dating
from the reign on Amenhotep III. The
sloping, outer walls surrounded a closed
area whose architecture was
dedicated to the service of
things sacred.

PYLON
The pylon
formed the façade
of the temple and
consisted of two piers closed
by a monumental gate, symbolizing
the horizon.

ESPLANADE
The esplanade or
colonnade which
preceded the pylon
was used to celebrate
the rites of entry,
which could be
attended by ordinary
citizens.

Hypostyle
hall

1st court

The campaniform capitals of the Ptolemaic period can be simple or multilobate. Several rows of papyrus umbels are carved on the bell of the capital, while their stems and the cord which binds them are carved on the shaft of the column.

RAMESSEUM (20th Dynasty)

The Osiride colossi which punctuate the façade of the Ramesseum ▲ *432* are an indication of the funerary nature of the Temple of Ramesses II.

HYPOSTYLE HALL
A raised portico opens onto the hypostyle hall which was reserved for divine appearances.

DIVINE APARTMENTS
These included the shrine of the ceremonial

barque, a vestibule lit by a light well and the naos containing the god's statue.

"DROMO"
The monumental causeway leading to the Temple of Khonsu was guarded by stone crio-sphinxes (sphinxes with rams' heads).

COURT
The court was the public part of the temple where the elite were admitted during festivals. It was surrounded by a double row of columns, whose papyrus capitals were decorated with closed buds.

TEMPLE OF THE ATEN AT TELL EL-AMARNA

The political and religious reforms of Amenhotep IV imposed the Aten as the unique and universal solar god. The king revived the principle of the cult of ancient Heliopolis in an open-air temple consisting of two main sections: the "jubilee house" (*per hai*), with a pylon and a sixteen-columned hypostyle hall, and the "discovery of the Aten" (*Gem Aten*), consisting of six consecutive courts with three hundred and sixty-five offering tables. The elongated proportions of the temple, which was constructed from small stone blocks (*talattat*) reflect a new architectural concept ▲ *378*.

| 2nd court | 3rd court | 4th court | 5th court | 6th court |

Necropolises were always set apart from the world of living and were situated outside the towns and cities, on the edge of the desert. The very first tombs consisted of an underground burial chamber and a superstructure for the purpose of funeral worship. The form of the proto-Dynastic tombs, constructed in perishable materials, was reproduced in the brick mastabas (bench-like tombs) of the Thinite period. From the 3rd Dynasty onward the use of stone and research into the superposition of several mastabas resulted in the development of the pyramids, which were still exclusively royal. During the Middle Kingdom mastabas were replaced by rock tombs.

CENOTAPH OF QUEEN MER-NEITH AT UMM EL-QA'AB
(1st Dynasty)
These so-called royal burials in the region of Abydos ▲ 386 are surrounded by secondary tombs.

The mudbrick superstructure, which no longer exists, was probably in the form of a tumulus.

The entrance was flanked by two funeral stelae.

Mudbrick vault with an overhanging arch.

SATELLITE TOMB OF A FAMILIAR
Familiars of the royal family were buried in small tombs near the royal sepulcher. Mudbrick vaults were constructed for the first time.

PYRAMID OF DJOSER AT SAQQARA (3RD DYNASTY) ▲ 346
To recreate the shape of the original tumulus, the architect Imhotep built a first, four-step, pyramid above an initial mastaba where several stages of construction are evident.

TOMB OF QUEEN MER-NEITH AT SAQQARA (1st Dynasty)
In the edifice above the underground burial chamber, several rooms contained the funeral paraphernalia. The façades echo the fortified, wood enclosure walls of the period. The structure was stuccoed and painted in symbolic colors. A false door in the façade overlooking the Nile allowed the soul of the deceased to escape.

BURIAL FIELDS
Private sepulchers, grouped together in vast cemeteries, were designed along the same lines. A rectangular stone or brick structure with sloping walls contained several decorated rooms, including a chapel with a stele, a false door, an offering table and the *serdab*, a sealed chamber which housed statues of the deceased. A shaft in the roof of the mastaba gave access to the burial chamber.

FUNERAL COMPLEX OF PEPY II
(5th Dynasty)
From the 4th Dynasty royal funeral complexes consisted of a "lower" or access temple linked by an ascending, covered causeway to the "upper" temple and pyramid. The funeral temple consisted of a public area, outside the enclosure wall, and a private area adjoining the pyramid. The king's three wives each had their own pyramid and funeral temple.

COVERED CAUSEWAY
The ascending causeway was covered along its entire length. The few inches left between the ceiling flags let in a little light.

TOMB OF PRINCE AMENEMHET AT BENI HASSAN ▲ *374*
(12th Dynasty)
A portico with two grooved columns precedes this new type of sepulcher, hewn out of the rock. A four-columned hall gives access, via a double door, to the sacred niche. The access shaft to the burial chamber runs along the south wall.

BONDING ON THE PYRAMID OF DJOSER
To ensure the solidity of the structure, Imhotep invented a system of bonding in which the layers of stone (consisting of 8-foot thick slabs) were inclined and parallel to the outer wall. During the final stage of construction a six-step pyramid was built around the entire structure.

● FUNERARY ARCHITECTURE IN PHARAONIC EGYPT

From the 18th Dynasty onward the places of worship and burial in royal tombs were clearly separated. The principle of the rock-cut tomb or hypogeum is simple: an axial corridor, sloping downward into the cliff, serviced a series of small and large pillared halls. During the Saïte period the structure of the tombs became more complicated and veritable funerary palaces were constructed. To prevent plundering, which had become a common occurrence, the tomb entrance was filled with sand and debris. Under the Ptolemies tombs were dug beneath towns and cities and the principle of separating the world of the living from that of the dead was abandoned.

NEW-KINGDOM ROYAL TOMBS IN THE VALLEY OF THE KINGS
The tomb of Amenhotep I was built according to the characteristic angular design of the 18th Dynasty.

From the 19th Dynasty onward an axial plan was adopted for tombs. A system of protective shafts replaced the granite portcullises of the pyramids.

ARTISAN'S TOMB AT DEIR EL-MEDINA
(19th and 20th Dynasties)
The artisans' tombs at Deir el-Medina ▲ 438 were individual or family tombs. A two-columned porch, surmounted by a small, constructed pyramid, opened onto a vaulted chamber beneath which lay the burial chamber. At the far end of the burial chamber was a niche containing a statue of the deceased.

TOMB OF THE VIZIER BOCHORIS AT SAQQARA
▲ *344* (16th Dynasty)

Like the Theban tombs of the same period, the tomb was based on the design of a rock temple but with a noticeably greater number of underground rooms and galleries.

TOMB OF PSUSENNES
(21st Dynasty)

The royal tombs of the Saïte period were all built within the enclosure wall of the Temple of Tanis ▲ *226*. These small tombs were built of limestone, granite and mudbrick.

NECROPOLIS OF KOM ES-SHOGAFA
(1st–2nd century BC)

The necropolis, with its complex arrangement of galleries around a circular shaft ▲ *192*, is a fine example of a collective tomb based on the Roman family principle.

GRAECO-ROMAN TOMB AT TUNA EL-JEBEL ▲ *377*
(c. 330 BC)

During the Graeco-Roman period tombs were built like funerary chapels. The false, vaulted walls of their façades were inspired by contemporary temples such as Dendera ▲ *388*.

● CIVIL ARCHITECTURE IN PHARAONIC EGYPT

Tiling in the palace of Ramesses II.

Floods and continual re-occupation have destroyed all trace of ordinary mudbrick dwellings. Stone was reserved for thresholds, column bases and door and window frames, while doors and columns were in wood. The layout of Egyptian houses, however prestigious or humble they may have been, was bi-polar, with the reception area separate from the living accommodation. All that remains today are the ruins of new towns built on the edge of the desert and suddenly abandoned, and the occasional remains of palaces which attest to the past splendor of these edifices.

ARTISAN'S HOUSE IN DEIR EL-MEDINA
(13th–20th Dynasties)
The consecutive rooms are rectangular in design. The living room, supported by two or three wooden columns, was preceded by a reception area. At the rear of the house a kitchen, with an oven and a cellar, opened onto a bedroom. Steps led up to the roof-terrace.

THE TOWN OF KAHUN
(12th Dynasty)
The town was built to accommodate the workforce used to construct the Pyramid of Senwosret III. It was surrounded by an enclosure wall and geometrically divided into districts, with a brick wall separating administrative workers and artisans.

THE VILLAGE OF DEIR EL-MEDINA
(19th–20th Dynasties)
Deir el-Medina ▲ 438 is an example of a village created from scratch, in response to a particular demand. It was built to accommodate the artisans working in the Valley of the Kings ▲ 417. The level of urban planning achieved by the Egyptians can be seen in the dense network of rows of adjoining houses, dissected by a north–south axis. The village was surrounded by an enclosure wall (426 x 164 feet). The houses were all built according to a similar layout. A warden's lodge stood at the town's only entrance.

1. Main entrance
2. Garden
3. Entrance hall
4. Living room
5. Bathroom
6. Bedrooms

7. Courtyard and grain silos
8. Outhouses and stables
9. Servants' quarters
10. Kitchens

HOUSE OF THE VIZIER NAKHT AT TELL EL-AMARNA
(18th Dynasty) ▲ 378
Like all prestigious dwellings, the house of Nakht stood in a vast enclosure which incorporated ornamental gardens. The outbuildings, reached through a service entrance, stood together in an area set apart from the house. The house itself consisted of private apartments and reception rooms.

THE PALACE OF RAMESSES III
(20th Dynasty)
The structure of the palace, which adjoins the funeral temple of Ramesses III at Medinet Habu ▲ 434, is organized around the throne room and echoes the principles of Egyptian houses.

CEILING IN THE PALACE OF AMENHOTEP III AT MALKATTA
The polychrome decoration, punctuated with floral motifs, alternates geometric spirals and heads of horned animals on a whitewashed, mortar revetment.

MILITARY ARCHITECTURE IN PHARAONIC EGYPT

Military architecture first appeared during the Archaic period and was developed during the Old Kingdom. The techniques of this type of architecture can be observed in the 12th-Dynasty Nubian fortresses built along Egypt's southern border to combat the threat from the kingdom of Kush. Built of mudbrick and strengthened by beams, they consisted of a glacis broken by a dry moat at the foot of the walls. The forts were designed to house a barracks, an administrative center and a temple. With the great conquests of the New Kingdom, Egyptian colonies were established in Lower Nubia and military structures became larger, more numerous and enriched by examples copied from the peoples of the Levant. They housed or defended Egyptian villages built in foreign lands.

FORTRESS OF BUHEN
The fortress stands at the northernmost point of a defensive line, dating from the Middle Kingdom, which stretched from the second cataract to the forts of Semna and Kumma in the south. These three mudbrick forts made use of the natural relief of the terrain which was partially recut.

Diagrammatic façade of a pre-Dynastic palace.

GATE IN THE ENCLOSURE WALL OF MEDINET HABU
(19th Dynasty)
This type of crenelated entrance tower ▲ *436* was based on Oriental examples. Their name (*migdol*) means "tower" in Hebrew. Here, it has no defensive role: apartments fill the two upper-level apartments. The outer façade of the sloping walls is reinforced by banquettes.

Plan of the
fortifications of
Buhen.

FORTRESS OF SEMNA

The fortress of Semna and its counterpart
Kumma, on the opposite bank of the Nile,
controlled access to Egypt from the
south. The bastioned wall, built on
constructed granite
foundations, follows the
relief of the terrain. The
defenses are
completed by a large
moat.

FORTIFICATIONS OF BUHEN

A low wall precedes
the moat. Then
comes a defense wall
with a glacis, built on
the slope of the moat
and flanked by semi-
circular bastions
pierced by a number
of loopholes. The
last fortification
(about 16 feet thick)
is punctuated at
regular intervals by
square towers. A
rampart walk,
protected by
crenelations, runs
around the top of the
two walls. Two oblong
towers protect the
main entrance and
stand either side of an
inner moat crossed
by a footbridge.

History of archeological excavations
Early travelers and the Egypt Expedition

From the time of the Crusades the Orient and Egypt became a popular destination for many travelers who wanted to see the lands of the Bible for themselves. The 16th-century fascination for the ancient world and the advances made in understanding led to an increased interest in past civilizations. Religious, diplomatic and business expeditions were joined by people in search of exoticism or with a thirst for discovery. One such military and scientific expedition, led by Napoleon Bonaparte in 1798, heralded the birth of archeology in Egypt. As well as leading his troops in a campaign to free Egypt from the Ottoman oppressor, Bonaparte also took with him a scientific and artistic mission led by Dominique Vivant Denon.

EGYPT EXPEDITION'S SCIENTIFIC MISSION

The Egypt Expedition's scientific mission consisted of several famous European scientists, sixteen cartographers and topographers, and more than 160 artists and technicians. Their task was to methodically collect information in areas as widely varied as architecture, geography, natural science and the humanities. This information was published collectively in 1809 as *La Description de l'Egypte* and consisted of eleven volumes of plates (three thousand drawings) and nine of text.

Following Champollion's decipherment of hieroglyphics in 1822, interest in the mysteries of Egyptian civilization increased even further. There followed a period during which European consuls organized the systematic plunder of the most important archeological sites, either on their own account or on behalf of their governments who wanted to enhance their country's museum collections. The most famous of these were the (Italian) French consul Bernadino Drovetti ▲ 468, the British consul Henry Salt ▲ 474 and the

PURVEYORS OF MUSEUMS

Swedish consul Anastasi. To ensure the success of their treasure hunt, they recruited such adventurers as Jean-Jacques Rifaud, who worked for Drovetti and who can be considered as the forerunner of modern archeology. He was the first to take interest in the less spectacular urban sites such as the houses of Arsinoe, and to try to identify the different layers he encountered, thus introducing the concept of stratigraphy.

Henry Salt (above) and Champollion (right).

CHAMPOLLION

As a member of the Franco Tuscan expedition (1828) Champollion ▲ 216 was not exempt from this thirst for scientific discovery. With the Italian Rossellini he combed the length and breadth of the Nile Valley as far as Abu Simbel ▲ 464, carrying out architectural and epigraphic surveys of the monuments they discovered.

They acquired bas-reliefs from the tomb of Sety I and several bronzes found in Thebes. On his return he submitted a report to the *pasha* of Cairo on the "conservation of the monuments of Egypt", which suggested that excavations should be controlled and sites protected from damage caused, in particular, by the Egyptian *fellaheen* (archeological

sediment in fact made excellent fertilizer for crops). At the same time (in 1821) John G. Wilkinson, the founding father of British Egyptology, compiled an inventory of the sites and drew the first plan of Thebes during his excavations in and around the city. Prussia was also affected by this passion for Ancient Egypt. In 1842 Frederick William IV

sent the philologist Karl Richard Lepsius to compile a catalogue of monuments and gather a collection of predominately epigraphic texts for the Ägyptisches Museum in Berlin ▲ 470. In 1866 he made a return visit. Champollion's German counterpart, Lepsius was the founder of the German School of Egyptology.

BELZONI

At the beginning of the 19th century the Italian Giovanni Battista Belzoni undertook several archeological investigations on behalf of Henry Salt. In 1817 he discovered the tomb of Sety I in Thebes ▲ 424 and, in 1818, the entrance to the Pyramid of Khafre (Chefren) ▲ 340. Drawings by Belzoni during his excavations (opposite and above). Drawing by Jean-Jacques Rifaud (left).

The director of excavations entering the Tomb of Amenhotep III, discovered in Thebes in 1898.

During the second half of the 19th century Auguste Mariette, or "Mariette Pasha" (1821–81), introduced a more systematic approach to field research and a hitherto non-existent concern for Egypt's national heritage. Mariette, a former grammar lecturer, was above all a committed field researcher who, from 1851 until his death, led numerous pioneering excavations. An important first discovery (the Serapeum at Saqqara) encouraged him to increase the number of on-site projects.

Although his methods may be questionable, he was instrumental in founding the Egyptian Department of Antiquities in 1859 (which centralized and supervised archeological research) and the Bulaq Museum in Cairo in 1863. From then on all antiquities found on Egyptian soil had to be preserved in the museum. This was a watershed in the history of Egyptian archeology.

GASTON MASPERO

When Mariette died in 1881 he was replaced as head of the Department of Antiquities by Gaston Maspero (1846–1916), professor of archeology at the Collège de France. Maspero continued his work in the field (excavation and restoration) and gathered around him an international team of researchers. Toward the end of the 19th century the first archeological organizations were created and, in 1890, Maspero founded the École d'Archéologie Orientale, forerunner of the IFAO. Two years later the British set up the Egypt Exploration Fund which was followed in 1898 by the German Deutsche Oriental-Gesellschaft. For more than fifty years, Egyptian archeology was a colonial affair and it was not until 1952 that an Egyptian actually became head of the Department of Antiquities which, until then, had been under French direction.

Bulaq Museum (left) and Mariette Pasha (right).

Birth of Egyptology

It was during this period that archeology became a science in its own right and not just a source of supply for epigraphists. The key figure in this development was incontestably the British archeologist Flinders Petrie (1853–1942), engaged by the Egypt Exploration Fund in 1882, whose methods gained a following and who formed an entire generation of researchers. As a prehistoric specialist he favored the less spectacular sites of the pre- and proto-Dynastic periods. He was a meticulous and methodical man who considered the slightest clue indispensable to an understanding of ancient civilizations. He drew plans and cross-sections of the smallest architectural structures, recorded successive levels of occupation and compiled indexes and made drawings of shards, flint tools and other objects he discovered. He was the first to realize that pottery, which developed in form and decoration over the ages, could act as a sort of "A–Z of ancient ruins" and provide chronological indicators of the different archeological layers. The concepts of typology and stratigraphy, which

are the central principles of modern archeology, were thus applied to Egyptology and enabled Petrie to establish comparative chronologies with neighboring civilizations. Petrie's methods were perfected throughout the 20th century and,

in 1958, UNESCO's Nubian rescue project provided an ideal opportunity for the further development of research specialisms, whether in specific periods of Egyptian history (Byzantine and Arabic civilizations) or indeed in particular areas of specialist information which contributed to the overall fund of archeological knowledge (palynology, paleontology and the study of ceramics).

The British archeologist Flinders Petrie (above) and the excavations of Dahshur, which took place in 1894 (left).

HISTORY OF ARCHEOLOGICAL EXCAVATIONS
RESCUE OPERATIONS

In 1954 Gamal Abd el-Nasser decided, for economic reasons, to build the Aswan High Dam, which would mean flooding the Nile Valley for a distance of over 312 miles, in other words the whole of Nubia as far as the second cataract. Christiane Desroches-Noblecourt and Sarwat Okasha called upon the international community to intervene, with a view to surveying and protecting the region that would be affected by the flooding. In January 1955 the director of UNESCO went to Nubia and, a few months later, the CEDAE (Centre d'Étude et de Documentation sur l'Égypte Antique) was established. An international rescue program was launched which involved carrying out surveys (to compile a complete inventory of sites under threat), making drawings, excavating specific sites and mounting rescue operations for the most important monuments.

Moving the blocks from the Temple of Abu Simbel.

The movable dam used to dismantle the flooded Temple of Philae.

PHILAE

The Temple of Philae, already partially flooded by the construction of earlier barrages, was rescued in the same way as the Temple of Abu Simbel. The stone blocks were simply dismantled and rebuilt on Agilkia, which was redesigned (with the help of dynamite) to reproduce the topography of Philae. The bas-relief texts made it possible to reconstruct the gardens of Isis to whom the temple was dedicated.

Some of the rescued monuments were given to countries taking part in the project. Others (the temples of Amada, Kalabsha, Abu Simbel and Philae ▲ 462), were moved and rebuilt well above the water level. Still others, such as the fortress of Buhen, were left to their fate.

Outline plan for dismantling the north wall of Abu Simbel.

ABU SIMBEL RESCUE OPERATION

In 1955 the CEDAE carried out photographic and photogrammetric surveys of the façades, paintings and epigraphic texts of Abu Simbel. Three rescue plans were considered. The first involved constructing a barrage to protect the site of Abu Simbel, while the second proposed raising each temple in a single block above the 200 elevation mark. The third (which was adopted) meant cutting the monuments into blocks and moving them 210 feet further up the cliff. The first stage of the operation involved getting the buildings out of the water. This was achieved by installing an 82-foot-high movable dam and pumping stations. The façades of the temples were then covered with sand to protect them from possible damage by falling rocks during the next stage: the leveling of the cliffs above the temples. During the actual dismantling of the monuments the blocks were often cut by hand because of the fragility of the sandstone, in spite of its being strengthened by injections of epoxy resin. Weighing over 11 tons each, 1,036 blocks were cut, numbered and transported further up the cliff. During reconstruction they were fixed to a concrete superstructure according to their original position and orientation. Each temple was then protected by a reinforced concrete vault to support the weight of the debris of rocks used to reconstruct the two hillocks which had originally surmounted them. It took three years and a 3,000-strong workforce to complete the operation. The temples were officially opened on September 22, 1968.

Marking the blocks of the Temple of Philae during the rescue operation.

A photogrammetric survey (left) of part of the entrance to the Temple of Ramesses II at Abu Simbel ▲ 464 and a photograph (right) of the same section. Photogrammetry makes it possible to determine the dimensions of a photographed object by measuring photographic perspectives. The process was used by UNESCO during the Abu Simbel rescue operation to facilitate the cutting and reconstruction of the temple blocks.

The monuments of Pharaonic Egypt are several thousands of years old and often badly disfigured by the ravages of time. The work of the archeological architect is slow and painstaking and consists of "unraveling" the architectural history of the monuments, curing the disorders from which they are suffering and restoring their original appearance. Restoring a monument is not simply a matter of patching up or rebuilding a badly damaged wall. It means taking it apart stone by stone in order to understand the circumstances in which it was constructed and the materials used. The work of the architect is therefore indissociable from that of the archeologist, and a piece of restoration often leads to a major archeological discovery.

Before undertaking any form of restoration work architects carry out systematic photographic and graphic surveys of each of the monument's façades. They then dismantle it, using a crane, stone by stone and layer by layer, from the top. Each of the dismantled blocks, as well as those found near the edifice, is recorded, numbered, photographed and stored in the so-called "stone museum".

SUBSIDENCE
The sandstone and limestone used at Karnak ▲ 404 contain high levels of sea salt. When the stone comes into contact with dampness the salt crystals lose their stability and re-crystallize on the surface of the stone blocks. The crust thus formed causes several inches of the stones to crumble or subside.

AREA OF EVAPORATION

sol

▨ CAPILLARY FRINGE
▥ WATER TABLE
▤ DAMPNESS CONTACT

> "ALTHOUGH AN ARCHITECT'S LIFE IS, OF COURSE, SPENT ON SITE, IT IS ALSO SPENT IN AN OFFICE OR LABORATORY."
>
> JEAN VERCOUTIER

CONSOLIDATING STONES

As a general rule, restorers consolidate crumbling stones with ethyl silicate injections and restick broken ones.

Any blocks which prove too badly damaged to be reused are replaced by new, made-to-measure blocks.

RECONSTRUCTING A FAÇADE

The fragments of carved stone are collected and identified. Once the blocks have been

CLEANING A STATUE

The surface of the statue is cleaned by means of a high-pressure jet, which is made up of a mixture of sand and water.

reconstructed, they are then assembled like a giant jigsaw puzzle. This was the method used to rebuild the sections of one of the walls of the tomb of Montuemhet in the Valley of Asasif, Thebes ▲ 425.

RE-ASSEMBLING A MONUMENT

Monuments are re-assembled in accordance with the Charter of Venice, which states that the final state of a building must be respected and must therefore incorporate all the

changes that it has undergone during its history. The stones found near the monument are sometimes used. Ruined foundations are replaced by red-brick masonry.

"TALATTAT"

During the restoration of the ninth pylon of the Temple of Karnak ▲ *404*, thousands of stones used in its foundations were found to have come from monuments dating from the Amarnian period ● *42* which were destroyed after the reign of Akhenaten. Twelve thousand of these standard-sized (10.2 x 9.8 x 19.7 inches), sandstone blocks (*talattat*) were saved. Most of them had extremely well-preserved carved and painted decorations.

RESTORING A STATUE

The various fragments found scattered inside the tomb of Montuemhet, in Thebes, were identified and assembled to reconstruct the statues shown above.

"WHITE CHAPEL" OF SENWOSRET I

The blocks of this 12th-Dynasty chapel ▲ *413* were reused in the 18th Dynasty foundations of the third pylon of the Temple of Karnak. They were discovered in 1938 by the architect Henri Chevrier. After patiently reconstructing the chapel on paper (anastylosis) he was able to rebuild the complete edifice.

RESTORING A SARCOPHAGUS

After the difficult task of identification, the wooden sarcophagus is painstakingly cleaned and reassembled piece by piece. The next stage is concerned with replacing the fragments of *pâte de verre* which together form the decoration.

SORTING "PÂTE DE VERRE" FRAGMENTS

The fragments of *pâte de verre* inlay found in a tomb are carefully sorted, identified and replaced.

CLEANING A MUMMIFIED CAT

Cats' mummies are often badly damaged. The sand must be cleaned away before they can be studied and sometimes X-rayed.

RESTORING COLORS

Carved and painted wall decorations are reproduced on transparent, plastic film as well as being photographed. Polychrome decorations are cleaned by micro-abrasion and the painted surface sprayed with a chemical fixative.

IDENTIFYING SHARDS

Pottery fragments and shards which have been found inside a tomb are carefully laid out so that they can be sorted, classified and identified.

COPTIC MONASTIC ARCHITECTURE

Desert monasteries and hermitages constitute one of the main components of Coptic architecture. This essentially monastic architecture, with its well-defended entrances, was built of sun-dried or burnt brick which blended remarkably well with the desert environment in which it evolved. Unfortunately its formal development remains obscure. The longstanding state of ruin of most of these complexes and the many modifications undergone by others over the ages make it impossible to obtain a precise impression of their original structure, which is also difficult to date.

TROGLODYTE HERMITAGE
This type of hermitage consisted of an open courtyard, reached via a flight of steps, which opened onto various rock-cut chambers. Large numbers of these hermitages, most of which were occupied during the 6th and 7th centuries, were discovered near Esna ▲ 446.

DETAIL OF STONEWORK IN THE KELLIA HERMITAGES
The bricks were laid in horizontal layers, or in a herringbone pattern, and covered with a clay revetment which was decorated with wall paintings.

"QASR"
Inside the enclosure wall of certain fortified monasteries – for example the Deir es-Suriani ▲ 208 (Wadi Natrun) – was a large square courtyard (*qasr*), reached via a drawbridge. *Qasr* were designed to withstand long sieges and consisted of cellars, kitchens, quarters (cells) and a chapel.

PULLEY LIFT
The pulley lift was another means of defending the entrance of a monastery. It was also used to hoist provisions over the walls as was the case, for example, at the Monastery of St Anthony ▲ 265.

MONASTERY OF ST SIMEON AT ASWAN ▲ *459*
The monastery, surrounded by a high enclosure wall, is one of the largest in Egypt. Its main buildings were a church, refectory and a multistoried structure containing the monks' cells and various outbuildings.

MEDIEVAL MONASTERY
The Deir Mari Girgis (Monastery of St George) ▲ *359* is situated on the edge of the desert and enclosed by a high wall. Apart from its religious function, it once served to protect the Christian peasants who farmed the surrounding land. Until the early 20th century their dwellings occupied the first court of the monastery. The second court housed the church with its five naves flanked by side chapels. The complex was covered by irregularly shaped domes and vaults of varying heights. The choir was located on the axis of the entrance to the church and consisted of three apsidal rooms (*haykal*) with iconostases and niches. A funerary enclosure and various outbuildings completed the complex.

WALLED HERMITAGE
Numerous examples of another type of (walled) hermitage ▲ *209* were discovered on the site of Kellia ▲ *209* which was inhabited during the 4th and 5th centuries.

The religious architecture of Muslim Egypt is characterized by three main types of mosque. The earliest of these was built around a central, open courtyard surrounded by arcades on four sides, with a deeper portico on the side indicating the direction of Mecca. Alongside this classic-style mosque (subsequently reserved for the great mosques), the mosque with *iwan* was a very different and specifically Egyptian type of mosque which became widespread during the second half of the 15th century. The third type, inspired by the mosques of Istanbul, was introduced during the Ottoman period.

Niche of the mihrab.

CLASSIC-STYLE MOSQUE
The classic-style mosque, governed by the direction of Mecca, was often subjected to ingenious distortions to ensure that it followed the alignment of the streets. The El-Aqmar (Gray) Mosque in Cairo (1125) ▲ *290* is the oldest example of this type of mosque.

OTTOMAN-STYLE MOSQUE
The Malika Safiyya Mosque in Cairo (1610) is a fine example of an Ottoman-style mosque with its characteristic, domed sanctuary preceded by a open, porticoed courtyard.

MINBAR AND MIHRAB
The carved wood or sometimes marble minbar is the "pulpit" from which the *imam* preaches. The mihrab, the niche indicating the direction of Mecca, is richly decorated with polychrome marble, painted tiles and an archway whose festooned voussoirs are in alternately colored stone (a technique known as *ablaq*),

MOSQUE OF AS-SALIH TALAI (1160) ▲ *299*
This perfectly regular, classic-style mosque is the only example of a mosque with a porticoed facade.

OASIS MOSQUES
In less densely built, urban areas mosques are more regular in design. The minarets of oasis mosques tend to be squat, and in this aspect they resemble those that can be found along the Mediterranean coast.

NUBIAN MOSQUE
The mudbrick mosque of the village of El-Khallassab, with its straight staircase leading to the minaret, inspired Hassan Fathi's design for the mosque of Qurna el-Gedida ▲ *442*.

MOSQUE WITH "IWAN"
The mosque with *iwan* became widespread throughout Cairo from the 14th century onward. It consists of a central, covered area opening onto four *iwan* (vaulted areas) of unequal depth. The layout is reminiscent of the great halls of the Mameluke palaces ● *116*, from which the term *qaa* layout is derived. Since they were built at a time when towns and cities were already dense, most mosques with *iwan* are fairly modest in size. They often have several outbuildings, like the Qijmas el-Ishaqi Mosque (1480) ▲ *300* in Cairo, a remarkable example of the adaptation of this layout to a triangular plot of land at the tip of an island.

● MINARETS

The tip of most minarets is surmounted by a brass crescent. On the minaret of the Imam as-Shafi'i Mosque – as formerly on the minaret of the Ibn Tulun Mosque – this has been replaced by a boat.

It is from the top of the minaret, a functional element attached to every Islamic religious building, that the *muezzin* issues his call to prayer. Generally speaking Egyptian minarets are characterized by three clearly defined, vertical sections. The first section is based on a square, the second on an octagonal and the third on a circular layout. Some scholars have associated this arrangement with the famous Alexandrian Pharos Lighthouse.

MINARET OF THE IBN TULUN MOSQUE (879)
▲ *312*
The minaret with its external, spiral staircase is the only one of its kind in Egypt. It was inspired by the great Mosque of Samarra, in Mesopotamia, where Ibn Tulun was born.

MINARET OF THE SULTAN HASSAN MEDERSA (1363)
▲ *309*
The minaret, one of the most elegant in medieval Cairo, stands about 260 feet high. Apart from a square base, its sections are octagonal.

MINARET OF THE FARAG IBN BARQUQ KHANQA (1411)
▲ *329*
The arrangement of the sections of this minaret defies the established order. The square section is followed abruptly by the circular section, while the transitional, octagonal section is at the top.

MINARET OF THE EL-MU'AYYAD MOSQUE (1419)
▲ *298*
This is in fact a pair of minarets which do not stand at a corner of the mosque but on either side of the entrance adjoining the Bab Zuwaila.

MINARET OF THE ISKANDAR PASHA MOSQUE (1556)
This was one of the earliest Ottoman minarets in Cairo. Although it no longer exists, its details were preserved for posterity in a diagram by Pascal Coste (1787–1879) ▲ *190*.

BALUSTRADES AND PARAPETS

Balustrades and parapets are a characteristic feature of Mameluke-style minarets. They appear in each of the sections and consist of stone panels with an openwork design or sunk or bas-relief carving based on a technique used for the first time on the screens of the Sangar el-Gawli Mausoleum.

STALACTITES

Stalactites form one of the principal decorative elements of minarets. These small, cellular pendentives were used in particular to decorate the transitional area between sections.

CROSS-SECTION OF THE SECTIONS OF THE FARAG IBN BARQUQ MINARET

MINARET OF THE ABU EL-DAHAB MOSQUE (1774) ▲ 295
Although in fact Ottoman, the minaret harks back to the Mameluke style and was mainly inspired by the unusual square minaret of the nearby El-Ghuri Mosque.

There were two main types of monastic establishment built in Muslim Egypt: the *khanqa* of the Mameluke period and the *takiya* of the Ottoman period. *Khanqa*, intended to accommodate the members of a Sufi brotherhood, were very often (like *medersa*) also an excuse to erect an impressive mausoleum. *Khanqa* and *medersa* were built along similar lines: a cruciform layout with *iwan* of unequal sizes. *Takiya* were closely based on the layout of the *medersa* of Istanbul.

"TAKIYA"
The *takiya* – introduced during the Ottoman period – was an independent building which consisted of a raised, open courtyard surrounded by an arcade and overlooked by domed cells. The *iwan* was located more or less along the axis of the entrance and its far wall indicated the direction of Mecca. The *takiya* could be combined with another religious establishment (a *sabil-kuttab*, for example) as with the Mahmudiya *takiya* of 1750 (right).

"KHANQA"
The Baybars el-Jashankir *khanqa*, which dates from 1310, is the oldest in Cairo. It is a fine example of the distorted open-court, cruciform layout (below) which developed in Egypt and which was characterized by a tendency to extend the axial at the expense of the lateral *iwan*. In this case, the difference in the size is particularly noticeable: the lateral *iwan* are much reduced, while the *iwan* containing the niche of the mihrab is the more spacious of the two broad axial *iwan*.

"SABIL-KUTTAB"
The *sabil-kuttab* was a specifically Egyptian form of architecture which fulfilled the dual function of providing free drinking water and offering local children a basic education. Although the *sabil-kuttab* was sometimes combined with other establishments such as mosques, mausoleums or *medersa*, it was also an independent building. Large numbers of *sabil-kuttab* were built during the Ottoman period and in c. 1800 there were around three hundred in Cairo.

"KUTTAB"
The Koranic school occupied the upper-floor loggia and was reached through a separate entrance. A teacher, paid by the establishment, taught the Koran, reading and writing to local children.

"SHAZARWAN"
Some fountains had a built-in cooling system which involved running the water over a carved marble plaque (*shazarwan*) placed at an angle in a support in the fountain (*sabil*) room.

The Baybars el-Jashankir *khanqa* ▲ 292 was designed to house around two hundred Sufis. Some resided in the adjoining living accommodation (which no longer exists) while others lived in the three-storied cell block which overlooked the courtyard.

● ISLAMIC FUNERARY ARCHITECTURE

In spite of opposition from orthodox Islam (according to which a simple tombstone is sufficient), a monumental style of funerary architecture developed within the city walls in Cairo during the Fatimid period. It was introduced by the Shi'ite rulers and initially took the form of independent, square mausoleums surmounted by a cupola. The early cupolas were built in brick and later in stone. From the 13th century onward mausoleums were often attached to a *medersa* (college of religious education), according to a formula adopted long before in Syria. As time passed royal sepulchers gave rise to the construction of huge funerary complexes, which combined several different types of structures, usually situated in the "cities of the dead" on the outskirts of the city.

KIOSK
The cenotaphs of important (especially religious) people are placed in square kiosks whose roofs are supported by four marble columns.

SIMPLE CENOTAPH
Simple cenotaphs mark the entrance to an underground tomb where the bodies are buried. They always consist of a horizontal stone flanked by two stelae, one of which ends in a "cap" indicating the rank and sex of the deceased.

FUNERARY COMPLEXES
These edifices sometimes achieve impressive dimensions, as in the case of the adjoining complexes of the Emir Qurqumas (1506) and Sultan Inal (1456).

INDEPENDENT, CUPOLATED MAUSOLEUM

Unlike their more modest predecessors, situated in necropolises on the outskirts of the city, these monuments often reached monumental proportions and were built within the city walls.

Although mausoleums have an invariable basic structure – a square building surmounted by a circular cupola resting on a (usually) octagonal drum – their cupolas and drums became the object of widely varying architectural techniques.

Cupola sculpted with a zig-zag or "herringbone" design.

Striated or ribbed cupola.

SCULPTED CUPOLAS

From the Mameluke period onward, cupolas on tombs and mausoleums were built of sculpted stone, an art which had no equivalent in the Muslim world. Striations were the first motif used but these were soon replaced by a "herringbone" design. Both were soon superseded by starbursts which were subsequently combined with various kinds of arabesques. This skilled art form disappeared with the Ottoman conquest.

Cupola decorated with starburst motifs.

Cupola decorated with arabesques.

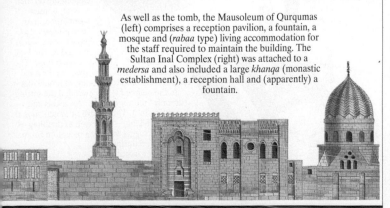

As well as the tomb, the Mausoleum of Qurqumas (left) comprises a reception pavilion, a fountain, a mosque and (*rabaa* type) living accommodation for the staff required to maintain the building. The Sultan Inal Complex (right) was attached to a *medersa* and also included a large *khanqa* (monastic establishment), a reception hall and (apparently) a fountain.

Contrary to many preconceived ideas of "Arab" houses as inward-looking spaces which are strictly private and always built around an open courtyard, Egyptian domestic architecture offers a wide range of different layouts which combine semi-public and private areas reserved for family life. For this reason many houses were not built with a courtyard, a feature reserved for the wealthiest households. However, all houses were organized around one central element: the main hall or *qaa*, which dictated the arrangement of the other rooms and was the center of the family's private life.

Layout of Beit as-Suhaymi ▲ 290.

OFFSET ENTRANCE
Access to houses was through an offset entrance with a stone porters' bench (*mastaba*).

COURTYARD
The entrance led into a courtyard, which was usually left unpaved. Opening onto the courtyard were various outbuildings: storerooms and stables, in particular, and sometimes an open reception room or *tahtabuch* for more modest visitors.

URBAN DEVELOPMENT
Courtyards in houses were a source of air and light as well as a semi-public area which compensated for the narrow streets and absence of public squares. The intensive urban development of the Mameluke period was accompanied by a reduction in the size of courtyards and the emergence of a vertical style of architecture.

"MAQAAD"
More important visitors were received in the *maqaad* (literally "the room for sitting in"). This north-facing, mezzanine loggia was mainly used during the summer months. It was reached via a staircase leading from the courtyard to the *qaa*.

"QAA"
Depending on their size, houses sometimes had several *qaa* (also known as *mandara*) situated on the first or second floor. The *qaa* was the focal point of family life: it provided the setting for meals and everyday activities as well as doubling as a reception room.

In the ceiling of one of the *iwan* was a north-facing air captor (*malqaf*), designed to capture the cool evening breezes. This ancient ventilation system was already in use in Pharaonic Egypt.

LAYOUT OF THE "QAA"

Qaa, which were sometimes impressive in size and always richly decorated, consisted of three sections. The slightly sunken, central section (known as a *durqaa*) usually had an ornamental basin with a fountain (*fasqiya*) and was lit by an octagonal lantern. It was flanked by two lateral *iwan* whose ceilings were not as high as that of the *durqaa*.

MAMELUKE "MAQAAD"

During the Mameluke period *maqaad* often took the form of huge loggias, like the one built in 1496 by the emir Mamay el-Saïfi. It opened onto an equally vast courtyard which is today the Midan Beit el-Qadi ▲ *288*. When houses were near a canal or lake the *maqaad* usually overlooked the water rather than the inner courtyard.

● "WAKALA"

Caravanserais (known as *khan, fonduq* or *wakala* depending on the period) were vast establishments which served as inns for traveling merchants, warehouses for imported merchandise and places in which to do business. They also provided accommodation for foreign residents and soldiers. Over the years their residential function was reinforced by the addition of a *rabaa*, a block of identical tenements, several stories high reached via a gallery.

ORGANIZATION OF A "RABAA WAKALA"
Caravanserais were organized around a large, central courtyard. The first floor was reserved for shops, some opening onto the street and others onto the courtyard. The accommodation for traveling merchants was on the upper floors. The *rabaa* proper might occupy several stories and had one or two separate entrances.

LAYOUT OF "RABAA" ACCOMMODATION
Rabaa accommodation consisted of duplex (or triplex) apartments. The main room (*riwaq*) overlooked the street or courtyard and was always on two levels. The first level also included the service areas (kitchen, etc.). The upper level(s) were occupied by bedrooms which opened onto the *riwaq*.

ENTRANCE
The entrance to the *wakala* was marked by a richly decorated, monumental gateway.

ARTS AND TRADITION

The River Nile and the marshes which were formed by its floods, the lakes of northern Egypt and the Faiyum, the Red Sea and the Mediterranean all provided the setting for navigation in Egypt. The scarcity of wood (acacia, sycamore and mulberry), coupled with the abundance of aquatic plants, were the determining factors in the construction of the many different and original types of boats used for fishing and hunting, transportation and war. Even divinities and the deceased took to the waters in their own sacred barques.

In 1954 one of the (dismantled) funeral barques of Khufu (Cheops) ▲ *335* was discovered. The 140-foot-long cedar-wood boat is a fine example of one of the methods of construction used by Old-Kingdom carpenters.

The keel-less hull was made of broad, jointed planks bound together with cords. On contact with the water the cords shrank and the wood swelled, thus ensuring that the boat was watertight.

From prehistoric times rafts were made from papyrus stems bound together with ropes made from plants. They were easily carried by hunters and fishermen and could be used in shallow water and marshes. The upswept prow and stern were the prototype for the characteristic design used over the centuries.

Drawings of boats were discovered on pieces of pottery from the Nagada period. They were probably made of papyrus and propelled by poles or oars. The prow and stern of this wooden pilgrim's boat (above), dating from the Old Kingdom, are made from papyrus clumps.

The transportation of Queen Hatshepsut's ▲ 409 two granite obelisks from Aswan to Thebes is illustrated in the bas-reliefs of the Deir el-Bahri. They were attached to a huge vessel made of sycamore with a specially reinforced deck to support their weight (410 tons), pulled by three rows of ten rowing boats.

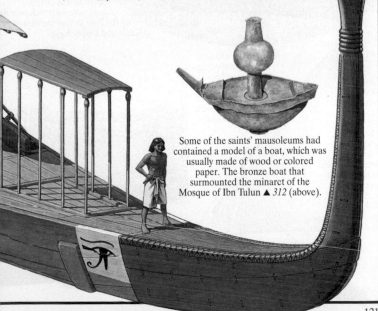

Some of the saints' mausoleums had contained a model of a boat, which was usually made of wood or colored paper. The bronze boat that surmounted the minaret of the Mosque of Ibn Tulun ▲ 312 (above).

121

There is evidence of the traditional use of ceremonial boats in Mameluke and Ottoman Egypt. During festivals such as the opening of the El-Khalig Canal ▲ *315*, the 15th-century sultans used an *ashari* or *dahabiya* (above), which was lavishly decorated for the occasio. In the 19th century the *dahabiya* was extremely popular among travelers sailir up the Nile to visit the sites of Middle and Upper Egypt.

Feluccas are still used for transporting stones and bricks used for building, sand, pottery and sometimes even animals.

Today transport vessels are made of iron rather than wood and traditional techniques are disappearing, except in the case of small fishing and pleasure boats.

The development of the Egyptian sail: with the increased transport of bulky freight, the central mast inclined toward the stern has been replaced by two or three masts; the hull has become much larger and a boom has been added to each sail to improve maneuverability.

Today there are more than four hundred of these fishing boats on Lake Manzala. Fish are caught with a rod, or with a net held flat just above the surface of the water, into which the mullet jump.

This simply designed, decked boat, or *zeheri,* is only found on Lake Manzala, whose shallow waters (you can stand up in them) require boats with a shallow draft. The *zeheri* enables fishermen to reach the marshy corners of this lagoon, which is teeming with fish. The vaulted cabin fitted with side ledges provides shelter for the crew in bad weather.

Felucca used for transporting stones.

Everyday life in Egypt is punctuated by rites of passage, as it is throughout the rest of the Muslim world. These mark the major stages in a person's life: birth, circumcision, marriage and death. In this respect religious and social ceremonies are still influenced by past rituals, which explains, in particular, the importance of funeral rites. The Copts, who have been in Egypt since time immemorial, still observe certain Pharaonic traditions as well as adopting Muslim customs such as circumcision.

Modern marriage ceremonies are becoming more "Westernized" and are often celebrated in public.

THE BRIDAL CARAVAN
The bride used to ride on a camel, while her dowry was carried by a caravan and thus exposed to public view. Today a car decorated with flowers and followed by a procession of vehicles has replaced this ancient tradition.

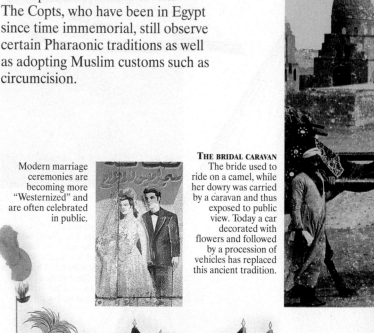

THE MARRIAGE CEREMONY
The signing – by the men – of the marriage contract (*katb el-kitab*) is followed by the payment of the dowry and, a week to ten days later, by a ceremony during which the day of the marriage (*khotba*) is arranged. On that day, according to tradition, the bride arrives in a procession to the sound of oboes and percussion instruments.

CIRCUMCISION
Boys are usually circumcized, between the ages of five and twelve, by a barber. It is the occasion of great celebration during which a procession is organized. Today the *mutahar* (boy to be circumcized) is dressed up, as if for a Western carnival.

COPTIC BAPTISM
Boys are baptized at forty days old and girls at eighty days. The ceremony is held earlier if the child is sickly. According to Coptic belief, if a child dies without baptism it will be reborn blind.

FUNERAL PROCESSION
The coffinless body of the deceased, wrapped in a white or green shroud, is carried by four close relatives. They are preceded by male relatives and friends and schoolboys carrying the Koran. The women of the family can be distinguished by a blue ribbon or scarf.

The social life of Egyptian people, whatever their religion or beliefs may be, is governed by religious festivals and pilgrimages. The only exception is Sham el-Nessim, which is a festival that marks the arrival of spring. The most festive period is Ramadan, the ninth month of the Muslim calendar (during which the Koran was revealed to the prophet Mohammed) and the month of the ritual fast. Another high point on the Muslim calendar is the last month of the year when the pilgrimage to Mecca is made. The worship of saints, whose anniversaries are commemorated by their *muled*, is another important and fairly characteristic aspect of popular Egyptian religion.

SHAM EL-NESSIM
This ancient festival corresponds to the first Monday after Easter. It is a day for family gatherings, traditionally celebrated in the open air, and a meal of *fshi* (salt fish), with eggs and green onions, is served.

"MULED"
The annual saints' festivals are the occasion for huge popular gatherings which may last for two or three days or as long as two weeks! From Cairo to the provinces, each town and village has its own *muled*, like the *muled* of El-Hagag celebrated in Luxor ▲ 397 (left), which is also the occasion for meetings of the Sufi brotherhoods. Muslim Egypt's most venerated saint is Sidi Ahmed el-Badawi who is buried in Tanta ▲ 211. The Coptic community also has its own *muled*.

Pilgrims (*hajj*) from Upper Egypt returning from
Mecca find the façade of their houses decorated with a fresco
consisting of conventional images of holy places, illustrations of
their journey, scenes from everyday life and symbolic animals.

"MULED" PROCESSIONS

Muled are celebrated by processions and dazzling displays of
lights in the towns and cities. The most impressive of these is
the procession that passes through Cairo on the occasion of
the Muled el-Nabi (festival of the Prophet's birthday).

"MAHMAL"

The *mahmal*, a richly decorated, empty litter
symbolizing the power of Egypt, was carried by
a camel at the head of the official caravan that
set out every year for Mecca. The tradition
ceased in 1926 when the Egyptian government
stopped sending the black carpet (made every
year in Egypt) which covered the four walls of
the Kaaba.

RAMADAN

Before the cannon announces
nightfall and the breaking of
the fast, tables are set out in
the streets of Cairo to serve the
iftar, the first meal of the day
during Ramadan.

The classic repertoire of Egyptian music and dance was compiled during the 19th century. Abdu el-Hamuli (1845–1901), who was the official singer of the khedive Ismaïl, revolutionized traditional music by making it accessible to the general public. Umm Kalsum, Farid el-Atrach, Mohammed Abd el-Wahab and Abd el-Halim Hafez, the popular idols of the Arab world, are his direct descendants, while Oriental dancers such as Leila Murad and Fifi Abdu have followed in the footsteps of the great singer and dancer, Almaza, the darling of 19th-century Egyptian high society. Ancient folkloric customs, together with a traditional orchestra and segregated dancing (the men in public and the women among themselves), are still practiced during the religious festivals and marriages.

"RABBABA"
The *rabbaba* is a wood instrument similar to the viol. There are two sorts: the two-stringed *rabbaba* of the *mughani* (singer) and the single-stringed *rabbaba* of the *shaer* (poet).

UMM KALSUM
Umm Kalsum (1898–1975) was a symbolic figure in the 20th-century Arab world. She sang of love, the glory of Egypt and the Muslim faith, and was extremely skilled at arousing the ecstatic emotion (*tarab*) experienced by Arabs when listening to poetry and music.

The *darbuka*, a drum made of skin and terracotta or metal, and the *dof*, which consists of skin stretched over a frame bordered with cymbals, are used to beat time for the dancers.

SAMIA GAMAL
Samia Gamal was a musical comedy star of the big screen during the 1940's and 1950's.

"OUD"
The *oud* is the ancestor of the lute, which dates back to early Egyptian antiquity. It is the key instrument of classical Arab music.

"QANUN" AND "NAI"
Together with the *oud*, the *qanun* and *nai* form the *taht*, the ancient orchestra which is today part of Egypt's classical repertoire. The *qanun*, which belongs to the cithara (zither) family, is placed horizontally across the player's knees and plucked with two finger guards worn on the index fingers. The *nai*, a reed flute even older than the *oud*, is the favorite instrument of the dancing dervishes.

Musical group from Slwa Oasis ▲ 256 celebrating a local festival.

129

During the 19th century it was difficult to gain access into private homes so Orientalist writers tended to concentrate on descriptions of streets and local life: craft trades, artisans and street sellers.

BASKETS
Baskets are woven from small palm leaves.

Although some of these are tending to disappear, the conviviality and industrious animation described by such writers as Gustave Flaubert, E.M. Forster and Lawrence Durrell can still be found at the heart of the crowds and traffic jams of modern towns and cities. Contemporary Egyptian writers such as Naguib Mahfouz, Yussef Idriss and Sonallah Ibrahim have used such settings as a background for their novels.

DONUT SELLER
Donuts are fried in oil and plunged into sugar syrup.

"FUUL" SELLER
The traditional Egyptian breakfast consists of well-boiled broad beans.

KNIFE GRINDER
The whine of blades against steel wheels is a familiar sound.

LICORICE-SYRUP SELLER
He rattles metal cups in his hand and carries a copper-plated metal pitcher slung on a strap across his shoulder.

PUBLIC SCRIBE
Love letters, business letters, legal letters: in spite of the increase in literacy, the public scribe is never short of customers.

MAT MAKER
Reed-fiber mats became popular during the 19th century, especially in Minuf, in the heart of the Delta region ▲ 205.

SHOE SHINER
Shoe shiners (often young children) work in stations, restaurants, barbers' shops and on street corners.

LIME-JUICE SELLER
The magnificently accoutered lime-juice seller.

POTTER
Clay pottery is made by both men and women.

IRONER
With his iron attached to his foot, he sprinkles the cloth with water as he works.

BARBER
He circumcizes young boys, shaves bridegrooms on their wedding day and gives the local men their daily shave.

MARQUETRY WORK
This craft is still used for tourist items and musical instruments.

> "WITH ITS TEA, THE ORIENT ENTERS MIDDLE-CLASS SITTING ROOMS; WITH ITS COFFEE IT ENTERS THE BRAIN."
>
> PAUL MORAND

"KANAKA"
The *kanaka* is used in the preparation of coffee.

During the Ottoman rule new products were introduced into Egypt: coffee appeared at the beginning of the 16th century, and tobacco arrived from Persia in the 17th century. Coffee soon became extremely popular in spite of the reservations that were expressed concerning this new beverage by certain religious authorities. The first cafés proved so successful that, in 1650, Cairo already had around 650 of these establishments and only a century later twice as many could be found. Nowadays there are around five thousand of them. These new meeting places have remained central to the social life of the urban male population in Egypt.

DRINKS
Coffee used to be drunk sweetened and scented with ambergris. Today it tends to be drunk *ziada* (which is extremely sweet) or *mazbut* (fairly sweet), occasionally *ariha* (with the merest hint of sugar) or alternatively *sada* (without any sugar) and sometimes scented with cardamom. Cafés also serve tea, which is not as heavy, and a variety of other infusions such as *karkade* (a hibiscus-based infusion), *yansun* (which is aniseed-based) and *erfa* (cinnamon-based). They do not serve alcoholic drinks.

STORYTELLERS AND MUSICIANS

In the past cafés were a place to listen to storytellers and musicians who used to turn up particularly just before major religious festivals. Nowadays customers can watch television and possibly an Egyptian or foreign film on video.

CAFÉS BY ANY OTHER NAME

Egyptian cafés were traditionally known as *qahwa*. Over the years and according to their particular function they have acquired different names. Some are still known as *nadi* (clubs), while others have become *cafitiria* (cafeteria) with a generally mixed clientele. The derivation of the term *horsa*, the cafés situated along the Mediterranean shore, remains unknown.

Cafés are an ideal place to while away the afternoon or evening hours. The choice of a regular café is based on political, professional and intellectual affinities.

Various board games such as backgammon, dominoes and draughts are played in cafés. It is also the place to hear the latest *nokat* (funny stories) and, of course, to smoke the hookah.

● FOOD "FUUL"

The aluminum *edra* has replaced the old copper pot of bygone days.

Fuul is an Egyptian specialty sold on corners by street sellers, and in shops. It is especially popular at breakfast time, although the Egyptians eat it at any time throughout the day. Traditionally *fuul* was simmered overnight on the embers of wood fires, particularly those used to heat the water pipes in the *hammam* (bath house). In fact *fuul* sellers used to leave their *edra* (the copper container in which the *fuul* was prepared) at the *hammam* in the evening and collect it the following morning.

1. Clean the broad beans and rinse under the cold tap. Dissolve the bicarbonate of soda in about 4 pints of water and soak the beans for 24 hours.

2. Rinse the beans and place in an earthenware casserole in twice their own volume of water. Cover and bring quickly to the boil.

5. Put the garlic purée into a dish and add the lemon juice and olive oil. Add the warm beans with some of their liquid.

6. Mix together and sprinkle with salt, chopped parsley and paprika.

134

INGREDIENTS

2 cups dried broad beans (Egyptian variety), 1 oz bicarbonate of soda, ³/₄ oz garlic, sea salt, 5 lemons, ³/₄ cup olive oil, table salt,

2 rounded tbs chopped parsley, paprika, radishes, spring onions, hard-boiled eggs.

3. Leave to simmer gently until completely cooked (approximately 2 hours), adding more boiling water if necessary.

4. Peel the cloves of garlic and place them in a mortar with some sea salt. Crush to a fine purée.

Serve hot with Arabic bread, radishes, spring onions and hard-boiled eggs.

The horse, which according to Arab legend was created from a handful of the south wind, was introduced into Egypt at the end of the Middle Kingdom during the Hyksos invasions. Under the pharaohs horses were mainly used as draft animals, and it was not until the Graeco-Roman period that a cavalry was formed. From the time of the Arab conquest the cavalry became the supreme military weapon and the horse, unlike its European counterpart, which was beginning to be used for agricultural labor, was reserved exclusively for fighting. Equestrian skill reached its peak during the Mameluke period, and at this time Arabic literature also acquired its great treatises on horsemanship.

**MAMELUKE
EQUESTRIAN SKILLS**
Once they had mastered the art of mounting bareback, the Mamelukes practiced vaulting onto their horse with and without a saddle, both with and without weapons. They continued their training with the twelve skills of classical horsemanship: use of the lance, use of the gourd, use of the mace, archery, swordsmanship, polo, jousting, hand-to-hand combat, the Mahmal ▲ *126*, hunting, use of the crossbow and racing.

Until the 18th century horses were reserved for warriors and members of the aristocracy. They only became more generally used during the 19th century, as illustrated by these drawings from *La Description de l'Egypte* (1809) showing different types of horsemen.

Illustrations from Ibn Ahnaf's *The Book of Horses* (1277): grooming (above) and schooling with the aid of a stick.

Arab tribesmen were less concerned with the training of the rider. Their traditional methods for rearing and schooling horses focused on the meticulous training of the animal, from which they required strength and obedience.

A pilgrim on his way to Mecca and a *muhasseb*, a member of the police responsible for the security of markets (above) Throwing the lance (right), one of the skills practiced by Mameluke horsemen.

● FALCONRY

The falcon, the symbol of the god Horus, occupied an important place in the imagery of Ancient Egypt.

In medieval Egypt, as in all eastern Arabic countries at that time, falconry was the most highly prized mode of hunting. Although birds of prey were used in Arabia well before the arrival of Islam, the art of falconry was mainly developed after the great conquests which brought the Arabs into contact with the Persians and Byzantines. With the first Ommiad caliphs, falconry became a veritable institution. Skills were passed on through the rural and nomadic populations, however, for falconry was not reserved merely for the privileged classes.

Birds of prey trained for hunting traditionally fell into one of two categories: "black-eyed" and "yellow-eyed" birds. The "yellow-eyed" birds used for hawking, such as the goshawk or *baz* (right), were low-flying hawks of the fist. The "black-eyed" birds belonging to the falcon family (above) are the only birds of prey with black irises. These high-flying hawks were used for hunting herons and cranes.

In Egypt the traditional techniques of falconry have survived in the regions bordering the deserts and are still as described in medieval texts.

EGYPT AS SEEN
BY PAINTERS

● EGYPT EXPEDITION'S SCIENTIFIC MISSION

L*a Description de l'Egypte*, which contained nine volumes of text and eleven volumes of plates (some three thousand illustrations), was the first systematic inventory of a country whose mysteries had intrigued travelers since the days of the 16th century. It was compiled from the endless notes, accounts and original sketches made by the scientists and artists who composed the Egypt Expedition's scientific mission. One such illustration is this view of the ruins on *Elephantine Island* (1), in which the figure in the foreground disappeared in the final reproduction; the remains from different periods (3) are another example, including jewelry and clothing whose color could not be restored for publication. One of the members of the mission was Dominique Vivant Denon (1747–1825), who was to be the creator of the Louvre Museum. Vivant published his own drawings including this watercolor of *Pompey's Pillar* (2) in 1802, several years ahead of his colleagues, whose work did not begin to appear until 1809.

1

2

3

During the 1830's the establishment of an "Oriental" school of artists was accompanied by a period of artistic or so-called "picturesque" voyages to the Orient and to Egypt in particular. One of the first arrivals in 1830 was Adrien Dauzats (1804–68), an architectural artist renowned for his exactitude. In 1845 he painted this *Outisde View of St Catherine's Monastery* (3), based on his traveling sketches, which was considered one of his most successful works. He was followed a few years later by the Scottish painter David Roberts (1796–1864), the best known of this first generation of painter-travelers. Roberts traveled in Egypt between September 1838 and June 1839 and, although he tended to concentrate on ancient monuments, he also drew several general views of Cairo (1) during his stay as well as interiors of mosques and medersat, including that of Sultan Hassan ▲ *308* (2) for which he had to obtain special official authorization.

1

2   3

The predominant themes of the Oriental artists were bazaars and interiors. The markets of Cairo were a favorite theme of the British watercolorist Charles Robertson (1844–91), who painted this street scene in the Khan el-Khalili (1) ▲ 286. They were also the subject of several paintings by Jean-Léon Gérôme (1824–1904) whose depiction of a Cairo carpet seller entitled *Le Marchand de tapis au Caire* (3) is an imaginary composition in which the background is based on photographs. Western artists painting official portraits were often inspired by the domestic interiors of their subjects. For example the English artist Frank Dillon (1823–1909) painted several watercolors of the residence of Sheikh el-Mahdi (2), an important religious figure. The skillfully painted interiors of his compatriot John Frederick Lewis (1805–76), lit by the light from courtyards or turned-wood screens, were set in the artist's own house in Cairo where he lived from 1840 to 1850. Lewis was the master of the genre, which included *The Midday Meal in Cairo* (4). These interiors, however, tend to be eclipsed by the abundant but seldom alluring imagery of the harem, which was so popular among the Orientalists.

1		2
3		4

Paul Klee (1879–1940) owes his very individual mastery of color and light to the Orient, which he discovered in the spring of 1914 during a brief stay in Tunisia. According to his journal, it was North Africa that gave his art a more definitive form: "I am obsessed by color... I am an artist." A journey to Egypt in 1928–9 proved no less decisive, as is evidenced by his painting, which became steadily more abstract and increasingly incorporated signs and symbols. New elements began to appear in the work of the German painter: horizontal streaks of color intersecting vertical or diagonal lines, a pictorial language composed of personal "hieroglyphs". *Ad Parnassum* (2), an oil painting completed in 1932, represents the sacred mountain of Apollo in the form of a pyramid. *Pyramid* (3), a watercolor painted in 1934, was directly inspired by the Pyramids of Giza ▲ *334*. It was three years after this that he produced the

famous pastel on cotton and jute, which was entitled *The Legend of the Nile* (4). Here Klee relived (as he confided in his journal) "the event from a distance", which represented "the point at which reality and the abstract meet". The work is the culmination of the symbolic language which he valued so highly. It uses a form of hieroglyphs representing barques, fish and aquatic plants against a background of blue rectangles of varying intensity and unusual luminosity. For Kees van Dongen (1877–1968) it was India that represented the artist's decisive encounter with the Orient of his dreams. His "Indian period" (1922–32) was contemporary with the period of Negro influence on the works of Picasso, Derain and Braque. In 1909 Van Dongen had attended a performance of the ballet *Cleopatra* in Paris, which had inspired a painting. In March 1913 he was profoundly affected by a visit to Egypt, so much so, in fact, that it was to transform his style. His lines became purer and his

forms became
increasingly
elongated. He
returned in 1928–9
after he had
completed several
new paintings.
Amongst these was
a work entitled *Cairo*
(1), a stunning oil
painting of the city
at night.

1	2
	3
	4

The 1920's saw the development of an Egyptian school of artists, headed by the Alexandrians Mohammed Naghi (1888–1956) and Mahmud Saïd (1897–1964). Naghi moved away from an early Impressionist influence to explore other styles, but returned to it toward the end of his life in this *View of the Nile in Cairo* (2) painted in 1942. The paintings of Mahmud Saïd, inspired by classical culture, are more realistic. They consist mainly of portraits which try to capture the sensuality and opulence of Egypt, as well as several landscapes which give a more personal and fantastic view of the country. This painting of Mersa Matruh (1) painted in 1950 belongs to his final period of lunar landscapes bathed in an unreal light.

EGYPT
AS SEEN BY WRITERS

ANCIENT SITES

FROM A NILE STEAMER

It is said that nobody can fail to be impressed by the first sight of the pyramids, but William Makepeace Thackeray (1811–63) also had other concerns.

❝At dawn in the morning we were on deck; the character had not altered of the scenery about the river. Vast flat stretches of land were on either side, recovering from the subsiding inundations: near the mud villages, a country ship or two was roosting under the date trees; the landscape everywhere stretching away level and lonely. In the sky to the east was a long streak of greenish light, which widened and rose until it grew to be of an opal colour, then orange then, behold, the round red disk of the sun rose flaming up above the horizon. All the water blushed as he got up, the deck was all red; the steersman gave his helm to another, and prostrated himself on the deck, and bowed his head eastward, and praised the Maker of the sun: it shone on his white turban as he was kneeling, and gilt up his bronzed face, and sent his blue shadow over the glowing deck. The distances, which had been grey, were now clothed in purple; and the broad stream was illuminated. As the sun rose higher, the morning blush faded away; the sky was cloudless and pale, and the river and the surrounding landscape were dazzlingly clear.

Looking a-head in an hour or two, we saw the Pyramids. Fancy my sensations, dear M——; – two big ones and a little one:

! ! !

There they lay, rosy and solemn in the distance – those old majestical, mystical, familiar edifices. Several of us tried to be impressed; but breakfast supervening, a rush was made on the coffee and cold pies, and the sentiment of awe was lost in the scramble for victuals.❞

W.M. THACKERAY, *NOTES OF A JOURNEY FROM CORNHILL TO GRAND CAIRO*,
PUB. SMITH, ELDER & CO., 1865

DAWN

Eric Newby (b. 1919) paid a visit to the pyramids at dawn.

❝Around 6.15 a.m., the terrible wind suddenly ceased, as if whoever was in charge had switched it off at the main, the sand fell back to earth where it belonged, the sky over the Gulf of Suez and Sinai turned an improbable shade of mauve, overhead the morning star shone down brilliantly out of a sky that had suddenly become deep indigo, and the Pyramids of Giza – two huge ones, of King Cheops and King Chephren, a lesser one of King Mykerinos and three little ones, one behind the other – appeared to rise up out of the ground with the rapidity of mushrooms in a slow-motion film, the only Wonders of the Seven Wonders of the ancient world – first designated by Antipater of Sidon in the second century BC, six of which were on the shores of the Mediterranean (the other, which was not, was the Hanging Gardens of Babylon) – to survive more or less intact.

Looking at them, under a sky that was now rapidly turning from mauve to apple green and lower down was the colour of honey, with the lights of Cairo glimpsed shining between them until they were either switched off or made invisible by the strengthening light of day, there was no doubt that these were among a select body of man-made wonders of any date which in spite of having all the attributes of follies and having suffered severely from over-exposure, actually came up to expectations, if for nothing else, for their shapeliness. **99**

ERIC NEWBY, *ON THE SHORES OF THE MEDITERRANEAN*,
PUB. HARVILL PRESS, 1984

A PATIENT PEOPLE

The work of excavating tombs was long and laborious, as Vita Sackville-West (1892–1962) was quick to note.

66 A patient people. I had watched them working at some excavations, a long stream of them, ascending and descending like the angels on Jacob's ladder, carrying little baskets of sand and rubbish on their heads. So must the children of Israel have laboured under the lash of the taskmaster, for even now in the twentieth century the taskmasters stood by, curling their knotted thongs round the ragged limbs of the laggards. Nothing could have given so poignantly the sense of cheapness and abundance of labour as the size of the little baskets; not much bigger than a punnet of strawberries, they were scarcely a load for a child, yet young men and women fetched them from out of the deep tomb, carried them up, and emptied them on the growing heap where the sun glared on the rocks. As they climbed and descended, they chanted a monotonous song; when the lash fell on them, they skipped into the air, but very good-humouredly, as though the lash were all in the day's work and fell with impartiality, more to keep the ranks on the move than to chastise the individual; so they gradually emptied the tomb which their forefathers had dug, and which time had silted up until the day should come for the curious foreigner to expose again the underground chambers, the rigid images of god and Pharaoh; only when the sunset whistle suddenly blew did they turn from beasts of burden into human beings, breaking their ranks and scattering like a flock of starlings at the clapping of hands. Then they ran and leapt over the rocks, some going away to ease themselves, others to drink thirstily from pannikins, but all joyful at their release, and childish in their demonstrations of pleasure. **99**

VITA SACKVILLE-WEST, *PASSENGER TO TEHERAN*,
PUB. THE HOGARTH PRESS, 1926

A PETRIE DIG

T.E. Lawrence (1888–1935) took part in a dig at this site, some forty miles south of Cairo in the middle of the desert.

66No one but I would have achieved a letter at all from a Petrie dig. A Petrie dig is a thing with a flavour of its own: tinned kidneys mingle with mummy-corpses and amulets in the soup: my bed is all gritty with prehistoric alabaster jars of unique types – and my feet at night keep the bread-box from the rats. For ten mornings in succession I have seen the sun rise as I breakfasted, and we come home at nightfall after lunching at the bottom of a 50 foot shaft, to draw pottery silhouettes or string bead-necklaces. In fact if I hadn't malaria to-day I could make a pretty story of it all: – only then I wouldn't have time. . . .

About the digging: 'we' have stumbled on what is probably the richest and largest prehistoric cemetery in Egypt, and in our first week have dug out about 100 graves: these contain wooden coffins and bedsteads, boxes of alabaster jars, dozens of pots of new and known types, some little ivory, (spoons and gaming pieces and scraps of caskets) a good many bronze implements, axes, adzes, chisels, and other trifles. Also a good many baskets, and the shrouds and cloths in which the bodies were wrapped. We have found very few flints, and those not of the best, since the bronze was in general use. The graves are usually about 5 feet deep, and as all the soil is pure sand, digging is merely child's play. Owing to a hitch in his arrangements the Professor has all his workmen here, and so twice as many graves are found than we can record properly: with plenty of time it would be delightful, whereas now we are swamped with the multitude. We have about 900 pots (complete: – all broken ones are thrown away) about 120 alabasters, and a matter of twenty bedsteads. Also we have preserved a number of bodies and skeletons complete by soaking them with boiling parafin wax. These will go to Museums. **99**

THE LETTERS OF T.E. LAWRENCE,
ED. BY DAVID GARNETT,
PUB. JONATHAN CAPE, 1938

LETTERS HOME

POMPEY'S PILLAR

Herman Melville (1819–91) recorded his impressions of Egypt in a journal. The following observations date from December 1856 and January 1857.

66At early morning came in sight of Alexandria Light house, and shortly after, saw Pompey's Pillar. Landed at 10. AM. Donkey to hotel, near which garden of the date palm. Pompey's pillar looks like huge stick of candy after having been long sucked. Cleopatra's

Needles – one of them down & covered over. Rode along banks of Canal of Mahammed, and to Garden of the Pasha. . . .

Alexandria. Seems Mcadamed with the ruins of thousand cities. Every shovel full of earth dug over. The soil, deep loam, looks historical. The Grand Square. Lively aspect. Arabs looking in at windows. The sea is the principal point. Catacombs by it. R.R. extension driven right through. Acres. Wonderful appearance of the sea at noon. Sea & sky molten into each other. . . . One down & covered. Sighing of the waves. Cries of watchmen at night. Lanterns. Assassins. Sun strokes. A daub of Prussian blue.**99**

HERMAN MELVILLE, *JOURNAL OF A VISIT TO EGYPT AND THE LEVANT*,
ED. HOWARD C. HORSFORD,
PUB. PRINCETON UNIVERSITY PRESS, 1955

CAIRO

Rudyard Kipling (1865–1936) wrote the following description to his children Elsie and John in February 1913.

66Cairo itself is a cross between Rome and Florence with touches of Cape Town thrown in. *But* it is cold – beastly cold and Mother and I are surprised and annoyed. The train that met us at Port Said was, as Sunshine T. remarked, exactly like a South African train – I looked for the big coat of arms and the springbuck on the outside. The men (there are no women in the street) are attired in long blue petticoats . . . When they do anything that requires exertion – such as pushing baggage trucks – they hold one end of the petticoat between their teeth. This has the great advantage of reducing them to silence. The colours of their garments are mostly blue or black, with occasional white or orange. We have not seen more than half a dozen women in the streets and they are of course veiled.

The nice thing is to see the camel again – passing unconcernedly between motor cars and trams. Cairo bristles with motor cars and all the luxuries. Our hotel here is full of the latest appliances down to a glorious lift, worked by an Arab in gold-embroidered jacket. It stuck this morning, when I was in it and the Arab panicked. The notice in the bedroom about bells says:–

> Once for the waiter.
> Twice for the chambermaid.
> Three times for the Arab!

This gives one a spacious feeling – as though, if one rang six times a Pyramid would enter. You never saw anything in the world so like their photographs as the Pyramids. We saw them this morning, across the Nile with the tawny grey desert behind 'em, and I only said:– 'Huh! Of course. Those are the pyramids.' Only when one looks at 'em for some time one realizes their enormous size. They dwarf the low hills behind 'em, and they change with the changing lights exactly like mountains. . . .

Our window attracts us . . . There are always camels or dahabeeyahs [large sailing boats] or donkeys to look at. Our balcony looks slap on to the great brown silent Nile. Somewhere round the corner is a barrack of English troops (Sunshine discovered it first) and we can hear bugles and drums.**99**

O BELOVED KIDS – RUDYARD KIPLING'S LETTERS TO HIS CHILDREN,
ED. BY ELLIOT L. GILBERT,
PUB. WEIDENFELD & NICOLSON, 1983

TOURIST AMENITIES

Evelyn Waugh (1903–66) found the service adequate in some areas but lacking in others during his visit to Cairo.

❝We arrived at Cairo in the late afternoon and went to look for an hotel. All the hotels in Egypt are bad, but they excuse themselves upon two contrary principles. Some maintain, legitimately, that it does not really matter how bad they are if they are cheap enough; the others, that it does not really matter how bad they are if they are expensive enough. Both classes do pretty well. We sought out one of the former, a large, old-fashioned establishment under Greek management in the Midan el-Khaznedar, called the Hotel Bristol et du Nil, where rooms even in the high season are only 80 piastres a night. My room had three double beds in it under high canopies of dusty mosquito netting, and two derelict rocking chairs. The windows opened onto a tram terminus. None of the servants spoke a word of any European language, but this was a negligible defect since they never answered the bell. . . .

The journey was unremarkable except to Juliet, who was not used to the ways of Egyptian porters. These throw themselves upon one's baggage like Westminster schoolboys on their Shrove Tuesday pancake, with this difference, that their aim is to carry away as small a piece as possible; the best fighter struggles out happily with a bundle of newspapers, a rug, an air-cushion, or a small attaché case; the less fortunate share the trunks and suitcases. In this way one's luggage is shared between six or seven men, all of whom clamorously demand tips when they have finally got it into the train or taxi. Juliet was shocked to see her husband and myself defending our possessions from attack with umbrella and walking-stick; when the first onslaught was thus checked and our assailants realised that we had not newly disembarked, we were able to apportion it between two of them and proceed on our way with dignity. . . .

One Friday, Solomon came to tell us about some religious dances that were to be performed in the neighbourhood; did we want to see them? Juliet did not feel up to it, so Geoffrey stayed at home with her and I went off alone with Solomon. We rode to the farther end of the plateau on which the pyramids stand, and then down into a sandy hollow where there were the entrances to several tombs. Here we left our camels in charge of a boy and climbed into one of the holes in the hillside. The tomb was already half full of Arabs; it was an oblong chamber cut in the rock and decorated in places with incised hieroglyphics. The audience were standing round the walls and packed in the recesses cut for the coffins. The only light came through the door – one beam of white daylight. The moment we arrived the dance began. It was performed by young men, under the direction of a sheik; the audience clapped their hands in time and joined in the chant. It *was* a dull dance, like kindergarten Eurythmics. The youths stamped their feet on the sandy floor and clapped their hands and swayed slowly about. After a short time I signed to Solomon my readiness to leave, and attempted to make as unobtrusive a departure as possible so as not to disturb these ungainly devotions. No sooner, however, had I reached the door than the dance stopped and the whole company came trooping out crying for 'bakshish.' I asked Solomon whether it was not rather shocking that they should expect to be paid by an infidel for keeping their religious observances. He said, rather sheepishly, that some tip was usual to the sheik. I asked where the sheik was. 'Sheik. Me sheik,' they cried, all running forward and beating their chests. Then the old man appeared. I gave him the piastres and they promptly transferred their attention to him, seizing his robes and clamouring for a share. We mounted our camels and rode away. Even then two or three urchins pursued us on foot crying, 'Bakshish! Bakshish! Me sheik!'

As we went back I asked Solomon, "Was that a genuine religious dance?"

He pretended not to understand.

'You did not like the dance?'

'Would they have done that dance if you had not brought me?'

Solomon was again evasive. 'English and American lords like to see dance. English lords all satisfied.'

'I wasn't satisfied,' I said.**

EVELYN WAUGH, *LABELS –*
A MEDITERRANEAN JOURNEY,
PUB. DUCKWORTH, 1930

THE DESERT

MOVEMENT AND SHADOW

English writer, traveler and social reformer Harriet Martineau (1802–76) wrote enthusiastically of riding in the desert.

Our first ride in the Desert, was full of wonder and delight. It was only about three miles: but it might have been thirty from the amount of novelty in it. Our thick umbrellas, covered with brown holland, were a necessary protection against the heat, which would have been almost intolerable, but for the cool north wind. – I believed before that I had imagined the Desert: but now I felt that nobody could. No one could conceive the confusion of piled and scattered rocks, which, even in a ride of three miles, deprives a stranger of all sense of direction, except by the heavens. These narrow passes among black rocks, all suffocation and glare, without shade or relief, are the very home of despair. The oppression of the sense of sight disturbs the brain, so that the will of the unhappy wanderer cannot keep his nerves in order. . . . The presence of dragon-flies in the Desert surprised me; – not only here, but in places afterwards – where there appeared to be no water within a great distance. To those who have been wont to watch the coming forth of the dragon-fly from its sheath on the rush on the margin of a pool, and flitting about the mountain watercourse, or the moist meadows at home, it is strange to see them by dozens glittering in the sunshine of the Desert, where there appears to be nothing for them to alight on: – nothing that would not shrivel them up, if they rested for a moment from the wing. The hard dry locust seemed more in its place, and the innumerable beetles, which everywhere left a net-work of delicate tracks on the light sand. Distant figures are striking in the desert, in the extreme clearness of light and shade. Shadows strike upon the sense here as bright lights do elsewhere. It seems to me that I remember every figure I ever saw in the Desert; – every veiled woman tending her goats, or carrying her water-jar on her head; – every man in blue skirting the hillocks; every man in brown guiding his ass or his camel through the sandy defiles of the black rocks, or on a slope by moonlight, when he casts a long shadow. Every moving thing has a new value to the eye in such a region.

HARRIET MARTINEAU, *EASTERN LIFE, PRESENT AND PAST*,
PUB. EDWARD MOXOM, 1848

THE DROMEDARY

Alexander Kinglake (1809–91) wrote the following lively account of his journey across the desert from Cairo to Suez.

**The 'Dromedary,' of Egypt, and Syria is not the two-humped animal described by that name in books of natural history, but is in fact of the same family as the camel, to which it stands in about the same relation as a racer to a cart-horse. The fleetness, and endurance of this creature are extraordinary. It is not usual to force him into a gallop, and I fancy from his make that it would be quite impossible for him to maintain that pace for any length of time, but the animal is on so large a scale, that the jog-trot at which he is generally ridden implies a progress of perhaps ten or twelve miles an hour, and this pace, it is said, he can keep up incessantly without food, or water, or rest for three whole days, and nights.

Of the two dromedaries which I had obtained for this journey, I mounted one myself, and put Dthemetri on the other. My plan was, to ride on with Dthemetri to Suez as rapidly as the fleetness of the beasts would allow, and to let Mysseri (who was still weak from the effects of his late illness) come quietly on with the camels, and baggage.

The trot of the Dromedary is a pace terribly disagreeable to the rider, until he becomes a little accustomed to it; but after the first half hour I so far schooled myself to this new exercise, that I felt capable of keeping it up (though not without aching limbs) for several hours together. Now, therefore, I was anxious to dart forward, and annihilate at once the whole space that divided me from the Red Sea. Dthemetri, however, could not get on at all; every attempt which he made to trot seemed to threaten the utter dislocation of his whole frame, and indeed I doubt whether any one of Dthemetri's age (nearly forty I think,) and unaccustomed to such exercise could have borne it at all easily; besides, the dromedary which fell to his lot was evidently a very bad one; he every now and then came to a dead stop, and coolly knelt down as though suggesting that the rider had better get off at once, and abandon the attempt as one that was utterly hopeless. 99

ALEXANDER KINGLAKE, *EOTHEN; OR TRACES
OF TRAVEL BROUGHT HOME FROM THE EAST*,
PUB. JOHN OLLIVIER, 1844

THE KNACK OF RIDING CAMELS
Edward Lear (1812–88) wrote to his wife Ann about the problems entailed in a relationship with a camel.

66Thus far we have come quite safely & with great pleasure. I wrote to you from Cairo – on the 12th – just before we were going to start, & I told you that I had already tried my camel, which conveyance both Cross & myself found admirably easy & pleasant. I cannot tell why people write such nonsense about the East as they do: regarding the camel, you have only to sit quite still when it rises, & hold fast by the saddle – & you are lifted up on the long necked monster – & away you go *just as if on a rocking chair*. – But the great beauty of the camelriding is the size of the sort of table you sit on – made up of pillows, & coats, & carpets & saddlebags: – we sit crosslegged – or opposite each other, or we turn round – just as we please, & we lunch or read as quietly as if we were in a room. Nothing can be more charming. As for the camels themselves – I cannot say much for them: – they *are* quite harmless & quiet, but *seem* the most odious beasts – except when they are moving. The sort of horrible way in which they growl & snarl if you only go 6 feet near them – is quite frightful – & if you did not know them – you would suppose they were going to eat you. They do the same to their own masters the Arabs – & appear to have the most unsociable disposition in the world – even among themselves. I give my camel a bunch of green morning & evening – but all attempts at making friends are useless: When I put the vegetable within a yard of him, he yells & grunts as if I were killing him – & after he has taken & eaten it he does just the same. – They all seem to say – 'Oh! bother you! can't you let me alone!' —— & are certainly uninteresting quadrupeds as to their social qualities. – Their pace is *just* 3 miles an hour – like clockwork: If you try to make them go faster – they growl: if you stop them or try to go slower – they growl also. – They will have their own way. It is a wonderful thing to see the long long strings of these strange creatures crossing the desert – silently striding along – laden with bales of goods. One & all have the same expression – 'I am going from Suez to Cairo to please you – but don't speak to me or come near me:– I shall go on well if you let me alone – but if you only look at me I'll growl – '– At night, when our tent is pitched, all the camels stride away – just where they please – looking for little thorny shrubs they feed on – till quite out of sight: but after sunset – when the Arabs call them, they all appear in 2s and threes – & are soon round the tent fires – where they are all tethered & have a lot of beans given them – & there they stay till morning. Most of them make a nasty noise as if they were sick all night long. – At sunrise, they are disturbed to be loaded, & then the groans & grumblings begin & go on till we are fairly off.**99**

EDWARD LEAR, *SELECTED LETTERS*,
ED. BY VIVIEN NOAKES,
PUB. CLARENDON PRESS, 1988

WOMEN IN EGYPT

EGYPTIAN CUSTOMS

Greek historian Herodotus (c. 480–c. 425 BC) writes entertainingly about the social mores of his day in Book Two of his "Histories", which is titled "Odd Practices of the Egyptians".

66About Egypt itself I shall have a great deal more to relate because of the number of remarkable things which the country contains, and because of the fact that more monuments which beggar description are to be found there than anywhere else in the world. That is reason enough for my dwelling on it at greater length. Not only is the Egyptian climate peculiar to that country, and the Nile different in its behaviour from other rivers elsewhere, but the Egyptians themselves in their manners and customs seem to have reversed the ordinary practices of mankind. For instance, women attend market and are employed in trade, while men stay at home and do the weaving. In weaving the normal way is to work the threads of the weft upwards, but the Egyptians work them downwards. Men in Egypt carry loads on their heads, women on their shoulders; women pass water standing up, men sitting down. To ease themselves they go indoors, but eat outside in the streets, on the theory that what is unseemly but necessary should be done in private, and what is not unseemly should be done openly. No women holds priestly office, either in the service of goddess or god; only men are priests in both cases. Sons are under no compulsion to support their parents if they do not wish to do so, but daughters must, whether they wish it or not. Elsewhere priests grow their hair long; in Egypt they shave their heads. In other nations the relatives of the deceased in time of mourning cut their hair, but the Egyptians, who shave at all other times, mark a death by letting the hair grow both on head and chin. They live with their animals – unlike the rest of the world, who live apart from them. Other men live on wheat and barley, but any Egyptian who does so is blamed for it, their bread being made from spelt, or *Xea* as some call it. Dough they knead with their feet, but clay with their hands – and even handle dung. They practise circumcision, while men of other nations – except those who have learnt from Egypt – leave their private parts as nature made them. Men in Egypt have two garments each, women only one. The ordinary practice at sea is to make sheets fast to ring-bolts fitted outboard; the Egyptians fit them inboard. In writing or calculating, instead of going, like the Greeks, from left to right, the Egyptians go from right to left – and obstinately maintain that theirs is the dexterous method, ours being left-handed and awkward. They have two sorts of writing, the sacred and the common. They are religious to excess, beyond any other nation in the world, and here are some of the customs which illustrate the fact: they drink from brazen cups which they scour every day – everyone, without exception. They wear linen clothes which they make a special point of continually washing. They circumcise themselves for cleanliness' sake, preferring to be clean rather than comely.**99**

HERODOTUS, *THE HISTORIES*,
TRANS. AUBREY DE SÉLINCOURT,
PUB. PENGUIN CLASSICS, 1954

AN ENGINEER'S WIFE

Freya Stark (1893–1993) was saddened to come upon the following example of an unemancipated marriage.

66We had done our work, and there were some hours to spare, and our hosts took us driving through the soft roads of this Arcadia, on which orange trees and mangoes and the feathery peppers threw their shade, – to where a small slope has the distinction, they told us, of generating the only water power in the flat Egyptian land. An engineer was in charge, and lived with his young wife in a brown detached villa as new as a new pin, with everything modern about it. We called, and found a drawing-room as polished as all the rest, with satin cushions of every size, shape and colour scattered wherever a cushion could be. On the middle of the sofa sat a doll, almost life-size and very richly dressed; we were left to admire it for a long time, while the engineer's wife got ready to receive us – not an everyday labour, as we saw when she came in, resplendent in Cairo fashions, with waved hair and face made up to match, and tea approaching behind her, in thin Japanese cups, shepherded hesitatingly by a very small maid.

As we talked, she told us what a lonely life she led: there was no one to call upon at all.

'Do you ever go walking?' said we, trying to find a bright side.

'Sometimes, when my husband has time. I could not go alone in the fields.'

There seemed nothing to be said; we admired the doll on the sofa.

She gave it a wistful little glance. 'I had it before I was married,' she said (I suppose she was about eighteen). 'I keep it. It is a sort of company.'

Poor young effendis. Their professions oblige them to live in country places, and

159

when they marry, their wives, surrounded by exported modernity in chilly splendour, have nothing in the world to do. No wonder they all ask to be transferred to a metropolis, where they may once more see a smile by the domestic hearth, and not feel that the whole social existence of their dear ones depends on them alone.**99**

FREYA STARK, *WEST IS EAST*,
PUB. JOHN MURRAY, 1945

THE ROOF GARDEN
Egyptian Nobel Prize-winning novelist Naguib Mahfouz (b. 1911) included the following description in Book 1 of the "Cairo Trilogy".

66The most amazing aspect of the roof was the southern half overlooking al-Nahhasin Street. There in years past she had planted a special garden. There was not another one like it in the whole neighbourhood on any of the other roofs, which were usually covered with chicken droppings. She had first begun with a small number of pots of carnations and roses. They had increased year by year and were arranged in rows parallel to the sides of the walls. They grew splendidly, and she had the idea of putting a trellis over the top. She got a carpenter to install it. Then she planted both jasmine and hyacinth bean vines. She attached them to the trellis and around the posts. They grew tall and spread out until the area was transformed into an arbor garden with a green sky from which jasmine flowed down. An enchanting, sweet fragrance was diffused throughout.

This roof, with its inhabitants of chickens and pigeons and its arbor garden, was her beautiful, beloved world and her favorite place for relaxation out of the whole universe, about which she knew nothing. As usual at this hour, she set about caring for it. She swept it, watered the plants, fed the chickens and pigeons. Then for a long time, with smiling lips and dreamy eyes, she enjoyed the scene surrounding her. She went to the end of the garden and stood behind the interwoven, coiling vines, to gaze out through the openings at the limitless space around her.

She was awed by the minarets which shot up, making a profound impression on her. Some were near enough for her to see their lamps and crescent distinctly, like those of Qala'un and Barquq. Others appeared to her as complete wholes, lacking details, like the minarets of the mosques of al-Husayn, al-Ghuri and al-Azhar. Still other minarets were at the far horizon and seemed phantoms, like those of the Citadel and Rifa'i mosques. She turned her face toward them with devotion, fascination, thanksgiving, and hope. Her spirit soared over their tops, as close as possible to the heavens. Then her eyes would fix on the minaret of the mosque of al-Husayn, the dearest one to her because of her love for its namesake. She looked at it affectionately, and her yearnings mingled with the sorrow that pervaded her every time she remembered she was not allowed to visit the son of the Prophet of God's daughter, even though she lived only minutes away from his shrine.**99**

NAGUIB MAHFOUZ, *PALACE WALK*,
TRANS. BY WILLIAM MAYNARD HUTCHINS
AND OLIVE E. KERRY,
PUB. DOUBLEDAY, 1991

THE EFFECTS OF LANGUOR

E.D. Clarke (1769–1822) wrote of the effects on visiting Europeans of the atmosphere of the city.

❝*Denon* speaks of the pleasurable sensations daily excited by the delicious temperature of *Caïro*, causing *Europeans*, who arrive with the intention of spending a few months in the place, to remain during the rest of their lives, without ever persuading themselves to leave it. Few persons, however, with whom we associated, were disposed to acquiesce in the opinion of this very amiable writer. Those who are desirous of uninterrupted repose, or who are able to endure the invariable dulness which prevails in every society to which strangers are admitted, may, perhaps, tolerate, without murmuring, a short residence in the midst of this dull and dirty city. The effect, whether it be of climate, or of education, or of government, is the same among all the settlers in *Egypt*, except the *Arabs*; namely, a disposition to exist without exertion of any kind; to pass whole days upon beds and cushions; smoking, and counting beads. This is what *Muillet* termed *Le vrai génie Egyptienne*; and that it may be acquired by residing among the native inhabitants of *Caïro*, is evident from the appearance exhibited by *Europeans* who have passed some years in the city.❞

E.D. CLARKE, *TRAVELS IN VARIOUS COUNTRIES
OF EUROPE, ASIA AND AFRICA, VOL. VI,*
PUB. T. CADELL & W. DAVIES, 1818

THE GROTESQUE

Gustave Flaubert (1821–80) wrote to his friend Louis Bouilhet from Cairo in December 1849.

❝I am sure that as an intelligent man you don't expect me to send you an account of my trip ... In a word, this is how I sum up my feelings so far: very little impressed by nature here – i.e. landscape, sky, desert (except the mirages); enormously excited by the cities and the people. Hugo would say: 'I was closer to God than to mankind.' It probably comes of my having given more imagination and thought, before coming here, to things like horizon, greenery, sand, trees, sun, etc., than to houses, streets, costumes and faces. The result is that nature has been a rediscovery and the rest a discovery. There is one new element which I hadn't expected to see and which is tremendous here, and that is the grotesque. All the old comic business of the cudgeled slave, of the coarse trafficker in women, of the thieving merchant – it's all very fresh here, very genuine and charming. In the streets, in the houses, on any and all occasions, there is a merry proliferation of beatings right and left. There are guttural intonations that sound like the cries of wild beasts, and laughter, and flowing white robes, and ivory teeth flashing between thick lips, and flat negro noses, and dusty feet, and necklaces, and bracelets! Poor you! The pasha at Rosetta gave us a dinner at which there were ten negroes to serve us – they wore silk jackets and some had silver bracelets; and a little negro boy waved away the flies with a kind of feather-duster made of rushes. We ate with our fingers, the food was brought one dish at a time on a silver tray – about thirty different dishes made their appearance in this way. We were on divans in a wooden pavilion, windows open on the water. One of the finest things is the camel – I never tire of watching this strange beast that lurches like a turkey and sways its neck like a swan. Their cry is something that I wear myself out trying to imitate – I hope to bring it back with me – but it's hard to reproduce – a rattle with a kind of tremulous gargling as an accompaniment.**99**

THE LETTERS OF GUSTAVE FLAUBERT,
ED. AND TRANS. BY FRANCIS STEEGMULLER,
PUB. FABER & FABER, 1981

BAKSHISH BOYS

Writing in the 1980's, William Golding (1911–93) does not lament the passing of the young hashish salesmen.

66An aspect of any Egyptian town that is bound to surprise a westerner – northerner – is how the children swarm everywhere. They seemed healthy enough to me as did the population generally. There were no ghastly cripples begging beside the road, no children too listless to move. Even so, the children stopped their playing as we approached and waited. They did not bother us, however, but only examined us curiously and from a distance. This is a change that has happened in the last ten years. It was not because we were 'convoyed' by Alaa and Rushdie, who look as Egyptian as anyone can. It is the result of a push by the authorities to get the bakshish boys off the backs of foreigners. Ten years before we had been plagued by them and they have been notorious for generations. But as far as my experience goes, from one end of Egypt to the other the bakshish boys are gone. So in Abu Tig we were able to walk free and unhindered. The streets were a little untidy but not dirty. There were small shops which seemed to stock only a few goods, except the tobacco kiosk which was loaded down with every kind of tobacco product. The Egyptians make 'hubble-bubbles' out of a can and a length of bamboo. Those who could afford the earlier, ornate versions of the hubble-bubble now smoke western style. But the average Egyptian if he is not dragging at his bamboo pipestem is smoking a cigarette. Everybody smokes hash now and then. Officially the police are supposed to stop it, but wink.**99**

WILLIAM GOLDING, *AN EGYPTIAN JOURNAL*,
PUB. FABER & FABER, 1985

AFTER THE WAR

Lawrence Durrell (1912–90) describes the atmosphere in Alexandria after World War Two.

66Even the war had come to terms with the city, had indeed stimulated its trade with its bands of aimless soldiers walking about with that grim air of unflinching desperation with which Anglo-Saxons embark upon their pleasures; their own demagnetised women were all in uniform now which gave them a ravenous air – as if they could drink the blood of the innocents while it was still warm. The brothels had overflowed and gloriously engulfed a whole quarter of the town around the old square. If anything the war had brought an air of tipsy carnival rather than anything else; even the nightly bombardments of the harbour were brushed aside by day, shrugged away like nightmares, hardly remembered as more than an inconvenience. For the rest, nothing had fundamentally changed. The brokers still sat on the steps of the Mohammed Ali club sipping their newspapers. The old horse-drawn gharries still clopped about upon their listless errands. The crowds thronged the white Corniche to take the frail spring sunlight. Balconies crowded with wet linen and tittering girls. The Alexandrians still moved inside the murex-tinted cyclorama of the life they imagined. ('Life is more complicated than we think, yet far simpler than anyone dares to imagine.') Voices of girls, stabbing of Arab quarter-tones, and from the synagogue a metallic drone punctuated by the jingle of a sistrum. On the floor of the Bourse they were screaming like one huge animal in pain. The money-changers were arranging their currencies like sweets upon the big squared boards. Pashas in scarlet flower-pots reclining in immense cars like gleaming sarcophagi. A dwarf playing a mandolin. An immense eunuch with a carbuncle the size of a brooch eating pastry. A legless man propped on a trolley, dribbling. **99**

LAWRENCE DURRELL, *CLEA*,
PUB. FABER & FABER, 1960

THE RUE ROSETTE

E.M. Forster (1879–1970) was sent to Alexandria in 1915 with the Red Cross, and he later published a history and a guide to the city.

66Of the three streets that dispute the honour of being Alexandria's premier thoroughfare the Rue Rosette undoubtedly bears the palm for gentility. The Bond Street (I refer to Rue Chérif Pacha) is too shoppy to be genteel, and the Boulevard de Ramleh competes from this particular aspect not at all. In its length, its cleanliness, and the refined monotony of its architecture, Rue Rosette outdoes either of its rivals. They are tainted with utility: people use them to get something or somewhere. But Rue Rosette is an end in itself. It starts in the middle of the town and no man can tell where it stops: a goal it may have but not one discoverable by mortal leg. Its horizon, narrow but uninterrupted, ever unrolls into a ribbon of blue sky above the wayfarer's head, and the ribbon of white beneath his feet corresponds, and right and left of him are the houses that he thought he had passed a quarter of an hour before. Oh, it is so dull! Its dullness is really indescribable. What seem at first to be incidents – such as the trays of worthies who project from the clubs – prove at a second glance to be subdued to what they sit in. They are half asleep. For you cannot have gentility without paying for it.
The poor street does not want to be dull. It wants to be smart, and of a Parisian smartness. Eternally well-dressed people driving infinitely in either direction – that is its ideal. It is not mine, and we meet as seldom as possible in consequence.**99**

E.M. FORSTER, *PHAROS AND PHARILLON*,
PUB. MICHAEL HAAG, 1983

BY TRAIN TO ASWAN

In an essay entitled "Nasser's Egypt", Gore Vidal (b. 1925) describes a meeting with a young poet named Ahmed, on the banks of the Nile, and then a conversation about the Egyptian economy on a train to Aswan.

❝'Are you German, sir?' A small, dark youth stepped from behind a palm tree into the full light of the setting sun which turned scarlet the white shirt and albino red the black eyes. He had been watching me watch the sun set across the Nile, now blood-red and still except for sailboats tacking in a hot, slow breeze. I told him that I was American but was used to being mistaken for a German: in this year of the mid-century, Germans are everywhere, and to Arab eyes we all look alike. He showed only a moment's disappointment.

'I have many German friends,' he said. 'Two German friends. *West* German friends. Perhaps you know them?' He pulled a notebook out of his pocket and read off two names. Then, not waiting for an answer, all in a rush, he told me that he was a teacher of Arabic grammar, that he was going to Germany, *West* Germany (he emphasized the *West* significantly), to write a book. What sort of book? A book about West Germany. The theme? He responded with some irritation: 'A Book About West Germany.' That was what the book would be about. He was a poet. His name was Ahmed. 'Welcome,' he said 'welcome!' His crooked face broke into a smile. 'Welcome to Luxor!' He invited me to his house for mint tea.

As we turned from the bank of the Nile, a long, haunting cry sounded across the water. I had heard this same exotic cry for several evenings, and I was certain that it must be of ancient origin, a hymn perhaps to Ikhnaton's falling sun. I asked Ahmed what this lovely aria meant. He listened a moment and then said, 'It's this man on the other side who says: will the ferryboat please pick him up?' So much for magic.❞

❝In the diner on the train south to Aswan I had breakfast with a young government official from the Sudan. He was on his way home to Khartoum. He had a fine smile and blue-black skin. On each cheek there were three deep scars, the ritual mark of his tribe – which I recognized, for I had seen his face only the day before on the wall of the Temple of Luxor. Amenhotep III had captured one of his ancestors in Nubia; five thousand years ago the ritual scars were the same as they are now. In matters of religion Africans are profound conservatives. But otherwise he was a man of our time and world. He was dressed in the latest French fashion. He had been for two years on an economic mission in France. He spoke English, learned at the British school in Khartoum.

We breakfasted on musty-tasting dwarfish eggs as dust filtered slowly in through closed windows, covering table, plates, eggs with a film of grit. A fan stirred the dusty air. Parched, I drank three Coca-Colas – the national drink – and sweated. The heat outside was already 110 degrees, and rising. For a while we watched the depressing countryside and spoke very little. At some points the irrigated land was less than a mile wide on our side of the river: a thin ribbon of dusty green ending abruptly in a blaze of desert where nothing at all grew, a world of gray sand as far as the eye could see. Villages of dried-mud houses were built at the desert's edge so as not to use up precious land. The fellahin in their ragged clothes moved slowly about their tasks, quite unaware of the extent of their slow but continual decline. In the fifth century B.C., Herodotus was able to write: 'As things are at present these people get their harvest with less labor than anyone else in the world; they have no need to work with plow or hoe, or to use any other of the ordinary methods of cultivating their land; they merely wait for the river of its own accord to flood the fields.' But all that has changed. Nearly thirty million people now live in a country whose agriculture cannot support half that number.❞

GORE VIDAL, *COLLECTED ESSAYS 1952–72*,
PUB. HEINEMANN, 1974

TRAVELING AROUND EGYPT

▲ Pyramids of Giza

▼ Temple of Wadi es-Sebua

▼ Necropolis of Thebes

▲ Temple of Philae on the island of Agilkia

▲ Deir el-Bahri

▼ Temple of Horus at Edfu

▲ Mineral formations in a lake near Siwa Oasis

▲ Cemetery in the Nile Delta ▼ Sand dunes

▲ On the shores of Lake Nasser

▲ Harvest   ▼ Valley of the Kings

▲ The Citadel, Cairo

▼ Market in Medinet el-Faiyum

▼ Cemetery in Aswan

ALEXANDRIA

"It is an arid desert, and between the two chains of mountains that it forms lies a wonderful land. To the west, the chain has the appearance of a line of sand hills; to the east it looks like the belly of a lean horse or the back of a camel. That, O Commander of the Faithful, is Egypt; all its wealth stems from the blessed river that flows through this land with the dignity of a caliph. It waxes and wanes as regularly as the sun and the moon."

Amr Ibn el-As

173

▲ ALEXANDRIA

1 RAS EL-TIN 2 ANFUSHI 3 ABU EL-ABBAS MOSQUE 4 FORT QAITBAY 5 TERBANA MOSQUE 6 EL-SHORBAGI MOSQUE 7 TOMB OF THE UNKNOWN SOLDIER 8 ATTARINE MOSQUE 9 MIDAN SAAD ZAGHLUL 10 NABI DANIEL MOSQUE 11 RAMLEH STATION 12 EL-QAID MOSQUE 13 ENGINEERING FACULTY 14 GRAECO-ROMAN MUSEUM

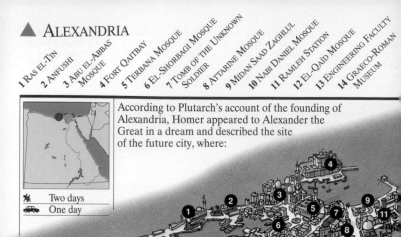

🚶 Two days
🚗 One day

According to Plutarch's account of the founding of Alexandria, Homer appeared to Alexander the Great in a dream and described the site of the future city, where:

"An island set in ocean deep, Lies off fair Egypt's rich and fertile land, And the name of the island is called Pharos". "Alexander's dream" was realized when the future capital of the Lagides and second largest city in the Roman empire, and the great commerical port of the late 19th and early 20th centuries, was founded in 331 BC on the site of the Ancient Egyptian village of Rakhotis. It was designed by the architect Dinocrates and lay between the Mediterranean coast in the north and Lake Mareotis (now Lake Mariut) in the south ▲ *203*. Although Alexandria has retained little of its ancient glory, it is still a legendary city which has been continually enriched by the many cultural influences exerted throughout its history. To many, it is the symbol of open-mindedness and cosmopolitanism.

EGYPT'S LEADING PORT. Since the construction of Heptastadion, a causeway built between Pharos and the mainland by Dinocrates, Alexandria has had two harbors. The EASTERN HARBOR is the oldest of the two, and was very active in the Middle Ages. During the Ottoman period it underwent a gradual decline caused by competition from the ports of Rosetta and Damietta, whose position at the mouth of two branches of the Nile meant they were directly linked with the hinterland. The WESTERN HARBOR, previously known as Eunostos ("safe return"), dates from the time of the Ptolemies and was the harbor that Mohammed Ali decided to develop. The creation of infrastructures and the improved links with Cairo following the

THE HARBORS OF ALEXANDRIA
Today the eastern harbor is only used by a few fishing boats and yachts. Boats can be hired for trips around the bay.

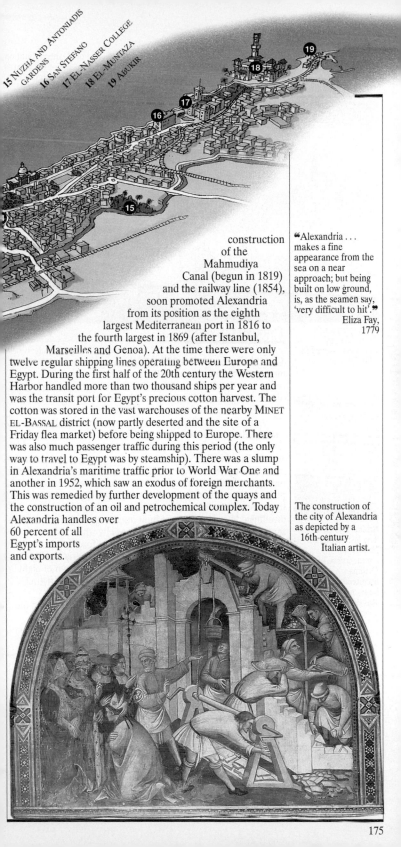

construction of the Mahmudiya Canal (begun in 1819) and the railway line (1854), soon promoted Alexandria from its position as the eighth largest Mediterranean port in 1816 to the fourth largest in 1869 (after Istanbul, Marseilles and Genoa). At the time there were only twelve regular shipping lines operating between Europe and Egypt. During the first half of the 20th century the Western Harbor handled more than two thousand ships per year and was the transit port for Egypt's precious cotton harvest. The cotton was stored in the vast warehouses of the nearby MINET EL-BASSAL district (now partly deserted and the site of a Friday flea market) before being shipped to Europe. There was also much passenger traffic during this period (the only way to travel to Egypt was by steamship). There was a slump in Alexandria's maritime traffic prior to World War One and another in 1952, which saw an exodus of foreign merchants. This was remedied by further development of the quays and the construction of an oil and petrochemical complex. Today Alexandria handles over 60 percent of all Egypt's imports and exports.

"Alexandria . . . makes a fine appearance from the sea on a near approach; but being built on low ground, is, as the seamen say, 'very difficult to hit'."
Eliza Fay, 1779

The construction of the city of Alexandria as depicted by a 16th-century Italian artist.

Fort Qaitbay, built on the site of the Pharos Lighthouse.

The capture of Alexandria by Bonaparte's army in 1798 (above).

SHARI' RAS EL-TIN
The last corbeled houses, so characteristic of late Ottoman architecture, can still be seen in the Shari' Ras el-Tin, as can some of the first European-style apartment blocks, with their profusion of Italianate decorations.

TURKISH QUARTER

The oldest part of Alexandria, lying along the causeway linking the former island of Pharos with the mainland, consists of the districts of Anfushi, Gumrok (the customs district) and Ras el-Tin ("cape of figs"). For a long time, these districts were collectively known by Western travelers as the "Turkish Quarter". They were only established, at the very earliest, during the 16th century. GUMROK, the oldest of the three, flourished as a result of the decline of medieval Alexandria, which lay further south on the site of the ancient city. Although the medieval city had became quite important during the Mameluke period, its population was decimated by plague in the 17th century and by 1658 the city was little more than a heap of ruins punctuated by a few dilapidated dwellings. New houses were built outside the city walls, and these constituted the nucleus of a new city which was to expand rapidly in the early 18th century before it, too, was hit by plague. When the French landed in Alexandria in 1798 the "Turkish Quarter" was little more than a small town of eight thousand inhabitants centered around the Gumrok district and subsisting mainly from fishing. The later urban development of RAS EL-TIN and ANFUSHI BAY dates from the reign of Mohammed Ali (1805–49), whose expansionist aspirations, which hinged on the development of a naval fighting force, led him to choose Alexandria as the center of his Mediterranean policy. This was the beginning of a period of major construction for the city. In 1818 the great pasha began to build the huge PALACE OF RAS EL-TIN, of which certain sections, especially the *haramlik*, were reminiscent of his native Macedonian architecture. The present palace, which was built in 1925 by Italian architects, houses the Admiralty and is closed to the public. A military hospital and camps were built to the east of the palace. In 1825 Mohammed Ali commissioned the French engineer

Lefèbure de Cerisy to construct an arsenal, whose workshops soon employed more than four thousand workers. Several years later he undertook the relocation of the cemeteries that were scattered along Anfushi Bay, so that the land could then be sold by lots and used for the establishment of a new district. The site revealed some of the most ancient necropolises in Alexandria.

RAS EL-TIN NECROPOLIS. Three hypogea were discovered in the gardens of the Palace of Ras el-Tin during the renovation work carried out on the building in 1913–14. Eight more were discovered in 1939–40. They date from the early 2nd to the 3rd centuries BC, and their design is significantly different from those of the neighboring Anfushi Necropolis. A quadrilateral well provided access to three long galleries. Within the galleries, dozens of burial niches had been hollowed out. Nowadays the necropolis is not open to the public.

ANFUSHI NECROPOLIS. The necropolis lies to the south of the esplanade leading to the Palace of Ras el-Tin and consists of five tombs, all dating from the first half of the 3rd century, discovered in 1901 and 1921. The first and most remarkable of the tombs is reached by way of a vaulted stairway hewn out of the rock, leading down into a square courtyard which is open to the sky and provides access to two tombs. The walls of the stairway and tombs have a painted stucco revetment imitating alabaster and marble. The vaulted ceiling of the funeral chamber is decorated with geometric trompe l'oeil designs reminiscent of the coffered ceilings in certain ancient villas. The funeral motifs are a fine example of the combined influence of Greek art and the traditional forms of Egyptian art.

SHARI' RAS EL-TIN. The long Shari' Ras el-Tin is one of the new streets which were built in the Turkish Quarter during the 19th century. It runs from the palace esplanade, crossing through the Turkish Quarter to arrive at the Midan Manshiya.

FORT QAITBAY. The fort (above) was built at the end of the 15th century on the site of the Pharos Lighthouse, which, because of its height, was one of the Seven Wonders of the World.

THE PHAROS LIGHTHOUSE
The lighthouse was built in the 3rd century BC and used until the time of the Arab conquest. Although restored several times by the Tulunids and Fatimids, the edifice disappeared during the 14th century. Each of its three stories was based on a different design. the first was square, the second octagonal and the third circular. This combination inspired the still very controversial theory of the early 20th-century scientist, Hermann Thiersch, which affirms that Egyptian minarets are the direct descendants of the Pharos Lighthouse.

**ABU EL-ABBAS
EL-MURSI MOSQUE**
The high, central
dome of the mosque
(79 feet beneath the
keystone) is
supported by eight
monolithic pink
granite columns
quarried, cut and
polished in Italy, and
flanked by four small
cupolas.

ABU EL-ABBAS EL-MURSI MOSQUE. The main mosque in
Alexandria is named after Sidi Abu el-Abbas el-Mursi, a holy
man from Andalusia who died in the 13th century. It stands
midway between Fort Qaitbay and the city center, in a square
set slightly back from the Corniche called the Midan el-
Gawamaa (Square of the Mosques). The square also contains
several other sanctuaries, including the ABU EL-FATAH, EL-
BUSEIRI, YAQUT and NASR AD-DIN mosques, which were
either restored or rebuilt when the square was renovated after
World War One. Although they tend to date from the 18th
century, the Abu el-Abbas el-Mursi Mosque was constructed
relatively recently, since it was started in 1928 and completed
in 1945 after work had been suspended during the war years.
It replaced a structure, built in 1767, which had been
destroyed by fire a few years earlier, and this has caused some
confusion over the age of the mosque. The building, which
covers an area of over 32,000 square feet, has an extremely
unusual octagonal design. Although such a design was not
unprecedented in the Islamic architectural tradition (the most
famous example being the Rocher dome in Jerusalem), it
tended to be reserved for mausoleums and had never been
used in Egypt. The building was designed by the Italian
architect Mario Rossi (1897–1961), who for many years
headed the architects' department of the Waqf ▲ *302* ministry
which commissioned the mosque, and who is said to have
converted to Islam shortly before his death. He also designed
several other Alexandrian mosques, including the Ras el-Tin
and Ibrahim el-Qaïd mosques.

TERBANA MOSQUE. The Terbana Mosque (1677) is one of the
few remaining ancient mosques in Alexandria. It stands on
the corner of the Shari' Terbana and the Shari' Suq el-
Tabakhin and is reached by following the
Shari' Ras el-Tin toward Manshiya. The
first-floor façade is occupied
by shops and a *sabil*
● *113*.

The entrance consists of a portal of bicolored bricks. Particularly worthy of note are the two enormous granite columns with Corinthian capitals, which stand to the left of the steps, and a number of ancient columns (some of which, unfortunately, are very badly damaged), which have come from other sites. The mihrab ● *108* is covered with Maghrebi-style ceramics.

THE JEWISH COMMUNITY Most of the synagogues belonging to Alexandria's Jewish community have been destroyed (above).

THE SUQ DISTRICT ★. As it nears Manshiya the last section of the Shari' Ras el-Tin, still known as the Shari' Faransa, becomes a busy shopping street. The district around the Shari' Ras el-Tin and Shari' Midan which runs parallel to it is Alexandria's traditional *suq* district. At the turn of the century mainly duty-free goods, including items of clothing, cloth, gold and silver jewelry, could be found on sale here. Each section of the *suq* has its own speciality. For example, the SUQ EL-MAGHARBA (Maghrebi *suq*) has row upon row of medicinal plants which are used to make infusions with healing or supposedly miraculous properties, while the SUQ EL-LIBIA (Libyan *suq*)

sells the famous embroidered costumes worn by the Bedouins. In the Shari' Midan one of Alexandria's few surviving *wakala* ● *118* attests to the age of these *suq*. It forms part of the EL-SHORBAGI MOSQUE COMPLEX, which was founded in 1757 and has a distinctive gallery on the second floor that overlooks the street. Some of the stonework of this architectural complex, which also includes shops and living accommodation, bears hieroglyphic inscriptions. The Shari' Midan was also renowned as the home of a large section of Alexandria's Jewish community. Many Jewish families lived in *okelles* ● *181* like the huge EL-LAYMUN OKELLE, built round a central courtyard with galleries leading to the apartments. There was a continuous Jewish presence in Alexandria from the time of its foundation (as evidenced by the Greek and Aramean inscriptions found in the necropolis of the Ibrahimiya district) to the period following World War Two when the community totaled about forty thousand. After this time, however, came the waves of emigration, in the years 1948, 1956, 1962 and finally in 1967 when the last Jews were expelled from Egypt in the aftermath of the June 1967 Arab–Israeli War. As one approaches Manshiya, the streets become increasingly narrow. This area is known as the ZANQAT EL-SITTAT (or "Ladies' Alley"). The confined space is packed with both shops and stalls which sell the cloth, trinkets and perfumes that find so much favor not only with native Alexandrian women, but also with increasing numbers of tourists. Popular myth would have it that men and women alike come here to enjoy the close contact imposed by the narrowness of the streets.

SHORBAGI MOSQUE The second-floor gallery looks over the shops at street level. A fruit market such as one might find anywhere in the city.

179

The Alexandria Stock
Exchange was destroyed by
fire in 1977.

MANSHIYA

The Manshiya district grew up around a
vast esplanade some 350 yards long, built on
the edge of the Turkish Quarter during the
1830's on the site of an old
training ground where
Bedouins and oasis-dwellers
came to sell their goods. The
successive names given to the
esplanade evoke the various
stages of its history. When it
was first built it was known as
the PLACE DES CONSULS
because the adjacent land was
divided up to provide sites for
the consulates of the major

**BRITISH
BOMBARDMENT**
In July 1882, after a
violent bombardment
which destroyed vast
areas of the city, a
British squadron
landed in Alexandria
and managed to wipe
out the army of
Colonel Orabi Pasha,
the leader of the
Nationalist Party and
Egyptian Minister
for War, who wanted
to put an end to
Anglo-French
economic control.

foreign powers. It became the MIDAN MOHAMMED ALI
following the inauguration (1873) of the equestrian statue of
the great pasha (by the French sculptors Jacquemart and
Cordier), which was placed in the center of the esplanade,
and then the MIDAN MANSHIYA when the area around the
esplanade was rebuilt after the 1882 bombardment. The only
building that did not have to be rebuilt was the Anglican
Church of St Mark, founded in 1844. Most of these buildings
have survived and form a remarkably homogenous
architectural complex rarely to be seen in Egyptian cities,
which are usually a hotch-potch of different architectural
styles and buildings from a huge variety of different periods.
Some are modern versions of the *okelle*, a type of apartment
block characteristic of Alexandrian architecture. The
ALEXANDRIA STOCK EXCHANGE, the nerve center of the city,
stood at one end of the square for almost a century. It was
burnt during the 1977 hunger riots and subsequently
demolished; since then the site has remained a piece of waste
ground. Manshiya, now known as MIDAN AT-TAHRIR
(Liberation Square), was the scene of President Gamal Abd
el-Nasser's famous announcement in 1956, informing the
people of Alexandria that the Suez Canal had been
nationalized.

"OKELLE". The *okelle* was a rental apartment block, organized in much the same way as a *wakala* ● *118*, which provided residential and commercial accommodation. The first floor opened onto the courtyard and street and was reserved for shops and workshops, while the upper floors were given over to living accommodation. Two examples of modern *okelle* are the PASSAGE MENASCE, built in 1883 and designed by Lasciac ▲ *281,* and the MONFERRATO BUILDING, also built in 1883 and designed by Piattoli, which are both situated in the Midan at-Tahrir. The interior of each of these huge edifices is dissected by a narrow, cruciform street.

"OKELLES"
These buildings housed Alexandria's ethnic minorities. In the 18th century, each European nation had its own *okelle*.

TRIBUTE FROM THE ITALIAN COMMUNITY. Manshiya opens onto the sea via the MIDAN ORABI, an enormous planted area which was formerly known as the "French Gardens" because they were established on land given to the city by France. At the end of the square, a monument in the form of an exedra (which is now dedicated to the Unknown Soldier) was a tribute given by the Italian community to the khedive Ismaïl. It was designed by the architect Verrucci and erected in 1937. In the period between the wars, the Italian population of Alexandria, which was second in size only to that of the Greek community, reached 25,000; yet although the Italians had been living in Egypt for quite a considerable time, they had never really become established there. They were usually Italian émigrés expatriated for one or, at most, two generations. During the first half of the 19th century, Italian immigration was essentially politically motivated. After the Risorgimento the reasons behind it became economic. The community was usually of modest status, commonly excelling in the field of construction work. Until the 1950's Alexandria, like many other Egyptian cities, had a good supply of monumental masons, cabinet makers, building contractors, architects and engineers. The tall, smoked-glass tower beyond the monument has housed the new French-speaking Léopold Sédar Senghor University since late 1990.

Midan Manshiya (below) at the turn of the century, now the Midan at-Tahrir (Liberation Square).

Map of 17th-century Alexandria.

The Attarine Mosque, where Saïd Mohammed, a friend of Abu el-Abbas ▲ *178*, is buried.

THE CITY CENTER

At the turn of the century the center of Alexandria, which for some time had been focused around the Midan Manshiya, shifted toward the new suburbs to the west of the city. From then on it developed on the site of the ancient city which had subsequently become the site of the medieval city after the Arab conquest. An amphitheater, fragmented ramparts and a few cisterns are all that remains of these successive occupations, although parts of the original layout such as the ancient Canopic Way, now the Shari' Hurriya (formerly the Shari' Bab Rosetta), survived and could still be seen in the 19th century. The so-called "Arab" fortifications, a huge five-mile-long perimeter wall fortified with towers which had protected the city since the 13th century, were still intact when the French landed in Alexandria and remained so until the declassification of fortifications decreed in 1885. The same was true of the famous Alexandria cisterns. In 1800 the engineers of the Egypt Expedition recorded over three hundred, while in 1846 Colonel Barthélemy Gallice counted 896. Today there are only half a dozen.

ATTARINE ANTIQUES DISTRICT ★. The district is reached by crossing the Midan Manshiya and taking the Shari' Ahmed Orabi, turning right into the Shari' Senwosret and finally into the Shari' Attarine. The district takes its name from the mosque on the corner of the Shari' Attarine and the Shari' Sidi-Metwali. This former church was dedicated to Saint

Athanasius in 370 and converted into a mosque at the beginning of the Arab conquest. In the early 19th century it was used as a naval hospital before being destroyed in 1830 and subsequently rebuilt. Behind the mosque lies the Suq el-Attarine (Perfume Market) where, at the end of the last century, perfumes and spices from Syria and Lebanon were sold. Today dealers sell antique and second-hand furniture, sometimes beautiful opalines, chandeliers, ancient weapons and more modern wrought-iron work. Lovers of French literature may be interested to know that it is not uncommon to come across an early edition on the shelves of the French bookshop *Librairie des Amis des Lettres*. One of the district's specialties are the roasted quail and pigeons on sale in the evenings in a tiny square only a few yards from the French bookshop. If you follow the Shari' Attarine in the direction of Cairo station and turn left into the Shari' Ismail-Mehna, you will come to an intersection and the amphitheater.

KOM EL-DIKKA. The Roman amphitheater was discovered in 1964 by archeologists from Warsaw University and the Graeco-Roman Museum. The discovery followed the demolition of the remains of a fort dating from the Napoleonic expedition, and the leveling of the artificial hill on which it was constructed. Its present horseshoe shape is the consequence of a series of modifications made between the 2nd and 4th centuries when it was converted into a church. Next to the amphitheater are the remains of two necropolises (13th–14th and 8th–9th centuries). The tombs had been incorporated into a recently discovered ancient Roman bath complex which was one of the biggest in Alexandria and indeed in Egypt.

THE AMPHITHEATER
The thirteen gray and white marble tiers of the terrace lead down to the arena. The buttressed wall of the semicircular passageway which ran beneath the early theater constitutes the perimeter of the new amphitheater. Nearby are the ruins of the Roman baths (above).

"CLEOPATRA'S NEEDLES"
Today the two obelisks that the Alexandrians called "Cleopatra's Needles", illustrated (left) by Vivant Denon, can be seen in London and New York. They used to stand near one of the towers of the Arab fortifications.

View of the rooftops of Alexandria with, in the foreground, the cupolas of the Nabi Daniel Mosque.

SHARI' NABI DANIEL. The first street on the right after the Amphitheater is the Shari' Nabi Daniel, which leads down to the Corniche. It is a perfect example of Alexandria's cultural and religious heterogeneity. On the left, below the street, are several columns which were probably part of the ancient Roman road. Nearby the NABI DANIEL MOSQUE houses the tombs of the khedivial family, including that of Saïd Pasha, the son of Mohammed Ali. As part of the controversy surrounding the location of the tomb of Alexander the Great, the so-called Soma, which is one of the great unsolved mysteries of Alexandrian archeological exploration, some

historians have maintained that it lies beneath the Nabi Daniel Mosque. Modern archeologists tend to situate the Soma about half a mile further east, in the Graeco-Roman cemeteries. A little further on, before you cross the Shari' el-Hurriya, is the elegant villa of the FRENCH CULTURAL CENTER and, below that, the huge ELIAHU HANABI SYNAGOGUE, the only synagogue which still holds religious services. It was founded in the late 19th century on the site of an earlier synagogue built in 1354 and destroyed by fire during the 19th century. It houses the combined treasures of the seven (now nonexistent) Alexandrian synagogues. The Shari' Nabi Daniel opens onto the Shari' Saad Zaghlul near the Midan Saad Zaghlul and the central tram station.

Midan Saad Zaghlul, the nerve center of Alexandria.

CINEMAS AND RESTAURANTS. Alexandria's liveliest entertainments spots, both by day and night, are found near the vast Midan Saad Zaghlul and the streets leading from the square to the Shari' Hurriya. The intercity bus terminus and the Ramleh (Ar-Raml) tram station make the MIDAN SAAD ZAGHLUL one of Alexandria's busiest thoroughfares. The square stands on land reclaimed from the sea when the city's new quays were built, beginning in 1907. It is dominated by a huge monument to the great nationalist leader Saad Zaghlul ▲ 281 by the Egyptian sculptor Mahmud Mukhtar ▲ 282. Several luxury hotels overlook the square, including the famous *Cecil Hotel* (1928), which provided the setting for part of Lawrence

The façade (right) and interior (below) of the Eliahu Hanabi Synagogue.

Durrell's ● *162 Alexandria Quartet*. The square also boasts two of the city's best-known coffee houses: the *Délices*, still run by the descendants of its Greek founder, and the *Trianon*, whose superb Art Nouveau-style frescos on wood have been recently restored. A little further on, in the Shari' Safiya-Zaghlul, leading up to Kom el-Dikka, are several of Alexandria's more prestigious cinemas. They include the *Strand* (owned for a long time by the founder of the Dores Studios, a portraitist who was extremely popular with prominent Alexandrians at the turn of the century), the *Rialto* with its name written in Greek lettering, the luxurious *Metro* built in 1950 by Metro-Goldwyn-Mayer (its décor, carefully maintained by successive managers, is well worth seeing) and the *Rio*, the only cinema with a second, open-air auditorium on the terrace. The *Elite* restaurant, the last gastronomic stronghold of French-speaking Alexandrians, is to be found in the same street. Its Greek *patronne*, who is known to her regulars as Madame Cristina, has had the walls covered with paintings, in the style of the bistros of Montparnasse. One of the paintings is a portrait of the poet Constantine Cavafy.

CAVAFY MUSEUM. Constantine Cavafy (1863–1933), the great poet born in Alexandria to Greek parents, is buried in the Greek cemetery near his house at no. 4 Shari' Sharm el-Sheikh. In 1933 his apartment was converted into a museum, a place of pilgrimage for his admirers where various rare editions of his books are on display. Visitors can also see family photos, his funeral mask and pieces of furniture which are supposed to have belonged to him but are probably copies. A new room is devoted to another Greek writer, Stratis Tsirkas.

GRAECO-ROMAN MUSEUM ★. The Graeco-Roman Museum is reached by way of the Shari' Safiya-Zaghlul and Shari' el-Hurriya. When it was founded in 1891 by the Italian archeologist Botti the museum occupied the five rooms of an apartment in the Shari' Rosetta. In 1894, in response to a growing interest in the history and archeology of Ancient Egypt, the khedive Abbas II decided to found a museum devoted to the ancient splendor of Alexandria. The newly established Graeco-Roman Museum received gifts from such great private collectors as Antoniadis, Gianaclis and Glymenopoulos and rooms were named after them until the Free Officers' coup in 1952. Since then the collection has been enriched by exhibits which have come mainly from excavations carried out in the city and its environs as well as from the Faiyum ▲ *361*, the Nile Delta ▲ *205* and Middle Egypt ▲ *371*. The museum's collection serves as an admirable illustration of the influence of Alexandrian culture throughout Egypt.

"You will find no other countries, no other seas. The city will always be with you: you will be walking along these same streets, growing old in these same, familiar districts and your hair will turn white beneath these same roofs. You will always find yourself in this city. As for leaving – vain hope – there is no boat, no road that you can take. As you have ruined your life in this corner of the earth, so you have destroyed it everywhere else in the world."
    Constantine Cavafy

Façade of the Graeco-Roman Museum.

Today the modern city stands on the site of ancient Alexandria and there are few visible remains of this former capital of the ancient world. The remains of Ptolemaic palaces, temples, baths and other public buildings are constantly being discovered and added to the collections of the city's Graeco-Roman Museum. Its twenty connecting rooms, arranged around a central garden containing statues, stelae, sarcophagi and a temple dedicated to Sobek, house the legacy of ancient Alexandrian civilization. The museum is a remarkable synthesis of Egyptian, Greek and Roman cultures, which echoes the symbolic cosmopolitanism of the city.

Bronze head of Hadrian with eyes in *pâte de verre*, found at Qena.

Marble statue of the god Harpocrates (naked and with a finger in his mouth), son of Isis. Found at Ras el-Soda.

Fragment of colored *pâte de verre* from the Roman period. Alexandria had a flourishing glass industry famed for its iridescent *millefiori* glass.

Plaster head (probably a Libyan) from Cyrenaica.

"TANAGRA"
The museum has a collection of terracotta figurines known as *tanagras*, named after the Greek town where a similar collection was discovered. They all come from Alexandrian necropolises, mainly Shatby, Hadra and Ibrahimiya.

ROMAN MOSAIC
Roman mosaic discovered at Thmuis in the central Delta region. It represents an aquatic scene with images of birds, frogs, eels, fish, crocodiles, hippopotamuses and Pygmies. In the center, beneath a windblown awning, a family group is being entertained by a dancer.

DIONYSIAC GOBLET
Silver-gilt goblet (1st century) with a Dionysiac harvest scene (showing cupids, satyrs and a nymph playing a lyre) engraved in relief.

"TANAGRA"
These figurines represent a wide variety of human figures and are a valuable source of information on Alexandrian social and religious life during the Graeco-Roman period.

Grotesque terracotta figurine.

The district was named after the (now destroyed) Bab Rosetta.

THE CISTERNS
Alexandria's network of cisterns impressed many Europeans and in particular elicited the following remark from Saint-Génis, a member of the Egypt Expedition: "Here the ingenuity of the Greeks, inspired by the most pressing of all needs when founding a city without [a natural source of] water, equaled the momentous efforts of the Ancient Egyptians in terms of the exacting nature of their undertaking, while endowing it with their natural taste for elegance. They succeeded in creating a second, subterranean city which was quite as vast as the first, and its remains are certainly one of the greatest and most beautiful works of Antiquity".

BAB ROSETTA DISTRICT

GREEK QUARTER. One of the most beautiful residential districts in Alexandria stretches along the Shari' el-Hurriya beyond the Graeco-Roman Museum. Its luxury villas and elegant residential blocks include the monumental MICLAVEZ BUILDING opposite the Town Hall (a prize-winner in the 1927 façade competition organized by the city) and the impressive ADDA COMPLEX, which was built in 1929 by the architect Nahman. It is undoubtedly the best maintained district in Alexandria; it is also the only district to have escaped the disfiguring modern construction suffered by the rest of the city. It used to be known as the Greek Quarter because, at the turn of the century, the wealthiest members of the Greek community chose to live in these streets, which are still named after the Ptolemies, Pharaohs, Abbasids and Fatimids. It was neither the only nor the oldest Greek quarter in the city, however. The first site of the city's largest foreign community, which could claim a population of over fifty thousand in the years between the wars, lay further east in the area around the Greek Orthodox patriarchate and the old Church of St Saba, in close proximity to which the Greek hospital (now used as warehouses) was built in 1887. Greeks of more modest status moved into the less expensive housing developments of Ibrahimiya.

REMAINS OF THE SHALLALAT GARDENS. Beyond the Greek Quarter the Shari' el-Hurriya opens onto a vast green area, which are the public gardens created by the Alexandria Town Council in 1905 on the site of the old fortifications around the Bab Rosetta. The debris was used to create relief and build the waterfalls (*shallalat*) after which the gardens were named. The remains of one of the rampart towers (the west tower) were excavated and incorporated into the design of the gardens, which also have the only CISTERN in Alexandria open to the public: the so-called IBN EL-NABI. The three levels of this square cistern

> "ALEXANDRIA SEEMS PAVED WITH THE CRUMBLING RUINS OF
> A THOUSAND CITIES. EVERY ACRE OF EARTH HAS BEEN TURNED
> AND TURNED AGAIN. THE GROUND APPEARS THICK WITH
> THE HUMUS OF ITS HISTORY."   HERMAN MELVILLE

are supported by granite columns taken from earlier
structures.

THE CISTERNS OF ALEXANDRIA. These enormous reservoirs
were constructed below ground level mainly when the city was
founded to ensure that its houses always had a fresh supply of
drinking water; some, however, were built at a later date.
They were all linked by a complex, intercommunicating
system of conduits and drew their water from a canal leading
from the Canopic branch of the Nile about 17 miles from
Alexandria, in the locality of Schedia. According to the
engineer and historian Ali Mubarak, many cisterns were
artificially filled with water brought in water skins and were
cleaned out once a year to ensure that they remained
hygienic. Most were filled in during the 19th century, although
a few were still being used in 1888 to supply water to private
citizens and public buildings. The five other surviving cisterns
in Alexandria are closed to the public. One of these is situated
nearby, on the corner of the Shari' el-Hurriya and a street that
takes its name from the Ptolemies, and was used as a shelter
during World War Two. Rumor has it that other cisterns still
exist and may be the cause of certain unexplained
disappearances.

FINE ARTS MUSEUM. The Fine Arts Museum, which is housed
in a villa in the district of Muharram Bey, is the subject of a
long-standing and so far unresolved controversy between the
Governorate, on which it depends in principle, and the
Ministry of Culture, which claims responsibility for the
supervision of the museum. The consequence of this,
however, is that most of its richly stocked collections are kept
in reserve and   are only occasionally brought
out for   temporary exhibitions.

The Museum of
Modern Art is housed
in a beautiful villa
donated in 1954 by
the Menasce family.

Engraving (1802) by
Louis Mayer of the
ancient columnated
mosque of the (now
nonexistent) Bab
Rosetta.

The tent occupied by the chie
engineer in charge of the
construction of the Mahmudiya
Canal. The plans for the canal were
drawn up by Pascal Coste

"Alexander found the Nile at Abukir (Canopic Mouth); then you had to go to Rosetta (ancient Bolbitine Mouth). So Mohammed Ali built a 45-mile-long canal, the Mahmudiya Canal, named in honor of Mahmud, the then ruler of Turkey, which was completed in 1820. It was badly constructed and its banks were continually collapsing, but the opening of the canal led to the rapid expansion of Alexandria and the decline of Rosetta."
E.M. Forster

MODERN ARCHITECTURE. The so-called "water traffic circle" is a must for lovers of modern architecture. Among the interesting old installations preserved by the Alexandria Water Company is the VILLA AGHION (1926), a fine piece of avant-garde architecture designed by the French architect Auguste Perret (1874–1954). On the way back to the Shari' el-Hurriya, which is particularly impressive just beyond the city walls, is the former GREEK HOSPITAL, built in 1945 by the French architect Jean Walter. Opposite the hospital is found the ENGINEERING FACULTY, built in 1950–2 by the architects' department of the Egyptian Ministry for Construction.

WALK ALONG THE MAHMUDIYA CANAL

From the point at which it leaves the Nile, the Mahmudiya Canal winds over a distance of about 50 miles before entering the roadstead of the western harbor. To some extent it can be seen as the successor to the canal which once brought water to Alexandria's cisterns and which was also constructed in the bed of the former Canopic branch of the Nile. The Mahmudiya Canal was built between 1817 and 1820 on the orders of Mohammed Ali, who envisaged a canal which would act as a navigable waterway to Cairo as well as supplying Alexandria's drinking water and irrigating the land of Bahayra province. The project was so important to Mohammed Ali that, having entrusted it for some time to a Turkish engineer who was soon overcome by the sheer scope of the task, he called upon the French architect Pascal Coste (1787–1879), who went on to complete the work, which was in fact his greatest construction project in Egypt. The Mahmudiya Canal can be reached from the Shallalat Gardens by way of a street that takes its name from the Suez Canal. At the turn of the century a number of Alexandrian families owned beautiful canal-side residences in luxuriant garden settings. Unfortunately almost nothing remains of these today, apart from the occasional palm-lined driveway leading to factories and warehouses in the now industrialized zone traversed by the canal. It is still possible to walk the entire length of the canal along the old paved road bordered by sycamores which runs along its banks. Although the walk may not be as romantic as it once was, it is still a very original way to discover the working-class and industrial districts of Alexandria.

NUZHA AND ANTONIADIS GARDENS. About 1½ miles upstream, the canal runs along the edge of the Nuzha and Antoniadis Gardens. The Nuzha district is steeped in history. In 268 BC the poet Callimachus lived and taught here, in c. AD 640 the Roman general Pompilius thwarted the King of Syria's attempt to capture Alexandria, while in the same year the cavalry of the Arab conqueror Amr Ibn el-As ● *66* pitched camp here before entering the city. The gardens were redeveloped by the Alexandria Town Council at the turn of the century. They originally belonged to a Marseilles trader by the name of Pastré before they were bought by the khedive Ismaïl. It was Ismaïl who opened them to the public. Today they comprise ZOOLOGICAL GARDENS, a small MUSEUM OF NATURAL HISTORY and a ROSE GARDEN. The magnificent neighboring property, also a public garden, used to belong to Sir John A. Antoniadis (1815–95), a prominent Alexandrian of Greek origin. The gardens could be visited during his lifetime and the entrance fee of two piasters was donated to charity. In 1918 his son gave the gardens to King Fuad, who in turn donated them to the city. Beyond the ANTONIADIS PALACE, which was the venue for the 1951 Anglo-Egyptian negotiations, a Roman tomb hewn out of the rock is of the same design as the tombs in the Anfushi Necropolis ▲ *177*, with three funeral chambers opening onto a central hall. It is impossible to know what type of paintings decorated the walls because the tomb is in a very bad state of disrepair. The originality of these remains lies in the total absence of Egyptian influence and its exclusively Greek architecture and decoration.

The massive Engineering Faculty, built in neo-Pharaonic style (1950–2) by the Egyptian Ministry for

Construction, has aged particularly well because it was so carefully finished.

Kom es-Shogafa ★

On the side walls of the vestibule two niches carved out of the rock contain statues of a man and

a woman which combine Egyptian (clothes and general bearing) and Greek (hair and headdresses) sculptural styles.

Take the Shari el-Khediwi from Ramses Station and turn left into the Shari' el-Awud as-Sawari. Continue past Pompey's Pillar and take the Shari' Bab el-Muluk on the right and then the Shari' el-Nasriya, which leads to the catacombs. The Kom es-Shogafa ("hill of tiles") is a rocky plateau situated between the ancient villages of Karmuz and Minia el-Bassal, now densely populated districts of Alexandria, where Christian catacombs and chapels were first discovered. The exploitation of the quarries, in addition to Mohammed Ali's ● *68* use of the hill as a bastion to defend the modern city, destroyed any remaining traces. In 1900, almost fifty years later, a donkey accident led to the discovery of another necropolis, an enormous hypogeum which is the largest in Alexandria and probably dates from the 2nd century AD. It is a remarkable example of the Alexandrian blend of Graeco-Roman and Egyptian styles.

INTERIOR. The catacombs were hewn out of the rock on three superposed levels. The dead were lowered by ropes down the central well of a spiral staircase. The vestibule has two semi-circular niches, each containing a bench surmounted by a shell carved in the vaulted upper half of the niche. This opens onto a rotunda built around a central well covered with a sort of domed kiosk supported by eight pillars. The adjoining burial chambers contain sarcophagi and niches for funeral urns have been hollowed out of the rock. On the left is the TRICLINIUM or banqueting hall where, on the days dedicated to remembrance of the dead, relatives and friends gathered for a funeral banquet in memory of their loved ones. The ceiling is supported by stone pillars and there are three stone couches (on which mattresses were piled) arranged in a semi-circle. The table, most probably wooden, stood in the center.

On the right is the so-called HALL OF CARACALLA, named in remembrance of that emperor's massacre of Christians invited to the amphitheater of Alexandria. Particularly interesting are the four tombs decorated with paintings on stuccowork where the bones of young men and horses were found. A staircase, decorated with a large relief carving of a shell, leads from the rotunda to the lower story, which consists of a vestibule and a burial chamber. Here the decoration is reminiscent of the Pharaonic tombs of Luxor and Saqqara in the Valley of the Kings. In the vestibule the capitals of the pillars are decorated with papyrus and acanthus leaves and the cornice with a winged sun flanked by two falcons. The statues have Greek hairstyles and headdresses and Egyptian clothes. A door set in the far wall leads into the funeral chapel, where both Greek and Egyptian religious symbols are found. On a bas-relief sculpture positioned on both sides of the door, two bearded serpents wearing the double crown of Upper and Lower Egypt rear up on their coils next to the serpent staff of Hermes and the pine cone of Dionysus. Above them two gorgons can be seen, which were probably intended to terrify unwelcome visitors. The burial chamber contains three enormous sarcophagi, hewn out of the rock and decorated with festoons of flowers, fruit and gorgons' heads. It is interesting that the representations of the Egyptian gods Anubis, Thoth, Ptah, Horus and Apis show a marked lack of understanding of both Pharaonic style and symbolism. The archeologist Gaston Maspero was struck by the Egyptian style of this funeral chapel, which caused him to comment: "Nothing is more curious to study than this hybrid form of documentation and the way in which it has been executed. The idea that comes immediately to mind as you examine it is that it was commissioned by members of the Egyptian nobility who were still deeply attached to their national form of worship. [. . .] However, if we remember the degree of popularity enjoyed by Isis throughout the Roman empire toward the end of the 2nd century AD, there is nothing to stop us supposing that this Egyptian décor housed the remains of a foreigner in some way associated with the worship of that goddess, perhaps an Isiac of Greek origin." Nothing remains of the structure that once surmounted the hypogea, except for a mosaic with geometric designs.

A passageway hewn out of the rock leads to a circular chamber supported by pillars. The tombs are arranged around the central chamber.

Some historians believe that Pompey's Pillar was part of the portico of the "sister" library of the Great Alexandria Library housed in the Serapeum. The 88-foot pillar is made of pink Aswan granite and tapers slightly from the 9-foot diameter of its base to one of 7½ feet at the top. It was dedicated in c. AD 297 by the prefect of Egypt to the emperor Diocletian for his victory in 296 over the Christian Achilles, who had usurped the title of emperor. On the west face of the granite base, the following four lines in Greek characters can still be deciphered: "To the most just of emperors, the divine protector of Alexandria, Diocletian the invincible: Postumus, prefect of Egypt." The pillar was wrongly named Pompey's Pillar by the Crusaders who believed that it marked the site of the tomb of the Roman general.

POMPEY'S PILLAR. By retracing your steps along the Shari' el-Nasriya and Shari' Bab-el-Muluk you come to Pompey's Pillar (El-Awud as-Sawari, "horseman's pillar") on the left. It is the most important surviving element of the SERAPEUM, the ancient temple of Serapis, which certain ancient writers described as the most beautiful in Alexandria and second only to the Capitol in Rome. The temple was built on a platform reached by a flight of one hundred steps. In the sanctuary was a richly decorated statue of Serapis, a Graeco-Roman deity combining the attributes of Osiris and Apis. Excavations carried out in 1943–4 in the southeast and southwest corners of the Ptolemaic enclosure yielded remains of the foundations of the temple containing plaques made of gold, silver, bronze, opaque glass and ceramic tiles which bore the inscription in Greek and in Egyptian hieroglyphics: "King Ptolemy [III Euergetes], son of Ptolemy and Arsinoe, divine siblings, [has dedicated] the temple and sacred enclosure to Serapis". The Serapeum was destroyed toward the end of the century during the reign of Trajan (98–117) and a new temple was probably built in the following decade, during Hadrian's reign. In 391 the Christians destroyed it and built a monastery and a church dedicated to Saint John the Baptist. These were destroyed in their turn, probably in the 10th century. The remains of Roman baths and various statues of the Sphinx and Ramesses II brought to Alexandria from Heliopolis (date unknown) can still be seen on the site of Pompey's Pillar. The function of the two long, underground galleries set with niches to the west of the pillar is not known for certain. One theory is that funeral urns were placed in the niches; another maintains that birds and other sacred animals were buried there. Another somewhat ludicrous hypothesis would have it that they were used as shelves for the books of the "sister" library of the Great Alexandria Library. They were most probably dedicated in some way to the worship of Serapis. From here, it is possible to regain the city center via the canal or the Sidi Gaber district.

Engraving (1820) depicting the entirely imaginary site of Pompey's Pillar with one of "Cleopatra's Needles" in the distance.

> "ALEXANDRIA, THE MORNING DEW, THE DOWN OF WHITE CLOUDS, SLANTING RAYS OF SUNLIGHT WASHED BY THE RAIN, THE HEART OF MEMORIES STEEPED IN HONEY AND TEARS."
>
> NAGUIB MAHFOUZ

THE CORNICHE ★

Alexandria did not have a corniche until the early 20th century. At the time the old isthmus residences faced inland while the rest of the bay was bordered by the remains of fortifications. Their declassification (1885) was followed by a seawall project, whose purpose was to reclaim a large area of land from the sea (a strip of land with an average width of about 100 yards). The new quays between Fort Qaitbay and Cape Silsila were begun in 1907 and completed ten years later. In 1934 the Corniche was extended as far as El-Muntaza.

CASINOS, BEACHES AND BEACH HUTS. Because Alexandria's beaches were either unsuitable or inaccessible, bathing (a popular pastime among European residents) was practiced throughout the 19th century in special bathing establishments. The most famous of these was the *Zuro*, later known as the *Cleopatra*, situated on the present site of the *Grand Trianon*. It had long, floating landing stages which lay at right angles to the beach, and wooden huts on stilts so that the women could bathe shielded from prying eyes. Although nothing remains of these establishments, they have to some extent been superseded by the many stilted "casinos" dotted along the Corniche. Nobody bathes here any more but people come to drink tea, even in bad weather, and for wedding celebrations. Dances were held here in the postwar years, especially at the *Ship* (now the *Saraya*), a casino that looked like a steamer, which was built in 1945 by the Alexandria Town Council but somewhat disfigured by successive renovation work. The development of the Corniche was accompanied by the construction of row upon row of beach huts, which were intended to offer the bathers the best possible facilities.

BEACH HUTS
The famous rows of beach huts (above) built along Alexandria's Corniche. They could be rented seasonally from the town council

and were initially a huge success. In 1945 demand was three times greater than the number of huts available because it was considered the "in thing" to have your own beach hut. Today the four thousand huts are enjoyed by a very different type of clientele for whom bathing in a swimsuit would be unthinkable.

DISCOVERY ON THE SITE OF THE NEW LIBRARY
In June 1993 the Egyptian Antiquities Department discovered the foundations of a Ptolemaic house on the site of the new library. A marble hand, two Ptolemaic heads and mosaics (one is shown above) were also discovered.

CAPE SILSILA AND THE SITE OF THE NEW LIBRARY. In the fall of 1989 the foundation stone of the new Alexandria Library was laid on Cape Silsila (formerly Lochias, the site of the palaces of the Ptolemies). The goal of the project's sponsor, UNESCO, was to reconstruct the "temple of learning" represented by the original Great Alexandria Library, whose 500,000 volumes will be part of the new library's data base. Founded by Ptolemy I Soter, the Great Library was the most important element of the Mouseion (museum) whose vast premises housed amphitheaters, laboratories, observatories, a refectory, a park and a zoo. It was the great intellectual achievement of the Ptolemaic dynasty, and the work conducted within its walls had a profound influence on Western thought. It appears that the museum and library, of which nothing now remains, were situated on the Canopic Way. The causes of the great fire that destroyed the library at the time of the conquest of the city by Amr Ibn el-As ● 66 in 640, and those responsible for it, remain the subject of heated historical debate.

ALEXANDRIA BY TRAM

One of the best ways of discovering Alexandria is by tram.
The main Ramleh line, which is also the oldest, leaves from
the Midan Saad Zaghlul in the city center and follows a route
which runs more or less parallel to the Corniche. It was
originally a railway line, built and operated by a British
company to service various coastal towns and villages
scattered among the dunes from which the name "Ramleh"
(*ar-raml*, "sands") is derived. At the time the area to the east
of the city had a population of at most five hundred
inhabitants, but the beauty of the site and the reputedly
therapeutic value of the climate soon encouraged prominent
Alexandrians to establish their summer residences there.
Over the years the Ramleh suburb became a permanent
residential district and the population increased to such an
extent that today only a few of the old villas have survived the
high-rise construction of the last few decades. The observant
visitor will, however, notice the few surviving remnants of
extravagant early 20th-century architecture. The Ramleh line
opened in 1863 and operated for the first year with horse-
drawn carriages. The following year steam engines were
introduced. The terminus was on the present site of the
Bulkeley Station, and there were departures every hour. In
1868 the line was extended to Schutz Station, and, twenty
years later, to San Stefano; in 1891 new stations (Saroit Pasha,
Laurens, Saraya) were added. In 1904 the line was electrified
and a new branch line was constructed to create a more direct
link between Bulkeley and San Stefano. Finally the line was
extended in 1910 to Victoria Station, which is now the
terminus.

STATION NAMES
Although a
committee was
formed in 1963 to
give "Egyptian"
names to all the
stations on this line,
most of them are still
known by their
original name, which
was often associated
with the district in
which they were
located, evoking the
topography and
cosmopolitanism of
Alexandria.

RAMLEH STATION AND "CLEOPATRA'S NEEDLES". The tram
terminus is in an extremely busy part of the city, invaded from
dawn until dusk by a host of street vendors and small
craftsmen such as the traditional shoe-shiners. Near the
present site of the station and opposite the modern *Hotel
Metropole*, the CAESAREUM once stood, a sumptuous temple
built by Cleopatra for Mark Antony and completed, after
their double suicide, by Octavian (Augustus), who dedicated
it during his lifetime to imperial worship. The temple was
sacked by Constantius II in AD 356, rebuilt, razed to the
ground once more and converted into a church before finally
disappearing in 912. It was here that
the

Imaginary
representation of
the site of the
Great Library.

Fort and harbor at Abukir.

HYPOGEUM AT MUSTAFA PASHA
There is a first-century tomb near the Mustafa Pasha Tram Station.

SHATBY CEMETERY
High walls surround the areas reserved for the members of each faith. View of the Jewish cemetery and the Suarez family mausoleum (below).

famous mathematician Hypatia was killed by being stoned to death in 415. Her murder marks the height of the persecution of nonbelievers by the Christians of Alexandria. In his writings, Pliny the Elder made mention of the obelisks (the deceptively named "Cleopatra's Needles") that decorated the temple, and which remained in Alexandria until they were transported to London's Embankment (in 1877) and New York's Central Park (in 1879), where they still stand. The pink Aswan granite "needles" had originally been erected in front of the temple of Heliopolis in Cairo by Thutmose III before being transported to Alexandria on the orders of Julius Caesar.

STATIONS. "MAZARITTA", the name of the first station on the tram line, is a corruption of "lazaretto" (built nearby by Mohammed Ali in 1831 and subsequently transferred to the other end of the city). En route to the station the line passes the IBRAHIM EL-QAÏD MOSQUE, which was built in 1951 by Mario Rossi. Shatby, named after a Muslim saint who died in 1272, is situated outside the old city walls. It is here that the cemeteries for members of the city's non-Muslim faiths (the main Muslim cemetery is at Bab Sidra) can be found, which were built in the mid-19th century near an ancient necropolis of little interest. IBRAHIMIYA services a district constructed on agricultural land belonging to Prince Ibrahim Ahmed, which was sold off in lots in 1888 by a real estate company. Sporting is named after the 100-acre Sporting Club, founded in 1889, and still remains one of the city's more fashionable districts. SIDI-GABER is the name not only of the tram station, but also of the railway station on the main Alexandria–Cairo line and the district surrounding the nearby mausoleum of Sidi Gaber (1145–1217), who was an Andalusian traveler. The tramline forks after MUSTAFA PASHA and BULKELEY stations, and merges again at San Stefano. The more direct, northern line passes through SABA PASHA, GLYMENOPOULOS, ZIZINIA, LAURENS, SARAYA and SIDI BISHR. Sidi Bishr is renowned for its unspoiled beaches, and it was here that the remains of the 2nd-century RAS EL-SODA TEMPLE were discovered in 1936. VICTORIA was named after Victoria College, founded by the British in 1899. The college was renamed the El-Nasser College after the Suez Crisis. In 1909 it moved its premises to the far end of the Ramleh line, but only after it had managed to ensure that the line would be extended to one of its entrances.

EL-MUNTAZA, EL-MAMURA AND ABUKIR GARDENS

EL-MUNTAZA. El-Muntaza lies about 15 miles east of
Alexandria along the Corniche. This vast estate was gradually
acquired by the khedive Abbas II who chose it as the site for
the SALAMLIK, one of his residences, built in 1892 and later

converted into a hotel. In 1932 King Fuad built the
HARAMLIK, a larger palace which was converted into a
museum after 1952 but which is now closed to the public.
King Farouk's contribution to El-Muntaza was the bridge to
the island where he built a tea-house. The complex is now
reserved for the Free Officers and their families. In the vast,
115-acre park asphalted pathways cross the gardens, follow
the edge of a pinewood and link pavilions and rotundas. The
luxury *Palestine Hotel* overlooks the beach. Next to the
El-Muntaza estate is the resort of EL-MAMURA with its ultra-
modern architecture, which was very popular in the 1960's.
ABUKIR ★. The fishing village of Abukir has a fine beach and
is renowned for its fish restaurants. Legend has it that ancient
Canopus took its name from the tomb of Canopus, one of
Menelaus' pilots who had returned from the Trojan War
and was buried near Fort Tawfiqiya. The few remnants
of the temples of Serapis and Isis, destroyed
by Theophilus, Bishop of Alexandria, are in
the Graeco-Roman Museum ▲ *186*. Reputed
to have miraculous properties, the relics of
Saint John and Saint Cyr (after whom
modern Abukir was named) were
transported to Canopus by Cyril, another
bishop of Alexandria. All that now remains
are the ruined baths near the fort, the Greek
catacombs, a granite statue and a recently
discovered statue of Isis.

ANCIENT CANOPUS
Canopus is associated
with the pleasure and
debauchery described
by Seneca (hence the
expression "Canopic
pleasures"): "There,
pleasure is given free
rein, there, as if a
certain licence were
due to the very place
itself, everything is
unrestrained".

**THE BATTLE OF
ABUKIR**
On July 25, 1799, the
French drove back
the Turkish army who
had landed in the Bay
of Abukir. But on
March 8, 1801, Sir
Ralph Abercromby
succeeded in
defeating the
Ottoman army, which
was forced to leave
Egypt in September.

These painted
carrioles are a feature
of Abukir.

Half a day

AROUND ALEXANDRIA

EL-MEX. Leave Alexandria via the Midan at-Tahrir and take the Shari' Bab el-Akhdar, which crosses the Minet el-Bassal district to the industrial suburb of Gabari, named after the venerable sheikh. The western cemetery of the ancient city, which stretched along this section of the coast, is now mainly submerged and eroded by currents. Some of the remains are in the Graeco-Roman Museum. Beyond the cemetery lies the former fishing village of El-Mex, a popular vacation resort with middle-class Alexandrians at the beginning of the century and now one of the city's industrial suburbs. Today the shoreline is occupied by warehouses, tanneries, oil refineries and a military camp. The extensively damaged remains of a small PTOLEMAIC NECROPOLIS, hewn out of the limestone rock and probably dating from the 1st century BC, was discovered in the El-Wardian district. Stone taken from the El-Mex quarries was used to construct both the ancient and modern cities of Alexandria.

EL-DIKHEILA. El-Dikheila lies on the coast road between Alexandria and Mersa Matruh. Excavations carried out near the military camp of El-Dikheila uncovered the remains of the ENATON

Detail of the interior of the Ptolemaic necropolis of El-Wardian.

MONASTERY, founded in the 5th century by a community of monks whose traces were also found further west in the desert near Lake Mariut and Wadi Natrun.

AGAMI. Agami, the Egyptian St-Tropez further along the coast road, is still the most fashionable resort on the Mediterranean coast and, from the end of June, welcomes several hundred thousand visitors and holiday-makers. The Cairo and Alexandria "smart set" still gather there every summer, but nowadays they are forced to share the resort with the middle and even the working classes as a result of the building boom experienced by Agami over the last decade. The resort was founded in the 1950's when two Alexandrians, Bianchi and Bless, acquired substantial areas of land on this virtually deserted site (only a few Bedouin families camped there),

Gabari Palace near El-Mex, which was built by the viceroy Saïd and subsequently used as a quarantine center.

which owed its beauty to the fig trees growing in abundance and the long bay with its small fort, built by the French army

1 ABUKIR 2 EL-MEX 3 LAKE MARIUT 4 ARAB TOWER 5 EL-DIKHEILA 6 AGAMI 7 ABUSIR 8 EL-ALAMEIN 9 SIDI ABD EL-RAHMAN 10 EL-DABA 11 MERSA MATRUH 12 SIDI BARRANI 13 SALLUM

during their Egypt campaign. Bianchi and Bless offered the land (fairly unsuccessfully) for sale in two lots which are still named after them. Throughout the next twenty years Agami comprised only a few stone villas (in the Bianchi district) and wooden chalets (in the Bless district) scattered among the dunes. With no running water or electricity, spending the summer there was more like going on safari than on holiday. For the early "settlers", modern Agami is barely recognizable. Few of the original buildings remain, most having been replaced by residential blocks, each one taller than the one before, where the apartments are extremely expensive. However, there is the occasional exception: for example, the VILLA LASHIN, built in 1962 by the architect Ali Azzam, or the award-winning (Aga Khan Foundation in 1980) BEIT EL-HALAWA (1975) designed by Abd el-Wahid el-Wakil, a disciple of Hassan Fathi ▲ *442*. The coast road passes through the resorts of Hannoville and Sidi Kheir, which are extremely popular in summer with local tourists, before it eventually reaches Abusir.

ABUSIR. Abusir is the site of the Ptolemaic temple of Taposiris Magna, probably built shortly after the foundation of Alexandria. All that remains of the temple, dedicated to Osiris, is the outer wall and the pylons. It appears that sacred animals were worshipped there, as is evidenced by an animal necropolis that was found nearby. Inside the walls can be found the remains of a Christian church and, below these, what is left of the public baths built by the emperor Justinian, a seawall, quays and a bridge. To the north of the hill the tower, which was built by Ptolemy II Philadelphus but is now ruined, has a square base surmounted by an octagonal and then a circular story. It is supposedly a replica of the destroyed Alexandrian Pharos Lighthouse. The BURG EL-ARAB, otherwise known as the Arab Tower, gave its name to the nearby village.

The Villa Lashin, whose design was inspired by the hull of a ship.

BURG EL-ARAB. At the center of Burg el-Arab, a village built on a small hill, is a sort of citadel which is in fact a carpet factory founded by the British after World War One. In close proximity to the village a quarry can be seen, which was exploited in ancient times.

KARM ABU MENAS

Today ruins are all that remain of this once bustling town. Its walls were covered with inscriptions made by pilgrims who had come here to find a cure for their pain or illness.

The 3rd-century Monastery of Abu Menas lies west of the city, midway between Alexandria and Wadi Natrun, on the road that used to lead to the Oasis of Amun and Cyrenaica. The site commemorates Saint Menas, an Alexandrian soldier serving in the army of Diocletian who, having refused to persecute the Christians and publicly declared his Christian faith, was martyred in 296. Legend has it that his remains were brought back from Phrygia by camel and buried at the spot where the animal stopped and refused to go any further. A spring whose waters possessed miraculous properties immediately welled up on the spot.

SAINT MENAS VINEYARDS. Today only ruins and desert remain where once vines and olive trees flourished in a fertile oasis whose four basilicas (discovered at the turn of the century by Monsignor Kaufmann) were reputedly the most beautiful in Egypt, famed for the richness of their marble, the majesty of their paintings and the splendor of their mosaics and gold. The impressive ruins of the sanctuary were destroyed in the 9th century by the Abbasid caliph el-Mutawakkil who dismissed the clergy, seized the ornamental tiling and plundered the treasure, thus beginning the acts of coercion perpetrated against the Copts during the Middle Ages.

BASILICA OF ARCADIUS. The most noticeable thing about the Basilica of Arcadius is its sheer size. It was built in the early 5th century and constitutes the heart of this vast monastic complex. The bases of the fifty-six marble columns that supported its roof can still be seen today. The gallery stood at the intersection of the transept and the main nave in an enclosed area containing the altar, the bishop's throne and the pews of the officiating priests. At the western end of the basilica stood a baptistry whose "corners" were rounded into semicircular, polychrome marble niches. This independent element, which was usually incorporated into the main structure, is the only example of its kind in ancient Christian architecture. A CHURCH to the west of the basilica (which it pre-dates) was built above the crypt containing the saint's tomb. Its capitals have a strong Egyptian and Byzantine influence. A staircase led down to the crypt from the central nave. To the west is an underground drain connected to the "miraculous" cistern which supposedly collected the curative waters but which in reality collected rainwater.

GRAPE PRESS
To the north of the site was a large monastery complex whose cells, shops, vast reception halls and a vat for pressing grapes (above) can still be seen today.

THERMAL BASILICA. In the 5th century another basilica was built to accommodate the growing numbers of pilgrims and infirm. The so-called "Thermal Basilica" was intended to house the source of the curative waters. Some of the heated baths and one of the pools (230 x 130 feet) attest to the size and importance of the structure. Pilgrims would fill their tiny terracotta flasks, usually stamped with the seal of Saint Menas (depicting the saint standing between two kneeling camels), at the source which rose beside the basilica.

Saint Menas

Saint Menas was believed to have healing powers. His fame spread following the recovery of the Emperor of Byzantium's daughter who suffered from elephantiasis and was cured by the waters of Saint Menas. From 363 onward the relics of the saint, above whose tomb Constantine erected the first basilica, became the focus for one of the most famous pilgrimages. Pilgrims came from all parts of Egypt and the Orient. The cult of Menas spread throughout the Mediterranean Basin and reached Gaul via Arles and northern Italy and the Rhineland via Rome. Under the 14th-century patriarch Benjamin II the relics of the saint were transported, after many mishaps, from Abu Menas to Cairo and placed in a church named after him.

Additional buildings. During the 5th and 6th centuries additional buildings were constructed around the second "Thermal Basilica". To the north a huge monastery, a veritable business complex, covered an area of almost 48,000 square yards. Ramparts strengthened by bastions surrounded the sanctuary, which was guarded by more than twelve thousand soldiers. An entire town, complete with houses and cemeteries, was excavated. The most surprising discovery was the house of one of the potters who made the flasks. The walls were covered with strange designs, and the workshop, shop, and remains of flasks, lamps and even toys were found.

Lake Mariut. Lake Mariut, ancient Mareotis, lies below sea level and separates Alexandria from the desert. It used to be linked to the River Nile by canals which brought products from all over Egypt to Alexandria.

Lake Mariut (below).

During the Middle Ages the waters of the lake dried up. In 1801, during the siege of Alexandria, the British breached the dyke which separated Lake Mariut from Lake Abukir (which no longer exists), flooding thousands of acres and destroying 150 villages.

203

THE COASTAL REGION

EL-ALAMEIN. Various tanks, pieces of artillery, uniforms and operational maps can be seen in the town's Military Museum. The Italian and German military cemeteries stand on the Tell el-Eisa Hill a few miles outside the town. Further along the coast, the village of Sidi Abd el-Rahman is renowned for its beautiful beaches.

MERSA MATRUH. Now the administrative capital of the Libyan Desert, Mersa Matruh is ancient Paraetonium where Alexander the Great stopped before moving on to the Oasis of Jupiter Amun ▲ 256. It was also the port where the Egyptian fleet lay at anchor during the war between Octavian (Augustus) and Cleopatra and Mark Antony. It is still possible to see the remains of Cleopatra's quay to the west of the ancient lagoon on which the town is built. On a hill to the north are the remains of a church dating from the early centuries AD.

Along the bay to the east, ROMMEL'S CAVE, now a museum, stands on a spit of land. The cave was Field Marshall Rommel's base and headquarters before the Battle of El-Alamein. One of the region's most beautiful beaches, Cleopatra Beach, lies 3 miles to the west. On a rocky islet about 50 yards offshore is CLEOPATRA'S BATH, a pool said to have been hewn out of the rock so that the queen could bathe in safety. In early June the Bedouin tribes of the Libyan Desert come to Mersa Matruh to honor their saint on the occasion of his *muled*. AGUIBA BEACH, 15 miles from Mersa Matruh, is one of the most famous beaches on this stretch of coast but the bathing is dangerous. EL-NAGUILA, an ancient Roman town whose remains can still be seen, was renowned for its gardens and figs. In 1916 EL-MAKTELA was the scene of a decisive battle between the British forces and the Sanusi Bedouins.

SALLUM. Sallum was once the ancient Roman port of Baranis, and the remains of wells in the town and surrounding area are still in evidence. Sallum is the last Egyptian town before the border with Libya. It is a trading center for Bedouin peoples from all parts of the region. The soldiers who were killed during the battle with Rommel's Afrika Korps are buried in the British and Commonwealth forces' military cemetery.

BATTLE OF EL-ALAMEIN
The Battle of El-Alamein ("the two worlds"), fought between Field Marshall Montgomery's Eighth Army under General Alexander and Rommel's Afrika Korps, lasted from October 23 to November 4, 1942. It stopped the German advance in North Africa and marked the beginning of their retreat. Military cemeteries and monuments to the memory of the soldiers killed at El-Alamein were built on the battlefield. About 66 miles from Alexandria is the memorial to the British and Commonwealth soldiers. The British cemetery with its impeccably aligned graves lies to the left of the road.

NILE DELTA

▲ CAIRO TO ROSETTA

1 CAIRO 2 DELTA BARRAGE 3 DEIR AMBA BARAMUS 4 DEIR ES-SURIANI 5 DEIR AMBA BISHOI 6 DEIR ABU MAKARYUS 7 SHAITANUF 8 EL-BAGUR 9 TANTA 10 KAFR EL-SHEIKH 11 TELL EL-FARAIN 12 DISUQ

DELTA BARRAGE: THE EARLY STAGES
Linant de Bellefonds, aware of the instability of the substratum, suggested constructing the barrage several miles downstream of the river's point of divergence. There were to be two barrages, one on the Rosetta branch of the Nile and one on the Damietta branch, with three navigable canals fed from a point above the barrage. Work began in 1834, but stopped the next year because of plague.

This itinerary leaves the main "agricultural route" between Cairo and Tanta and crosses an ancient, wooded landscape which provides a striking contrast to the vast cotton-producing regions of the eastern Delta.

DELTA BARRAGE. The Delta barrage, or El-Qanatir el-Qahiriya, was constructed at the southern tip of the Nile Delta, about 12 miles downstream from Cairo, to control the supply of water to Lower Egypt. The idea was first conceived in 1833 and the project study initially entrusted to Linant de Bellefonds (1799–1883), a French naval officer who had joined the staff of Mohammed Ali. The site was closed by a plague epidemic two years later. In 1842 Bellefonds was replaced by another French engineer, Dieudonné-Eugène Mougel. Construction began in 1843 and lasted for almost twenty years, through three khedivial reigns. The barrage was completed in 1863 but was so badly designed that it had to be constantly repaired and, by 1883, it was very nearly abandoned. However, a group of British engineers, led by Sir Colin Scott-Moncrieff, came to the rescue, which is a matter of some historical interest since, at the time, the Delta barrage was the largest hydraulic construction in the world.

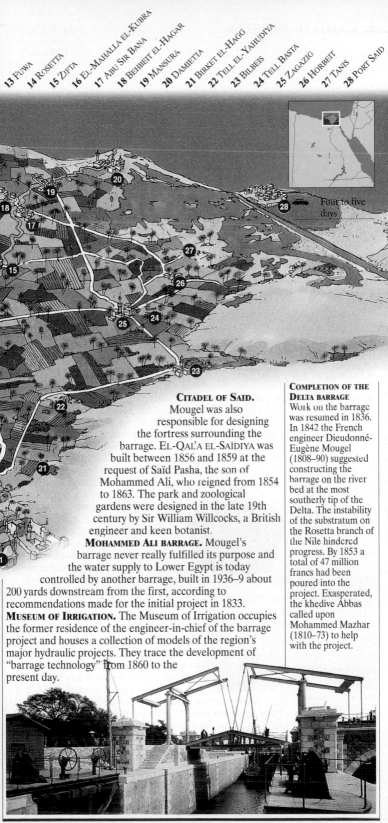

Four to five days

CITADEL OF SAÏD.
Mougel was also responsible for designing the fortress surrounding the barrage. EL-QAL'A EL-SAÏDIYA was built between 1856 and 1859 at the request of Saïd Pasha, the son of Mohammed Ali, who reigned from 1854 to 1863. The park and zoological gardens were designed in the late 19th century by Sir William Willcocks, a British engineer and keen botanist.

MOHAMMED ALI BARRAGE. Mougel's barrage never really fulfilled its purpose and the water supply to Lower Egypt is today controlled by another barrage, built in 1936–9 about 200 yards downstream from the first, according to recommendations made for the initial project in 1833.

MUSEUM OF IRRIGATION. The Museum of Irrigation occupies the former residence of the engineer-in-chief of the barrage project and houses a collection of models of the region's major hydraulic projects. They trace the development of "barrage technology" from 1860 to the present day.

COMPLETION OF THE DELTA BARRAGE
Work on the barrage was resumed in 1836. In 1842 the French engineer Dieudonné-Eugène Mougel (1808–90) suggested constructing the barrage on the river bed at the most southerly tip of the Delta. The instability of the substratum on the Rosetta branch of the Nile hindered progress. By 1853 a total of 47 million francs had been poured into the project. Exasperated, the khedive Abbas called upon Mohammed Mazhar (1810–73) to help with the project.

Deir es-Suriani, Deir Abu Makaryus, Deir Amba Bishoi and Deir Amba Baramus (top to bottom).

DEIR AMBA BISHOI
Legend has it that Father Bishoi was led to the ascetic life through the call of an angel, and founded the community which inhabits the monastery bearing his name. The building is distinguished by its well-preserved entrance loggia and a mill which stands to the northeast. The Deir Amba Bishoi and Deir Amba Baramus are the only two monastries with baptisteries.

REMAINS OF KELLIA
All that remains of the mudbrick architecture of Kellia (made from sand compressed with saline soil) are a few mounds covering the hermitages that have escaped the bulldozers.

THE MONASTERIES OF WADI NATRUN

In the early 4th century AD a monastic order, which favored retreat beyond the Nile Valley, was founded in the western Delta region. The solitude of the desert retreat soon became the Christian heroic ideal and the image of the "white martyr" replaced the "red martyr" of the persecutions which marked the reign of Diocletian in the early 4th century and ended in AD 313 when Constantine made Christianity the official religion of the Roman empire ● 74. In 325 Saint Amun founded the first monastic establishment at Nitria (El-Barnudji) with a view to practicing the doctrine of renouncement, austerity and prayer advocated by the Scriptures to obtain eternal salvation and escape the temptations of the secular world.

THE RETREATS OF WADI NATRUN. Five years later Saint Makarios, who aspired to a more rigorous form of asceticism, decided to found the eremitic retreats of Scete, now Wadi Natrun, which comprises four functioning monasteries: Deir Amba Baramus, Deir Amba Bishoi, Deir Abu Makaryus, founded in the 4th century, and the 6th-century Deir es-Suriani. On the death of a Desert Father whose life was considered to have been exemplary, a chapel was built in front of his cell, and the first monasteries came into being.

DEIR AMBA BARAMUS. Deir Amba Baramus, or Monastery of the Romans (named after the Roman monk Arsenius who lived there), was Wadi Natrun's first religious community. The western section, the nucleus of the monastery, contains the church dedicated to the Virgin Mary whose nave is divided by 19th-century wood paneling. The south wing has some beautiful Corinthian pillars and the northeastern section contains the living accommodation, library and garden. Some beautiful frescos have also been uncovered.

DEIR ES-SURIANI. Deir es-Suriani, or Monastery of the Syrians, was named after the Syrian merchants who acquired it at the beginning of the 8th century for the community of Syrian monks living in Egypt at the time. The community remained in Egypt until the 16th century when Syria fell to the Turks. The great EL-ADRA CHURCH is dedicated to the Virgin Mary and its frescos tell the story of her life. The iconostasis (the so-called "Door of Symbols") of the sanctuary consists of six leaves, each with seven ebony panels inlaid with ivory representing (from top to bottom) the seven periods of the Christian era. The library contains several hundred manuscripts and over three thousand printed works.

DEIR ABU MAKARYUS. From the 6th century the Deir Abu Makaryus, or Monastery of St Makarios, assumed considerable importance as the official residence of the bishops of Alexandria, the heads of the Coptic Church, who were forbidden to reside in Alexandria itself by the Byzantine rulers. It was here that Wadi Natrun's first library, widely dispersed in the 17th century, was founded. The dungeon-tower, the most developed of the towers, is truly remarkable. It incorporates no less than four churches and a wine vat. The second-floor church has an iconostasis and sculptures dating from the 4th and 5th centuries.

THE KELLIA HERMITAGES. The community of Kellia, founded by Saint Amun, consists of 1,500 hermitages (cells) arranged in five clusters over a distance of about 12 miles. Situated about one third of the way along the track linking Nitria with Wadi Natrun, the Kellia hermitages were originally a staging post before becoming an ascetic retreat, although they did not break all ties with the secular world. Abandoned toward the 9th century, the site was rediscovered in 1964 by Guillaumont. However, cultivation has changed the landscape where once there was little more than shrubs and bushes. The two 5th-century ecclesiastical centers of Qasr Waheida and Qusur Isa are, apart from the church of the White Monastery (440), the earliest monastic buildings that can be dated with any certainty.

209

Between the barrage and Tanta the landscape becomes fragmented: enclosed fields separated by hedges and large villages hidden among the trees. The tiny region of Batn el-Baqara ("belly of the cow"), which lies between the two branches of the Nile and the ancient Bahr Firuniya, gives an idea of what the landscape must have looked like before the major hydraulic projects of the 19th century changed the face of agriculture.

SHATANUF. According to French-speaking Egyptians Shatanuf is a corruption of "Châteauneuf" and was named by the soldiers of Napoleon Bonaparte. In fact it is an ancient village whose name was of Coptic origin. ASHMUN, an industrial center renowned for its ceramics, lies off the main route. Its brickworks produce the polychrome bricks which give the regional architecture its distinctive appearance.

EL-BAGUR. El-Bagur is an unprepossessing town whose only claim to fame is to have been the birthplace of Sheikh Ibrahim el-Baguri (1783–1860), rector of El-Azhar ▲ 294 and a renowned theologian. He is better known today, however, as the organizer of the first student demonstration to be held in modern times, against military conscription during the reign of Saïd (1854–63). Since 1826 SHIBIN EL-KOM has been the capital of Minufiya province. President Anwar el-Sadat ● 71 was born (1918) a few miles away in MIT ABU EL-KOM.

TANTA

Tanta, which nestles at the heart of the rich Gharbiya province, is both the provincial capital and one of the largest towns in the Nile Delta (335,000 inhabitants in 1986). During the Byzantine period this ancient city was the seat of a bishopric, but little evidence is left of its long history. Today the town is especially famous for the mausoleum of Egypt's greatest Muslim saint, Sidi Ahmed el-Badawi, born in Fez, Morocco, in 1199. In 1237 he was told in a vision to go to Tanta, where he began to lead the life of an ascetic. He installed himself on the

"We left Mehallet-Kebir this morning, and took the road to Tanta. [. . .] Travelers often make endless detours to cover a relatively short distance. Here you count miles in terms of the number of hours' walking they represent and assess routes in relation to the number of villages along the way. As you get further away from the Nile, the landscape becomes less wooded; in some places there is not a tree in sight, with cultivated fields stretching as far as the eye can see and a few palms, mimosa, sycamores, willows and the occasional vine providing the only shade near the houses and villages.**"**
Joseph Michaud

roof of a house (which is why his disciples became known as Sutuhiya, or Ashab el-Sath, "people of the terrace") where he remained without eating or drinking for forty days. He died on June 8, 1276, and was buried in the house on top of which he had lived. Several years later his disciple and successor, Abd el-Al, built a *qalua* (a sort of cell to which ascetics could retreat) above his tomb, and this was later converted into a *zawia* (a center for religious teaching). The first mosque, which incorporated the mausoleum, was not built until the 18th century, but all that remains today is the minaret and the *maqsura* (the bronze grille surrounding the catafalque). It bears an inscription, dated 1773, which traces the saint's genealogy. The present building dates from the reign of Abbas (1848–54). The MUSEUM OF TANTA contains several collections ranging from Pharaonic times to the present day.

Xois. Not far from KAFR EL-SHEIKH (the town's Egyptian name), capital of the Sixth Nome of Lower Egypt, the village of Pa-Khasu ("village of the pothole") stands on the site of the remains that have managed to survive. Excavations have revealed the *agora* of the Graeco-Roman town, with its public baths and pottery workshops. On the road between Tanta and Alexandria a lake to the west of the El-Khandaq el-Gharbi Canal marks the site of ancient NAUCRATIS (el-Nibeira), originally a Pharaonic village that later became a Greek military fortress and then a commercial center. Imau, the capital of the Third Nome of Lower Egypt, is situated not far from here on the KOM EL-HISN.

THE TANTA PILGRIMAGE
Three *muled* are celebrated in honor of Sidi Ahmed el-Badawi. The first, or "great *muled*", which coincides with the *muled* of the Prophet ● *126*, gave rise to the Tanta pilgrimage. The other two, the "little *muled*" and the "*muled* of the month of Ragab",

were introduced later by the sheikhs of the various branches of the Ahmediya Brotherhood, founded after the death of Ahmed by his successor. Because the three festivals were also huge agricultural fairs, their dates were later incorporated into the old Nilotic calendar inherited from Pharaonic Egypt and preserved to the present day by the Coptic liturgy. They were replaced by similar fairs, in particular at Disuq ▲ *212* and Damanhur (between Alexandria and Cairo), and became part of a cycle of traveling fairs which were a blend of popular piety and agrarian rites. The pilgrims would start their pilgrimage to Mecca with a visit to the saint of Tanta, which became known as "the gate of the Prophet" (Bab el-Nabi).

THE TARBOOSH
In 1820 Mohammed Ali introduced a new regulation headgear for the soldiers of his reformed army. The red felt hat known as the tarboosh replaced the Mameluke and Ottoman turban and, for more than a century, became the national headgear of modern Egypt. It was initially imported from Tunis and Fez but, as it became increasingly widely worn by members of the state services, demand grew to such a point that it was decided to manufacture the tarboosh in Egypt. A Moroccan was brought in to manage the factory, the workers came from Tunis and wool was imported from Europe. At the height of its activity the factory was producing sixty dozen tarbooshes per day.

TELL EL-FARAÏN. Tell el-Faraïn, or Pharaohs' Hill, is near the village of Shaba (7½ miles from Disuq). According to Herodotus, "Leto" (Buto) was the seat of an important oracular divinity during the Persian period. On one of the site's three *tells* is the enclosure wall of the temple of

the serpent-goddess Wadjet, symbol of Lower Egypt and mistress of the site. The town was divided into two sections known as Pe and Dep, and occupied the other two hills.

DISUQ. Like Tanta, Disuq is a place of pilgrimage and is mainly renowned for its patron saint, Sidi Ibrahim el-Disuqi (1235–78), founder of the Burhamiya, or Disuqiya, the brotherhood named after him and one of the four largest in Egypt, who are distinguished by their green turbans. He is thought to have been Sheikh el-Islam during the reign of El-Zahir Baybars, who had a *zawia* built for him where he taught and was buried. The present 19th-century mosque is a vast edifice, covering an area of almost 24,000 square yards, whose prayer hall is adorned with seventy white marble columns. Further west the route follows the winding course of the Rosetta branch of the Nile and offers the double advantage of enabling visitors to journey across a beautiful landscape and visit the town of Saïs.

SAÏS. Saïs, or Zaou, the capital of the Fifth Nome of Lower Egypt, lies north of the town of Sa el-Hagar on the right bank of the Damietta branch of the Nile.

It has been a religious center since the beginning of the Pharaonic period and houses the sanctuaries of Neith, its principal divinity, and various associated divinities. Saïs was one of the compulsory destinations for funerary rites. It became a bishopric during the Christian era and remained active until the 12th century. The site is somewhat disappointing since all that remains of the Pharaonic capital are mudbrick walls and a few scattered blocks of stone.

FUWA. Fuwa is an ancient town which probably stands on the site of ancient Metelis. Its position opposite the mouth of the Alexandria Canal made it the offloading point for maritime and river traffic, and it became such an important trading center that in the 15th century many European countries established consulates there. The gradual silting-up of the canal, however, diverted trade to Rosetta and indirectly brought about the decline of Fuwa. Prospects improved slightly in the 19th century when the construction of the Mahmudiya Canal ▲ *190* restored some of Fuwa's former activity, but it was the opening of a large tarboosh factory that really revitalized the town. Yet, like most of the factories established by Mohammed Ali, it fell into disuse during the reign of Saïd, and the town had to diversify into other areas of industrial activity (rice-growing and flour-milling). Its location, off the main road networks, has meant that Fuwa has remained a sleepy little town (114,000 acres in 1986) but this has enabled it to retain a certain old-fashioned charm. Fuwa was also the birthplace of Saad Zaghlul ● *70* ▲ *281*.

VISITING FUWA. The MOSQUE OF NASR AD-DIN, founded by Hassan ben Nasr Allah el-Ustadar, a Mameluke emir born in Fuwa in 1365, gives some idea of the town's medieval grandeur. The oldest mosque in Fuwa is the MAUSOLEUM OF SIDI ABD ALLAH EL-BURULLUSI. It was renovated in 1860 by Mohammed Pasha, brother of Ismaïl. The ABU EL-NAGA MOSQUE (opposite), on the banks of the river, is in an advanced state of ruin.

BRIDGE OF MUTUBIS. Built in the 1940's along the lines of the Mohammed Ali barrage ▲ *207*, this is the most northerly of the barrages which cross the Nile.

PALM GROVE OF ROSETTA. The vast palm grove of Rosetta stretches from the shores of the Nile to Lake Idku. Its dates (there are several carefully selected and artificially sown varieties) ripen a month later than in other regions and are reputedly Egypt's best.

TELL EL-FARAÏN
Several architectural elements from the reign of Ramesses II and a stele donated by Shoshenq V (AD 38) stand side by side with a number of objects from the Late Period. Recent soundings around the *tell* have revealed the remains of a pre-dynastic civilization.

ROSETTA

Rosetta, the "city of a thousand palm trees", is situated about 9 miles from the mouth of the Nile. It is one of the most attractive of the Delta cities and has the richest selection of monuments. According to Arab chroniclers it was founded in AD 870 by Ibn Tulun ● *66* ▲ *312*. In fact the site has been occupied since prehistoric times and the town's Arabic name (Rashid) is derived from the Ancient Egyptian via the Coptic name (Rikhit). Its foundation by Ibn Tulun corresponds to a relocation of the town, slightly further south. Rosetta, for a long time a town of modest proportions, housed the garrison responsible for defending the Boghaz (mouth of the Nile) which today lies about 7 miles away. The town began to assume greater importance during the Ottoman period, reaching its peak in the 17th century when it benefited from the developing trade with Constantinople and the Aegean, and remaining prosperous until the 19th century. With the construction of the Mahmudiya Canal ▲ *190* it began to move into slow decline and once again became a small town (52,000 inhabitants in 1986) relying for its livelihood on traditional fishing and food industries. But this relative decline has in fact meant that Rosetta has preserved its architectural heritage.

The minaret of one of the many mosques, and a café in Rosetta.

THE OTTOMAN TOWN. Built along the river, the town has maintained a regular, almost orthogonal, urban development and offers a remarkable overview of domestic Ottoman architecture. Twenty-two of the thirty-eight houses originally classified by the Committee for the Conservation of Arab Monuments have survived. Bought and restored by the Egyptian Department of Antiquities, they were all built between the 16th and 18th centuries and form a homogenous series of buildings in terms of their layout, exterior design and interior decoration. Rosetta's houses are characterized by their height (two or three stories above the first floor), which contrasts with their relatively narrow façades overlooking the street, and the use of visible brickwork which is often outlined with mortar to create polychrome patterning in black, red and white. The layers of bricks are intersected by horizontal wood clamps which are also visible.

MOSQUES. The mosques of Rosetta are also characteristic of the region. The (often tiny) courtyard has been reduced to a simple square which has been made into a garden and forms a small atrium at the center of the extremely simple prayer hall. Only the entrance and the mihrab are richly decorated, with polychrome marble or tile mosaics. Everything of interest can be seen by taking a few leisurely walks around the town. The northwest district has four of the most beautiful houses in Rosetta: the AMACIALI, HASSIBA GHAZAL and MAKKI HOUSES (today occupied by a women's aid organization) and the partially restored THABET HOUSE, which is a training center for carpenters and wood turners. The SHEIKH QINDIL

MOSQUE is a particularly delightful sanctuary. The main market street runs from the Midan el-Gumhurriya through the old part of the town. The ARAB KELI MUSEUM occupies an 18th-century house and traces the history of Rosetta. The EL-MAHALLI MOSQUE (1721) has a distinctive prayer hall whose beamed ceiling is supported by ninety-nine columns taken from other sites. The EL-GINDI MOSQUE is of the same type but smaller, while the ruined ZAGHLUL MOSQUE is Rosetta's largest and oldest mosque. The AZZUZ BATHS (a beautiful 18th-century *hammam*) have remained intact with all their original installations. At the southern end of the town is the EL-ABBASI MOSQUE, built in 1809, while the Turkish tiles and finely carved marble columns of the DUMAQSIS MOSQUE (1704), which is situated in the Shari' Port Said, are of particular interest.

FORT QAITBAY. This small fort was built in about 1470 on the banks of the River Nile by the Sultan Qaitbay to defend the Boghaz. Its twin, Fort Rashid (renamed Fort Julien by the French), was built across the river. It was here that the French army captain Bouchard discovered the Rosetta Stone in 1799.

THE HOUSES OF ROSETTA ● *116*
The many large doors and windows of the houses are covered by turned-wood grilles or *mashrabiya* work. The doorway opening onto the street is wide enough to allow a fully loaded camel to pass through since in most of the houses, which were mainly owned by merchants, the first floor was used for business, with shops, cellars, warehouses, stables and sometimes a *mandara* for receiving customers. There is often a well, fed by an underground cistern, which sometimes opens onto the street via a *sabil* ● *113*.
The living accommodation was on the upper floors, with the second-floor *salamlik* reserved for the men and the third-floor *haramlik* for the women and family. All the houses are built according to the same layout.

Egyptian belongs to the family of Hamito-Semitic (or Afro-Asiatic) languages. When it first appeared in c. 3150 BC Egyptian writing contained all the theoretic principles that would last throughout its development until it disappeared in the 4th century AD.

Jean-François Champollion (le Jeune) was born in Figeac in 1790. Fascinated by Egypt from an early age, he went on to study Oriental languages (Hebrew, Coptic and Arabic) and was the first to interpret Egyptian hieroglyphs (1822) from the Rosetta Stone. He dedicated his entire life to improving his knowledge of the Ancient Egyptian language and civilization. In 1826 he founded the Department of Egyptology of the Louvre Museum and, in 1831 (one year before his death), he was appointed professor of the Collège de France by Louis-Philippe.

MONUMENTS DE L'EGYPTE ET DE LA NUBIE PAR CHAMPOLLION LE JEUNE

"MONUMENTS DE L'EGYPTE ET DE LA NUBIE"
This collection of Champollion's work in Egypt was published between 1835 and 1845 by his brother.

THE ROSETTA STONE
This bilingual decree by Ptolemy V Epiphanes (196 BC) was discovered in Rosetta in 1799 by a French officer of the Egypt Expedition. It was written in hieroglyphs, demotic script and Greek.

Lettres Grecques	Signes Démotiques	Signes Hieroglyphiques
A	ʊ . ʊʊ .	🦅 🦜 ⟩ 🦆 ⟨ 🕊 ⎰ ⎱ 👁 ⟿
B	⊔ . ⩊ .	⎰ ⎱ 🐦

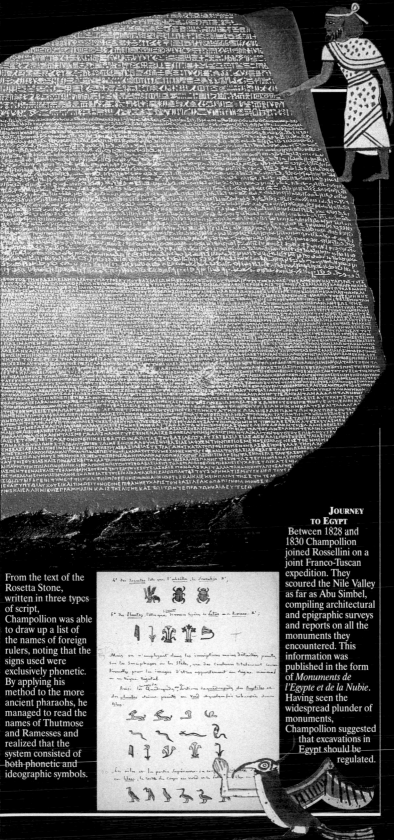

From the text of the Rosetta Stone, written in three types of script, Champollion was able to draw up a list of the names of foreign rulers, noting that the signs used were exclusively phonetic. By applying his method to the more ancient pharaohs, he managed to read the names of Thutmose and Ramesses and realized that the system consisted of both phonetic and ideographic symbols.

JOURNEY TO EGYPT

Between 1828 and 1830 Champollion joined Rossellini on a joint Franco-Tuscan expedition. They scoured the Nile Valley as far as Abu Simbel, compiling architectural and epigraphic surveys and reports on all the monuments they encountered. This information was published in the form of *Monuments de l'Egypte et de la Nubie*. Having seen the widespread plunder of monuments, Champollion suggested that excavations in Egypt should be regulated.

HIEROGLYPHS READ HORIZONTALLY FROM RIGHT TO LEFT

HIEROGLYPHS READ HORIZONTALLY FROM LEFT TO RIGHT

The hieroglyphs are not aligned in sequence, one after the other, but arranged in the form of an imaginary square.

HIEROGLYPHS READ VERTICALLY FROM RIGHT TO LEFT

HIEROGLYPHS READ VERTICALLY FROM LEFT TO RIGHT

There are no spaces between words and no punctuation.

DECIPHERING HIEROGLYPHICS

Egyptian hieroglyphs were written from right to left or from left to right, horizontally or vertically. The direction from which the hieroglyphs should be read is indicated by the direction in which the "living" symbols, represented in profile, are facing.

Detail (above) of a color plate from *Monuments de l'Egypte et de la Nubie*, showing bas-reliefs from the Temple of Amenhotep III at Wadi Hellal. A detail from the manuscript of Champollion's *Grammaire égyptienne* is shown at the bottom of the page.

HIERATIC SCRIPT

Hieratic script is a cursive form of hieroglyphics, used during the early dynasties for everyday documents. It was written with a calamus (reed pen) on papyrus, leather or pottery. From the 21st Dynasty it was used to transcribe religious texts on papyrus.

DEMOTIC SCRIPT

Demotic script is a simplified form of hieratic script. It became the popular form of writing during the 25th Dynasty. Like hieratic script it is always written horizontally, from right to left.

COPTIC SCRIPT

Coptic script was the last stage in Pharaonic Egyptian writing and the only written language used between the 3rd and 17th centuries AD since when it has been reserved for the Coptic liturgy. It was written using the Greek alphabet with seven additional symbols taken from demotic script.

, ϩΕυ, ϩΗΕ   *Pêcher ou poissons*

, ΠΙS.
. φS   *Voler, s'élever en haut*

The ruins of Iseum, the ancient town of Hebet or Per-Hebet, meaning "the house of the god Hebet" (Horus), look like a huge pile of stone blocks and are for the most part inaccessible.

The port of Talkha at Mansura.

The first of the two itineraries from Cairo to Damietta follows the right bank of the Nile, while the second crosses the river at Mit Ghamr to Zifta and follows the left bank to Damietta.

ZIFTA. The town of Zifta is proud of having been the scene of an unusual event. In the spring of 1919, at the Congress of Versailles, the world powers confirmed the British protectorate of Egypt and rejected the Egyptian demand for independence ● 70. In Zifta a demonstration of secondary-school students was supported by the entire town and a revolutionary group proclaimed independence. The incident lasted only a few weeks as British troops eventually surrounded the town.

ABU SIR BANA. Modern Abu Sir Bana is named after the ancient town of Busiris mentioned by the Greek historian Herodotus (although nothing remains of the Temple of Osiris to which he referred).

EL-MAHALLA EL-KUBRA. El-Mahalla el-Kubra ("the great warehouse"), already an important trading center in the 10th century, developed significantly in the 14th century when the administrative reforms of the reign of the sultan Barquq made it the capital of the central Delta region. It was relieved of this function in the 19th century and entered a decline from which it did not recover until the 1930's when the establishment of the Misr Group factories made it the largest industrial textile center in Egypt. Today it is Egypt's fourth largest city (359,000 inhabitants in 1986). It still has many of its mosques although, unfortunately, most are damaged. The GAMIA EL-NASSER, or Victory Mosque, in the old town, was founded at the time of the Arab conquest, while the nearby KHAWKHAT EL-YAHUD ("the postern of the Jews") has replaced one of the oldest synagogues in Egypt. The 13th-century EL-MITWALI MOSQUE is remarkable for its sheer size, and the Coptic Church of SUEIQAT EL-NASARA for its two superposed structures (although only the lower of the two is of any great age).

BEHBEIT EL-HAGAR. The ruins of Iseum are situated midway between Semenud and Mansura. The temple probably dates from the Saïte period, while the monument (the sanctuary of Isis) was mainly built by Ptolemy II and completed by Ptolemy III. A block of stone used in the construction of the Iseum in Rome suggests that it was destroyed during the first century AD. The temple was surrounded by a mudbrick wall built during the Ptolemaic period and an avenue of sphinxes would once have led to the main entrance. Today gardens cover the area between the enclosure wall and the inscribed blocks of stone. The western façade of the temple is decorated with images of the Nile and dedicated to Osiris ▲ *386*. A colonnade, with Hathor capitals, bounded to the south by a flight of steps leading to the roof, precedes the sanctuary of Isis (for which it is at present proving difficult to reconstruct the layout). In a rear chapel, the god Osiris is depicted as a king with divine attributes, not as a mummy.

SEMENUD. The town has retained the Greek name (Sebbenytos) of the Egyptian town of Tchebnetcheret (the Divine Calf), capital of the Second Nome of Lower Egypt. It was the birthplace of the historian Manethon ● *66*, author of the first history of Egypt, according to whom it was the land of the 30th-Dynasty pharaohs. The few, scattered blocks of stone on the ancient *tell* to the west of the town are not really worth visiting.

MANSURA. Today the town of Mansura is the capital of Daqahliya province and an important industrial center. It was founded as a fortified camp in 1219 by the Ayyubid sultan El-Malik el-Kamil to oppose the Crusaders after the capture of Damietta in 1218. Built along the River Nile and the Bahr el-Saghir ("little river"), one of its former branches, it was surrounded by water and made an ideal entrenched camp. In July 1221 an offensive led by John of Jerusalem was stopped before the city walls and the crusade of Louis IX of France ended at Mansura after a long and fruitless siege punctuated by skirmishes (1249–50). The French king was taken prisoner on April 7, 1250 and released a month later in return for the restoration of Damietta and payment of a ransom. With the end of the Crusades the town was able to pursue a more peaceable existence. It became a provincial capital during the Ottoman period and its rapid expansion in the second half of the 19th century made it one of the leading cotton centers in the Delta region. About 19 miles southeast of Mansura, two important *tells* mark the ancient sites of MENDES (Tell el-Rub' in the north) and THMUIS (Tell el-Tmei in the south). Mendes, capital of the Sixth Nome of Lower Egypt and an important town from the time of the Old Kingdom to the 29th Dynasty, was superseded by Thmuis in the 1st century AD. Among its ruins are the enclosure wall of the temple (dedicated to Be, the god of fertility embodied in the form of a ram) dominated on one side by a monolithic naos (over 25 feet high) in pink granite. The site of Thmuis is littered with shards, architectural stone fragments and remains of mosaics.

EL-MUAFI MOSQUE
The El-Muafi Mosque (below) stands in the heart of the old town of Mansura. The mosque, built by El-Salih Ayyub in 1188 and refurbished at the end of the 16th century, houses the mausoleum of Sidi Abd Allah el-Muafi. The small, old house to the south (the so-called house of Ibn Loqman) is said to have been the prison of Saint Louis (Louis IX). It is in fact all that remains of a public kitchen used during the *muled* to prepare and distribute food to the town's inhabitants.

During the siege of Mansura (1249) the Muslims used gunpowder for the first time. They made incendiary devices and sowed terror among the ranks of the Crusaders.

Unlike Mansura, Damietta is an ancient town, renowned for its textile industry during the Byzantine period. Its wealth and its strategic position on the eastern mouth of

DAMIETTA. Damietta was one of the main Muslim objectives during the Arab conquest of Egypt. During the first two centuries of Arab domination, the Byzantines launched frequent naval attacks against the town and it was after one such raid, in 853, that Damietta was fortified for the first time. Protected by its walls, the city expanded rapidly and became extremely prosperous during the Fatimid period as a result of the growth of the textile industry.

Damietta is in fact famed for its brocades and its *tiraz* industry. The wearing of this extremely expensive ceremonial garment, reserved for princes and monarchs, was probably a revival from the Sassanid empire. The extremely complex figurative, floral and geometric designs of the silk embroidery decorating these linen or cotton robes often included epigraphic borders which make some of these garments not only works of art but also valuable historic documents. During the Crusades the town was the focus of a bitter and drawn-out struggle. It was subjected to a long and unsuccessful siege on the accession of Salah ad-Din as part of an attack launched by Amaury I of Jerusalem in December 1169. In 1218 the Crusaders succeeded in capturing the town and occupied it for almost three years. But they failed to resist El-Kamil, who withdrew to the fortified town of Mansura, and were forced to surrender it to the Muslims in 1221. Recaptured by Saint Louis in 1249,

the Nile made it a key town during the Crusades. Damietta never recovered its early prosperity and today it is a modest-sized town (ninety thousand inhabitants in 1986) by Egyptian standards.

just before the death of El-Salih, Damietta came under Christian control once more until the French king was defeated at Mansura in 1250. The following year, the Bahrite Mamelukes, convinced that the town was too vulnerable, destroyed its fortifications. In 1261 Baybars closed the Boghaz to ocean-going vessels for the same reason. Damietta fell into decline and was abandoned in favor of a new town which was founded a little further south on the site that it still occupies today.

VISITING DAMIETTA. The ABU EL-MAATI MOSQUE can still be seen in the old town of Damietta. The mosque is surrounded by a huge cemetery where pigeon enthusiasts discuss turtle- and ring-doves at the pigeon market held there every week. Pigeon fancying is still a highly regarded sport in Egypt and its techniques perpetuate the memory of the prestigious pigeon post organized by the Mameluke sultans to maintain communications between Egypt and Syria, the two provinces of their empire. Damietta was one of the main staging posts on the Cairo–Palestine route. The fragile-looking boxes on reed racks which adorn the balconies of Damietta are in fact the urban equivalent of the earthen pigeon lofts seen in rural areas. The MADBULIYA MOSQUE, founded by Qaitbay in the 15th century for Sidi Ibrahim el-Madbuli, is a fine example of a medersa from the Mameluke period.

MONASTERY OF ST DAMIENNE. In addition to its monastic buildings and accommodation, this 6th-century Coptic complex also has four churches, although only one is of any great age. Saint Damienne, the daughter of a governor of the Delta region, vowed to remain celibate and retreated with forty companions to a palace built for her by her father. She and her companions were martyred during the great persecutions of the reign of Diocletian for refusing to pay homage to the emperors. Her festival, celebrated from May 5 to 20, is the occasion of a vast gathering. In the far north of the region, the RAS EL-BARR ("cape of the world") dominates the Boghaz of Damietta.

ABU EL-MAATI MOSQUE
The Abu el-Maati Mosque was built during the Fatimid period on the site of the Gamia el-Fath (Mosque of Conquest), founded when the town was captured by the Muslims, and has several points in common with the Amr Ibn el-As Mosque in Cairo ● *325.* It stands outside the modern town on a hill whose ruins mark the site of the first town. The mosque has been closed down and is falling into ruins.

BUBASTIS
Although the area of archeological interest extends along both sides of the road, the most remarkable remains lie to the north. At the western end the remains (from north to south) of a palace, a pre-Dynastic tomb, various cemeteries (Old Kingdom, Coptic and Muslim) and cat cemeteries have been identified. Of the two chapels dedicated to Qa'a, only the white limestone pillars of the chapel of Pepy I (to the south) are still standing. At the eastern end the ruins of several Middle and New Kingdom palaces, a New Kingdom necropolis and two tombs belonging to the viceroy of Kush stand near a pile of basalt blocks marking the site of the Temple of Bastet.

CAIRO TO TANIS

The itinerary from Cairo to Zagazig follows the Ismaïliya Canal and makes a pleasant excursion that can be extended to the isthmus of Suez. The route passes through Heliopolis ▲ 285 and the village of MUSTURUD where the Holy Family is said to have stayed in Egypt, now a place of pilgrimage from August 5 to 22.

BIRKET EL-HAGG. This dried-up "pilgrims' lake" was, for many centuries, an assembly point for the pilgrimage to Mecca. It was for these pilgrims that Sultan Barsbey built the EL-KHANQA MOSQUE in 1427.

TELL EL-YAHUDIYA. Tell el-Yahudiya ("the hill of the Jews") lies about 12 miles northeast of Heliopolis. From the 20th Dynasty the site was named after territory owned by Ramesses III and a sanctuary dedicated to Re. It was extended during the Middle Kingdom and the Second Intermediate period. The great enclosure wall has been attributed, without evidence, to the Hyksos. The high priest of Jerusalem, Onias IV, who sought the protection of Ptolemy VIII, is said to have built a temple to Yahweh in the disused sanctuary in 160 BC. Today the site is of little interest.

BILBEIS. Situated on the boundary of the eastern Delta region, this ancient city has always been one of the region's fortresses. Captured during the Arab conquest, the city's strategic importance increased with the creation of the Hejaz route. During the Crusades it became the rallying point for the Muslim armies leaving for Palestine. At the entrance to Bilbeis are the barrage built during the reign of Baybars and the EMIR EL-GEISH MOSQUE (640, renovated in 1593).

TELL BASTA. The ruins of Tell Basta extend on either side of the road to the northeast of Zagazig. Its Greek name, Bubastis, echoes the Egyptian name Per-Bastet, meaning "House of Bastet". It was the capital of the Twelfth Nome of Lower Egypt until the 18th Dynasty, and became capital of Egypt in the 22nd and 23rd Dynasties. The sacred animals of its principal divinities, the cat for Bastet and the Pharaoh's rat for Atum, were buried by the thousands in special cemeteries.

ZAGAZIG. The capital of Sharqiya province was originally a
camp which housed the workers requisitioned around 1830 to
construct barrages on an ancient branch of the Nile, the Bahr
Moïs. The center of the town has retained some beautiful
examples of 19th-century architecture and the museum has
some interesting regional collections. About 2 miles west of
Abu Kebir, HORBEIT has been recognized as the Pharaonic
town of Shednu (Pharbaethos in Greek),
and about 2 miles southeast of Horbeit,
ABU YASSIN was the late necropolis of the
sacred bulls of Pharbaethos. The
excavation of the mausoleum of the bulls
by the OAU (Organization of African
Unity) in 1938 discovered several granite
sarcophagi, which can still be seen today.
TELL TUKH (one mile south of Tukh el-
Qaramos), ancient Bekhnu or Dekyt, is
thought to have been active from the
time of the New Kingdom. The first
excavations of the site revealed structures
built on sand embankments forming a
rectangular rampart and a temple
surrounded by a brick enclosure wall.
The activity of the *sebakhin*, increased by
important discoveries (the Zagazig
treasure in 1905), has cleared the
northwestern part of the site and only a
tiny part of the ramparts can still be seen.
Between the villages of KHATANA and QANTIR (about 4 and 5
miles north of Fakus), a series of *tells* marks the sites of the
ancient Pharaonic cities of Avaris (capital of the Hyksos) and
Piramesse (the estate of Ramesses). Avaris already existed at
the time of the Middle Kingdom. It was colonized by the
Canaanites and became the capital of the kingdom of the
Hyksos. Ramesses II came from Avaris, and decided to build
temples and palaces there. His successors preferred the site of
Tanis, stripped the nearby town of its monuments and reused
them elsewhere. In El-Husseiniya, the
TELL NABASHA occupies the site of
the ancient Imet, eastern Buto.

The name of Bilbeis
(above) is derived
from the Coptic
"Phelbes". Views of
the eastern Delta
with one of the
region's many pigeon
lofts (below).

TANIS
The Temple of Amun
has been reduced to a
pile of granite blocks
by the extensive
exploitation of
limestone used to
manufacture lime.
The reconstructed
entrance, a statue of
Ramesses II and a
head
(below).

TANIS

Tanis (Djane in Egyptian, Zoan in Hebrew and Tanis in Greek), capital of the Fourteenth Nome of Lower Egypt, appears with some certainty to have been founded at the end of the 20th Dynasty and became capital of Egypt in the 21st and 22nd Dynasties ● 43. Psusennes I made it the replica of Karnak, while his successors increased the number of sanctuaries dedicated to Theban deities. Although the town occupied a large area during the Ptolemaic period, the gradual submersion of the region led to its decline during the Roman occupation. Tanis was a bishopric until the 5th century and little more than a village by the end of the 7th. In the 14th century the region was almost deserted. The development of San el-Hagar, founded in 1821, was largely a result of the land reclamation policy.

EXCAVATIONS. Although it was mentioned in the Bible, Tanis was not identified with San el-Hagar until the map produced in 1722 by a French priest, Father Claude Sicard ▲ 264. Auguste Mariette ● 96 ▲ 350 excavated the great temple between 1859 and 1864 and his work laid the foundations for the erroneous theory that Tanis was Piramesse (the estate of Ramesses), which had already been identified with Avaris, the Hyksos capital. In 1884 Flinders Petrie ● 96 excavated the site for five months. In 1939 Pierre Montet discovered the miraculously preserved royal necropolis of the kings of the Third Intermediate period, which he worked until 1946. In 1964, after the interruption caused by the Suez Crisis ▲ 234, Jean Yoyotte resumed excavations which were taken over in 1985 by Philippe Brissaud, who steered the mission's activities toward their present direction. After the MUSEUM (note, in particular, the exhibits outside) visit the central part of the *tell* from west to east.

GATE OF SHOSHENQ III. The avenue leading to the main temple is bordered by carved stone blocks and fragmented colossi of Ramesses II. The huge gate has no foundations and is made of inscribed stone blocks brought from other sites. On the right is a pink granite triad of Re, Ramesses and Ptah-Tatenen. Beyond are the remains of the columns of Ramesses II.

ENCLOSURE WALLS. Part of the double enclosure (two successive and independent mudbrick walls), lies to the left of the gate. The corners of the enclosure of Psusennes I, built around the temple, can be seen from the hill that it formed. A bigger enclosure was built in the 30th Dynasty.

In his tomb (detail above) Psusennes I, protected by a golden mask, lay on a silver leaf inside a silver coffin contained in an anonymous Ramesside sarcophagus in black granite. This was enclosed in another huge granite sarcophagus inscribed with the name of Merneptah.

TOMB OF OSORKON
As well as the vault of the king and his son, the tomb also contained four limestone rooms with painted walls. One of these rooms, whose walls were decorated with the "Field of Cyperus" (detail above), contained the tomb of Takelot II.

THE GREAT TEMPLE. The Great Temple of Amun is nothing more than a heap of granite blocks. In the absence of any remains we are left to imagine the rows of pylons preceded by obelisks, and colonnaded courtyards with palm capitals. The scattered monuments include a recumbent colossus of Ramesses II, said to favor procreation.

THE ROYAL NECROPOLIS. The necropolis lies, surprisingly, within the enclosure of Psusennes. It appears that the 21st Dynasty ranged its tombs against a sandy hill. The 22nd Dynasty extended the complex until the reign of Shoshenq III, who leveled the area and enclosed the tombs in a mudbrick platform on which he built his own tomb. The tombs of (north to south) Shoshenq III, Amenemope, Psusennes I and Osorkon II, and three anonymous tombs, built of reused materials (especially Ramesside granite), can still be seen.

TOMB OF PSUSENNES I. A vertical shaft leads to an antechamber decorated with images of protective spirits and one of the king worshipping Osiris. It contained the sepulcher of an unknown 22nd-Dynasty king, Heqakheperre Shoshenq. Two chambers opening toward the east contained the kings Psusennes and Amenemope (south chamber, intended for Queen Mutnedjemet). Another chamber contained the sepulcher of Ankhefenmut, while a blind chamber contained that of the General Wundebawdjed.

TOMB OF OSORKON. The granite vault contained the huge granite sarcophagus of Osorkon II and the sepulcher (found intact) of his son, Prince Hornakht.

TOMB OF SHOSHENQ III. The rectangular tomb, built of limestone blocks from the 21st Dynasty (including inscribed blocks taken from private tombs), consisted of a central shaft and a chamber containing two granite sarcophagi (the king's had been taken from another site). Only the chamber is decorated, with scenes from the *Book of the Dead* and the *Book of Night*. To the north of the Great Temple the remains of a TEMPLE OF NECTANEBO, dedicated to Khonsu, were excavated. To the east, beyond the enclosure of Psusennes, stands the TEMPLE OF THE EAST, a kiosk-like structure with ten or so palmiform columns (Ramesses II usurped by Osorkon II). To the south, opposite the gate of Ptolemy I, is a 30TH-DYNASTY TEMPLE. To the southwest of the precinct a 21st Dynasty temple dedicated to Mut was discovered and named the TEMPLE OF ANTA. It had been rebuilt during the Saite and Ptolemaic periods.

Recent excavations have revealed the remains of the town and two other temple complexes. A large enclosure and the outline of a temple dismantled during the Ptolemaic period were discovered at the southern end of the *tell*. Further west a later necropolis, built on the site of a Third Intermediate period cemetery, was identified. In the center of the *tell* a line of granite blocks marked the site of a (destroyed) temple, which was almost as vast as the Great Temple of Amun.

GEOGRAPHY OF THE ISTHMUS OF SUEZ

The fault that is today occupied by the Gulf of Suez and the Red Sea was formed at the end of the Eocene, during the folding process which created the Sinai peninsula. The fault was filled by the waters of the Mediterranean during the Miocene and the connection with the Indian Ocean was established toward the middle of the Pliocene. Less is known about the formation of the isthmus separating the Gulf of Suez from the Mediterranean. It is the result of a slow upthrust affecting the whole of the eastern Delta. It could have begun at the end of the Pliocene, but was never completed.

Geologically speaking the isthmus is almost indistinguishable from the Arabian Desert, of which it forms the northern extremity. In the north the aridity is slightly tempered by the proximity of the coast and the presence of lakes and marshland, today being reclaimed. The plateau slowly rises toward the south until the rocky sub-stratum surfaces between the Bitter Lakes and Suez.

SUEZ CANAL

CANAL FROM THE NILE TO THE RED SEA. A legend based on Greek and Latin texts (Strabo and Pliny) attributes the first project for the construction of a direct link between the River Nile and the Red Sea to Senwosret I. There is no supporting archeological evidence for this, however. It was not until the Saïte period and the reign of Necho II (610–595 BC) that the first canal was dug from the Pelusian branch of the Nile to the northern end of the Bitter Lakes. It was restored and completed almost a century later by Darius I (522–486 BC) and traces of this canal can still be seen today along the Wadi Tumilat, between Saft el-Hinna and Ismaïliya. It was extended to the Red Sea during the reign of Ptolemy II Philadelphus (285–46 BC), abandoned at the beginning of the Roman occupation and re-excavated during the reign of Trajan (AD 98–117). A new point of supply was established on the Nile a few miles north of Cairo, and it was this canal that was restored by Amr Ibn el-As ● 66 and became known as the "Canal of the Commander of the Faithful". In AD 767 the Abbasid caliph El-Mansur closed the canal to cut off supplies to the insurgent towns of the Hejaz.

EARLY PROJECTS. The engineers of the EGYPT EXPEDITION ● 94 were the first to develop the full-scale project of a direct link between Pelusium and Suez. By opening up the Suez route, Napoleon Bonaparte hoped to "deal a blow to England which was as fatal as the discovery of the Cape of Good Hope had been to the Genoese and Venetians". However, the leveling of the site, begun in January 1799 under the supervision of Charles Le Père, only lasted a few months. An error in calculating one of the positions led Le Père to conclude that, at high tide, there was a significant difference in level (about 33 feet) between the two seas and that, as a result, locks would have to be incorporated into the ship canal. In spite of opposition from theorists, Le Père's hypothesis was accepted unquestioningly for almost fifty years. It was supported by the Saint-Simoniens (a group of revolutionary French intellectuals) who arrived in Cairo in 1833 and who saw the Suez Canal as the first in a series of similar interoceanic links which would promote economic and financial exchanges. However, Mohammed Ali preferred to involve the group's twenty or so engineers and technicians in the Delta barrage ▲ *206* project. In 1835 a plague epidemic closed the site and dispersed the Saint-Simoniens, although they did leave behind them disciples such as Linant de Bellefonds ▲ *206* and Ferdinand de Lesseps. Lesseps, then French vice-consul in Alexandria, was attracted by their views and convinced of the feasibility of the Suez Canal project. He adopted their idea of forming a public company and launching a public loan to raise funds for its completion.

RESEARCH ASSOCIATION. The creation of a transit service and the establishment of the Overland Road (transit via Egypt of the India packet) in 1839 revived enthusiasm for the Mediterranean–Red Sea link. In Paris the Saint-Simoniens formed an association in 1846 to research the Suez project, which brought together English, German, Austrian and French industrialists and entrepreneurs. In 1847 the leveling work carried out by Bourdaloue confirmed that there was no significant difference in level between the two seas. Linant de Bellefonds compiled the technical report. The implementation of the project was delayed by Turkish opposition, British skepticism and the illness of Mohammed Ali. The khedive Abbas, who succeeded his grandfather in 1849, was not particularly pro-European, as he was afraid of a further increase of their influence in the region.

The Suez Canal, built between 1859 and 1869 to link the Mediterranean and the Red Sea, was one of the major construction projects of the 19th century and the first in a series of similar links that would revolutionize the world geography of trade. It covers a distance of over 100 miles between Port Said and Suez, crossing the sands of the northern coastal region and then the series of lagoons formed by Lake Timsah and the Bitter Lakes (which are an extension of the Gulf of Suez) separating the eastern Delta region from the Sinai peninsula.

The political situation was altered by the accession of Saïd (1854) who, unlike his predecessor, was very open to European ideas and counted Ferdinand de Lesseps among his friends. He immediately approved the Suez project, presented for the first time on November 15, 1854, and ratified the act of concession a fortnight later. The pilot study estimated that a total of 2,613 million cubic feet of earth would have to be excavated: 600 million on land by manpower and 2,013 million in water by dredgers. The total cost was estimated at two hundred million francs.

PORT-SAID - Palais de la Compagnie du Canal de Suez

The act of concession granted the Universal Company of the Suez Ship Canal the right to manage and develop the canal for ninety-nine years from the time it was filled with water. The profits were to be shared between the founders (10 percent), the Egyptian government (15 percent) and the shareholders (75 percent).

FERDINAND DE LESSEPS
Ferdinand de Lesseps (1805–94), son of a diplomat who was French consul-general in Egypt, spent part of his boyhood in Alexandria and was a friend of the sons of Mohammed Ali. He returned to Egypt as a trainee at the French Consulate in Cairo in 1833 and was vice-consul in Alexandria from 1834 to 1838 where he met the Saint-Simoniens and learned about their Suez Canal project. The accession of his childhood friend, Saïd, to the throne of Egypt offered him an unexpected opportunity.

A mobile machine used during the excavation of the Suez Canal.

THE CANAL PROJECT

Work on the canal began on April 25, 1859, near Port Said, but soon ran into political and financial difficulties. Lesseps was forced to launch a Europe-wide campaign to sell half of the four hundred thousand 500-franc shares issued. He managed to sell the remainder to Saïd, who became the holder of 44 percent of the capital. This concerned the British and the Turks, who succeeded in having work on the project suspended. The intervention of Napoleon III brought the crisis to an end. From 1860 twenty thousand Egyptian *fellaheen* worked day and night. They were requisitioned by the army (many traveling long distances) and were replaced every month. The freshwater canal was completed in 1862 and in November of the same year, the waters of the Mediterranean entered Lake Timsah. Ismaïl, who succeeded Saïd in 1863, was less enthusiastic about the project. The Turks reminded him that had not approved the work on the canal and would not allow him to use enforced labor. Lesseps once again appealed to Napoleon III. An international commission, formed in March 1864 to resolve these differences, pronounced in favor of the company. The sultan issued a decree on March 19, 1866, approving the concession and the work was completed three years later.

CELEBRATIONS
The ceremonial inauguration of the Suez Canal at Port Said, preceded by an extravagant firework display and a ball attended by six thousand people, was the start of celebrations that lasted several weeks and included the opening of the Cairo Opera House built by the khedive Ismaïl.

THE FINAL BLOW
On November 17, 1869 Ali Pasha delivered the final blow which breached the barrage of the Suez plain reservoir and let the waters of the Mediterranean flow into the Red Sea.

AT ANCHOR IN THE BITTER LAKES
The convoy left Port Said for the new town of Ismaïliya where it dropped anchor for the night before continuing its journey to the port of Suez.

INAUGURATION CELEBRATIONS
Lavish celebrations were held to commemorate the inauguration of the Suez Canal. Among the khedive Ismaïl's six thousand guests were several of the crowned heads of Europe, including the Empress Eugenie, the Emperor of Austria, the Prince of Wales, the Prince of Prussia and the Prince of the Netherlands, as well as a host of journalists, artists and businessmen. When the sluices closing the Bitter Lakes were opened and the waters of the Mediterranean flowed to Suez, the first convoy of forty-eight ships bedecked with flags sailed through.

PORT SAID

"There is nothing worthy of note about Port Said. It admits to a bad reputation and has, for its size, an even larger stock of improper photographs than Brussels or Buenos Aires.**"**

Richard Curle

The town of Suez was badly damaged by the three "canal wars", especially the last. A reconstruction campaign has been underway for several years. A street in Suez.

THE THREE SUEZ CANAL WARS

NATIONALIZATION. The Suez Crisis erupted during the summer of 1956 against a background of international tension. On July 19, 1956, the United States announced that, contrary to pilot agreements negotiated in Cairo, they would not be making a financial contribution to the Aswan High Dam ▲ *460*. Great Britain and the World Bank also withdrew from the agreement. On July 26, 1956, President Nasser responded by announcing the nationalization of the Suez Canal. A series of negotiations and talks were held throughout the summer to no avail. On October 29 the Israelis invaded Sinai, on the pretext of dismantling Palestinian bases. France and Great Britain issued an ultimatum to the two parties which stipulated a ceasefire and withdrawal to a distance of 10 miles on either side of the canal. Israel, which had not reached the ten-mile limit, agreed to the ceasefire while Egypt rejected it. The French and British bombed the canal towns and airlifted troops into Port Said. Under pressure from the United States the three aggressors accepted a ceasefire and authorized the deployment of an international security force, which had evacuated the canal zone by March 1, 1957.

THE FRONT LINE. In spring 1967, after several months of tension running high, Syria called upon her Egyptian ally in accordance with the joint defense agreement signed by the two countries. At the end of the month Jordan, which had just suffered a series of Israeli attacks, also signed a joint defense agreement with Egypt. At the beginning of June 200,000 troops were on a war footing in Egypt and Syria and ready to face the 264,000-strong Israeli force. On June 5 the Israeli government took American diplomats unawares by launching a huge air attack on Egyptian, Syrian and Jordanian airports, followed by a ground offensive the next day. When the ceasefire was signed on June 8, Egypt had lost Sinai and the Suez Canal was in ruins, while Syria was cut off from Golan and Jordan from the left bank of the River Jordan. In spite of an armistice negotiated under the auspices of the United Nations, Egypt and Israel installed themselves on either side of the Suez Canal and began a war of attrition punctuated by isolated incidents. For the next eight years the Suez Canal became the front line between the two armies and was closed to navigation.

BREAKING THE DEADLOCK. On October 6, 1973, Egypt initiated the hostilities by launching a surprise attack on the Suez Canal and the reputedly impregnable fortified defense (the so-called Bar-Lev Line) constructed by the Israelis on the east bank. The Badr plan, prepared down to the last detail during the previous two years, was carried out to perfection in the first few days of the conflict, but the Israeli counter offensive, launched on October 8, was swift and equally effective. When the ceasefire was signed on October 22 the Egyptians had recaptured a large part of Sinai but the Israelis still held the canal zone between Ismaïliya and Suez. Neither side was the victor. Egypt, however, was able to reestablish her sovereignty over both

The main attraction of Port Said is its port, which consists of four huge harbors and an outer port. It is worth a visit just to see the ships waiting to go through the Suez Canal. The distinctive green-domed offices of the Suez Canal Company (above right), built in 1967.

PORT TAWFIQ
Port Tawfiq lies southeast of Suez and is linked to the town by a jetty. It stands on an artificial peninsula created from the sand excavated during the construction of the Suez Canal.

banks of the canal with the first disengagement agreement, which was signed in January 1974.

A MAJOR TRADE ROUTE. It took two years to clear the canal of the accumulated wreckage and rubble of eight years of war. The canal was reopened to shipping on June 5, 1975, and gradually reestablished its position in international trade, but only after extensive redevelopment. The increased tonnage of cargo ships meant that the channel had to be widened. The first phase of the work, completed in December 1980, extended the overall length of the canal to 122 miles, and the width was expanded to 399 yards (208 yards for the channel) with a maximum draft of 56 feet. A new phase was begun in 1990 to deepen and widen the channel so that it could now accommodate ships with a draft of up to 68 feet.

Today the former villa of Ferdinand de Lesseps in Ismaïliya is used to receive the Egyptian government's VIP guests.

The bazaar of Suez in about 1870.

Ismaïliya, founded in the 1860's, was named in honor of the khedive Ismaïl on the initiative of Ferdinand de Lesseps, who lived there until work on

the canal was complete. A street in early 20th-century Ismaïliya and the Suez Canal (above).

THE CANAL TOWNS

SUEZ. Suez was built in the 15th century when Qolzum, whose ruins form a *tell* at the entrance to the freshwater canal, was abandoned. The town developed during the 19th century when it was used by the British as a staging post on the route to India, and a railway line linking it with Cairo (constructed in 1857) contributed to its further expansion. The town was badly damaged during the wars with Israel and most of its factories (fertilizer and refineries) were destroyed from the 1960's onward. Today they are being rebuilt with financial aid from Saudi Arabia.

ISMAÏLIYA. Ismaïliya, which now has more than 500,000 inhabitants, was founded on the shores of LAKE TIMSAH (Crocodile Lake) during the construction of the Suez Canal. It consisted mainly of houses for the engineers and technicians working on the site. In a Pharaonic-style building Ismaïliya's MUSEUM OF ANTIQUITIES houses collections put together by the French conservationist Jean Clédat. The Rammeside stelae which used to stand in the Garden of Stelae are now in the Port Said Museum.

PORT SAID. Port Said was originally nothing more than a camp consisting of huts on stilts, founded in 1859 by Saïd Pasha to house the Suez Canal workforce. The sand excavated during dredging was used to fill in part of Lake Manzala and level the reclaimed land. By the late 19th century it was already an important port and all the major maritime powers had a consulate there. The new Port Said MUSEUM houses Pharaonic, Graeco-Roman, Coptic and Islamic antiquities. On the other side of the canal is PORT FUAD, founded in 1925.

SINAI

▲ SINAI

BEDOUINS

The Bedouins were the original inhabitants of Sinai and still represent the largest section of the total population (200,000) of the peninsula. They belong to different tribes governed by customary laws. Tribal confederations, in both North and

South Sinai, manage their interests and organize their social life. This mainly sedentary population is today being marginalized by new economic trends and the development of their territory. Although their nomadic lifestyle may have disappeared they continue to maintain their traditional activities and there is a thriving Bedouin craft industry.

SINAI

Bordered by the Mediterranean in the north, the Gulf of Suez in the west and the Gulf of Aqaba in the east, the Sinai peninsula covers an area of almost 24,000 square miles between Africa and Asia. It is the other face of Egypt, a far cry from the Pharaonic sites of the Nile Valley. Sinai is an area of contrasts. The northern coastal plain, where most of the peninsula's population is concentrated, stretches from the Suez Canal ▲ 228 to the Gaza Strip and gradually gives way in the south to a limestone plateau, the El-Tih Desert. South of El-Tih are the Sinai Mountains, a vast range of crystalline mountains rising to heights of over 6,500 feet. Here, traditional farming and stock breeding are carried on in the many oases of its *wadis*. Finally the Red Sea, where the mountains fall steeply into the turquoise waters, is teeming with marine life, whose beauty and variety is equal to that of the famous tropical reefs found in the Southern Hemisphere. While he was visiting Egypt in 1850, Gustave Flaubert wrote: "The sea bed with its wealth of different shells and corals was more colorful than a primrose meadow, while the surface of the sea shimmered and sparkled with every possible shade of color, blending from chocolate to amethyst, from pink to lapis-lazuli and the palest of pale green. It was truly unbelievable . . . ."

CLIMATE. The climate is varied, although aridity is the common factor in these vast desert wastes. There is a very definite Mediterranean influence in the north where the coastal strip has a much higher winter rainfall and temperatures are much cooler than the regional average. The central plateau is the most arid region, while in the fall and early spring the Sinai Mountains often suffer torrential and devastating rainstorms. In mid-winter the highest peaks are regularly covered in snow. The Gulf of Aqaba has a fairly constant climate throughout the year, with milder winters resulting from the temperature of the Red Sea (68 to 77 degrees Fahrenheit) and cooler summers resulting from the north-northeasterly winds which blow down this natural corridor.

FAUNA. Sinai's once richly varied fauna has become much impoverished. Gazelles, oryx and jackals are now rare and leopards have completely disappeared. However, original species such as the hyrax (a strange rodent-like creature) and the ibex (a type of wild goat) still populate the peninsula. Steps have been taken to safeguard the wildlife of Sinai and special reserves have been created. Camels, the traditional symbol of the Bedouin way of life, are now gradually being replaced by Japanese jeeps.

LOOKING TO THE FUTURE: PROJECTS AND PROSPECTS. Since it was restored to Egypt in 1982 Sinai has been the subject of a number of tourist, agricultural and industrial development projects. In fact Egypt sees this vast territory as a potential solution to its problem of overpopulation. Work is currently underway on the El-Salam Canal, which will link the Nile with North Sinai and ultimately irrigate about 495,000 acres. This is surely an indication of the intention to populate this previously neglected region and make it productive. Now that there are real prospects of peace in the region, Sinai should also be able to resume its traditional function as a bridge between Egypt and Lebanon, Syria and Israel.

GETTING TO SINAI. There are several ways of getting to Sinai by means of public transport, including bus and taxi, but visitors who are short of time may prefer to fly. However, given the vast distances that have to be covered, the best solution, if possible, is to have your own vehicle. Good road maps are available and the road signs in Sinai are better than anywhere else in Egypt. If you plan to leave the main highways, it is essential to have a four-wheel drive. Alternatively you can join one of the excursions organized by local Bedouins, and these can be either in their own vehicles, by camel or on foot.

> "Historically, the Sinai is a paradox. This seemingly worthless, underpopulated, undercultivated, static piece of gritty real estate has been the most besieged territory in the world – at last count, the battleground for at least fifty invading armies since recorded history began."
>
> Burton Bernstein

239

SOUTH SINAI

The first route into South Sinai suitable for motor vehicles was opened in 1929 by King Fuad who wanted to visit St Catherine's. The route followed the Suez Canal before winding up into the mountains and continuing along a track as far as El-Tor, today the regional capital of the Governorate of South Sinai. It was used by pilgrims on their way to St Catherine's as well as servicing the quarantine center for the pilgrimage to Mecca. The center was set up in El-Tor at the end of the 19th century when sea routes to places of pilgrimage gradually replaced the traditional *darb el-hajj* route across the center of the peninsula. Until the Israelis invaded Sinai in June 1967 ● *71* the peninsula remained a marginal area which was virtually cut off from the rest of Egypt, the real frontier of the country being the Suez Canal ▲ *228*. The 1979 Camp David Agreements and the restoration of Sinai to Egypt marked the beginning of a new era, symbolized by the opening of the Ahmed Hamdi Tunnel (named after an officer killed during the 1973 Arab–Israeli War) in 1980. The tunnel, which is about 10 miles north of Suez and about 88 miles from Cairo, was intended to open up Egypt's Asiatic territory. On the Sinai side the road heads south along the Suez Canal.

Aïn Musa. "They took us to the oasis of the Springs of Moses which is the starting point of the desert routes and where our tents, which had left Cairo two days before us, had been put up beneath the slender palm trees." (Pierre Loti, *Le Désert*, 1896). Aïn Musa (Springs of Moses), the largest oasis in South Sinai, was planted with palm trees, mimosa and tamarisk and fed by a hot (104 degrees Fahrenheit) spring. According to the Bible the oasis was the site of Marah (which in Hebrew means "bitter") where Moses is said to have thrown a piece of wood into the bitter-tasting waters and made them sweet (Exodus 15, 24–5). Until the freshwater canal between the valley and Suez was built, in 1863, Aïn Musa constituted one of the main freshwater supplies for the town and the ships that docked there, as well as

Moses receiving the Ten Commandments.

"And the people murmured against Moses, saying, What shall we drink? And he cried unto the Lord; and the Lord shewed him a tree, which when he had cast into the waters, the waters were made sweet."

(Exodus 15, 24–5).

one of the main way stations on the Sinai route. The members of the Egypt Expedition recorded a total of nine springs and during the 19th century the oasis was a popular vacation resort among foreign diplomats. Today it is a mere shadow of its former self. Only one of its sources is still maintained, and a good proportion of the pools are now filled in; the palm grove remains only partly cultivated. The wreckage of the successive Arab–Israeli wars fought in this region is the only legacy from an era which sealed the fate of this once prosperous oasis.

RAS EL-SUDR AND QAL'AT EL-JUNDI. Ras el-Sudr is the second most important town on the Gulf of Suez after El-Tor. It originally developed as a result of the oil industry, but now it is becoming increasingly popular as a tourist center mainly because of its proximity to both Suez and Cairo. A road leads northeastward from Ras el-Sudr to Qal'at el-Jundi, the former citadel of Salah ad-Din, at a distance of about 30 miles. The 12th-century citadel, which was built to protect the route of pilgrimage and also to repel the attacks of the Crusaders, stands at the top of an outlier of the Jebel el-Raha several hundred yards above the vast expanses of the El-Tih plateau. For centuries it stood forgotten among the surrounding rocks, until it was rediscovered in 1909 by the French geologist Jules Barthoux, who was traveling from Suez to El-Tor. Among the buildings that can be found enclosed by the walls of the citadel are cisterns and shops with particularly beautiful, vaulted rooms which have been hewn out of the rock. There is also an old observation post.

THE WILDERNESS
The biblical description of Sinai as the "wilderness" always evokes the image of Moses leading the Jews out of Egypt along the valleys known as "the most ancient routes in the world". These routes took them to Mount Sinai (Jebel Musa, or the Mountain of Moses) where the prophet received the Ten Commandments. The Bible seems to have identified the spot (which subsequently became mythical) where over the centuries scholars, holy men and women and pilgrims have come to seek salvation. Until the early 20th century the route of the Exodus was the subject of many scientific and theological debates. It is now widely thought that Moses led the Children of Israel from Goshen (the eastern Delta) via the Bitter Lakes to the Isthmus of Suez, along the Gulf of Suez and Wadi Feiran to Mount Sinai.

The Oasis of Feiran extends almost 3 miles and includes a truly magnificent palm grove and a number of orchards.

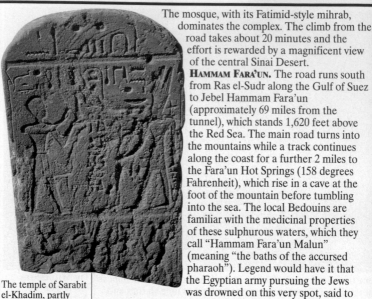

The mosque, with its Fatimid-style mihrab, dominates the complex. The climb from the road takes about 20 minutes and the effort is rewarded by a magnificent view of the central Sinai Desert.

HAMMAM FARA'UN. The road runs south from Ras el-Sudr along the Gulf of Suez to Jebel Hammam Fara'un (approximately 69 miles from the tunnel), which stands 1,620 feet above the Red Sea. The main road turns into the mountains while a track continues along the coast for a further 2 miles to the Fara'un Hot Springs (158 degrees Fahrenheit), which rise in a cave at the foot of the mountain before tumbling into the sea. The local Bedouins are familiar with the medicinal properties of these sulphurous waters, which they call "Hammam Fara'un Malun" (meaning "the baths of the accursed pharaoh"). Legend would have it that the Egyptian army pursuing the Jews was drowned on this very spot, said to be haunted by the spirit of the pharaoh.

The temple of Sarabit el-Khadim, partly built into the rock, probably dates from the Middle Kingdom. It has a number of upright stelae dedicated to Hathor and the rulers of the Nile Valley.

TEMPLE OF SARABIT EL-KHADIM. The main road follows the Wadi Tayiba ("pleasant valley") for about 20 miles before rejoining the coast at Abu Zenima, a small oil and mining center. To the south of the town the road running along the Wadi Matalla to the temple of Sarabit el-Khadim is surfaced for the first 22 miles and then replaced by a track for about 7½ miles. The temple is situated at the top of a hill about 45 minutes' walk from the track. It was dedicated to Hathor, "Mistress of the Turquoise", and was built to protect the many mines in the area from which the Egyptians of the Old Kingdom extracted turquoise and copper during winter campaigns. Visitors are shown round by the Barakat family, who have been the temple guardians for as long as anyone can remember.

Remains of Qal'at el-Jundi. Texts carved on some of the stone lintels recount the history of the fortress.

MAGHARA TURQUOISE MINES. Abu Rudeis, which is situated about 103 miles from the tunnel, is an oil center to the south of Abu Zenima. From here a track follows the Wadi Sidri for about 13½ miles to the Maghara turquoise mines. The entrance to the mines is marked by stelae dedicated to the rulers of the Old Kingdom.

WADI MOQATTEB. From the mausoleum of Sheikh Suleyman, south of the mines, the track heads southeast for about 4½ miles before joining the Wadi Moqatteb, otherwise known as the Written Valley. The valley has derived its name from the

Nabatean inscriptions which are cut into the sandstone face of its western slopes. About 6 miles further on the track joins the Wadi Feiran road leading to St Catherine's Monastery. These two excursions can be combined by using the road between Sarabit el-Khadim and the turquoise mines, but should not be undertaken without a guide and four-wheel drive.

Beyond Feiran (left), the road follows the Wadi el-Sheikh to the Watia Pass gorge, bordered by granite cliffs, before emerging onto the plateau of St Catherine's Monastery. The typical mountain village of St Catherine looks incongruous in this desert landscape. The village has almost four hundred inhabitants, mainly Bedouins originating from the Jebaliye ("mountain") tribe, who are said to be the descendants of two hundred Walachian and Bosnian families sent by Justinian to defend the monastery when it was founded.

THE SINAI MOUNTAINS

About 27 miles south of Abu Rudeis the main road continues toward El-Tor while a secondary road turns eastward toward the Oasis of Feiran and St Catherine's.

OASIS OF FEIRAN ★. The oasis of Feiran lies midway between the Red Sea and St Catherine's and is an ideal place to break your journey. It is the largest oasis in South Sinai and lies at the narrowest point of the valley at the foot of the Jebel Serbal, which rises to a height of 6,790 feet to the south of the oasis. This is traditionally the site of Rephidim, where the Jews stopped on the last stage of their journey before reaching Mount Sinai (Exodus 17, 1–16). The oasis flourished in the early centuries of the Christian era and a bishop's palace was founded there in 400. In the 7th century the conquering army of Caliph Omar brought about its decline by putting an end to its religious ascendancy in favor of St Catherine's. The ruins of ancient Pharan stand on a hill, El-Meharret, at the center of the oasis. At its foot is a small hermitage, a dependency of St Catherine's. Today Feiran has about 650 inhabitants, mainly Qararsha or Awlad Saïd Bedouin.

▲ St Catherine's Monastery

The first thing you see as you approach the monastery, built between 527 and 565 on the orders of the emperor Justinian on the site of the "Burning Bush", at an altitude of 5,150 feet, are its gardens surrounded by cypresses and its impressive walls. It has the double distinction of being the smallest diocese in the world and the oldest working monastery. It is named after Saint Catherine, an Alexandrian martyr who died in 307. Her body was supposedly carried away by angels and discovered five centuries later at the top of the mountain which today bears her name.

The monastery belongs to the Greek Orthodox Church and most of the monks are Greek. Although the principal church and the site of the "Burning Bush" are open to the public, the monks guard their tranquillity and do not allow visitors into the treasure-house, the museum or the library, which has the largest collection of manuscripts in the world after the Vatican Library.

During times of instability and unrest, the normal access route to the monastery was closed and a basket-and-pulley was used to hoist visitors and provisions over the walls.

A short ascent opposite the entrance leads to a vantage point overlooking the interior of the monastery. It is a heterogeneous complex consisting of buildings from different periods and even includes a 10th-century mosque built as a mark of allegiance to the Muslim powers that had promised to protect it. Inside the Byzantine-style church, originally dedicated to the Transfiguration of Christ, a fine collection of icons from different periods gives some idea of the extent of the monastery's treasures.

"And Mount Sinai was altogether on a smoke, because the Lord descended upon it in fire: and the smoke thereof ascended as the smoke of a furnace, and the whole mount quaked greatly. And when the voice of the trumpet sounded long, and waxed louder and louder, Moses spake, and God answered him by a voice.**"**
(Exodus 19, 18–19)

It was on Mount Sinai (Jebel Musa, or the Mountain of Moses) that Moses received the Ten Commandments. It lies south of St Catherine's Monastery and rises to a height of 7,497 feet. It can be reached along a track to the east of the monastery walls or via a flight of three thousand steps hewn out of the rock to the south. Both lead to an amphitheater (known as the "Seventy Elders of Israel") where St Stephen's Hermitage stands in a garden planted with cypresses. A flight of some 750 steps leads to the summit where a chapel built in 1934 is reminiscent of the original (AD 363) rebuilt by Justinian in 530.

It is advisable to take the gently sloping track to the top of Mount Sinai and leave the steps for the descent.

There is a breathtaking view from the chapel (above) and on a clear day you can see the Gulf of Aqaba and the coast of Saudi Arabia. To the southwest Mount Catherine (Jebel Katherina), the highest point on the Sinai peninsula, dominates Mount Sinai from a height of 8,650 feet.

COLORED CANYON
The Bedouins who live on the site accompany visitors

who want to see the canyon's remarkable colored rock formations. At the foot of cliffs which are barely a yard apart in places, the sandstone and limestone strata form swathes of color ranging from pink to brown and from yellow to green.

GULF OF AQABA AND THE RED SEA ★

The road continues eastward toward the Gulf of Aqaba through 44 miles of breathtaking landscapes, where the combined effect of the limestone mountains and sedimentary deposits has produced some remarkable variations of form and color, as well as some truly spectacular views. About 56 miles from St Catherine's Monastery, a main intersection leads southward toward Dahab, Sharm el-Sheikh and Ras Mohammed and northward to Nuweiba and Taba on the Israeli border.

DAHAB. The "Bedouin village" of Assalah forms the southern half of Dahab. Its palm-fringed bay is bordered by cafés, restaurants and campsites, which offer basic facilities at competitive prices. A little further on, the Israeli-built village of Dahab is a business and administrative center. The many beaches and diving sites that can be reached from both villages include the famous "Blue Hole" about 5 miles from Assalah.

SHARM EL-SHEIKH. About 12½ miles from Ras Mohammed is the peninsula's most developed tourist center, which all underwater enthusiasts must visit. Sharm el-Sheikh is divided into two parts, the southern half where the town stands on a cliff overlooking the port, and Na'ama Bay, situated 4½ miles to the north, which is the center for hotels and diving clubs. The 10-mile stretch of coast between Sharm el-Sheikh and Ras Nusrani has many diving sites randomly dotted along its length, and these are easily accessible from the road. Beyond Ras Nusrani the main road heads northward and the diving sites are reached along coastal tracks.

RAS MOHAMMED. Ras Mohammed (*ras* is the Arabic word for "cape" or "head") is the most southerly point of the Sinai peninsula. It was declared a conservation site in 1983 and became a national park in 1989 in order to protect and preserve the region's marine and desert flora and fauna. Foxes and gazelles have been reintroduced and the park also has a large migratory and sedentary bird population. The mangrove forests in the south provide an ideal habitat and have the most northerly growing mangroves in the Northern Hemisphere. The park is renowned for its diving sites where a pair of flippers and a snorkel are all you need to discover the wonders of its underwater marine life. Among the shoals of multicolored fish, the lucky diver may encounter the Napoleon fish (up to 6 feet in length but the most peaceable of diving companions), the reef shark, the manta ray or the green turtle. Maps of the park are available at the entrance.

Nuweiba. From Dahab the road cuts through the mountains, rejoining the coast in sight of the port of Nuweiba from where there is a daily ferry service to the Jordanian port of Aqaba. Nuweiba lies either side of the Wadi Watir delta, with the port and Muzeina Bedouin fishing village to the south and 2½ miles to the north the tourist and Tarabiin Bedouin villages, separated by the remains of an 18th-century Turkish citadel. The road running westward between the two will take you to the Colored Canyon. It follows the Wadi Watir to the oasis of Aïn el-Furtaga where a track, to the right, runs along the bottom of the valley for 7½ miles and comes out onto a plateau above the canyon. Nuweiba also has a number of beaches and diving sites.

Taba. For six years Taba was the stumbling block in Israeli–Egyptian relations. It was only restored to Egypt in 1989 following international arbitration. Plans for the development of a major resort on the Israeli–Egyptian border are currently under consideration. At present Taba has restaurants and beach cafés and one luxury hotel. The frontier post (about 100 yards from the hotel) can be crossed on foot and there is a bus service to Eilat.

Return route via Darb el-Hajj. The road leading westward from between the fjord and the Geziret Fara'un (Pharaoh's Island) winds for about 19 miles along a *wadi* to the central plateau of the Sinai peninsula, the El-Tih Desert. It follows the ancient pilgrim's route, which crossed the peninsula to the Hejaz mountains in present-day Saudi Arabi. The route, which was much frequented until the early 20th century, was used for an annual pilgrimage, accompanied by an army escort to protect the *mahmal* ● *126*. Today it is still

the main overland link between Egypt, the Arabian peninsula, Lebanon, Syria and Israel, via the port of Nuweiba. The Bedouin village of El-Thamad, the first settlement on the route, is gradually becoming an important way station. Nakhl lies at the center of the peninsula and has for a long time been a crucial staging post. A road leads from the center of Nakhl to El-Arish, 94 miles to the north. About 37½ miles west of Nakhl the road climbs to the top of the Mitla Pass and then down toward Suez in the west across dunes dotted with the wreckage of armored vehicles, evidence of the conflicts that have taken place in the area.

There are some truly beautiful landscapes between Nuweiba and Taba. The road borders a sea whose transparent colors range from deep blue to turquoise. On the opposite shore is the Saudi Arabian and Jordanian coast and the port of Aqaba. About 6½ miles before you get to Taba the road climbs above the fjord, where the turquoise waters of the inlet are dominated by cliffs. After crossing the bed of the Wadi

Morakh, Geziret Fara'un (Pharaoh's Island) can be seen beyond a hill, dominated by its recently restored fortress, begun in 1170 by Salah ad-Din.

THE SUEZ CANAL AT EL-QANTARA
In 1916 El-Qantara was the departure point for the Palestine railway line that ran along the Mediterranean coast toward Gaza and Jerusalem. It was built for military purposes by the British and linked Cairo and Jerusalem until 1948. It continued to run as far as Gaza between 1948 and 1967. It was dismantled at the time of the Israeli invasion and its lines and sleepers used to construct the Bar-Lev Line, a defensive rampart erected by Tsahal along the Suez Canal during the occupation. A mobile bridge (above), destroyed in 1967, enabled trains to cross the canal at El-Firdan, about 12½ miles south of El-Qantara.

NORTH SINAI

The route across North Sinai, known as the "Ways of Horus", has linked Egypt and Palestine since ancient times and served as both an invasion and trade route. Before the Suez Canal was built, the isthmus acted as a bridge between Africa and Asia.

EL-QANTARA. El-Qantara ("the passage"), which lies about 22 miles north of Ismaïliya ▲ *236* between the Bitter Lakes and Lake Timsah in the south and the marshlands of the ancient Pelusian branch of the Nile in the north, has always been a place of passage into Sinai. Dissected by the Suez Canal, El-Qantara el-Garbiya in the west and El-Qantara el-Sharkiya in the east are two fairly uninteresting towns which suffered during the Arab–Israeli conflicts from 1956 to 1973. A ferry service links the two towns. About 3 miles outside El-Qantara the road runs north to El-Arish (100 miles) and south to Ismaïliya (25 miles).

PELUSIUM. The ancient site of Pelusium, about 19 miles north of El-Qantara, can be reached via a minor road which turns off near the village of BALUZA, whose name is reminiscent of the ancient port. Pelusium dates from the time of the Hyksos invasion in c. 1700 BC. The Hyksos were going to found their capital on the site of Pelusium, on the mouth of a branch of the Nile, and then decided to settle further up the Delta. However, an important port was established at Pelusium and became, under the Ptolemies, the eastern counterpart of Alexandria. As a major Egyptian port it fell prey to invaders and gradually declined as the Pelusian branch of the Nile moved and dried up. In 1118 it finally fell to the Crusaders led by King Baldwin I of Jerusalem and was burned and razed to the ground. The only remains that can be seen at Tell el-Farama, the site of ancient Pelusium, are several hundred yards of the outer walls and the Aswan granite columns scattered on the ground on the site of the ancient port.

LAKE BARDAWIL. Beyond Baluza the road runs eastward, parallel to the coast, along the shores of Lake Bardawil, which can be reached via a number of minor roads. The 52-mile-long lagoon occupies half the northern coastline of the Sinai peninsula and is separated from the sea by a narrow sandbank only a few dozen yards wide in places. It is an important staging post for migratory birds who rest there when crossing the Mediterranean. It is classified as a protected site and is considered one of the richest waterfowl reserves in the Mediterranean Basin. Fishing plays an important part in the region's economy and employs 15 percent of the working population. The fishing season is at its height between January and May when the 999 gaily colored fishing boats, according to local tradition, are dotted across the glittering waters of the lagoon. Sole constitutes the main catch and is exported as far afield as Europe. The lake supposedly takes its name from the nearby tomb of Crusader King Baldwin, even though the king's remains were

Legend attributes the name of Lake Bardawil to the Crusader King Baldwin I of Jerusalem, who died at El-Arish in 1118. His body was embalmed and his entrails buried near the lagoon, beneath a small mound of stones known as the Turbet el-Bardawil.

"The Bedouins wear a tunic with pointed sleeves which sweep the ground and which they tie behind their backs so that they can walk unhindered; the tunic is fastened at the waist with a broad, embroidered leather belt in which they insert a curved dagger.... Some throw a brown-and-white-striped woollen blanket over the tunic; they drape a piece of soft, dark-colored cloth elegantly over the tarboosh and turban covering their head, to protect them from the heat of the sun. They are all tanned ... and all have noble features."
Valérie de Gasparin, 1850

EL-ARISH
The capital of North Sinai, which has one of the most beautiful palm groves in Egypt, today has a population of 70,000. Until fairly recently, the less wealthy Cairenes used to holiday in palm beach huts rented from the Bedouins. Today hotels and villas occupy several miles of the seafront. The population of this important commercial center on the main Palestine

later taken back to Jerusalem.

EL-ARISH. Today the capital of North Sinai is being extensively developed. FUAKHARIYA, the oldest part of the town, which used to stand on a hill overlooking the palm grove, has the remains of a Pharaonic fortress, rebuilt by the Ottomans in 1560, occupied and restored by Bonaparte's troops in 1799 and destroyed by British bombardments during World War One. The remains of the fort can be seen at the end of the Shari' Suq el-Khamiss ("Thursday market") where a Bedouin market is held every Thursday morning. There is a permanent exhibition of the arts and traditions of the Bedouins of the Sinai peninsula near the zoological gardens on the outskirts of El-Arish.

RAFAH. The 27-mile trip to Rafah can easily be made from El-Arish. As you approach the border with the Gaza Strip the rapidly changing landscape resulting from much heavier rainfall and more developed agriculture can be considered as an "introduction to Palestine". About 19 miles from El-Arish the village of SHEIKH ZUAYED holds a Bedouin market every Tuesday morning. About 6 miles further on, at a point where an arch stands above the road, a minor road leads to the coastal village of EL-FAIRUZ, built on the site of Yamit, an Israeli settlement which symbolized the resistance of Jewish settlers during the Israeli withdrawal in 1982. A few miles further on the town of Rafah is dissected by the border and partly inhabited by Palestinian refugees

route is made up of Egyptians, Palestinians and Bedouins. Some of the town's inhabitants claim to be descended from the Bosnian soldiers sent by Süleyman the Magnificent to build the fortress in 1560.

from the 1967 war, some of whom cross the border every day to work in the Gaza Strip. There is a Saturday market in Rafah.

RETURN JOURNEY BY THE INLAND ROUTE. From El-Arish a road leading south (follow the signs to Ismaïliya) into the interior offers an opportunity to see the desert which was once the preserve of nomadic tribes. A few grazing camel herds are a reminder of a way of life that has virtually disappeared. The road, which forks west to El-Arish (37½ miles), skirts round the Jebel Maghara with its open-cast coal mines, passes through the village of Bir Gifgafa and crosses the Khatmia Pass before heading down toward the Suez Canal across some beautiful sand dunes. There is a ferry service to Ismaïliya.

DESERTS

Ten days

LIBYAN DESERT

The Libyan Desert stretches from the eastern bank of the Nile to the Libyan border over an average distance of 500 miles, and covers two thirds of the total surface area of Egypt. It is an inhospitable region with hardly any rainfall, high summer temperatures and treacherous winds. The Ancient Egyptians likened this vast desert to the sea and the oases to islands. In fact several deep depressions in the Libyan plateau actually lie below sea level and have created the five great oases: Siwa, Farafra, Baharia, Dakhla and Kharga. These low-lying areas make it easy to reach the water table, which lies above an impermeable layer of clay. Kharga, the largest of the five oases, stretches for nearly 120 miles.

POPULATION. In ancient times foreign influence (Egyptians, Greeks, Romans and Libyans) destroyed the basic stock of the indigenous oasis-dwellers. During the Islamic period the population was further modified by slaves brought from Darfur (Sudan). According to Roman records the Kharga Oasis in fact became a vast slave market which sold oasis-dwellers into slavery in the Nile Valley. Aspects of Bedouin culture have survived among the population (which has been sedentary for centuries), that place particular emphasis on blood ties, animist beliefs grafted onto Islam and a poetic tradition which speaks of nostalgia for the desert in a language similar to classical Arabic. Unlike the Sinai tribes ▲ *238*, who have inherited the traditions of the Arabian peninsula, the Bedouins of the Libyan Desert (with the exception of Siwa) live according to the traditions of the Egyptian civilization handed down by the original oasis-dwellers. However, their main forms of activity, driving caravans and collecting tributes from sedentary populations (in return for their protection), have died out.

The date palm is ideally suited to this desert region, which produces a wide variety of dates.

254

10 BALAT
11 KHARGA
12 TEMPLE OF NADURA
13 BAGAWAT
14 AIN UMM EL-DABADIB
15 AIN UMM LABAKHA
16 QASR EL-ZAIYAN
17 NEW BARIS
18 DUSH

CARAVAN ROUTES. Since the time of the Old Kingdom the desert has been crossed by a network of caravan routes linking Egypt with her neighbors. Ivory, ebony, rhinoceros hide, panther skins and slaves were brought into Egypt across this harsh and arid wasteland. In order to protect the borders and control the wealth arriving from Libya and Darfur, the Egyptians colonized the western oases, while the Greeks built Ptolemaic temples and the Romans constructed fortresses.

CROPS. Crops were cultivated in the oases of the Libyan Desert between the 1st and 4th centuries AD. These included olive trees, grown for their oil, vines, thought to have disappeared with the arrival of Islam (the vineyard which exists today dates from the reign of Mohammed Ali), corn, barley, millet, cotton and cardamom. However, the date

The palm date, and the papyrus.

palm so characteristic of this desert region is rarely mentioned. Of the fifty or so varieties of dates produced in Egypt, the oases grow mainly tamars, faligs, hamrawis and, best of all, the delicious saïdis.

MONASTIC CELLS. Christian mummies dating from the second half of the 3rd century AD were discovered in the oases of the Libyan Desert. This new religion was introduced very early on and began to develop within the lower strata of Egyptian society. The environment of the desert was favorable to the creation of monastic cells, which were often the victim of attacks by Barbarian tribes such as the Blemmyes. The Arab conquest finally put an end to Christianity in the desert region.

FAUNA. In Pharaonic times the donkey was Egypt's most widely used pack animal. It was gradually replaced in caravans by the dromedary, introduced into Egypt in 525 BC during the invasion led by the son of Hystaspes, later Darius I, King of Persia, who reigned from 521 to 486 BC. The country's population of camels has decreased significantly, owing to the development of the railway and the automobile.

Sand dunes cover 40 percent of the total surface area of the Libyan Desert. They can reach heights of up to 500 feet and change shape and direction with the winds. The pure, clean lines and gentle slopes of these sand mountains can be treacherous, gradually engulfing anything that lies in their path.

255

SIWA OASIS

To reach the Siwa Oasis from Cairo, take the toll expressway that crosses the desert to Alexandria and turn off left toward Burg el-Arab ▲ *201*. Siwa is situated nearly 190 miles southwest of Mersa Matruh, and the road linking them has a surprisingly good surface. For those who like the desert, the "oasis route" runs south from Giza ▲ *334* to Siwa and south-southwest to the oases of Bahariya, Farafra, Kharga and Dakhla. Siwa lies 187½ miles from the shores of the Mediterranean and 312½ miles from the Nile in a depression about 60 feet below sea level. Several million years ago the Libyan Desert was entirely covered by the waters of the Mediterranean, and there are still some salt-water lakes, such as El-Zeitun. Although these may add to the mystery of the landscape, it is the freshwater springs (nearly three hundred of them) flowing beneath palm- and olive-shaded paths that constitute the true beauty and wealth of the oases. Dates and olives are gathered by *zaggala* (stick bearers) who must remain celibate until the age of forty. The oases' ten thousand inhabitants are divided into nine tribes who are all descended from the Zenatiya Berbers. In spite of extensive intermarriage they continue to speak the Berber Siwi dialect. The Berber influence is also apparent in the craftsmanship which is unique throughout Egypt. The women continue to embroider yellow, orange and green geometric designs on *milaya* (large shawls), although synthetic materials have replaced traditionally woven cloth.

SHALI. This fortified town, whose outer wall was pierced by only three gates, was founded in 1203 following a violent Bedouin attack which left only forty survivors in the entire oasis. The steep, winding streets of Shali (the Berber word for "town") have been abandoned since 1926 when, for three days and nights, the rains beat down on the *karshif* (salt-caked mud) houses, making them uninhabitable.

TEMPLE OF AGHURMI. Of the many visitors who came to Siwa in ancient times to consult the oracle of Jupiter Amun (Darius), it was Alexander the Great who, in 331 BC,

CRAFTSMANSHIP
Traditionally the women of the Siwa Oasis used to wear all their wealth in the form of heavy silver jewelry: bracelets and different sorts of necklaces as well as rings and chains. Today these items of jewelry are becoming increasingly rare and their precious metal content is decreasing. Siwa is also renowned for basketwork and embroidered cloth. A wedding dress (above) embroidered with colored threads and decorated with buttons.

The Siwa Oasis has many lakes and over three hundred (freshwater or therapeutic) springs.

All that remains of the Temple of Umm el-Ubeyda is one wall, richly decorated with funeral scenes.

immortalized both the oracle and the oasis. The young Macedonian had just been proclaimed pharaoh in Memphis and was greeted as such by the high priest of the oracle. The temple stands to the northwest of the rock of Aghurmi, the ancient town. Cartouches of Amasis dating from the 26th Dynasty have been deciphered in spite of their very damaged condition, and these have established the date of the construction of the monument as the 6th century BC. At the foot of the rock of Aghurmi there is a second Temple of Amun, built during the 30th Dynasty and known as UMM EL-UBEYDA.

JEBEL EL-MAWTA. The ancient site of Jebel el-Mawta ("mount of the dead") was unknown to the 19th-century explorers. This huge limestone mass contains tombs from the 26th Dynasty and Ptolemaic period. The most beautiful sepulcher belongs to Si-Ammon, a rich oasis-dweller of Greek origin, and dates from the 3rd century BC. The image of the sky-goddess Nut with a halo of sycamore leaves (to the right

TEMPLE OF JUPITER AMUN
Although the houses which concealed the edifice (below) were cleared away in 1970, the temple is in an advanced state of disrepair. It is still possible to make out the Egyptian-style Ismaïl Hellenized by two Doric demi-columns (only one remains). Two rooms lead to the sanctuary where a corridor less than 32 inches wide must have been used to hide the priest who delivered the oracle.

of the entrance) is particularly impressive. The tombs were plundered by the Romans and subsequently reused. The oasis-dwellers were obliged to use them as shelters during the Italian air raids at the beginning of World War Two.

CLEOPATRA'S POOL. The most famous spring at Siwa Oasis is the Aïn el-Hammam, otherwise known as "Cleopatra's Pool". The dark-green waters are collected in a circular pool, carpeted with algae and moss. Other well-known features of the Siwa Oasis include the sand baths where it is believed that rheumatism sufferers can relieve their pain by being buried up to their necks in the sands of JEBEL DAKRUR.

FARAFRA
Farafra, which lies on a plain rather than in a depression, is surrounded by a stone wall (above). About 19 miles to the north is the so-called White Desert where huge, dazzlingly white limestone formations assume weird and wonderful shapes (below).

EL-AREG

A hard track (nearly 190 miles long) linking the Bahariya and Siwa oases was opened in 1991 (military authorization must be obtained before using it). It passes through the uninhabited oases of SITRA (90 miles from Bahariya), NUA MISSA (125 miles) and BAHREIN (nearly 140 miles) before reaching El-Areg. About 160 miles from Bahariya the track joins the foothills of a plateau which it follows northward. After 5 miles leave the track and turn due east (follow the tire marks in the sand). After 4½ miles on a rocky plateau, you reach the top of the depression. Although the descent to the oasis is easy, the ascent is a much more delicate operation because of the soft sand. Unlike the other oases in the desert El-Areg ("the lame man") cannot be seen from a distance. Its green palms are surrounded by high, white cliffs in which the Romans dug out forty or so tombs. The harsh brilliance of the sheer, white rock rises steeply from a mother-of-pearl carpet of fossilized shells covering the bottom of a depression. Purity of color and a sense of vastness and space make this one of the most striking oases in Egypt.

BAHARIYA

Although Bahariya is the nearest oasis (225 miles) to the Egyptian capital, it has been least affected by modern development in spite of its proximity to an important iron mine. Its palm groves cover a 60-mile long, undulating basalt depression which is quite literally overflowing with hot springs. According to the Arab archeologist Ahmed Fakhri, El-Bawiti (which has

16,000 of Bahariya's 26,000 inhabitants) is the site of the most beautiful of these springs, the AÏN EL-BISHMU. Unfortunately many of the lovely freestone basins which contained the soft waters have been replaced by concrete tanks. The few archeological remains in the oasis (which converted to Christianity in the 4th century) are virtually inaccessible.

FARAFRA

Farafra has all the features of a traditional oasis: groups of palm trees emerging from a sea of sand dunes and mysterious, narrow alleyways bordered by blind walls. The inhabitants have a reputation for being skilled hunters and kill jackals, hyenas, gazelles and even fennecs.

DAKHLA

The villages of Dakhla ("inner") Oasis, which lies in a rocky landscape punctuated by sand flows, have preserved their traditional architecture. The oasis extends over a distance of about 40 miles and most of its archeological sites are near the Kharga–Dakhla–Farafra road.

DEIR EL-HAGAR. A winding track leaves the road 4½ miles before El-Qasr and leads to the ruins of Deir el-Hagar ("monastery of the rock"), which lie in a shallow depression. The temple dedicated to the Theban Triad, which was one of the few Roman ruins in the oasis, was damaged by an earthquake.

EL-MUZAWAKA TOMBS. The tombs of Pelusis and Petosiris, hewn out of the Jebel el-Muzawaka, are decorated with scenes of traditionally Egyptian funeral rites. Petosiris, however, is dressed in Greek clothes and the ceiling is decorated with a bull from the Persian Mithras cult.

EL-QASR. This ancient fortified town, about 17 miles from Mut, was established in the Middle Ages on the foundations of a Roman village. It is one of the oldest inhabited sites in the oasis.

BALAT. Balat, with Mut and El-Qasr, is one of the three villages of Dakhla Oasis. Nearby, excavations are presently being carried out by the Institut Français d'Archéologie Orientale (IFAO) on the complex of AÏN ASIL and the necropolis of Qila el-Dabba. A row of five mastabas, which comprised the main elements on the site, were discovered during a *khamsin* (sandstorm) by the archeologist Ahmed Fakhri. The mastaba of the governor Medunefer, who was a contemporary of Pepi II, was still intact and revealed some beautiful funeral paraphernalia, which included gold jewelry.

EL-QASR
The four- and five-story houses which border the narrow, winding village streets have carved doors, locks and lintels. The oldest lintel (1518) decorates the Beit Ibrahim. The mosque has retained its Ayyubid minaret (below) and stands next to a medersa housing several ancient texts. Small, individual mausoleums (above) stand side by side in the Muslim cemetery.

These stones, known as "melons", can be seen between Assiut and the Kharga Oasis.

EL-BAGAWAT
The 120 Nestorian chapels built between the 4th and 10th centuries are scattered across the sandy slopes of Jebel el-Teir, about 1¼ miles northwest of Kharga. Only five of these domed, mudbrick monuments still have their painted decorations.

KHARGA OASIS

The capital of Kharga ("outer") Oasis, which, at 116 miles long, is the largest of the five oases, is also called Kharga. The oasis can be reached from Dakhla or via the new DESERT ROAD (completed in 1991), which follows the right bank of the Nile toward Assiut (244 miles). Make sure you don't miss the badly marked turnoff at Koreimat (56 miles from Cairo) and then continue due south, crossing the Nile at Assiut and then following a resurfaced road for 150 miles until you come to Kharga. The region, known as New Valley, is also serviced by an airline. Most of the archeological remains in the Libyan Desert are to be found in this oasis along the road running north–south between Kharga and Baris.

NEW VALLEY. In 1959 the Egyptian government announced its desert colonization program, which aimed to develop agriculture in the oases and exploit the region's industrial potential as well as its natural resources of ore and water. The "New Valley" project was centered around the town of Kharga and included the oases of Dakhla and Farafra, thus covering an area of roughly 176,800 square miles, with a population of 120,000. In 1967 Hassan Fathi ▲ *442* launched the New Baris project but the expected population movement just did not happen, no doubt because of the *fellaheen*'s age-old mistrust of the desert. Development initiatives have therefore been focused on more reliable ventures, with tourism benefiting from substantial investments and the promotion of such events as the "Pharaoh's Rally". Mining is centered around the phosphates of Abu Tartur, between Dakhla and Kharga. A new museum in the Shari' Gamal-Abd el-Nasser houses Pharaonic objects discovered at Balat by the IFAO.

TEMPLE OF HIBIS. The temple, which stands about 1¼ miles north of the present capital, is the only Persian temple of any size in Egypt. It was built by Darius I, according to Egyptian architectural tradition, with a quay, an avenue of sphinxes, monumental entrances and three hypostyles leading into a naos. The eight-columned pavilion with its extremely beautiful capitals dates from the reign of Nectanebo II (30th

Dynasty), while the main entrance, decorated with Greek legal inscriptions, was built by the Ptolemies. In spite of these additions, the edifice has a fine unity of style.

EL-BAGAWAT. Christianity, the official religion from the reign of Constantine until the Islamic conquest, spread rapidly through the oases and gradually replaced the social structure of the Pharaonic period. Pagan temples were replaced by monasteries, churches, chapels and monastic complexes. However, the worship of the dead continued to be practiced with the same degree of fervor, as evidenced in the 120 Nestorian chapels of El-Bagawat. In ancient times religious and political opponents of established power were banished to the oases. One such opponent was Nestorius, a heretical bishop who was exiled to El-Bagawat for having maintained that of the two natures of Christ (divine and human) only the human was earthly and suffered on the cross. From this it followed that Mary, mother of the "human" Christ, was not the mother of the Son of God. Cyril, Bishop of Alexandria, opposed this doctrine and Nestorius was condemned and removed from office in 431 by the Council of Ephesus. He died twenty years later.

TEMPLE OF NADURA. About 1¼ miles northeast of Kharga is the ruined Temple of Nadura, built by the Romans during the reign of Antoninus Pius or his predecessor Hadrian (117–38). Although it was badly eroded by the wind, a scene representing female musicians playing percussion instruments and sistra can still be made out on the few remaining wall sections. This would seem to suggest that the temple was in fact not dedicated to the Egyptian god Amun but to his divine spouse.

DARB EL-SINDADIYA. To defend themselves against attack from hostile tribes, all too frequent before the reign of Mohammed Ali, the inhabitants of the Western Desert lived in underground fortresses. In the ancient village of Darb el-Sindadiya the mudbrick houses have palm-trunk beams. The dark, narrow streets wind around the spring of Aïn el-Dar, which

AÏN UMM EL-DABADIB
The village of Aïn Umm el-Dabadib is dominated by trapezoid towers. In the distance are the sandy slopes of the north escarpment of the oasis. The village once had a very sophisticated irrigation system, built by the Romans, which consisted of four underground aqueducts each 3 miles long, running from the escarpment to the fort. The aqueducts can be reached via the air shafts, dug every 30 or 40 yards and covered at ground level with huge, flat stones.

FORTRESS OF AÏN UMM LABAKHA
The fortress's round towers make it look more like a castle. The beauty of its proportions is enhanced by the sand-covered cliffs.

Markets in the town of Kharga.

has dried up. This 10th-century site is now used to stable animals and should be visited with a guide.

AÏN UMM EL-DABADIB ★. A rough track runs south from Kharga across the foothills of Jebel el-Sheikh before turning north to Umm el-Dabadib. Another track (17½ miles) skirts westward round JEBEL EL-SHEIKH and JEBEL EL-TARIF to Kharga. This expedition should be undertaken with a guide as the going is often difficult across the sand dunes. Under Diocletian, the temples, surrounded by vast, square mudbrick enclosures, were replaced by fortresses which sometimes had a church outside the walls. Communities grew up around the churches with their attendant houses, necropolis and crops. This was how the Romano-Byzantine village of Aïn Umm el-Dabadib was founded. The site is typical of the caravan oases, which were situated near a spring at the end of the caravan routes and also served as staging posts on the Libyan Desert routes. They had the cisterns and irrigation systems so vital in places where water is scarce. The Ptolemies exploited the agricultural wealth of the oases and were succeeded by the Romans, whose irrigation systems were unsurpassed. At El-Deir water is drawn using a system of hand-operated levers and directed along drainage channels leading from the well in the courtyard of the fort to irrigate the crops.

AÏN UMM LABAKHA ★. The Romans built Aïn Umm Labakha at the other end of the caravan route about 19 miles from Aïn Umm el-Dabadib. Leave the road about 2 miles north of Munira and head westward, skirting south round the village of Aïn Sabba and then leaving the track altogether to head across country toward a cliff about 3 miles to the northwest. The Roman fort can be seen at the foot of the escarpment.

EL-DEIR. The Roman fortress of El-Deir lies about 15 miles north of Kharga. Follow the Assiut road northward to Munira (10 miles). Turn right (eastward) about 200 yards before the road checkpoint and follow the track, which is an old tarmacked road. The last mile or so can only be negotiated in a four-wheel drive. El-Deir ("the monastery"), an impressive rectangular structure supported by twelve towers, stands at the foot of JEBEL UMM EL-GHANAYIN.

QASR EL-GHUEIDA. This is one of the few temples (250–80 BC) in the oasis which was constructed and decorated entirely during the Ptolemaic period, between the reigns of Ptolemy III and Ptolemy X. The outline of its fortifications, built by the Greeks at the intersection of the Sudan and Libyan routes, can be seen to the east of the road. The wooden roof covering the hypostyle has disappeared, exposing the columns with their Composite capitals. The flat roof of the naos and the vaulted roof of the lateral chapels were a characteristic architectural feature of oasis temples. Qasr el-Ghueida was dedicated to the Theban Triad: Amun, Mut and Khonsu.

QASR EL-ZAIYAN. In the village of Qasr el-Zaiyan (15 miles south of Kharga) is a small temple dedicated to Amenebis, god of the town of Tchnonemyris, which was built under the Ptolemies and flourished until the Byzantine period. A Greek inscription commemorates the restoration of the temple during the reign of the emperor Antoninus (138–61). .

DUSH. Beyond the village of Baris a track leads eastward (56 miles) to the temple and excavations of Dush. About 1½ miles to the north is the unfinished and now abandoned "show town" of NEW BARIS designed by the architect Hassan Fathi ▲ 442. The remarkable religious, military and civilian complex of Dush developed, to a large extent, as a result of the slave trade. It is situated at the end of the Darb el-Arbaïn ("the road of forty days", the time it took to travel from Sennar in the Sudan back into Egypt). At Dush the caravans either headed for Kharga and rejoined the Nile Valley at Assiut or turned off toward the Nile at Esna. The IFAO has been excavating the site since 1967. The temple, entirely cleared of sand, is in pure Pharaonic tradition. Built during the reigns of Domitian and Trajan (1st century) it was decorated during the reign of Hadrian (2nd century). The sanctuary, which comprises two interconnecting rooms with a vaulted ceiling, is flanked by two chapels. On the outside of the far wall are images of Osiris-Huy (Serapis) and Isis. The wall, which has a window communicating with the interior, constituted the (gold-plated) back wall of an adjoining chapel. The fortress and its civilian buildings are also Roman, but stratigraphic studies show that the site was occupied from the beginning of the Ptolemaic period.

THE "DUSH TREASURE"
The site of Dush, whose garrison controlled the Sudan route, was abandoned in the 5th century. Its temple was excavated by the archeologists of the IFAO. During the winter excavations of 1988 they discovered the "Dush treasure", which consisted of 2½ pounds of gold hidden in a vase. Among the bracelets, necklaces and gold plate was the high priest's diadem.

MONASTERY OF ST ANTHONY

In spite of successive restorations, the monastery has retained its original appearance, surviving the Arab conquest as a result of its isolated position. The

intellectual life of the monastery flourished between the 12th and 15th centuries until it was plundered in 1454 by Bedouin servants. Today it still has about one hundred icons (the oldest dating from the 9th century) housed in the library and the seven churches whose white domes stand out against the green of the palm groves. In the Church of the Virgin Mary a wooden iconostasis, inlaid with ivory crosses and motifs, separates the nave from the sanctuary.

Map of the deserts of Lower Thebaid, produced in 1717 by an icon artist using information provided by Claude Sicard, who was given the task of locating and drawing the monuments of Ancient Egypt by Philippe d'Orléans. The map includes plans of the monasteries of St Paul (right) and St Anthony (left).

ARABIAN DESERT

The Arabian Desert is an arid, mountainous region which lies between the Nile and the Red Sea. Several thousand nomadic Bedouins (the Ababdeb and the Bichariya) live amidst the austere beauty of its mountains and gorges, a mineral world of metamorphic rocks where a few thorn-bushes and sebaceous plants manage to grow. The fauna is also limited since the hordes of gazelle that once populated the region have been decimated by hunters, while social change has got the better of the herds of dromedaries. However, rodents and foxes can survive in this vast, empty wasteland, which every spring welcomes huge flights of migrating birds, especially storks. All forms of life depend on the winter precipitation (less than 118 inches per year), which often falls within the space of a few hours. The Arabian Desert is also a vast mining region which has been exploited since ancient times, its quarries providing the building materials for many great edifices in Upper Egypt and Rome. Since the advent of Christianity it has also served as a refuge for anchorites seeking communion with God in the solitude of the desert. Two monasteries were built by the disciples of Saint Anthony and Saint Paul on the sites where the saints had chosen to live. Today these fortresses are occupied by Coptic Orthodox monks. Leave Cairo via the Katamia road, which joins the coast road north of Aïn Sukhna. Turn south in the direction of Hurghada. About 20 miles west of Ras Za'farana, on the road between the coast and the Nile Valley, a track forks off to the Monastery of St Anthony. The Monastery of St Paul can be reached by way of the tarmacked road which leaves the main Suez–Hurghada route about 15½ miles south of Ras Za'farana.

From the top of the promontory, the magnificent view of the monastery complex of St Paul compensates for the mass of recent concrete constructions outside the walls.

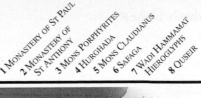

1 MONASTERY OF ST PAUL
2 MONASTERY OF ST ANTHONY
3 MONS PORPHYRITES
4 HURGHADA
5 MONS CLAUDIANUS
6 SAFAGA
7 WADI HAMMAMAT HIEROGLYPHS
8 QUSEIR

MONASTERY OF ST ANTHONY.

Saint Anthony the Great was born in 251 near Beni Suef and orphaned at the age of eighteen. He sold all his worldly possessions and retired into the mountains of the Arabian Desert. The founder the Desert Fathers died at the age of 105 and is buried beneath the ancient church of the monastery. About 300 yards away is the cliff cave in which he lived. The monastery (Deir Mari Antonios), built by his disciples in 361–3, is the oldest monastery in Egypt and has retained its original appearance in spite of successive restorations.

MONASTERY OF ST PAUL.

Saint Paul was born into a wealthy Alexandrian family in 228. In his attempt to find his way in life he sought refuge in the Arabian Desert where he remained alone for eighty years, wearing garments made out of palm fibers and living on the half-loaf of bread brought to him every day by a raven. It was Saint Anthony who revealed his saintliness to him. The 5th-

Five days

265

❝Walked and walked for hour after hour across the plains, in the burning sun and the icy wind, continually crushing the pale, embalmed plants [beneath our feet]. The desert is both as monotonous and as changing as the sea. The day before yesterday it was monumental blocks of granite; yesterday smooth, flat sand, and today we are entering a region of millstones and are surrounded by a new and surprising world of hitherto unseen landscapes. A gloomy maze of valleys, made of these yellowish and white stones, has just opened up before us; the horizontal layers of rock look like regular courses in a wall built by a human hand. You have the impression of walking through a destroyed city, walking along streets, giant streets, between ruined palaces and citadels.❞
Pierre Loti

TEMPLE OF SERAPIS
On the site of Mons Porphyrites a flight of steps leads to the temple whose various elements (pediments, architraves, bases of Ionic columns) lie scattered on the ground.

century Monastery of St Paul has three churches. It was plundered several times during the 15th and 16th centuries and abandoned for a long time before being reinhabited by monks from the Monastery of St Anthony. In St Paul's Church the knightly saints, Saint George, Saint Theodorus and Saint Michael the Archangel, are depicted on horseback fighting devils. The icons include an image of Saint George of Cappadocia, dressed in a purple habit, mounted on a white horse. The monastery also has such ancient, illuminated manuscripts as the Coptic version of the Divine Liturgy and the Commentary on The Epistle of Saint Paul the Apostle to Titus by Saint John Chrysostom. Outside the monastery there can still be seen an ancient grain mill, olive press and the pulley that was used to hoist visitors and provisions over the walls during times of unrest.

IMPERIAL QUARRIES. The Arabian mountains had two Roman penal colonies or "quarry farms", enterprises involved in the extraction from these desert quarries of monoliths weighing several hundred tons used in the construction of temples.

The quarries were exploited by a private entrepreneur, known as the "quarry farmer", but were supervised by an imperial representative and a soldier such as the centurion Avitus, who commanded the first cohort of the Sicilian cavalry. The emperor Claudius is generally considered to have been the first to exploit these mines. The archeological sites of Mons Porphyrites and Mons Claudianus can be reached via the Red Sea coast or the Nile Valley. The first route follows the coast in the direction of Hurghada, a small resort with an underwater diving center. At RAS GHARIB a long mountain ridge known as the JEBEL EL-ZEIT, or Mountain of Oil (petroleum), runs parallel to the shore. In the second millennium BC the Egyptians exploited two mines here to extract galena (natural lead sulphide) or kohl, which was applied around the eyes. Mons Porphyrites is reached by turning off the main coast road just over 11 miles north of Hurghada and following a newly tarmacked road for about half a mile and then a well-marked track to the right. After nearly 18 miles you suddenly leave the track and head northward for about 7 miles. A Roman discharge ramp will become visible at the foot of a fairly steep slope. Head into the mountains along the Wadi Sidri (which runs from east to west) and after 5 rather stony miles you eventually come to an ancient Roman site shaded by four acacia trees. Follow the valley to the left, which runs west and then south for 4½ miles, and you will finally arrive at the Roman camp of Mons Porphyrites.

MONS PORPHYRITES. The stone on this site is a pinkish-purple porphyry which comes from JEBEL ABU DUKHAM ("father of smoke"). In the arid valley of Abu Ma'mmal, between the Nile and the Red Sea, the Romans built a veritable town, with a fort, two temples, stables, cisterns and wells. Five columns arranged in a semi-circle, which form the remains of a cistern with a circular roof and *saqia* (water wheel), stand among the smooth stones of the *wadi*. The castellum (fort) and baths were built against a rock opposite the cistern. A flight of steps leads to the remains of the Temple of Serapis. A stele, discovered in 1823, provides the only surviving evidence of a Christian church, which was commissioned and undoubtedly financed by a high-ranking official by the name of Flavius Julius.

MONS CLAUDIANUS ★. Turn onto the Port Safaga–Qena road and follow it for about 24 miles. A roadside stopping-place with a refreshment stall indicates the direction (due north) of the Mons Claudianus. Follow the badly maintained, tarmacked road for about 14 miles. At the end of the tarmac take the second *wadi* to the right of the track after some trees and small houses. The Roman fort stands to the left of the *wadi*, about 1½ miles from where you turned off. The Roman penal colony of Mons Claudianus, nestling at the foot of JEBEL FATIRA, supplied Rome with black granite columns, some of which still support the Pantheon today, while others can be seen in Trajan's forum. According to certain archeologists the workforce consisted of *damnati in metallum* (men sentenced by common law) and included early Christians. The grandiose ruins of the penal colony are in keeping with the scope of the undertaking. The fort, with its massive walls flanked by beautifully rounded towers, and the outline of the inner buildings which housed the Roman garrison can be seen from a distance, like a mirage in this arid valley. Today hot springs still well up inside the ruins. This was an extremely sophisticated complex for a penal colony in the middle of the desert. A bath is set into the ground and underground heating systems called hypocausts lead to the *sudatoria*

otherwise known as the "sweating baths". Outside the walls stables big enough to house horses and bullocks were covered with a thatched roof supported by thirty or so pillars. A flight of twenty steps leads up to the Temple of Mons Claudianus, which was begun during Hadrian's reign, but never completed.

QUARRIES. The actual quarries are on the opposite slope of the *wadi*. The fragments of granite and geometric designs carved in the rock illustrate the method used to extract the columns. Quarriers dug oblong holes along the line to be cut and drove in wooden wedges which were then soaked with water. As the wood expanded, the granite shattered. A cracked column rests on a thick layer of granite fragments, and makes the quarry look as though it has been only recently abandoned.

Port of the popular resort of Hurghada.

MONS CLAUDIANUS QUARRIES
The perfectly cylindrical shaft of a polished granite column lies between the fort and *wadi*. On the opposite slope of

the mountain an apparently perfect column (200 tons) cracked as it was transported and was abandoned on the spot. The columns were dragged across the desert by draught animals and then transported down the Nile to Rome where they arrived more than a year later.

The Wadi Sakait emerald mines were exploited by the pharaohs and Mameluke sultans.

Detail of the cartouche of Irwywrta (17th Dynasty), one of the rock carvings in the Wadi Hammamat.

WADI HAMMAMAT. In Pharaonic times Wadi Hammamat, at the foot of Jebel Hammamat, was known as the Valley of the Rohamnu. Its quarries, exploited since the time of the Old Kingdom, provided much of the *bekhen* (hard stone) used to build the temples of Thebes and Upper Egypt. The deposits lie in long, narrow layers midway between the Nile and the Red Sea. On the northern bank of the *wadi* is the classic *bekhen*, a sort of sandstone schist with reddish reflections, whereas the stone in the *wadi* bed is of inferior quality. A third type of stone, more finely grained and lighter in color but with a dull finish, was also used. Extracting the stone and transporting it across the desert to build the sacred edifices of the pharaohs was a glorious undertaking which deserved to be recorded for posterity. To this end a number of hieroglyphic tablets were carved along the southern slope of the Wadi Hammamat gorge over a distance of 2½ miles (milestone 96 on the Qift–Quseir road, opposite the wooden hut selling Egyptian antiques). The rock carvings, representing men, hunting scenes and dancing, are next to some truly remarkable inscriptions dating from the Old to the New Kingdom. The thirty-seven Middle Kingdom inscriptions include the stele of Senwosret I, carved during the reign of Senwosret I by Ameni, an inspector of naval recruits and infantry commander. It confirms the vast size of some of the expeditions, which involved over seventeen thousand free men crossing these desert gorges to build monuments to the greater glory of the pharaoh. Among the representations of animals and hieratic inscriptions, an early Aramean alphabet and eight inscriptions illustrating the period of the New Kingdom, there are scenes dedicated to Min-Amun executed in a more classical style.

TRADE ROUTES. Once the ancient trade routes with Punt (southern Arabia and the coast of Somalia), the routes linking the Nile with the Red Sea coast have been much less frequented since the construction of the Suez Canal. Spices and perfumes were brought to the Egyptian ports of Myos Hormos (Abu Shar el-Kibli), Leukos Limen (Quseir) and Berenice.

GOLD MINES. Gold was found in the quartz seams of the mountain ranges of the Arabian Desert, in the region of Qift (otherwise known as Koptos). Iron ore and emeralds were two of the other resources to be found in the Arabian Desert which were mined during ancient times.

❝The sand leads us to Kosseïr [Quseir]. It is as if the sand from the shore has been blown into this broad valley by the wind; it is like the abandoned floor of a gulf. From a distance you can see the foremasts of the ships which are laid up like those on the Nile.❞

Gustave Flaubert

CAIRO

ANTIQUITY

To protect the south side of the city, Salah ad-Din (below) erected

Bounded in the west by Jebel Moqattam and in the east by the River Nile, the site of modern Cairo had not always been the chosen location for the foundation of a capital. There are in fact three major landmarks in the city's evolution: HELIOPOLIS ▲ *285*, the capital (in c. 3100 BC) of the first, short-lived, united kingdom of Upper and Lower Egypt; MEMPHIS ▲ *332*, which as the majestic capital of the Old Kingdom has perhaps the most legitimate claim to the title of the "great ancestor" of modern Cairo; and the Fort of Babylon ▲ *318*, built by Trajan (98–117).

FROM FUSTAT TO EL-QAHIRA

a fortified wall (which was never completed) to enclose El-Qahira and Fustat. He also constructed the dyke at Giza to guard against flooding.

The capture of the Fort of Babylon by the armies of Amr Ibn el-As in 640 marked the beginning of the various stages of the construction of the "Mother of the World" (Umm el-Dunya), as Cairo was called by its chroniclers and inhabitants, as well as the establishment of Islam in Egypt. Amr founded a mosque at the apex of the Nile Delta, where he began to build the first Arab settlement in Egypt. Centered around the mosque, FUSTAT ▲ *324* ("encampment"), as it later became known, had the outward appearance of a military camp, in which the various Arab tribes that made up his army were divided into *khittat* (districts). With the emergence of the Abbasid dynasty a new military and administrative district known as EL-ASKAR ("army") was established to the north of Fustat, now the modern district of Sayyida Zeinab ▲ *314*. The Abbasid governor of El-Askar, Ahmed Ibn Tulun, who was of Turkish origin, sought to free himself from the control of Baghdad. In 868 he founded, around the mosque named after

Two Mameluke horsemen practicing with lances (below).

View of the aqueduct, built by Salah ad-Din, which brought water from the River Nile to the foot of the Citadel.

16TH-CENTURY CAIRO

With the Ottoman conquest Egypt became one of the provinces of a vast empire whose capital was Istanbul. The spice and later coffee trade ensured Cairo's remarkable prosperity throughout the 16th and 17th centuries. A 16th-century French map of Cairo (left).

him, the new district of EL-QATAI' ("the wards", a reference to the districts allocated to the various contingents of his army). El-Qatai' was recaptured and burned by the Abbasids, gradually abandoned and finally used as a "quarry" for the construction of the Fatimid capital of El-Qahira (originally Kahira, "The Triumphant One"), built on the site of the "Islamic City" and, for the first time, fortified.

THE MEDIEVAL CITY

Salah ad-Din (Saladin) commissioned the Citadel. It took 89 years to build (1116–1207) and became the new seat of power, opening up the city of El-Qahira which became (and continues to be) populated by craftsmen, laborers and *harafish* (beggars). In the 16th century the Ottoman governors who occupied the Citadel pursued the construction projects begun by the Mameluke sultans.

THE MODERN CITY

Mohammed Ali ● 68 began the major construction work, which entailed draining the lakes of El-Ezbekiya ▲ 274 and building new roads, and the Cairo of today finally began to take shape. His successors carried out a series of projects to extend the city which involved building new districts such as Heliopolis ▲ 285 in 1905, mostly financed by private foreign interests. Today Cairo has a population of twelve million (one quarter of the entire population of Egypt), with an average density of 130,000 inhabitants per square mile and as many as 250,000 in some districts.

NAPOLEON BONAPARTE IN CAIRO
After defeating the army of Murad Bey at the Battle of the Pyramids (below) in 1798, Bonaparte remained in Egypt until returning to France in November 1799. The most

tangible evidence of the French presence in Cairo was, on Bonaparte's orders, the shutting of the gates which closed each *hara* (district) at night.

The Obelisk of Senwosret I (left) is one of the few remaining monuments of the so-called Thinite ● 39 period of the city of Heliopolis.

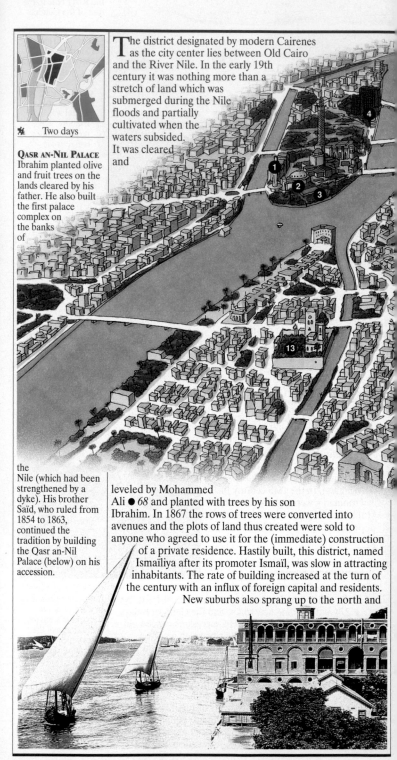

Two days

QASR AN-NIL PALACE
Ibrahim planted olive and fruit trees on the lands cleared by his father. He also built the first palace complex on the banks of

The district designated by modern Cairenes as the city center lies between Old Cairo and the River Nile. In the early 19th century it was nothing more than a stretch of land which was submerged during the Nile floods and partially cultivated when the waters subsided. It was cleared and

the Nile (which had been strengthened by a dyke). His brother Saïd, who ruled from 1854 to 1863, continued the tradition by building the Qasr an-Nil Palace (below) on his accession.

leveled by Mohammed Ali ● 68 and planted with trees by his son Ibrahim. In 1867 the rows of trees were converted into avenues and the plots of land thus created were sold to anyone who agreed to use it for the (immediate) construction of a private residence. Hastily built, this district, named Ismaïliya after its promoter Ismaïl, was slow in attracting inhabitants. The rate of building increased at the turn of the century with an influx of foreign capital and residents. New suburbs also sprang up to the north and

northeast
with the extension
of the tram network,
begun in 1897.

BAB EL-HADID

RAMSES STATION. First built in 1856, the main railway station was reconstructed in traditional Arabic style in 1892. Its façade was refurbished in the same style in 1955 and its esplanade renovated the following year, when a statue of Ramesses II, standing above a fountain, replaced the famous statue depicting the *Awakening of Egypt* by the sculptor Mahmud Mukhtar ▲ *282* erected in 1928.

RAILWAY MUSEUM. The museum, founded in 1933, stands at the far end of the station and houses seven hundred exhibits (scale and life-size models). At the station end of the SHARI' EL-GUMHURRIYA stands Cairo's last *sabil-khuttab* ● *113*, the SABIL EL-WALDA (Fountain of the Queen-Mother), built in 1869 by the Italian architect Ciro Pantanelli (1833–84).

SHARI' IMAD AD-DIN. Cairo's first investment properties were built along the main thoroughfare of the city center, formerly the theater and nightclub district. The oldest are the KHEDIVIAL BUILDINGS (1910) inspired by Haussmann. Several of Cairo's largest clubs were situated in the Shari' Imad ad-Din, including the CLUB DES PRINCES built in 1897 by Lasciac ▲ *281*. All that remains of the original décor with its distinctive masonic symbolism are heads crowned with a diadem, reminiscent of the Statue of Liberty.

BAB EL-HADID
The Bab el-Hadid (Railway Gate) once gave its name to the square in front of the station (now Ramses Square) and to one of Cairo's old districts. It also inspired the title of a film by Yussef Shahin. Shahin (above) with actress Hind Roustom during shooting.

THE "DIANA" CINEMA
Of the several cinemas in the Shari' Imad ad-Din, the *Diana* (1933), a fine example of pure Art Deco, is undoubtedly the best preserved.

CAIRO OPERA HOUSE
The Cairo Opera House, which opened in 1871 with a performance of Verdi's *Aïda*, was destroyed by fire in 1971 and replaced by a car park.

EL-EZBEKIYA

Equestrian statue of Ibrahim Pasha in the Midan el-Opera.

Some of the arcaded buildings in north El-Ezbekiya still remain in the Shari' Wagh el-Birka and the Shari' Mohammed Ali.

A VAST LAKE
Following the Egypt Expedition, most of Cairo's European residences and several royal palaces, including one belonging to Mohammed Ali, were built on the shores of what was once the lake of El-Ezbekiya (below).

Once a vast lake, El-Ezbekiya is today one of the most important communications centers in Cairo. The area was drained in 1837, and took shape from 1868 onward. The northern section was sold by lots and arcaded buildings constructed in accordance with a rigidly enforced plan. In the center the khedive Ismaïl had the El-Ezbekiya Gardens designed along the lines of Parisian parks by Delchevalerie, a horticulturalist from Paris. They had many attractions, including a waterfall, bandstands, cafés-concerts and carousels. The khedive, who was particularly fond of entertainment, also had a circus, theater and opera house built in the southern part of the gardens, all within a few months. Finally, he ordered several new streets to be built through the old districts, including the Shari' Clot-Bey, which was intended to give easy access to the station, the Shari' Abd el-Aziz, which led to the Abdin Palace ▲ *281,* and the Shari' Mohammed Ali, the road to the Citadel ▲ *304.* Almost fifty

years later the Shari' el-Azhar and Shari' el-Geish were built to open up the old center of Cairo.

HOTELS AND DEPARTMENT STORES. These elaborate projects made El-Ezbekiya the favorite haunt of European visitors and residents for many years afterward. A number of countries initially had their consulates here and it was also Cairo's leading café, brasserie and hotel district, with such establishments as the NEW

HOTEL (now the *Hotel Continental*) and the famous SHEPHEARD'S. Tourists who were not so wealthy stayed in the many boarding houses in the SHARI' CLOT-BEY where the nights were reputedly extremely "hot". Several department stores, SEDNAWI (1913), TIRING & STEIN (1908), OMAR EFFENDI (1911) and the CICUREL chain, were opened on the edge and in the neighborhood of El-Ezbekiya.

MODERN EL-EZBEKIYA. Since the 1960's the El-Ezbekiya Gardens have become neglected and dusty. They were dissected by the extension of the Shari' 26 Yulyo, and were gradually encroached upon by a number of different buildings.

MIDAN EL-ATABA EL-KHADRA

Cairo's largest fresh food market is held in the Midan el-Ataba el-Khadra or Ataba ("threshold") Square, situated (as its name suggests) between the old and modern cities. Beneath the arcades of the adjacent buildings, traders sell all kinds of bric-a-brac. Since the 1930's the northern side of the square has traditionally been the preserve of the booksellers.

POSTAL MUSEUM. Situated on the second floor of the Central Post Office, the museum is a hotch-potch of artefacts, pictures and documents illustrating the ways in which messages have been sent in Egypt over the centuries.

THE "GROPPI" CAFÉ. The SHARI' ADLI is worth a visit; if only to stop off at one of Cairo's three *Groppi* cafés (the second is in the Midan Suleyman-Pasha and the third in Heliopolis), founded by a Swiss caterer who settled in Cairo in the 1920's.

TURN-OF-THE-CENTURY ARCHITECTURE. In the same street, the widely diverse styles of a group of more or less contemporary buildings reflect the heterogeneity of turn-of-the-century Cairene architecture: a SYNAGOGUE (1907) of Secessionist inspiration standing next to a block of rented apartments of Italianate design (GATTEGNO), and the ST DAVID'S BUILDING, a neo-Gothic, brick apartment block. Next to these are the head office of the government-controlled building society (1905) and the neoclassical CLUB RISOTTO (1899).

SHARI' QASR AN-NIL. The buildings in the Shari' Qasr an-Nil are more recent (1930–50) and therefore taller. The IMMOBILIA (1937) was, for over a decade, the tallest building in Cairo. Two impressive 1930's apartment blocks, the BAEHLER and the SEDNAWI, stand either side of the far end of the Shari' Qasr an-Nil where it leads into the MIDAN TAL'AT HARB, officially renamed in 1952 but still generally known as the MIDAN SULEYMAN-PASHA.

"SHEPHEARD'S" This famous hotel, the epitome of European colonialism, was destroyed by fire during the riots of January 26, 1952.

The Egyptologist Auguste Mariette (1821–81) was instrumental in the foundation of Cairo's Museum dedicated to Pharaonic antiquities, which provided an indispensable complement to the Egyptian Department of Antiquities established by the viceroy of Egypt, Saïd Pasha, in 1859. The original collection was housed in the suburb of Bulaq and then transferred to Giza in 1891 before re-crossing the Nile in 1902 to its present building in the Midan at-Tahrir (Liberation Square). This tailor-made museum encompasses every aspect of Ancient Egyptian civilization. The concealed basement area is as large as the section open to the public and houses an equally large collection of treasures.

On the west wall of the so-called treasure-chamber of the Tomb of Tutankhamun are twelve turquoise monkeys, the benevolent spirits of the First Hour of the sun's nocturnal voyage.

Chair belonging to the royal princess and queen, Sitamun, Daughter of Amenhotep III. It is decorated with five plaster and gilt scenes in relief and two sculpted heads in front of the arm rests.

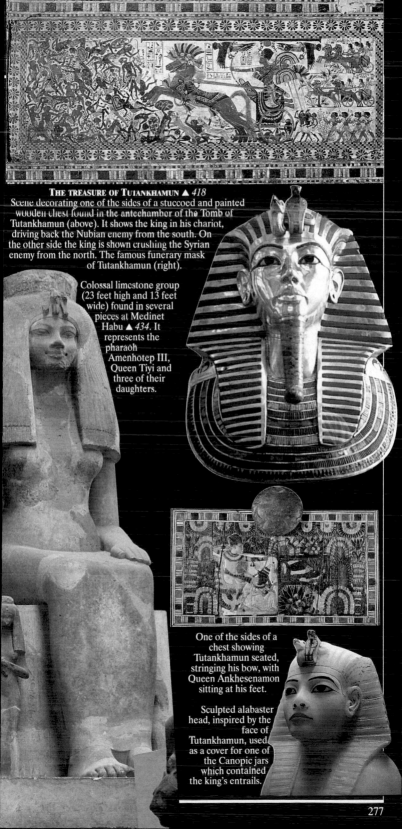

THE TREASURE OF TUTANKHAMUN ▲ 418
Scene decorating one of the sides of a stuccoed and painted wooden chest found in the antechamber of the Tomb of Tutankhamun (above). It shows the king in his chariot, driving back the Nubian enemy from the south. On the other side the king is shown crushing the Syrian enemy from the north. The famous funerary mask of Tutankhamun (right).

Colossal limestone group (23 feet high and 13 feet wide) found in several pieces at Medinet Habu ▲ 434. It represents the pharaoh Amenhotep III, Queen Tiyi and three of their daughters.

One of the sides of a chest showing Tutankhamun seated, stringing his bow, with Queen Ankhesenamon sitting at his feet.

Sculpted alabaster head, inspired by the face of Tutankhamun, used as a cover for one of the Canopic jars which contained the king's entrails.

HEAD OF NEFERTITI
Quartzite head thought to be of Nefertiti found near the Palace of Merneptah in Memphis. It was part of a group of several sculpted elements ultimately intended to form a statue.

RAHOTEP AND NOFRET
Painted limestone statues of the high priest Rahotep, one of the sons of Snefru, and his wife Nofret, from the mastaba of Rahotep at Meidûm ▲ 357.

Akhnaton, l'hérétique...

Etrange personnage!

BLAKE AND MORTIMER
In the Amarnian room, Mortimer and Professor Ahmed admire a statue of Akhenaten from Karnak.

HEAD OF NEFERTITI
Unfinished head in brown quartzite, from a sculptor's workshop at Tell el-Amarna ▲ 378.

INSPECTION OF CATTLE
A model (representing cattle inspection by the owner and his scribes) from the tomb of the chancellor Meketre to the south of the Temple of Deir el-Bahri ▲ 426.

Rebuilt after 1952, the Midan at-Tahrir is an important communications center. The freeways of the 6 October Bridge, a major overpass, end at the square, which is also the terminus for a number of bus routes.

MIDAN AT-TAHRIR

Over the years the Midan at-Tahrir (Liberation Square), which was for a long time peripheral to the city center, has become a major communications nucleus. Several important public buildings stand on the approaches to the square. The MUGAMAA ("conglomerate") or Central Government Building (1950) is the nerve center of Cairene bureaucracy. All government ministries and departments have offices and representatives there. In 1960 the LEAGUE OF ARAB STATES moved into premises designed by Mahmud Riad (1905–86), who also designed the offices of the ARAB SOCIALIST UNION which, after its dissolution in 1977, became the headquarters of the National Democratic Party.

THE AMERICAN UNIVERSITY. This private establishment, founded in 1920, occupies the Khayri Palace, which formerly housed the Gianaclis cigarette factory and then the first Egyptian University.

THE GEOGRAPHICAL SOCIETY. Founded by Ismaïl, the society has a library, a cartographic collection and a series of relief maps of Egypt. It also houses an ethnographical museum with a collection of objects depicting everyday life in 19th-century Egypt. Situated in the same complex, the PARLIAMENT building was built in only a few months after the unilateral Declaration of Independence on February 28, 1922, by the British government.

THE GEOGRAPHICAL SOCIETY
The Geographical Society was founded by the khedive Ismaïl as the scientific

instrument of his imperial aspirations in East Africa. In reality it was used as a staging post by the European explorers who came in search of the sources of the Nile, and later by the many geographers whose research it financed during the interwar years (as illustrated by its well-stocked library, consisting mainly of works in French). The main hall (above).

Boats on the Nile: detail of an engraving in the Geographical Society collection.

ABDIN

ABDIN PALACE. The construction of this vast palace, on the outskirts of the old city, was begun by Ismaïl on his accession in 1863. The khedive wanted to transfer the seat of government from the Citadel to a more open site. The work was supervised by two French engineers, De Curel and Rousseau, and lasted for ten years. Initially constructed with a traditional wooden framework, the palace was destroyed by fire on several occasions. Between 1909 and 1911 it was entirely rebuilt in stone by Antoine Lasciac (1856–1946), who, for more than fifty years, was one of the key figures in Egypt's architectural circles. Various alterations made during the 1930's by Verrucci included a luxurious Byzantine throne room.

BEIT EL-UMMA. Built at the turn of the century, this eclectic residence was the home of the nationalist leader of modern Egypt and founder of the Wafd party, Saad Zaghlul (1857–1927). When it became a museum, the so-called Beit el-Umma (House of the People) was carefully preserved in its original state. With its Art Nouveau dining room, Louis XV reception rooms, "Arab" living room, Turkish baths and magnificent library, the villa is a rare example of the tastes and lifestyle of the early 20th-century Egyptian political elite. The nearby SAAD ZAGHLUL MAUSOLEUM, built in neo-Pharaonic style between 1928 and 1931, was based on plans by the Egyptian architect Mustafa Fahmi.

GARDEN CITY

In spite of the sweeping curves of its boulevards, this residential district, designed in 1906, does not really resemble a "garden city". Its promoters, the Bacos, who were property developers of Syro-Lebanese origin, acquired what was left of Ibrahim Pasha's estate on the banks of the Nile at a very reasonable price. Apart from a few villas constructed in 1910 most of the buildings date from between 1925 and 1935, a period which saw the spectacular development of the Art Deco style in Egypt. Among the most remarkable are the VILLA WAHBA, designed in 1925 by the French architect Edrei, and three large apartment blocks by the Italian architect Mazza.

After 1952, the Abdin Palace (above) was opened to the public. The curious collection of clocks and watches put together by Farouk I was of particular interest. Today the palace houses various government departments and can no longer be visited.

THE "WAFD"
In 1919 a *wafd* (delegation) headed by Saad Zaghlul (left) declared its intention of visiting London to try to secure Egyptian independence. The delegation was not received by the English, but it gave its name to the Wafd nationalist party led by Zaghlul. Certificate of subscription (above) for the construction of the Saad Zaghlul Mausoleum.

When the Abdin Palace was built, a broad esplanade was created in front of the main façade.

281

Abu el-Ela Bridge,
Gezira.

GEZIRA

This 14th-century island with its changing shoreline
remained uninhabited until 1830 when Mohammed Ali
built a palace and quarters for the royal guard at its
northern tip. Because of the precariousness of its
construction the complex soon became known as As-
Zamalik, which in Turkish means "makeshift dwelling".
Since it could only be reached by boat it was
intermittently occupied and it was not until the
accession of Ismaïl that it was extensively refurbished.
The shores of the island were raised to prevent
flooding, a jetty was constructed to facilitate access and
most of the land was cultivated. In the center of the
island the khedive built a palace surrounded by
botanical and zoological gardens with exotic plants, a fine
menagerie of African wildlife, fountains and various
pavilions, including the monumental GEZIRA
SALAMLIK. The island became the
favorite residence of the khedive and in
1872 was linked to Cairo by the Qasr an-
Nil Bridge, which was guarded at either
end by lions sculpted by André
Jacquemart (1824–96). Although Gezira
has lost the elegance it had during the interwar years, it still
has some very fine buildings, including some impressive villas
in a wide variety of architectural styles.

MUKHTAR MUSEUM. The Mukhtar Museum, designed by
Ramesses Wissa Wassef for the sculptures of Mahmud
Mukhtar (1891–1934), one of the greatest Egyptian sculptors,
houses eighty-five works in bronze, stone, marble, basalt,
granite and plaster. In the Shari' at-Tahrir renovation work is
currently being carried out on the building (designed in 1936
by Mustafa Fahmi ▲ *281*) which houses the PLANETARIUM, the
MUSEUM OF EGYPTIAN CIVILIZATION and the GEZIRA
MUSEUM, whose collection includes thousands of objets d'art
collected by the royal family, housed in the Agricultural
Pavilion of the Gezira Exhibition Grounds.

OPERA COMPLEX. This cultural complex (left), a gift to Egypt
from Japan in 1988, was inaugurated in 1993. It comprises two
concert halls, the *hanager* (multi-purpose exhibition and
theater areas) and the Museum of Modern Art which, when it
opened in 1991, housed thirteen thousand works by Egyptian
artists. In the ANDALUSIAN GARDENS, or MASPERO GARDENS,
near the Ramesses Bridge, is an obelisk discovered at Tanis
▲ *226*.

GEZIRA SPORTING CLUB. In 1882 the British established their
first institution in Egypt on a piece of land given to them by
the khedive Tawfiq. The Gezira Sporting Club, which was
based on London's Hurlingham Club, was reserved for British
officers. Although now half its original size, it is still very
exclusive.

THE GEZIRA CENTER FOR MODERN ART. The museum is
housed in a *salamlik* ● *116* that was once owned by Ibrahim
Pasha, and contains a modern art gallery as well as the
Mohammed-Khalil collection. The collection includes works
by major Impressionist painters such as Monet, Van Gogh
and Gauguin, which were acquired in Paris from 1919
onward.

The Gezira *salamlik*
(above) where the
Empress Eugenie
stayed during her visit
to Cairo, now the
Marriott Hotel.

CAIRO TOWER
The 614-foot tower
was built in 1961
with the three
million dollars paid
by the Americans to
President Nasser as
compensation for
their refusal to
participate in the
construction of the
Aswan Dam.

LE NIL

PARTIE du GRAND CAIRE

RODA

Roda Island was formed earlier than Gezira. It has not changed significantly since the time of the Arab conquest (7th century) when some impressive buildings were constructed: an arsenal, a Nilometer and a fortress. The last Ayyubid sultan even decided to transfer the seat of his government to the island and, to this end, had a new fortress, palaces and barracks built in 1240. Under the Mamelukes the seat of government returned to the Citadel and Roda became a district of beautiful waterside residences built in garden settings by the ruling classes. The few remaining examples of this trend, which continued into the 20th century, include the MANISTERLI SALAMLIK, built in the middle of the 19th century and originally part of the home of a Turkish official, and the MANYAL PALACE. Built between 1901 and 1933 by Mohammed Ali Tawfiq in the "neo-Islamic" style, it comprised five different buildings, one of which was a mosque. The present Manyal Gardens represent a tiny part of the gardens created, at enormous expense, by Ibrahim and which originally covered most of the island. They disappeared as a result of the post-Zamalik urbanization during the 1930's.

Map of Roda Island made by members of the Egypt Expedition.

The Manyal Palace was converted into a museum in 1955. Since 1964 part of the grounds has been occupied by Club Méditerranée chalets and a swimming pool.

NILOMETER

The Nilometer or *miqyas* was first constructed in 715 and completely rebuilt in 861. It consisted of a stone-lined well connected to the river bed which was used to measure the rise in the water level that occurred during August and September, as well as to regulate the distribution of water and determine the tribute to be paid by Egypt to the caliph. The central, calibrated column acted as a graduated scale, with its nineteen divisions corresponding to so many cubits.

"AL-AHRAM"
Since 1968 the
newspaper has had its
offices in a twelve-
story, luxury
apartment building
(above). In addition
to its daily paper the
Al-Ahram group
prints and distributes
around ten different
editions, including an
international edition
printed in London
and New York. It also
owns a publishing
house which
specializes in
translation and
scientific
encyclopedic
publications.

Detail of the
fountain of the
Shubra Palace
(below).

THE INNER SUBURBS

BULAQ. During the Ottoman period Bulaq was an extremely
busy port with many warehouses. Today the ruined
caravanserais and the SINAN PASHA MOSQUE (1571) are
surrounded by slums. The EL-BALAH WAKALA (date
caravanserai), now a combined cloth, military surplus and
scrap-iron market, is a dealers' paradise.

THE PRESS DISTRICT. On the outskirts of
Bulaq, halfway between Ramses Station
and the Egyptian Museum, is the "press
district" where several leading Egyptian
dailies have their offices. The most
famous of these, *Al-Ahram* (*The
Pyramids*), was founded in 1876 by the
Takla brothers, Lebanese refugees who
fled to Cairo to escape the Ottoman
repression of the first "Arab nationalists". With a daily
circulation of almost one million copies and over six thousand
employees, including one thousand journalists, the unofficial
Al-Ahram has become the jewel in the crown of the largest
newspaper group in the Arab world as well as one of the
leading international newspapers.

SHUBRA. This densely populated suburb, linked by a tram
service to the city center since 1903, has developed along the
Shari' Shubra which, in the early 19th century, was one of the
few roads in Cairo suitable for motor vehicles. It was built by
Mohammed Ali to facilitate access to his favorite residence
where pavilions were scattered in a garden setting. The most
extravagant of these pavilions was a NYMPHAEUM, a large
ornamental lake fed by a central fountain and surrounded by
a colonnade (1826).

AS-SAKAKINI. Sold by lots in the 1880's, the As-Sakakini
district, named after the Syrian family who owned the land,
also owes its development to the tram service. At the center
of this radially designed district is the palace built by Habib
Sakakini in 1897. It is characterized by its overornate exterior
and, among other curiosities, one of Cairo's first ever lifts.
Temporarily closed for restoration, it houses the collection of
the Hygiene Museum.

THE OUTER SUBURBS

The spa town of Helwan was the first realized example
of the 19th-century idea of building cities in the
desert. Today it is an important industrial
center. At the turn of the century a Belgian
finance group founded the city of Heliopolis to the
north of Cairo while the garden city of Maadi was
established to the south at about the same time. Such
initiatives had previously been the prerogative of private

developers. Since the first plan for the development of Cairo in 1958, the authorities have focused on the urbanization of the eastern desert plateau as the best way to prevent the progressive loss, through building, of the agricultural land surrounding the capital to the north and west. This has resulted in the creation of the suburbs of Medina Nasr and Medina el-Moqattam. The eastward extension of the city was again incorporated into the 1970 and 1981 urban planning programs and gave rise to the construction of such new towns as 10 Ramadan, 6 October, 15 May (named after victories against Israel) and Medina el-Sadat.

HELIOPOLIS

Heliopolis, or Misr el-Gadida (New Cairo) as it is known by the Cairenes, is a unique example of urban development which owes a great deal to the personality of its promoter, Baron Empain. After successfully developing Cairo's first tram network, for which he obtained the concession in 1894, the baron had the idea of building a new town in the desert on land bought cheaply from the Egyptian government in 1905. It was several decades before the project, which was for prestige rather than profit, became viable. Heliopolis is different from other contemporary developments in every aspect: within an area of 6,250 acres, it is a composite urban development based on a garden-city layout with buildings which combined the French architectural tradition (apartment blocks above arcades built flush with the façade) with the neo-Arabic style used by the development company. A hierarchy of districts and types of housing to suit the future population (manual workers, office workers, and the wealthy middle class) was established, and strict building regulations were imposed on potential buyers. Palm groves, advanced infrastructures for the time such as a sewer system which Cairo did not have, sports facilities, schools and hotels helped to make Heliopolis a cohesive urban development which has retained most of its original characteristics.

"EXOTIC" ARCHITECTURE
As well as the villas and arcaded apartment blocks which line the main streets (above), other monumental constructions include the *Heliopolis Palace Hotel* (detail below). With its eight hundred bedrooms, it was once the largest hotel in the Middle East; today, however, it houses the central offices of the Egyptian Presidency and is not open to the public. In the city center the neo-Byzantine basilica containing the tomb of Baron Empain was designed by Marcel (1860–1928), who also designed a series of villas in different architectural styles.

THE "HINDU VILLA"
Baron Empain stayed in this extravagant building, inspired by the temples of India, during his visits to Heliopolis.

285

🕐 One day

Cover of *El-Suqariya*, a novel by Naguib Mahfouz.

EL-HUSSEIN MOSQUE
In principle the mosque is out-of-bounds to non-Muslims. It is the

main focal point for religious gatherings, especially Friday prayer meetings and the major Islamic festivals.

EL-HUSSEIN AND KHAN EL-KHALILI

The El-Hussein and Khan el-Khalili districts are as popular with tourists as they are with the Egyptians, particularly during Ramadan and the *muled* ● *126* of El-Hussein (629–80), the grandson of the Prophet and holy martyr of the Shi'ites who was killed by the Ommiads at the Battle of Karbala.

THE EL-HUSSEIN MOSQUE. The mosque, entirely rebuilt under the khedive Ismaïl, was erected on the site of the cemetery of the Fatimid caliphs. Remains of the cemetery were discovered during work carried out on the mosque's foundations earlier this century. Inside are forty-four white marble columns, the wood ceiling is supported by arches and pierced by three lanterns. To one side of the mosque is the MAUSOLEUM, the oldest part of the complex (built in 1154 and modified in 1236), containing the remains of El-Hussein. It is surmounted by a cupola whose ceiling is decorated and inlaid with gold. The complex has two minarets, one to the southwest dating from the same period as the mosque, and the other built in a different style which is contemporary with the mausoleum.

AHMED PASHA "SABIL-KUTTAB". Built in 1864, the *sabil* ● *113* has a rounded façade surmounted by a wooden canopy.

KHAN EL-KHALILI. The Khan el-Khalili was named after the great *khan* (caravanserai) ● *118* built in 1380 by the Emir Djaharks el-Khalili. It can be reached via the Shari' Sikka el-Badistan opposite the minaret of the El-Hussein Mosque. A series of early 20th-century housing blocks have replaced two great *wakala* ● *118,* one of which was the famous carpet *wakala.* The first narrow street on the left leads to the *El-Fishawi Café,* or *Café of Mirrors,* which, at the turn of the century, was the meeting place for Cairene artists, writers and intellectuals, and is the favorite haunt of the writer Naguib Mahfouz (pictured opposite). Half the café was demolished in 1968 when the Midan El-Hussein was extended.

SHARI' EL-BADISTAN. The long, narrow Shari' el-Badistan and the Shari' Khan el-Khalili are the district's two main thoroughfares. Once two gates controlled access to the streets, but now only the west gate remains.

EL-GHURI GATE. In 1511 the sultan El-Ghuri replaced the Khan el-Khalili with a larger *khan* whose gate and wide,

2 SUHAYMI MOSQUE
22 SAÏD EL-SAADA MOSQUE
23 EL-USTADAR MOSQUE
24 BAB EL-FUTUH
25 QITASBAY SABIL-KUTTAB
26 ODA BASHI SABIL-KUTTAB
27 QARA SUNQUR MEDERSA
28 SULEYMAN AGA SABIL
29 EL-JASHANKIR MOSQUE
30 EL-HAKIM MOSQUE
31 BAB AN-NASR
32 MUSAFIRKHANA MOSQUE
33 ODA BASHI WAKALA
34 MUHARRAM MOSQUE
35 EL-AHMEDI MOSQUE
36 EL-HUSSEIN MOSQUE
37 AHMED PASHA SABIL
38 BAB EL-BADISTAN
39 EL-SILAHDAR WAKALA
40 AYYUB MEDERSA

"EL-FISHAWI" CAFÉ
Naguib Mahfouz, winner of the Nobel Prize

EL-SILAHDAR "WAKALA". El-Silahdar *wakala* was constructed in 1837 on the site of an older *wakala* and restored in 1985. The second floor of the *wakala* houses numerous workshops reached along an external gallery. Most of the items sold in the streets below are made on the upper floors of the district's *wakala*. The Shari' el-Badistan becomes the SHARI' EL-MUIZZ, which is bordered from end to end by *wakala,* including the former slave market, the EL-GALLABA WAKALA. The Shari' el-Muiz crosses the SHARI' EL-MUSKI, built in 1845 to link El-Ezbekiya ▲ 274 with the El-Hussein district. On the corner of the two streets stands the SHEIKH MUTAHAR MOSQUE, built by Abd el-Rahman Katkhuda in 1744. It still has its original entrance, minaret and *sabil-kuttab*.

vaulted entrance can still be seen today.

for Literature, is one of the "regulars" at the *El-Fishawi Café.*

ASHRAFIYA MEDERSA. The complex was constructed in 1425 by the sultan El-Ashraf Barsbey, and comprises a mosque-medersa, a mausoleum and *sabil-kuttab*. Inside the complex, the *iwan* of the *qibla* has a remarkable marble-covered floor, while the west *iwan* has a wood ceiling inset with ivory and an inlaid *minbar*.

SHARI' EL-MUIZZ

Detail (above) of the minaret of the An-Nasir Mohammed Medersa.

This three-mile-long street forms the kasbah, the backbone of the city. During the time of the pharaohs it linked Heliopolis ▲ 285 and Memphis ▲ 332. In the 10th century it was incorporated into the city founded by the Caliph el-Muizz (931–75) after whom it was named.

AS-SALIH NAGM AD-DIN AYYUB MEDERSA. Built between 1242 and 1250 this is one of the first Ayyubid medersat and one of the few to have survived from this period. All that remains is a wall surmounted by a minaret. To the north of the medersa is the nearby KHUSRU PASHA SABIL-KUTTAB (1535).

SHARI' BEIT EL-QADI. This 19th-century street was built on the site of the Zahiriya Medersa (1263). On the left as you leave the Shari' el-Muizz is the QAA MUHIB AD-DIN or UTHMAN KATKHUDA PALACE ● 116, once a Mameluke residence (1350). The street leads into the MIDAN BEIT EL-QADI (the Judge's House, which stands on the site of the former courthouse). To the south the so-called MAMAY MAQAAD is the only surviving element of a house built in 1496. Today it stands in isolation and consists of a five-arched colonnade and a doorway. The great porch on the eastern side of the square was one of the entrances to the house.

THE COMPLEX OF SULTAN QALA'UN. The complex, built along the Shari' el-Muizz in 1284 by Sultan el-Mansur Qala'un comprises a mosque-medersa, a mausoleum and a *mauristan* (hospital), which was replaced by a modern hospital in the 1920's. The main entrance, surrounded by Gothic columns and surmounted by an inscribed lintel, opens onto a long corridor. To the left the mosque-medersa comprises a rectangular courtyard with four *iwan*. The mausoleum stands opposite the medersa and consists of a partially covered entrance hall and a funeral chamber. The entrance to the *mauristan* was at the end of the corridor.

THE COMPLEX OF SULTAN AN-NASIR MOHAMMED. To the right of the Qala'un minaret are the medersa and tomb of An-Nasir Mohammed, the son of Qala'un, who died in 1340. The Gothic-style entrance came from the 13th-century Christian Church of St John of Acre, destroyed by Sultan El-Ashraf Khalil, brother of An-Nasir. Built in 1295, it was the first cruciform medersa in Cairo.

THE COMPLEX OF SULTAN BARQUQ. Built in 1384 by Sultan Barquq, who ruled from 1382 to 1399, the complex comprises a medersa, a *khanqa* ● *112* and a tomb. The façade has a distinctive stone entrance, a plain cupola and a minaret with three balconies. The bronze-plated entrance door with its polygonal decorations opens onto a square chamber. A corridor links the chamber with an extremely regularly designed courtyard where a central fountain is surrounded by four *iwan* with almost symmetrical façades. A door next to the north *iwan* leads to the tomb of the sultan's daughter. The sultan is buried in the Eastern Cemetery ▲ *327*.

KAMILIYA MEDERSA. The medersa of Sultan el-Kamil (1180–1238), built in 1225, is the second largest medersa in the world after that of Zinki in Damascus. During the Mameluke period, it became the prototype for the development of some of the most beautiful examples of Cairene urban architecture. All that remains of the original edifice is the monumental entrance and the west *iwan*, the rest having been replaced by more modern buildings.

ABD EL-RAHMAN KATKHUDA "SABIL-KUTTAB". The street forks just beyond this series of monuments. The Shari' an-Nahassin, on the left, leads to the Bab el-Futuh ▲ *291* and the Shari' Tombukshiya to the Bab an-Nasr ▲ *292*. In the angle of the fork the Katkhuda *Sabil-kuttab* (1744) can be found, a blend of Mameluke and Ottoman architecture and one of the most spectacular *sabil-kuttab* ● *113* in Cairo. One of the square, faïence plaques decorating the first-floor chamber represents a view of Mecca (right), while the second-floor chamber has a carved wood loggia overlooking the street, whose decorated wood roof is supported by fine wooden pillars.

QALA'UN MAUSOLEUM
The funeral chamber is in the shape of a square enclosing an octagon described by eight monolithic granite pillars and columns (four of each), all richly decorated (left). The mihrab is surrounded by columns and has a revetment of marble and mother-of-pearl mosaic panels (above).

The fountain of the Barquq Medersa is virtually identical to that of the Sultan Hassan Medersa ▲ *309*.

Bab el-Futuh (right), the
Gate of Conquest.

BEIT AS-SUHAYMI
The *qaa* (chambers)
of this 17th-century
house ● *116* are in
two different styles:
the more or less
enclosed, classic style
of the great *mandara*

in the east wing to the
right of the entrance,
where the lantern is
the only source of
light, and the more
open style of the
salamlik (reception
suite) ● *116* in the
west wing, whose
wide, turned-wood
bays overlook the
courtyard. The
tahtabuch on the first
floor and the *maqaad*
on the second floor
(rooms reserved for
the menfolk and their
guests) both look
onto the courtyard.
The *maqaad* faces
north to take
advantage of the
cooler air, while the
south-facing
tahtabuch is ideal for
receiving guests or
relaxing in winter.
Opposite the *maqaad*
the harem chamber,
with its Turkish
faïence, *mashrabiya*
and wood paneling, is
a true museum piece.

SHARI' DARB EL-QIRMIZ. In 1973 the German Archeological
Institute in Cairo undertook the restoration of the Islamic
monuments in the Shari' Darb el-Qirmiz. In the space of 165
yards, there are five buildings dating from the 14th and 18th
centuries: the Katkhuda *Sabil-kuttab*, the Beshtak Palace, the
SHEIKH SINAN MAUSOLEUM (1585–6) and the Sabiqiya
Medersa. The restoration of the street won the 1983 Aga
Khan Award for Architecture.

BESHTAK PALACE. Built by Emir Beshtak
in 1334, the palace has distinctive
projecting windows covered with
mashrabiya. The proportions of the main
qaa (chamber) on the second floor, its
pointed arches, stained-glass windows
and gilt and painted wood paneling make
it one of the most beautiful chambers of
its period. The palace houses a museum
which traces the history of the city of
Cairo. A small, outer door leads to the
13th-century BESHTAK or EL-FIJL
MOSQUE on the first floor of the palace.
SABIQIYA MEDERSA. The Sabiqiya
Medersa, otherwise known as the
Mithqal Medersa, was built in 1368. A
vaulted passage runs beneath the
medersa and into a narrow street leading
to the Midan Beit el-Qadi.
EL-AQMAR OR GRAY MOSQUE. The
mosque, built in 1125 on the site of a Coptic monastery, is one
of the few surviving examples of Fatimid architecture. Its
design is extremely interesting, with the thickness of the
outer wall compensating for the constraints imposed by
the direction of *qibla*, the geometry of the layout and the
direction of the street. The residual space was occupied by the
entrance hall, the staircase to the minaret and
two rooms opening onto the courtyard. On the
corner of the Shari' el-Muizz and DARB EL-
ASFAR is the BEIT MUSTAFA
GAAFAR (1713), which today
houses the Egyptian
Antiquities
Organization.

BEIT AS-SUHAYMI. Beit as-Suhaymi, the most impressive of what was once a large group of houses reached via a network of narrow streets and culs-de-sac, was built in 1648. It was bought in 1796 by Sheikh Ahmed as-Suhaymi who extended it by converting several of the adjacent houses. The various parts of the building have separate staircases and in the region of thirty *qaa*.

SULEYMAN AGA EL-SILAHDAR MOSQUE AND "SABIL". The complex (1839), which comprises a *sabil*, medersa and mosque, has a single façade overlooking the street. The distinctive, rounded façade of the *sabil*, which conforms to no particular school, is in inscribed marble. The complex is surmounted by a Turkish-style canopy decorated in relief.

EL-HAKIM MOSQUE. The second largest Fatimid mosque after El-Azhar ▲ *294* was begun in 990 by the Caliph El-Aziz and completed in 1013 by his son El-Hakim (who reigned from 996 to 1021), founder of the Egyptian Druze sect. It was abandoned, converted into a market, then into an Islamic museum and finally restored in 1981 by the Indian Bahai sect, which completed the modification of the small remaining section of the original edifice. An interior staircase leads to the remains of the city's 12th-century ramparts and a well-preserved rampart walk.

BAB EL-FUTUH (GATE OF CONQUEST). In 1087 Badr ad-Din el-Gamali (1010–94), the vizier of El-Mustansir, sent for three Syrian architect-brothers from Edessa to build the three main gates of the city: the Bab el-Futuh, Bab an-Nasr and Bab Zuwaila ▲ *298*. The Bab el-Futuh consists of a huge block of stone pierced by a huge vaulted opening and flanked by two rounded towers. The squat proportions of the vault result from the base being about 16 feet below street level.

Detail of the porch of the Bab el-Futuh.

EL-AQMAR MOSQUE
This was the first mosque in Cairo to have a decorated stone façade and a shell-like sculpted pediment.

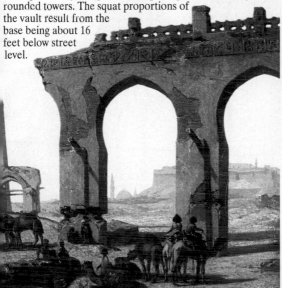

EL-HAKIM MOSQUE
The architectural features of this huge mosque (395 x 370 feet) are similar to those of the Ibn Tulun Mosque ▲ *312*: a large courtyard surrounded by porticos in two or three naves and a hypostyle prayer hall. The El-Hakim Mosque in the 19th century (left) and after it was restored in 1981 (above).

Entrance to the
Baybars el-Jashankir
khanqa (above).

QAITBAY "WAKALA"
Each first-floor bay
of the *wakala* is
occupied by a stall
which backs onto a
shop opening onto
the interior. The
windows of the
second and third
floors each represent
separate apartments.
The entrance (above
and right), in the
center of the façade,

has maintained its
monumental aspect
in spite of the fact
that the ground level
has risen.

SHARI' EL-GAMALIYA

BAB AN-NASR (VICTORY GATE). The two
square towers flanking the gate, built at the
same time as the Bab el-Futuh, have an
upper story with barbicans and
machicolations.

QAITBAY "WAKALA". Built in 1480 by Sultan
Qaitbay, the *wakala* ▲ *118* is one of the most
interesting examples of Circassian civil
architecture. The extremely regular external façade of the
edifice is created by the repetition of the identical, vertical
bays consisting of a first-floor opening, a *mashrabiya* panel
surmounted by a lattice window on the second floor and a
group of three windows on the third floor. Inside the four
main sections of the building surround a fairly large
courtyard. The first floor (whose openings have slightly
pointed arches) is in stone, while the upper floors are brick.

BAYBARS EL-JASHANKIR "KHANQA". Baybars el-Jashankir only
ruled for one year. He was executed by An-Nasir Mohammed
whose power he had usurped and his name was removed from
the façade of the *khanqa* (1306–10), one of the oldest in
Cairo. As well as a funeral chamber it also contains a *ribat*
(monastery) designed to house soldiers. The minaret is one of
the few to have a revetment of turquoise faïence. The
QITASBAY SABIL-KUTTAB opposite dates from 1630.

QARA SUNQUR MAUSOLEUM. The mausoleum was part of a
medersa built in 1300. A section of the façade still exists today
and the coat of arms of Emir Qara Sunqur, master of polo to
Sultan Qala'un, can be seen above one of the windows.
Next to the BAB HARA EL-MABAYDA, one of the old
city gates, is the ODA BASHI SABIL-KUTTAB (1673)
whose façade is decorated
with green and blue tiles
and surmounted by a
wood canopy.

ZULFIQAR "WAKALA". The separate accommodation for traveling merchants above this impressive *wakala* (1673) is reached through an entrance next to the *sabil-kuttab*. During the 17th century coffee was sold in the *wakala*. Today the first floor, which used to be a storage and wholesale warehouse, contains workshops which make furniture from recycled wood. The upper floors comprise over sixty apartments. The windows of the interior and exterior façades have been modified and the *mashrabiya* work replaced by simple windows.

THE GAMAL AD-DIN EL-USTADAR MEDERSA. Reached via the Shari' Wakala el-Tuffah, the medersa was built in 1408 on the site of one of the gates (Gate of the Wind) of the great Fatimid Palace. This probably explains its unusual design, with the dimensions of the *qibla* chamber reduced to a minimum and the building extended in the opposite direction. Beyond the medersa is the *mashrabiya* façade of the 17th-century BAZARAA WAKALA, the sole survivor of the street's several cloth and tobacco *wakala*, which still existed at the turn of the century.

TATAR EL-HIGAZIYA MEDERSA. South of the Ustadar Medersa in Atfa el-Qaffasin, the Tatar el-Higaziya Medersa was built between 1348 and 1360 by Qunad Tatar el-Higaziya, daughter of the sultan An-Nasir Mohammed, near the so-called "Palace of the Emeralds". Its plain façades and interior design, however, make it look more like a private residence. On the corner of Atfa el-Qaffasin and the Shari' el-Gamaliya the MAHMUD MUHARRAM MOSQUE (1539) can be found, and on the corner of the Shari' Darb el-Tabalawi is the MARZUQ EL-AHMEDI MOSQUE, built in the 7th century.

MUSAFIRKHANA PALACE. The palace stands in the Shari' Darb el-Tabalawi and has a second entrance in the Shari' Darb el-Masmat. Built between 1779 and 1788, this fine example of an Ottoman residence was the birthplace of the khedive Ismaïl in 1830. It was bought by Mohammed Ali at the turn of the century and used for receiving important guests, hence the name "Musafirkhana" ("House of Guests"). Today it houses artists' and sculptors' studios. It has several rooms decorated with various types of intricately carved *mashrabiya* panels, while the interiors of the rooms, especially the second-floor harem chamber, are full of richly decorated and painted wood paneling.

Bab an-Nasr and, in the background, the minaret of the El-Hakim Mosque.

"In the maze of narrow, winding streets, beneath the endless, overhanging balconies in finely carved wood lattice-work, we are forced to slow our pace as we join the tightly packed throng of people and animals . . . An occasional encounter with the more delightful face of the Orient as, above the tiny houses decorated with *mashrabiya* and arabesques, you catch a sudden glimpse of tall minarets soaring skyward in the dusk."

Pierre Loti

Two doors of the Musafirkhana Palace open onto the courtyard; the windows are closed with wood lattice (above). The palace is situated in the Qasr el-Shawq district, which existed before the city was built.

1 INAL EL-YUSUFT MOSQUE **2** EL-MU'AYYAD MOSQUE **3** RADWAN BEY KASBAH **4** QAITBAY PALACE **5** MAHMUD EL-KURDI MOSQUE **6** FARAG IBN BARQUQ ZAWIA **7** BAB ZUWAILA **8** AS-SALIH TALAI MOSQUE **9** NAFISA EL-BEIDA WAKALA **10** MOHAMMED ALI SABIL **11** EL-FAKAHANI MOSQUE **12** EL-GHURI MEDERSA **13** BEIT SHABSHIRI **14** EL-GHURI MAUSOLEI

EL-AZHAR

🐾 One/two days

THE UNIVERSITY OF THE ARAB WORLD
The El-Azhar Mosque-University used to house around ten thousand students. Today students are taught in faculties and the mosque is reserved strictly for prayer.

Until the turn of the century El-Azhar, which took its name from the mosque built by General Gawhara in 971, was one of the most famous districts in Cairo. Since then it has undergone many changes, particularly with the construction of the SHARI' EL-AZHAR in the 1920's, which divided the city in two. Almost from the outset the El-Azhar Mosque served a dual purpose as a place of worship and learning. The desire of successive rulers to make their mark has meant that the present building, which is very different from the original porticoed mosque, is a mixture of architectural styles from different periods. The mosque has six entrances and five minarets. The main entrance, the 18th-century BAB EL-MUZAYINI (Barbers' Gate), so called because students used to be shaved beneath its porch, opens onto a tiny courtyard which leads into the AQBUGHAWIYA MEDERSA (built in 1340 and now a library) on the left and into the TAYBARSIYA

15 EL-ISHAQI MOSQUE
16 EL-AZHAR MOSQUE
17 BEIT SITT WASSILA
18 EL-AYNI MOSQUE
19 BEIT EL-HIRAWI
20 BEIT ZEINAB KHATUN
21 TARABAY AS-SHARIFI MOSQUE
22 AYTMISHI MOSQUE
23 ALIN AQ PALACE
24 EL-MU'AYYAD MAURISTAN
25 KHAYRBAY MOSQUE
26 UMM EL-SULTAN SHA'BAN MEDERSA
27 BEIT ER-RAZZAZ
28 EL-MARIDANI MOSQUE

MEDERSA (1310) on the right. The QAITBAY ENTRANCE (1469), surmounted by a minaret, opens onto a vast central courtyard (275 x 112 feet) surrounded by porticos supported by more than three hundred marble columns which have come mainly from ancient monuments. The prayer hall, to the east, is larger than the courtyard (262 x 164 feet) and consists of several rows of columns whose arrangement conceals the various alterations. Although the mihrab has been modified several times, the Kufic inscription decorating the interior is original. The section of the hall behind the mihrab was added by Abd el-Rahman Katkhuda in 1753. At the northern end is the tomb-medersa of Gawhara Qunqubay (1440).

ABU EL-DAHAB MOSQUE. The mosque (1774), built in typical Ottoman style with a central cupola ● 108, consisted of a mausoleum and a *takiya*. Today it provides living accommodation for the students of the El-Azhar University.

QAITBAY "WAKALA" AND "SABIL-KUTTAB". Built in 1447, four years before the identical *wakala* built by the same sultan near the Bab an-Nasr ▲ 291, the Qaitbay *wakala* and *sabil-kuttab* is in a sorry state today. Only the wing overlooking the street and *sabil-kuttab* are used. The ABLUTIONS FOUNTAIN on the corner is part of the complex. The BEIT ZEINAB KHATUN ● 116 at the far end of the Shari' Atfa el-Azhari, which runs along the side of the El-Azhar Mosque, was built in 1468 and refurbished in 1713. The characteristics of the two periods are illustrated by the difference in style between the first-floor rooms, which reflect the severity of Mameluke architecture, and the more extravagant style of the Ottoman period in the second-floor rooms. Opposite the Beit Zeinab Khatun and beyond the El-Ayni Mosque, two old houses stand at the far end of the Shari' Atfa el-Ayni: the BEIT SITT WASSILA, probably built before 1637 and now in ruins, and the BEIT EL-HIRAWI (1731), which was recently restored by the French mission set up in 1983 to help preserve Islamic Cairo.

The five minarets of the El-Azhar Mosque (left and above).

❝[Their minarets] have small balconies and columns which are so intricately carved that you can see through them; some are a long way off and some quite close pointing skyward above your head.❞

Pierre Loti

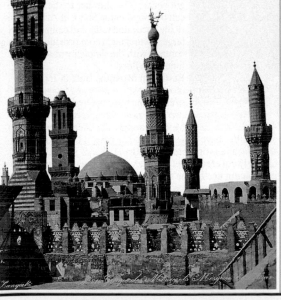

EL-GHURI COMPLEX

The complex, built by the sultan El-Ghuri (1501–16), the last great Mameluke sultan, comprises five buildings: a medersa and mausoleum, which stand opposite each other in the Shari' el-Muizz, a *sabil-kuttab* ● *113*, a *maqaad 116* and a *wakala* ● *118*.

The central courtyard of the El-Ghuri *wakala*, the interior of the mosque and the entrance (below).

EL-GHURI "WAKALA". Built in 1504–5, this is the most complete and best-preserved *wakala* in Cairo. The regularity of the external façade and the uniformity of the windows of this stone edifice are extremely impressive. The first floor has a few small, high, square windows, while the upper stories have three rows of different types of windows, arranged in groups of three. This last row is closed by *mashrabiya* panels, each the width of three windows. The great door with its trilobate arch leads into a central courtyard where the surrounding sections of the building echo its external regularity, with the exception of the first floor, which consists of wide arcades intersected by a gallery. Today the *wakala* houses a craft center.

EL-GHURI MAUSOLEUM. The mausoleum (1503–4), distinguishable from the mosque by its unfinished cupola and a *sabil-kuttab*, includes a funeral chamber to the right and, to the left, a prayer hall with three *iwan* ● *116* evenly distributed around the central, raised and covered part of a lantern, which was once part of a *khanqa* ● *112*. The SABIL-KUTTAB forms the front section of the mausoleum and is a particularly fine example of Mameluke architecture. It has three latticed bays framed by moldings and surmounted by stone panels, while the interior is richly decorated with marble floors and walls and a ceiling with rounded, painted and gilt beams. The entrance to the MAQAAD can be found in the Shari' el-Azhar. The richly decorated walls and ceiling of this large, rectangular room provide a striking contrast with the simplicity of the limestone floor.

EL-GHURI MOSQUE. Built in 1504, the mosque has four *iwan* and a central, sunken courtyard open to the sky. The two large *iwans* are pierced by large Moorish arches; the lateral *iwans*, which are smaller, have raised arches. The base of the bicolored stone façade is occupied by cloth merchants' shops. The formerly covered street between the mosque and the mausoleum used to be the home of the famous silk market. An enormous entrance with a trilobate arch decorated with stalactites opens onto a corridor lit by a central well. The interior decoration has distinctive polychrome marble dados (whose rectangular design is reproduced to infinity), flagging laid in geometric patterns and gilt and painted wood paneling. The southern section of the Shari' el-Muizz is the extension of the main thoroughfare that crossed the city to Old Cairo ▲ *320* and which is now intersected by the Shari' el-Azhar.

> **"STREETS OF PRIVATE HOUSES ARE LIKE TUNNELS FROM MEETING OVERHEAD OF PROJECTING WINDOWS . . . SOMETIMES HIGH BLANK WALLS – MYSTERIOUS PASSAGES – DIM PEEPS AT COURTS AND WELLS IN SHADOW."** HERMAN MELVILLE

BEIT GAMAL AD-DIN
A typical 17th-century residence of a Cairene notable. The house was saved from demolition by the Cairo Conservation Committee, which classified it as an historic monument in 1899. The external façade has two projecting *mashrabiya* panels overlooking the street. The entrance is through a curved arch set deep in the ground (detail below).

BEIT SHABSHIRI
The small, interior courtyard of the house (above) is overlooked by four richly decorated façades with projecting *mashrabiya* panels, lattice windows and galleries. The harem chamber occupies the entire east wing of the house. It is well lit by large, lateral bays covered with *mashrabiya*, which overlook both street and courtyard.

BEIT GAMAL AD-DIN EL-DAHABI. The only surviving house in this once extensive residential district, no. 6 Hara Hoch Qadam was built in 1637. The rectangular, interior courtyard is surrounded by four architecturally distinct façades. The second-floor harem chamber is remarkable for its balanced proportions and the almost perfect symmetry of its spatial organization. The *mashrabiya* walls of the north *iwan* adjoin the loggias at mezzanine level. This allowed the womenfolk to be present and yet remain unseen when (male) guests were received. On the corner of the Shari' el-Muizz and the Shari' Hara Hoch Qadam, the EL-FAKAHANI MOSQUE, constructed in 1145 and rebuilt during the 17th century, still has its original carved wood doors.

HARA EL-RUM. To the east of the Shari' el-Muizz, the Hara el-Rum or "Christian Quarter" was originally located outside the city walls. It became part of the city when the walls were moved during the 11th century and, until the 19th, was the seat of the Coptic patriarchate and housed several churches and monasteries. Today all that remains are the Church and relatively recent MONASTERY OF ST TADROS, and the 6th-century El-Adra (CHURCH OF THE VIRGIN), which was entirely rebuilt after the district was ravaged by fire during the 11th and 14th centuries. At the end of Atfa el-Tateri the 17th-century BEIT SHABSHIRI can be recognized by the projecting *mashrabiya* work on its façade. Although small, the house includes all the elements of a grand aristocratic residence: *tahtabuch*, *maqaad*, various *qaa* (six on three floors) and several staircases which give separate access to each part of the house.

EL-MU'AYYAD MOSQUE

The prayer hall of the mosque looks directly onto a courtyard which has been converted into a shady garden (right and below). The arcades incorporated into the walls of the garden are surmounted by blind niches in the form of Persian-style arches reminiscent of the El-Azhar Mosque ▲ 294.

The El-Mu'ayyad Mosque was built by Sultan el-Mu'ayyad on the site of a prison in which he had endured such suffering that he vowed, if he ever regained his freedom, to replace it with a mosque. The fulfillment of this promise gave rise to one of the most beautiful mosques in Cairo. Although the prison was demolished, the site was still used for executions and the heads displayed in accordance with tradition. It was here that the sultan Selim had his enemy Tomanbay, the last of the Mameluke sultans, hanged in the 16th century. Exterior of the mosque (right), the sanctuary (center right) and the prayer hall with the mihrab and minbar (far right).

TUSSUN PASHA "SABIL". The *sabil* ● 113 was built in 1820 by Mohammed Ali in memory of his son, Ahmed Tussun, who died at the age of twenty. Its marble-clad, rounded façade surmounted by a wooden canopy observes the criteria of contemporary Turkish architecture. The rooms of the *kuttab* are scattered throughout the building.

NAFISA EL-BEIDA "WAKALA". This 18th-century *wakala* ● 118 specialized in the manufacture and sale of sweetmeats. Today various structures have encroached upon the large, rectangular courtyard. The *rabaa* section is still inhabited and has around fifty apartments accessible via an interior passageway. The southern section of the building is occupied by a *sabil-kuttab* ● 113 with an overornate façade.

EL-MU'AYYAD OR RED MOSQUE. The mosque was built (1415–20) by Sultan El-Mu'ayyad against the south wall of the city. The bronze-plated entrance door, which bears the titles and name of Sultan Hassan, is from his medersa ▲ 309. An entrance hall leads into the mausoleum containing the tombs of the sultan and his son. Its walls are completely covered with a polychrome marble revetment forming several geometric patterns. The prayer hall looks directly onto the courtyard, which has been converted into a garden. The columns of the hall are surmounted by two rows of superposed arches which are reminiscent of the great Ommiad mosque in Damascus, where El-Mu'ayyad was governor. The mihrab has a remarkably fine central, marble-covered decoration and festooned archstones, while the minbar is decorated with polygonal panels inlaid with mother-of-pearl and ivory. The two minarets, which stand on the two salient angles of the BAB ZUWAILA (1092), offer a panoramic view of Cairo. To the east is the outline of the city wall and its towers buried beneath the rubble.

AS-SALIH TALAI MOSQUE ★. The mosque, which stands to the south of the Bab Zuwaila, was founded in 1160 by the emir As-Salih Talai, vizier to the last of the Fatimid caliphs. Around the interior courtyard the columns supporting the arches of the porticos are surmounted by ancient capitals from Christian churches. A subtle combination of stained glass and stuccowork decorates the windows in the upper part of the wall of the *qibla*. The wooden minbar (1300) is engraved with star motifs repeated to infinity. Opposite the mosque, all that remains of the FARAG IBN BARQUQ ZAWIA, which was built in 1408, are two reception rooms, one of which is used as a mausoleum.

All that remains of the palace (above) built by Radwan Bey in 1650 is the triple-arched *maqaad* ● *116*. The *wakala*, to the north, is now occupied by a sawmill and the courtyard is used as a wood depot.

RADWAN BEY KASBAH. Opposite the Bab Zuwaila is Cairo's only surviving example of a covered market. It was built during the 17th century by the emir Radwan Bey who dominated Egypt's political life for a quarter of a century and renovated the district, building *rabaa* (apartment blocks), a *wakala*, two *zawia*, a *sabil* and a palace. The market is a covered street whose wooden roof is pierced by lanterns which let in a soft, filtered light. Today it is occupied by manufacturers of tent fabric who have given the market its name (Khayamiya, which means "tentmakers' bazaar"). The living accommodation above the first-floor shops and stalls is virtually abandoned. On the left, beyond the Radwan Bey Kasbah, is the MAHMUD EL-KURDI MOSQUE, built in 1395, which comprises a mosque-medersa and a mausoleum. About 20 yards to the south, the INAL EL-YUSUFI ATABAKI MOSQUE also includes a mausoleum and a *sabil-kuttab*. Built in 1392–3 it is in the same style as the Mahmud el-Kurdi Mosque-Medersa with two *iwan* and a covered courtyard. The difference lies in the shape of the minaret and the minor decorative details. The interior of the second of the two mosques is better preserved with painted ceilings and marble-clad walls.

AS-SALIH TALAI MOSQUE
The five Persian arches of the freestone façade of the mosque (above) are closed to the street by *mashrabiya* panels which were added in 1303. When the mosque was built in 1160 the shops, which are today below the building, were at street level.

EL-MIHMANDAR MOSQUE
The mosque is reached through a gateway with a lobed arch decorated with stalactites (above).

UMM EL-SULTAN SHA'BAN MEDERSA
The medersa contains the mausoleums of the sultan and his mother. Each tomb has a door with sculpted wood panels (above) leading into the prayer hall.

DARB EL-AHMAR

The districts surrounding the Shari' Suq el-Silah and Shari' Darb el-Ahmar were established in the 12th century. They reached the peak of their urban development under the Mamelukes when they were centered around particular activities and markets such as the Suq el-Silah (Weapons Market).

EL-ISHAQI MOSQUE ★. This cruciform mosque ▲ *108* was built in 1480–1 by the Emir Qijmas el-Ishaqi, head of the Sultan Qaitbay's stables. It stands above street level and the lower level is occupied by shops. The complex includes an ablutions room and a drinking fountain in a building across the street, linked to the mosque by a covered gallery surmounted by *mashrabiya* work. The entrance is decorated with marble and Koranic inscriptions and leads into a square entrance hall with a painted wood ceiling surrounded by an epigraphic frieze. A lattice window looks onto the mausoleum. The wall of the *qibla* is decorated with red and white marble and the beautifully carved minbar is inlaid with ivory.

EL-MIHMANDAR MOSQUE ★. Built in 1324–5, the mosque comprises a central courtyard and four *iwan*. The west *iwan* has a mezzanine loggia with a turned wood balustrade and stained-glass windows. The wood ceilings have decorated beams. The mausoleum, in the northeast corner, has a fluted-stone exterior.

EL-MARIDANI MOSQUE ★. The mosque was founded in 1339–40 by Prince Altanbugha el-Maridani. The work was carried out under the supervision of Ibn el-Suyufi, chief architect to Sultan an-Nasir Mohammed. The central courtyard, surrounded by porticos, is separated from the prayer hall by an attractive wood lattice. Inside, four rows of raised arches are supported by ancient columns. The mihrab, inlaid with geometrically arranged green, red and yellow marble, is one of the most beautiful in Cairo, while the carved minbar is a work of art in its own right. The wall of the *qibla* has a marble revetment and a series of stained-glass, gemel windows with rounded arches. The arch of the main entrance in the Shari' el-Tabbana is decorated with stalactites.

QAITBAY PALACE. All that remains of this luxurious palace, built in 1485, is the *maqaad*, which consists of three Gothic arches resting on two ancient columns.

BEIT ER-RAZZAZ. This grand, 15th-century palace with two courtyards was built by Sultan Qaitbay and converted by Ahmed Katkhuda er-Razzaz in 1778. The present entrance is near the ablutions fountain, which stands between the PALACE and the SULTAN SHA'BAN MEDERSA built in 1369. A passageway leads into an irregularly shaped courtyard surrounded by buildings. On the right the QAITBAY ENTRANCE leads to the upper floors, which consist of several *qaa*, including a beautiful harem chamber. Its originality lies in the carved openwork of the huge vertical wood bays which reach from floor to ceiling. The part of the building overlooking the second courtyard has a first-floor reception room and second-floor *maqaad*.

EL-MARIDANI MOSQUE
Unusually, the wall of the *qibla* is separated from the rest of the mosque by a turned and carved wood screen (above). It is one of the earliest examples of *mashrabiya* work in Cairo.

The Beit er-Razzaz has two entrances. Today one of them is actually inside the shops on the Shari' el-Tabbana.

AQSUNQUR OR BLUE MOSQUE. The mosque was founded in 1346 by the Emir Shams ad-Din Aqsunqur, a member of Sultan an-Nasir Mohammed's entourage, and was restored and slightly modified in 1652 by Ibrahim Aga el-Mustahfizan who had the interior walls covered with blue tiles, thereby giving the mosque its alternative name. The arches of this porticoed mosque are supported by square and octagonal pillars rather than columns, which lends it a very distinctive appearance. The porticos were originally covered by groined vaults instead of the usual wood ceiling, but some of these have been replaced. The first of the mosque's three mausoleums, at the northwest corner, is dedicated to the son of Sultan an-Nasir Mohammed. The second, between the minaret and the south entrance, has the same tiled decoration and is dedicated to Ibrahim Aga, while the third is of more recent construction and contains the tomb of Aqsunqur.

THE BLUE MOSQUE
The Iznik tiles used to cover the interior of the mosque were imported from Istanbul and Damascus. The mihrab is in polychrome marble, while the minbar, the oldest marble minbar in Cairo, is inlaid with precious stones. The minaret offers a panoramic view of the city.

THE WAQF. The Waqf is a religious foundation which converts or acquires property in perpetuity for religious or charitable purposes. The income from a Waqf building is used to ensure the continuation of the foundation. During the Mameluke period the Waqf became widespread and resulted in the creation of a private version of the foundation. The ingenious exploitation of the system has enabled major construction companies to participate effectively in the urban development of the city.

THE OMAR AGA WAQF. The complex (1621) occupies the west façade of the street and comprises, from north to south, a *sabil-kuttab*, a mausoleum, an ablutions fountain and a *rabaa*.

KHAYRBAY MOSQUE. Khayrbay, governor of Aleppo during the reign of El-Ghuri, was made commander-in-chief of the army during the conquest of Syria by Sultan Selim I into whose hands he delivered the country. His complex comprises a mausoleum, built in 1502, a mosque and a *sabil-kuttab* added in 1520. The mosque is built according to the irregular layout of a medersa with *iwan*, with the prayer hall occupying a central position flanked by two *iwan*, although the direction of Mecca is not strictly observed. The funeral chamber, surmounted by a cupola, is surprisingly high.

ALIN AQ PALACE. Built in 1293, the palace is also known as the Palace of Khayrbay (Khayrbay lived there after being appointed Pasha of Cairo under the Ottomans). All that remains of this once luxurious palace are the freestone walls of the four façades pierced by arched windows. The main entrance in the Shari' Bab el-Wazir is a wide, rectangular opening decorated with stalactites and flanked by two stone benches.

TARABAY AS-SHARIFI MAUSOLEUM AND GATE. About one hundred yards further on in the Shari' Bab el-Tureb is the Tarabay as-Sharifi Mausoleum and Gate built in 1503 on the site of the Bab el-Wazir (Cemetery Gate). The *sabil-kuttab* to the right of the gate used to lead to a medersa (which no longer exists), while the façade of the beautifully constructed mausoleum is composed of vertical panels crowned with stalactites.

AYTMISHI MOSQUE. Built in 1383 by Seif ad-Din Aytmish el-Baghasi, a member of Sultan Barquq's entourage, the structure comprises a *sabil-kuttab* on the corner where only the first floor remains, a mosque and a mausoleum. The mosque consists of a single *iwan* leading off a central area with a wood ceiling pierced by a lantern. The mausoleum is surmounted by a small dome of a type virtually exclusive to Cairo. It is decorated with raised ribs which are vertical at the base and become suddenly helicoidal.

EL-MU'AYYAD "MAURISTAN". The impressive ruins of the El-Mu'ayyad *mauristan* (1418) are reached by following the Shari' el-Tabbana southward into the Shari' el-Mahgar and turning right into the Shari' Sikka el-Kumi. The *mauristan* replaced the 14th-century Ashrafiya Medersa founded by Sultan Sha'ban and was once a huge building which covered a vast area. Today much of this area is occupied by apartment blocks. It was Cairo's second largest hospital after the one founded by Sultan Qala'un ▲ 289. Inside the ruins huge arcades, whose façades are pierced by arched windows surmounted by oculi, can still be seen around a courtyard.

An arch in one of the walls surrounding the courtyard of the ruined El-Mu'ayyad *mauristan*.

THE CITADEL

The Lions' Tower (below), today transformed into the Military Museum.

The site, formed by the foothills of Jebel Moqattam, was first occupied in 810 when the governor Hatim Ibn Hartama built the so-called "Dome of the Wind" pavilion. Since then the Citadel has continually attracted the attention of the governors of Egypt. In 1176 Salah ad-Din ▲ *270* enclosed it with fortifications to protect it against attack by the Crusaders. The Mameluke sultans made it their headquarters and built a number of structures, including the vast QASR EL-ABLAQ PALACE and an 11,000-foot aqueduct with four pumping stations. During the Ottoman period, the Citadel became a real city with two residential districts occupied by Janissaries and *azab* (celibates). It became the main residence and seat of government of Mohammed Ali, who modified the walls and constructed civil and military buildings as well as the mosque named after him. The Citadel has three distinct sections, each surrounded by walls punctuated with towers and gates: the Lower Enclosure (El-Azab), the Northern

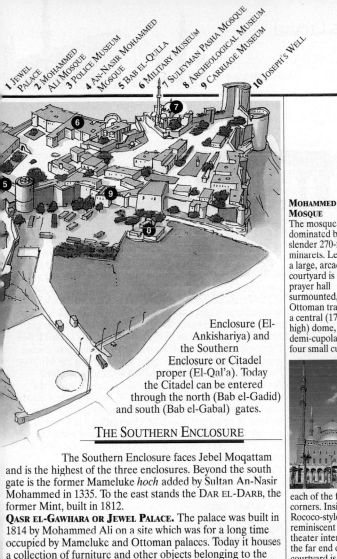

Enclosure (El-Ankishariya) and the Southern Enclosure or Citadel proper (El-Qal'a). Today the Citadel can be entered through the north (Bab el-Gadid) and south (Bab el-Gabal) gates.

THE SOUTHERN ENCLOSURE

The Southern Enclosure faces Jebel Moqattam and is the highest of the three enclosures. Beyond the south gate is the former Mameluke *hoch* added by Sultan An-Nasir Mohammed in 1335. To the east stands the DAR EL-DARB, the former Mint, built in 1812.

QASR EL-GAWHARA OR JEWEL PALACE. The palace was built in 1814 by Mohammed Ali on a site which was for a long time occupied by Mameluke and Ottoman palaces. Today it houses a collection of furniture and other objects belonging to the family of the viceroy whose apartments and courtroom were in the palace.

MOHAMMED ALI OR ALABASTER MOSQUE. This monumental mosque (1830–57) dominates the city from the site previously occupied by the Mameluke palace, QASR EL-ABLAQ (1315). Mohammed Ali sent to Istanbul for the Greek architect Yussuf Bushnaq, who achieved only a pale imitation of the Ottoman

MOHAMMED ALI MOSQUE
The mosque is dominated by two slender 270-foot minarets. Leading off a large, arcaded courtyard is a vast prayer hall surmounted, in the Ottoman tradition, by a central (170-foot-high) dome, four demi-cupolas and four small cupolas on

each of the four corners. Inside, the Rococo-style décor is reminiscent of a theater interior. At the far end of the courtyard is a clock, a gift from Louis-Philippe of France to Mohammed Ali.

▲ THE CITADEL

An-Nasir Mohammed
Mosque

The great interior courtyard of the An-Nasir Mohammed Mosque

is surrounded by a double row of stone arcades in alternate red and black bricks, supported by ancient Pharaonic, Byzantine and Coptic columns.

BAB EL-AZAB
The Bab el-Azab (below), which opens onto the Midan Salah ad-Din, was built by Abd el-Rahman Katkhuda in 1754. Today it is surrounded by 19th-century walls. It was on a road somewhere between the Bab el-Azab and the upper part of the Citadel that Mohammed Ali ordered the massacre of five hundred Mameluke chieftains on March 1, 1811.

mosques. However its position makes it Cairo's most famous and most frequented mosque.

AN-NASIR MOHAMMED MOSQUE ★. Built by Sultan an-Nasir Mohammed in 1335, it is the only well-preserved Mameluke building in the Citadel. The mosque has two minarets and two entrances. The first entrance, inscribed in an arch decorated with stalactites, was reserved for the sultan, while the second, in the form of a trilobate arch, was situated opposite the Bab el-Qulla and used by the soldiers stationed in the Citadel. The marble panels covering the interior of the mosque were removed and sent to Istanbul by Sultan Selim I when he conquered Egypt in 1517. Their absence accentuates the characteristically sober interior decoration of Mameluke architecture. A gateway opposite the mosque leads onto the esplanade of the POLICE MUSEUM, which occupies the old Artillery School built in 1830 on the site of the Lions' Tower. The museum traces the history of the Egyptian police force from Pharaonic to modern times. On the left is the MILITARY PRISON, built by the British in 1880 and used until 1983.

JOSEPH'S WELL. The 270-foot well was carved out of the rocky hillside by Salah ad-Din in 1183 to ensure the Citadel's water supply. The water was brought up by two pumping stations. A spiral staircase with observation windows winds around the outside of the well. The additional width (about 6 feet) of the upper section is taken up by an access ramp for the first pumping station.

THE INNER WALL. The wall separating the Northern and Southern Enclosures was built by the Mameluke sultan Baybars el-Bunduqari (1223–77) to isolate his palace from the rest of the Citadel.

NORTHERN ENCLOSURE

The Northern Enclosure is surrounded, for the most part, by the fortifications erected by Salah ad-Din and rebuilt by Mohammed Ali. The wall incorporates twenty or so towers and two gates: the Bab el-Gadid (1826) and the Bab el-Qulla, the central gate built in the 16th century and modified by Mohammed Ali, who added the upper sections reserved for the guards. This part of the Citadel has for a long time been used as a military camp and garrison. Behind the Bab el-Qulla, in the open space in front of the Harem Palace, stands a statue of Ibrahim Pasha (one of Mohammed Ali's sons) which is a copy of the one in the Midan el-Opera ▲ 274. To the left of the gate is the DIWAN, which is the equivalent of a ministry of education, built during the reign of Mohammed Ali.

THE HAREM PALACE. The palace (1827) consists of three wings whose interior decoration and painting reflect the Levantine style adopted by Mohammed Ali. It was the residence of the royal family until 1874 when the khedive Ismaïl transferred the seat of government to the Abdin Palace ▲ 281. It was used as a military hospital during the British occupation and, in 1946, was converted into a museum which traces the military history of Egypt. In the central wing visitors can see the former alabaster-covered *hammam*, while the exit in the left wing leads into a courtyard where the statue of Colonel de Sèves (previously in the Midan Suleyman Pasha ▲ 275) now stands. On the right, halfway between the palace and the Suleyman Pasha Mosque, stands the 16th-century tomb of Sheikh Mohammed el-Kahaki and, on the left, part of the wall built by Salah ad-Din and circumscribed by the later, 19th-century wall.

SULEYMAN PASHA MOSQUE ★. Built in 1528 by an Ottoman governor, Suleyman Pasha (who had no connection with Colonel de Sèves), the Suleyman Pasha Mosque is not only Egypt's first cupolated Ottoman mosque, but also its most beautiful. It stands in a small garden, which is enclosed by an outer wall, and can be reached by way of a courtyard whose arcades are surmounted by small cupolas. The prayer hall has a large central cupola and three demi-cupolas, all richly decorated with floral and geometric motifs. The extremely fine, marble-covered mihrab illustrates the influence of Mameluke art. The mosque is also known as the Sariya el-Gabal Mosque after the Fatimid saint, Sayyid Sariya, whose tomb stands at the eastern end of the surrounding wall. Several of its rooms are surmounted by cupolas and decorated with 19th-century naive designs.

CARRIAGE MUSEUM. Housed in the building used as the British Officers' Mess during the colonial period, the museum has a collection of eight carriages, the majority of which date from the reign of the khedive Ismaïl; indeed, the collection includes the carriage he used for the opening of the Suez Canal ▲ 232 in 1869. To the south of the museum, the BURG EL-TURFA (1207) is one of the few towers in Cairo which is open to the public. Columns from the Ottoman period and the remains of a 15th-century minaret can be seen in the open-air archeological museum.

The dome of the Suleyman Pasha Mosque, decorated with Koranic verses.

The French officer Colonel de Sèves (1788–1860) (left) was employed by Mohammed Ali to reorganize the Egyptian army. He was promoted to general and converted to Islam, taking the name Suleyman Pasha.

Interior of the Suleyman Pasha Mosque (below).

"... the immense city of Cairo, with its citadels and towers, and walls, and minarets stretching away for miles, the splendid ancient city, and beyond it, modern Cairo, with its turmoil of tramways, railroads, and other modernities."
Wilfred Scawen Blunt

1 EL-YUSUFI MOSQUE   **2** AS-SAYYIDA ZEINAB MOSQUE   **3** SANGAR SALAR MOSQUE-MAUSOLEUM   **4** SARGHATMISH MEDERSA   **5** AHMED EFENDI SABIL   **6** IBN TULUN MOSQUE   **7** TAGHRI BARDI MEDERSA   **8** GAYER-ANDERSON MUSEUM   **9** UMM ABBAS SABIL-KUTTAB   **10** SHEIKHU MOSQUE   **11** SHEIKHU KHANQA   **12** SUNOUR SAADI MAUSOLEUM

MIDAN SALAH AD-DIN

The Midan Salah ad-Din, built in the 12th century at the same time as the Citadel, became a parade ground around which a number of great monuments were constructed.

MAHMUDIYA MEDERSA. Founded in 1567–8 by the governor Mahmud Pasha, this medersa has four different façades.

The interior is about 65 feet square and consists of two *iwan* and a long, narrow courtyard.

QANIBEY EMIR AKHUR MEDERSA ★. The medersa (1503), whose façade overlooks the square, comprises a *sabil-kuttab*, an entrance at the top of a flight of steps and a mausoleum with a high-pitched cupola decorated with geometric and floral motifs. The building is entirely of stone and consists of a central courtyard open to the sky and four *iwan*. Near the Citadel, the HARA DARB EL-LABBANI was bordered on either side by houses whose upper stories overhung the street. Today only one of these remains, the (probably) pre-18th-century BEIT ALI EFENDI LABIB, situated at no. 4, on the right. This former residence of Hassan Fathi ▲ *442* is now owned by the Aga Khan Foundation.

EL-GAWHARA EL-LALA MOSQUE ★. Although small (about 2,000 square feet), the mosque (1430) comprises an ingeniously designed medersa, *sabil-kuttab* and mausoleum where every inch of space has been used to advantage.

AR-RIFA'I MOSQUE. The mosque was founded in 1869 on the site of the Sheikh ar-Rifa'i *zawia* (1122). Designed by the architect Mustapha Fahmi ▲ *281* and completed in 1912 by Max Herz Pasha, it covers a

The wooden minbar inlaid with mother-of-pearl, and detail of the interior decoration (above) of the Qanibey Emir Akhur Medersa.

One of the streets leading off the Midan Salah ad-Din (right). In the distance is the Mahmudiya Mosque.

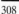

MIDAN ▲
SALAH AD-DIN

13 DERVISH THEATER
14 AR-RIFA'I MOSQUE
15 EL-GAWHARA EL-LALA MOSQUE
16 QANIBEY MEDERSA
17 MAHMUDIYA MEDERSA
18 SULTAN HASSAN MEDERSA
19 QAITBAY SABIL-KUTTAB
20 QANIBEY EL-MOHAMMEDI MOSQUE

rectangular area of about 75,350 square feet and has four monumental façades. As well as the tomb of Sheikh ar-Rifa'i the mosque also contains those of King Fuad (1868–1936), his mother, and Mohammed Reza Pahlavi (1919–80), the last Shah of Iran.

SULTAN HASSAN MEDERSA. Founded by Sultan Hassan, son of An-Nasir Mohammed, the medersa (1356–63) is one of the finest examples of Mameluke architecture. A corridor leads from the entrance hall into an almost square courtyard surrounded by four *iwan*, in the center of which is an ablutions fountain. The four doors leading to the medersa correspond to the four Muslim orthodox schools. The *iwan* of the *qibla* is decorated with stuccowork friezes inscribed with Kufic script and has a mihrab, flanked by eight marble columns and preceded by a marble *dikka* (platform), and a minbar. Behind the minbar the mausoleum, surmounted by a once gold and silver-plated cupola, houses the tombs of Sultan Hassan's two sons (the assassinated sultan's body was never recovered); there is also an ancient wooden Koran case inlaid with ivory.

SHARI' SUYUFIA. Part of the ancient thoroughfare which

Everything about the Sultan Hassan Medersa is impressive: its area (about 850, 350

square feet), its façade surmounted by a projecting cornice, its monumental entrance (39 x 125 feet) and its sober interior where every corner is perfect.

Remains of the Emir Qusun Palace, which still has a vaulted entrance decorated with stalactites.

"MAQAAD" OF THE EMIR TAZ PALACE
The *maqaad* appears to have been added by Ali Aga Dar el-Saada who built the *sabil-kuttab* (1677) at the southern end.

The cupola of the Hassan Sadaqa Mausoleum is covered with plaster decorations.

used to cross the city to Old Cairo, it extends beyond the Ibn Tulun district in the direction of the Imam as-Shafi'i cemetery.

EMIR QUSUN PALACE. The palace, which stands to the west of the Sultan Hassan Medersa, was built between 1330 and 1337 by Emir Qusun and has been renovated several times, in particular by Yashbak Min Mahdi. The existing ruins cannot be visited because they are in a bad state of disrepair.

EMIR TAZ PALACE. The palace, built in 1352 by Emir Taz on his marriage to the daughter of Sultan An-Nasir Mohammed, was significantly modified at the end of the 19th century when it became the first Egyptian girls' school. Today it is used as an educational supplies depot and the interior has been badly damaged. The *qaa* overlooking the west entrance and the entrance itself have collapsed, while the courtyard was divided in two by a wall built in the 19th century at the same time as most of the buildings surrounding the northern section.

EL-ABAR "ZAWIA". The *zawia* (1248) stands on the corner of the Shari' Suyufia and the Shari' Qaraqol el-Manshiya. It was originally part of a complex consisting of a *khanqa* and a medersa, of which only the mausoleum remains. This now forms part of the façade of the Emir Taz Palace and houses the tombs of Sheikh Ala ad-Din el-Abar and his wife.

QIZLAR "SABIL-KUTTAB" AND "RABAA". The façade of this complex, founded in 1618 by Ali Aga Dar el-Saada, consists of a *sabil-kuttab* entirely surrounded by identical bays (each corresponding to a *rabaa*) pierced at first-floor level by wide openings and, on the upper floor, by pairs of superposed, oriel windows.

HASSAN SADAQA MAUSOLEUM. The mausoleum houses the tombs of its founder, Sunqur Saadi, and Hassan Sadaqa. It was part of a complex (1315) consisting of a medersa which no longer exists, a *takiya* ● *112* and a *ribat* (monastery) which was replaced during the 19th century by a Dervish theater.

DERVISH THEATER. The theater, also known as Sama Khana, is dedicated to the dancing dervishes of the Mawlawiya sect. It was restored between 1979 and 1989 by the Italian Cultural Center and houses an Italian-Egyptian restoration training center and an exhibition hall. The 19th-century building includes some older sections. Excavations have revealed the remains of the Sunqur Saadi Medersa, which were used as foundations. The interior includes a monastery complex and a huge circular chamber with a special women's gallery, whose walls and dome are decorated with flowers and landscapes. The first floor is all that remains of the YUSSUF BEY SABIL-KUTTAB (1772) on the opposite side of the Shari' el-Muzafar, while on the corner of the Shari' el-Helmiya the El-Muzafar Mausoleum (1322) forms part of the adjacent building.

DERVISH THEATER
The monastery cells of the Sufis occupied a vast complex built around gardens.

SHARI' SALIBA

In the Shari' Sheikhu, to the west of the Midan Salah ad-Din, the QAITBAY SABIL-KUTTAB (1479) is, unlike its contemporaries, completely autonomous: an innovation which became popular during the Ottoman period. On the corner of Shari' Sheikhu and Shari' Darb el-Samak stands the QANIBEY EL-MOHAMMEDI MOSQUE (1413). The interior consists of a single *iwan* whose wide arch opens onto a covered courtyard with a wood ceiling.

SHEIKHU MOSQUE AND "KHANQA" ★. The mosque and *khanqa* were built (1349–55) opposite each other by Emir Sheikhu. The absence of any decoration accentuates the strength of the architectural form. The design of the mosque combines the characteristics of mosques with *iwan* and porticoed mosques ● *108* as it consists of two porticoed *iwan* and a central courtyard open to the sky. At the northeast corner of the *khanqa* stands the EMIR ABDALLAH SABIL-KUTTAB (1719). The 19th-century UMM ABBAS SABIL-KUTTAB, built by the mother of the khedive Abbas, has replaced the Sheikhu *sabil*.

TAGHRI BARDI MEDERSA. The complex, founded in 1440 by

Emir Taghri Bardi el-Rumi, comprises a medersa, a *sabil-kuttab* and a mausoleum surmounted by an impressive stone cupola decorated with interwoven fluting.

SHEIKHU "KHANQA"
The *khanqa* was designed to house needy pilgrims. The courtyard (left) is surrounded at second-floor level by wooden galleries leading to the study cells on the west and south sides. The other two sides consist of two *iwan*, one of which is reserved for prayer.

▲ IBN TULUN MOSQUE

IBN TULUN MOSQUE
The mosque's main mihrab consists of a stone niche surrounded by a simple frame. Others were added

subsequently in the prayer hall, including a marble mihrab with a wooden arch, flanked by four columns.

The Ibn Tulun Mosque before it was restored in 1918.

EL-QATAI'. In 868 Ahmed Ibn Tulun seized power and founded the city of El-Qatai' ▲ *271*. He erected a fortress-like mosque on a small hill in the center of the new city, as well as a huge castle on the Jebel Moqattam, at the foot of which lay a vast *midan*. In 1069, following a terrible famine, the city was sacked and abandoned. In 1168 Cairo was besieged by the Francs and the vizier Shawar ordered Fustat and El-Qatai' to be burned. Today the Ibn Tulun Mosque is all that remains of this legendary city. The site, upon which a vast lake lay until the mid-19th century, was occupied by the Mamelukes who built palaces, mosques and medersat. It was totally transformed following the draining of the lake, after which modern buildings were constructed.

IBN TULUN MOSQUE. Built in 876–9 by Ahmed Ibn Tulun on the Jebel Yashkur, this is the oldest original mosque in Cairo. It was converted into a military hospital by Ibrahim Pasha in the 19th century, and was subsequently used as a salt warehouse and a beggar's prison before being classified as a historic monument in 1882. It was restored, in 1918. The rectangular building is entirely constructed in brick (including the strange-looking merlons on top of its walls) and surrounded by a "rampart" walk. It is a porticoed mosque ● *108* (the porticos rest on pillars) consisting of five naves on the *qibla* side and two on the other three sides. The plaster of the intrados of the arches is decorated with inscribed geometric designs. The long foliate frieze which runs the length of the porticos is surmounted by a carved wood inscription of Koranic verses. The minaret, a square tower with an external, spiral staircase, is the only one of its kind in Egypt. Faithfully restored by the sultan Lajin in the 18th century, it is reminiscent of the minaret of the Samarra Mosque in Mesopotamia, which is believed to have been the inspiration behind the design of the Ibn Tulun Mosque.

GAYER-ANDERSON MUSEUM. The museum houses the private collection of Major Gayer-Anderson and includes furniture, silks, glassware, crystal, carpets, carved wood paneling and embroidered Arab costumes. It was founded in 1937 in two ancient residences, the BEIT EL-KIRIDILIYA (1632) and BEIT AMNA BENT SALIM (1540), reached via a narrow, private street. The first has a *sabil* at the southwest corner and a *maquad* with a monumental entrance. The *qaa* situated between the two buildings has been furnished in its original style. The second residence has a small courtyard with a single-arched *maqaad* and a magnificent *qaa* with an extremely high ceiling which runs the length of the house. Several third-floor rooms have been organized to accommodate the collections and include a reconstruction of a Syrian room. Beyond the Ibn Tulun Mosque the Shari' el-Khalifa leads to the cemeteries ▲ *326*.

SARGHATMISH MEDERSA. The medersa was built in 1356 by Emir Seif ad-Din Sarghatmish against the northwest wall of the Ibn Tulun Mosque. It has a central courtyard open to the sky, formed by four *iwan* surrounded by study cells. The cupola, supported by wooden pendentives, covering the main *iwan* in front of the mihrab, was rebuilt in 1940 to replace the original which had been destroyed. The mausoleum is situated next to the west *iwan*. In front of the medersa are the recently renovated MOSQUE AND MAUSOLEUM OF EL-KHODARI, built in 1767. Inside, the arcaded prayer hall has a painted wood ceiling.

SANGAR SALAR MOSQUE AND MAUSOLEUM. The complex (1304) is situated to the west of the Sarghatmish Medersa, in the Shari' Abd el-Magid el-Labbani. It houses two similar mausoleums, one dedicated to its founder, Emir Alam ad-Din Sangar el-Gawli, and the other to his comrade, Emir Seif ad-Din Salar. A staircase leads (right) to the mausoleums along a corridor surmounted by groined vaults and (left) to the mosque with its single *iwan*. The eastern gate of the courtyard opens onto the Qal'at el-Kabch district.

Napoleon Bonaparte visiting the French Institute in Egypt.

SULTAN MUSTAFA "SABIL-KUTTAB"
The façade of the circular *sabil* is pierced by large bays covered by bronze grilles. The interior is decorated with polychrome marble and faïence revetments. The *kuttab* is surmounted by a finely carved wood canopy.

MIDAN AS-SAYYIDA ZEINAB
The square was built during the second half of the 19th century during the reign of the khedive Ismaïl. It was renovated and extended after the canal which crossed it was filled in and has been constantly changing ever since. It owes its popularity to the presence of the As-Sayyida Zeinab Mosque (above and right), which is an important place of pilgrimage for Muslims. During the *muled* (anniversary of the birth) of Sayyida Zeinab, thousands of the faithful from all over Egypt gather in the square.

During the Ommiad period the modern working-class district of QAL'AT EL-KABCH was one of the most exclusive districts in Cairo. It experienced its Golden Age during the reign of Sultan An-Nasir Mohammed who carried out extensive renovations and constructed a water supply. At the end of the 14th century the district was destroyed and abandoned as a result of a power struggle between Prince Yalbugha and Sultan Sha'ban. Land and property were subsequently divided into plots and today buildings stand on sites once occupied by gardens.

QAITBAY MEDERSA. The medersa is situated in a square on the Shari' Qal'at el-Kabch. Founded by Sultan Qaitbay in 1475, one year after the construction of the mausoleum-medersa ▲ *328* on which it was based, it is characterized by a profusion of stalactites and honeycomb decorations, especially on the façade and below the balconies of the minaret. Inside there are four *iwan* and a courtyard covered by a wood ceiling. The wood casing of the mihrab is decorated with intricately carved polygonal stars. On the left, in the Shari' Abd el-Magid el-Labbani, the two stone benches in front of the (now condemned) wooden entrance of the YUSSEF BEY SABIL-KUTTAB (1634) are a favorite resting place for peddlers. The stone consoles that used to support the second floor can still be seen. Opposite the *sabil* the mosque founded by Sultan el-Malik el-Zahir Jaqmaq is named after Lajin el-Seifi who rebuilt it in 1449. Behind the mosque is a recently created GARDEN, reached via the Shari' Qadri opposite the Sarghatmish Medersa, which won the 1992 Aga Khan Award for Architecture.

AS-SAYYIDA ZEINAB MOSQUE. The mosque houses the shrine of Sayyida Zeinab, granddaughter of the Prophet and patron saint of Cairo, whose primitive mausoleum is said to be contemporary with that of El-Hussein ▲ *286*. The mosque, renovated in 1549 and rebuilt by Abd el-Rahman Katkhuda in 1761, used to have a columned prayer hall and was surmounted by small, flat domes. It was entirely rebuilt at the end of the 18th century and extended and restored in 1884 and again in 1942. The main façade, minaret and cupola are typical of the Mameluke architectural style.

314

The interior is richly decorated with arabesques and inscriptions, while the colonnaded prayer hall has a painted wood ceiling and is surmounted by a cupola in front of the mihrab. The mausoleum, to the west, is also surmounted by a cupola supported by a pendentive of stalactites. The cenotaph is surrounded by a finely worked bronze grille. Opposite is the SULTAN MUSTAFA SABIL-KUTTAB (1759).

BEIT AS-SINNARI. The Beit as-Sinnari is reached by taking the first street on the right after the *sabil*, turning left into the Shari' Hassan el-Kashef and then right into a narrow alleyway named after a former president of the French Institute, Gaspard Monge (1746–1818). Built in 1794 by Prince Ibrahim Katkhuda as-Sinnari, the house was requisitioned in 1798 (as were the now nonexistent houses of Hassan Kashef and Qasim Bey) as a residence for the scientists and scholars of the Egypt Expedition's scientific mission.

The building has all the characteristic elements of Cairene houses ● *116* of that period. To the north the *tahtabuch* forms a wide loggia which opens onto a courtyard, and is surmounted by a *maqaad* with a separate entrance. The harem suite comprises several rooms and *qaa* which are interconnected by a series of stairways and passages. The main *qaa* overlooks both the street and the

courtyard, while the huge *mashrabiya* bays of the second *qaa*, to the west, look onto the courtyard.

SHARI' PORT SAID OR EL-KHALIG. Today it is difficult to imagine the former charm of this district, which was totally transformed by the urban development of the early 20th-century. The El-Khalig Canal was first dug during the Pharaonic period to link the Nile and the Red Sea and was subsequently filled in and re-dug many times. In the 14th century it was rebuilt and opened to navigation by An-Nasir Mohammed and soon became a popular place for boating. The canal, fed by the Nile opposite Roda Island ▲ *283*, crossed the city from north to south. It was navigable almost all year, when the waters of the Nile were high.

During the Nile floods (between August 10 and 20), a special ceremony was held to let the water into the canal by breaking the small dyke at its mouth. The event was followed by a great public celebration during which the Cairenes took to the stretch of water between the Nile and the El-Khalig Canal. In 1897 the canal was filled in once again to make way for a tram line. It was replaced by the Shari' el-Khalig el-Masri, which was later widened and renamed Shari' Port Said.

THE FRENCH INSTITUTE IN EGYPT
On July 12, 1798, Napoleon Bonaparte landed in Alexandria with 38,000 men, including a scientific mission consisting of a team of mathematicians, engineers, scientists, economists, artists and writers. The leading members of the mission formed a society, based on the French Institute, with the aim of studying the resources and development of Egypt. The results of their work were published in *La Description de l'Egypte* (1809), which included more than three thousand illustrations.

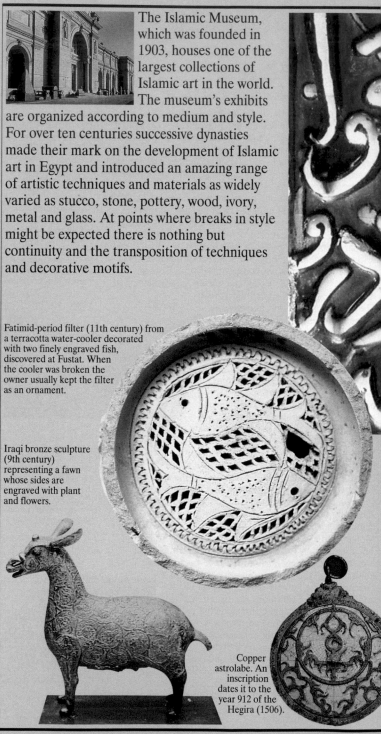

The Islamic Museum, which was founded in 1903, houses one of the largest collections of Islamic art in the world. The museum's exhibits are organized according to medium and style. For over ten centuries successive dynasties made their mark on the development of Islamic art in Egypt and introduced an amazing range of artistic techniques and materials as widely varied as stucco, stone, pottery, wood, ivory, metal and glass. At points where breaks in style might be expected there is nothing but continuity and the transposition of techniques and decorative motifs.

Fatimid-period filter (11th century) from a terracotta water-cooler decorated with two finely engraved fish, discovered at Fustat. When the cooler was broken the owner usually kept the filter as an ornament.

Iraqi bronze sculpture (9th century) representing a fawn whose sides are engraved with plant and flowers.

Copper astrolabe. An inscription dates it to the year 912 of the Hegira (1506).

Elaborately worked
bronze lamp
(Mameluke period)
from the Sultan
Hassan Medersa
▲ 308.

Detail of a wood-
paneled room, inlaid
with decorative motifs
in mother-of-pearl.

Glass lamp (14th
century) from the
Sultan Hassan
Medersa ▲ 308,
decorated with
Koranic verses and
phrases honoring the
sultan.

Page from an Arabic manuscript (1582)
describing the beneficial effects and medicinal
properties of certain plants and herbs.

Ancient Coptic religious community (above)

BABYLON
At the time of the Arab conquest in 640, Babylon was a large fort with huge towers, bastions and a 40-foot-high outer wall with a moat. It had a port, and two Nilometers, and was linked to the Red Sea by a canal which had existed in the days of Ancient Egypt. The Nile, which now lies 400 yards or so further west, flowed at the foot of these fortifications, whose remains can still be seen today. The fort

was also known as Qasr el-Shamaa (Castle of the Candle), *shamaa* (candle) being in fact a corruption of the Coptic word *khemi* (Egyptian).

Remains of the Fort of Babylon (above).

THE COPTS

Traditionally, the Apostle Mark is said to have preached Christianity in Egypt in c. AD 40. Within the context of the Roman and Byzantine occupations, Egypt became one of the main theaters of a schismatic activity which culminated in the appearance of Arianism in Alexandria in c. AD 318. As the object of Roman persecution, Christianity in Egypt took to the desert and gave rise to the cenobite monasticism preached by Saint Pachomius at the beginning of the 3rd century. During the reign of Constantine (324–37) the Egyptians converted en masse but, in response to Byzantine oppression, adopted the Monophysite doctrine which affirms the one, primarily divine, nature of Christ. This hostility toward Byzantium helps to explain the ease with which the Persians (in 619) and later the Muslim armies ● 66 were able to capture Memphis and Babylon. A century later there was a major movement to convert to Islam, but this was accompanied by major uprisings against Arab domination in 725 and 739. Egypt remained predominantly Christian until the mid-9th century, but between the 12th and 14th centuries the present proportion of a 90-percent Muslim population was established. The Delta has a small Coptic population concentrated in Middle Egypt, between Minya and Assiut. Social and religious life is centered around the church, presided over by priests (who are allowed to marry), but it is the monasteries, especially Deir Amba Baramus ▲ *208*, which constitute the focal points of the Coptic community and the seat of its episcopal hierarchy.

🚶 Half a day

Exterior, interior and icons in El-Muallaqa (St Mary's Church).

OLD CAIRO

FORT OF BABYLON. The name Babylon is a corruption of the ancient name Pi-Hapi-n-On, meaning "the home of Hapi" (the Nile god). The site of Old Cairo is believed to have been occupied, well before the arrival of the Romans, by an important settlement which was the forerunner of the towns founded subsequently on the site.

EL-MUALLAQA OR ST MARY'S CHURCH. El-Muallaqa, dedicated to the Virgin Mary, is said to have been built between the end of the 3rd and beginning of the 4th century. The name Muallaqa ("suspended") is derived from the fact that its floor was constructed on two of the

319

**GATE OF
ST GEORGE'S
CONVENT**
A wooden gate
leads onto a small
courtyard and
St George's Convent,
today inhabited by
thirty or so nuns.

towers of the ancient Roman fortress, covered with palm
trunks and a layer of stone. The church originally consisted of
the southeastern section or "upper church", now appearing as
an addition. The main church is said to have been built
between the 5th and 6th centuries. Destroyed in the 9th and
rebuilt in the 11th century, the church became the seat of the
Coptic patriarchate until the 14th century. The set of twenty-
nine steps leading to the entrance so impressed 14th- and
15th-century travelers that it became known as the "staircase
church". The interior is divided into four naves by three rows
of marble columns and has seven sanctuaries, six in the two
side aisles and one in the upper Church of St Mark. In front
of the central sanctuary is an 11th-century pulpit supported by
fifteen marble columns. A wooden staircase leads to the
chapel of the Ethiopian saint, Takla Haymanot, built on one
of the bastions of the fortress. The craftsmanship of the 10th-
and 13th-century iconostases, in cedar, ebony and walnut
inlaid with ivory, is truly remarkable, as is the collection of
over one hundred icons, the oldest of which dates from the
8th century. Other objects belonging to the church, such as
icons and manuscripts, are preserved in the Coptic Museum.
THE GREEK CHURCH OF ST GEORGE. A long set of steps leads
to one of the few round churches which still exist in the East,
built on part of the outer wall and the Roman towers.
Although rebuilt in 1904 and extensively restored after several
fires, it has retained some of its beautiful stained-glass
windows.
COPTIC QUARTER. A huge, studded
wooden gate opens onto Hara Mari
Girgis, a narrow street which still has its
original paving stones.
ST GEORGE'S CONVENT. The
convent is situated at no. 17 Hara
Mari Girgis. Only the chapel, the
oldest part (10th century) of the
convent, can be visited. Its old wooden ceiling has been
replaced, but it still has several original wood fixtures,
including three doors, one 23 feet high, with beautiful
decorations in relief.
KENISET MARI GIRGIS OR ST GEORGE'S CHURCH. A
small porchway, beyond no. 9 Hara Mari Girgis,
leads into Atfa Mari Girgis. St George's Church,
on the right, was founded in 684 by Athanasius,
a wealthy scribe, and rebuilt in 1857. The
church has one ancient section, the Qaa el-
Arsan (wedding chamber), which dates from
the 4th century. Formerly reserved for the
Coptic marriage ceremony, the chamber
houses some real works of art: turned-wood
lattice windows, walls decorated with
paintings and elements in relief, and a
ceiling painted with colored frescos.
EL-ADRA OR CHURCH OF THE VIRGIN.
The 9th-century Church of the Virgin,
rebuilt in the 18th century, stands at
the far end of Atfa Mari Girgis.
**ABU SARGA OR THE CHURCH OF
ST SERGIUS.** The Church of St
Sergius is a typical example of

**CHURCH OF THE
VIRGIN**
In Coptic and Arab
manuscripts from the
17th century onward,
the church (above)
was known as
Keniset el-Adra
Qasriyet el-Rihan
(Church of the
Virgin and the Pot of
Basil). It can no
longer be visited as it
was ravaged by fire
in 1975.

The tower of the
Church of the Virgin
(right).

"THIS COUNTRY IS A PALIMPSEST, IN WHICH THE BIBLE IS WRITTEN OVER HERODOTUS, AND THE KORAN OVER THAT."

LADY DUFF GORDON

Coptic churches and monasteries. Its façade is no different from those of the neighboring houses. Founded at the end of the 4th century and rebuilt at the beginning of the 11th century, it stands on a crypt that is said to have sheltered the Holy Family during their flight from Egypt. It is a place of pilgrimage for Christians of all denominations and is named after Saint Sergius and Saint Bacchus, soldiers martyred during the reign of Maximian. The church, built along the lines of an Eastern basilica with a single nave, three sanctuaries separated by iconostases and two side aisles delimited by arches resting on columns, houses some extremely fine examples of marquetry work inlaid with ivory, especially in the sanctuaries. The

The 14th-century Arab geographer Maqrizi (1364–1442) described Sitt Barbara, or St Barbara's Church (above), as the largest and most beautiful Coptic church of its time. Most of the woodwork is now in the Coptic Museum and the only piece remaining in the church is a 13th-century carved wood iconostasis inlaid with ivory (left).

original altar can be seen in the Coptic Museum.

SITT BARBARA OR ST BARBARA'S CHURCH. The church, originally constructed between the 4th and 5th centuries and rebuilt during the 11th century, still has an ancient chapel in which the relics of Saint Cyrus and Saint John (to whom it was originally dedicated) are preserved. It also has some remarkable wood paneling, some of which is in the Coptic Museum, and a series of icons. At the far end of Hara Sitt Barbara, the CONVENT OF ST BARBARA stands in a pleasant garden setting with a view of the ancient fortifications and part of the cemeteries. The convent comprises several buildings, including a school built in 1960 by the architect Ramesses Wissa Wassef.

BEN-EZRA SYNAGOGUE. The synagogue was built on the site of the 8th-century Church of St Michael, which was in turn built on the ruins of an ancient synagogue said to have been founded in c. 605–562 BC by Jews led back into Egypt by Jeremiah, on the very spot where Moses prayed in the 13th century BC. In 1115 the Rabi Abraham Ben-Ezra persuaded the Coptic patriarchate to restore the land, without tribute, to the Jewish community and had the synagogue rebuilt. Its recently restored, relatively simple exterior contrasts with the intricacy and richness of the interior decoration, the 12th-century woodwork in particular. During reconstruction work carried out in 1894 a GENIZA (a repository for documents) was discovered. It had been designed to store all the documents containing a reference to God and which could therefore not be destroyed without

The Ben-Ezra Synagogue houses a large number of antiques, including several ancient Torah (above).

321

In 1910 Marcos Simaïka Pasha, aware of the very specific nature of an art belonging to a period which extended from early Christian times to the Arab conquest in the 7th century, collected funds by subscription and founded Cairo's first Coptic Museum on land belonging to the Coptic Church. The simple lines of the building are emphasized by the elaborately carved *mashrabiya* work from ancient palaces and houses. A new wing was added in 1947 to accommodate the collection of Coptic antiquities put together by Gaston Maspero (1846–1916), which had previously been exhibited in the Cairo Museum.

One of the five pieces of a linen and wool wall hanging (above) whose central section represents Leda and the swan.

Detail from a parchment of magical texts.

Wall fresco.

Painted wooden icon (18th century) showing the two Coptic saints, Abrakaad and Ogbani, who are wearing animal masks.

SAINT ANTHONY AND SAINT PAUL
Painted wooden icon (18th century) illustrating a visit by Saint Anthony to the white-bearded Saint Paul. Beside him is the raven which brought him bread every day in its beak.

Bronze oil lamp of the type used to illuminate Coptic churches, with a handle in the form of an imaginary animal.

Details from a piece of Coptic fabric (4th or 5th century) on which flute players (above), dancers and Amazons carrying shields are embroidered with wool and silk threads.

Detail of a 3rd- or 4th-century linen curtain showing a centaur inside a medallion.

Napoleon Bonaparte is said to have built the first windmills in Egypt (their remains can still be seen today) on the plateau of Fustat (above). Their number was subsequently increased, reaching seventy-five by the end of the 18th century. They survived until 1982 when they began to disappear as the area (which today has thirty thousand inhabitants) began to be populated.

sacrilege. According to legend, the scribe Ezra concealed Moses' incomplete Torah there. Among the (now widely dispersed) documents more than 250,000 are said to have dated from 1002 to 1266, including at least 7,000 of great historical value. They constitute a valuable source of information on Cairo during the Fatimid period seen through the eyes of the Jewish community of Fustat.

FUSTAT AND THE ARAB CONQUEST. When he arrived in Egypt in 640 Amr Ibn el-As ● *66* pitched camp in a large vineyard on the banks of the river to the north of the Fort of Babylon and thus founded Fustat ("encampment"), the first Arab settlement in Egypt. Legend has it that as he was striking camp to move on to Alexandria, Amr discovered a pair of doves nesting on his tent and ordered them to be left untouched. Upon his return the tent was replaced by a mosque around which the *khittat* (districts) were established, as a result of the military concessions granted to each of the ethnic and tribal groups represented among the thousands of soldiers who had fought in the campaign. For three centuries Fustat continued to expand, incorporating the old Fort of Babylon and the town of El-Askar ▲ *270* and finally becoming part of the city of El-Qatai' ▲ *312*. It reached the height of its glory at the end of the 9th century when it (and not Alexandria) became one of the major commercial centers and one of the largest cities (with 120,000 inhabitants over an area of 750 acres) in the Mediterranean Basin. In 1175 the vizier Shawar ordered the city to be razed to the ground to prevent it falling into the hands of the Crusaders. Today all that can be seen is the black smoke from the kilns of the potters who have moved onto this vast wasteland. The last of the several excavation projects carried out at Fustat between the Amr Ibn el-As Mosque and the Greek Orthodox cemetery were the Gayraud excavations which began in 1982 at Istabl Antar, a former powder magazine built on top of the plateau.

AMR IBN EL-AS MOSQUE. The mosque stands in the Shari' Mari Girgis about 350 yards north of the Coptic district. Built by Amr Ibn el-As in 642, it was Africa's first mosque. It was originally a simple rectangle (197 x 118 feet) of clay bricks with a low ceiling supported by palm trunks. It was used for teaching long before the El-Azhar Mosque ▲ *294* was built and could hold up to five thousand students. The mosque has been destroyed, rebuilt and renovated many times, particularly in 1798 by Murad Bey, who gave it its present form: a parallelogram (394 x 360 feet) with four porticos supported by 150 white marble columns, 8 doors and 3 minarets. It was extensively restored and almost entirely rebuilt in reinforced concrete in the 1970's.

Icon depicting Saint Mercurius.

CHURCH AND CONVENT OF ST MERCURIUS. The Church and Convent of St Mercurius or Abu Seifein are situated to the north of the Amr Ibn el-As Mosque, outside the Roman fortifications but inside the rectangle formed by the Coptic, Maronite, Anglican and Protestant cemeteries. After several fires this extremely ancient church was used as a sugar-cane warehouse before being reconsecrated in the 11th century. Inside a painting of Christ and the twelve Apostles hangs in front of the 10th-century sanctuary whose wooden dome is supported by demi-cupolas decorated with biblical scenes. The walls of the second-floor Chapel of St George have revealed several layers of paintings from different periods. A staircase on the north side of the church leads to a crypt where Saint Barsum is said to have lived for twenty years during the 14th century. The 6th-century convent, one of the oldest in Egypt, was entirely rebuilt in the 10th century. Today it is occupied by nuns and is not open to the public. Its wealth of artistic treasures, including an extraordinary collection of icons, makes it a real school of Coptic art.

Details of marquetry work (below) from the Church of St Mercurius.

CHURCH OF AMBA-SHENUDA. The 7th-century church was converted into a mosque in the 11th century. Three centuries later it was restored and reverted to its original function. It has three naves, separated by two rows of marble columns. The iconostasis, in red cedar inlaid with ivory, contains a series of seven extremely valuable icons. It also possesses a triptych of Greek origin and a 14th-century glass lamp.

✻ One day

THE COMPLEX OF SULTAN QAITBAY
The complex was once made of of several buildings, but now only the mosque and the medersa (interior, above), which houses the tomb of the sultan, remain.

KHUND TUGHAY MAUSOLEUM
Khund Tughay, also known as Umm Anuk, favorite wife of An-Nasir Mohammed and mother of his son Anuk, died in 1348. Today all that remains of the original complex, which consisted of a *khanqa* with two *iwan* and a mausoleum surmounted by a cupola, is the vaulted *iwan* and the drum of the cupola with its (now largely destroyed) richly decorated faïence frieze.

The area (about 2,500 acres), cultural wealth and ancient history of Cairo's Muslim cemeteries make them an important part of the city. Their position on its immediate outskirts, extending for a distance of about 7 miles from north to south, constitutes a barrier to Cairo's eastward expansion.

A CITY WITHIN A CITY. At first glance the cemeteries are characterized by a rich and varied use of space and building styles, and it would be no exaggeration to refer to them in terms of cities and urban planning. The plots on which the tombs are built can vary from a few square yards to several hundred square yards or more. They form a network which combines a regular, orthogonal framework born of a desire for order and economy of space with a remarkable freedom and complexity of organization: two extremes which not only coexist but interpenetrate.

The diversity of the plots has given rise to a similar diversity of architectural forms: the tombs can be simple stone parallelepipeds decorated with two stelae, mausoleums surmounted by cupolas in garden settings, intricately carved wood "kiosks" or even "towns" with several buildings.

LIVING AMONG THE DEAD. Cairo currently has two necropolises and four cemeteries used by Muslims. Together they represent 6.4 percent of the surface area of Cairo itself and 3.6 percent of its suburbs. The vast "City of the Dead" is also inhabited by the living. The two great necropolises have a permanent population of 179,000 inhabitants, of whom almost 20,000 live inside the perimeters while the rest live on the outskirts of these two great burial sites. It is worth taking a closer look at two of Cairo's cemeteries in particular: the Mameluke Cemetery, to the east of the medieval city, and the Southern or Imam as-Shafi'i Cemetery.

THE MAMELUKE TOMBS

THE FUNERARY COMPLEX OF SULTAN QAITBAY
The buildings which comprised the funerary complex of Sultan Qaitbay were surrounded by a wall.

The Eastern Cemetery contains the tombs of the Circassian Mamelukes, including those of five sultans: Barquq, El-Ashraf Barsbey, El-Ashraf Inal, Abu Saïd Qunsua and Qaitbay. There were twenty-one other monuments, made up of the tombs of Mameluke princes and princesses and nine mosques.

SOUTHWEST OR AZROMOK COMPLEX. The tomb of EL-ASHRAF AZROMOK (1505), recognizable by the blue enamel ribs of the cupola, is reached by carrying straight on after the flyover at the end of the Shari' El-Azhar and taking the first street on the right, the Shari' Qarafet Bab el-Wazir. By retracing your steps, the SULTAN MOHAMMED KUZ EL-ASSAL (said to have existed only in the popular imagination) cupola or "honey pot" can be seen on the right. Further north the street takes the name of the Sultan Ahmed, and, 100 yards or so further on, on the left, stands the monument of KHUND TUGHAY (1348). Opposite the monument is the cupola of the PRINCESS TOLBIYA MAUSOLEUM (1363), Sultan An-Nasir's principal wife. To the north the TOMB OF GUZAL (1403) stands on the right while, on the left, behind the *hochs*, is the TOMB OF AZDUMUR and, as you turn into the Shari' el-Afifi, the TOMB OF TASCTUMUR (1334). Three hundred yards or so further on a tiny square leads to the ROYAL CHAPEL, dedicated to the sons of Mohammed Ali. The complex, which occupies an area of about 242,000 square feet, was designed in 1894 by Fabricius Bey. It includes several different types of tombs, from the simple marble tombstones in the gardens reserved for the princesses to the chapel surmounted by a cupola housing the tombs of the khedives Tawfiq and Abbas Helmi.

Two different views of the Sultan Barsbey Complex (above). The Sultan Inal Complex and Ounas Mausoleum (opposite page).

QAITBAY MAUSOLEUM
The overall harmony of the proportions of the last mausoleum to be built in this Mameluke wasteland by Sultan Qaitbay (1418–96) is striking. The richly decorated prayer hall with its marble-covered floor and a detail of the mihrab (above).

QAITBAY CEMETERY

The Qaitbay Cemetery is reached by following the Shari' el-Afifi westward. On the right between two apartment blocks, the QAITBAY GATE leads into the heart of a suburb established at the end of the 19th century on the waste ground surrounding the Mameluke tombs. It extends from the Qaitbay to the Barquq complex and in 1986 had a population of 17,255 (compared with 2,287 in 1897). To the north lies a small square bordered on the west by the QAITBAY MOSQUE. The building, which consists of a mosque-medersa, a *sabil-kuttab* and a mausoleum, is only the central unit of a remarkable complex linked by some historians with a "royal suburb". By continuing northeast you come to the 15th-century SHEIKH YUSSEF TAKIYA on the left, while directly opposite, on the other side of the street, a block of houses conceals a brick cupola, the QOBBET KHANDIJA UMM EL-ASHRAF (1430).

SULTAN BARSBEY COMPLEX. A 985-foot-long wall, pierced by a double row of windows, identifies the complex of Sultan Barsbey (1432), who reigned for sixteen years (1422–38). The complex covered an area of about 32,000 square feet and consisted of four buildings situated on either side of the central street. On the east side, the medersa and *khanqa* share the same façade and are linked by an interior communicating passage leading from the main entrance, although each has a separate, secondary entrance. The other buildings, about 300 yards from the first two, are a *zawia*

(whose ruins can still be seen today) dedicated to the poor and, opposite, the 16th-century Qobbet ar-Rifa'i convent surmounted by a cupola. Beyond the complex lies a flatter and less densely built-up area where the tombs of Gani Beik el-Ashrafi (1430) and Qurqumas (1511), which until 1981 stood in front of the El-Hakim Mosque ▲ *291*, are surrounded by railings.

SULTAN BARQUQ "KHANQA". This was the first and largest monument to be built (1400–11) in the necropolis. The square building (50,000 square feet in area) is surmounted by two symmetrical minarets and two symmetrical cupolas at both ends of the northeast façade. Between them a smaller, third cupola heightens the central mihrab. The north cupola houses the tombs of the sultan and his sons, while the south cupola contains the tombs of his wives. The northern corner of the building is occupied by a triple-arched SABIL-KUTTAB on the two loggia sides, which offers a general view of the complex. The northern section of the cemetery consists of a network of roads, small squares and gardens laid out in the 1950's, which provide the setting for the two adjoining burial sites: the EMIR QURQUMAS MEDERSA AND MAUSOLEUM (1506–7), mainly inspired by the COMPLEX OF SULTAN QAITBAY, whose equerry he was, and the Sultan Inal Complex (1451–6). The cupola at the center of a five-road intersection is all that remains of the last monument in this necropolis, that of SULTAN QUNSUA ABU SAÏD, who reigned for a year in 1798.

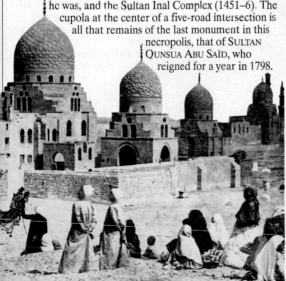

SULTAN INAL COMPLEX
There is no comparison between the sultan's eight year reign and his magnificent tomb (detail above), which comprises a

mausoleum, a *khanqa*, a mosque, a medersa, a *zawia* and a *sabil*.

Exterior view of the
Mameluke tombs.

This broad avenue,
which runs between
two rows of "palace-
tombs", is the main
thoroughfare through
the Imam as-Shafi'i
Cemetery. With its
interwoven
patchwork of old and
more recent
residential blocks,
which have filled
every available space,
and the constant
noise of passing
traffic, the cemetery
is a busy place. The
hubbub reaches its
peak on Fridays when
visitors come to the
cemetery and one of
the largest
fleamarkets in Cairo
is held.

**EL-SULTANIYA
MAUSOLEUM**
The mausoleum
(1350) houses the
tomb of the mother
of Sultan Hassan
(1347–61) ▲ 309.
The recently restored,
rectangular structure
consists of a vaulted
iwan flanked by two
identical cupolas.

SOUTHERN CEMETERY

The Southern Cemetery has been Cairo's main burial site
since the Arab conquest in 640. Today it covers an area of
around 1,375 acres and contains twenty-six monuments to
ascetics, canonists, holy men and descendants of the Prophet,
as well as the forty-seven funerary monuments of the emirs
and sultans from the Ikhshidid, Fatimid, Mameluke and
Ottoman periods. Since the early 1980's the necropolis, which
once formed a continuation of the city, has been cut off by a
network of motorways, freeways and flyovers which has
surrounded it and cut through it, leaving only a few links in
the north.

IMAM AS-SHAFI'I CEMETERY. The BAB EL-QARAFA, built in
1499 by the sultan Qaitbay, marks the entrance to the
cemetery at the intersection of the Shari' Salah Salim freeway
and the Imam as-Shafi'i Avenue. Take the Shari' el-Qadiriya,
named after the descendants of Sheikh Abd el-Qader el-
Ghilani who settled (date unknown) around the ZEIN AD-DIN
YUSSEF MEDERSA AND MAUSOLEUM (1298), the first
monument on the right. The Shari' el-Qadiriya bends slightly
to the right and then to the left before joining the Imam as-
Shafi'i Avenue.

IMAM AS-SHAFI'I MAUSOLEUM. The south end of the avenue
leads into a small square formed by the demolition of tombs
and *hochs*. On the right stands the tomb of Imam as-Shafi'i,
the founder of one of the four orthodox schools of Sunni
jurisprudence and creator of the social philosophy of Islam, a
retiring man who devoted himself to prayer. He died in 820.
The rectangular mausoleum, commissioned by Salah ad-Din
● 66 and built in 1211, is one of the largest in Egypt and
measures 49 feet along the inside and 67 feet along the
outside wall. The stone structure supports a wood cupola
which is similar to the Rocher dome. It houses the
cenotaphs of the imam, the sultan el-Kamel Ayyub
(1218–38) and Sayyed Mohammed Abd el-Hakam, who
shared the former tomb of the imam. The present
structure is very different from the
original.

EL-BASHA "HOCH". Turn
right as you leave the
avenue and join
the Shari' el-

Imam el-Leisi (which runs parallel to the avenue) via a network of narrow streets. Follow it northward, turning right after about 300 yards, and you come to the tiny, white-painted mausoleum of MOHAMMED EL-HASSWATI (1160), whose square tomb is surmounted by a brick cupola. To the north the five cupolas of the El-Basha *hoch* can be seen outlined against the sky. The royal chapel, which dates from 1820, contains the khedivial tombs of Tussun, Ibrahim, Abbas and Farouk, Mohammed Ali's sons and grandsons who succeeded him on the throne of Egypt, as well as the tombs of their wives, children and servants.

All that remains of the Menufi *iwan*, once part of a magnificent late 13th-century edifice, is the huge cupola and vaulted *iwan*.

MAMELUKE CEMETERY

The Mameluke Cemetery lies to the south of the Citadel and is part of the Southern Cemetery. As you leave the Imam as-Shafi'i Cemetery, turn right into a narrow alleyway about 50 yards after the NUR AD-DIN MOSQUE (1575). This leads to the Mameluke Cemetery, which is devoid of roads and where the tall, isolated minarets serve as landmarks among the ruins. The first of the twelve funerary monuments is the EL-SULTANIYA MAUSOLEUM (1350), while further on, on the right, stands the EMIR QUSUN MINARET (1335), which is all that remains of what was one of the first burial complexes built in the cemetery under the Bahrid Mamelukes. To the west is a complex comprising the small BADR AD-DIN EL-QARAFI MAUSOLEUM (1300) surmounted by a cupola, and the 14th-century south minaret, the EL-RIHAN IWAN (1534), the stone cupola of the SUDUN MAUSOLEUM (1504) and the small, brick cupola of the EL-SAWABI MAUSOLEUM (1286) stand around a small square.

TOMBS OF THE MAMELUKES
The El-Basha *hoch* (above) also houses the tombs of the Mamelukes that Mohammed Ali had assassinated on his accession ● 68.

About 100 yards further on, on the left, are two 14th-century mausoleums, both named after TANKHIZBUGHA, while beyond these, on the left, the solitary MENUFI IWAN stands at the corner of a recently built mosque. As you leave the cemetery you can see two monuments perched on the Jebel Moqattam: the GAHINA EL-KHALWATI KHANQA and the EL-GUYUSHI MASHHAD.

The Gahina el-Khalwati *khanqa* (left), built in 1538, is the more northerly of the two funerary monuments on Jebel Moqattam. The other, the El-Guyushi *mashhad*, was built in 1085 by the Fatimid vizier Badr el-Gamali (also known as Emir el-Guyushi) who governed Egypt between 1074 and 1094. It is considered the most important shrine of the Fatimid period.

Artist's impression of the site of Memphis as it might have looked in about 800 BC.

The ruins of the ancient city of Memphis are situated on the left bank of the River Nile about 19 miles south of Cairo. Although most of the visible remains are not particularly spectacular, Memphis really should be visited before the Pyramids of Giza and Saqqara for two reasons: firstly, because these sites are in fact the two main necropolises of Memphis; and secondly, because Memphis played a key role in Egyptian history for over three thousand years. The city was founded by the first 1st-Dynasty king Menes (or Narmer) and, although it was not the capital as such (this is too modern a concept), it has almost always been the center of Egypt. Its role as such has been favored by its geographical location on the boundary between Lower and Upper Egypt and almost at the apex (point of divergence) of the Nile Delta. As a result Memphis and its immediate environs became known, among other things, as the juncture of the Two Lands. The name Memphis was derived from the Greek form of the Egyptian *Men-neter*, which was an abbreviation of the name of the Pyramid of Pepy I at Saqqara and its dependency. The main part of the ruins, which corresponds in general terms to the city's largest sanctuary, the so-called Sanctuary of Ptah and its dependencies, are situated near the village of MIT RAHINA. Part of the village is perched on a vast, high hill (*kom* or *tell* in Arabic) formed from accumulated and stratified archeological layers. To the east of the hill can be found the buildings of the village of BEDRASHEIN.

Memphis is also known to the Egyptians as "Hout-ka-Ptah", or "Castle of the *ka* of Ptah", which could possibly be the origin of the word "Egypt" (via the Greek *Aïguptios*).

COLOSSUS OF RAMESSES II.
Isolated remains are all that can be seen of the city of Memphis. In a building at the entrance to the site is a statue of the pharaoh Ramesses II. This huge limestone colossus (right) used to stand before the gates of the Sanctuary of Ptah; today it lies upon the ground. A princess stands at the knee of the pharaoh, who is dressed in a loincloth and is wearing the *pschent*, the double crown of Upper and Lower Egypt. A colossus of the same pharaoh, discovered lying next to the first, was transported to Cairo in 1955, where it now stands, in Ramses Square ▲ *273*. Behind the kiosk containing the colossus an OPEN-AIR MUSEUM houses various monuments from the site: statues, monumental stelae including one belonging to the 26th-Dynasty king Apries, and a beautiful 18th-Dynasty sphinx known as the "alabaster sphinx". On the other side of the road are the remains of the embalming tables used for the Apis Bulls (26th Dynasty). The best preserved of these is in alabaster and decorated with lions' heads. It is over 17 feet long and almost 10 feet wide.
SANCTUARY OF PTAH. Further west, below the village of Mit-Rahina, a short walk brings you to the site of the Sanctuary of Ptah, built during the reign of Ramesses II. All that remains of this vast edifice, which is on the scale of Karnak ▲ *404*, are the bases of columns and walls standing in mud. However, research is still being carried out on the site of Memphis and some important archeological and historical results are currently emerging.

The Great Pyramid,
the largest of the
three Pyramids of
Giza, is the only one
of the Seven Wonders
of the World (as
defined by classical
antiquity) to have
survived to the
present day. With its
two neighbors and
the Sphinx, ever
watchful at the foot
of the plateau, the
Great Pyramid
continues to fire the
imagination of all
those who see it. It
owes its survival to
the simplicity and
perfection of its
design.

PYRAMIDS OF GIZA

The "Pyramids" are situated on the desert plateau which
marks the boundary of the vast urban complex of Giza
(pronounced with a hard "g"), which is in fact a suburb of
Cairo. Today there is a tendency to refer to the "Pyramids of
Giza" even though the Egyptian name for the site is *El-
Ahram* ("the Pyramids"), a name which was also used by
Western visitors prior to the meteoric rise of the village of
Giza. Although the site extends beyond the plateau of Giza
and despite the fact that there are many other pyramids in the
Libyan Desert (in an area extending from Abu Rawash in the
north to Lisht ▲ *356* in the south), the exclusivity of the name
is justified by the sheer magnificence of these three pyramids,
which have been renowned since classical antiquity and even
from the time of the Ancient Egyptians. The pyramids are in
fact the tombs of three 4th-Dynasty pharaohs: Khufu (Cheops
in Greek), Khafre (Chephren) and Menkaure (Mycerinus).
PYRAMIDS. The Egyptian pyramids, from the Pyramid of
Khufu (an unrivaled architectural masterpiece) to the more
modest pyramids belonging to less powerful or less ambitious
pharaohs, were tombs reserved for the pharaohs of the
Old Kingdom (3rd–6th Dynasties)
and part of the Middle Kingdom

❝I know that
philosophers may
groan or smile at the
thought that the
greatest monument
ever created by
mankind is a tomb;
but why see the
Pyramid of Cheops
merely as a pile of
stones and a
skeleton.❞
François René de
Chateaubriand

(11th–12th Dynasties) and their queens. They are the principal element of a large architectural complex which, in addition to the actual pyramid, consisted of a funerary or "upper" temple, a small pyramid or "annex" (of religious or symbolic significance), and a causeway leading to a valley or "lower" temple which stood at the foot of the plateau, on the edge of the desert, and was linked to the Nile by a dock and a canal. The perfect and to some extent elementary design of the Pyramids of Giza in particular was the product of a long process which took place over several centuries incorporating various stages of development: superposed mastabas and the so-called "step" pyramids ● 84. The form of the monument also has several levels of symbolic significance. The pyramid was in fact the means by which the dead pharaoh rose to the firmament and joined the sun, far from the shadows of the tomb. It was also seen as an emanation of this heavenly body, the mineral concretization of the sun's rays. These are only two interpretations from an entire spectrum of symbolic images that the Ancient Egyptians associated with the pyramid. In spite of the many remaining obscurities (a situation which is not helped by the lack of any pre-5th Dynasty inscriptions in these sometimes gigantic monuments), there is still sufficient information to identify the occupants of the pyramids, even though most traces of them and their funeral paraphernalia have long since disappeared from the monuments they commissioned.

PYRAMID OF KHUFU. The pyramid is 755 feet square at its base, was originally 482 feet high (it lost 33 feet when the apex was removed) and has a total superposed volume

AVENUE OF THE PYRAMIDS
Once a pleasant, tree-lined avenue (left) led to the Pyramids of Giza. Today they are reached via a very ordinary and seemingly endless approach road, which has developed haphazardly and uncontrolledly, with its constant stream of traffic, hotch-potch of apartment blocks and bars interspersed with a few fields, and the gilt grandiloquence of the *Mena House Hotel*, formerly one of the grand palaces which marked the main staging posts on the India and Far East route.

WHAT IS A PYRAMID?
An Egyptian pyramid is nothing more than a tomb, in spite of what may have been or may be said by those lovers of false mysteries, the so-called "pyramidologists" and the adherents of a similar bogus form of Egyptology. But this is neither disheartening nor disappointing if it is considered within the context of Ancient Egyptian culture and its view of life, death and the divine monarchy. Nor does it detract from the often huge merit of those who designed and constructed these monuments.

DÉPOSÉ

CORRIDORS AND GALLERIES
A descending gallery leads from the entrance of the pyramid to an unfinished underground chamber hewn out of the living rock of the plateau. At one point it intersects an ascending corridor that widens and

opens out, a little further on, into the 28-foot-high Grand Gallery with its striking corbeled courses.

(assuming it were solid) of about 88 million cubic feet. According to tradition the entrance was on the north side and the corridors were aligned with the circumpolar stars ever-present on the horizon to ensure immortality. The present ENTRANCE, lower than the original entrance, is linked by a passageway to the "real" access corridor. There is "nothing to see" in the pyramid apart from the pyramid itself, whose interior construction and remarkable atmosphere (although the stale air can sometimes be tiring) make it a true architectural masterpiece.

INSIDE THE PYRAMID. The layout of the chambers and passageways inside the pyramid has been modified over the years. The descending gallery intersects an ascending corridor that opens out into the Grand Gallery. From the bottom of the gallery a horizontal passage leads into the so-called QUEEN'S CHAMBER (these traditional names have no factual basis). At the top of the Grand Gallery a sort of antechamber with granite portcullises leads into the main chamber, known as the KING'S CHAMBER. The precision and perfection of its construction make the chamber, which is almost 20 feet high, 34 feet long and 17 feet wide, an unrivaled piece of architecture. It is entirely sheathed in granite and the ceiling consists of granite monoliths. Above the chamber five "discharge" compartments were built to relieve the enormous weight above the ceiling. There is no doubt that this was the burial chamber of Khufu himself. The king's lidless granite sarcophagus is still in the chamber, although entirely empty, most probably plundered toward the end of the Old Kingdom. The architectural complex of Khufu is not limited to these underground chambers. The funerary or "UPPER" TEMPLE with its basalt flagging can still be seen on the east side of the pyramid. Recent (1992–3) discoveries have also made it possible to excavate part of the valley or "lower" temple, as well as a so-called "annex" pyramid in the village of Nazlet el-Saman.

SOLAR BARQUE. The so-called "Solar Barque" is preserved in an unprepossessing building, on the south side of the pyramid, above the 100-foot boat pit in which it was discovered, completely dismantled, in 1954. It

Climbing to the top of the pyramid was for a long time an obligatory if dangerous pastime among (even some of the most illustrious) tourists. This is now strictly forbidden.

took several years to restore the 140-foot, cedar-wood barque to its original elegance, complete with cabin and long oars. All the elements are joined with ropes and pegs, with not a nail in sight. The significance of such grandiose vessels is still the subject of much discussion. They may have actually been used, in particular for the king's funeral, or they may have been a representation of the Night- and Day-Barques of the Sun: a promise of immortality or at least of resurrection. Near the Pyramid of Khufu are two other monuments which, although they cannot be visited and are relatively unattractive, form part of the history of the site. The TOMB OF QUEEN HETEPHERES, the mother of Khufu, is one of the few royal tombs left untouched by grave robbers. The funerary treasures, discovered by an American expedition led by George Reisner, can be seen in the Cairo Museum ▲ 276. Also near the Great Pyramid, the temple of one of the smaller

Akhet-Khufu (the Ancient Egyptian name for the monument and architectural complex, meaning "the Horizon of Khufu") dates, like its two neighbors, from c. 2500 BC (it is impossible to give a more precise date for these early periods).

Although the climb to the top of the Pyramid of Khufu (Cheops) was perilous, it still proved a very popular undertaking among travelers and tourists. Each block of stone measured between 2 and 3 feet and the climb was far from easy.

The Pyramid of Khufu (surmounted by a pyramidion made of a single granite or basalt block) stood 479 feet high and covered an area of 12 acres. It consisted of 2½ million stone blocks, each 35 cubic feet, arranged in 201 courses.

In the center of the King's Chamber (33 feet long by 16 wide and 16 high) the pharaoh once lay in his sarcophagus surrounded by his now non-existent treasures. In spite of the many precautions taken by the tomb builders to obstruct and conceal the corridors, grave robbers managed to find their way into the tomb on several occasions.

"Suddenly the corridor rose steeply. The torch illuminated an imposing gallery, about 26 feet high, with corbeled upper courses. Breathing became easier and we might have been at the entrance to a magnificent temple were it not for the steps carved in this slippery slope. But they were only shallow notches about three feet apart and we advanced with great difficulty, often falling, unless supported by the Bedouins who climbed like cats along this eerie corridor. The dry stone blocks are so marvellously positioned that you would not get a pin between them."
Edouard Schuré

Drawings by Belzoni ● 95 showing the exposed entrance of the Pyramid of Khafre and the interior of the great burial chamber which he discovered in 1818.

(queens' or princesses') pyramids in the complex of Khufu was later converted into the SHRINE OF ISIS, "Mistress of the Pyramid" and *paredra* of Osiris, "Lord of Su-menu", whose own shrine was situated not far from the Sphinx, on the edge of the desert.

PYRAMID OF KHAFRE. Although the pyramid of Khafre (Chephren) is not quite as big (originally over 470 feet high, today over 446 feet) as his father's, it is nonetheless a striking sight with its white "cap" at the apex, the remains of the dazzling limestone casing which once completely covered the pyramids of both Khufu and Khafre. The interior is less complicated but just as impressive as that of Khufu. The Pyramid of Khafre, however, is renowned not so much just for itself but for the entire pyramidal complex: the partly preserved ascending causeway (descending if you approach it from the pyramid) and, lower down, at the entrance to the valley (where there is now a Sound and Light Auditorium), the impressive and extremely well-preserved valley or "lower" temple. Abu Hol, the Great Sphinx, which has become indissociably linked with the Pyramids, is also a "must" for all visitors to Egypt.

THE SPHINX. The Sphinx of Giza was undoubtedly carved out of a rocky spur which suggested its shape. Although it has long been the victim of erosion, and damage from upsurges of underground water, it has been cleared of sand and restored several times since antiquity, and remains one of the undisputed wonders of a civilization renowned for its architectural achievements. This colossus of Khafre (240 feet long and 65 feet high) is both the guardian and symbol of royalty. Other meanings have been attributed to it over the ages. During the New Kingdom it was seen as a representation of Re-Harakhti, the falcon-headed sun god, or Horem-Akhet (Horus on the Horizon, Harmachis in

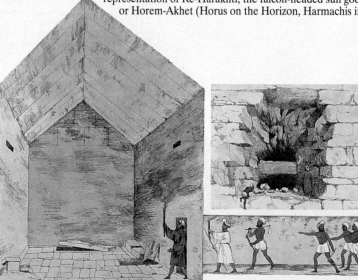

Greek), whom everyone came to worship and entreat. Young princes raised in Memphis came here either to meditate upon the concept of power or in search of legitimacy. Legend has it that the future Thutmose IV built a stele between the feet of the Sphinx following a dream that he had there in which the god Harmachis asked him to clear away the sand from his feet in return for his royalty. During the New Kingdom the Sphinx was also seen as a representation of the Syro-Canaanite god Hurun: an illustration of the ambient cosmopolitanism and the cultural and religious parallels of the period.

PYRAMID OF MENKAURE. The Pyramid of Menkaure (Mycerinus), which is much smaller than the other two, is beautifully constructed, distinguished by its red granite lower courses and extremely well-preserved underground chambers. An enormous stone sarcophagus that was found inside the pyramid and sent to England in the 19th century was unfortunately lost when the ship transporting it sank off the coast of Spain. Visitors who are leaving Menkaure are reminded of the semi-legendary tradition that the pyramid was built by Nitocris, the queen of the last of the 6th-Dynasty pharaohs (who is sometimes confused with the Saite courtesan Rhodopis). Until the 19th century it was generally believed that the pyramid was haunted and that as it approached noon the ghostly figure of a beautiful, naked woman would appear and cause the downfall of overzealous visitors.

"View of the Sphinx, Abu Hol (Father of Terror). The gray of the sand, the Pyramids and the Sphinx are steeped in a deep rosy hue; in the intensely blue sky eagles glide and circle slowly round the summits.**"**
Gustave Flaubert

Head of the Great Sphinx,
by Luigi Mayer (1755–1803).

Oedipus, oil on canvas
by Jean-Léon Gérôme (1824–1904).

Profile of the Head of the Great Sphinx,
by Frederik Ludvig Norden (1708–42).

*View of the Head of the Great Sphinx and the
Second Pyramid,* by L.F. Cassas (1756–1827)

For a long time the Sphinx
(which dates from c. 2500 BC)
remained engulfed by sand. In
1853 Auguste Mariette ● 96
began to clear it, a task which
was completed over forty
years later. *The Sphinx*
(right), by David
Roberts.

"... NOT A HIDEOUS COMPOUND ANIMAL ... BUT A SACRED SYMBOL OF THE UNION OF THE STRONGEST PHYSICAL WITH THE HIGHEST INTELLECTUAL POWER ON EARTH."

HARRIET MARTINEAU

The Sphinx, watercolor
by Emile Prisse d'Avenue (1807–79).

Head of the Great Sphinx and the Pyramids of Giza, print by David Roberts (1796–1864).

The Sphinx and the Pyramid of Giza, drawing
by Louis-Amable Crapelet (1822–67).

"Simoon" in the Desert, print
by David Roberts (1796–1825).

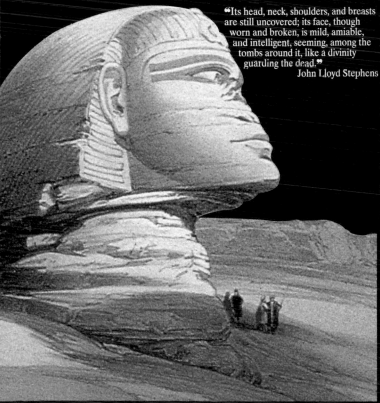

"Its head, neck, shoulders, and breasts
are still uncovered; its face, though
worn and broken, is mild, amiable,
and intelligent, seeming, among the
tombs around it, like a divinity
guarding the dead."

John Lloyd Stephens

343

🚗 🚶 One/two days

HARRANIA
The architect
Ramesses Wissa
Wassef ▲ *282* trained
young artists (in
whom he recognized
spontaneity and an
innate sense of

beauty) who, from
early childhood, had
revived an extremely
ancient tradition and
achieved total
mastery of design and
color in their carpets.
His work was
continued after his
death and the carpets
produced in his
workshop are
unrivaled, in spite of
many imitations.

SAQQARA

With Giza ▲ *334,* Saqqara is one of the two main necropolises
of Memphis ▲ *332.* Its monuments cover every period of
Egyptian history, including the Archaic period (these are now
engulfed by sand), the 3rd Dynasty and the Christian era.
Stretching across the desert is a string of non-royal pyramids
and cemeteries which also depended on Memphis. Although
these sites may not feature on many tourist itineraries (some
are in any case military zones and therefore out of bounds),
they are an important part of understanding Ancient Egypt
and especially the Old Kingdom. North of Giza, at the point
where the Nile Delta begins to diverge, the remains of the
Pyramid of Djededfre, the son of Khufu, can be seen at ABU
RAWASH. To the south is the site (out of bounds) of ZAWIYET
EL-ARYAN with its unfinished pyramid, which is in fact a vast,
preliminary excavation.
ABUSIR. The Abusir cemetery contains the pyramids of the
principal 5th-Dynasty pharaohs: (from north to south)
Sahure, Niuserre, Neferirkare and
Neferefre, all closely associated with the
worship of the solar god Re (who forms part

of each of their names). The pyramids are of average size and badly preserved although some still have their causeway (access ramp) and part of their funerary temple. The vast TOMB OF PTAHSHEPSES, situated between the Pyramids of Sahure and Niuserre, has been excavated and restored by an expedition from Czechoslovakia, which has worked regularly on the site for many years. The tomb is well worth a visit. A short walk across the desert brings you to the site of the sun temples of ABU GHUROB, to the north of Abusir. The TEMPLE OF NIUSERRE is open to the sky and has a central obelisk (known as a *benben*) symbolizing the light of the sun. Much further south are the Pyramids of Dahshur ▲ *354*.

NECROPOLIS OF MEMPHIS
Generally speaking the various branches of the Necropolis of Memphis correspond to a fairly recent (19th-century) breakdown which linked each site to a modern village in the valley, although these subdivisions are not always well founded. For example, north and central Saqqara are more closely linked to Abusir than to South Saqqara. And it should not be forgotten that the site is in the desert "west of Memphis".

GETTING TO SAQQARA. Most people travel to Saqqara by road. Alternatively you can cross the desert on horseback from the Pyramids of Giza. As you turn west at Bedrashein (not far from Memphis) it soon becomes obvious, whether you are following the road along the canal or the main highway leading toward Upper Egypt, that the region is becoming an albeit distant and partly agricultural suburb of Cairo. The landscape becomes increasingly urban: factories, poultry farms, houses, highways, private villas and "carpet schools" (which are nothing

more than workshops and shops centered around the mass tourist industry). The village of HARRANIA, a few miles from the main pyramid route is an interesting place to stop. It is the home of the famous carpet weavers who work in the Wissa Wassef ▲ *282* workshop (which also has a shop). As you leave the road which follows the canal and fork right (toward the west), the plateau will gradually come into view with the summit of the Step Pyramid over to the left. Once through the ticket barrier the road (which soon becomes a track) takes you into the heart of this vast site whose archeological and artistic wealth is truly overwhelming. As there are usually only a few hours allowed for this visit, it is important to be selective and well organized. The many monuments at Saqqara are often some distance apart, but you will find it extremely rewarding if you take your time walking across the plateau.

Necropolis of Abusir: the pyramids of Niuserre and Neferirkare (right), and the Pyramid of Sahure.

The funeral complex of Djoser with the remains of the Monastery of St Jeremiah in the foreground.

JUBILEE CHAPELS
The pavilions and chapels (in fact a series of décors and façades whose stone

doors are permanently open onto passageways suitable for ghostly processions) were built by Imhotep to immortalize Djoser's jubilee celebrations.

STEP PYRAMID. The visit usually starts with the Step Pyramid and vast funeral complex of Djoser, the 3rd-Dynasty pharaoh. The complex is truly remarkable, if only for its building materials, as this was the first monumental structure to be built entirely of stone. It is also one of the most ancient monuments in Egypt, and even the world, as it dates from c. 2500 BC. Imhotep, the highly talented architect and master of works of Djoser, was also a vizier, doctor of medicine and literary scholar. Over the centuries the figure of Imhotep assumed a superhuman dimension, becoming a sort of demigod of medicine and healing whom the Greeks associated with Asclepius (Aesculapius). The Step Pyramid of Djoser is the culmination of an entire stage of development. Originally the pharaoh's tomb looked like a huge mastaba which was subsequently altered several times until it looked like several superposed mastabas, hence the six "steps" of the pyramid. Small stone blocks replaced the mudbrick used in the construction of previous royal tombs. The pyramid stands above a vast network of underground galleries, with stelae and blue-tiled chambers. Only the so-called Saïte gallery, refurbished for technical reasons at a later date, can be visited.

THE FUNERAL COMPLEX OF DJOSER. The funeral complex, the only one of its kind in the world, includes a funerary temple (now in ruins), situated on the north (and not the east) side of the pyramid. This is less interesting, however, than the impressive statue of Djoser (the original is in the Cairo Museum ▲ 276) which can be seen through two holes drilled in the wall of the *serdab* (hiding place). The temple and pyramid stood in a vast, rectangular precinct (1,820 feet long, 100 feet wide and about 33 feet high) whose redans and beautiful, honey-colored limestone can still be seen near the southeast corner. Here, too, is the only entrance into this vast complex. A long, narrow colonnade leads into the courtyard dominated, on the right, by the Step Pyramid and, on the left, by the southern mass of the enclosure wall.
Incorporated into the

wall is the access shaft to the SOUTH TOMB (reminiscent of the ancient royal burials of Abydos) whose apartments, which are decorated in the same way as those of the pyramid, are unfortunately closed to the public. From the top of the walls there is a magnificent view of south Saqqara with the Pyramids of Dahshur to the south. An inset in the courtyard side of the wall is decorated with a frieze of cobras.

JUBILEE CHAPELS. Back across the courtyard is the purely symbolic (and to some extent fictitious) complex built in beautiful bonded stone, a permanent monument to Djoser's royalty and so-called *heb-sed* (jubilee) celebrations. Royal jubilees, which were usually held to celebrate the thirtieth anniversary of a monarch's reign, dated back to early Pharaonic times. They were usually held in temporary structures built for the occasion. Djoser wanted to immortalize the occasion with permanent structures, hence the Jubilee Court and chapels and the simulated structures representing buildings associated with the dual monarchy of Upper and Lower Egypt: the House of the South and House of the North, whose capitals are decorated with the heraldic plants of both kingdoms.

PYRAMID OF UNIS. A flight of steps on the south side of the enclosure wall brings you down into the precinct where you can walk along the "streets" of tombs to the pyramid of the last of the 5th-Dynasty pharaohs. The pyramid, which has lost most of its outer casing, was the first to have its chambers and underground galleries decorated, or rather inscribed. In fact the regular columns of blue-painted hieroglyphics inscribed on the walls are the earliest known version of the so-called Pyramid Texts. The only other pyramids containing these texts (those of Tety, Pepy I, Mernere, Pepy II and the queens of Pepy II) are all at Saqqara and date from the 6th Dynasty. Only the texts of Unis and Tety are accessible. Follow the ruins of the covered causeway which once linked the pyramid and Upper Temple to the Valley Temple to see the remains of the reliefs which once decorated its walls.

The funeral complex of Djoser (above), workmen on the site of the Saqqara excavations and the reopening of the Step Pyramid in 1987.

THE FUNERAL COMPLEX OF DJOSER You will be encouraged to take your time when visiting the vast architectural complex of the Pyramid of Djoser if you spare a thought for the difficult and painstaking task of excavating, studying and partially restoring it. The French architect Jean-Philippe Lauer (left, standing behind the wall), the master of works for almost seventy years and undisputed pyramid expert, returns to work on the site every winter.

▲ SAQQARA

Colonnaded entrance

South tomb and "cobra" wall

This vast funeral complex is the work of the architect Imhotep, minister of Djoser, the 3rd-Dynasty pharaoh who founded the capital of Memphis. The complex was innovative in its use of stone as a building material and in the form of its pyramid. The systematic excavation of the site was begun in 1927 by the Egyptian Department of Antiquities and continued by Jean-Philippe Lauer, who also instigated a large-scale restoration program.

Granite statue of King Djoser, found on the Saqqara site.

Imaginary reconstruction of the construction of the Step Pyramid.

South court | Heb-sed (jubilee) court | Step Pyramid | North court | Enclosure wall

ENCLOSURE WALL
The outer wall, punctuated with redans and the traditional decoration of false doors, encloses an area of about 37 acres.

COLONNADED ENTRANCE
The first court is reached along a covered gallery supported by engaged semi-columns, sometimes joined in pairs. The so-called "fasciculate" columns represent the stems of plants bound in bundles.

"COBRA" WALL
On the interior façade of the enclosure wall is a series of "dummy" doors with their blinds rolled up, surmounted by a frieze of protective cobras.

"HEB-SED" (JUBILEE) PAVILION
The solid stonework is surmounted by an arched roof. Slender columns with double-arched capitals decorate the façade which is preceded by a low wall.

Although the causeway no longer extends as far as the Valley Temple (whose few remains can be seen near the barrier closing off the site), it is still flanked, about midway along, by mastabas: the rock-cut TOMB OF NEFER with its fresh-looking, colored scenes (limited access: ask for information) and the impressive, constructed tombs of NYANKH-KHNUM and KHNUMHOTEP with their perfect colors. The MONASTERY OF ST JEREMIAH (Apa Jeremias) lies to the southeast, beyond the "boundary" represented by the causeway of Unis. Many of the architectural elements of the building have been taken from Pharaonic monuments.

CEMETERY OF THE NEW KINGDOM.
Excavations begun by an Anglo-Dutch mission about twenty years ago, in a vast area to the west, revealed a cemetery of the New Kingdom (late 18th and 19th Dynasties). Some impressive and often superbly decorated tombs, which have lain forgotten beneath the sand since they were plundered by 19th-century grave robbers, are being gradually uncovered. They include the TOMB OF HOREMHEB, the general who became king. He was one of the successors of Amenhotep IV (Akhenaten) who, after becoming pharaoh, had a tomb constructed in the Valley of the Kings ▲ *417* where he was buried. However, his Memphite tomb remained an important monument for funeral worship. The surviving reliefs are remarkable for their blend of idealization and "realistic" observation of scenes of mourning, tributes and prisoners of war. It is also possible to visit the so-called Persian Tombs, more than 65 feet deep, which date from the 26th (Saïte period) and 27th Dynasties. On the way back to the Pyramid of Djoser are the TOMBS OF PRINCESS IDUT (6th Dynasty) and the VIZIER MEHU, both decorated with beautiful scenes in relief. In an area to the northwest, where MARIETTE'S HOUSE once stood (it has since been destroyed), a tent serves as a makeshift cafeteria.

SERAPEUM. The Serapeum was a vast religious complex which extended from the eastern edge of the site to

One of the granite sarcophagi (above), which contained the mummified bulls. Mariette recorded twenty-four, placed in chambers dug on either side of an underground corridor.

AUGUSTE MARIETTE
Auguste Mariette or "Mariette Pasha" (1821–81) was one of the pioneers of Egyptian archeology and founder of the Egyptian Department of Antiquities and the first Cairo Museum. His many discoveries at Saqqara included the famous Serapeum, the catacombs of the Apis Bulls, which he excavated in 1850 and of which he made several drawings (right and top left).

the tombs of the Apis Bulls, via a long avenue of sphinxes. To a certain extent it also represented the religious, intellectual and cultural convergence of two civilizations: Egypt and Greece. The Serapeum (the Latin form of the Greek "Serapeion") is dedicated to Serapis, a hybrid or "synthesized" divinity created by the early Ptolemies in an attempt to bring Egyptians and Greeks closer together. Serapis is, as it were, a compound of Osiris and Apis, the sacred animal of Ptah; hence the association between the Serapeum and the tombs of the Apis Bulls. A very badly damaged HEMICYCLE (a semicircle of Greek statues),which includes such illustrious figures as Plato, Heraclitus, Homer, Hesiod and Pindar, stands near the entrance to the catacombs. It is a fine example of the Graeco-Egyptian relationship, which was more than just a close association.

MASTABA OF TI. Near the tombs of the Apis Bulls is the remarkable 5th-Dynasty mastaba of Ti, the largest in the necropolis. The decorations in the courtyard, vestibule and chapels depict the activities of a high-ranking figure of the Old Kingdom. Other mastabas which are well worth a visit include the TOMBS OF PTAHHOTEP and AKHETHOTEP, to the

Scene from the tomb of Nefer and Qa'a-Hay depicting the making and baking of bread.

SERAPEUM
This is one of the most incredible sites in Egypt: mummified bulls were buried in monolithic sarcophagi in vast underground chambers. The practice went on for centuries and, in the tombs open to the public, until the early Christian era.

NEW DISCOVERIES
The recently
discovered tomb
of the vizier Aper-El
(below). The domed
interior of the
Pyramid of Mernere,
discovered by the
Archeological
Mission at Saqqara, is
decorated with stars
(below, bottom).

northwest of the Pyramid of Djoser. Further south is the
"Street of Tombs", which lies beyond the PYRAMID OF
USERKAF (5th Dynasty) and PYRAMID OF TETY (6th Dynasty)
where the walls of the burial chambers are inscribed with
Pyramid Texts. Then there are the MASTABAS OF MERERUKA
(sometimes known as Mera), which has reliefs and a
magnificent statue set within a niche, KAGEMNI (or Memi)
and ANKHMAHOR. The latter is also known as the "Doctors'
Tomb" because some of its images represent surgical
operations. This is the end of the "standard" tour of the site.
But Saqqara is not just a cemetery of the Old Kingdom
(although monuments from this period tend to be in the
majority) and the later Egyptian and Greek periods are well
represented. There are also the cliff tombs, which include, for

example, the tomb of the vizier
Bakenrenef (Bocchoris) excavated by the
Pisa Mission, and the many animal
necropolises (for the cows that bore the
Apis Bulls, dogs, cats, ibis, baboons and
falcons) associated with shrines which
flourished here in the later centuries BC.
The New Kingdom is also represented on
the site. For example, the cliff just north
of the road, dominated by an official rest
house, contains a series of New-Kingdom
rock tombs dating mainly from the 18th
Dynasty. For ten or so years the French
Bubasteion Mission (named after the
shrine of the goddess Bastet, which stood
on the site at the time of the Serapeum)
has been excavating the tombs of such
important figures as the CHANCELLOR
MERY-RE and the VIZIER APER-EL (the
jewelry from the tomb is on display in the
Cairo Museum) from the reigns of
Amenhotep III and Amenhotep IV
(Akhenaten). Finally it should be
remembered that the site of Saqqara
extends much further south. Two groups
of monuments are well worth a visit, even
though they are not on most tourist
itineraries. On the edge of the desert are
the PYRAMIDS OF DJEDKARE-ISESI and

TOMB OF APER-EL
~~e~~ burial chamber
~~…~~per-El was
~~…~~red, at a great
~~…~~ the
~~…~~ Mission.
~~…~~
~~…~~he

PEPY I and, further west, the PYRAMID OF MERNERE. The
chambers of the last two (6th-Dynasty)
pyramids are inscribed with Pyramid Texts
and are being studied and restored by the
French Mission at Saqqara. The mission,
which is also excavating the religious
complex of Pepy I, has made a recent
discovery of pyramids belonging to the
king's wives to south of the complex.
Much further south the site of the
MASTABA EL-FARA'UN (Pharaoh's
~~…~~ch) can be found, as well as the
~~…~~al sarcophagus-shaped funerary
~~…~~ent of the 4th-Dynasty pharaoh
~~…~~f, and the PYRAMIDS OF
~~…~~his queens.

MEMPHIS
TO THE FAIYUM

1 CAIRO
2 GIZA
3 PYRAMID OF SENWOSRET III
4 RED PYRAMID
5 PYRAMID OF AMENEMHET II
6 BENT PYRAMID
7 PYRAMID OF AMENEMHET III
8 PYRAMIDS OF MAZGHUNA
9 PYRAMID OF SENWOSRET I
10 PYRAMID OF AMENEMHET I
11 MEIDUM PYRAMID
12 PYRAMID OF SEILA
13 AITFIH
14 ILLAHUN PYRAMID
15 SEDMENT EL-JEBEL
16 IHNASIYA EL-MEDINA
17 BENI SUEF
18 DISHASHA

One day

DAHSHUR

"As the Nile widens out once again and flows between the slopes of Jebel Moqattam and a curtain of date palms, all the pyramids are visible. The Pyramid of Giza is almost out of sight, the old Pyramid of Saqqara is level with the boat and the Pyramids of Dahshur are drawing closer. Cairo has completely disappeared."
Eugène Fromentin

The site of Dahshur stands on the left bank of the Nile, about 16 miles south of Giza, in a restricted military zone. It is hoped, however, that the recent re-allocation of land will enable the site to be opened to the public in the not-too-distant future. The site includes two 4th-Dynasty stone pyramids and three 12th-Dynasty mudbrick pyramids, both groups lying parallel to the Nile, as well as the remains of necropolises and an Old-Kingdom town.

PYRAMID OF SENWOSRET III. The original 12th-Dynasty monument, now a 98-foot-high mudbrick hillock with a central (excavated) crater, had a limestone revetment and stood 328 feet square and 256 feet high. An outer access shaft, opening to the west, led to the granite-lined funeral apartments (robbed during Antiquity and today inaccessible) whose burial vault contains a red granite sarcophagus. An underground corridor to the northeast linked the four tombs dug to the north of the pyramid where Jacques de Morgan discovered the jewelry of the princesses Sat-Hathor and Mereret, now on display in the Cairo Museum ▲ 276.

Surrounded by a brick enclosure wall, the FUNERARY COMPLEX (annex tombs, north and west chapels) was probably inspired by that of Djoser. Outside the enclosure wall, to the south, was the vaulted chamber which housed the cedar-wood barques and their sled (Cairo Museum). The east temple is in ruins. Scattered across the mountainside to the south are (inaccessible) Old-Kingdom tombs and the remains of the town of the Pyramid of Snefru.

"WHITE" PYRAMID OF AMENEMHET II. The extensively damaged limestone pyramid (12th Dynasty) had eight sand-filled strengthening walls arranged in the shape of a star. The (inaccessible) north entrance opened onto a straight corridor which led down to the split-level funeral chamber, closed by two granite portcullises, which contained a sandstone sarcophagus set in the floor. Inside the rectangular enclosure wall, all that remains of the funerary temple to the east are a few scattered blocks and a paved way leading eastward. The several tombs (including that of Princess Khnumet) to the west contained jewelry and diadems which can now be seen in the Cairo Museum. To the north of the complex is the Old-Kingdom necropolis excavated by Jacques de Morgan, while the limestone blocks and remains of a paved way to the south could belong to a Middle-Kingdom pyramid.

PYRAMID OF AMENEMHET III. The original 12th-Dynasty monument consisted of a pyramid (341 feet square and 266 feet high), surmounted by a black granite pyramidion (Cairo Museum). The underground chambers which open to the east were lined with Tura limestone. They formed a complicated system of three sets of chambers: the royal burial chamber containing a red granite sarcophagus, decorated with projections and redans; the queens' chamber; and a suite of rooms of indeterminate use to the south.

Two gates (east and west) were set in the niched, inner enclosure wall. The east funerary temple has virtually disappeared; only its paved way has survived. To the north of the way traces of mudbrick (probably priests') dwellings were discovered. A line of twelve tombs, between the two enclosure walls to the north of the pyramid, have provided some valuable discoveries, including a wooden statue (Cairo Museum) of the *ka* of the 13th-Dynasty king Auybre-Hor. Private tombs dug during the Old Kingdom lie to the southwest. The two tombs of the second, older group of pyramids were constructed during the 4th Dynasty by King Snefru.

RED PYRAMID. The so-called Red Pyramid, to the north, is the earliest example of a "true" pyramid. Built from blocks of the local red stone and originally covered with Tura limestone, it was 722 feet square and stood 325 feet high. The access corridor to the tomb is on the north side and opens onto a suite of three rectangular rooms.

PYRAMID OF AMENEMHET III
The monument looks like a pile of mudbricks emerging from a mound of bricks and sand. The fragility of its construction, indicated by the restoration carried out during the Pharaonic period (supporting beams, limestone blocks) explains why the pyramid was

abandoned in favor of the Pyramid of Hawara ▲ *370* where the pharaoh was buried.

The so-called Red Pyramid is relatively well preserved. Its limestone pyramidion and the remains of the funerary temple were recently discovered to the east.

BENT PYRAMID. At the southern edge of the site this dual-angled pyramid still retains much of its limestone outer casing. Its name is derived from the inexplicable change in its angle of inclination: from 54° 27' to 43° 22' at a height of 160 feet. It has two entrances, each leading to two (inaccessible) series of chambers. The (still visible) brick walls of its upper temple once housed two stelae which stood either side of an offering table set in the floor. The lower temple, surrounded by a brick enclosure wall, consisted of a four-roomed antechamber, a court and, at the far end, a ten-pillared portico leading to six chapels.

The northeast corner of the Bent Pyramid at Dahshur.

MAZGHUNA. About 3 miles south of Dahshur a track leads westward from Mazghuna to a site occupied by two pyramids from the end of the 12th and 13th Dynasties, which are now nothing but heaps of rubble.

The pyramids of Amenemhet I and Senwosret I stand about one mile apart on opposite sides of a *wadi*. They are very badly damaged and look like two mounds of sand on the edge of the plateau. The Pyramid of Senwosret, to the north, looks like a 65-foot-high hill and is a larger version of the Pyramid of Amenemhet.

LISHT

Midway between Dahshur and Meidum the site of Lisht lies on the *jebel* to the northwest of the villages of Lisht and Maharraqa. The remains of Old-Kingdom and 11th-Dynasty tombs are obscured by the ruins of Itytawi, a residential town founded by the two first 12th-Dynasty kings.

PYRAMID OF AMENEMHET I. The pyramid was partially constructed from limestone blocks taken from Old-Kingdom monuments. The (inaccessible) north entrance, which lay behind a false granite door (Cairo Museum) at the back of a chapel, opened onto a corridor leading to an access shaft. The water level in the flooded burial chamber makes it impossible to visit. A few scattered blocks are all that remains of the funerary temple, built on a lower terrace to the east. Inside the double enclosure wall royal tombs lay to the west of the complex and several mastabas, including that of the vizier Antefoker, to the east. Outside the southwest corner of the wall, the (intact) tomb of Senebtisi and a number of papyri were discovered.

The entrance of the Meidum Pyramid, on the north side, is about 65 feet above the ground. A descending corridor leads to a rock-cut antechamber once closed by a wooden

door. Beyond the chamber, a square shaft leads to the rectangular tomb (plundered during the New Kingdom) with its vaulted and corbeled roof.

PYRAMID OF SENWOSRET I. The pyramid still has part of its limestone outer casing. It is built on a central strengthening framework of stone cross-walls in which the cavities formed by the walls are filled with stone blocks. On the pyramid's north side a chapel concealed the entrance to the (inaccessible) corridor which was lined with limestone and blocked with granite. The flooded burial vault makes excavation impossible. The monument, in the center of the funeral complex, is surrounded by a double limestone (inner) and brick (outer) enclosure wall. Between the two walls are nine pyramids belonging to the royal family. The funerary temple on the east side was based on the design of the Old-Kingdom temples. Part of the paved way of the lower temple has been discovered. The mastabas outside the complex include that of Imhotep, chancellor and high priest of Heliopolis, containing two magnificent statues of Senwosret I.

MEIDUM

The pyramid, reached via the road about 5 miles southwest of the village of Meidum, is known as El-Ahram el-Kaddab ("the false pyramid"). It is thought to have been begun by King Huni (3rd Dynasty) and completed by Snefru (4th Dynasty). It was originally a seven-step pyramid, but another story was probably added prior to the smooth, limestone revetment which made it a "true" pyramid. It was undoubtedly used as a quarry, which accounts for its present appearance: a sort of terraced tower emerging from a huge mound of debris. The limestone funerary temple, located in the center of the east side, consists of two offset rooms leading to an open court where two arched stelae stand on either side of an altar. The outer wall once enclosed two tombs, one to the north and the other to the south, most probably the satellite pyramid. An open way

THE GEESE OF MEIDUM

Many tombs dating from the Old Kingdom to the Roman period are scattered north-to-south across the hillside around the pyramid complex. The nearby necropolis is divided into three sectors: the west, northwest and, of particular interest, the north sector with mastabas nos. 1 to 17 from the reign of Snefru. The mastaba of Neferma't and Atet (no. 16) has provided some fine inlaid reliefs and the famous "geese of Meidum" (below).

PYRAMID OF SENWOSRET II AT ILLAHUN
The pyramid was built around a 40-foot-high limestone core. Limestone walls in the shape of a star form the framework of the mudbrick structure, which was originally covered with a limestone revetment and surmounted by a black granite pyramidion. It would have been about 157 feet high and 351 feet square with an angle of inclination of

42° 35'. Each side was separated by a sand-filled trench. The monument was surrounded by a niched enclosure wall, partly constructed and partly dug. The (inaccessible) entrance to the southwest opened onto a complex system of four access shafts and two tombs. The deeper, vaulted tomb is lined with granite and contains a sarcophagus.

running east–west for a distance of 230 yards used to lead to the enclosure wall of the pyramid town, Djed-Snefru, to the east. To the south of the way the remains of a construction ramp are still visible.

GERZA AND RIQQA. The site lies on the left bank of the Nile about 3 miles north of Meidum and less than 1½ miles north-west of the village of Riqqa, which has a brick and cement works. Gerza ("Grgt" in Pharaonic Egyptian and "Kerke" in Greek) gave its name to the second half of the pre-Dynastic Nagada (Gerzean) period. The necropolises, spread over a distance of almost 3 miles, were divided into two groups: Gerza and Riqqa. The pre-Dynastic Gerzean tombs were oval pits dug in the sand in which the dead were laid on their side, surrounded by funerary paraphernalia. The nearby cemeteries of Riqqa, to the south, contained the New-Kingdom tombs.

SEILA. Situated about 7 miles to the west of the Meidum Pyramid on the Jebel er-Rus, the three-step Pyramid of Seila is covered with limestone debris. It should have had four steps and probably dates from the 3rd or 4th Dynasty. Its function remains unknown. It is one of a group of seven monuments of this type scattered throughout Egypt. The excavation of Coptic priests' tombs revealed thousands of papyri (some religious) as well as white linen robes.

ABUSIR EL-MELEQ. Turn west off the main Cairo–Beni Suef road at Ishmant and continue for about 6 miles. In addition to pre-Dynastic remains, the site of Abusir el-Meleq had sepulchers from the Hyksos period and, in the secondary necropolis of Ihnasiya el-Medina, priests' tombs from the Saite period. Osiris was worshipped here, and blocks from a temple built by Nectanebo II were used to build the mosque. In 750 the last Ommiad caliph, Marwan II, fled Baghdad but was killed by the Abbasid usurpers. He is buried nearby.

ATFIH. The town of Atfih stands about 2 miles east of the Nile on the ancient site of Aphroditopolis. The Egyptian name "Tp-yhwt", meaning "the first of the cows" (Hathor), became "Petpeh" in Coptic, from which the Arabic "Atfih" was derived. Although infrequent, past excavations have discovered animal necropolises and Ptolemaic family tombs. The recently discovered sepulchers of cows in huge limestone tombs are not open to the public.

ILLAHUN

The Pyramid of Senwosret II stands about 2 miles northwest of the village of Illahun, on the right bank of Joseph's Canal (regulated by two barrage-bridges which have replaced the dam built by the Middle-Kingdom pharaohs). The village lies midway between Beni Suef and Medinet el-Faiyum ▲ *368*. The ancient town of Ro-hent became Lahone ("mouth of the canal") in Coptic. A mudbrick enclosure wall (in addition to that of the pyramid) surrounded the remains of a red granite funerary temple to the east, eight mastabas and the Queen's Pyramid to the north, and four access shafts in the south, three of which led to tombs. The tomb of Princess Sat-Hathor contained a fine collection of gold and silver jewelry, including a beautiful diadem (Cairo Museum). The remains of the lower temple were discovered to the east. The pyramid complex is at the center of a huge complex of buildings.

Necropolises dating from the pre-Dynastic to the Roman period are scattered across the hillsides around Illahun. Beneath a hillock, to the west, the architect of the pyramid, the chancellor Inpy, was laid to rest in a 12th-Dynasty mastaba. The town of Kahun, which was founded by Senwosret II to accommodate the pyramid workers, lay about half a mile to the west, across a *wadi*.

SEDMENT EL-JEBEL. Sedment, which is situated about 8 miles northwest of Ihnasiya, is the seat of a major Coptic pilgrimage. During the 15th century the large Coptic monastery, founded two centuries previously, was abandoned. The present monastery, Deir Mari Girgis ● *107*, was built in 1914.

BENI SUEF

The recently completed museum stands on the edge of the town. The first floor is devoted to Pharaonic (royal statues, Canopic jars, sarcophagi, sphinxes) and Graeco-Roman (funerary stelae, *tanagras*) antiquities which have mostly come from the nearby sites of Abusir and Heracleopolis Magna. However all the second-floor exhibits, comprising Coptic and Muslim antiquities, have come from the Cairo museums.

BENI SUEF
At the turn of the century Beni Suef was a small village. Today it is an average-sized town (over 150,000 inhabitants), the capital of the governorate of Beni Suef and an important agricultural center.

A necropolis from the
Third Intermediate
period, excavated to
the southeast,
contained limestone
tombs. Numerous
fragments from the

IHNASIYA EL-MEDINA

Outside Beni Suef a secondary road leaves the main road and
heads west (10 miles) to Ihnasiya el-Medina, also known as
Ihnasiya Umm el-Kimam ("mother of the shards"). Nen-nesu
or Hwt-nen-nesu ("house of the royal child"), capital of the
Twentieth Nome of Upper Egypt, became the Greek town of
Heracleopolis Magna and then Hennes in Coptic and Ahnas
in Arabic. The site increased in importance during the 9th
and 10th Dynasties when its princes controlled a large part
and then the whole of Lower Egypt before being ousted by
the Theban princes. During the Graeco-Roman period the
capital of the nome of Heracleopolis worshipped a local ram-
headed god, Herishef, who became Arsaphes, or Heracles in
Greek. The ancient site covers an area of 165 acres, but there
are no buildings between the town in the northeast and the
villages to the west and south. The TEMPLE OF HERISHEF, built
by Ramesses II, stood in a depression to the southwest. Its

scattered blocks were hewn out of fine
quartzite, but the present state of the site
makes it difficult to see the original
layout: a columned court, a columned
portico with palm capitals and decorated
with two seated colossi of Ramesses II, a
hypostyle hall with twenty-four columns,
which opened onto a pronaos and the
sanctuary. Recent excavations to the
south, near the Roman ramparts, have
revealed an Archaic period cemetery,
bricked-up officers' tombs from the First Intermediate period
and a necropolis from the Third Intermediate period.

Roman period
provide evidence of
buildings arranged
round a forum which
was later bordered by
churches. The four
granite columns at
Kenissa are thought
to belong to a temple
later converted into a
church.

DISHASHA. The necropolis is situated on the west bank of
Joseph's Canal, about 6 miles south of Ihnasiya el-Medina.
Turn west off the Beni Suef–El-Minya road at Biba (Coptic
church). Dishasha village lies about 14 miles northwest. A vast
necropolis dating from the end of the Old Kingdom contains
rock tombs and mastabas. Two are of particular interest: the
rock tomb of Inty, whose chapel, cut out of three niches, is
decorated with Old-Kingdom scenes and texts, and the tomb
of Iteti, with its pillared canopy, rock-cut chapel and vaulted
ceiling, and
vertical access
shaft.

THE FAIYUM

At less than an hour's drive from Cairo, the
Faiyum offers an extremely rapid and restful
change of scenery. Since 1993 it has been
linked to the capital by a four-lane toll
expressway and can easily be visited in a day,
although a longer stay is certainly justified.
The Faiyum is in fact a microcosm of Egypt,
bringing together the most beautiful aspects
of the country's landscapes: fields and palm
trees, water and desert, mountains and
ruins. Its several outstanding natural
features include the vast salt lake BIRKET
QARUN. The many, mainly Ptolemaic and
Roman, archeological sites may not have
the imposing splendor of the sites of
Upper Egypt, but they do have the
charm of isolated and almost
forgotten ruins. The Faiyum, in spite
of appearances, is not in fact an
oasis. Although it is surrounded by
desert, the vast depression (692
square miles) in which it
lies is linked to the
Nile by one of its

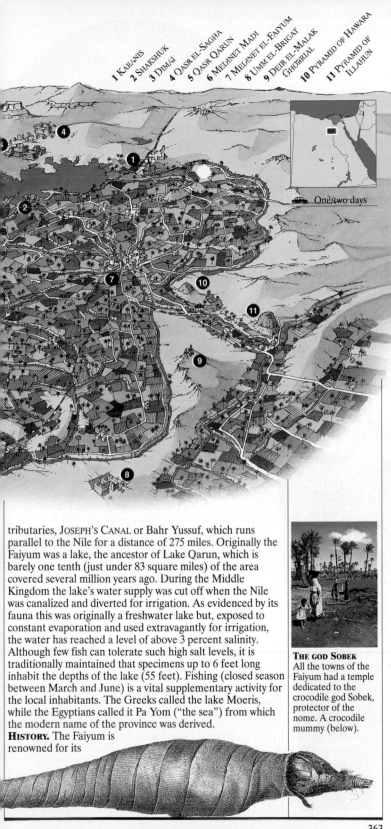

One/two days

tributaries, JOSEPH'S CANAL or Bahr Yussuf, which runs parallel to the Nile for a distance of 275 miles. Originally the Faiyum was a lake, the ancestor of Lake Qarun, which is barely one tenth (just under 83 square miles) of the area covered several million years ago. During the Middle Kingdom the lake's water supply was cut off when the Nile was canalized and diverted for irrigation. As evidenced by its fauna this was originally a freshwater lake but, exposed to constant evaporation and used extravagantly for irrigation, the water has reached a level of above 3 percent salinity. Although few fish can tolerate such high salt levels, it is traditionally maintained that specimens up to 6 feet long inhabit the depths of the lake (55 feet). Fishing (closed season between March and June) is a vital supplementary activity for the local inhabitants. The Greeks called the lake Moeris, while the Egyptians called it Pa Yom ("the sea") from which the modern name of the province was derived.

HISTORY. The Faiyum is renowned for its

THE GOD SOBEK
All the towns of the Faiyum had a temple dedicated to the crocodile god Sobek, protector of the nome. A crocodile mummy (below).

363

prehistoric remains, with Neolithic man in particular leaving traces of early populations of hunters and fishers. During the Old Kingdom the marshlands and reed beds of To-She ("land of the lake") were rich with fauna and were a favorite hunting-ground for the pharaohs and nobility. Crocodiles abounded, the embodiment of the god Sobek who, until the end of the Roman occupation, remained the protector of the nome. Each town dedicated a temple to him and he was worshipped as Suchos, Soknopaiou, Petesuchos and Pnepheros. But this fertile region could not remain purely a place of leisure and enjoyment and, on the initiative of Senwosret II, the powerful rulers of the Middle Kingdom began a systematic development of the land with irrigation systems, canals and a dam on the Joseph's Canal. The Faiyum became the most fertile region in Egypt and received particular attention from its principal benefactor, Amenemhet III, who was so enchanted by its beauty that he abandoned his pyramid at Dahshur ▲ 354 in favor of one he had built at Hawara. The inhabitants of the Faiyum deified the pharaoh who was worshipped for the next two thousand years.

GRAECO-ROMAN PERIOD. Many centuries later the Faiyum had a second protector, Ptolemy II Philadelphus (3rd century BC), the first of the Lagides to adopt the Egyptian tradition (convenient from the dynastic point of view) of marrying his own sister. He named the most beautiful province of Egypt after this beloved sister, Arsinoe, a name which it kept until the end of the Roman Empire. Ptolemy II transformed the Faiyum by settling the Greek veterans of his army there. This new population brought prosperity to the province by developing and perfecting its irrigation system. At the time the surface area under cultivation (almost 618 square miles) represented 10 percent of fertile Egypt. Although the present level of the lake is 33 feet lower, which has released half its surface area, the area of cultivated land in the modern Faiyum is less than it was in the nome of Arsinoe. The province, which was closely associated with the city of Alexandria, was always regarded by the Ptolemies as a sort of experimental region, under Greek control, for the development of crops and the introduction of new species such as the apricot tree.

The Roman occupation gradually reduced Arsinoe's golden age to nothing. Subjected to a colonial-type economy and overwhelmed by a system of absurd and ruinous taxation, the *fellaheen* were forced to leave their villages. The province, which began to decline in the middle of the 3rd century, was finally and completely ruined by the 4th and only recovered some of its former glory during the reign of Mohammed Ali (1805–49).

PAPYRUS. According to a custom particularly associated with the nome of Arsinoe, human and crocodile mummies were covered with a thick binding of used or new papyrus. This layer, made up of all kinds of texts (including everyday writings, letters, accounts and exercises) was complemented by the discovery of piles of old archives. Together they provide a detailed description of every aspect of the daily life of the nome.

ARSINOE-CROCODILOPOLIS
The Greek veterans brought into the Faiyum by Ptolemy II settled in the ancient towns of the province as well as founding new towns around Lake Moeris and on the boundary of the cultivated lands.
A plan (1823) of Arsinoe-Crocodilopolis (above), one of the largest of these new towns.

TEMPLES OF KARANIS
The TEMPLE OF THE SOUTH (below) is the older of the two temples of Karanis. Built of stone, it is dated by a still-legible, Greek inscription on the lintel of the main doorway in which the name of the original dedicatee, Nero, has been altered to that of his uncle, Claudius. The temple includes

three rooms linked by a wide vestibule. The TEMPLE OF THE NORTH is almost a total ruin, but pools and steam rooms of the Roman baths can still be seen.

DIMAI
The ruins of Dimai are both striking and mysterious. They are buried beneath great tumuli, red with shards of glass and pottery and strewn with all kinds of fragments.

KOM USHIM: RUINS OF KARANIS. After the Avenue of Pyramids follow the signs for Alexandria and then turn onto the road to the Faiyum. The NEW MUSEUM OF ANTIQUITIES is due to be built at this intersection to replace the museum in the Midan at-Tahrir ▲ 280. After crossing expanse of desert, as the road begins to be bordered by the ruins of Karanis lie over to the left. A small museum houses relics from excavations in the region. Of all the towns in the nome of Arsinoe, Karanis is undoubtedly the one for which there is the most information, because of the well-preserved state of the everyday objects and papyrus. The town was founded during the reign of Ptolemy II around a temple dedicated to Petesuchos, a crocodile god. As it spread northward a second temple was built. After a period of decline the town prospered until the 3rd century BC before finally disappearing in the early 5th century.

SHAKSHUK. About 2 miles after Karanis turn right and follow the signs for the inn known as the *Auberge du Lac*, once a favorite winter resort and hunting lodge with King Farouk, along a road which follows the shores of Lake Qarun. The village of Shakshuk stands at the far end of a small bay and its main street forms a corniche below which brightly colored fishing boats, decorated with images and prayers, bob at their moorings.

DIMAI. Although it is possible to travel overland by four-wheel drive to Dimai (there is a track opposite Karanis), the best way to approach the arid shores and

mudbrick walls of SOKNOPAIOU NESOS ("the island of the crocodile god") is across the lake from Shakshuk. This former fishing village and caravanserai, on the northern boundary of the nome, was the first to be deserted by its inhabitants. A processional way whose remains can still be seen to the south of the site led from the gates of the TEMPLE OF SOBEK to the god's primordial habitat. About one hundred yards outside the walls, the cellars used for storing oil and wine still have their vaulted ceilings. The remains of two temples, one built of stone and one of brick, can still be seen inside the precinct. A few miles east is the limestone TEMPLE OF QASR EL-SAGHA which, although never completed, has retained its seven chapels. It is one of the few examples of Middle Kingdom religious building, but there is no indication as to its function.

DIONYSIAS. After Shakshuk take the road which runs parallel to and sometimes along the shores of the lake. Follow it for a few miles and then take the direction of QASR QARUN, leaving the point of the lake on your right. Turn left after crossing a canal and follow a road bordered by large dovecotes until, about 8 miles after the village of El-Shawasna, the roof of the Temple of Dionysias comes into view. This was the most westerly town in the nome and may have been a staging post on caravan routes from the Libyan Desert. It was founded in c. 3rd century BC and, because of its strategic position and incursions by the Bedouin tribesmen known as the Blemmyes, was fortified by the emperor Diocletian. A Roman fort similar to those in the Kharga Oasis ▲ 260 housed a large garrison.

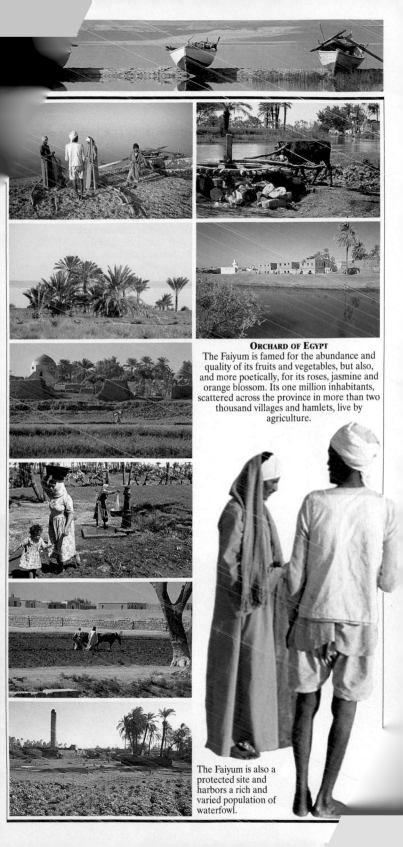

ORCHARD OF EGYPT

The Faiyum is famed for the abundance and quality of its fruits and vegetables, but also, and more poetically, for its roses, jasmine and orange blossom. Its one million inhabitants, scattered across the province in more than two thousand villages and hamlets, live by agriculture.

The Faiyum is also a protected site and harbors a rich and varied population of waterfowl.

To the south, the avenue leading to the Temple of Narmuthis is guarded by sphinxes and lions.

When Leo Africanus visited Medinet el-Faiyum in the early 16th century he described it as "civilized and well populated; it has many craftsmen, especially weavers".

The first excavations (1948) uncovered thermal baths, ho... decorated with frescos and glassworks which are today on... more engulfed by sand. Unusually for the Faiyum the so-called "TEMPLE OF STONES" dedicated to Sobek still has its roof, while in the shadowy interior fourteen rooms are arranged either side of a central corridor leading to three chapels.

MEDINET MADI: NARMUTHIS. Continue southward from Qasr Qarun. Archeologically speaking Medinet Madi (ancient Narmuthis) is considered to be the most interesting site of the Faiyum, although it is so vast that it has not yet been completely excavated. Narmuthis stood next to a Middle Kingdom city and its Ptolemaic extension. The Middle Kingdom temple, dedicated to Sobek, Ernutet (the serpent goddess associated with Isis) and Horus, was built by Amenemhet III and extended by the Ptolemies. Like the rest of the site it is under threat from the sand. Its interior walls are covered with hieroglyphics and bas-reliefs depicting Amenemhet III and his son, Amenemhet IV, presenting offerings to the gods. The far end of the temple is extended by a small Ptolemaic temple which would have been linked to the city's north gate by a processional way and porticos.

MEDINET EL-FAIYUM

Medinet el-Faiyum, known first as Crocodilopolis and then Arsinoe, is the modern capital of the province. It stands at the center of the Faiyum basin and is the point of convergence for road, canal and rail networks.

Medinet el-Faiyum is crossed by Joseph's Canal and eight tributary canals and has been described, by its more enthusiastic reviewers, as the Venice of Egypt. The city where the writer and

...er Maxime Du Camp marveled at ...aars [which were] of a cleanliness ...sual for the East" has all the charm of ...ural Egyptian town. Bridges and ...ootbridges link quays which are bustling with trade. Among the main attractions are the huge wooden waterwheels (built by the Greek settlers) which creak and groan as they raise water from one level to another. The great stone obelisk (more like a stele) which stands at the city's north entrance was erected in honor of Senwosret I (12th Dynasty). Not much remains of the ancient capital of the nome at Kiman Fares, a few miles outside Medinet el-Faiyum, as the site has been extensively developed. This was the home and principal place of worship of the crocodile god, Sobek, and a sacred lake harbored enormous crocodiles which, according to Strabo, were fed on meat and honey cakes and adorned with gold by the priests. The city has a substantial Coptic community, but during the 1980's became a stronghold of Muslim fundamentalism.

UMM EL-BRIGAT: TEBTUNIS. Head south out of Medinet el-Faiyum and turn left, after the bus station, toward Itsa. The brick remains of a ROMAN AQUEDUCT lie scattered in the fields. At Tutun a sign on the right indicates the direction of Umm el-Brigat. The road follows the edge of a broad canal and after about 4 miles comes to the site and modern village of Umm el-Brigat. Although partially covered by sand, the extensive remains of ancient TEBTUNIS are extremely impressive, and enhanced by this beautiful setting.

DEIR EL-MALAK GHOBRIAL. Several ancient monasteries,

TEBTUNIS
The ruins lie on the edge of the desert. Tebtunis, founded during the 22nd Dynasty, was developed by Greek and Roman settlers. It was here, in the late 19th century, that a *fellaheen* discovered the first papyri scrolls in Greek, Latin and demotic script. A broad and still partially paved way crosses the ruins under the watchful gaze of two huge limestone lions. All that remains of the vast temple complex are some of the lateral rooms in beautiful, honey-colored stone.

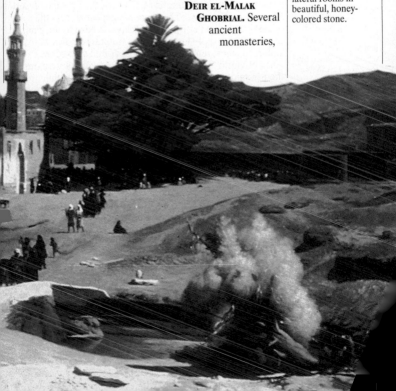

Detail of a fresco depicting Adam and Eve, from one of the many Coptic monasteries of the Faiyum.

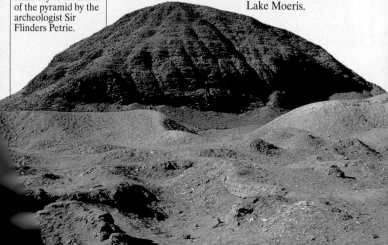

A MAGNIFICENT FIND
An exceptional discovery gave an added dimension and restored some of the former glory to the Faiyum which suffered so much over the ages. In 1888 a total of 146 magnificent portraits painted on wood were discovered during excavations carried out in the Roman cemetery to the north of the pyramid by the archeologist Sir Flinders Petrie.

situated at the southern edge of the Faiyum, are evidence of a Christian presence which dates back to the 3rd century. The monasteries (there were still thirty-six in the Middle Ages) are today being given a new lease on life by a revival of Coptic monasticism. The oldest and most interesting to visit is the DEIR EL-MALAK GHOBRIAL, or the Monastery of the Archangel Gabriel, built on the high slopes of the Jebel Naqlun. The mystical associations of this austere, arid landscape, so close to the cool freshness of trees and plots of green vegetables, go back a very long way.

According to the Christian historian Abu Salih, Jacob, the grandson of Abraham, settled here. The original monastery was probably built in the 4th century AD by the Bishop Aur, acting upon the instructions of the Archangel Gabriel, who had commanded him to build a sanctuary in these mountains where people "would gather in crowds more numerous than doves in a dovecote". In fact between the 4th and 6th centuries the monastery was the center of the religious life of the Faiyum, with Saint Samuel numbering among its many illustrious visitors. Before it was rebuilt in 1968, all that remained was a church with six Corinthian columns supporting a beautiful wood ceiling decorated with geometric designs. Just below the ridge of the mountain, southeast of the monastery, cells hewn out of the rock (the work of Bishop Aur) enabled monks to retreat in accordance with the eremitic tradition of the Egyptian desert.

PYRAMID OF HAWARA. (The route is signposted from the obelisk of Medinet el-Faiyum.) Today it is hard to imagine that the Pyramid of Hawara and its funeral complex were among the most renowned and most visited sites of the Ancient World. The brick infrastructure is all that remains of the pyramid, once covered in bonded stone, while the labyrinth where Herodotus claimed to have counted three thousand rooms (the site, he said, defied description) has been reduced to a confused expanse of shards. The legend associated with the complex was linked with that of its founder, Amenemhet III, who was also said to have created Lake Moeris.

EL-MINYA TO THEBES

▲ EL-MINYA TO THEBES

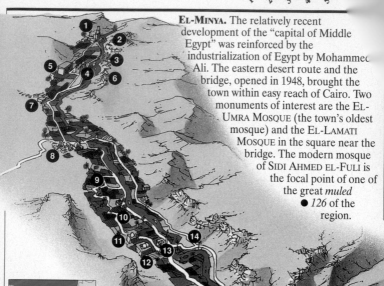

EL-MINYA. The relatively recent development of the "capital of Middle Egypt" was reinforced by the industrialization of Egypt by Mohammed Ali. The eastern desert route and the bridge, opened in 1948, brought the town within easy reach of Cairo. Two monuments of interest are the EL-UMRA MOSQUE (the town's oldest mosque) and the EL-LAMATI MOSQUE in the square near the bridge. The modern mosque of SIDI AHMED EL-FULI is the focal point of one of the great *muled* ● 126 of the region.

🚗 Two to four days

The minaret of the El-Lamati Mosque and the Muslim cemetery of El-Minya at the foot of the Libyan mountain range.

The municipal museum, currently being refurbished, houses a collection of Egyptian antiquities.

TIHNA EL-JEBEL. Acoris was the Greek name for the Pharaonic town of Dehenet ("the forehead") whose name was undoubtedly inspired by the promontory around which the town has developed. Tihna el-Jebel is one of the sites where, under the Lagides and then the Romans, the Pharaonic and Greek cultures co-existed: the ancient gods were honored with Greek names, the dead were buried according to Egyptian tradition and their epitaphs were written in Greek or Latin. The temple is reached via the steeply sloping sacred way, once lined by altars, statues and columns. Amun and Suchos (the Greek name of the crocodile god Sobek ● 61 ▲ 362) were the two main divinities of the temple. The hieroglyphic inscriptions are in the name of Nero. On the columns several calligraphic Greek texts, written in ink, give thanks for the Nile floods: "(Year) two and (year) one of our Lords Diocletian and Marcus Aurelius, the welcome waters, regenerating and life-giving with their fertile mud, rose to the sanctuary of Suchos, Amun, Hermes and

Hera and the gods who share their temple, amidst general happiness and rejoicing" (based on a translation by Bernand). To the right a chapel, perched on the cliff, combines the Egyptian (images of the gods) and Greek (dedication) styles. The cross in the niche at the back of the chapel is an indication that the building was used for Christian worship. About 100 yards southwest of the temple, amidst the rubble of collapsed houses, are the remains of a GREEK-STYLE TEMPLE dedicated to Zeus-Helios-Serapis, a part-Greek, part-Egyptian god of the Ptolemies. A relief representing the Dioscuri standing either side of Helena, high up behind the promontory, was meant to protect boatmen passing along the Nile below. The necropolis stretches along a valley to the east.

DEIR EL-ADRA. The "Monastery of the Virgin" stands on the cliff opposite the town of SAMALUT on the so-called JEBEL EL-TEIR (Bird Mountain) where the Holy Family is said to have stayed. The church, which according to tradition was founded by the Empress (Saint) Helena, mother of Constantine, stands above a tomb from the Archaic period. During pilgrimages (January 29 and August 22) the

One of the ancient mosques of El-Minya.

monastery, no longer inhabited by monks, becomes an encampment for the Faithful. To the north are the ancient quarries, which spared the speos of Merneptah and a low relief of Ramesses III.

ZAWIYET EL-MAYTIN. The remains of a 3rd-Dynasty pyramid, a mound of red shards and the façade of the tomb of Nefersekheru (18th–19th Dynasty) are more or less all there is to see at Zawiyet el-Maytin or Kom el-Ahmar (Red Hill), the modern name of Hebenu, the capital of the Sixteenth Nome of Upper Egypt. The walk along the Arabian mountains (currently being quarried by dynamite) is extremely beautiful and runs along the edge of one of the largest Muslim cemeteries in Egypt.

"The steep banks of the river often consist of broad, straight lines one above the other. The white mountain (*sharab*) is covered with rounded hillocks striped with gray, striped like the back of a hyena; at other points it is a smooth, white cliff."
Gustave Flaubert

373

BENI HASSAN

Beni Hassan could be described as a typical Middle-Kingdom necropolis. The time had passed when high-ranking government officials were buried near their king (Saqqara ▲ 344, Giza ▲ 334): the upheavals of the First Intermediate period (2140–2022 BC) gave a certain independence to local governors (nomarchs) and it was from then on that they tended to be buried in their own nome. Twelve of the thirty-nine great rock-cut tombs are decorated and five of these are truly remarkable, not only for their architectural beauty, but also for their vast, vaulted chambers and their choice of columns. Champollion ▲ 216 classified the columns with cut-off corners as "proto-Doric" and believed he had discovered the ancestor of the Greek Doric order. The name of Baqet, one of the architects, was found. These tombs are also remarkable for the richness and originality of their décor. The tombs of Amenemhet (no. 2), "prince of the Oryx Nome", Khnumhotep III (no. 3), "the hereditary lord", Khnumhotep I (no. 14), Baqit III (no. 15) and Khety (no. 17) feature traditional scenes of agricultural life, hunting in papyrus thickets, pilgrimages by boat to Abydos ▲ 386 and Busiris, and the presentation of offerings to the deceased who is represented in "heroic" proportions, seated on a chair. The desert hunting scenes on the north wall of tomb no. 2 depart from the classical repertoire and, on the north wall of tomb no. 15, include the hunting of four fantastical creatures: a "Sethian" animal, a griffin, a serpent-headed quadruped and a unicorn. These creatures are clearly a representation of the belief that the desert was the home of the evil forces of chaos and that hunting in the desert helped to preserve cosmic order. The training of men in violent sports and military exercises was a constant preoccupation of the suzerains of the Oryx Nome, who had to maintain their power by force (the east walls of tombs nos. 2, 15 and 17 depict scenes of the fortress under siege). In tomb no. 2 (on the north wall) Asiatic tribesmen, led by their chief Abisha, have come, with their donkeys, to sell kohl (of which the Egyptians used a great deal). This is the most famous representation of these nomadic Bedouins, who lived and traveled along the eastern borders of Egypt. There are two biographical inscriptions in the necropolis that are essential to an understanding of the political and economic situation of Egypt at that time, when the country was emerging from over a century of serious upheavals. One of these is a thirty-two-line inscription on the interior uprights of the door of tomb no. 2; the other is an inscription of 222 columns of text which can be found within tomb no. 3.

"SPEOS ARTEMIDOS". The Cave of Artemis, situated in a *wadi* (Batn el-Baqara) about 2 miles to the southwest of Beni Hassan, was hewn out of the rock for the lion-goddess Pakhet ("she who scratches"), alias Artemis, by Hatshepsut. These *wadi* mouths were the preserve of wild beasts who sometimes left the desert and made incursions into the valley.

ANTINOE. Antinoe was founded by the emperor Hadrian in AD 130 . Little is known of the town's Pharaonic past, of which the temple dedicated by Ramesses II to the god Shepsy, the avatar of Thoth of Hermopolis, is the only visible legacy. All that remains of Hadrian's town is a pile of shards interspersed with architectural fragments. It was used as an ancient quarry and capitals from Antinoe have been found in a 15th-century mosque in Cairo. Legend has it that Salah ad-Din ▲ *271* had the enclosure wall dismantled and used it to build the wall of the capital. The mosque in the village of Sheikh Abada is said to have been built on the site of the house of Mary the Copt, who was the Prophet's concubine. The early Christians established orthodox monasteries in the mountain quarries.

One of the views of Antinoe that appeared in *La Description de l'Egypte* ● *140* ▲ *315*. The triumphal arch which stood on the site at the time of the French expedition has since disappeared (used in the construction of a sugar refinery).

THE FOUNDATION OF ANTINOE
Founded by Hadrian on October 30, AD 130, Antinoe is said to have been built in memory of his favorite, Antinus, who threw himself in the Nile to save the emperor from a deadly omen.

"Phlegon gathered the architects and engineers of my entourage together on the shores of the river; sustained by a sort of lucid intoxication, I led them along the rocky hillsides; I explained my plan, the construction of the forty-five sections of an enclosure wall; I marked the position of the triumphal arch and the tomb in the sand. Antinoe was about to be created.**"**
Marguerite Yourcenar, *Memoirs of Hadrian*

Gayet's excavations a Antinoe (left).

DEIR ABU HENNES. Deir Abu Hennes (St John's Monaste[...] to the south of Antinoe, is famous as the orthodox monaste[...] founded in the quarries exploited during the reign of Amenhotep III. Crosses, Greek and Coptic graffiti and praye[...] niches attest to the presence of this eremitic community centered around the tiny church which is traditionally thought to date from the time of Empress Helena.

MELLAWI. Before El-Minya became the regional capital at the beginning of the 19th century, Mellawi was an important town whose revenues were dedicated to Mecca. The streets of the old town have retained their original layout with two fine ancient mosques standing next to each other at the center: the EL-YUSUFI MOSQUE (1623), whose columns and capitals came from ancient sites in the region (including Antinoe), and the EL-ASQALANI MOSQUE, which dates from 1779. The Mellawi Museum houses an admirable collection of antiquities which have come mainly from the necropolis of Tuna el-Jebel. They include bronzes, ibis mummies and sarcophagi, plaster coffin masques (which are in fact portraits), and huge sarcophagi from the necropolises of Meir and Assiut and a fine head from a New-Kingdom royal statue.

BIRTH OF HERMOPOLIS
The word for "eight" in Ancient Egyptian is *shmun*. It was one of the town's two ancient names and has survived in the modern name of Ashmunein. It refers to the eight "ancestors of very early times" who formed four couples of frog-males and serpent-females, the incarnations of the primordial waters, spatial infinity, shadows and the invisible. A muddy hillock emerged from the primordial waters. On it grew a lotus with golden stamens and petals in lapis-lazuli. In the form of four bulls, the males fertilized the flower which opened and revealed a child, a finger held to its mouth: the sun was born which, in its turn, would create the world.

HERMOPOLIS

With the other Ancient Egyptian cities of Heliopolis ▲ 285, Memphis ▲ 332 and Thebes ▲ 394, Hermopolis shares the rare privilege of being one of the "birthplaces of the world". As well as being a "cosmogenetic" capital it was also the capital of the Fifteenth (Hare) Nome of Upper Egypt. Its patron was the god Thoth, incarnated in the form of the ibis and baboon, the scribe who presided over all forms of knowledge: language and sacred writings, laws, the measurement of time and the calendar. He became Hermes in the Greek pantheon, the Trismegistus of the hermetic texts.

REMAINS. The ruins of the city lie in the center of the plain at the point where it widens out. Huge columns surmounted by Corinthian capitals lend a particular charm to the site. They are the remains of a basilica (built on the site of a 3rd-century Ptolemaic temple), the town's monumental covered market during Ptolemaic and Roman times. Earlier remains are rare and we can only guess at the layout of the great temple of Thoth. The two colossal quartzite baboons at the entrance to the site, bearing the name of Amenhotep III, would certainly have stood before a gateway. The great column bases, sculpted with the cartouches of Philip III Arrhidaeus, belong to a portico that was still standing at the time of the Egypt

The so-called "Ptolemaios" funeral temple at Tuna el-Jebel.

Expedition. Among clumps of tamarisk to the west, a small pylon marks the entrance to a temple dedicated to Amun-Re, built by Ramesses II, using limestone *talattat* ▲ *402* taken from Tell el-Amarna, and decorated during the reigns of Merneptah and Sety II. The two scenes in the gateway show Sety II being welcomed by Amun-Re and Thoth (with the head of an ibis). To the south of the site the large peasant houses of the village, built on the rest of the *tell*, have great charm and character. The mosque, built from the debris of the ancient town, replaced a church.

Tuna el-Jebel

On the surface Tuna el-Jebel consists of the chapels of the Ptolemaic and Roman tombs belonging to the notables of Hermopolis. Below ground is the necropolis of the sacred

baboons and mummified ibis offered to Thoth. Well before the cemetery the northwest boundary stele of the town of Akhenaten stands alone on the face of a low cliff. The king and Nefertiti, along with three of their daughters, are shown worshipping the solar disk.

Tomb of Petosiris. The originality of the family tomb of Petosiris, the high priest of Thoth and contemporary of Alexander the Great, lies in the combined Egyptian and Greek styles of its décor. The tombs found beyond the Tomb of Petosiris are characterized by the same blend of styles, with the Greek ornamental front sometimes replacing the (Egyptian) grooved cornice and the capitals varying from Pharaonic composite to Corinthian.

Tomb of Isadora. Isadora drowned during the reign of Hadrian. The sculpted shell decorating her tomb is echoed in the lines of Greek verse painted on the wall: "In fact, it was the nymphs, oh, Isadora, the nymphs, daughters of the river, who built this chamber for you. Nilo, the eldest daughter of the Nile, began the work, fashioning a shell like those he [the Nile] harbors in his watery depths" (based on a translation by Perdrizet). The Roman access shaft to the west of the tomb is 112 feet deep.

Necropolis of sacred animals. The galleries of the *ibiotaphon* extend for several hundred yards. Here, as elsewhere, the cult of the animal incarnation of a particular divinity became widespread during the last centuries of pagan worship.

El-Bersha. During the 11th and 12th Dynasties the nomarchs of the Fifteenth Nome of Upper Egypt were buried at El-Bersha. The tombs have fallen prey to quarriers and are in an advanced state of disrepair. Of the ten tombs on the site only one is open to the public: the Tomb of Thuthotep, famed for its scene depicting the transporting of a colossal statue.

Sheikh Saïd. During the 5th and 6th Dynasties the governors of Hermopolis were buried at Sheikh Saïd. The names of the princes can still be seen in the ruined necropolis.

Tomb of Petosiris
Inside the tomb (whose entrance is seen below) the religious and funerary scenes are executed in accordance with Egyptian principles, while scenes of everyday life interpret the traditional repertoire in Greek style (vestibule). In the chapel the plinth decorated with bearers of offerings is a true masterpiece.

The sacred animal necropolis contains chapels (the best preserved is in the name of Ptolemy I), stone baboon sarcophagi and corridors filled with jars where there are two mummified ibis (above, left and right).

BOUNDARY STELAE
To mark the boundaries of his new city Akhenaten had fourteen monumental stelae carved in the cliffs, three on the west bank and eleven on the east bank. The scenes show the royal family worshipping the solar disk, while the texts praise the divine star, outline the construction program and undertake not to exceed the boundaries defined by the stelae.

TELL EL-AMARNA

Virtually everything there is to say has been said about what has become known as the "Amarnian experience". Hypotheses and fantasies aside, it basically concerned a king and queen involved in a political experience which was, to a certain extent, at variance with tradition. Their decision to identify a single, sufficient god, concentrated within the solar disk, their creation of a new city on land which, according to the texts, did not belong to any divinity, their adoption of the esthetic principles which characterized all their works and, finally, the brutal return to orthodoxy by their successors, with a *damnatio memoriae* which left no stone standing, are the main features of what was an exceptional period in Egyptian history.

AKHETATEN. In his fifth regnal year Amenhotep IV changed his name to Akhenaten, meaning "favorable to the Aten" (the solar disk) and founded his capital, Akhetaten ("Horizon of the

Aten"), in the vast cirque of Tell el-Amarna, which covers an area of 6 miles (north–south) by 2 miles (east–west). The king built temples for his new cult, palaces for himself and the royal princesses, administrative buildings, houses for his subjects and a village for the necropolis workers, marking the perimeters with fourteen BOUNDARY STELAE. The necropolis is divided into two sections which lie to the north and south of the cirque. Of particular interest in the north are the tombs of HUYA (no. 1), MERYRE (no. 2), AHMOSE (no. 3), another MERYRE (no. 4) and PANEHSY (no. 6) and, in the south, of PARENNEFER (no. 7), TUTU (no. 8), MAHU (no. 9) and AY (no. 25) who became pharaoh and succeeded Akhenaten. To the attentive visitor scenes from the everyday life of the ancient city are revealed in the reliefs of the tombs. The royal couple form the leitmotif and are shown "in their public appearances and in the privacy of the palace, accompanied by their daughters, breathing, eating, walking, at leisure, making offerings and worshipping, beneath a huge sun whose rays are vibrant with life. These epiphanies of the Trinity are the central theme of huge compositions showing the foundation festivals, offerings placed in open sanctuaries, visits to sanctuaries, the receiving of tributes, the rewarding of ministers, the dedication of the worshippers and the activities of their subjects, living images with a wealth of picturesque detail" (P. Vernus and J. Yoyotte, *Les Pharaons*).

MEIR AND EL-QUSIYA. During the Old and Middle Kingdoms, the notables of Cusae (modern El-Qusiya) were buried in the necropolis of Meir. Cusae was the capital of the Fourteenth Nome of Upper Egypt and the town of the goddess Hathor ● 62 who became the Greek goddess Aphrodite Urania. Recent renovation work in the tombs has restored the texture and color of their images. The hallmark of this necropolis, especially in the CHAPELS OF SENBI AND UKHHOTEP, is the extremely realistic style in which traditional scenes are represented. Here, more than anywhere else, one is aware of the artists' sense of the present, of details that surprise and amuse. The hirsute herdsman (below), bent like his staff, verges on caricature.

KOM DARA. Kom Dara is the name of a huge brick construction (over 393 feet square) covered with sand and bordered by the houses on the outskirts of the village. Whether mastaba or pyramid ● 82, this Old-Kingdom tomb is the largest in its necropolis.

Tell el-Amarna as it is today.

"Each of these streets . . . was conceived, traced by Akhenaten. We watched, together, as each of the buildings was constructed. Now, all I have to do is close my eyes and I see its towering temples and houses, its living gardens and its network of streets."
Andrée Chedid
Nefertiti et le Rêve d'Akhenaten

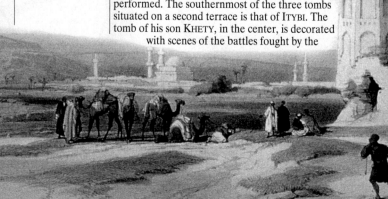

"From the time of
the Arab conquest to
the reign of
Mohammed Ali,
Assiut prospered
owing to its position
at the end of the
caravan
route
from
Nubia, Sannar,
Dongola and Darfur.
Its markets sold 'gold
dust, elephants' tusks,
ebony, musk, civet,
ambergris, ostrich
feathers, various
types of gum and a
host of other
expensive
merchandise. But its
most valuable
commodity was the
two or three thousand
black slaves that the
caravans brought
back to sell in
Egypt'."

Benoît de Maillet
*La Description de
l'Egypte*

ASSIUT

Assiut, Syut to the Ancient Egyptians, was the fief of the jackal gods Wepwawet ("Opener of Ways") and Anubis, after whom the Greeks renamed it Lycopolis ("city of the wolf"). Although the geographical position of the capital of the Thirteenth Nome of Upper Egypt meant that it was of strategic interest in the recurrent struggles between Upper and Lower Egypt, it never played a role of any national importance. The modern city center stands squarely on the *kom* of the ancient city and nothing is directly known about the monuments buried beneath several feet of accumulated ruins.

FAMOUS NAMES. Plotinus, the neo-Platonist philosopher, was born in Lycopolis in 205. He left the provincial capital for Alexandria and became a disciple of Ammonius, founder of the famous neo-Platonist school. From there he went on to Rome where he taught a doctrine based on the "union of the soul with God through ecstasy and contemplation". Some two hundred years later the town became the birthplace of one of the greatest saints of Christian Egypt: John of Lycopolis, a carpenter who withdrew to the desert of the nearby mountains. Among those drawn by his gift of prophesy was the Roman emperor Theodosius who learned of his forthcoming victories over the tyrants (Magnus Clemens) Maximus and Eugenius, his death and the succession of his sons to the Empire. John died in 394.

MODERN ASSIUT. Today Assiut is a large town, the seat of a governorate and capital of the province of Saïd (Upper Egypt), with the third largest university in Egypt (whose students occasionally give the government cause for concern). The covered market, on top of the *kom*, has a certain charm. The museum of the former Assiut College houses a modest collection of antiquities from all periods, which come from the region's various sites.

NECROPOLIS OF ASSIUT. The TOMB OF HAPIDJEFA, Prince of Assiut during the reign of Senwosret I, was dug on the first terrace of the cliff, but he died and was buried in Nubia, and his tomb in Assiut remained empty. A long inscription lists the ten clauses of the contract concluded with the priests to ensure that his funeral cult was properly performed. The southernmost of the three tombs situated on a second terrace is that of ITYBI. The tomb of his son KHETY, in the center, is decorated with scenes of the battles fought by the

NECROPOLIS OF ASSIUT
This extensively damaged necropolis is famous for the wealth of documentary and historic detail of the texts of its four largest tombs. A plan of the tombs and some of the decorative details (left), as recorded by the authors of *La Description de l'Egypte*.

kings of Heracleopolis against the Theban princes, while the TOMB OF (another) KHETY, to the north, has images of the hydrological work carried out by the owner to use the Nile floods to best advantage. The view from the terrace takes in modern Assiut (whose suburbs are encroaching onto agricultural land) and, to the north, one of the largest Muslim necropolises in Egypt.

DEIR DURUNKA. About 6 miles south of Assiut, on the road which runs parallel to the Libyan mountains, a town suddenly appears on the cliff face. Its buildings, constructed in recent years by the Coptic orthodox see of Assiut, are evidence of the importance of the pilgrimage of the Virgin of Deir Durunka (August 22). The Holy Family is believed to have stayed in the site's oldest CHURCH, which stands in an ancient quarry in the middle of the cliff. Its monastery is the most famous in a region where Christianity is particularly deeply rooted. The churches of several nearby

"Two o'clock. The sun, already high in the sky, takes [Assiut] from behind. The entire town is steeped in grayish purple and stands in a vast stretch of pale lilac water. Behind the town the lofty, unyielding silhouette of a mountain is bathed in the same light, completely immersed and indistinct in the softest and most even tones of purplish-gray imaginable. One senses, in the distance that separates the town and the mountain and in the sudden change of tone, the vast expanse that lies between them. In fact you can see water flowing around the town. To the right, to the left, a vast, double lake. A bridge links the two branches . . . A huge town, a city of mud walls and monumental constructions; pyloned houses, clean, regular and new-looking; the streets are dusty but free of rubbish."
Eugène Fromentin, 1835

The great temple that once stood at Qaou el-Kebir is lavishly illustrated in *La Description de l'Egypte* (above). In 1821 it was washed away when the Nile altered its course. Its blocks were reused for a palace in Assiut.

The entrance and interior of the church of the Red Monastery.

The god Min at the Temple of Athribis.

monasteries were dedicated to Saint Athanasius, Saint John the Baptist, Claudius, Philotas and Moncurius. About 300 yards to the north a rectangular opening, clearly visible against the white rock face, is traditionally believed to be the hermitage of Saint John of Lycopolis.

ABU TIG. Abu Tig is derived from the Greek *apotheke* (shop, warehouse). The town stands at the center of a region whose agricultural landscape has a very particular charm. Land re-allocation has had a different effect on the plain of Abu Tig where the boundaries between the (often terraced) fields appear as irregular curves rather than as the straight lines seen on the plains in the rest of the valley. The region gives some idea of the cultivated face of Egypt from Antiquity to the construction of the Aswan High Dam.

EL-BADARI. The term "Badarian" was derived from the village of El-Badari. The nearby cemetery in fact revealed a considerable amount of material (dating from between 5500 and 3800 BC), which made the Badarian stage (during which the inhabitants of the Nile Valley perfected their stock-breeding and agricultural skills) the earliest stage of the pre-Dynastic period.

QAOU EL-KEBIR. The two names of the Pharaonic town known as Antaeopolis (town of Antaeus) in Graeco-Roman times are translated as "The Two Sandals" and "High Mountain". The (now non-existent) great temple that once stood at Qaou el-Kebir is mentioned in *La Description de l'Egypte*: "Travelers will be amazed, as we ourselves were, at the sight of these beautiful columns and palm capitals (visible from the river through groups of palm trees of the same height), standing, as it were, amongst the trees whose image they faithfully reproduce." The NECROPOLIS can still be seen, perched high on the mountain. Three 12th-Dynasty tombs (two Wakhas and an Ibu) are the most interesting monuments on the site. The rock-cut CHAPEL consists of several porticoed terraces opening onto a series of underground rooms. The long access ramps from the valley add to the monumental aspect of the complex. Most of its tombs are later (30th Dynasty), from the Roman period.

TAHTA. Commemorative scarabs are evidence of the gift made by Amenhotep III to his queen Tiyi of a 150-acre domain at Djarukha, in the region of Tahta, her family home. It was inundated during the Nile floods and the royal sovereigns used to sail aboard the royal barque (the *Shining Sun*). Blocks found in the fields by local *fellaheen* are all that remain of the temple, dedicated to Horus, that once stood at Tahta.

WHITE MONASTERY. According to the life of Shenute as told by his disciple, Besa, the Coptic abbot was born in 348, took monastic orders at the age of seven and soon withdrew into the desert where he lived as a hermit. He took part in the Council of Ephesus in 431 and died in 466. He built the Deir el-Abyad or White Monastery, of which only the church has survived. The building materials for the monastery were provided by local temples as Shenute vented his fury against the pagan gods. The age, size and state of preservation of the church make it an important landmark in the history of ancient Christian art: a nave with a basilican layout, reused columns and, to the east, a "tri-conical" sanctuary. Several fires have detracted from its original splendor. The festival of "Amba Shenuda" is held on July 14.

RED MONASTERY. The 6th-century Deir Amba Bishoi is also known as the Red Monastery because of the burnt brick from which it was built. It lies about 2 miles north of the White Monastery and, like the latter, only the church remains.

AKHMIM. On his pilgrimage to Mecca in the 12th century Ibn Jobeir passed through Akhmim and was greatly impressed by one of its temples: "Apart from its walls, this huge temple is supported by forty columns ... The ceiling of the entire temple is made of stone paving admirably arranged to form a

"And the angel said to Apa Bgoul: 'When you rise in the morning, put the robe that you find before you on the little boy Shenute, ... the Lord Jesus has sent it to you so that you may dress him in it; for verily I say unto you, he will be a just and chosen man ... he will build a monastery, he will be an inspiration and a

protector for anyone who comes to him in his dwelling-place and his church will last for generations'.**"**
Vie de Schnoudi (based on the translation by Amélineau)

The White and Red monasteries (above).

383

NECROPOLIS OF EL-HAWAWISH
The Old-Kingdom tombs of this necropolis are decorated with figures and scenes from everyday life. A butchery scene (right).

GIRGA
❝It is an unremarkable, modern town; as big as El-Minya and Mellawi, smaller than Assiut and less pretty than all of them. The name Girga or Dgridga comes from the great monastery, built before the town existed and dedicated to Saint George, pronounced "Gerge" in the local dialect ... The Nile washes against the buildings of Girga and each day demolishes them a little more ... The town's only interest is its position, equidistant from Cairo and Syene, and the richness of the surrounding region.❞
Dominique Vivant Denon

single unit ... Inside and outside ... the figures are all different in shape and appearance; there are figures horrible to behold, of inhuman aspect, which make those who look upon them tremble with fear, filling them with apprehension and wonder" (based on a translation by Gaudefroy-Demombynes). In the 14th century El-Khatib destroyed the temple and built a college, the remains of which are found inside the houses: its granite columns have been transformed into millstones and the limestone is used in the lime kilns. Akhmim is the town of the ithyphallic god Min who, as well as being the god of fertility, was also master of the deserts between the Nile and the Red Sea. The Greeks recognized him as Pan and duly called the town Panopolis: "The Pans and Satyrs who live near Chemmis [Akhmim] were the first to learn of the death of Osiris and spread the news. This was how the sudden fear that grips a multitude became known as panic" (Plutarch). The ancient history of the town which, during the Pharaonic period, was called Ipu or Khent-Menu, is told by its necropolises. The Arabian mountains open up into a cirque, delimited to the south by the NECROPOLIS OF EL-HAWAWISH where the governors of the province were buried from the 4th to the 11th Dynasties. To the north the EL-SALAMUNI PROMONTORY contains the rock-cut tombs of the Graeco-Roman period. About two-thirds of the way up the slope a gate

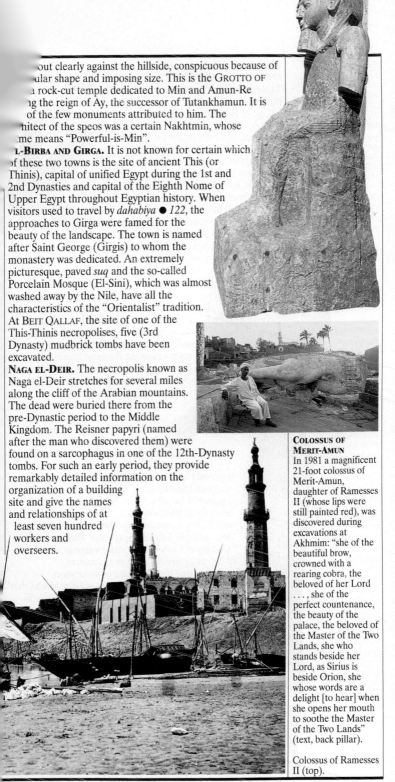

...out clearly against the hillside, conspicuous because of ...ular shape and imposing size. This is the GROTTO OF ... a rock-cut temple dedicated to Min and Amun-Re ...g the reign of Ay, the successor of Tutankhamun. It is ... of the few monuments attributed to him. The ...hitect of the speos was a certain Nakhtmin, whose ...me means "Powerful-is-Min".

L-BIRBA AND GIRGA. It is not known for certain which of these two towns is the site of ancient This (or Thinis), capital of unified Egypt during the 1st and 2nd Dynasties and capital of the Eighth Nome of Upper Egypt throughout Egyptian history. When visitors used to travel by *dahabiya* ● *122*, the approaches to Girga were famed for the beauty of the landscape. The town is named after Saint George (Girgis) to whom the monastery was dedicated. An extremely picturesque, paved *suq* and the so-called Porcelain Mosque (El-Sini), which was almost washed away by the Nile, have all the characteristics of the "Orientalist" tradition. At BEIT QALLAF, the site of one of the This-Thinis necropolises, five (3rd Dynasty) mudbrick tombs have been excavated.

NAGA EL-DEIR. The necropolis known as Naga el-Deir stretches for several miles along the cliff of the Arabian mountains. The dead were buried there from the pre-Dynastic period to the Middle Kingdom. The Reisner papyri (named after the man who discovered them) were found on a sarcophagus in one of the 12th-Dynasty tombs. For such an early period, they provide remarkably detailed information on the organization of a building site and give the names and relationships of at least seven hundred workers and overseers.

COLOSSUS OF MERIT-AMUN
In 1981 a magnificent 21-foot colossus of Merit-Amun, daughter of Ramesses II (whose lips were still painted red), was discovered during excavations at Akhmim: "she of the beautiful brow, crowned with a rearing cobra, the beloved of her Lord . . ., she of the perfect countenance, the beauty of the palace, the beloved of the Master of the Two Lands, she who stands beside her Lord, as Sirius is beside Orion, she whose words are a delight [to hear] when she opens her mouth to soothe the Master of the Two Lands" (text, back pillar).

Colossus of Ramesses II (top).

385

Abydos stands apart among the famous cities of Ancient Egypt. It was not the city of a dynastic god and creator of the universe, nor a political or administrative capital, nor an important economic center. It was a holy city, the city of Osiris who was murdered by his brother and enemy, Seth, and became regent of the World of the Dead. It was the city where, according to the legend that finally prevailed over all the others, the god was buried. Kings built cenotaphs there and the great and not-so-great erected stelae in their name, all hoping, at least after their death, to make the pilgrimage by boat to Abydos. Khenti-Imentiu ("Chief of the Westerners") was the principal god of Abydos, the "Westerners" being the deceased who, like the sun which sets in the west, crossed the Nile to the left (west) bank and were laid to rest in their tombs. He was gradually superseded by Osiris.

ABYDOS

TEMPLE OF SETY I. The site of Abydos is vast. Virtually nothing remains of the ancient town which lies beneath the village of Beni Mansur, of the metropolitan temple which stood at the place known as Kom el-Sultan, or of the desert necropolises.

The fame of Abydos is based on one monument: the cenotaph-temple of Sety I, the only royal structure built on the god's territory which is still well preserved. The bases of the walls are all that remains of the two courts built by Ramesses II. Today visitors enter the temple via the portico which precedes the first hypostyle hall. Among the temple's special features are the SEVEN AXIAL CHAPELS dedicated, from left to right, to Sety I deified, Ptah, Harmachis (Horus on the Horizon), Amun-Re (central chapel), Osiris, Isis and Horus. These rooms and the suite of rooms leading off the chapel of Osiris are decorated with reliefs which number among the most beautiful in Egyptian art. Following the hiatus of the Amarnian experience ● *42,* ▲ *378,* the reign of Sety I (and at Abydos in particular) marks the birth of what was to become the Ramesside style. Along the right-hand wall of the corridor opening off the left wall of the second hypostyle hall a sculpted tableau gives a selective list of seventy-six pharaohs to which Sety I pays homage: one of the few "royal lists" compiled by the Egyptians. This so-called "Gallery of Lists" is of greater value as a self-view of Egyptian history than as a means of reconstructing the royal line of succession.

OSIREION. The strange structure of huge blocks that Sety I had built behind his temple was supposedly the fictitious tomb of Osiris. According to Strabo: "At the far end [of the temple] is a well into which you descend via spiral galleries formed by monoliths of extraordinary size and structure. A canal diverted from the great river flows to this place where it is surrounded by a sacred wood of acanthus, dedicated to Apollo." This artificial underground island may have contained the sarcophagus and Canopic jars of the god. The complex was covered by a mound planted with trees, a distinctive feature of Osirian sanctuaries. The smaller and less well-preserved cenotaph-temple of Ramesses II lies about 200 yards to the north of that of his father.

> "OSIRIS IS WORSHIPPED AT ABYDOS. IN HIS TEMPLE, IT IS FORBIDDEN TO SING OR PLAY THE TRUMPET OR THE LYRE IN HONOR OF THE GOD, AS IS THE CUSTOM FOR THE OTHER DIVINITIES." STRABO

ROYAL BURIALS. In the desert about 2 miles to the southwest are the tombs of the 1st- and 2nd-Dynasty kings whose capital was at This. These great mudbrick rectangles are divided into blind rooms where offerings were placed and where skeletons of men and lions were found, possibly sacrificed during the funeral ceremony. The place is known as UMM EL-QA'B ("mother of the pots"). During the New Kingdom the tomb of one of the kings was transformed into the tomb of Osiris and became a

ERECTION OF THE "DJED" PILLAR
Sety I performing the ceremony of the erection of the *djed* pillar, symbol of Osiris, in the presence of the goddess Isis.

place of sacrifice, always accompanied by the ritual breaking of small terra-cotta pots. SHUNET EL-ZEBIB ("storehouse of dates"), a huge high-walled rectangle at the western end of the site, is also an early dynastic tomb.

HIW. Today nothing remains of the ancient capital of the Seventh Nome of Upper Egypt, where Amun of Thebes and Hathor were worshiped.

QENA. Modern Qena developed as a result of the opening up of the Wadi Qena toward the Red Sea (which became the main commercial route between Upper Egypt and the east-coast ports) and because of its famous mosque. On his return from Mecca the Maghrebi Abd el-Rahim settled in Qena and founded a Sufi center which attracted students from all over Upper Egypt. After his death in 1195 the mosque built above his tomb became a place of pilgrimage. The great modern mosque of Sheikh el-Qenawi, in the main square, is evidence of the "saint's" importance, and his *muled* is the largest between Cairo and Aswan.

Detail of the capitals
of the Temple of
Hathor.

An inscription,
combining traditional
eulogies and precise
dimensions, describes
the attributes of the
main temple: **"The
king of Upper Egypt
himself constructed
the temple [of the
goddess] in beautiful,
shining sandstone; it
is one hundred and
twelve cubits long and
seventy-five and one
fifth cubits wide. It is
truly magnificent to
behold with its overall
height of twenty-
three and one third
cubits, its chapels,
chambers, chapel of
the New Year,
staircase, columns
and upper chapels."**
(based on a
translation by
Sylvie Cauville)

The ceiling of the
Court of the New
Year (above right).

DENDERA

"Re opened his eyes inside the lotus as it emerged from
primordial chaos and his eyes began to weep and droplets fell
to the ground: they were
transformed into a beautiful woman
who was named Gold of the Gods,
Hathor the Great, Mistress of
Dendera" (based on a translation
by Sylvie Cauville). And so Hathor
was born. She presided over
amorous pursuits; music, dance and
enjoyment were her preserve and it
was through them that she was
honored. This pan-Egyptian
divinity also took the form of a
fierce lioness who killed humans, a
celestial cow and life-giving flood
waters. Dendera was only one of

her many temples, but it is today among the best preserved
and the best known in Egypt. Virtually everything inside the
mudbrick enclosure wall is designed to evoke divine
influence. The entrance is through a huge gateway preceded
by public fountains. The monuments are all relatively recent
since, as in many sanctuaries throughout Egypt, the ancient
temples of Dendera were entirely rebuilt during the
Ptolemaic and Roman periods.

TEMPLE OF HATHOR. The main temple, which was begun
during the reign of Ptolemy XII Auletes (80–51 BC) and
continued until the reign of Nero (AD 54–68) remained
unfinished. Today visitors enter directly via the pronaos with
eighteen columns arranged in the form of a sistrum, the

instrument associated with the goddess, whose head, with its cow's ears, is reproduced on the capitals. The astronomical ceiling is decorated with the daily course of the sun, the lunar cycle, the decans, the Twelve Hours of the day and night and the signs of the zodiac. Along the walls is the sinuous body of the sky-goddess Nut who swallows the solar disk in the evening and gives birth to it in the

morning. After this comes the HYPOSTYLE HALL flanked by six rooms which were the service chambers where offerings were received. The priests arranged these offerings on huge tables in the offering hall. This led into the vestibule with the "robing room" and finally the central SHRINE of the "Great Seat". The huge granite naos with bronze doors inlaid with gold, which housed the goddess' statue, is no longer there. The sanctuary also contained the sacred barques of Hathor, Horus, Isis and Harsomtus who are represented on the walls (the goddesses with women's heads and the gods with falcons' heads). The sanctuary is separated from the rest of the temple and protected from the outside world by a corridor and the ELEVEN DIVINE CHAPELS that it services. The chapels are dedicated (from the left as you face the sanctuary) to Hathor, Isis, Sokar (the falcon-headed funeral god of Memphis associated with Osiris), Harsomtus (son of Hathor and Horus), the next four chapels to Hathor, the ninth to Horus of Edfu and the last two to Hathor. Crypts are built into the walls of the temple on three sides and at three levels. Some are richly decorated and one, entered through chapel no. 8, is mainly devoted to the representation and the description of the divine statues and the sacred objects of the temple.

CLEOPATRA AND CAESARION
The exterior back wall of the temple has become famous for its representation (in a style which, it is true, does not distinguish them from other kings and queens) of the legendary Cleopatra and the son she bore Caesar, Ptolemy XV Caesar, known as Caesarion.

"This monument seems to me to have something primitive about it, the character of a temple *par excellence*. . . . Nothing simpler and more precisely calculated than the few lines which compose its architecture. Since the Egyptians borrowed nothing from other cultures, they did not add 'foreign' ornaments or superfluous elements to what was dictated by necessity. Their principles were order and simplicity, and they elevated these principles to the very highest level.**"**
Dominique Vivant Denon

COPTIC BASILICA
Inside the temple, to the left of the entrance, are two *mamissi*. Between them is the Coptic basilica which was added in the 5th century.

FESTIVAL OF THE NEW YEAR. The tower of the central shrine ends in the Court of the New Year and the Pure Place, which lies beyond through the right-hand door of the vestibule. Every temple had these two rooms, used for the New Year ceremonies, which involved the presentation of offerings in the court and the exposure of the divine statues in the Pure Place. On the ceiling, as in the pronaos, are images of Nut swallowing and giving birth to the sun, whose rays light up the temple, symbolized by the face of Hathor. The procession ascended the stairs to the roof: the king was followed by the priests bearing symbols and portable chapels, who were in turn followed by the divinities bearing offerings. Once on the roof they made their way to the chapel whose twelve columns represented the face of the goddess turned toward the four points of the compass. The divine statues were exposed to the sun's rays and were recharged with its divine energy for another year (the hippopotamus-goddesses on the columns personified the twelve months of the year).

RESURRECTION OF OSIRIS. On the roof the six chapels, in two groups of three, are dedicated to the basic myth of the resurrection of Osiris, who was murdered and cut into pieces by his brother Seth. Isis searched Egypt for the pieces and put them together to recreate the body of her husband. She then bore him a son: Horus, the supreme royal heir. These chapels guaranteed the annual resurrection of the god during a festival held as the waters of the Nile subsided. This ancient ritual, described in every detail on the walls, was a commemorative ceremony which involved the creation, by re-enacting the gestures, of a replica of Osiris's body from a paste in which barley was the main ingredient. The image, sprinkled with pure water, germinated and was later buried in one of the chapels. All the provinces, which each possessed a reliquary containing a piece of the god's body, were invited to attend. The process was so delicate and so decisive that, in order to ensure its success, the powers of the protecting spirits were invoked, whose assembled hosts can be seen in the chapels. One of the chapels contained the molding of the famous zodiac, bought by France in 1823 (Louvre Museum ▲ 476). A staircase (a metal one has replaced the original) leads to the roof of the pronaos, which offers a view of the various monuments on the site, the desert (where the necropolis was located) and countryside beyond.

"MAMISSI". On the way back to the entrance of the temple, two *mamissi* stand on the left. The first, dating from the reign of Nectanebo I (380–63 BC) is the oldest building on the site. The second is unfinished and bears the cartouches of Trajan and Antoninus Pius (138–61). Both of these *mamissi* are dedicated to the birth of the divine heir Harsomtus, son of Hathor and Horus. The scenes decorating the exterior south wall, against which a Coptic basilica (far left) was built in the 5th century, are true masterpieces of bas-relief carving from the later period. They are skillfully executed, and their attention to detail is quite meticulous.

The sacred lake is the most beautiful of Egypt's surviving temple lakes. During the festival of the resurrection of Osiris 34 barques and 365 tiny "boats", each containing a candle, were set afloat on its waters.

The town of El-Ballas still produces the large earthenware jars (used for carrying water) for which it is famed (above). However, plastic (Egypt is one of the world's largest per capita consumers) will soon replace this age-old craft industry.

QIFT. The ruins of ancient Koptos, in the center of Qift, give little idea of the importance of the town during antiquity. It rebelled during the reign of Diocletian and was razed to the ground. The geographical position of Koptos guaranteed its economic prosperity before it was superseded, during the Mameluke period, by Qus and, in modern times, by Qena. The town stands at the mouth of a *wadi* which opened it up to the desert. Koptos and its god Min ● *63* both date from the beginning of Egyptian history. In Koptos Min was the protector of the gold mines, quarries and caravan routes. All that remains of his temple are a few foundations and fragments of the enclosure wall. The best preserved

One of the gates (right) of the Temple of Harwer in Qus.

Pilgrims from the Maghreb, Cairo and Alexandria passed through Qus on their way to Mecca. The age and beauty of its mosque are an indication of its prosperity. Detail of the decoration of the mosque and a ruined palace (below).

monuments are concentrated in the southern part of the town: a solitary gateway dating from the reign of Claudius, the uprights of a door set in a farmyard (Ptolemy XII and Caligula) and the chapel of the legendary Cleopatra with an image of three concentric naos containing the sacred barque. North of the suburbs of the modern town is the small TEMPLE OF EL-QAL'A, which dates from Roman times, dedicated to Isis and Harpocrates.

NAGADA. Nagada made a valuable contribution to Egyptian prehistory. Excavations revealed a vast cemetery of small, rectangular tombs just below the surface of the sand. The deceased lay curled up on their side, surrounded by pots, schist offering basins and terracotta figurines. Since this discovery the last stages of prehistory in Upper Egypt (3800–3100) have been known as I, II and III.

QUS. The two ruined gates of the TEMPLE OF HARWER (Horus the Elder) are all that remains of the ancient town of Apollinopolis Parva, the rival of Koptos in the Fifth Nome. The opening of an alternative route to the Red Sea during the 13th century meant that Qus replaced Qift as Upper Egypt's main commercial center trading with Africa, India, Arabia and the Yemen.

THEBES

▲ THEBES

1 TEMPLE OF AMUN-RE
2 KARNAK: TEMPLE OF MONTU
3 TEMPLE OF MUT
4 TEMPLE OF LUXOR
5 BIRKET HABU
6 MALKATTA
7 MEDINET HABU
8 TEMPLE OF AMENHOTEP III
9 TEMPLE OF HOREMHEB
10 DEIR EL-MEDINA

Restitution of the Theban region to the Middle Kingdom.

The celebrated Egyptian city of Thebes was described by Homer as "the city of a hundred gates" because so many of its temples had the monumental entrances favored by contemporary Greek architecture. Known to the Ancient Egyptians as Waset, Thebes was twice the Egyptian capital. It was from Thebes that Ahmose restored the unity of Egypt and inaugurated the New Kingdom, one of the most glorious periods in the history of the Two Lands. Even when it was not the capital, Thebes nonetheless played a key role in the history of Egypt. From the Middle Kingdom to the end of antiquity it was the sacred city of Amun-Re, the supreme god and source of Pharaonic legitimacy, and one of the main spiritual, intellectual and economic centers in Ancient Egypt.

Six days

CITY OF THEBES. The ancient city of Thebes stood at the center of a vast cultivated region, bordered to the east and west by the arid peaks of the Arabian and Libyan mountains. It was divided by the Nile into two very distinct parts. The city proper lay on the east bank now occupied by the town of Luxor (from the Arabic El-Uqsur, meaning "the palaces"). It was built entirely of mudbrick and consisted of a series of districts, suburbs and villages organized around the temples of Karnak and Luxor and linked by a *dromos*, a straight, paved way bordered by sphinxes. On the west bank the necropolis, funerary temples and embalming rooms, which were known during the Roman occupation as *memnonia*, were built into the cliff.

Foundations of houses, some of the few remains of the city of Thebes.

395

THE CORNICHE
The Temple of Luxor
is situated on the
Corniche, whose
promenade has just
been entirely rebuilt
by a Chinese
company. It owes its
somewhat irregular
layout to the fact that
it was built on the site
of a quay which
followed the line of
the river. To the east
of the Corniche a
garden has recently
been restored after
years of neglect. It is
surrounded by
bazaars which were
relocated here as part
of a campaign to
smarten up the town.

The first pylon: the
temple entrance is
flanked by two colossi
of Ramesses II and
one of the two
original obelisks.

THEBES: EAST BANK

By the mid-19th century Thebes was a shadow of its former
self. It was nothing but a small town ranged against the
Temple of Amenhotep III, a pile of ruins amidst a pile of
more ancient ruins, which was under threat from the Nile
floods and the lime kilns. Luxor, a town of 11,000 inhabitants
in 1900, now has a population of 150,000 and is governed by a
special statute which grants it an administrative autonomy
unique throughout Egypt. The center of the town revolves
around the Temple of Luxor. About 2 miles to the north lies
the ruined Temple of Karnak. Some sections of the ancient
paved way bordered by sphinxes, which used to link the
temple to Luxor, have been excavated.

"EGYPTOMANIA". Following the successive waves of
"Egyptomania" that swept Paris and London, and even
reached the United States, there was an understandable
attempt in this Ancient Egyptian capital to bring official
buildings into line with a traditionally "Egyptian" form of
architecture, especially after the discovery of the Tomb of
Tutankhamun. The National Bank of Egypt near the
Winter Palace, the spa south of the *Novotel*, the police
station and the 1960's railway station are just a few examples.
During the period when Upper Egypt was visited by train,
the neo-Pharaonic stations of Edfu ▲ *448* and Kom Ombo
▲ *452* were obligatory stops on the
itinerary.

COLONIAL ARCHITECTURE. At the
northern end of the temple site are
two ocher-colored houses belonging to
the descendants of one of Luxor's old
Coptic families. These houses have
probably survived because they were
sequestered after the 1952 revolution.
The center of Thebes still has a few
Art Deco and Italianate apartment
blocks near the station and, in the
Shari' el-Markaz, neo-Arabic-style
wooden balconies. At the airport
road intersection are three
tropical-style, "Nubian"
sandstone buildings with huge
wooden verandahs: the villa of the
head of Luxor Town Council, the
"rest-house" of the Egyptian Ministry
of Irrigation and the Anglican Coptic
School.

TEMPLE OF LUXOR

This monumental complex was linked to Karnak by the long, straight *dromos* completed during the reign of Nectanebo I. The paved way, which is extremely well preserved in front of the temple, crossed the city and ended before a huge sandstone gate, of which only the eroded remains can be seen today. The gate opened onto a forecourt in the corner of which stands a small Roman chapel of burnt brick, dedicated to the god Serapis during the reign of Hadrian. The Temple of Luxor used to be called Ipet Resyt, which has often been translated as "Harem of the South". More broadly speaking it was a southern palace where the god resided like a king, attended by his servants, the priests. The temple was first excavated in 1881 by Gaston Maspero and the work was continued by his successors. Over a century later, during the excavation of the court of Amenhotep III (whose columns were in danger of collapsing), workmen found five carefully preserved royal statues from the New Kingdom buried in the sand about 3 feet below the level of the courtyard. Another twenty or so statues of pharaohs and divinities from different historical periods were discovered buried haphazardly beneath them. They are on display in the Luxor Museum, in a room shaped like a tomb.

Although the site was cleared by Gaston Maspero ● 96 in 1881 and studied by his successors, the Temple of Luxor has not yet been completely excavated because the Abu el-

Hagag Mosque stands on a solid mass of earth in the corner of the first court.

ABU EL-HAGAG MOSQUE. The mosque, dedicated to Sheikh Yussef Abu el-Hagag, is one of the oldest in Luxor. The sheikh, who came from Baghdad in the 12th century, was descended from the Prophet via Hassan, son of the Prophet's daughter Fatima. The Fatimid-style mosque has survived several attempts to demolish it and release the site. It has a beautiful mudbrick minaret to which a second was added in the early 20th century by the khedive Abbas Helmi.

"MULED" OF ABU EL-HAGAG. The *muled* ● 126 of Abu el-Hagag is the most important annual feast in Luxor and one of the best known in Upper Egypt. It is held on the fourteenth of the month of Sha'ban, the presumed date of the sheikh's arrival in the town. The *muled* is characterized by a procession of *feluccas* ● 122 carried by the Faithful, which is thought to be a ritual dating back to the ancient procession of the sacred barque of Amun from the Temple of Luxor to Karnak. For the Faithful the boats represent the one used by Abu el-Hagag on his journeys. Another special feature of the *muled* is a dish of minced meat, onions and crushed corn.

THEBAN TRIAD: AMUN, MUT AND KHONSU

The development of the domain of Amun-Re is linked to that of Thebes, the capital of Egypt from the 18th Dynasty. Each pharaoh recorded his devotion in stone. Karnak was first discovered in the 16th and studied from the 18th century, with the Donati excavations (1759) and Napoleon Bonaparte's Egypt Expedition (1798). The first Egyptologists appeared with Champollion (1828) while the excavation of the Temple of Amun, directed by Mariette (1858), marked the beginning of systematic research.

SACRED BARQUE OF AMUN
During the Beautiful Feast of the Valley and the Festival of Opet, Amun journeyed in his sacred barque carried by thirty priests. The vessel, in gilt and inlaid wood and decorated at the prow and stern with divine symbols, supported an openwork naos surmounted by a dais.

Temple of Montu

Eastern temple

Temple

Sacred lake

Seventh pylon

Eighth pylon

TEMPLE OF LUXOR
The Temple of Luxor, linked to Karnak by a *dromos* (1½ miles) built by Nectanebo, was where the Feast of Opet was celebrated. During the reign of Amenhotep III, the edifice consisted of a south sanctuary preceded by a peristyle court and a colonnade. The entrance pylon and first court were added by Ramesses II.

Ninth pylon

Tenth pylon

Temple of Khonsu

Temple of Opet

PLAN OF KARNAK
The largest enclosure in the center, with its nine gateways, was dedicated to Amun. The enclosure to the north contains the Temple of Montu, whose original layout is reminiscent of the Temple of Luxor. To the south, and linked to the Temple of Amun by a *dromos*, lies the temple of his wife Mut.

PYLON AND COURT OF RAMESSES II. The great pylon form.
the façade of the temple was preceded by colossi and two
obelisks, of which only one remains. The other was
transported to Paris in the 19th century and now stands in t
Place de la Concorde. On the walls are scenes of the Battle
Kadesh, fought by Ramesses II against the Hittites in Syria. /
chapel whose façade has four fasciculate granite columns
stands in the corner of the first court behind the pylon. It was
a triple shrine for the sacred barques of Amun, Mut and
Khonsu, which were brought in through a western side door
in direct line with the way leading from the quay. In the
northeastern corner of the court the massive structure of a
Coptic church (whose walls are still standing) provides the
foundations of the ABU EL-HAGAG MOSQUE: three very
different places of worship whose proximity makes a striking
historical summary. Although the south side of the court,
where "closed" papyrus columns alternate with pink granite
colossi, was open to the public, this was as far as they could
go. From here they watched the arrival of processions which
then moved on into the part of the temple built during the
reign of Amenhotep III.

THE COLONNADE. Two huge, black granite colossi representing
Ramesses II seated on his throne and wearing the double
crown of Upper and Lower Egypt mark the entrance to the

The chapel which
served as a shrine for
the sacred barques
dates from the reign
of Hatshepsut and
was reused on this
site by Ramesses II.

**COURT OF
RAMESSES II**
On the south side of

the court, alternate
"closed" papyrus
columns and pink
granite colossi create a
powerful
effect. The statues
on the left show
Ramesses II walking
majestically. At his
side his queen,
Nefertari, scarcely
reaches to his knee.

great colonnade whose interior decoration dates from the
short reign of Tutankhamun ▲ 418. The young king's face
appears in the sculpted groups (usurped by Ramesses II) at
the entrance to the hall. Although the side walls have been
reduced to less than one third of their original height, their
decoration is extremely interesting because it depicts the
first of Thebes' two most important religious festivals, the
OPET FEAST (the name of the month in which it was held,
the second month of the season of the Nile floods). The king
had to take part in the feast at least in the first year of his
reign since it confirmed that he was indeed the son of Amun-
Re. Originally, during the reign of Hatshepsut, six chapel-
shrines served as a "way station" for the sacred barques
during their overland journey from Karnak to Luxor.

Only the return journey was made along the Nile. But from the reign of Amenhotep III, the festival was continually extended in size and duration (from eleven days to over three weeks) and both journeys were made by river. On the west wall of the columned court are scenes depicting the progress of the outward journey and, on the east wall, the return journey to Karnak. After it had passed through the colonnade, the procession of sacred barques entered the Court of Amenhotep III.

COURT OF AMENHOTEP III. The Court of Amenhotep III, with its fasciculate porticos, is virtually complete. The south side of the court opens onto a long hall, the pronaos of the temple. Two of the side chapels set in the back wall housed the barques of Mut and Khonsu, which

ended their journey here. A central door led into an outer hall where there are signs of a large axial niche, remains of frescos and traces of the chapel (which venerated the insignia of the Roman legion that pitched camp around the temple in AD 301). The frescos represented a speech made by the emperor Diocletian at the time of his reorganization of the defense of Upper Egypt. In front of the niche, a canopy supported by four columns (of which only two remain) surmounted the altar. A door appears to have been recently pierced at the back of the niche to allow access into the temple. The door led into the offering hall whose decorations have retained some of their original colors. In the center of the next hall is a chapel built by Alexander the Great who is represented on its walls as a pharaoh, a status conferred on him after his victory by the priests of Amun of Siwa Oasis ▲ 256. The sacred barque of Amun ended its journey here and was placed on a pedestal, while Amun of Karnak entered all the side chambers of the eastern part of the temple. Today visitors enter beneath the Roman arch added to the entrance by Amenhotep III.

"MAMISSI". The ceremonies culminated in the next room, the so-called *mamissi* or "birth room", with the symbolic annual union of the queen mother and Amun-Re. Ancient texts explain how the god charmed the queen with his scent. The aim of this union was to engender the newborn child and consequently the king himself and his *ka*, which was the expression of his specific function: his royalty. This ceremony symbolized the

The great colonnade, seen from the Court of Amenhotep III.

THE PROCESSION OF SACRIFICIAL BULLOCKS
In the southwest corner of the Court of Ramesses II are reliefs showing the procession of sacrificial bullocks brought to the temple by shaven-headed priests dressed in pleated linen robes (above). At the head of the procession the pharaoh's many sons are recognizable by their long sidelocks. The scene depicts their entry into the temple. The pylon is shown from the front while all its original statues are seen in profile.

Detail from a papyrus scroll representing one of the sacred gods of Karnak.

"TALATTAT"
Talattat are the blocks of stone of equal size used for building during the reign of Akhenaten ● *42* and reused in

the construction of more recent edifices. The Luxor Museum has a wall (59 feet by 10 feet) of *talattat* blocks originally used in one of Akhenaten's temples at Thebes. The blocks were taken from the ninth pylon of the Temple of Karnak. The wall (detail right) was painstakingly reconstructed and shows Akhenaten and Nefertiti paying homage to Aten.

rebirth of the king's royal person and the confirmation of his power, since he was simultaneously re-engendered and recognized by Amun-Re. So when the pharaoh emerged from his temple, he appeared rejuvenated and invested with new strength and wisdom. Although the annual cycle would be repeated, he would remain the guarantor of order. The world would continue to function and Egypt would prosper.

APARTMENTS OF AMUN OF LUXOR. The rooms at the far end of the temple constituted the apartments of Amun of Luxor. They were arranged around the great transverse colonnaded hall. In the axial sanctuary chamber traces of the platform which supported the divine naos can still be seen. It may seem strange to the modern mind that Amun could reside simultaneously at Karnak, Luxor and in other temples. Amun was in fact omnipresent throughout the world and was represented in these sanctuaries in a special "concentrated" form. He could only be apprehended in his multiple aspects, each one of which was not only a reflection but also a part of the Great Whole. The Great Whole could not be expressed directly: his inconceivable magnitude, his power and his nature could only be glimpsed through symbols.

TOWARD KARNAK. The ancient route to the Temple of Karnak follows the SHARI' EL-MARKAZ, the main street, which runs parallel to the Corniche. This busy street is bordered by bazaars, restaurants and cafés with brightly colored signs. Near the Pharaonic-style police station is the oldest mosque in Luxor, the EL-MEKASHKESH MOSQUE, which contains the 10th-century remains of a saint who had come to Upper

Egypt to spread the teaching of Islam. The mosque has been restored many times and is often visited by pilgrims because of the miraculous powers attributed to the saint who, according to tradition, was a monk before converting to Islam. Opposite the mosque is the Franciscan Church and its adjacent schools (girls on the right and boys on the left), founded in 1889 and run by Franciscan nuns. Beyond the courthouse and the Coptic church stands the great Coptic basilica.

LUXOR MUSEUM

The Luxor Museum, which is situated midway between Karnak and Luxor on the Nile Corniche, is a useful complement to a visit to the two temple sites. In the great basement rooms, to the right of the entrance, are the remarkable discoveries made in 1989 in the great Court of Amenhotep III. These include an amazing quartzite reproduction of a life-size royal statue of Amenhotep III, which stands on the sled on which it was moved. Other fine statues include the goddesses Iwnit and Hathor

and, on a single pedestal, a group depicting Horemheb kneeling before Amun. On the first floor is an extremely fine basalt statue of Thutmose III, found in the "Hiding Courtyard" at Karnak, followed by an alabaster group representing the god Sobek and Amenhotep III. Against the wall the great stele of King Kamose depicts the decisive Theban victory over the Hyksos, which heralded the birth of the New Kingdom. On the second floor are scenes reconstructed from the *talattat* blocks taken from the ninth pylon, and a fine head of Amenhotep IV (Akhenaten) also taken from the edifices built by this king to the east of the great Temple of Amun-Re. Near the ramp is a colossus of Senwosret I in the guise of Osiris, which is thought to have come from the façade of the Middle Kingdom temple at Karnak. At the intersection, the Shari' el-Markaz becomes the SHARI' EL-KARNAK and, after crossing a small bridge, the remains of the recently excavated *dromos* that once linked the Temple of Luxor to the Temple of Karnak gradually come into view, lower down, in the middle of a village. From the ruined Temple of Mut, on the left-hand side, a second *dromos* leads to the gateway of the tenth pylon. It passes the great *pisé* enclosure wall, the gateway of Ptolemy III Euergetes and several houses which can be seen on the left before it finally arrives at the domed tomb of two saints (Sidi Ahmed and Sidi Ali). A road running past the Department of Antiquities leads to the main entrance of the temple.

"Anyone who has drunk of the waters of the Nile, seeks to return to the Nile, for no other water can slake their thirst. Anyone born in Thebes seeks to return to Thebes for no other city in the world can compare with Thebes. Anyone born in a street in Thebes seeks to return to that street; in cedarwood palaces, they long for a hut built of clay; amidst the scent of myrrh and perfumed unguents, they long for the smell of dried cow-dung burning on the fire and the aroma of fried fish ... Would that I were a swallow or crane with powerful wings to fly in the face of my guards toward the land of Kemi. I would build my nest on the marbled columns of the Temple of Amun, amidst the dazzling, golden brilliance of the obelisks, the scent of incense and the aroma of fatted sacrificial victims."

Mika Waltari
The Egyptian

A SACRED PLACE
Only priests and those who served the god were allowed into the inner sanctum of the temple, which was a veritable "holy city" enclosed by a high mudbrick wall. The temple was not so much a place of worship for the ordinary rank and file as one where mysterious ceremonies involving precise and complex rituals were held, with a view to maintaining cosmic harmony. All that ordinary Thebans saw of the temple were its gates, its enclosure wall and the paved access ways. What could be more impressive than the permanent presence of this awesome, hidden power?

TEMPLE OF KARNAK

GREAT TEMPLE OF AMUN-RE. The ancient name of Karnak, Ipet Sut ("the most hallowed of places"), designates the "center of the world" where Amun, the creator of the universe, first created himself and then all things and living beings. He combined the power of the Theban demiurge (Amun) with that of the supreme sun-god of Heliopolis (Re). He was the guarantor of the continued survival of the universe that he had created and therefore of the kingdom ruled by his "beloved son" pharaoh, the only official priest. Mankind, by worshipping in the temple, could help preserve the cosmic harmony so essential to life, and encompassed by the Egyptian concept of *ma'at* ● *63* which signified truth, order and justice. All this was part of the pharaohs' duty. Their watchword was "Life, Stability and Strength".

ORGANIZATION OF THE TEMPLE. Amun resided in his temple and was served by a hierarchy of priests who not only performed the sacred rites but also carried out the intellectual and material tasks associated with the running of the most important sanctuary in Egypt. Among other things, this involved managing a vast agricultural domain. A total of eighty thousand people served the temple during the reign of Ramesses III and the High Priest of Amun was a prominent figure who attended all the important events in the life of the kingdom. For more than two thousand years, from the end of the second millennium BC, the pharaohs erected monuments at Karnak as an offering to their divine father Amun-Re to ensure his good offices. Each one modified, embellished and extended Karnak, often demolishing the edifices of his predecessors to dedicate a new building, while Amun-Re, present in the small gold statue which stood in a monolithic kiosk (naos) in the depths of the temple, shone in the darkness.

ARRIVING AT THE TEMPLE: THE QUAY. Karnak is reached along an access road built on the site of the canal that once linked the Temple of Amun to the Nile. All that remains of the dock (now filled in) is the quay and the central raised dais. In ancient times the quay and its approaches were planted with trees and groves. Below the quay to the right (south of the dais) and beyond a Roman dock in red brick are two parallel paved ramps bordered by stone parapets, built during the reign of Taharqa ● *44*, which once led down to the river bank. Beyond the ramps lies the CHAPEL OF ACHORIS, a columned structure with screenlike walls received the sacred barque of Amun on the occasion of its ceremonial voyages. The western *dromos* leading to the temple entrance is bordered by crio-SPHINXES, creatures with the body of a lion (the epitome of vigilance and guardianship and the symbol of royalty) and the head of a ram (the symbolic animal of Amun and the embodiment of physical strength and procreant energy). Nestling between the feet of the god is a statue of his son Ramesses II. To the right, just before the entrance, are the remains of a Roman chapel dedicated to imperial worship.

"I know that Karnak is the horizon above the earth, the glorious first ascension, the sacred eye of the Master of the Universe": an inscription by Hatshepsut ● *426* on one of the obelisks.

Details of the great enclosure wall.

THE "DROMOS"
The sphinxes lining the processional way were thought to protect the journey of the sacred barques leaving the temple.

HYPOSTYLE HALL
One can only imagine the splendor of the axial aisle when twelve papyrus columns supported the 82-foot-high ceiling. Light flooded in through the high traceried windows, which opened onto the central nave, while the side aisles remained in the shadows. Here and there a fine pencil of light penetrated the few square openings pierced in the stone ceiling. This "thicket" of giant papyri symbolized the force of life which abounds near its creator. Their "roots" plunged into the water of the *nun* (underground water table), while their stems thrust upward and their corollas opened toward the sky of the blue-painted ceiling.

COLUMN OF TAHARQA
The giant papyrus column is all that remains of the kiosk of Taharqa, which stood in the center of the temple's first court.

The steps of the chapel, front colonnade and walls are red brick. Inside are pedestals (once surmounted by statues) inscribed with the names of Roman emperors. The emperors, often represented in the guise of pharaohs on the bas-reliefs of later temples, were honored during the first three centuries AD. The great temple entrance has lost its granite lintel (weighing about 440 tons), whose fragments lie strewn on the ground. It is flanked by two sandstone piers attributed to Nectanebo I. The building was never completed, and the walls have a rough appearance. The pylon, the largest in Egypt, is thought to have once stood about 105 feet high. The piers of a pylon represented the mountain chains which bordered the fertile valley (the only inhabitable part of the region), the two horizons between which the sun (often carved on the cornice in the center of the entrance) ran its course. The pylon protected the temple entrance and gave access to the sacred area. Near the top of the gateway, to the right, an inscription commemorates the visit of the members of the Egypt Expedition ● *140* in 1799.

FIRST COURT. The KIOSK OF TAHARQA, in the middle of the first court, has one remaining column. At its center is the alabaster pedestal on which the sacred barque of Amun-Re rested. The sides of the court are bounded by colonnades from the Bubastite period. At the foot of these columns are traces of a row of rams, the remains of the eastern section of the *dromos* which was removed when the court and kiosk were built. Behind the pylon, to the right, a pile of mudbrick is all that remains of the ramp used to build the edifice. Above the ramp, in the stone façade, a Coptic niche and rows of horizontal holes into which floors were fitted are the legacy of one of the monasteries built inside the temple from the 7th century onward. On the left of the court is the edifice built by Sety II whose three chapels served as a way station for the sacred barques of Amun, Mut and Khonsu. The CENTRAL CHAPEL, preceded by two royal statues (only the pedestals have survived), accommodated the barque of Amun, which was decorated on the prow and stern with rams' heads. At the far end of the building are three niches which held royal devotional statues. On the right is the CHAPEL OF KHONSU, whose sacred barque was decorated at both ends with a falcon's head surmounted by a crescent moon and disk. On the left is the CHAPEL OF MUT, whose barque was decorated with the statue of a woman wearing the crowns of Upper and Lower Egypt. To the south of the court, a temple built by Ramesses III includes a pylon preceded by colossi, a court and covered halls. It has no shrine, but three rooms which accommodated the barques. At the far end of the great court are the damaged piers of the second pylon, built by Horemheb. The shattered statue of Pinedjem I has been reinstated in front of the entrance. The pylon's gateway,

An impression of strange strength and beauty is created by the superhuman proportions of the hypostyle hall which formed the antechamber (pronaos) of the temple. It was here that the sacred barques gathered before leaving the temple and where part of the coronation ceremonies were held, strikingly depicted in the bas-reliefs decorating the walls. The far wall of the right side aisle includes a scene showing Ramesses II receiving his "jubilees" (promising many years on the throne) from the hands of Amun-Re.

Detail of a fresco
representing the
procession of the
sacred barque.

THUTMOSE III
A row of royal colossi
representing
Thutmose III stands
along the west wall of
the "Wadjyt Hall".
The king is standing
with his arms crossed
and is wearing the
tight-fitting costume
of the *sed,* or jubilee,
celebrations. This is a
reminder of the
original function of
the hall, which was
used for one of the
stages of the
coronation ceremony:
the apposition of the
crowns of Upper and
Lower Egypt.

rebuilt during the Ptolemaic period and flanked by two colossi
of Ramesses II, leads into the great colonnaded hall begun by
Sety I and completed by Ramesses II.

COURT OF THE OBELISKS: THE TEMPLE GATE. As you leave the
great hypostyle hall through the gateway of the badly
damaged third pylon, you come into a narrow court where
several symmetrical obelisks once stood. This was the main
point of intersection of the two main axes of the temple, just
in front of the entrance to the covered halls. Only one of the
obelisks erected by Thutmose I remains, alongside the granite
plinths of two of its neighbors, erected by Thutmose III. The
eastern gate of the temple, built by the architect Ineni, was
preceded by a lightweight canopy supported by two gold-
plated columns. As you pass through the gateway of the
pylon, you are left to imagine the dark, covered halls. The
first, "Wadjyt ('verdant' or 'flourishing') Hall", was
refurbished several times. The colossi of Thutmose I are a
reminder of its original function: the apposition of the crowns
of Upper and Lower Egypt. It was then converted for a short
time into a narrow court where Queen Hatshepsut erected
two magnificent obelisks. Thutmose III, who wanted to
overshadow his co-regent, restored the columned hall.

BARQUE SHRINE AND PALACE OF MA'AT. The next pylon leads
into the inner part of the temple and the central chapel-shrine
built of huge granite blocks whose final
stage (which can still be seen today) dates
from the time of Philip III Arrhidaeus,
half-brother and successor of
Alexander the Great. It is preceded by
a vestibule comprising two pillars
carved with the symbolic plants of the
Two Lands: the papyrus (north) of
Lower Egypt and the lotus (south) of
Upper Egypt. The chapel has two
sections: a vestibule to the west and
then the shrine proper, whose
central pedestal is extremely well
preserved. It was here that the
sacred barque of Amun-Re rested
when the god was not traveling. The
walls are decorated, on four
registers, with scenes showing the
king making offerings to Amun-Re
represented in his two most
common guises (as a king walking
and as an ithyphallic, mummiform
being). The reliefs on the south wall
of the chapel have retained some of
their colors. The sacred barque is
represented as it appeared during the
ceremonies of the "Beautiful Feast of
the Valley", which took the divine
procession to the west bank of the
Nile. The chapel stands in the center of a
monumental complex known as the
"Palace of Ma'at", which included a
suite of offering halls. In front of
a stele (in the form of a false
door) inlaid with lapis lazuli and

a huge offering table (neither of which have survived), the god received his "meal" in the form of an offering of food which was recovered and redistributed by the priests once he had "eaten his fill". As you make your way round the outside of the chapel, from south to north, you come across a door with black granite uprights which opens onto a series of small rooms. The first shows the ritual purification of Hatshepsut by Horus and Thoth. The water they pour over her is represented by a double line of "crosses of life". In the upper register is the "royal ascent" of the queen accompanied by the gods. The queen's effigy and name have been hacked out, another example of Thutmose III's campaign against the memory of the queen who, for more than twenty years, had overshadowed him by retaining the regency entrusted to her on the death of her husband, Thutmose II.

"MIDDLE KINGDOM COURT": THE LOST SANCTUARY. Below the chapel, to the east, is an area which today resembles a sort of court. It is in fact the site of a former sanctuary and its annexes, built at the time of the foundation of the temple during the Middle Kingdom. The monumental complex, constructed in fine limestone by Senwosret I, constituted the heart of the temple and was hallowed for as long as the latter was in use. It disappeared into the limestone kilns of the inhabitants who occupied the site when the temple was abandoned. A court must have preceded the series of gates (the "Gates of the Hereafter", of which only the granite thresholds have survived) while a huge alabaster platform is probably all that remains of the naos, the kiosk which contained the god's statue. The daily rites of worship were performed here. Every morning the duty priest broke the seal affixed the previous night and opened the wooden shutters of the naos. The officiating priest dressed and prepared the god, reciting the appropriate prayers and making offerings while he ministered to his "needs". He then withdrew, discreetly removing every trace of his footsteps on the thin layer of sand on the floor. Everything in this dark, silent place was steeped in an air of mystery and respect.

Colossal statue of Ramesses II.

OBELISKS OF HATSHEPSUT
The north obelisk erected by Hatshepsut is still standing while its companion lies on the ground (detail left). In the inscription on the base the queen prides herself on the fact that these monoliths were extracted in seven months. Their upper section and pinnacle were entirely plated in electrum, an alloy of gold and silver.

The two pillars decorated with the papyrus and the lotus, the symbolic plants of the Two Lands.

THE "AKHMENU" AND ITS ANNEXES. Since the walls have been destroyed it is possible to pass directly into the annexes built by Thutmose III against the east wall of the temple. The most prominent feature of this monumental complex is the great columned hall, known during antiquity as the "Akhmenu" ("jewel of monuments"). It is better to approach it through the entrance to the complex, which lies to the south between two polygonal columns. One of the Osiride colossi that flanked the entrance is still standing. In the southern part of the complex a long corridor leads to a series of small side rooms. The first seven were used to preserve the ritual offerings of food and the last two were split-level magazines. A square hall decorated with images of the sacred barques of Amun, Mut and Khonsu leads back to the great hall. The great hall of the Akhmenu has retained its stone revetment

and most of its original wall-paintings, particularly its azure ceiling scattered with gold stars. On the right of the entrance is the "Chamber of the Ancestors", a tiny chapel dedicated to the royal ancestors of Thutmose III, whose walls have been restored using casts made from the original blocks in the Louvre Museum in Paris. The room is basilican in design and comprises a raised, central "nave" illuminated by high windows and two side aisles whose roof is supported by columns in the form of ancient jubilee tent-pegs, a reference to the function of the monumental complex. The mysterious ceremonies associated with the jubilee celebrations were in fact performed here, beginning in the southern suite of rooms, which could be reached through the side door opening onto a well-preserved, eight-columned hall. This was the chthonian part of the complex associated with the journey through the Underworld in which the god Sokar, the main participant in the nocturnal regeneration of the sun, interceded. The ceremonies took place inside the great hall of the Akhmenu where the sacred barques were placed. The fifteen bays of the great hall are noticeably unequal. The central bay is much wider than the others and the texts are arranged symmetrically on the architraves along its axis, which is aligned with the great solar axis of the temple. An axial door to the east opens onto a series of three rooms ending in a narrow door whose raised threshold once stood above an alabaster pedestal. This discrete side entrance is like the doorway to a hidden crypt and leads into a vestibule with four well-preserved, fasciculate columns whose walls are decorated with flora and fauna: the "botanical garden" of Karnak. It is situated opposite the secret sanctuary which consisted of a long hall with niched side walls (most of the niches have since been destroyed). By contrast, the immense red quartzite pedestal which supported the naos at the far end of the hall is well preserved. In front of it stands a huge, granite offering table. To the north of the Akhmenu are three parallel chapels.

A staircase on the right leads to the "upper room", which is open to the sky and where a central altar is aligned with the four points of the compass. The room symbolized the victory of the sun, which, having journeyed through the Underworld, rose in the east in the form of the scarab beetle Khepri, pushing the shining disk between its front feet. The union with the solar disk, one of the

closing ceremonies of the jubilee, was performed here and was repeated on the occasion of each new annual cycle. During this ceremony the divine and royal statues were exposed to the rays of the rising sun so that they assimilated its vital energy.

EASTERN BUILDINGS. A wooden gallery runs across the rear of the temple toward the east. Along the axis the nearby ruins of the small TEMPLE OF THE HEARING EAR can be found, so called in ancient times because it was here that the Thebans were able to present their prayers to Amun. The single, axial obelisk which used to stand on the site of the sanctuary is now in Rome. It is one of the largest of its kind.

SACRED LAKE. A tour of the temple takes you, a little further south, to the vast stretch of water known as the sacred lake. To the east, below the stands used for the Sound and Light Show, is the area where the temple priests lived. By following the edge of the lake you come to the remains of a temple built by Taharqa. At one corner of this crumbling edifice with its misshapen walls is the huge granite scarab beetle representing the god Khepri, whose pedestal is engraved with the name of Amenhotep III.

SACRED LAKE
Water from the sacred lake, thought to be a resurgence of the *nun* (primordial water), was used for ablution, purification and the preparation of offerings in the rooms on the far side of the lake. The lake was also the scene of the "sacred voyages" made by statues of the gods in small boats.

AKHMENU
The ceiling of the Festival Court of Thutmose III is supported by two rows of ten columns and a row of thirty-two pillars. It has retained much of its polychrome decoration.

411

Gateway of the seventh pylon, flanked by statues of Thutmose III.

Statue of the god Amun in the four-columned hall in the Temple of Khonsu.

PROCESSIONAL WAY. The north–south axis of Karnak consists mainly of a series of pylons and courts. The entrance is through the side gate of the first court, the so-called "Hiding Courtyard", which was the scene of an amazing discovery in the early 20th century of thousands of statues and bronzes. These had been removed from the inner rooms of the temple during the Ptolemaic period to release space and facilitate the restoration of the walls, and hidden beneath the pavement of the court where they remained for thousands of years. The finest of the statues can be seen in the Luxor ▲ *403* and Cairo ▲ *276* museums. To the south lies the seventh pylon, built by Thutmose III. Two obelisks used to stand in front of the south façade until the western obelisk was removed in AD 330 on the orders of Constantine. Today it stands in Istanbul, not far from the Church of St Sophia, on the site of the Constantinople Hippodrome where it was relocated. A little further on stand the eighth and ninth pylons, built by Hatshepsut and Horemheb respectively. Inside the ninth pylon tens of thousands of *talattat* were discovered, which had come from edifices built to the east of the temple by Amenhotep IV (Akhenaten) at the beginning of his reign. About one hundred of these blocks have been reassembled and are on display on the second floor of the Luxor Museum. On the east side of the next court is a jubilee structure, built by Amenhotep II, comprising a porticoed façade and an axial ramp. Finally the tenth pylon, begun by Amenhotep III and completed by Horemheb, marks the southern boundary of the site. Huge statues of Amenhotep III once stood in front of it.

TEMPLE OF KHONSU. The Temple of Khonsu, built by Ramesses III, is certainly the most complete and the most revealing of Karnak's architectural structures. Its main entrance was through the great gateway built by Ptolemy III, set in the southern section of the enclosure wall. The edifice is virtually intact. Engraved on the cornice is a solar disk flanked by two protective cobras facing each of the two horizons. It is framed by two great, extended wings which symbolize its heavenly flight. The entrance to the court of the temple is through the gateway of the pylon, which is on the whole well preserved. Beyond the covered hypostyle hall are the remains of a central pedestal for the barque of Khonsu and, beyond that, a four-columned hall with a central altar. The shrine is situated right at the back of the temple. The Temple of Khonsu offers visitors the opportunity to see the most secret part of the temple, no longer possible in the Temple of Amun. It is also a very good example of the general layout of an Egyptian temple, in which the rooms become progressively smaller from the entrance to the inner sanctum: the shrine containing the god's statue.

TEMPLE OF OPET. The remains of the Temple of Opet lie to the west and at right angles to the Temple of Khonsu. The later section, built during the Ptolemaic period, is the best preserved. Its external decoration was never completed. In the temple forecourt is a statue of the lioness Sekhmet and nearby an altar and a pool. This layout was linked to the healing powers of the goddess whose help was solicited by those who were sick and infirm through their prayers and magic.

OPEN-AIR MUSEUM. A visit to Karnak should be complemented by a walk to the Open-Air Museum, which can be reached before leaving the site through the north gate of the first court of the Temple of Amun. It has a collection of monuments mainly discovered during excavations carried out inside the third pylon. First of all, blocks from the "RED CHAPEL" of Hatshepsut, a beautiful building which served as a shrine for the barque of Amun and whose site is today occupied by the chapel of Philip Arrhidaeus, are presented course by course on ledges. Further on, in the shade of some trees, the magnificent "WHITE CHAPEL" of Senwosret I, the most elegant and ancient structure in Karnak, has been reconstructed from the blocks of stone recovered. Built in the style of a jubilee kiosk, it has a roof, openwork sides and two entrances, and stands on a raised platform. Its delicately carved scenes show the king making offerings to Amun-Re and Amun in his ithyphallic form. The different nomes (the administrative areas of Egypt) are listed in the form of columns on the parapet. Thus the entire region is represented on the chapel of the king who took possession of it, the pharaoh and guarantor of the order established by Amun. A little further north the "ALABASTER CHAPEL" OF AMENHOTEP I, the oldest known barque shrine, has been rebuilt. Inside the shrine, the king is shown presenting offerings to the sacred barque. Finally, beyond the reconstruction of the summit of a small limestone pylon constructed by Thutmose II is that of the "Festival Court" built by Thutmose IV, which used to be situated in front of the fourth pylon on the site of the eastern side of the hypostyle hall.

Detail of a fresco in the Temple of Khonsu.

THE "RED CHAPEL"
The shrine of the sacred barque was built by Hatshepsut entirely in red quartzite, apart from its black granite foundations and doors. The queen is depicted throughout as a pharaoh (below) and is either alone or precedes Thutmose III, intentionally stressing her ascendancy over her co-regent.

TEMPLE OF MUT
In the courts of the Temple of Mut rows of strange statues of Sekhmet stand among clumps of alfa-grass. There must have been at least one for each day of the year.

❝Walking into Karnak was like walking into one of Piranesi's Prisons, solidified suddenly into stone, and grown to natural, nay to heroic size . . . . Beyond the aisle, a vast space littered with fallen masonry lay open to the sky. Cavernous openings, porticos, colonnades, blocks of masonry; obelisks, statues of Pharaohs, some upright, some prone; and beyond them, beyond this magnificent desolation, shrilled the thin piping of the frogs . . . It crushed the mind, since it was not the human mind that had conceived it as it now appeared, but such inhuman factors as time upon earth.❞

Vita Sackville-West

TEMPLE OF PTAH. The sunken path opposite the north entrance of the great hypostyle hall runs past two chapels dedicated to the "Divine Votaresses of Amun" and leads to the Temple of Ptah, the great god of Memphis who also had a shrine in Thebes. The statue of Sekhmet (his wife), found on the site, has been reinstated in one of the rooms at the back of the temple. The light filters down onto the statue of the powerful woman who was once no stranger to the innermost chambers of the great Temple of Amun-Re.

TEMPLE OF MONTU. The Temple of Montu, the warrior god of Thebes, lies beyond the gate of the great precinct situated opposite the entrance to the Temple of Ptah. The edifice, built by Amenhotep III, is fairly extensively ruined and is not open to the public. It is possible, however, to admire the huge Ptolemaic gateway of the precinct, opposite which there was once a *dromos* and a quay.

TEMPLE OF MUT. South of the tenth pylon and less than 450 yards from the Precinct of Amun is the Temple of Mut, the wife of the great god of Thebes. The now-ruined temple, built by Amenhotep III, has a special romantic charm. On the sides of a ruined colonnade are reliefs representing the god Bes, a bearded and beneficent dwarf and, in the court, rows of strange statues of Sekhmet. The temple is surrounded on three sides by the waters of the crescent-shaped sacred lake (Asheru), which shine and sparkle through clumps of reeds. Beyond the lake is the TEMPLE OF RAMESSES III, preceded by "walking" royal colossi. To the left of the great entrance, in the northeast corner of the precinct, another badly ruined temple, dating from the reign of Amenhotep III and dedicated to Amun Re, still has some of its painted scenes. Outside the Precinct of Mut is the recently excavated *dromos* which once linked the temple entrance to the great paved way (1½ miles long) which led to Luxor.

MODERN BUILDINGS. On the left as you leave the temple is the Franco-Egyptian Center which, since 1967, has been responsible for the conservation, study and restoration of the temples. The traditional, Nubian-style residence of the permanent CNRS (Centre National de la Recherche Scientifique) mission which constitutes the French team stands lower down on the shores of the Nile. The Epigraphic Survey of the Oriental Institute of the University of Chicago, generally known as Chicago House, has a research library renowned for its photographic collection, which includes an important 19th-century section. Chicago House, founded in 1924 by James Breasted and based in Luxor, gathers information on the sites of Upper Egypt using photogrammetric techniques.

CROSSING THE RIVER

All the other important remains in Thebes are found on the opposite bank, which is reached, as in ancient times, by boat. The crossing, which is today one of the main attractions of a visit to Luxor, once had symbolic significance. For the Ancient Egyptians, the westward crossing was not so much a journey to the shores of the Dead (an unthinking, modern interpretation) but more the voyage to the land of Life.

THE GODDESS SEKHMET
Inside the right-hand (south) chapel of the Temple of Ptah stands a black granite statue of Sekhmet, the wife of Ptah. The lion goddess (whose name means "powerful") sometimes unleashed her anger against mortals, especially on the last five days of the year, and was only appeased by long prayers recited by priests. She also possessed healing powers.

THEBES: WEST BANK

"Every sarcophagus is broken and the bones of the kings of Egypt are scattered. In one I picked up a skull.... Among the paintings on the walls was represented a heap of hands severed from the arms, showing that the hero of the tomb had played the tyrant during his brief hour on earth. I dashed the skull against a stone, broke it in fragments, and pocketed a piece as a memorial of a king."

John Lloyd Stephens, 1837

For the Ancient Egyptians the west was not the direction of finality and death but rather the way to the "kingdom of the West" where the deceased could be admitted by Osiris to the Day of Judgment. It was also the direction taken by the setting sun before it journeyed through the Underworld. When it disappeared into the shadows the heavenly body was gradually regenerated and reappeared each morning as a new being. These two aspects of rebirth (Osirian and solar) are represented in all the funerary monuments, tombs and temples on the west bank of Thebes. The Egyptians who cultivated this fertile valley believed that the kingdom of Osiris resembled this earthly kingdom of fields, canals and agriculture. It was a sort of familiar, earthly paradise where the deceased could enjoy a happy life for eternity. They could only recover their completeness, temporarily lost at the moment of death, by gathering together all the various elements which made up their identity during their earthly life: their body, their *ka* (vital energy which was both preserving and creative), their *ba* (spiritual element), their *ankh* (immortality), their shadow and their name.

FUNERARY RITES. The body, in particular, was essential to the life that mummification aimed to preserve. The mortal remains, brought by boat from the east bank, were prepared more or less carefully, depending on the family's financial resources. Specialist priests, imitating the rites originally performed by Anubis on the body of Osiris, removed the entrails which were preserved in four Canopic jars (whose stoppers represented each of the four sons of Horus) and placed in the tomb near the sarcophagus. Once the body was cleaned, dried out with natron and coated with ointments, it was tightly bound in strips of cloth. There were many embalming rooms between the Nile and the Theban necropolis.

VALLEY OF THE KINGS

The royal necropolis, known in ancient times as "the Place of Truth", is a logical place to start a visit to the west bank. None of the tombs in the western valley is open to the public and only the present Valley of the Kings enables visitors to discover the very singular world of the 18th- and 19th-Dynasty pharaohs. The mountain of Thebes at the far end of the valley in fact forms a

natural pyramid both in terms of its shape and its function since it contains sixty or so royal tombs.

THE GREAT ROYAL HYPOGEA. Today it is only possible to visit about a dozen of the great royal tombs. They are opened in turn from year to year to limit the amount of damage caused by the vast numbers of visitors and enable restoration work to be carried out. The tomb of Ramesses II (a large part of which has collapsed) and that of his father, Sety I, are not open to the public. The latter tomb is famed not only for the quality but also for the extent of its decoration (details above and right), which must be protected and preserved. The royal tombs were entirely hewn out of the living rock, sometimes penetrating deep through alternating layers of limestone and flint.

"THE BOOK OF THE DEAD"
Sacred texts containing the formulae to be pronounced in the presence of the guardians of the gates of the Twelve Hours of the night were placed in the tombs. These formulae were found in the chapters of what is known today as *The Book of the Dead* but which the Egyptians called *The Book of the Coming Forth by Day*.

Although one of the smallest in the necropolis, the Tomb of Tutankhamun is undoubtedly the most famous of the Egyptian tombs as a result of the extraordinary discoveries made there in the early 20th century. It had been protected by a particular set of circumstances. An attempt to plunder it during antiquity had proved unsuccessful; the thieves must have been surprised and the tomb closed up again. The debris from the later excavation of the nearby hypogeum of Ramesses VI covered and disguised the entrance to such an extent that the tomb remained exceptionally well concealed from would-be plunderers for centuries. In 1922 Howard Carter directed excavations on the site under the sponsorship of Lord Carnarvon. He was about to abandon his search when a small flight of steps suddenly appeared . . .

THE SITE
Having explored the Valley of the Kings fairly unsuccessfully for several years, Howard Carter decided, and with good reason, to concentrate on the ancient workers' huts located at the foot of the Tomb of Ramesses IV.

LORD CARNARVON
For several years Lord Carnarvon (1866–1923) financed excavations in the Valley of the Kings which ended with the discovery, by Howard Carter, of the Tomb of Tutankhamun. He died before the tomb had been completely excavated, a task which took almost ten years.

Howard Carter (1873–1939) began his career in Egypt as a draftsman. In 1899 he was appointed inspector general of monuments in Upper Egypt.

DISCOVERY OF THE TOMB

When the door of the tomb was cleared on November 4, 1922 the fact that it had been re-sealed gave rise to fears that the tomb had been plundered. One can imagine Carter's amazement when, on November 25, he got his first glimpse of the priceless contents of the sepulcher: "At first, I could see nothing. The flame of the candle flickered as hot air was released from the chamber. Then, as my eyes grew accustomed to the darkness, shapes gradually began to emerge: strange creatures, statues, and, everywhere, shining gold. For a few seconds – which must have seemed like an eternity to my companions – I was speechless." Carter had just discovered the greatest treasure ever bequeathed by Pharaonic Egypt.

INSIDE THE TOMB

Everything a king could possibly need in the Hereafter was arranged in these small rooms: dismantled chariots, furniture, chests, vases, statues and various kinds of food. The initial impression created by so many objects piled up in this cramped space was that of a strange collection of bric-a-brac rather than a logical arrangement.

THE FUNERAL MASK

On the forehead were carved Nekhbet (the vulture) and Bruto (the serpent), the symbols of the Two Lands governed by the king. On the chin was the beard symbolizing Osiris and, around the neck, a three-tiered necklace of gold and blue faience.

THE MUMMY

Inside the third sarcophagus was a mummy whose hands – covered in gold, crossed on its chest and sewn to the linen shroud – held a flail and crook, the emblems of Osiris. On the outer linen shroud was a representation, decorated with gold elements, of the flight of the Ba (the spiritual element).

The items were obviously of more value for their physical, effective presence than for the way in which they were arranged. In the tomb they were fulfilling their role mystically, just as ordinary objects fulfilled their role in the world of the living. Today the treasure of Tutankhamun can be seen in the Cairo Museum ▲ 276.

THE SARCOPHAGUS

The wooden chests which slotted inside one another, and the successive sarcophagi, or coffins, formed protective layers around the royal mummy. The first coffin was in gilt wood and measured just over 7 feet. The second coffin (6½ feet), covered in gold and inlaid with glass to imitate precious stones, symbolized Osiris. The third and final coffin (6 feet) was wrapped in a reddish linen shroud. It was in solid gold and represented the pharaoh as a boy. The neck and chest were encircled by a neckpiece of seeds and flowers sewn on papyrus. Inside the coffin was a mummy whose head was covered with a gold mask representing Tutankhamun with the attributes of Osiris.

Plaster revetments evened out the irregularities of the walls. The occasionally carved but mainly drawn decorations were painted and it was not uncommon for this type of tomb ornamentation to be completed at the time of the king's death. A large royal tomb had a main staircase (carefully sealed after the burial) and then a descending corridor. During the 18th Dynasty this led onto an interior gallery which was sometimes interrupted by a huge well and might also make several sharp turns before reaching the burial chamber. During the 19th Dynasty the route was generally more rectilinear in design. The burial chamber, situated at the furthest point on this route, housed the sarcophagus containing the royal mummy. Furniture was arranged around it and in small adjoining rooms. The most logical visitor's route from the entrance to the end of the Valley of the Kings cannot take into account the chronological order of the tombs.

TOMB OF RAMESSES IX. This is the first tomb (no. 6) on the route. Its corridor is flanked by four rooms decorated with scenes from the sacred books, while beautiful astronomical images are painted on the blue background of the ceiling. Priests dressed in panther skins are depicted in the furthest room. A four-pillared room precedes the burial chamber where only the mark of the sarcophagus remains on the floor.

TOMB OF MERNEPTAH. The tomb (no. 8) of the son and successor of Ramesses II has a steeply sloping corridor which crosses the first room. In a pillared side room opening off the first, the king is depicted in the presence of various gods. The corridor crosses another room before finally reaching the vaulted burial chamber, which contains a pink granite sarcophagus.

TOMB OF RAMESSES VI. This is one of most complete and best preserved tombs (no. 9) in the necropolis. The first section of the corridor is decorated with images from the *Book of Gates*. The sky goddess Nut (who swallows the solar disk in the evening and gives birth to it each morning) is depicted among the various constellations on the great vault of the sarcophagus chamber.

TOMB OF RAMESSES III. On either side of the entrance to the tomb (no. 11) are two sculpted heads of Hathor, goddess of the Theban necropolis. The decoration of the small side rooms is remarkable for the sheer variety of scenes represented: the preparation of offerings, sailing boats, Nile gods, divinities of the various nomes and two blind harpists singing the king's praises. The next rooms have scenes from the *Book of What is in the Underworld* and the pillared room from the *Book of Gates*. The sarcophagus has been removed from the eight-pillared burial chamber and is today housed in the Louvre Museum ▲ *476* in Paris.

TOMB OF RAMESSES I. The short reign of the founder of the 19th Dynasty explains the small size of his tomb (no. 16). The funeral chamber is decorated entirely with scenes depicting the king in the presence of various divinities and extracts from the *Book of Gates*.

TOMB OF HOREMHEB. In the lower part of the tomb (no. 57), where the scenes are depicted against a blue-gray background, it is possible to see the various stages of the wall paintings. Once the general outline had been established, the drawing was painted in red and then corrected in black by a more expert hand before the different colors were added.

TOMB OF AMENHOTEP II. The scenes in the first rooms of the tomb

TOMB OF RAMESSES III
The variety of scenes depicted in the side rooms is remarkable. The next rooms have scenes from the *Book of What is in the Underworld*, the pillared room from the *Book of Gates* and the corridor from the *Litany of Re*. The goddess Hathor, the Nile god, and Ramesses III (opposite, below).

423

The portico of the
fasciculate,
colonnaded façade of
the extremely well-
preserved Temple of
Sety I occupies the
entire western side of
the second court.

(no. 35) show the king in the presence of Osiris, Anubis and
Hathor. The extremely stylized decoration of the funeral
chamber (painted in black against an ocher background) is
reminiscent of the writing on a huge papyrus and evokes the
Book of What is in the Underworld. The mummy was still in its
sarcophagus when the tomb was discovered. In ancient times
the small side room to the right was used to conceal nine
royal mummies from further plunder following the
desecration of their respective tombs.

TOMB OF SETHNAKHT. The Tomb of Sethnakht (no.14) was
originally the Tomb of Queen Tawsert (wife of Merneptah-
Siptah and then of Sety II). Sethnakht extended it and
covered the parts decorated by the queen with plaster, but
these are now showing through in places, especially in the
corridor. In the funeral chamber decorated with scenes from
the *Book of Gates* are a few remaining fragments of the
sarcophagus. The nearby TOMB (no. 15) OF SETY II has a
particularly fine carved decoration at the entrance to the
corridor evoking the *Litany of Re* and the *Book of What is in
the Underworld*.

TEMPLE OF SETY I

Stretching to the north and east at the end of the road to the
Valley of the Kings is Thebes' oldest necropolis, the
necropolis of Tarif, or Antef (after the 11th-Dynasty princes
who founded it). Some of the tombs, most of which have been
destroyed, can still be seen along the side of the road
leading to the Temple of Sety I. Once through the
present gate of the precinct, the ruined gate of
the axial
pylon
which
opened
onto the

first court can be seen on the left. On the south side of the court are the remains of a palace. To the north of the temple the mudbrick walls of a complex of vaulted magazines have been rebuilt to a height of about 3 feet. The walls of the annexes have virtually been leveled. Inside the mortuary temple the ceremonies designed to guarantee the survival of the king in the Hereafter were performed. The road continues south along the side of the necropolis of Dra-Abu el-Naga, which lies on the slopes of the Western Desert. None of the sometimes well-preserved tombs belonging to 18th-Dynasty priests and scribes is open to the public.

ASASIF NECROPOLIS

After skirting round the necropolis Dra-Abu el-Naga the road continues westward into the Valley of Asasif where only two of the 25th- and 26th-Dynasty tombs can be visited.

TOMB OF PASABA. The tomb of Pasaba, the steward of Nitocris, the Divine Votaress of Amun, has a long flight of steps leading to a pillared court where there is a bee-keeping scene on one of the pillars. The first court leads into a second, which in turn leads to the underground rooms and the gallery opening onto the tomb. To the west of the tomb is the pylon of the TOMB OF MONTUEMHET, one of the largest tombs in Thebes, which is currently being restored.

TOMB OF KHERUEF. The Tomb of Kheruef (no. 192), steward of Queen Tiyi during the reign of Amenhotep III, stands about 100 yards southeast of the tombs mentioned above. Although it is very badly damaged it has a series of raised reliefs which are truly remarkable not only for their expressive quality but also for their portrayal of movement in the figures participating in the festival of the erection of the *djed* pillar.

TEMPLE OF SETY I
The central entrance opens onto a six-columned, hypostyle hall (above) whose walls are decorated with scenes in which Sety I and Ramesses II make offerings to Amun-Re. The shrine lies on the axis of the temple. The north entrance opens onto a court with a solar altar, while the south leads to a suite of rooms dedicated by Sety I to his father, Ramesses I, and completed by Ramesses II.

Senenmut, chief steward and architect to Queen Hatshepsut, had his own figure included in the statue niches of the central corridor of the temple. His tomb (no. 353) lies to the north of the road as you leave the temple.

MURALS
Beneath the double portico situated between the complex of Anubis and the ramp is a series of scenes depicting the birth and education of the queen, her accession and divine ancestry. Beneath the opposite portico, south of the ramp, are the celebrated scenes of the maritime expedition sent by the queen to the land of Punt

(modern Somalia). Scenes on the low wall forming the southern boundary of the portico show the houses on stilts (above) and flora of these distant lands, as well as the amply proportioned Queen of Punt. (The present relief is a cast of the originals which can be seen in the Cairo Museum ▲ 276.)

DEIR EL-BAHRI

Deir is the Arabic word for "monastery". It is often used in Thebes to designate the site of an ancient Coptic monastery built on the ruins of a Pharaonic structure. The far end of the Valley of Asasif is blocked by the cliff of Deir el-Bahri at the foot of which a series of three temples was built.

TEMPLE OF MENTUHOTEP I. The Temple of Mentuhotep, built during the Middle Kingdom, is the oldest temple in the group and stands on the left. It is characterized by its outer porticos and its ramp leading to a terrace whose center was once occupied by a massive pyramidal, or more probably mastaba-type, structure ● *82*. Behind the temple lay a court open to the sky and a hypostyle hall built against the cliff. A long underground corridor led deep into the mountainside to the tomb. In the rocky spur which closes the mountainous cirque to the left of the temple is the (inaccessible) entrance shaft which led to the cache of royal mummies (including the mummy of Ramesses II) discovered by Gaston Maspero ● *96* in 1881.

TEMPLE OF HATSHEPSUT. The temple stands on the axis of the present access road, formerly the site of the ancient *dromos* which once crossed the entire Asasif depression to the Nile Valley. Several of the limestone sphinxes which stood along its edge are now in New York's Metropolitan Museum. The first part of the uprights is all that remains of the entrance to the first court. To the left of the ramp, beneath one of the square-pillared porticos that border the terrace to the west, is a carved scene depicting the transportation of two great obelisks that the queen had brought by river from the Aswan quarries to Karnak ▲ *404*.

426

Detail (far left) of the great corbeled vault, painted with a starry blue sky, of the shrine in the Temple of Hatshepsut, and detail (left) of a wall painting.

Detail of a scene depicting the queen's birth.

The ramp leads to a second court also bordered by a double porticoed façade of square pillars. The precinct situated in the northwest corner is dedicated to Anubis, the jackal-headed god who presided at the embalming ceremony and who is represented on the walls of the twelve-columned vestibule. In the center of the far wall is the narrow, vaulted corridor which led to the shrines. The north side of the court is occupied by a polygonal-columned portico, while to the south is a monumental annex, with its own access ramp, dedicated to Hathor. The THIRD TERRACE (not open to the public) consists of a central court bordered by a colonnade on three sides and, to the north, a smaller court with a square solar altar in the center. On the other (south) side of the central court is a suite of vaulted rooms dedicated to the royal funeral cult. The SHRINE OF THE TEMPLE was built into the side of the cliff. Its last room and vestibule were additions dating from the Ptolemaic period.

TEMPLE OF THUTMOSE III. Scarcely anything remains of the temple built by Thutmose III between those of Mentuhotep I and Hatshepsut. Only the first section of the ramp, the remains of the terrace and fragments of the walls and columns are still visible. It was designed to dominate the Temple of Hatshepsut and must have been a fine edifice, judging by the decorated blocks; two are in the Luxor Museum ▲ 403.

The extremely powerful architectural composition of the temple, designed as a series of terraces and horizontal porticos which stand out against the vertical rock face, was probably inspired by the nearby Temple of Mentuhotep.

The funeral temple of Queen Hatshepsut (1490–68), on the west bank of the Nile, was built by the architect Senenmut. This hemi-speos, which lies along a southeast/northwest axis, was inspired by the nearby Temple of Mentuhotep whose terraces and porticos it has reproduced. Its originality lies in the way in which the edifice blends with the natural surroundings. Discovered in 1743, it was the subject of several research programmes. The first excavations, carried out by the Egypt Exploration Fund in 1893, were followed by excavations, consolidations and restorations by the American (1911) and Polish (1961) missions.

"PROTO-DORIC" COLONNADE
The sixteen-sided columns of the north portico of the second terrace evoke the Greek architectural tradition, causing them to be wrongly described as "proto-Doric". However the abacus (with no capital), molding and groove are typically Egyptian.

HATSHEPSUT
This painted limestone head of Queen Hatshepsut, now in the Cairo Museum ▲ 276, came from an Osiride statue of the upper terrace portico.

EXPEDITION TO THE LAND OF PUNT
The painted bas-reliefs of the south portico of the first terrace tell the story of the trading expedition to the land of Punt (Somalia) during the ninth regnal year. The King of Punt and his wife are accompanied by bearers of offerings.

The figures are realistically portrayed, with the Queen of Punt easily recognizable by her obesity.

HATHOR CAPITALS
The columns of the chapel of Hathor are decorated with capitals representing the goddess of the Theban necropolis. The cow's ears, the sistrum and the house of Horus are the attributes of the goddess.

From left to right: an agricultural scene (Tomb of Menna), the presentation of offerings by envoys from the land of Punt (Tomb of Rekhmire), four agricultural scenes (Tomb of Menna) and a barber's scene (Tomb of Userhet).

NECROPOLIS OF SHEIKH ABD EL-QURNA

After leaving the Asasif, the road runs past the hill of Khokha and turns south to necropolis of Sheikh Abd el-Qurna, which lies beyond the ruined temples of Ramesses IV and Thutmose III. The necropolis has dozens of tombs belonging to 18th-Dynasty dignitaries and stretches across the surrounding hills. The entire area is dotted with hundreds of holes, interspersed with the houses of the village.

TOMB ARCHITECTURE. Although they vary in terms of detail and size, the tombs of these dignitaries are built according to a general principle that differs from that of royal tombs. Their doors, which originally had a movable leaf, opened toward the east where the light of the rising sun symbolized rebirth. The upper section was surmounted by a small mudbrick pyramid (the remains of some of these can still be seen). The façade sometimes opened through a series of closely placed doors, which meant that the first vestibule remained accessible. In the court in front of the façade stood the biographical stelae of the deceased. Inside the tomb a vestibule wider than its depth opened onto a long, narrow room, at the end of which a niche contained statues of the deceased and his relatives. The rest of the tomb was inaccessible and consisted of a rock-cut corridor leading to an underground tomb which housed the sarcophagus and the funeral paraphernalia. It is impossible to predict the number of tombs open to the public. The six tombs that are generally open give a complete and varied idea of the beauty of this necropolis.

TOMB OF RAMOSE. The Tomb of Ramose (no. 55), vizier and governor of Thebes during the reign of Amenhotep IV, is preceded by a court and is famed for the quality of the bas-reliefs in the vestibule. On the east wall the beauty of the outlines and the fine texture of the braided hair illustrate the degree of refinement of the art of the period. The south wall is painted with scenes depicting the funerary procession. The construction of the tomb was interrupted when Ramose had to follow the king to Tell el-

Amarna. The various stages of the drawing, carving and painting of the scenes are can be seen on the walls.

TOMB OF USERHET. The Tomb of Userhet (no. 56), a royal scribe during the reign of Amenhotep II, lies to the south of the Tomb of Ramose. The most remarkable scene shows Userhet in a chariot, hunting desert animals with a bow.

TOMB OF NAKHT. About 100 yards to the north a path climbs steeply to the tomb (no. 52) of the scribe and astronomer of Amun during the reign of Thutmose IV. On the west wall, to the right of the door, are scenes depicting fishing, hunting and the harvest in the Nile Delta where Nakht probably had an estate. To the left of the door is one of the most beautifully painted scenes (the funerary banquet) in Thebes, but there are no illustrations of the astronomical activities of Nakht.

TOMB OF MENNA. About 50 yards further up the path, the Tomb of Menna (no. 69), an inspector of estates during the reign of Thutmose IV, contains some extremely realistic agricultural scenes and very detailed funeral scenes.

TOMB OF REKHMIRE. About 100 yards to the south a path climbs to the tomb (no. 100) of the governor of the town and vizier during the reign of Thutmose III. On the west wall, to the left of the door, are scenes of foreign tribute from Punt (Somalia), Khefti (Crete), Kush (Sudan) and Retenu (Syria), while those in the chapel illustrate Rekhmire's economic and administrative activities. Beyond these, scenes showing the polishing of statues, the making of bricks and goldsmiths and carpenters at work provide a great deal of information on the various attitudes, tools and accessories which characterized these trades.

TOMB OF SENNEFER. Near the Tomb of Rekhmire is the Tomb of Sennefer (no. 96), whose title was "Mayor of the Southern City" (Thebes) during the reign of

TOMB DECORATIONS
On the walls of the vestibule, painted scenes illustrate the private life and professional activities as well as the funeral procession and banquet of the tomb owner. These images are a remarkable source of information on the civilization of Ancient Egypt both in terms of the wealth of details provided and the meaning and degree of sophistication of representation. At the far end of a narrow room opening off the center of the vestibule was a niche containing statues of the deceased and his relatives.

BATTLE OF KADESH
Beneath the east portico of the second court of the Ramesseum is one of the finest-known representations of the Battle of Kadesh (Syria) where Ramesses II fought the Hittites in 1299 BC. The scene depicts Ramesses II's heroic counterattack. Standing in his chariot the young king fires arrows with deadly precision at the fleeing Hittites, many of whom are drowning in the Orontes. On the left the river reaches Kadesh, which is surrounded by ramparts and water. The intact banner means that the city was not captured. There were other encounters during the Hittite war until the first great peace treaty was concluded in the twentieth year of Ramesses' reign. To the east of the portico other episodes of the Battle of Kadesh are illustrated on the first pylon.

Amenhotep II. Its upper section is inaccessible. A long, underground corridor leads to the tomb, whose ceiling is painted with luxuriant vines and grape clusters, while the walls are decorated with scenes of offerings made to Sennefer by his daughter, the singer of Amun Muttawi.

RAMESSEUM

Below the necropolis the monumental complex of the Ramesseum, built by Ramesses II, stretches along the edge of the fertile valley. It was started at the beginning of his reign and took twenty years to complete. It has been used as a quarry since antiquity. As the walls of the façade have been pulled down the entrance leads straight into the inner area of the second court.

SECOND COURT. The court is flanked to the east and west by pillared porticos with engaged Osiride statues of Ramesses. The king is shown with his arms crossed, holding his scepters and tightly wrapped in a shroud (in imitation of Osiris), being summoned to rebirth in a new life. Beneath the eastern portico is an illustration the Battle of Kadesh. In the last register, at the top of the wall, is the grand procession of the annual festival of Min. The entrance to the second court of the Ramesseum was blocked by the fall of a huge granite colossus on whose shoulder an inscription

...s Ramesses as the "sun of
...". The statue must have stood
...ally about 69 feet high. On the
... side of the court was a royal palace
...se lower wall sections and column
...s can still be seen. The interior of the
...ple is reached via the east side of the
...urt, beyond the very badly damaged
...rst pylon.

HYPOSTYLE HALL. The central part of the
hall (whose ceiling is well preserved) was
lit by traceried windows. Behind the
façade, on the interior (south) wall of the
hall is a scene showing the capture of the
Syrian fortress of Dapur. Across the hall,

at the far end of the west wall, Ramesses II receives his
scepters from Amun-Re. Below this scene is a procession of
Ramesses' many sons. On the walls of the next room are the
sacred barques of the Theban Triad and the royal barque
which came here in procession from Karnak during the
"Beautiful Feast of the Valley". In the mysterious shadows of
the shrine (which now no longer exists) the king's statue was
placed in the presence of a statue of Amun, the source of all
life. This annual union invested the dead king with new
energy. On the ceiling of the hall are images of the months
and seasons of the year. In the center Thoth, master of both
writing and time, is represented as a baboon on top of a *djed*
pillar, the symbol of renewal.

SMALL TEMPLE. On the north wall of the Ramesseum is a
small temple dedicated to Ramesses' mother, Tuya, and wife,
Nefertari. Its foundations date from the reign of Sety I and it
has retained some of its original paving and column bases.

ANNEXES. The mudbrick annexes of the Ramesseum, which
extend for a distance of 20 yards or so around the shrine, are
better preserved than in other Egyptian temples. They give a
clear idea of the magazines, workshops and service chambers
built inside the sacred
precinct.

ANNEXES
The wealth of the
temple, such as
cereals, cloth,
earthenware jars and
precious metals, was
stored in the
magazines (some still
have their original
vaults) in the
northwest section of
the Ramesseum. A
sacerdotal necropolis
was founded here in
the 10th century BC
and the chapel walls
and entrances to the
burial shafts of the
many tombs scattered
across the site make it
difficult to distinguish
the original layout of
the annexes.

OSIRIAN ROOMS
The south door of the second hypostyle hall leads into a first chamber, which in turn leads into a small, two-columned room decorated with scenes of the king's coronation renewed in the Hereafter. The next room is a sort of vestibule which has a long bench (where offerings were probably placed) and opens onto two connecting rooms. A second door in the vestibule led into the Osirian chapel proper, which was linked to the other world by the false door carved on the far wall.

MEDINET HABU

The road runs alongside the ruined temples of Thutmose IV, Merneptah, Ay and Horemheb before reaching the monumental complex of Medinet Habu. The entrance, with its square towers, glacis and rounded merlons, imitates the gateways of oriental fortresses: a reminder of battles fought by Ramesses III during a troubled period in Egyptian history. This fortified entrance was part of a square, mudbrick building which no longer exists.

CHAPELS OF THE "DIVINE VOTARESSES OF AMUN". Inside the complex, on the left, are the adjoining funerary chapels of the "Divine Votaresses of Amun" who were 25th- and 26th-Dynasty queens and princesses. Each chapel has a court leading to a shrine covered, unusually in Egypt, by a vault of bonded stone.

SMALL TEMPLE. Opposite the chapels, to the north, is the Small Temple (18th Dynasty). The main part of the temple (built on a substructure) dates from the reign of Thutmose III and can still be seen today. At the far end, the shrine is preceded by a central barque shrine and surrounded by a gallery with a series of windows set in the outer wall. The temple originally possessed its own mudbrick enclosure whose tone gates, built by Taharqa, have survived. Over the centuries a series of additions were made to the east side of the temple. A kiosk dating from the reign of Nectanebo I was added to the court and small pylon built by Taharqa. This was followed by the construction of a Ptolemaic pylon on which the outer lintel of the gateway has retained part of its painted decoration. Finally a pronaos preceded by a court was begun during the reign of Antoninus Pius. The walls of this unfinished complex were built from reused blocks, as demonstrated by the fragments of bas-reliefs which can be seen on the inner walls. The temple stands on the sacred hill of Djeme, the site of the sepulchers of the eight primordial divinities of Hermopolis and joint creators of the world. Subtle and complex connections, based on the myths of the origins and renewal of creation, linked Amun-Re to this site where important ceremonies were held every year.

GREAT TEMPLE. The virtually intact pylon of the Temple of Ramesses III stands at the center of the site. It is decorated with scenes depicting the king adopting the traditional stance of the "massacre of the enemy". The north façade of the temple evokes the war fought by Ramesses III against the "Sea Peoples" in the Nile Delta. In the FIRST COURT, in front of each pillar of the north portico, is a colossus of the standing king. Across the court is the outer colonnade of the palace with the king's "Window of Appearances". A ramp leads to the SECOND COURT, whose southwest corner is also decorated with battle scenes. However, the quality and state of preservation of the images of the sacred barques of the Theban Triad, in the western section of the north wall, are far superior. Although most of

the inner rooms have lost their ceiling, the lower section is intact. A series of hypostyle halls led, along the central axis of the temple, to the sanctuary. In the north section, near the second hypostyle hall and the staircase leading to the terrace, is the entrance to the complex dedicated to Re-Harakhti. It is arranged around an open courtyard which used to have a central solar altar. On the lintel of the west portico, the king is shown in front of a group of chattering baboons (animals devoted to the rising sun), worshipping the solar barque. On the south side of the central axis is the suite of Osirian rooms.

ROYAL PALACE. The overall layout of the royal palace built against the temple is clearly visible. The central hypostyle hall

One of Ramesses I's sons (west wall of the main court of the Great Temple), the sacred barque of the Theban Triad (west wall of the hypostyle hall) and the pharaoh on the River Nile (right-hand side chapel).

Ramesses III chose the sacred site of Medinet Habu to build his jubilee and funeral temple. Although inspired by the Ramesseum it is unlike other religious edifices in that it is surrounded by a fortified enclosure wall. Following the death of Ramesses III it became the administrative center of the priests of Amun. After the excavations of Mariette and Morgan in 1859, it was not until the work carried out by the Oriental Institute of Chicago (1927–60) that the site became the subject of extensive research which involved a systematic study of the temple.

"MIGDOL" FORTIFIED ENTRANCE

Of the two gateways in the enclosure wall, only the east gate has survived. The first floor consists of solid masonry, pierced by a central gateway. The upper floors house apartments reached via a ramp situated beyond the gateway.

18TH-DYNASTY BARQUE SHRINE
The oldest building on the site is a square-pillared, peripteral temple. It was built by Queen Hatshepsut and completed by Thutmose III as a shrine for the sacred barque of Amun during the Beautiful Feast of the Valley.

MAIN PART OF THE TEMPLE

ANNEXES

NAVAL BATTLE
The bas-reliefs on the north outer wall depict the first great naval battle in history. It shows Ramesses III defeating the Sea Peoples who swept along the eastern Mediterranean coast in c. 1200 BC, destroying the Hittite empire and the coastal towns and cities. The Philistines were driven back by Ramesses III and settled on the Palestinian coast to which they gave their name.

SHOPS
Shops were vaulted and built in brick.

ENCLOSURE WALL

PRISONERS
These faience panels from the Palace of Ramesses III show Egypt's traditional enemies taken prisoner by the pharaoh. They can be recognized by their dress and headgear: a Libyan, a Nubian, a Syrian prince, a Bedouin and a Hittite.

The Temple of Medinet Habu covers an area of 20 acres. A text written during the reign of Ramesses III states that 62,626 prisoners of war worked in the temple.

TOMB OF SENNEDJEM
On the east wall of the tomb was a beautifully painted image of the "fields of Ialu", a sort of map of the kingdom of the Hereafter (detail above). On the west wall the deceased and his wife adore twelve gods, including Osiris (right), in a naos. On the south wall

Nephthys and Isis, in the form of birds, watch over the mummy. All the scenes have the characteristic yellow background of most of the many tombs of Deir el-Medina.

(the bases of the columns can still be seen) opens to the north toward the first court of the temple, while a door to the south leads to the throne room. The throne dais, behind which the "false door" stele once stood, is still in place. Beyond this are three apartments consisting of a vestibule, chamber and washroom. This was above all a symbolic residence where the dead king would continue to be present and be served within his mortuary temple.

ENCLOSURE WALLS AND ANNEXES. The second enclosure wall of Medinet Habu is the wall of the Temple of Ramesses III, which surrounds a complex of annex buildings. The remains of the houses of the Coptic town of DJEME, which occupied the entire site, gives the outer enclosure wall an irregular outline.

DEIR EL-MEDINA

The workmen's village of the royal necropolis, situated in the little valley behind the hill of Qurnet Murai, has been completely excavated. The master quarriers, masons, painters and sculptors who worked on the royal tombs lived within the enclosure wall with their families. They could reach the Valley of the Kings via the mountain path which passed above the cliff of Deir el-Bahri. Their houses, clustered together on either side of the village street, consisted of a main room in which there was a sort of bench with steps and a second, smaller room. Beyond this was an open kitchen with a stove and often a cellar hewn out of the rock. A small flight of steps led to the terrace.

TEMPLE. The temple dedicated to Hathor and Ma'at that stands to the north of the village was completely rebuilt during the Ptolemaic period. It consists of a small court and

438

Interior of the Tomb of Pashed (left), from the Ramesside period.

LAYOUT OF A TOMB
The tombs of Deir el-Medina tended to follow the same basic layout. An entrance in the form of a small pylon opened onto a court at the far end of which was the funerary chapel in the form of a small, steep-sided pyramid (one has recently been restored near the two tombs open to the public). In front of the chapel stelae and statues of the deceased were protected by a canopy. The access shaft to the tomb was dug either in the floor of the court or the chapel.

pronaos (whose columns have composite capitals), a central sanctuary and two side chapels. The south wall in the left of the two chapels is engraved with a beautiful scene depicting the weighing of the heart in the presence of Osiris. The heart of the deceased (the seat of thought), placed on one pan of the scales, should be balanced by the light feather of Ma'at (goddess of Truth). The result was recorded by Thoth. A monstrous creature, Ammit "the Devourer", waited by the scales for those who were rejected, while the successful candidates could attain the Kingdom of the Blest. To the north of the temple lies the Great Pit, an excavated site over 130 feet deep which yielded almost five thousand *ostraca* ● *59*. These have provided very useful information on life in Deir el-Medina during the Ramesside period. Only two of the tombs in the hillside necropolis to the west of the ancient village can be visited.

TOMB OF SENNEDJEM. The Tomb of Sennedjem (no. 1), a servant in the royal necropolis during the 19th Dynasty, was discovered intact in 1886. It has a beautiful vaulted ceiling decorated with vignettes from the *Book of the Dead*.

TOMB OF INHERKAU. The tomb (no. 359) of the "foreman of the mayor of the Two Lands" consists of two vaulted rooms. The second is decorated with vignettes from the *Book of the Dead* superposed on three registers. Inherkau is shown adoring the Phoenix and the cat of Heliopolis slaying the serpent Apophis.

The ruined temple of Deir el-Medina dedicated to Hathor and Ma'at, the two goddesses of the necropolis.

COLOSSI OF MEMNON

After several hundred yards the road leading back to the Nile passes the famous Colossi of Memnon (the Greek form of the name of Amenhotep III). These two huge, pink quartzite statues representing the king seated on his throne (which bears the symbol of the union of Upper and Lower Egypt) have not always stood alone on the plain as they do today. They once stood before the façade of the mudbrick pylon of a huge mortuary temple. Few of its remains can still be seen but its layout has been established by taking soundings. The temple was demolished during antiquity and a number of its blocks reused in Karnak and in some of the temples of the west bank.

A number of Greek inscriptions (which can be seen on the lower part of the colossus) were carved by the illustrious visitors who came to hear the famous "singing" statue of the Roman period. Some are dated and the oldest originates from the reign of Nero. While most visitors were content to write simple prose, some have composed elaborate poems.

VALLEY OF THE QUEENS

Only a few of the eighty tombs on this site at the southern edge of the Theban necropolis are open to the public. During the 18th Dynasty it received the remains of princes and princesses, while in the 19th Dynasty certain queens were also buried here. Unfortunately the famous TOMB OF NEFERTARI (no. 66), decorated with scenes of exceptional high quality, is not accessible. The TOMB OF AMENHIKHOPESHEF (no. 42), a son of Ramesses III, shows the young prince accompanied by his father in the presence of Thoth, Ptah and other divinities. At the far end of the tomb is the sarcophagus and the remains of a still-born baby. The TOMB OF QUEEN TITI (no. 52), probably one of the wives of a 20th-Dynasty king, consists of an entrance corridor where the queen is depicted with sidelocks, the sign of extreme youth. Several divinities are represented, including Ptah in his naos, Thoth, Atum,

THE "SINGING" COLOSSUS
According to Strabo the northern colossus lost the upper part of its torso as a result of an earthquake in 27 BC. For a long time afterward it emitted a strange musical sound at dawn, a phenomenon caused by the effect on the stone of the marked change in temperature. It stopped singing when Septimus Severus repaired the upper part of the statue.

QURNA
Most of the population of the west bank is concentrated in a series of hillside villages near the tombs. The largest of these villages is Qurna, which continues to flourish in spite of damage to the tombs, the ban on further building and a number of rehousing projects.

Isis and Nephthys. In the second chamber the queen presents an offering to the Hathor cow as it emerges from the sacred mountain. In the furthest chamber offerings were placed before the gods. On the far wall Osiris is depicted between Neith and Selqit, Nephthys and Thoth. The TOMB OF KHAEMWESE (no. 44) shows the young prince dressed in a linen robe and wearing a necklace, with the characteristic sidelock of princes. He first makes a lone offering to the gods and is then presented with his father to the guardians of the gates of the Hereafter.

MALKATTA. A track leads south and skirts round the western edge of Medinet Habu. After about half a mile the sparse remains of the mudbrick walls of the various monumental complexes of the Palace of Malkatta, Amenhotep III's royal residence, can be seen on the right and then the left of the track. It is the only known Theban palace and certainly the only one to have been built on the west bank. The construction of the vast lake (Birket Habu) to the east of the palace created the regularly spaced mounds that extend for about 1¼ miles. Near the far end of the ancient lake is the small Roman temple of Deir Shelwit, built at the end of the 1st century AD.

441

When villagers from Qurna make the journey to Mecca, their houses are decorated with images of pilgrimage. The lion is often featured, symbolizing the difficulties of the journey and the courage of the pilgrim. Appropriate Koranic verses, prayers and the pilgrim's name complete the decorations. The interior of the house is also decorated with paintings and *surah*. Garish banners, which combine Pharaonic and Islamic images, are hung on the walls of the town.

HASSAN FATHI
The Egyptian architect Hassan Fathi (1900–89), winner of the 1980 Aga Khan Award for Architecture, researched and completed several projects in the region.

QURNA

Qurna is a fine example of traditional Egyptian rural architecture. The houses, built of mudbrick mixed with straw and cemented together with mortar made from mud, seem to blend with their surroundings. The mud revetment is earthcolored in the plains and ocher in the mountains. Facades are decorated with brick crenelations and raised and rounded corners. The flat roofs are made of planks supported by palm beams or trunks and covered with an insulating layer of earth. The façades are roughcast in bright colors, made from iron oxide-based paints (yellow, ocher, red and blue).

QURNA EL-GEDIDA (NEW QURNA). One reason given for the relocation of the inhabitants of Qurna (still very much on the agenda) was the deterioration of the tombs. The best known of the many projects generated by the proposal was Hassan Fathi's pilot scheme, completed in 1948. It was not, however, appreciated by the mountain-dwellers, who made their living from tourism and the sale of (genuine or fake) antiques favored by the location of their villages, and they refused to leave. The project was inspired by traditional Nubian housing and makes generous use of vaults and *pisé* domes, architectural features that are used in the rest of Egypt only for tombs. Some buildings were eventually inhabited, but only after some major alterations. Finally the project overlooked the fact that rural dwellings must be flexible and able to be constantly altered, which is virtually impossible in New Qurna where now only the mosque remains intact.

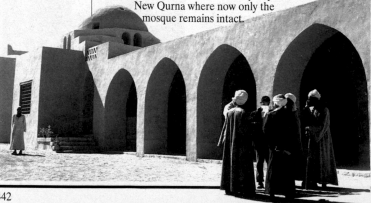

THEBES
TO ASWAN

THEBES TO ASWAN

ARMANT. The village of Armant (the ancient Greek settlement of Hermonthis), which stands near the Nile about 12½ miles south of Thebes, is steeped in history. The flourishing Middle Kingdom town, with its large necropolis, was extended during the 18th Dynasty by the construction of huge temples (now destroyed). Much later Cleopatra VII made it the capital of the nome. It was still flourishing at the beginning of the Christian era but was subsequently neglected. Although nothing much remains of the Temple of Cleopatra (its blocks were used in the 19th century to build the Armant sugar refinery), the temple dedicated to the local god Montu, represented here in the form of a Buchis bull, has survived. Buchis bulls, the earthly representation of the god, were buried in the sacred vaults of the Bucheum near the Temple of Montu. Among the scattered blocks and foundations which still exist (pylon of Thutmose III) is the image of a rhinoceros. The four sanctuary towns of Hermonthis, north Karnak ▲ *404*, Medamud and Tod, situated in the vicinity of Thebes and dedicated to Montu, enclosed an area known as the "Palladium of Thebes", the ancestral land placed under the god's protection.

Detail of hieroglyphs and general view of the ruined Temple of Tod.

Today little remains of the Temple of Cleopatra at Armant, since most of the blocks were reused to build the local sugar refinery.

TOD. Across the Nile from Armant, on the edge of the Arabian Desert, the village of Tod stands on an ancient site which is still mostly buried beneath its houses. Although the first religious settlement dates back to the Old Kingdom, the temple (as it stands today) and sacred lake date from the Ptolemaic period. At the back of the temple, in the area of the pronaos, are scenes commemorating its foundation. On the right the chapel-shrine of Thutmose III, designed to receive the sacred barque of Montu, houses a statue of the falcon-headed god surmounted by a solar disk, two *uraei* and two tall feathers. A vast hoard of treasure consisting of gold and silver ingots, silver chalices and lapis lazuli was found in four chests buried beneath the

🚗 ✈ Three days

original Middle Kingdom sanctuary. The pieces are now on display in the Cairo Museum ▲ 276 and the Louvre ▲ 476 in Paris.

JEBELEIN. To reach Jebelein (whose name, derived directly from Ancient Egyptian, means "the two mountains"), cross the Nile from the east to the west bank at El Shagab, about 17½ miles south of Luxor. The (higher) east mountain is dominated by the Tomb of Sheikh Mussa and has a Ptolemaic temple dedicated to the goddess Hathor. The remains of a mudbrick structure (a 20th-Dynasty fort) can be seen on the summit of the mountain, but the main reward for the effort spent climbing up this limestone mass is the magnificent view from the top. The ancient town of CROCODILOPOLIS used to lie on the small plain at the foot of the mountain, but now only the necropolis remains, on the west mountain opposite. The tombs, which were built between the Middle Kingdom and the Ptolemaic period, have been repeatedly plundered and the site is strewn with debris. Across the Nile from Jebelein, at MOALLA, there are openings on the hillside which mark the entrances to tombs dating from the First Intermediate period and belonging to dignitaries who achieved a degree of independence from a centralized power weakened at the end of the Old Kingdom. A text from the tomb of the nomarch Ankhtifi explains the administration of the region during the famine that had occurred during this time.

> "The alien and mysterious Nile, that gigantic serpent that winds so fabulously, so ungraspably, back through history."
> Rose Macauley,
> *Pleasures of Ruins*

ESNA

A barrage lies just outside the town of Esna, which stands on the west bank of the Nile. The town's Greek name was Latopolis because the fish (*lates*), the embodiment of the goddess Neith, was its sacred animal. Esna became increasingly important during the 18th Dynasty when Egypt developed its commercial relations with the Sudan, and an Esna–Derr route was established. The original temple of Esna was built during the reign of Thutmose III. There was a renewal of interest in the town during the 26th Dynasty. Under the Ptolemies and the Romans it became the capital of the Third Nome of Upper Egypt and a second temple was built. Most of the edifice has remained unexplored since the modern town has developed on the site of the ancient city, and its roof, surrounded by modern urban development, is on a level with the floors of the houses. The temple was dedicated to the ram-god Khnum who, at the dawn of time, fashioned mankind from the mud of the Nile on his potter's wheel. His divine companions included the lioness Menhyt (his consort), Nebtu (the goddess of the countryside), and the god Heka (the manifestation of vital energy). A special place was reserved for the androgynous divinity Neith (represented armed with a bow and arrows) who, according to local mythology, was the primordial creator of the world.

TEMPLE OF ESNA
The hypostyle hall, the only part of the temple that has survived, dates from the reign of the Roman emperor Claudius. An image of the god Bes at Esna (below).

The necropolis of El-Kab. The entrances to the excavated tombs can be seen on the mountainside.

Coptic statues found among the ruins of the Temple of Esna, which was converted into a church.

HYPOSTYLE HALL. The scenes and texts in the hypostyle hall, executed between the Graeco-Roman period and the reign of Decius in AD 250, were never completed. The style of the period is reflected in the bas-reliefs, whose figures have a more rounded appearance. The rectangular hall (the roof is still intact) opens to the west through an entrance flanked by columns. Inside, a wide variety of scenes illustrating the surrounding countryside is depicted on the capitals of twenty-four columns, while the shafts are reserved for images of the town's three main festivals: the creation of the universe by Neith, the raising of the sky by Khnum, and his victory over the human rebels. The columns support a ceiling, on which all these events are circumscribed by the course of the sun and the constellations. Outside the hall, on the frame of one of the lateral doors of the façade, two cryptographic texts dedicated to Khnum and Neith use only two (ram and crocodile) hieroglyphs.

Fresco from the tomb of
Paheri, grandson of
Ahmose and nomarch
of Nekheb,
representing scenes
from everyday life.

EL-KAB

From the pre-Dynastic period
two religious centers developed
in the region of El-Kab, one on
either side of the River Nile. On
the east bank, near the shores of
the river, stood the ancient
Egyptian city of Nekheb (the
Greek city of Eileithyiapolis) and,
on the west bank, ancient Nekhen
(the Greek city of Hieraconpolis)
also known as Kom el-Ahmar ("the
red hill") where vast pre-Dynastic
cemeteries stretch across the desert.
Nekheb el-Kab, one of the oldest
towns in Upper Egypt, was placed
under the protection of the vulture-
goddess Nekhbet. She was also known
as "the white goddess" because she
offers the White Crown of the south to
the pharaoh and presides over royal and
divine births. When the capital was
moved to Memphis, El-Kab lost its
importance even though it was the
birthplace of the noble Middle Empire
families who reconquered the country
after the Hyksos invasion ● 40. Two
sectors of El-Kab lie on a vast plain
situated at the mouth of a *wadi*. The first,
the town proper, includes temples, a
mamissi (birth house) and a sacred lake
(now a large depression to the east of the
town) protected by a thick brick enclosure
wall (1,740 feet square) with lateral gates.
Today visitors use the west entrance, which
provides the opportunity to see various
architectural elements. In a smaller enclosure is
the main temple dedicated to Nekhbet, a
religious establishment dating from the Old
Kingdom which was maintained and then converted
at the beginning of the New Kingdom until the 30th
Dynasty. In front of this crumbling temple the remains
of the *mamissi* dedicated to Nekhbet (the embodiment of
Hathor) can still be seen. The second sector is centered
around the necropolis, on a rocky outcrop. The most
important tombs (those of Ahmose, Renni, Paheri and Se
date from the 18th Dynasty and the Ramesside period.

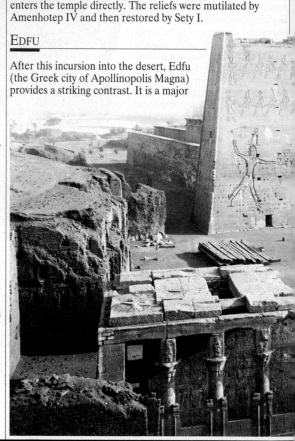

THE GOD HORUS
The Temple of Edfu is inhabited by the falcon-headed god Horus, also depicted crowned with a solar disk whose two spread wings represent the falcon soaring in the skies. As the protector and divine symbol of royalty, the falcon is associated with Re, the solar star, and becomes the guarantor of universal cosmic harmony. The Temple of Horus at Edfu is a fine example of a typical temple layout which is best understood by working inward from the entrance to the sanctuary (or naos) situated in the darkest and most secret recesses of the temple. As well as being a place for the daily worship of the god, the temple was also the focal point of the great annual festivals which constituted the official ceremonies of Horus, as evidenced by the Egyptian calendar. The festival of the coronation guaranteed the annual renewal of Horus' royal status and reaffirmed the power of his earthly representative, the pharaoh, and was held on the esplanade in front of the first pylon. Every year a falcon was chosen for the occasion from a sacred aviary in the Temple of the Falcon (now destroyed).

TEMPLE OF THOTH. Leave the tombs on the left and follow the *wadi* (about 1½ miles) to the Temple of Thoth. The chapel was built by Setau, viceroy of Nubia, during the reign of Ramesses II at the place known locally as El-Hammam ("the bath"). A nearby cave-temple in the mountainside is dedicated to Nekhbet, who was transformed into the lioness Hathor-Tefnut. According to an ancient myth, the disappearance of the moon is linked to the lioness' flight into the desert, from where she was brought back into Egypt after being pacified by the god Thoth. A flight of steps carved out of the rock leads to the Ptolemaic speos. Two vestibules lead into a small, rock-cut chamber with a vaulted ceiling. The temple was converted into a Coptic monastery during the Christian era. Further along the *wadi* is the crag known as "Vulture Rock", which is covered with drawings and inscriptions, some dating from prehistoric times. Beyond the rock is the TEMPLE OF AMENHOTEP III, dedicated to Nekhbet-Hathor. The portico of the façade has disappeared, and one enters the temple directly. The reliefs were mutilated by Amenhotep IV and then restored by Sety I.

EDFU

After this incursion into the desert, Edfu (the Greek city of Apollinopolis Magna) provides a striking contrast. It is a major religious and commercial center which stands at the nucleus of the road network and the end of the desert and gold-mine routes. The pile of rubble to the west of the Temple of Horus is probably the original site of the village of DJEBA. Although French and Polish teams were keen to excavate the site and have uncovered Old Kingdom mastabas and Byzantine houses, the nerve center of the town is undisputedly the temple of the falcon-god Horus.

TEMPLE OF HORUS. Access to the site is from the back of the temple. There has been a succession of structures built on this sacred site from prehistoric times (when the falcon-god was housed in a wicker hut) to the New Kingdom. The temple owes its imposing appearance to Ptolemy III Euergetes who began to rebuild the original temple completely in 237 BC. The work was not completed until 57 BC. Today visitors pass beneath the pylon and cross the court bordered on three sides by a colonnaded portico. Beyond the court is the FIRST HYPOSTYLE HALL (or pronaos) whose façade honors Horus and Hathor and whose gates were opened only for festivals. The high priest used to enter the temple through this gate and purify himself in the "ROBING ROOM" (on the left of the entrance to the pronaos) before taking the papyrus bearing the day's order of worship from the library (on the right of the entrance). The SECOND HYPOSTYLE HALL, darker than the first, opens, on the west side, onto the "CHAMBER OF THE NILE" (which contained the pure water from the well used for the priests' ablutions) and

EDFU
The Temple of Edfu, one of the best-preserved temples in Egypt, stands in the center of the town (details above).

The court of the temple is bordered to the south, east and west by identical colonnaded galleries with "open" capitals. The columns in the same gallery are all different.

HYPOSTYLE HALL
On the columns were images of the various divinities of the nome to whom offerings were made and who represented all the sanctuaries of Egypt. The south and west walls illustrate the ritual of the founding of the temple. The king is seen choosing the site with the goddess Seshat (crowned with a star), marking out the boundary with a cord and stakes, digging the foundations and filling them with sand before dedicating the divine residence to its master, Horus.

the "laboratory" (where the ointments and perfumes were prepared for the daily anointment of the statue). On the opposite (east) side it opens onto the treasure-house where valuable and religious items were kept. Then comes the OFFERING HALL where food offered to the god was placed on dressers and altars and from where staircases led up to the temple terrace. On certain occasions (transitional periods such as the Festival of the New Year) the god had to be united with the solar disk in the "Court of the New Year", which opened off the so-called "Pure Place" (whose ceiling traced the voyage of the solar barque through the Twelve Hours of the day). The statue, the god's earthly medium, had to be recharged with divine energy by being carried up the side staircase to the temple terrace; here it was exposed to the sun's rays before being taken down again by the opposite staircase. The bas-reliefs on the walls of these staircases show the procession of priests and standard-bearers carrying the cases containing the god's statues up to the court of the New Year on one side and down again on the other. The vestibule opens onto the SANCTUARY and its stone naos, which also contained the sacred barque of Horus. The god (his statue) residing in the temple enjoyed the services of the priests who woke him each morning, dressed him, offered him meals and sang hymns in his honor. They returned in the evening to prepare the god for the night's repose. A corridor ran round the outside of the naos to various CHAPELS reserved for special rites, for storing the cloth used to clothe the god's statues and to welcome divinities, including Hathor, who usually resided in Dendera ▲ 388. Her visit to her husband, the Horus falcon, for a fortnight every year was an occasion for great public celebration, and the two gods emerged regenerated from this encounter (the "Feast of the Beautiful Meeting").

eave the darkness of the sanctuary and make your
ay to the inner, eastern section of the enclosure
vall on which the sun-god is depicted destroying his
enemies. These events were performed as part of an
annual ritual known as the "Triumph of Horus",
which ended with Horus seizing power and
taking possession of his earthly heritage. The
ritual of the "ten harpoons" (which ended with
the slaying of the hippopotamus, the symbol of
Seth, enemy of the sun and Horus) and Horus
sailing victoriously on the sacred lake of Edfu
(now buried beneath the village to the east of
the temple) were the two main elements of the
festival. Another annual ritual performed in the
MAMISSI situated in the forecourt of the great
temple was the birth scene of the divine child
Harsomtus, the son of Horus and Hathor, in the form of the
god "Horus who unites the Two Lands", embodied on earth
by the pharaoh Horus.

JEBEL SILSILA. About 90 miles south of Edfu, the Nile flows
between the rocky shores of Jebel Silsila ("the mountain of
the chain"). According to legend, the river was once barred at
this point by a chain stretching between two rocks on either
side of the river. Jebel Silsila marks the boundary of the
Egyptian region of Nubia where the Nile was believed to rise
and where the Nile god was worshipped. The site was
quarried early on in history because of the excellent quality of
the sandstone and the proximity of the Nile. The vast
sandstone quarries on the eastern shore provided the stone
for the monuments of Dendera ▲ 388, Thebes ▲ 394, Esna
▲ 446, Edfu and Kom Ombo. Three thousand workers toiled
to provide stone for the Ramesseum ▲ 432. Quarrymen's
marks and inscriptions provide evidence of the gargantuan
tasks carried out by the Pharaonic workforce: the great
STELE OF AKHENATEN, for example, hewn out of the rock
north of the shore. Amenhotep IV (Akhenaten) ▲ 378
worshipped Amun here (at the beginning of his reign) and the
inscription below the stele indicates that a large workforce
brought back stone for the sanctuary of Karnak ▲ 404. Closer
to the shore are the remains of a
great (unfinished) sandstone
sphinx and a chapel of
Amenhotep III.

JEBEL SILSILA QUARRIES
Many of the (mostly open) quarry faces are as much as 65 feet high. The stone was quarried from a straight or echeloned face (above). The quarry on the eastern shore was worked from the 18th Dynasty to the Graeco-Roman period. The quarry was abandoned in AD 200 and was only reopened in 1906 when the Esna barrage was built.

View of the rock-cut grottos at the entrance to the ancient quarries.

WEST BANK

The west bank can now be reached along the road which runs from Edfu, along the canalized section of the Nile, to the old Aswan ▲ 456 dam. Although it, too, has quarries, it is first and foremost the site of a speos and the Nile shrines. The largest SHRINES were built by Sety I, Ramesses II and Merneptah and there is also a stele of Ramesses III with its hymn to the Nile. The kings made offerings during the festivals held in honor of the Nile floods.

SPEOS OF HOREMHEB. The façade of the speos (with its five openings formed by four pillars) is visible from a distance. At one time a flight of steps climbed from the river to a forecourt. The speos itself consists of a vaulted, transverse hall whose far wall opens onto the sanctuary containing seven statues, including Amun (in the center) and Horemheb. The decoration was completed during the reign of Ramesses II. On the southwest wall Horemheb is shown being suckled by the goddess Taweret (represented by a hippopotamus, the embodiment of the Nile and its life-giving floods) who imparts her divine strength and power in her milk, thus enabling him to vanquish the Nubian enemy. As you leave the speos of Horemheb, follow the river south to the great stelae which consecrate offerings from Ramesses III, Ramesses V and Shoshenq I to the gods of Thebes, Heliopolis and Memphis. Beyond the stelae some of the small chapels which line the route (the chapel of Sennefer, for example) are in fact tombs, although most are commemorative monuments erected in honor of the Nile.

KOM OMBO

The road continues southward along the east bank to Kom Ombo, passing through the villages of New Nubia, where some of the Nubian refugees were relocated when their homes and villages were drowned following the construction of the Aswan High Dam ▲ 460. The region is typically Nubian, with its brightly colored houses, its fields of sugar cane and, as you approach Kom Ombo, orange groves.
TEMPLE OF KOM OMBO. The Temple of Kom Ombo can be seen from a distance. It is situated on top of a

hillock, on the ancient site of Ombos, which was occupied from prehistoric times. The elevated position of the temple offers a splendid view (from the terrace, facing away from the sanctuary) of the modern village of Kom Ombo, which lies to the east, opposite the island of Mansuria on a bend in the Nile. The great temple has some impressive ruins. When it was abandoned by the priests, it was engulfed by sand (the color of the stone is an indication of the level of sand on the inside). The Copts who inhabited it destroyed some of the reliefs, before the edifice was used as a quarry. Finally the Nile completed its destruction by eroding part of the temple's ancient terrace. In spite of the ravages of time and mankind, it is difficult to remain indifferent to the beauty of the site. One very singular feature of the temple's layout and elevation is the double row of doors leading to a DOUBLE SANCTUARY, which is emphasized by a wall-cum-screen separating the two sections. The northern section is dedicated to the falcon-god Harwer, or "Horus the Elder", and the southern section to the crocodile-god Sobek. The two gods are accompanied by their "families": Harwer's wife Tesentnefert ("the Good Sister") and son Panebtawy ("Lord of the Two Lands") and Sobek's consort Hathor and son Khonsu, although the two triads often tend to merge and combine in an extremely complex theology. The overall layout is that of a divine temple during the Ptolemaic period. A few foundations are all that remain of the PYLON whose southern section develops the theme of the king entering the temple, followed by spirits bearing the products of the land of Egypt and the Sobek triad. Beyond the pylon and inside the court the king is shown leaving his palace escorted by standards. In the southwest corner of the court a staircase once led to the roof terrace.

The paved COURT has a columned portico and central altar. As you approach the sanctuary there is a scene showing the purification of the king in one of the intercolumniations of the façade of the pronaos. Three

A crocodile relief on one of the temple walls.

CITY OF GOLD
The name Kom Ombo (the ancient Greek settlement of Ombos) is derived from the Ancient Egyptian word *nubt*, which means "city of gold". In fact the town occupied a strategic position at the mouth of the *wadis*, which led to the regions in which gold was mined.

OFFERINGS
It was the pharaoh's duty to uphold the worship of the gods and present them with offerings in return for their protection. These offerings are usually depicted in the lower register of temple decorations.

SURGICAL INSTRUMENTS
On the inner face of the second enclosure wall is a unique illustration of several surgical instruments. These Roman instruments should be related to the healing powers usually associated with Harwer.

columns with composite capitals flanking the door of the PRONAOS are inscribed with the motifs of the lotus (south) and the papyrus (north), the symbols of the Two Lands. Inside the pronaos the arrangement of the capitals echoes this duality with the exception of one (southwest) column, while the intercolumniations illustrate the king's coronation. The ceiling is decorated with astronomical images, and the scenes on the walls of the hall show the king's purification and his consecration of the temple. On the west wall of the papyrus-columned HYPOSTYLE HALL, between the two doors of the central axis, is an inventory of the sacred places of Egypt, the gods of the main towns and the local and national festivals. In the next room the construction and foundation of the temple are prefaced by a scene showing the goddess Seshat "stretching the cord". This is followed by the purification of the newly erected temple where the king is shown throwing grains of natron. Traces of circles on the paving in front of the entrance to the hall indicate the original position of the offering table. In the OFFERING HALL, a lion goddess, appointed to oversee the offerings made on each day of the year, was accompanied by bull- or ram-headed spirits. Only the south staircase leading to the roof terrace (where the temple statues were exposed to the sun) remains. In the last room before the sanctuary were the statues of the gods and the temple-builder kings who were worshipped there. Although the "Court of the New Year" (to the north of the last room) no longer exists, part of the ceiling of the "Pure Place" (where the statue was dressed for the Festival of the New Year) still remains, decorated with two images of the sky-goddess Nut. On the body of the first are winged solar disks and, on the second, the different phases of the moon, while a barque of the night sails between the two. The pedestals that once supported the sacred barques and some of the chapels of the sanctuary can still be seen. To the south of the temple the CHAPEL dedicated to HATHOR by Domitian houses the crocodile mummies from the nearby crocodile necropolis (about half a mile to the southeast) and some recently discovered sarcophagi. The *mamissi* near the pylon of the temple has been largely destroyed.

ASWAN AND NUBIA

ASWAN

Aswan is situated about 130 miles south of Luxor on what was once the southern border of Ancient Egypt. It lies on the east bank of the Nile at a point where the river cuts its way through the granite rock of the first of the cataracts

The brightly painted houses of the village of Aswan are sometimes decorated with drawings and scenes illustrating the pilgrimage to Mecca made by the owners.

surrounding the ISLAND OF SEHEL, where Anukis (daughter of Khnum) was worshipped. About 250 inscriptions (dating from the 4th Dynasty to the Ptolemaic period), engraved on the rocks of the island, commemorate particular expeditions and events: for example, the famine which raged for seven years during the reign of Djoser was ended only by the intervention of the god Khnum. At Aswan the green, fertile belt of the Nile Valley is interrupted and replaced in mid-desert, behind the great dam, by the vast LAKE NASSER. Sandstone is replaced by granite in the form of two rocky barriers which hold back the Nile and also harbor the quarries

10 KERTASSI   **11** KALABSHA   **12** MAHARRAKA   **13** DAKKA   **14** WADI ES-SEBUA   **15** AMADA   **16** ABU SIMBEL

exploited early on in history by the great builder-pharaohs.

Khnum is the lord of the cataract and master of a gulf which was believed to be the source of the Nile floods. From ancient times Aswan was a huge market situated at the crossroads of the routes from Africa, the western deserts of Egypt and India.

This frontier trading-post, visited by people from a number of different countries, was also an important strategic point. It has served as a base for Roman garrisons, for the Turkish troops of the Ottoman sultan Selim in 1517, for the army of General Kitchener during the conquest of the Sudan (1896–8) and is now a major garrison for the modern Egyptian army.

ELEPHANTINE ISLAND. Syene, the Ancient Egyptian name of Aswan, was derived from "syenite" (the name was wrongly applied to granite and today reserved for another type of rock). It is the modern counterpart of the first market town situated on the island of Elephantine (from the Egyptian word *abu* meaning "elephant") so called because of the extensive trade in ivory during antiquity. The island, with its Nubian villages, is reached by *felucca*. The ancient quays and landing-stage on the eastern side of the island once gave access to the temples of Thutmose III and Amenhotep III, destroyed in 1822 by the Turkish government. Only the Roman NILOMETER remains. Near the Nilometer the ELEPHANTINE MUSEUM houses objects discovered on the island and in the surrounding area, including prehistoric schist basins and the mummies of the sacred rams of Khnum, with their richly decorated and gilt casings. The ruins of the ancient city were discovered beyond the museum, in the south part of the island. They include the temples dedicated to Khnum and Satis by Queen Hatshepsut and the temple built in honor of Hekayib (governor of Elephantine Island during the 6th Dynasty and deified posthumously) by his successor Sarenput I (whose tomb is at Gharbi Aswan). Several chapels containing statues represent the largest complex devoted to private worship.

✵   Four days

NILOMETER
The Nilometer on Elephantine Island was described by Strabo in the 1st century AD as "a steeply graded staircase that plunges down into the river". The graduated scale on the walls was used to measure the flood levels which were certified by inscriptions in demotic script, Greek, Arabic and French.

457

Mummies from the ram necropolis found nearby can be seen in the Elephantine Museum.

KITCHENER'S ISLAND. Geziret el-Nabatat or Plantation (formerly Kitchener's) Island is also reached by *felucca*. It is famed for its botanical gardens, which include many African and Asiatic species.

GHARBI ASWAN

KITCHENER'S ISLAND
The British general Horatio Kitchener (1850–1916) was sent to Egypt in 1883 to reorganize the Egyptian army, which he then led against the Sudanese Mahdi. After his victory in 1898 he discovered an island off the shore of Aswan where he planted a wide variety of exotic plants, which are still flourishing today.

Detail (right) of frescos in the Tomb of Sarenput I (12th Dynasty).

On the side of the hill known as Qubbet el-Hawwa (named after the *marabut* buried there) are two rows of rock-cut tombs belonging to the princes and dignitaries of Elephantine.

Opposite the town of Aswan, on the west bank, the steep cliff of Gharbi Aswan (west Aswan) is surmounted by the tomb of a *marabut*, QUBBET EL-HAWWA, erected in honor of a local saint.

HYPOGEA OF THE PRINCES OF ELEPHANTINE. The tombs of dignitaries who held office between the end of the Old and the Middle Kingdoms can be seen halfway up the cliff. They are reached by flights of steps equipped with a form of chute for hoisting sarcophagi from the Nile to the tomb entrance. When the tombs, discovered between 1889 and 1969, were excavated they revealed texts describing expeditions into the Sudan and Central Africa. They are also of interest from the architectural point of view, with the huge speos highlighting the veining and colors of the rock. They include the TOMBS OF SABNI AND HIS FATHER, MEKHU, who died during the reign of Pepy II on a voyage to Lower Nubia (probably assassinated by local tribesmen). His son organized an expedition to bring back the prince's body and punish the inhabitants. On the left section of the door Mekhu and his wife receive offerings. THE TOMB OF SARENPUT II is remarkable for its six-pillared chamber and the niches containing a statue of Sarenput in the guise of Osiris. THE TOMB OF HARKHUF, the great 6th-Dynasty explorer who traveled to Central Africa and brought back a "dwarf" (who was probably a Pygmy) for the king, contains a text giving details of the letter from the king thanking Harkhuf for his present. The TOMB OF HEKAYIB AND HIS SON has a double-columned façade as well as reliefs which depict hunting and fishing scenes and a bullfight.

The most richly decorated TOMB is that of SARENPUT I. The limestone entrance with images of the deceased opens onto a six-columned chamber. Sarenput is featured on the shaft of the columns on either side of the central axis. He can also be seen at the entrance and on the far wall of the chamber followed by his sandal-bearer and his dogs, hunting with his family and being entertained by singers. On the same bank the TOMB OF THE AGA KHAN is a reminder of the latter's presence in Aswan. The forty-eighth imam, Mohammed Shah Aga Khan (who died in 1957) is buried here.

MONASTERY OF ST SIMEON. The Monastery of St Simeon lies about twenty minutes' climb from the Mausoleum of the Aga Khan. However, a better line of approach is to follow the path which runs along the ridge (about fifty minutes' walk), for it offers a magnificent view of Aswan. The monastery was built in the 6th century in honor of a local saint, Amba Hadra (or Amba Samaan), but the problems of keeping it supplied with water, along with repeated Bedouin attacks, led to its being abandoned at the end of the 12th century. It has all the features of a Coptic monastery ● *106*: the church built according to the classic layout of a nave flanked by side aisles and dissected by a transept leading to the choir (whose vaulted ceiling had a fresco showing Christ seated on a throne, surrounded by angels) and the sacristies, monks' cells, attics and tombstones. It was one of the largest Coptic monasteries in Egypt.

EAST BANK. On the east bank the town of Aswan and its bazaar stretch along the Corniche, which is the departure point for the road to the granite quarries. En route it passes

the FATIMID CEMETERY whose high-domed mausoleums commemorate the saints of Islam and, in particular, Sayyida Zeinab ▲ *314*. In the northern sector of the quarries, exploited from the 6th Dynasty to the Graeco-Roman period, is the so-called UNFINISHED OBELISK, which, had it been completed, would have weighed over 1,320 tons and stood some 118 feet high. To extract the blocks (often carved on three faces) the Egyptians chipped out holes along the line of the stone to be removed into which they inserted wooden wedges. These wedges were kept well soaked and, as they swelled, they shattered the block of stone. To the south two lidless Graeco-Roman sarcophagi and an unfinished royal colossus lie in the sand.

MONASTERY OF ST SIMEON
Once one of the great Coptic monasteries in Egypt, the Monastery of St Simeon was surrounded by a high enclosure wall made of brick with stone foundations.

The veritable forest of cupolas surmounting the tombs of venerated and important people in Aswan's vast Fatimid cemetery is an impressive sight.

"What a pity the pyramid-builders did not immortalize themselves in a more productive way. If they had thought of it they could have used the Aswan granite on the spot for anticipating the building of the High Dam. Their architects and engin-eers would have been equal to this gigantic job, and then Egypt would have already enjoyed, for more than 4,500 years, the extra acreage that the High Dam is now going to give her."
Arnold Toynbee, 1965

HIGH DAM
A barrage of gravel, earth and rocks almost a mile deep at its base, 2½ miles long and 375 feet above the level of the water retains the vast artificial lake (which stretches for about 312 miles beyond the Egyptian border) formed by its construction. A huge hydroelectric power station has been built on the right bank.

Construction work in progress (above).

TEMPLE OF WADI ES-SEBUA
The eight pairs of sphinxes lining the *dromos* of the Temple of Ramesses II (below) evoked the

name of the site: the Valley of the Lions. They led to a pylon flanked by two colossi of Ramesses II. An Osiride court precedes the excavated part of the temple.

FIRST DAM. The first dam, built in Aswan granite and inaugurated by the British in 1902, soon proved unequal to the task of controlling irrigation downstream. It was widened and heightened several times but was finally replaced by the High Dam.

HIGH DAM. The construction of the Aswan High Dam (Sadd el-Aali) was overshadowed by political difficulties. The initial financing was to have come from the United States but in the end it was built and brought into use by Russian capital and engineers.

SAVING THE TEMPLES. The shores of the Nile between Aswan and Abu Simbel were lined with temples. An international rescue operation organized by UNESCO saved these divine residences from the flood waters. Some were transferred to museums in Berlin, Leiden, Madrid, New York and Turin, while others remain in situ, on the west bank (now LAKE NASSER), as proof of the value of these Nubian edifices.

KALABSHA. The Temple of Kalabsha, originally situated over 30 miles from Aswan, now stands about 6 miles from the first dam. Most of the temple was built during the reign of Augustus, although the remains of a chapel at the northwest corner date from Ptolemy IX. The temple is dedicated to the god Merwel (the Greek god Mandulis), the Nubian version of Horus associated with Isis, goddess of Philae. Its layout is the same as that of the Temple of Edfu ▲ *448*. Starting from the pylon, a double enclosure wall in brick and stone delimits the divine complex. The pylon, reached via a ramp, opens onto a courtyard with colonnades on three sides. On the façade of the pronaos intercolumniations alternate with columns whose capitals take the form of the lotus, papyrus and vines. The naos (later converted into a church) consists of three adjoining rooms. The roof beyond the first room of the sanctuary offers a good view of the site and the nearby TEMPLES OF KERTASSI and BEIT EL-WALI (governor's house), a speos preceded by a court whose walls celebrate the military victories of Ramesses II.

CONSTRUCTION OF THE FIRST DAM
The first dam or El-Khazzan ("the reservoir") was built between 1898 and 1902 (left). It was 100 feet high, about 88 feet deep at its base and 1½ miles long.

WADI ES-SEBUA. Wadi es-Sebua ("valley of the lions") is the site of the ancient temple of Wadi es-Sebua and the temples of DAKKA and MAHARRAQA. The Graeco-Roman temple of Dakka, dedicated to the god Thoth of Pnubs, was begun in the 3rd century BC by the Ethiopian king Arkamani. Several Ptolemies and Roman emperors worked on the temple, which was finally completed by Augustus. The axis of the temple, runs parallel with the river. A great pylon leads into the complex where the sanctuary lies beyond the pronaos and two rooms. The TEMPLE OF WADI ES-SEBUA was completely dismantled and rebuilt 2½ miles to the west. The small Temple of Horus which originally stood there is now destroyed and only the Temple of Ramesses II remains.

AMADA. The southern section, comprising the Temple of Derr and the Tomb of Penne (a governor), has developed around the TEMPLE OF AMADA, a hemi-speos dedicated to Amun-Re and Re-Harakhti by Thutmose III and Amenhotep II. The speos part of the temple was detached from the ground and lifted in one 990-ton block which was then moved 2 miles across the desert on rails to its new site about 330 feet above the first. In 1966 the constructed part of the pronaos was dismantled, course by course, and then reassembled and rebuilt near the speos. The TEMPLE OF DERR, which had originally stood on the east bank, was dedicated to Re-Harakhti by Ramesses II. The TOMB OF PENNE (Penne was the governor of the region which lay between the first cataract and the second) was located in a necropolis containing Middle Kingdom and New Kingdom tombs at Aniba.

"But I am left with the impression that the Nile itself, with its great flow of water and its ever green banks and eternal youth is the really interesting thing, far finer than its monuments. These are interesting as part of the river's history, not the Nile because of them."
Wilfred Scawen Blunt

TEMPLE OF MAHARRAKA
The temple, which dates from Roman times and was dedicated to Isis and Serapis, was never completed. The most important remains are those of the hypostyle hall.

461

PHILAE

According to tradition it is from Philae ("Pilak" in Egyptian), the smallest of the islands, that the goddess Isis watches over the tomb of Osiris on the neighboring island of BIGA, declared sacrosanct because its earth was considered part of the god's mummified body. Only priests and temple servants were permitted to live on the island to perform the sacred rites of Isis and Osiris.

TEMPLE OF ISIS. The Temple of Isis and Horus the Child (Harpocrates) dominates the group of monuments erected on the island between the 26th Dynasty and the Roman period. Beyond the *dromos* scenes on the great pylon show the sovereign addressing the divinities Isis, Horus and Hathor. Two granite lions, once joined to two obelisks, stand guard. Inside the gate of the first pylon an inscription attests to a visit by members of the Egypt Expedition in 1799. The central court opens, to the east, onto a series of rooms and, to the west, onto a *mamissi* comprising a pronaos and three rooms

where Isis the Elder is worshipped as the mother of Hathor. The second pylon, slightly offset to the east, opens onto a pronaos (later converted into a Coptic church) with a decorated ceiling on which the vulture of Upper and Lower Egypt circles in the central bay while the barques of night and day sail down the lateral bays. The sanctuary is composed of several rooms and forms an independent suite. The granite naos still exists. A staircase in the first room leads to the roof and the Chapel of Osiris, where the sacred rites of the god were performed and whose walls are covered in devotional scenes based on the myth of his death and resurrection. As you leave the naos continue westward to the 2nd-century GATEWAY OF THE EMPEROR HADRIAN and the source of the Nile. A vulture and a falcon are perched above a grotto where the Nile god is depicted entwined by a serpent, pouring water from two vases. To the north is a temple dedicated to Harendotes and, to the south, a Nilometer.

TEMPLE OF HATHOR. The columns of the temple dedicated to Hathor by Ptolemies VI (Philometor) and VIII (Euergetes II) have scenes of harpists, flutists, monkeys playing the lyre and the god Bes playing a small drum, distractions designed to placate the goddess. The nearby KIOSK OF TRAJAN received the sacred barque of Isis when the goddess returned to the island. Although unfinished, it is remarkable for its capitals.

Philae seen by a traveler: (from top to bottom) a reconstruction of the island and its monuments during the Graeco-Roman period; the flooded Temple of Isis; rescuing the temples; the island of Agilkia today (right).

The pronaos of the great temple of Abu Simbel with its pillars and engaged statue of Ramesses II, invaded by the sand.

Scenes of the famous Battle of Kadesh, engraved on the walls of the pronaos.

"In front of the small temple are six colossi which are more impressive from a distance than close to. They are about thirty feet high and carved out of the rock like the great temple, which is decorated with a huge statue whose head and shoulders alone are visible above the sand. I could see even from a long way off that it was superbly carved. A row of hieroglyphs runs along the frieze."
Giovanni Battista Belzoni

ABU SIMBEL

The delightful islands of Aswan and Philae are the prelude to the grand finale of a voyage up the Nile: the great rock temples of Abu Simbel. While air links offer a quick and easy way to reach the site (built 175 miles from Aswan), with the added bonus of an aerial view of the vast Lake Nasser, the road crosses a relatively flat and dazzlingly colored stretch of desert. In 1968 the Egyptian government, in association with UNESCO, undertook a truly "Pharaonic" task. The two speos of Ramesses II and Nefertari were cut into sections, strengthened, dismantled and reconstructed on the summit of a rocky outcrop of the Libyan mountains which overlooks the Nile at this point. The original site, at the foot of the cliff, was completely submerged following the construction of the Aswan High Dam.

TEMPLE OF RAMESSES II. The more southerly speos sets the tone with its façade (108 feet high x 125 feet wide) of four colossal statues of Ramesses II facing the east. The smiling king sits enthroned, wearing the double crown of Upper and Lower Egypt. His subjects, including princesses, princes, the queen mother and his first queen Nefertari, are depicted on a much smaller scale, standing at his feet. The power of Ramesses II extending over the enemies of Egypt is represented on the sides of the thrones where the conquered nations are placed to the north or south according to their geographical position. As if to greet the rising sun, twenty-two baboon statues stand upright above the cornice and look down on the falcon-headed sun-god Re who receives an offering from Ramesses II. In the darkness of the PRONAOS a colossal Osiride statue Ramesses II supports the roof, glorifying the perpetuity of royal power in the Hereafter. He wears the White Crown of Upper Egypt in the southern half of the pronaos and the Red Crown of Lower Egypt in the northern half. On the walls are scenes of Ramesses II's military victories, including the famous Battle of Kadesh proclaimed by the Egyptians as a glorious victory over the Hittites. The scenes show the king holding a council of war and the troops leaving the Egyptian camp for Kadesh, situated on the banks of the River Orontes. The inevitable confrontation is directed, from his chariot, by the king who then charges into battle and brings back prisoners whose hands and genitals have been cut off to help assess their numbers. The pronaos leads into a series of (sometimes unfinished) rooms: magazines where ritual items were kept and rooms with benches on which offerings were placed. The

RELOCATING THE TEMPLES
The delicate rescue operation of Abu Simbel lasted for three years (1963–6). The two temples were disengaged from the cliffs in which they were carved, dismantled into 1,036 numbered blocks, transported and reassembled in an artificial cliff according to the original layout, in a new setting which recreated their original environment.

vestibule, covered with offering scenes, opens onto another room with a central door leading into the sanctuary and two others opening onto side chapels. In the sanctuary are four seated statues carved out of the rock: Re-Harakhti (red), Ramesses II deified (red), Amun-Re (blue) and Ptah (white). The divine patrons of Egypt's three great cities (Heliopolis, Thebes and Memphis) surround the deified king. Twice a year (on October 20 and February 20) at daybreak, the sun's rays fell on and "revitalized" the statues in the sanctuary. Only Ptah, the source of chthonian life, remained in the shadows. At the center of the sun's regenerating light the king was reinvigorated with divine energy. On either side of the façade two chapels (one of which contains a solar altar) are dedicated to the worship of the sun, while three stelae stand at the southeast corner of the façade. One of these, the so-called "Marriage Stele", illustrates the marriage of Ramesses II with the daughter of the king of the Hittites.

TEMPLE OF NEFERTARI. The façade of the Temple of Nefertari echoes the theme of the royal colossus of Ramesses II, which

alternates with statues of his first queen Nefertari, in the guise of Hathor-Satis, and their children. The pronaos, whose six Hathor pillars replace the Osiride pillars of the speos of Ramesses II, is decorated with scenes which show the king massacring the various enemies of Egypt in the presence of Nefertari while the queen herself makes offerings to the goddesses Mut and Hathor (far wall). Three doors in the pronaos open onto the vestibule preceding the sanctuary set deep in the hillside. Inside this rocky "womb" the goddess Hathor appears as the Hathor cow, protecting the breastplate of Ramesses II, while on the south wall the king glorifies his own image and that of his deified queen. On the north wall Nefertari performs the rites of divine worship under the watchful eye of Mut and Hathor.

EGYPT IN THE MUSEUMS OF THE WORLD

In 1824 the French refused the collection put together by the Piedmontese French consul in Egypt, Bernadino Drovetti (1776–1852). It was subsequently acquired by Charles Felix of Savoy, King of Piedmont and Sardinia, who decided to found the first great Egyptian museum. Since then the 5,300 pieces (which came from surface excavations and date mainly from the New Kingdom) have been exhibited at the Accademia delle Scienze in Turin. It was not until the Italians Schiaparelli and Farina, who were following in the footsteps of Mariette, Maspero and Petrie, undertook systematic archeological excavations and scientific studies that the different stages of Egyptian history, from prehistory to the Coptic period, were explored.

Treasure from the tomb of Kha.

EGYPTIAN MUSEUM, TURIN

After Cairo, the city of Turin has the largest collection of Egyptian antiquities in the world. Its rooms are organized according to themes or by provenance. A magnificent collection of colossal statues representing gods, kings and nobles, acquired by Drovetti in 1815, came from the Temple of Amun at Karnak. Ernesto Schiaparelli's early 20th-century excavations at Deir el-Medina ▲ *438* discovered the (intact) 18th-Dynasty tomb of the architect Kha and his wife, complete with all the funeral paraphernalia, furniture and statues which were intended to accompany the deceased on their voyage into the Hereafter. There is another intact (although anonymous) tomb from the 5th Dynasty, as well as the richly painted 11th-Dynasty tomb of Ity from Gebelein.

The Turin museum houses a fine collection of ceramics, amulets, papyri and cloth as well as a number of figurines made of wood.

STATUE OF RAMESSES II
Next to the 18th- and 19th-Dynasty royal statues is one of the masterpieces of Egyptian art: a seated statue of Ramesses II, wearing a pleated tunic with, on his left, the sculpted image of his wife.

One of the rooms in the Turin museum,
painted by Dellcani (1881).

ARCHEOLOGICAL MUSEUM, FLORENCE AND THE VATICAN MUSEUM

The National Archeological Museum in Florence possesses a comprehensive collection of Egyptian antiquities. Its exhibits consist mainly of pieces which were brought back from Ippolito Rossellini's expedition to Egypt with Champollion ▲ 216 in 1828, and the later discoveries of Ernesto Schiaparelli.

The Vatican Museum in Rome founded in 1839 by Pope Gregory XVI houses, amongst other treasures, a head of the pharaoh Mentuhotep IV (11th Dynasty) and a colossal granite statue of Queen Tuy, mother of Ramesses II. Much of the Vatican's Egyptian collection (like that of the Capitol museums) has come from excavations carried out within the city of

Rome, which highlights the importance of the cult of Isis, introduced from Egypt at the time of the Roman conquest.

HEAD OF MENTUHOTEP
This sandstone head of the pharaoh Mentuhotep is one of the key exhibits in the Vatican's Egyptian collection.

CHAPEL OF ELLEJISSA
Following the Nubian rescue operation which was mounted by UNESCO during the 1960's, the museum at Turin acquired Nubia's most ancient rock chapel. It was built at Ellejissa by Thutmose III in 1450 BC, restored two centuries later by Ramesses II and converted into a church with the advent of Christianity.

EGYPT IN THE MUSEUMS OF ITALY
Italy has collections of Egyptian antiquities in Bologna, Naples, Palermo and Trieste, as well as in Turin, Florence and the Vatican.

USEFUL INFORMAITON
MUSEO ARCHEOLOGICO NAZIONALE DI FIRENZE
Via della Colonna, 38
Florence
Hours: 9am–2pm

MUSEO GREGORIANO EGIZIO
Cortile del Belvedere
Citta del Vaticano
Vatican, Rome
Hours: 9am–2pm

MUSEO EGIZIO DI TORINO
Via Accademia delle Scienze, 6
Turin
Hours: 9am–2pm

In 1846 Frederick William IV, King of Prussia, chose a small island in the River Spree, in the center of Berlin, as the site for the city's Egyptian Museum, which would house, in particular, the 1,500 pieces brought back from an expedition led by the Egyptologist Karl Richard Lepsius (1810–84). The pieces were added to Berlin's existing collection of Egyptian antiquities, formed thirty years earlier by Frederick William III. Its director was Giuseppe Passalacqua, an adventurer from Trieste who had brought back a surprising number of antiquities from the Nile Valley.

HISTORY OF THE EGYPTIAN MUSEUM, BERLIN

The Egyptian Museum of Berlin was opened in 1850 and run under the joint directorship of Karl Richard Lepsius ● *94* and Giuseppe Passalacqua until the death of the latter in 1865. From the end of the 19th century two Egyptologists, Johann Peter Adolf Erman and Ludwig Borchardt, promoted the study of Egyptology and enriched the museum's collection. Erman began to write a dictionary of the Egyptian language in Berlin while Borchardt carried out excavations in Egypt where he discovered the famous limestone bust of Queen Nefertiti at Tell el-Amarna ▲ *378*. The museum also received donations of pieces discovered during the excavations financed by two patrons of the arts from Berlin: Baron von Bissing and the wealthy merchant James Simon.

During World War Two the museum collections, stored in the city and the neighboring provinces, sustained considerable losses. All the sarcophagi and mummies were destroyed, as were one hundred crates of exhibits and over five hundred stone items. Five warehouses remained undamaged. The contents of three of these, recovered by the Russians, were returned to the Bodenmuseum in East Berlin in 1958. The contents of the other two warehouses, which were returned to West Germany by the Allied troops, formed the nucleus of the Egyptian Museum of West Berlin, opened in 1967.

USEFUL INFORMATION
ÄGYPTISCHES MUSEUM
Schlossstr. 70
14059 Berlin
Hours: 9am–5pm
Closed: Friday

ÄGYPTISCHES MUSEUM UND PAPYRUSSAMMLUNG BODENMUSEUM-MUSEUMSINSEE
10178 Berlin
Hours: 9am–5pm
Closed: Monday

There are also important collections at Leipzig, Munich (efficient acquisitions policy), Hamburg, Hanover, Heidelberg and Hildesheim.

SARCOPHAGUS OF KEN-HOR
Painted wood sarcophagus from the Third Intermediate period, surrounded by its funeral paraphernalia.

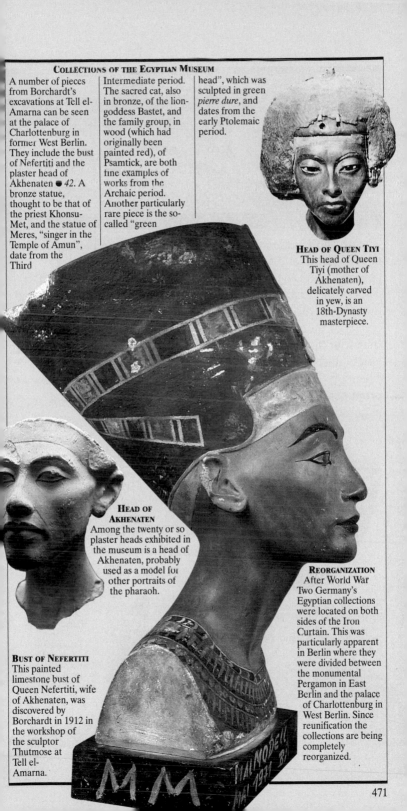

COLLECTIONS OF THE EGYPTIAN MUSEUM

A number of pieces from Borchardt's excavations at Tell el-Amarna can be seen at the palace of Charlottenburg in former West Berlin. They include the bust of Nefertiti and the plaster head of Akhenaten ● 42. A bronze statue, thought to be that of the priest Khonsu-Met, and the statue of Meres, "singer in the Temple of Amun", date from the Third Intermediate period. The sacred cat, also in bronze, of the lion-goddess Bastet, and the family group, in wood (which had originally been painted red), of Psamtick, are both fine examples of works from the Archaic period. Another particularly rare piece is the so-called "green head", which was sculpted in green *pierre dure*, and dates from the early Ptolemaic period.

HEAD OF QUEEN TIYI
This head of Queen Tiyi (mother of Akhenaten), delicately carved in yew, is an 18th-Dynasty masterpiece.

HEAD OF AKHENATEN
Among the twenty or so plaster heads exhibited in the museum is a head of Akhenaten, probably used as a model for other portraits of the pharaoh.

BUST OF NEFERTITI
This painted limestone bust of Queen Nefertiti, wife of Akhenaten, was discovered by Borchardt in 1912 in the workshop of the sculptor Thutmose at Tell el-Amarna.

REORGANIZATION
After World War Two Germany's Egyptian collections were located on both sides of the Iron Curtain. This was particularly apparent in Berlin where they were divided between the monumental Pergamon in East Berlin and the palace of Charlottenburg in West Berlin. Since reunification the collections are being completely reorganized.

471

The decision made in 1906 to create an Egyptian Department of Antiquities at the Metropolitan Museum in New York, coincided with the first American expeditions to Egypt, and to Thebes and Lisht in particular. As well as being mainly supplied by the discoveries made during these excavations, the museum's collections were also enriched by the reproductions of more than four hundred copies of wall-paintings made by the team of epigraphists accompanying the expeditions. Lord Carnarvon, Theodore M. Davis and Albert Gallatin are three of the prominent names associated with the sales, donations and bequests made by private collectors to the Metropolitan Museum.

Head of Queen Tiyi, wife of Amenhotep III (18th Dynasty).

Pink granite sphinx representing Queen Hatshepsut. The Metropolitan has fourteen monumental sculptures and nine Osiride capitals from the Temple of Deir el-Bahri ▲ 426.

USEFUL INFORMATION
METROPOLITAN MUSEUM OF ART
1000 5th Avenue
New York
Hours: 9.30am–5.15pm
Fri. and Sat.: 9.30am–8.45pm
Closed on Monday
BROOKLYN MUSEUM
200 Eastern Parkway
Hours: 10am–5pm
Wed. to Sunday

Fragment of a wall painting, showing fishing with a net, from a Theban tomb.

The museum has a fine collection of Old- and Middle-Kingdom sarcophagi, including this 21st-Dynasty, painted wood sarcophagus.

Limestone funeral stele of Senu (18th Dynasty).

Reconstruction of the temple at Dendera (1st century BC), a gift from Egypt in recognition of the American contribution to the Nubian rescue operation ● 98.

OTHER UNITED STATES MUSEUMS

The Brooklyn Museum in New York also possesses a significant collection of Egyptian antiquities, as well as a major center of Egyptology: the Wilbur Library. Also worth a visit are the Museum of Fine Arts in Boston (one of the largest museums in the United States), the Philadelphia University Museum, the Walters Art Gallery in Baltimore, the Oriental Institute Museum and Field Museum of Natural History in Chicago, the Cleveland Museum of Art and the museums of Detroit, Kansas City, New Haven and St Louis.

473

The magnificent neoclassical building of the British Museum, which superseded Montagu House, stands in Bloomsbury, in the heart of London. Among its many other treasures it houses one of the four or five leading collections of Egyptian antiquities in the world. Like the other major European collections, it was initially based on an older, existing collection, and formed from the shrewd acquisitions of those veritable "forwarding agents" of antiquities who enjoyed more or less unrestricted access to Egypt and its treasures during the first half of the 19th century: in particular the British consul in Cairo Henry Salt (1780–1827) and the adventurer Giovanni Battista Belzoni (1778–1823).

HISTORY OF THE BRITISH MUSEUM collection

Systematically organized and scientifically conducted excavations, particularly under the aegis of the Egypt Exploration Fund (later the Egypt Exploration Society), made it possible to build up varied and comprehensive collections. The reliefs and statues of Deir el-Bahri ▲ 426 are one such example. The British archeological missions were extremely active on a number of sites and kept the museum supplied with coherent archeological material, not just "beautiful objects". In this respect, the material from the site of Qasr Ibrim (in Nubia), is particularly interesting.

ORGANIZATION OF THE COLLECTION
Exhibits are organized on the basis of an outstanding, revised presentation. Generally speaking, statues, reliefs, sarcophagi and heavy pieces, with some extremely dark and evocative side galleries, are on the first floor, while smaller items and thematic classifications are on the second.

BUST OF RAMESSES II
Most of the major exhibits were either purchased by or donated to the museum during the 19th century: for example the granite bust of Ramesses II (right), taken from the Ramesseum ▲ 432 by Belzoni and the "royal list" of Abydos, as well as paintings and small, luxury, funerary items.

Mock Canopic jars in painted wood, made in the 21st Dynasty. By this time the internal organs were being embalmed and then replaced in the mummified body.

THE PAPYRUS COLLECTION

The museum has an entire series of important papyri, including an account of the enquiry into the plundering of the royal tombs during the reign of Ramesses IX (Abbott Papyrus), the mathematical Rhind Papyrus and the great Harris Papyrus.

"BOOK OF ANI"

The museum also has some splendid examples of *Books of the Dead*: for example the 19th-Dynasty, painted papyrus book of the scribe Ani (left), and the books of Hunefer and Nakht.

ROSETTA STONE

This huge, black basalt stele is one of the "jewels" of the museum's collection. It is inscribed with the bilingual text, in Greek and Egyptian (hieroglyphs and demotic script), which provided the key for the deciphering of Egyptian writing.

USEFUL INFORMATION
BRITISH MUSEUM
Great Russell Street
London WC1

Opening hours:
10am–5pm
Sunday: 2.30–6pm

Closed on public holidays.

475

New-Kingdom "horse" ring in gold, cornelian and *cloisonné*.

Jean-François Champollion, sometimes described as founding father of Egyptology, became the first curator of the Egyptian Department of Antiquities of the Louvre Museum, founded by Charles X in 1826. On the second floor of the south wing of the Cour Carrée, the architect Fontaine designed the rooms destined to house one of the most prestigious collections of Egyptian art in the world. The pieces which comprised the first acquisition, approved by the king in 1824, were presented against a décor which reproduced Egypt's legendary magnificence and grandeur. Champollion gave precedence to the historical and scientific view, imposing a new concept of museology which broke with the traditional esthetic demands of the period.

HISTORY OF THE LOUVRE COLLECTION

When Champollion ▲ 216 died in 1832, the department already had a considerable number of exhibits which had come mainly from the purchase of the collection of the British consul in Alexandria, Henry Salt, in 1826, and of the second collection of Drovetti, the French consul in Egypt, in 1827. Drovetti's first collection, refused by France in 1824, is now in the Egyptian Museum in Turin. The antiquities that Champollion brought back from Egypt in 1828, although few in number, were extraordinarily high quality. The second half of the 19th century heralded a new type of acquisition from the French excavations in Egypt carried out by Auguste Mariette ● 96. The foundation of the Cairo branch of the French Institute in 1880 strengthened the links between archeological missions and national institutions. The more recent additions mainly resulted from the transfer of reserve collections from the Bibliothèque Nationale in 1922 and the Musée Guimet in 1946, as well as from donations from private collectors.

Quartzite statue of Nefertiti: a fine example of the humanization of figures during the Amarnian period.

MADJIA SARCOPHAGUS
The painted wood sarcophagus found at Deir el-Medina ▲ 438 is an example of the new type of sarcophagus used at the time. Various objects, pieces of furniture and items of jewelry were found during the same excavations.

USEFUL INFORMATION

MUSÉE DU LOUVRE
34, quai du Louvre
Opening hours:
9am–6pm
Monday and
Wednesday:
9am–10pm
Closed on Tuesday.

Paris

PECTORAL OF RAMESSES II

The brilliance and prosperity of the New Kingdom is reflected in the sumptuousness of the exhibits, as illustrated by the gold cup of the Egyptian general Djehouty and the pectoral of Ramesses II.

TREASURES OF THE LOUVRE

Remains from the royal tombs of the Nile Valley exhibited in the Louvre include the pink granite sarcophagus of Ramesses III and a fragment of a wall-painting representing Sety I and the divinity Athor. The Archaic period is represented by a number of illustrated papyri and bronze statues. The museum also has some fine pieces from the Saite period: the Posno Horus, the life-sized limestone statue of the Apis Bull from Mariette's excavations at Memphis in 1852, and some fine examples of the Faiyum portraits. With the remains of Christian churches and the famous linen and wool weaving, the Louvre's Coptic rooms cover the eight most productive centuries of Christian art in Egypt.

SEATED SCRIBE

The museum has a collection of Old-Kingdom statues of which the oldest are in limestone and archaic in their rigidity. The "seated scribe" (in limestone, alabaster and rock crystal), found at Saqqara, is a fine example of their stylistic development.

CHANCELLOR NAKHTI

Outstanding among the Middle-Kingdom pieces are the remains of funerary items and the magnificent acacia statue of the chancellor Nakhti, found in the provincial necropolis of Assiut.

As well as the leading national museums, which have entire wings and series of rooms devoted to Egyptian antiquities, there is an impressive number of smaller museums and foundations throughout the world which have their own Egyptian collection, put together from purchases and donations. As it would be impossible to provide an exhaustive list, here are some of the best known.

FRANCE

In Paris, apart from the Louvre, the small collections of the Musée Rodin, the Petit Palais and the Bibliothèque Nationale are well worth a visit. The Clot-Bey (doctor to the *pasha* of Egypt in the 19th century) collection in Marseilles has been transferred from the Château Borély to the magnificent building of La Vieille Charité in Le Panier district. The collection of Egyptian antiquities in the new art museum in Grenoble, where Champollion grew up and began his research, includes the stele of the Princess of Bakhtan. The Musée des Beaux-Arts in Lyons also has a fine collection of objects which have come mainly from the excavations of Coptos but also from the collections of such national institutions as the Musée Guimet and the Louvre. In Strasbourg the collection of the Palais Universitaire (the University Institute of Egyptology) is, unusually for France, an extremely valuable university collection built up primarily during the German Imperial period (1870–1914) but also during the period when the university sponsored the French excavations at Tanis (limited access).

Statue of a bearded man (Nagada period), Musée des Beaux-Arts, Lyons.

COLLECTIONS IN THE FRENCH MUSEUMS

Nantes: Musée d'Archéologie

Avignon: Musée Calvet (currently being refurbished)

Cannes: Le Suquet

Orleans: Musée Historique et d'Archéologie de l'Orléanais

Toulouse: Musée Georges-Labit

Bas-relief from the Temple of Kalabsha ▲ 460 in Nubia, showing Augustus in Egyptian dress (Musée Champollion, Figeac).

A small exhibition of objects on loan from the Louvre Museum can be seen in the recently converted Musée Champollion in Figeac, originally the house where the Egyptologist was born.

Wooden model of a boat (12th Dynasty) and heads of Semite prisoners (20th Dynasty) in the Kunsthistorisches Museum, Vienna.

Faiyum portrait (2nd century). Pushkin Museum, Moscow.

OTHER LEADING EUROPEAN MUSEUMS

BELGIUM
In Brussels the collections of the Musées Royaux d'Art et d'Histoire were put together from major Belgian excavations and purchases. The Queen Elisabeth Foundation has made Brussels one of the international centers of Egyptology.

AUSTRIA
The Kunsthistorisches Museum in Vienna has a very large and long-standing collection of stelae, reliefs and statues, including a remarkable

13th-Dynasty statue of the Sobekemsaef and Theban sarcophagi. There are also some fine reliefs from the tomb of Meryre (presented in major exhibitions devoted to Amenhotep III in the United States and Paris), recently discovered at Saqqara ▲ 344 by the French Bubasteion mission.

THE NETHERLANDS
The large collection in Leiden was put together by the Swedish consul Giovanni Anatasi at the beginning of the 19th century. It

consists mainly of pieces from Thebes ▲ 394 and Memphis ▲ 332 and includes, in particular, the magnificent reliefs from the Tomb of Horemheb and the statues of Maya.

Funerary statuette in polychrome wood. Gulbenkian Museum, Portugal.

Make-up dish in the shape of a fish. Barbier-Mueller Museum, Geneva.

Obelisks appeared on the European scene in 1585 when the Vatican obelisk was erected opposite St Peter's in Rome. However, they tended to lose their specifically Egyptian characteristics. On October 22, 1836 the Luxor obelisk, a gift from the Egyptian government to France, was erected in the Place de la Concorde during a ceremony attended by the people of Paris.

THE OBELISKS OF ROME
The city of Rome has five obelisks (right and left). The obelisk of Ramesses II from Heliopolis ▲ 270, which used to stand in the center of the Circus Maximus (above), today stands in the Piazza del Popolo.

THE OBELISK OF CONSTANTINOPLE
The 197-foot obelisk of Thutmose III (far right) broke as it was being unloaded in Constantinople. Only the upper section (85 feet) was erected by Theodosius the Great on the site of the Roman hippodrome, today the At Meydani.

"CLEOPATRA'S NEEDLES"
In 1877 John Dixon built a cylindrical metal container surmounted by a deck and fitted with masts and sails, to transport one of "Cleopatra's Needles" from Alexandria to London. The second of the two obelisks, a gift from the Egyptian government to the United States in 1879, today stands in New York's Central Park.

PRACTICAL INFORMATION

◆ EGYPT IN THE MOVIES "THE MUMMY" – FROM KARL FREUND TO SHADIE ABD EL' SALAM

The Ten Commandments (1923), directed by Cecil B. De Mille.

Cecil B. De Mille's Cleopatra (1934).

The rows of slaves move apart as the procession advances. The huge sphinx is pulled by hundreds of pairs of arms. Cleopatra (Elizabeth Taylor), brought back to Rome by Caesar, makes a spectacular entry into the city. And so begins the last of the great Egyptian epics: Cleopatra (1963) directed by Joseph Mankiewicz.

THE GREAT EGYPTIAN MYTH

The big names in the movie world have taken on the great Egyptian myth with varying degrees of taste and success: from Ernst Lubitsch's The Wife of Pharaoh (Germany, 1921) to Howards Hawks' Land of the Pharaohs (United States, 1955). Cecil B. De Mille, master of the epic genre, directed Cleopatra (1934) and two versions of The Ten Commandments (1923 and 1956). However, there were more serious productions. The Mummy (United States, 1932), starring Boris Karloff (famed for his interpretations of Frankenstein)and directed by Karl Freund, was undoubtedly

one of the most successful movies about Egypt. Gabriel Pascal achieved a veritable tour de force when he screened Caesar and Cleopatra in London during World War Two. Scenes shot on location were added after the war. The papier-mâché sphinx in whose shadow Caesar met Cleopatra had to be transported by boat to the land of its illustrious and authentic ancestors.

"EGYPTIAN" AND "ORIENTAL" PRODUCTIONS

This "affair" with Ancient Egypt coincided with a fascination for an imaginary Orient which began as silent movies took

their first, faltering steps. However, the exotic, colonial theme was soon exhausted and the movie world was inundated by a wave of "Egyptian" and "Oriental" fiction which included a dozen or so versions of Cleopatra and The Mummy and, in the second, George Fitzmaurice's The Son of the Sheikh (1927), with Rudolf Valentino in the title role, as well as several versions of The Arabian Nights and Jacques Becker's Ali Baba and the Forty Thieves (1954). Pasolini's version of The Arabian Nights (1974) was somewhat more eclectic. Nor

did Egypt itself escape this wave. The first full-length movie in the history of Egyptian cinema was Victor Rossetto's The Land of Tutankhamun. The first real images of Egypt where produced by the French Lumière brothers when one of their cameramen landed in Alexandria on March 10, 1897, and shot thirty-five films in the region. In 1907 the Alexandrian directors Aziz & Dorès shot short documentaries which they screened in a cinema equipped by Gaumont and which still exists as the Strand.

From left to right: Dawud Abd el' Sayed's El-Kit-Kat, Asma el-Bakri's Proud Beggars (1991), based on a novel by Albert Cossery, Yussef Shahin's The Land and Pier Paolo Pasolini's The Arabian Nights.

Alexandria – Why? (1978), directed by Yussef Shahin, who also directed *The Sixth Day* (1986), based on a novel by Andrée Chedid and starring Dalida, and *Adieu Bonaparte* (1985) with Michel Piccoli.

Karl Freund's *The Mummy* (1932).

The Son of the Sheikh (1927).

Jacques Becker's *Ali Baba and the Forty Thieves* (1954).

TODAY'S EGYPTIAN CINEMA

Today Egypt is establishing itself as the main movie maker in the Arab world. It produces, on average, between sixty and eighty movies a year, not counting television series, filmed theater and the *Fawazir* (charades) of the month of Ramadan which have been widely exported for the last decade. While Egyptian musical comedies have delighted several generations of moviegoers throughout the Arab world since the 1930's, the West's experience of Egyptian cinema has been mainly through the work of Yussef Shahin with

movies such as *Alexandria – Why?* (1978). Shahin also directed *The Land* (1969), a major militant movie set in pre-Revolutionary Egypt. Another great Egyptian moviemaker, Salah Abu Seif, is known for his neo-Realist approach. One of his major works, *El-Qahira Talateen (Cairo, 1930's)* tells the story of a provincial law graduate in Cairo who can only obtain a ministry post by agreeing to marry the mistress of the relevant head of department. After a long period of stagnation, dominated by

so-called "commission" movies, Egyptian cinema is re-establishing itself in its own right. A new generation of directors, including Mohamed Khan and Khairy Bishara, is making movies which examine the problems of a developing urban society. Cairo and its surrealist everyday existence often play the leading role.

One of the most successful of these movies, Dawud Abd el' Sayed's *El-Kit-Kat* (named after a district in Cairo), tells the story of a debauched *sheikh* with a passion for marijuana. The most remarkable movie is undoubtedly Shadic Abd ol' Salam's *The Mummy* (1969), inspired by Maspero's discovery of the cache of royal mummies at Deir el-Bahri.

Cecil B. De Mille, at the foot of the *papier-mâché* sphinx used in his version of *Cleopatra* (1934).

The "Land of the Pharaohs" is an ideal winter vacation destination. The mild temperatures and fine weather make visiting archeological sites and deserts much easier. The Red Sea is at its best in spring and fall, and the Mediterranean in summer. Egypt is both accessible and affordable and the Egyptian people are very hospitable. Following a drop in tourism over the past two years due to the political events affecting the country, the Nile Valley has now regained its popularity as a holiday destination.

VISAS

Visitors to Egypt must have a visa. These can be obtained by post, although it is easier to go and get one in person. Visas are issued for three months but are only valid for one month if obtained in Egypt.

◆ A 14-day extension can be obtained free of charge at the Mugamaa ◆ 527 (Central Government Building) in Cairo.

◆ To obtain a visa, you need a valid passport and a photograph. The cost is £15/$15.

For visa applications, Egyptian consulates are usually open Monday–Friday, 10am–noon.

EGYPTIAN CONSULATES:
◆ UK:
2 Lowndes Street
London
SW1X 9ET
Tel. 0171 235 9777
◆ US:
1110 Second Avenue
New York, NY 10022
Tel. (212) 759 7120
◆ AUSTRALIA:
125 Monaco Cres.
Red Hill
Canberra ACT 2603
Tel. 062 950 394

◆ CANADA:
454 Laurier Ave,
E. Ottawa
Ontario K1N 6R3
Tel. 613 234 4931;
3757 Côte des
Neiges
Montreal
Quebec H34 1V6
Tel. 514 937 7781

◆ Visas can be obtained at the airport on arrival in Egypt and are less expensive.

◆ If you are booking a package tour, your travel agent will usually obtain your visa for you.

VISA FOR SINAI

A special 14-day visa (issued free of charge) enables you to visit the region between Sharm el-Sheikh and Taba as well as the biblical sites.

INSURANCE

Avoid doubling up on insurance

◆ Some credit cards (American Express, Visa) offer an insurance scheme. Consult your insurance company to avoid over-insuring for medical cover and repatriation.

◆ On package tours, insurance is not always included. If not, you can always take out additional insurance to cover theft or loss of luggage, repatriation and third-party liability.

◆ N.B. Even if you are only buying a plane ticket, do take out a cancellation insurance, which means your money will be refunded if you have to cancel your vacation for any reason.

PHOTOGRAPHY

ASA 100 and 200 films are on sale everywhere (£E 12). Flashes may not be used in museums or tombs. ASA 1000 films are not very common and it is advisable to take these with you.

◆ An additional charge for cameras (£E 10 in museums and £E 5 in tombs) is payable at the entrance.

◆ For the best quality, have your films developed when you return home.

HEALTH

◆ There is some risk of malaria between June and October. Ask your doctor about the best form of preventive treatment.

◆ Make sure you have something to hand to combat the "Pharaoh's curse", (upset stomach).

◆ Don't swim in the Nile or canals as you could contract bilharzia, a serious parasitic disease which affects the liver.

VACCINATIONS
There are no compulsory vaccinations for Egypt but:
◆ A vaccination against hepatitis A and B is advisable.
◆ For further information on vaccinations, cost and the countries for which they are required, ask your general practicitioner.

MOSQUITOS
Mosquitos can be irritating in the evening, especially in the Delta region. Make sure you take an insect repellent, citronella, or some form of insect repellent device.

Stylized sun (Tell el-Amarna).

Path leading to Mount Sinai.

MOVIE CAMERAS

These must be declared on arrival and departure. Films are not very common. The same conditions apply as for cameras, but charges are higher in museums (£E 100) and tombs (£E 25) and an additional charge is made for movie cameras (£E 30) at the entrance to sound and light shows. Movie cameras may not be used at the Aswan High Dam or in the Valley of the Kings.

CARE OF PHOTOGRAPHIC EQUIPMENT

Egypt is a dusty country. When you are not using your camera keep it in its case. Take a special cleaning brush with you. In the event of a sandstorm, wrap it in a plastic bag.

INDISPENSABLE ITEM
A torch and spare batteries for visiting tombs.

N.B.
Because of the present political situation, it is not advisable to visit Middle Egypt (El-Minya and Assiut), which is the stronghold of the Islamic Fundamentalist groups.

USEFUL INFORMATION

An international student identity card costs about £5/$16 and entitles the holder to a 50 percent reduction when visiting archeological sites and museums as well as on certain train journeys.
For further information contact:
◆ INTERNATIONAL STUDENTS HOUSE 229 Great Portland Street London W1
◆ The card can also be obtained from the University of Cairo on Roda Island.

YOUTH HOSTEL CARDS
There are Youth Hostels in the major towns and cities but, although they are the least expensive form

of accommodation, they are often some way from the city center and conditions are fairly basic. You may be asked for your card.
For a list of Youth Hostels, contact:
◆ UK: Tel. 0707 324 1780
◆ EGYPTIAN YOUTH HOSTEL ASSOCIATION 1 Shari' el' Ibrahim Cairo Tel. 354 0527

AN ABSOLUTE "MUST"
Climbing the austere and magical, rocky slopes of Mount Sinai at dawn is an unforgettable experience.

TAKING ACCOUNT OF THE CLIMATE

WINTER
◆ From December to March northern Egypt can be cold and wet.
◆ Afternoons in the south are warm, but the nights can be cold.

SUNSHINE
The sun shines all the year round. Only the Mediterranean coast has overcast days in winter.

HEAT
Temperatures begin to rise in April and remain high until October. They do, of course, vary according to latitude and reach a maximum of 120°F in the south.

SANDSTORMS
These occur mainly in March and April. The most formidable is the *Khamsin*.

HUMIDITY
Because of the low level of humidity, the intense summer heat is more bearable in the south than in the Delta region, where temperatures are in fact lower.

CLOTHING
Dress to suit the climate and customs.
◆ In winter warm clothing is essential as the north winds can be bitterly cold.
◆ Avoid blunders: while shorts are quite acceptable on archeological sites, they are less so in towns where a more discreet, modest style of dress is appropriate.
◆ Some form of sun hat is a must.
◆ Woolen clothing insulates against both cold and heat.

IN °F	CAIRO		ASWAN	
	MIN	MAX	MIN	MAX
JANUARY	48	64	50	73
FEBRUARY	48	66	51	79
MARCH	51	75	57	88
APRIL	57	82	66	97
MAY	64	90	73	102
JUNE	68	95	79	108
JULY	70	97	79	106
AUGUST	22	97	79	106
SEPTEMBER	70	90	75	102
OCTOBER	64	86	72	99
NOVEMBER	59	79	63	88
DECEMBER	50	70	54	77

Kubri at-Tahrir (At-Tahrir Bridge), Cairo.

Pyramids of Giza.

CALENDARS

COPTIC CALENDAR
According to tradition this solar calendar is very similar to the Ancient Egyptian calendar and is still used by Egyptian *fellaheen* as the basis for their agricultural work throughout the year. Its months correspond, broadly speaking, to the months of the Gregorian calendar, although Christmas falls on January 7 and the New Year begins on September 11.
◆ Coptic months:
Tubah (Dec.–Jan.)
Amshir (Jan.–Feb.)
Barmahat (Feb.–Mar.)
Bacshon (April–May)
Baunah (May–Jun.)
Abib (Jun.–July)
Masri (July–Aug.)
Nasi (Aug.–Sept.)
Tut (Sept.–Oct.)
Babah (Oct.–Nov.)
Hatur (Nov.–Dec.)

MUSLIM CALENDAR
This 12-month lunar calendar is based on the exile (*Hijra* from which "Hegira" is derived) of the Prophet Mohammed from Mecca to Medina in AD 622. Because each year is eleven days behind the previous one, festivals – including the "Muled el-Nabi" (the Prophet's birthday) – are not fixed.
◆ Islamic months:
Moharram
Safar
Rabia el-awal
Rabia el-thani
Gamad el-awal
Gamad el-thani
Ragab
Shaaban
Ramadan (month of fasting)
Shawal
Zul Qeda
Zul Hegga

EGYPT FOR UNDER £500/$800
◆ It is possible to spend a week in a 4-star hotel in Cairo or Luxor for between £490 ($770)and £730 ($1160) per person, depending on the season, including a return flight.
◆ Prices are equally attractive for the Red Sea. In summer they drop to £440 ($700) per week at Hurghada (flight, 4-star hotel and diving included).
◆ Allow between £440 ($655) and £1250 ($1875) for a week's cruise on the Nile, and between £560 ($844) and £1375 ($2062) for ten days.

WOMEN IN EGYPT
Egypt is among the most liberal countries in the Arab world as regards the status of women. A lack of respect toward a woman in a public place is immediately condemned. Foreign women can therefore visit Egypt safely, provided they do not cause offence by being unsuitably dressed.

ISLAMIC FESTIVALS AT THE END OF THE 20TH CENTURY			
THE PROPHET'S BIRTHDAY	BEGINNING OF RAMADAN	AID EL-KEBIR	YEAR OF HEGIRA
JUL. 19, 1997	JAN. 10, 1997	APR. 19, 1997	1417
JUL. 8, 1998	JAN. 1, 1998	APR. 9, 1998	1418
JUN. 27, 1999	DEC. 20, 1998	MAR. 29, 1999	1419
	DEC. 9, 1999	MAR. 17, 2000	1420

WHEN TO GO
◆ The best time to visit archeological remains is between November and March. The same applies for oases and deserts.
◆ The Red Sea is at its best in spring and fall, as is the Delta region (take account of hotels closing out of season).
◆ Avoid Sinai in winter as nights in the mountains are bitterly cold.
◆ Avoid Cairo and Alexandria in summer, at Easter and during the New Year festivals.
◆ Finally, prices drop significantly in summer and in November–December, except in Cairo and Alexandria.

TELEPHONE
To call Egyptian towns and cities from abroad, dial the international code of the country you are calling from (UK 00, US 011) followed by the code for Egypt (20) and the code for the town or city (Cairo 2, Alexandria 3 . . .).

AVERAGE BUDGET
For a week's vacation, including personal expenditure but not transport:
◆ On a package tour allow between £300 ($475) and £370 ($590) per person.
◆ For an individual vacation allow (per person):
£910 ($1440) for a 5-star hotel,
£670 ($1060) for a 4-star hotel,
£490 ($770) for a 3-star hotel.

The Egyptian pound (£E) is worth about £0.21/$0.29 (May 1996) and the cost of living in Egypt is about one third of that in the West. All Egyptian notes are printed in English on one side and Arabic on the other. Travelers' checks and credit cards are a useful method of payment, although Western currency is accepted in most places. There are practically no autotellers.

MONEY

The Egyptian pound (£E) consists of 100 piasters (pt.). There are notes for £E 100, 50, 20, 10, 5 and 1, notes and coins for 50 and 25 piasters, and coins for 20, 10 and 5 piasters.
£1 (sterling) = £E 4.70
(May 1996)
$1 = £E 3.40
(May 1996)

FOREIGN CHECK CARDS

Only accepted in certain tourist stores such as jeweler's, papyrus institutes.

CREDIT CARDS

Visa, American Express and Mastercard are accepted in the major hotels and restaurants and many stores.
A charge of between 3 percent and 5 percent may be made, depending on where they are used.
N.B. It is extremely difficult to change money with a credit card, except at branches of the Bank of Cairo and large hotels.

BANKS

Egyptian banks are closed on Fridays and Saturdays. During the week and on Sundays they are open from 8.30am to 2.30pm, and often from 6.30pm to 8.30pm.

◆ Banks in all major hotels offer a 24-hour, 7-day service (at the standard rate of exchange).

◆ You can only obtain foreign currency at the airport on the return journey (you will need to keep the receipts).

N.B. The £E cannot be exchanged and Egyptian currency may not be taken out of the country. It is therefore better to spend all your Egyptian currency before you leave.

FOREIGN CURRENCY

Foreign currency is accepted in many tourist stores.

TRAVELERS' CHECKS

These are changed in all banks (passport essential) and accepted in many tourist stores. They are extremely useful.

BY AIR

Although air services to Egypt have increased since the decline of the Muslim Fundamentalist action, most flights operate to and from Cairo, although there are now an increasing number of flights to Luxor, Hurghada and Sharm el Sheikh. (Egyptair also organizes some charter flights).

◆ It takes 4½ to 5 hours to fly from London to Cairo.

◆ The flight time from New York to Cairo is 10½ hours.

AIRLINE COMPANIES
UK
British Airways (0181 759 2525) and Egyptair (0171 437 6309) both offer daily direct flights to Cairo, and Britannia has a direct charter to Luxor/Murghada/Cairo. Air France

fly to Cairo from London with a stopover in Paris: CSA do the same with a stopover in Prague; and El Al's London to Cairo flight stops over in Tel Aviv; KLM have an Amsterdam stopover; Olympic Airways fly to Alexandria and Cairo via Athens; and Turkish Airlines fly to Cairo via Istanbul. The excursion fare with Egyptair is £285 roundtrip.

US
EGYPTAIR, (800 334 6787 or 212 315 0900) fly nonstop from New York to Cairo. First class tickets are available at a cost of $6246 roundtrip, $3966 business class and $1499 coach class. TWA (800 221 2000) fly nonstop to Cairo. Combined business/first class fare is $3966 roundtrip, $1499 coach.

BY ROAD FROM ISRAEL

BY BUS
Several bus companies operate services (2–5 per week, depending on the season) between Cairo and Tel Aviv. The journey takes between 7 and 9 hours, but allow an additional 2½ hours for customs formalities at the border post of Rafah. It is advisable to obtain a visa before you leave.

◆ You can obtain a 14-day visa for Sinai (free of charge), returning

by the same border post.

SERVICES (◆ 528)
◆ Sinai bus company: terminal in Abbassiya Square in Cairo. The Cairo-Tel Aviv-Cairo service (Mondays and Wednesdays) costs £15/$25 single and £28.40/$45 return and can be paid in £E. Agent in Egypt: East Delta Bus Company.

◆ The Israeli company Egged operates the same service from Tel Aviv.

Prices are similar. For information (Israel) telephone (972) 3 (preceded by 0 if calling from Israel) 537 55 55. Agent in Egypt: Travco Travel.
◆ Galilee Tours: 142, Mayarkon, Tel Aviv. Tel. (972) 3 (preceded by 0 if calling from Israel) 22 13 72. Same service, twice per week. Agent in Egypt: Benu Travel.
◆ Israeli bus company: daily service from Eilat (bus station) to Taba.

BY CAR
The northern frontier post at Rafah is open until 4pm (noon on Thursdays) and closed on Fridays and Saturdays. Allow 2½ hours for customs formalities and registration of vehicle. The southern frontier post at Taba is theoretically open 24 hours. The same conditions apply as for Rafah.

Vienna

CARPATHIANS

GREECE
Istanbul
Athens
Black Sea
CAUCASUS
TURKEY
SYRIA
Mediterranean
CYPRUS
Baghdad
Beirut
Damascus
IRAQ
Port Said
Jerusalem
Alexandria
Tel Aviv
Suez
SAUDI
ARABIA
Cairo
SINAI
Luxor
Medina
Aswan
Red Sea
Mecca
Jidda
EGYPT
Nile
Atbara
SUDAN
Khartum

BY SEA
◆ Services from Italy have been temporarily suspended.
FROM JORDAN
A ferry service operates twice per day between Aqaba (Jordan) and Nuweiba, leaving Aqaba at 10am and 6pm. The crossing lasts 3 hours and costs £19/$30 (£E 100). Prices for cars vary depending on size and type. For further information, contact: Egyptian Company for Navigation, 20, Shari' Tal'at Harb, Cairo. Tel. (02) 574 68 36 / 574 57 55 / 575 69 98.

INDIVIDUAL VISITS TO EGYPT
ESSENTIALS

◆ An international driving licence, valid for one year, can be obtained from AA and RAC stops and the automobile associations. Take your driving licence, a passport-sized photograph, and £3/$4.50.
◆ Insurance: assistance and repatriation.
◆ Money: Egyptian and American/British currency, travelers' checks and credit cards.
◆ Special permits: essential for traveling in the desert and visiting certain archeological sites classed as military zones. These can be obtained (with some difficulty) from the Egyptian army – C.I.A. branch, Kobri el-Obba (just before the An-Nasir Mohammed Mosque), Heliopolis – or from a travel agency specializing in "desert and oasis" excursions.

ACCOMMODATION

◆ It is essential to reserve accommodation before you leave – directly or through a local tour operator.
◆ On arrival in Cairo, confirm reservations for the other places you will be staying.

TRANSPORT

Always check return flights and connections at least 72 hours before departure.

More than seventy tour operators organize package tours to Egypt. The major companies – Airtours, British Airways Holidays, Goldenjoy Holidays, Hayes and Jarvis, Kuoni, Nouvelles Frontières, Thomas Cook and Thomson Holidays – devote several dozen pages of their brochures to Egypt, while some of the smaller operators – Africa Travel Centre, Trailfinders – even publish special brochures on the Land of the Pharaohs. Other operators, catering for a more specialized market, organize excursions (Bales Tours, Exodus Expeditions, Explore Worldwide, Tracks Africa) and diving (Divers Lodge, Oonasdivers, Twickers World).

NILE VALLEY

THE NERVE CENTER OF EGYPTIAN TOURISM
The Nile is the backbone of Egypt and, since most of the country's archeological heritage is found along its shores, there has been a substantial increase in the number of cruises along the "sacred river". This is undoubtedly the best way to visit Egypt for the first time.

NILE-BASED TOURS
Until recently organized tours tended to focus on Cairo and the Nile Valley. New "packages" have been developed which combine visits to the Pharaonic sites with trips to Sinai and the Red Sea.

1-WEEK PACKAGE
All tour operators organize a basic 1-week package which usually includes 3 nights in Cairo with visits to Memphis, Saqqara and the Pyramids of Giza, a journey to Luxor or Aswan and, from there, a 4-night cruise stopping at Karnak, Luxor, Esna, Edfu and Kom Ombo.
Prices vary (from £610/$960 upward) depending on the number of excursions and the level of comfort on the boat. The journey from

Cairo to Luxor (or Aswan) is usually made by air, although some companies offer an overnight train journey (with sleeping car).

THE CLASSIC TOURS
◆ 9-day tour:
1 day traveling to Cairo, 2 days in Cairo (Pyramids), 5-day cruise in Upper Egypt (4 nights),

1 day return travel from Cairo.
The fairly rapid pace is ideal for tourists with not much time and who want to acquire a general impression of Egypt.

◆ 11-day tour:
1 day traveling to Cairo, 2 days in Cairo

(Pyramids), 7-day cruise in Upper Egypt (6 nights), 1 day return travel from Cairo.
The great classic tour includes a visit to the temple of Dendera in the above itinerary. There is also a 12-day roundtrip tour (with a 7-day cruise) starting from either Luxor or Aswan.

◆ 15-day tour:
1 day traveling to Cairo, 2 days in Cairo (Pyramids), 11-day cruise in Upper Egypt (10 nights), 1 day return travel from Cairo. This tour incorporates visits to the sites of Middle Egypt: Tuna el-Jebel, Ashmunein, Tell el-Amarna and Beni Hassan. It is not available in winter due to the low level of the Nile.
◆ All the above tours offer an optional visit to Abu Simbel.
◆ The packages may be modified by individual agencies: 1 night in Abu Simbel, a 2-day visit to Alexandria, 3

additional days in Cairo with a visit to the Delta region (Tanis) and the Suez Canal (Ismaïliya).

EXTENSIONS
Travel agencies also offer 3- and 5-day extensions (or longer on request) to the classic tours, in towns and cities such as Cairo, Luxor and Aswan (Egyptology tour), or Hurghada and Sharm el-Sheikh (with a trip to St Catherine) on the Red Sea coast.

Cruise boats on the Nile.

Hotel Cataract, Aswan.

Felucca boatman in Upper Egypt.

THE ALTERNATIVE NILE

◆ In view of recent political events, some tour operators organizing tours in Middle Egypt have suspended visits to such towns as Tell el-Amarna, Tuna el-Jebel, Beni Hassan and El-Minya.

◆ For tourists in search of "authenticity", other agencies offer a cruise on a *dahabiya*, a 19th-century sailing boat. Each boat can take up to seven people and can only be hired by groups for between £955 ($1515) and £1240 ($1965) (per person, per week). These cruises have the advantage of passengers being able plan their own itinerary.

11-DAY TOUR

15-DAY TOUR

Cruise

LAKE NASSER

The Lake Nasser cruise allows you to visit the temples of the Lower Nubia. There are three luxury cruise boats: *Eugénie, Nubian Sea* and *Tania* (reservations can be made through Kuoni, Jet Tours and Clio). To enjoy this beautiful cruise at its most peaceful you are recommended to go soon, as there are currently twenty more cruise boats being built.

HOTELS

VACATIONS AT AFFORDABLE PRICES

As well as being more economic, hotel vacations enable you to visit the area around Cairo, Luxor or Aswan. Although most operators offer four- and five-star hotel accommodation, the Egyptian hotel structure is very different from that of Europe or the United States. Luxury hotels have a more limited range of facilities and prices are more affordable (from £485/$770 per week).

◆ Excursions can be reserved from your hotel.

◆ The only exception is the Abu Simbel excursion which is liable to be cancelled at any moment due to tourist numbers and/or weather conditions. It is advisable to reserve before you leave.

◆ Some tour operators offer Mediterranean vacations in Alexandria.

◆ The leading tour operators are represented on all the major sites and can make on-the-spot reservations.

THE RED SEA

DIVERS' PARADISE

Vacation facilities on the Red Sea coast at Hurghada and Sharm el-Sheikh are being extensively developed. They are mainly organized by tour operators specializing in diving (Divers Lodge, Oonasdivers, Scuba Safaris, Twickers World). Packages include the flight, as well as the accommodation and diving in one of the best locations in the world for under £485 ($770) per week at certain times of year. These vacations are becoming so popular that Jet Tours has opened its own Eldorador hotel-club in Hurghada ◆ 502.

"FELUCCAS"

Sailing down the Nile in a *felucca* ● 122 is a truly unforgettable experience. Mini-cruises (3–4 nights) from Aswan to Luxor can be organized direct with the *felucca* boatmen as these cruises are not strictly official. The price (£E 30 per person for a minimum of six people) includes full board: the boatman does the cooking and you sleep on board.

◆ Unfortunately, these cruises are probably going to be banned in the near future for security reasons.

There is no shortage of local transport in Egypt, as it is criss-crossed by bus, train and air services. Traveling by train and bus is cheap but requires patience. There are a few express services between Cairo, Alexandria and Luxor. Air links are the most efficient, but tend to substantially increase the cost of the vacation.

LONG-DISTANCE BUSES

Main services between Cairo and major towns and cities:
◆ Cairo–Alexandria and Port Said: "Super Jet" (Midan at-Tahrir). Leaves every 30 mins. Price £E 17– 25. Journey time: 2½–3 hours. Tel. 77 26 63
◆ To Sinai: "East Delta" (Midan Abbassiya). 7 buses a day to Sharm el-Sheikh (£E 35) and Nuweiba (£E 55). Tel. 76 22 93
◆ To Upper Egypt: "Upper Egypt". Daily departure from Midan at-Tahrir or Midan Ahmed-Helmi in Giza. Journey time: 10–15 hours for Luxor and Aswan (£E 50). Tel. 574 66 58 or 76 02 61
◆ Buses run between Alexandria and Mersa Matruh, and Luxor and Hurghada. Journey time: 5 hours.
◆ Make reservations in advance and check times.

CAR RENTAL

Prices vary, depending on the type of car, between £E 130 and £E 400 per day for between 62½ and 75 miles.
◆ Allow an additional £E 30–60 per day for an extra driver.
◆ Avoid driving if possible as traffic is difficult.

SUBWAY

There is a north–south line in Cairo which is useful for getting to the Coptic district. Price £E 1.

CITY BUSES

There are no maps of bus routes, stops are badly indicated and buses are crowded. Further information can be obtained from the bus station in the Midan at-Tahrir.

TAXIS

Taxis are plentiful and inexpensive. They have an orange number plate. The journey across Cairo costs £E 15–25, double for taxis parked in front of hotels. You can rent a taxi for £E 15 per hour.
◆ Communal taxis operate between districts and towns. Terminals are outside stations and in the major squares. Ask the driver where he is going. From the center of Cairo to the Pyramids: £E 0.50.

BOATS

There is a boat service three times a week between Hurghada and Sharm el-Sheikh. Journey-time: 6 hours (£E 100).

INTERNAL AIRLINES

Egyptair and Air Sinai operate services between the major towns and cities.

Bus station, Midan at-Tahrir in Cairo.

Although air travel is more expensive than other forms of transport, it is more reliable. For further information, contact:
◆ Egyptair (London) Tel. 0171 437 6309 (New York) Tel. (800) 334 6787
◆ Air Sinai (in Egypt) Tel. 578 03 22 or 578 03 23
The frequency of flights varies according to the time of year. Check on arrival.

TRAINS

◆ Daily services between Cairo and Alexandria: 8am, 9am, 2pm, 6pm and 7pm. Journey time: 2–2½ hours (£E 20). Sleepers make the journey twice per day and cost £E 35 including a meal.
◆ Sleepers are to be recommended if you are traveling south by train. There are 2 departures daily from Ramses Station at 7.30pm (arriving in Luxor at 5.45am and Aswan at 10.35am) and 8pm (arriving in Luxor at 6.15am and Aswan at 10.55am). Price: £E 250 (single) and £E 470 (return). Compartments have 2 bunks and a wash basin. Dinner and breakfast are served in the compartment.
◆ Return from Aswan at 3pm and 3.30pm and from Luxor at 10pm and 10.30pm. Reserve places before you leave for Egypt.
◆ Express trains run on the same route for half the price, but the journey is exhausting (12 hours to Luxor, 23 hours to Aswan). Two departures every morning.
◆ In summer there is a daily service from Cairo to Mersa Matruh via Alexandria.

Route	Frequency of flights	Flying time	Round trip–£/$
Cairo–Alexandria	Several flights/day (not Tue.)	30 mins	£83/$124
Cairo–Luxor	Several flights/day	50 mins	£140/$210
Cairo–Aswan	Several flights/day	1¼ hrs	£193/$290
Cairo–Hurghada	Several flights/day	1 hour	£152/$228
Cairo–Kharga	2 flights/week (Wed.–Sun.)	1 hour	£/152$228
Cairo–Sharm el-Sheikh	2 flights/day	30 mins	£160/$240
Luxor–Aswan	Several flights/day	30 mins	£53/$80
Luxor–Hurghada	2 flights on Thur.	30 mins	£63/$94
Luxor–Sharm el-Sheikh	Flights on Mon., Thur., Sat.	40 mins	£81/$121
Luxor–Kharga	Flights on Weds., Sun.	30 mins	£63/$94
Aswan–Abu Simbel	Several flights/day	30 mins	£85/$128

EL DARB EL AHMAR ST

The first thing you notice about signs in Egypt is that they are in short supply. More information is obtained by speaking to local inhabitants than by referring to official signs. However some progress has been made in recent years and it is always useful to be able to recognize a few of the basic signs.

Taxi and sign for gas station.

TRAINS/ STATIONS/ TICKETS
All destinations are indicated (in Arabic and Latin letters) inside the station, as are the "ticket" and "reservation" windows.

PUBLIC TRANSPORT
Bus terminals are usually situated outside railway stations and in main squares. They are rarely signposted and you have to be guided by the numbers of buses and minibuses. Routes are not indicated and it is essential to obtain first-hand information.
◆ Cairo subway stations are indicated by a large, red "M".

STREET PLANS
Plans of the local district are found in the main Cairo subway stations and sometimes in the railway station in major towns and cities. Otherwise use your own maps.

BANKS/BUREAUX DE CHANGE
These opulent-looking buildings, with their name in large letters on the façade, are easily recognizable. The day's exchange rates are given on a board at the entrance.
◆ There are virtually no autotellers.

Post office.

HOSPITALS/POLICE/ TOURIST OFFICE/ POST OFFICE
These are rarely signposted.
◆ The TOURIST POLICE are found everywhere, on archeological sites and in towns. Their offices are signposted in English.
◆ Telephone centers are easily recognized: they have the same sign as in Europe.

Subway ticket (top); Cairo subway sign (above center); letter boxes (right); speed limit and direction sign (left); street sign (below, center).

NAMES OF TOWNS
The name is given in Arabic and English at the entrance to the town and on the milestones along roads.

STREETS
Street names, when they exist, appear in Arabic and English on a blue plaque. Otherwise . . . ask someone.

ROADS
Only the direction is indicated, except on freeways between Cairo and Alexandria or the Suez Canal.

MUSEUMS AND SITES
Only the main sites are signposted on the roads, and very often at the last minute. Ask as you go along.

Egypt is a hospitable country and has an efficient tourist infrastructure. There is a wide range of hotels and restaurants in all categories where service is reasonably efficient, provided you are not in a hurry. Finally remember that bargaining is expected in the markets and many of the stores. Egyptians value this type of exchange and, generally speaking, enjoy contact with foreign visitors.

ACCOMMODATION

HOTELS

◆ The major hotel chains (Hilton, Sheraton, Marriott, Sofitel, Novotel, P.L.M. and Mövenpick) are represented in Cairo, Alexandria, the Nile Valley and on the Red Sea coast.

◆ Prices are much more affordable than in Europe: between £240 ($385) and £425 ($675) per week for full board in a luxury hotel.
NB: Only 4- and 5-star hotels have the same level of comfort as their European counterparts. Below this, the differences are very noticeable.

OPENING TIMES

In Egypt most hotels are open round the clock.

RESERVATIONS

It is better to make advance reservations and confirm at least the day before.

◆ NB: Abu Simbel (2 hotels) and Middle Egypt (not recommended at present because of the political situation) are sometimes unable to accommodate the large numbers of tourists during peak periods.

VACATION VILLAGES

The villages are situated on the Mediterranean beaches (Sidi Abd er-Rahman, Mersa Matruh) and the Red Sea coast (Hurghada, Safaga, Sharm el-Sheikh, Dahab, Nuweiba). They all have a range of watersports facilities.

YOUTH HOSTELS

Most of the large towns have youth hostels. It costs around £E 10 per person (breakfast is often included) for a double room and £E 5 for a meal. They are closed between noon and 2pm (or 10am and noon) and at night (11pm at the latest).

RESTAURANTS

There are any number of restaurants, from tiny local restaurants to luxury restaurants (including those in the big hotels). For reasons of hygiene it is best to avoid buying sandwiches (falafel) from street sellers. Prices range from around £E 7 in the many "eating-houses" to £E 70 in luxury hotels and restaurants. Lunch is served between noon and 3pm and dinner between 7pm and 11pm. Many restaurants stay open all day.

◆ It is advisable to reserve a table on Thursday evenings, which is the Egyptian "night out".

AVERAGE HOTEL PRICES (IN £/$) – SINGLE-DOUBLE ROOM / MEALS PER PERSON			
Per night	Breakfast	Lunch	Dinner
5–star hotels	£6	£11	£15
£79–98/$127–157	$10	$18	$24
4–star hotels	£4	£9	£10
£39–59/$63–94	$6	$14	$17
3–star hotels	£3	£6	£6
£24–31/$39–49	$4	$9	$10
2–star hotels	£1	£2	£3
£5–6/$8–9	$2	$4	$5
1–star hotels	£1	£2	£2
£3–4/$5–6	$2	$3	$3
◆ In Upper Egypt prices may drop noticeably in summer.			

CULINARY SPECIALTIES

There are a number of different starters (mezzeh): tahina, a sesame seed paste sometimes mixed with aubergines (baba ghanug); chick peas (hummus); stuffed vine leaves. Mulukhiya is a soup often flavored with garlic and served with rice. Taamiya or falafel are little balls made of fried broad beans mixed with herbs and sprinkled with sesame seeds. Kushari, rice with lentils and macaroni, is served with a tomato and onion sauce. Rice accompanies kebabs (grilled meat), koftas (grilled minced meat), shawarma (thin slices of meat) and pigeon (hamaam).

◆ Pastries include the semolina-based basbussa, baklava (almond-flavored flaky pastry) and konafa (made with vermicelli pasta). Umm-ali is a flaky pastry which is cooked in milk flavored with almonds and raisins, and spiced with cinnamon.

DRINKS

◆ Egyptian wines – Cru des Ptolémées (white), Rubis d'Egypte (rosé) and Omar Khayyam (red) – are inconsistent and often disappointing.

◆ There are two brands of beer: Stella (light) and Export (strong).

◆ Mineral water (Baraka, Mineral) is very cheap.

◆ There are various fruit juices (guava, mango, orange, lemon and strawberry) depending on the season. Try assab (sugarcane juice).

◆ Karkadé, the national drink, is a decoction of flowers from the hibiscus family and an excellent antidote to high blood pressure. Tamr hindi (tamarind juice) may be added.

◆ Tea is served black, rarely with mint, and is sweet.

CAFÉS

The atmosphere in Egyptian cafés is friendly, becoming positively animated in the evening. Customers drink tea, Turkish coffee and anise, watch television, play dominos and *tawla* (backgammon), the national game, and smoke the *shisha*

(hookah) amidst lively discussions and raised voices.

WATER INTAKE

This is not a problem except when in the desert. In summer drink at least 4–4½ pints of water per day.

HYGIENE

♦ In large towns and cities, the tap water is drinkable although highly chlorinated. Sealed, bottled water is preferable!

♦ In rural areas make sure you boil or filter water or disinfect it chemically. If you are going into the desert, take water purifying tablets.

♦ Although food is strictly controlled in the big restaurants, this does not apply elsewhere. Be wary of raw vegetables

and fried food and eat well-cooked meat.

♦ Avoid staying out in the sun too long, iced drinks during the day and air conditioning.

♦ If you do suffer from the "Pharaoh's curse" eat white rice

and yoghurt flavored with lemon.

PHARMACIES

Pharmacies are found throughout Egypt and medicines are very cheap. They sell the all-important sun creams but do not always stock insect repellents.

SAFETY

Muggings and attacks are rare and there is a general feeling of safety. If you do have problems, contact the tourist police.

OPENING HOURS

♦ Offices and administrative departments are closed on Friday, the day of general prayer.

♦ In the towns many shops close on Sunday. On other days they are usually open from 9am to 2pm and 5pm to 10pm. In tourist areas they stay open all day.

POST OFFICES

Open daily from 8am to 2.30pm, except Fridays.

♦ Stamps can also be bought from hotel shops and postcard sellers at a slightly higher price.

♦ Letters and postcards cost the same: 80 piasters.

♦ They take between 4 and 10 days to reach their destination. Receiving mail is even more unreliable: between 3 days and 3 weeks!

COMMUNICATION AND INFORMATION

TELEPHONE

♦ The telephone service is good, except in the western oases.

♦ There are telephone centers in all Egyptian towns. Operators know the codes, just give the number you want. You pay for the first three minutes (Cairo to Europe costs £E 23.5) and each additional minute (£E 7). Cairo to the US on AT&T costs $5.35 for the first minute and $1.05 for each additional minute.

♦ There is a reduction of 25 percent for calls made between 10pm and 8am.

♦ Some telephone boxes take phone cards (£E 20 or 40) which can be bought from the centers.

♦ Finally, it is easy to call from hotels although it costs 30 percent more.

CODES FOR COUNTRIES OUTSIDE EGYPT

UK: 0044
US: 001
AUSTRALIA: 0061
CANADA: 001

TO CALL EGYPT FROM ABROAD

20 + code for the town + number

CODES FOR EGYPTIAN TOWNS

Cairo	2
Alexandria	3
Luxor	95
Aswan	97
Sharm el-Sheikh	62
The Faiyum	84
Ismaïliya	64
El-Minya	86

Port Said	66
Suez	62
Police	122

Information: 140 in Cairo, 10 throughout the rest of the country.

♦ Dial 0 before these codes if you are calling from within Egypt.

TOURIST OFFICES

Tourist offices can supply (rudimentary) maps of the main towns and a few tourist brochures.

FOREIGN PRESS

European newspapers and magazines are on sale throughout Egypt. A daily paper will usually be two days old.

♦ Radio: you can tune in to the BBC.

♦ Television: international channels in English (CNN and Super Channel) are available in the major hotels.

LOCAL PRESS

♦ Egyptian newspapers are also available in French and English.

♦ English language papers: *Egyptian Gazette* (daily) and *Egypt Today* (monthly).

♦ Egyptian television (Channel 2) broadcasts daily news bulletins in English (10pm).

◆ LIVING IN EGYPT

LOCAL EVENTS

Although there may be a generally festive atmosphere within the town, religious festivals are essentially a family occasion.

COPTIC FESTIVALS
Coptic Christmas (January 7). Coptic Easter (variable).

MUSLIM FESTIVALS
Because most of the Muslim festivals are part of the lunar calendar, their dates change each year ◆ 486.
◆ *Muled el-Nabi*: anniversary of the Prophet's birth (month of Rabia).
◆ The *aïd el-saghir* (little festival), also known as the *aïd el-fitr*, marks the end of Ramadan and lasts for three days. It is celebrated by the giving of presents and family outings.
◆ The *aïd el-kebir* (great festival) is also known as the *aïd el-adha* (festival of the sacrifice). A sheep's throat is cut in memory of Abraham's sacrifice.

COMMUNAL FESTIVALS
◆ *Sham el-Nessim* (festival of spring) is held the day after the Coptic Easter.
◆ The processional festival of the *Muled of Abu el-Hagag* (Luxor) is a legacy from Pharaonic times.
The saint is carried in procession through the town, in a barque, from his mosque in the Temple of Luxor.
◆ The festival of Abu Simbel occurs on February 22 and October 22 when the sun's rays penetrate the depths of the temple.
◆ These festivals can mean a change of itinerary due to sites being closed or religious services being held.

PUBLIC VACATIONS
January 10 – New Year's Day
July 23 – anniversary of the 1952 Revolution
October 6 – anniversary of the 1973 Arab-Israeli War

THE EGYPTIAN PEOPLE

Egyptians are hospitable and love to communicate. English, and sometimes French, is spoken in the major towns. You will find people warm and friendly provided you bear the following points in mind:

DON'T . . .
◆ Criticize religion.
◆ Get irritated with an official who is taking a long time.
◆ Try to "chat up" a woman in a public place.
◆ Refuse an item after fixing and agreeing a price.
◆ Take photographs of "street scenes" without asking people's permission.
◆ Walk around towns in clothes which are too short or considered indecent.

(This applies especially to women.)
◆ Make fun of Egypt (its organization, cleanliness, *baksheesh* . . .). The Egyptians love their country (and are quite aware of its weaknesses).

HOWEVER . . .
◆ Small gifts (photos, perfumes) are appreciated.

EGYPTIAN PRICES
Egyptians pay less to get into archeological sites (15 times less) and for air travel (70 percent less). For everything else, prices are – theoretically – more or less the same.

SOME PRICES

SITE OR MUSEUM ENTRANCE: £E 4–10

1 COFFEE OR TEA: £E 1 – 3, DEPENDING ON THE ESTABLISHMENT

1 LITER OF GASOLINE (FOUR-STAR): £E 1

1 EGYPTIAN NEWSPAPER IN ENGLISH: £E 0.40
Le Progrès Egyptien

1 LARGE BOTTLE MINERAL WATER: £E 2
Baraka

1 POSTCARD: £E 0.50

1 PACKET OF EGYPTIAN CIGARETTES: £E 1.50

1 PLANE TICKET – CAIRO–ASWAN. LUXOR–CAIRO: £E 850

BARGAINING

Prices are set in the shops (apart from the *suqs*) in large towns and cities, hotel shops, jewelers', papyrus institutes and restaurants. In other places bargaining is expected. Depending on the store keeper or stall holder prices can range from single to triple figures. Never get irritated when you bargain as there is a certain pleasure to be had from the discussion.

BAKSHEESH

This is usual for a service rendered (car park attendants, shoe attendants in mosques). Taxi and barouche drivers always expect a tip over and above the agreed price. Service in hotels and restaurants is included (12 percent), but it is usual to "round up" the total amount of the tab.

◆ You should ask for small change (50 pt. and £E 1 notes) which is useful for small tips.

CHILDREN

On archeological sites there are always children begging for pens, sweets, samples of perfume and – more directly - *baksheesh*.
A few tips:
◆ Never give money.
◆ Never give anything to a child who hasn't asked.
◆ Never give anything if children are in groups as this can cause fights.

Street grocery store, Aswan.

ENTERTAINMENT

Cairo and Alexandria, with their clubs, cabarets, casinos and movie theaters, represent a certain *joie de vivre* and liberality within the Arab world.

MOVIE THEATERS

The major movie theaters in Cairo are to be recommended. Their traditional décor (wide screen) is delightful. The most famous – the Metro, Radio and Miami – are located in the city center, in the Shari' Qasr an-Nil and Shari' Tal'at Harb. But there is also the Rivoli (Shari' 26 July), the Lido and the Pigalle (Shari' Imad el-Din) and the Tahrir (Shari' at-Tahrir).
◆ As a general rule performances are at noon, 3pm, 6pm and 9pm.

BELLY DANCING AND CABARETS

Egyptian belly dancers still continue to fire the imagination.
◆ Many, including the most famous (Fifi Abdou, Lucie, Hendeya and Dina) have abandoned the

cabarets near the Pyramids in favor of the major Cairo hotels where they enjoy greater prestige.

◆ There are still a few cabarets where you can see good displays of Oriental dancing. But apart from Cairo and a few hotels in Alexandria, you would be advised to give them a miss. In the south dancers tend to shake their bodies rather than dance.

◆ You can usually have supper during the performance, which never begins before midnight or 1am.

NIGHTCLUBS

Hotel nightclubs are the preserve of the younger members of the Cairene and foreign (Kuwaiti, Saudi) bourgeoisie . . . and tourists.

DANCING DERVISHES

This is an absolute "must". Performances are given (free of charge) in the El-Ghuri medersa (just before the El-Azhar Mosque) on Wednesdays and Saturdays at 9pm. The Sufi (Muslim mystics) dancers spin and whirl in their full, flared robes.

Dancing dervishes.

Several tour operators offer alternative vacations for those who want a more direct experience of Egypt. So why not leave the beaten tourist track of the Nile Valley and explore the deserts and oases in a four-wheel drive, on a mountain bike, on foot or by camel? Discover the other more intimate, more severe but equally enchanting face of Egypt, the Egypt of vast dunes, magnificent stretches of sand and limestone, unexpected oases and Pharaonic and Roman remains. The splendor of the landscapes, of the light and color will leave a lasting impression. There is only one condition: you must be physically fit.

6-day circuit (Northern Oases)
6-day circuit (4 Western Oases)
12-day circuit
7-day circuit
2-day circuit (The Faiyum)

HEALTH

The desert routes are only suitable for people who are in good health and do not suffer from cardiac or respiratory problems (regardless of age).

CLOTHING

◆ Lightweight, comfortable clothing for the daytime and warm (woolen) clothing for the nights, which are cold.
◆ Footwear should be closed and high fitting as you may come across scorpions and/or horned vipers.
◆ Finally, a hat (or *shesh*) and sunglasses are essential.

DESERTS AND OASES

The oases are situated in the Libyan (or Western) Desert.

Distance from Cairo:	
Siwa	470 miles
Bahariya	251 miles
Farafra	364 miles
Dakhla	462 miles
Kharga	376 miles
The Faiyum	75 miles

White Desert.

El-Areg Oasis.

FOOD

It is important to have a regular water intake. Biscuits and dried fruit (dates) are useful.
◆ Way station restaurants serve "rustic" but generous meals.

ADMINISTRATIVE CONDITIONS

Those traveling individually must obtain a special permit before crossing the desert.

SAFETY

You are strongly advised not to leave the main highways without first consulting a travel agent, since the desert, beautiful as it may be, is also treacherous. No insurance policy covers accidents which occurs in Egypt other than on the itinerary fixed before departure.

INSURANCE

N.B. Not always included in the basic price of the package. It is advisable to have your own insurance (e.g. Europ Assistance).

Palm and tamarisk.

Camping in Wadi Rayan.

ACCOMMODATION

Oases have small hotels or "resthouses" which are reasonably comfortable, clean and pleasant.
◆ El-Wadi el-Gadeed Tourist Resthouses Kharga Oasis
Tel: (088) 90 07 28
This is, so to speak, the "headquarters" of the few resthouses in the Libyan Desert.
◆ The telephone number is given for information only as connections in the region are unreliable.
◆ Other resthouses:
– Siwa Oasis: Hotel Arous el-Waha
– Bahariya Oasis: The Governorate Bungalow Complex
– Farafra Oasis: Small hotel near the bus terminus
– Dakhla Oasis: Dar el-Wafeeden Hotel, Mubearz Hotel
– Kharga Oasis: Bulaq Tourist Resthouse, Baris Resthouses
◆ Alternatively, you can sleep in the desert under canvas. Bring your sleeping bag.

SEASONS

These are spring (N.B. sandstorms in March and April), fall and winter vacations.

Summer temperatures limit excursions into these desert regions.

DESERT CLIMATE (IN °F) MIN/MAX TEMPERATURES – KHARGA					
JAN. 43•75	FEB. 46•79	MARCH 52•82	APR. 59•88	MAY 70•39	JUNE 77•104
JULY 75•106	AUG. 77•106	SEPT. 72•100	OCT. 66•90	NOV. 54•84	DEC. 48•75

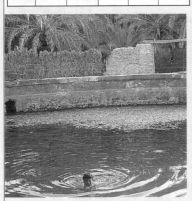

Cleopatra's Pool, Siwa Oasis.

WATER

HOT SPRINGS
The oases of the Libyan Desert – Kharga, Dakhla, Farafra and Bahariya – all have a number of hot, sulphurous springs (102˚F–113˚F) which are relaxing and good for rheumatism.

COLD SPRINGS
Siwa Oasis has some three hundred springs. You can swim in Cleopatra's Pool and the Fantasy Land spring. Women are advised not to swim as this may be misconstrued by the local inhabitants.

TOUR OPERATORS

In the UK, desert tours can be arranged by:
TOP DECK TRAVEL (Tel. 0171 370 4555) and THE IMAGINATIVE TRAVELLER (Tel. 0171 937 3028) as well as NOUVELLES FRONTIERES (Tel. 0171 629 7772) and WESTERN AND ORIENTAL TRAVEL (Tel. 0171 221 8677).
The Imaginative Traveller offers a Western Desert Safari, visiting the oases of Kharga, Dakhla and Farafra, and travel through the White Desert. They also organize a Camel Safari into the Sinai Desert.
In the US desert tours can be arranged by:
ARCHEOLOGICAL TOURS (Tel. 212 986 3054), GENESIS TOURS INTERNATIONAL (Tel. 800 888 8167), MISR TRAVEL (Tel. 212 582 9210), Niki Tours (Tel. 213 464 8427) SPHINX TOURS (Tel. 201 882 9300) and OVERSEAS ADVENTURE TRAVEL (Tel. 617 876 0533)

◆ ADVENTURE TRAILS:
OASES AND DESERTS

The abandoned village of Aghurmi, Siwa.

Roman fortress of Aïn Umm Labakha.

◆ Tour operators take every possible precaution (specially trained teams, rescue vehicles) to deal with any problems that may arise.
◆ Most of the "adventure trails" require you to be able to adapt to basic conditions (simple accommodation and food) and have a good team spirit: you will be asked to help set up camp and prepare meals.
◆ The difficulties specific to each package are explained in the brochures.

TOUR OPERATORS ON THE SPOT

You can choose from a wide range of excursions of varying lengths in four-wheel drive vehicles.
◆ Would-be participants can devise their own itinerary and submit it to the agency, which takes care of the administrative side of things. These excursions require a minimum of between 3 and 6 participants, depending on the route. The cost of equipment, maintenance and the various permits required means that this type of excursion is quite expensive in spite of the fairly rudimentary levels of comfort. Allow £400/$700 per person for a 6-day excursion in the Oases and £730/$1150 for a longer, 12-day excursion. Services offered: full board under canvas (take your own sleeping bag) or in a hotel.
◆ The excursions are supervised by specially trained desert guides who speak several languages.
◆ High standards of safety are guaranteed: continuous radio contact and a back-up (maintenance) vehicle.
◆ The best "adventure trail" specialist is Siag Travel, organizers of the Pharaohs' Rally.
Siag Travel (May Sedky)
Sakkara Road
PO Box 107
Ahram Giza
Tel. 385 60 22 / 385 30 02 or 30 05
Fax: 384 08 74
◆ Another "adventure trail" specialist:
Pan Arab Tours
55, Shari' El-Gumhurriya–Cairo
Tel. 590 21 33
Fax 362 09 71

ADVENTURE TRAILS

LIBYAN DESERT FROM CAIRO
The Libyan Desert, with its oases and Roman and Pharaonic remains, is opening up to tourism. The "trails" (between 950 and 1,250 miles) follow the desert tracks. Allow between £1350/$2100 and £1580/$2500 per person for 12 days.
◆ 6 days: Bahariya Oasis, the White Desert, Farafra, Dakhla and Kharga oases. Return via Luxor by air. The "trail" can be done in the reverse direction.
◆ 7 days: Wadi Rayan, Bahariya Oasis, dunes of Ghard, Dakhla Oasis, Aïn Amur (well), Roman ruins of Aïn Umm el-Dabadid, Kharga Oasis, Necropolis of El-Bagawat.
◆ 12 days: Wadi Rayan, Bahariya Oasis, Allam el-Ghard, Aïn el-Sukhna (hot springs), Qara and Siwa oases, the "great ocean of sand", Aïn Dallah, Farafra Oasis and the White Desert.
ARABIAN DESERT
The Arabian Desert is more rocky than its Libyan counterpart. There is a choice of two "adventure trails":
◆ 2 days (from Luxor): Wadi Qena, Wadi el-Atrash, Mons Porphyrites and the Roman quarries.
◆ 2 days (from Hurghada): Wadi Barud, Roman ruins of Mons Claudianus and the gold mines of Wadi el-Fatira.
LINKS WITH THE OASES
By bus
◆ Upper Egypt Co. Midan Ahmed-Helmi (behind Midan Ramsès) Cairo
Tel. 574 66 58
or behind Midan Tahrir, opposite the Ramsès Hilton Hotel
Tel. 76 02 61
Services between Cairo and Kharga, Dakhla, Bahariya and Farafra oases. Reserve in advance.
◆ Many services have been suspended due to Muslim Fundamentalist action in Assiut. Contact bus company for further information.
◆ West Delta Company
Midan Ahmed-Helmi
Tel. 76 55 82
Cairo–Siwa via Alexandria and Mersa Matruh. Reserve in advance.
◆ Egyptair
Cairo–New Valley (Kharga), Wednesdays and Sundays.
◆ 4-wheel drive hire
Max-Rent-a-Car
Europcar
27, Shari' Lebanon Mohandissine
Tel. 347 47 12 / 13.

The Sinai peninsula ▲ *237* is a mountainous triangle bordered toward its apex by the gulfs of Suez and Aqaba. With its multicolored sand, sandstone canyons, ocher cliffs and pink granite mountains, it is a region of spectacular landscapes that seem to come to life with the play of light. These natural splendors are enhanced by the biblical tradition. The ultimate destination of any journey to this arid peninsula must surely be St Catherine's Monastery ▲ *244* which stands alone, in the middle of the desert, at the foot of Mount Sinai.

ST CATHERINE AND MOUNT SINAI

The 6th-century monastery of St Catherine stands at the foot of Mount Sinai (7,497 feet) and Mount Catherine (8,650 feet).

◆ The church and garden of the monastery are open to the public between 9.30am and noon but are closed on Fridays, Saturdays and Sundays. Visitors must be suitably dressed.

◆ The 3-hour walk to the top of Mount Sinai (Mountain of Moses) is well worth the effort. The best times are early in the morning, so you can watch the sunrise from the summit, or late in the day. The climb can either be made along a camel track, on foot or by donkey, or via a path of over three thousand steps hewn out of the granite by the monks.

◆ It is worth staying an extra half a day to climb Mount Catherine (5 hours' walk) and visit the monasteries of the Holy Apostles and Forty Martyrs on the way.

◆ Near St Catherine is the so-called Blue Desert with its rocks painted by Jean Vérame.

◆ There is overnight accommodation in the village of St Catherine.

SINAI: THE EXCURSIONIST'S PARADISE

The diversity of Sinai's landscape makes it an ideal destination for excursions on foot, by camel, in a 4-wheel drive or on a mountain bike. South Sinai is the most beautiful part of the peninsula and the main excursion centers are Sharm el-Sheikh, Dahab, Nuweiba and Taba.

◆ The most popular excursions include Aïn Musa (the Springs of Moses, whose waters are said to have been purified by Moses' staff); the desert crossing (by four-wheel drive) to Sarabit el-Khadim, and the ascent of Mount Sarabit (2,635 feet) to the Temple of Hathor which stands among the turquoise mines; the crossing of the so-called "Biblical Mountains" to the Oasis of Feiran; the Colored Canyon and, finally, Taba via the desert and The Fjord (with its magnificent view of the Red Sea, Pharaoh's Island and the fortress of Salah ad-Din).

◆ The excursions can be booked through tour operators or directly, on the spot. Alternatively they can be done individually in a hire vehicle.

On the shores of the Red Sea.

Windsurfing regatta.

The flora (coral reefs) and fauna (multicolored fish) of the Red Sea are unequalled throughout the world, except in the Maldive Islands. The clear waters and excellent conditions make it possible to dive virtually all year round. Today the Red Sea is becoming an increasingly popular vacation destination. Diving holiday companies offer one-week packages which include flight, hotel, full board and diving.

A FAST-DEVELOPING TOURIST REGION

The Red Sea, with its two main towns, Hurghada ▲ 267 and Sharm el-Sheikh ▲ 248, is an exceptional and inexpensive vacation destination which is becoming increasingly popular among diving enthusiasts. To meet the increasing demands of tourism, the region has launched a major development program to provide hotel facilities ranging from basic boarding houses to luxury hotels. The Red Sea currently has 18,000 hotel rooms, a figure which is expected to double by the year 2000.

◆ All hotels provide basic diving equipment, so there is no need to take your own equipment unless you are a purist.

MAIN DIVING "SPOTS"

◆ The submerged part of the cliffs of Ras Mohammed ▲ 248, a nature reserve at the most southerly point of the Sinai peninsula, descend to a depth of 1,970 feet. It is an underwater wonderland of coral and multicolored fish. Access to the site is restricted. For further information contact diving clubs.

◆ Tower (197 feet) and Temple (65 feet) owe their names to their exceptional underwater "architecture".

◆ Geziret Shadwan.

◆ Most of the best "spots" are located midway between Hurghada, on the west coast, and Sharm el-Sheikh, at the mouth of the Gulf of Aqaba.

◆ The sites near Dahab include the famous "Blue Hole" (a sheer cliff 262 feet underwater reserved for experienced divers) and the dark, narrow "Canyon" which, although

DIVING SITES

imposing at first sight, in fact offers easier access.

TIPS

◆ The "spots" are accessible to divers of all levels. Beginners can discover the beauties of this underwater landscape with a mask and snorkel. The view is breathtaking with visibility to a depth of around 100 feet. More experienced divers can enjoy the magnificent spectacle of the underwater cliffs.

◆ All divers should wear shoes and even a diving suit. The reefs are razor sharp, some corals are poisonous and the sting of the famous stonefish is deadly.

◆ There are a few sharks in the Red Sea, but they do not usually attack.

◆ Diving instructors give special courses which provide students with an international diving licence.

◆ Hotels organize mini-cruises for divers which include a picnic and a night on board with night diving. These can be booked on the spot.

AS WELL AS DIVING

◆ For non-divers, the Hurghada and Sharm el-Sheikh diving centers also have glass-bottomed boats which give an insight into the marine life of the Red Sea.

◆ The beauty of the landscape, flora and fauna is an ideal subject for underwater photography. Courses can be booked and equipment hired on the spot.

Diving.

Windsurfing.

MIN – MAX AIR TEMPERATURES AND MAX WATER TEMPERATURES (IN °F)											
	JAN.	FEB.	MAR.	APR.	MAY	JUNE	JULY	AUG.	SEPT.	OCT.	NOV.	DEC.
HURGHADA (RED SEA)												
AIR	50•70	50•70	54•73	61•79	70•86	75•88	77•90	77•91	73•88	68•84	61•79	54•73
SEA	66	68	70	73	77	79	81	81	77	73	70	68
ALEXANDRIA (MEDITERRANEAN)												
AIR	48•64	48•66	52•70	55•75	61•81	68•82	73•86	73•88	70•84	64•82	59•75	52•68
SEA	63	61	63	64	70	73	77	79	79	75	72	66

FROM DIVING TO WINDSURFING

In the wake of sub-aqua centers, windsurfing centers are springing up along the western Red Sea coast. In 1994 a windsurfing center was opened in Hurghada by the Blue Lagoon travel company, while the town of Safaga (40 miles to the south) specializes in windsurfing and regularly hosts high-level competitions.

If you don't like diving, windsurfing or sunbathing, a Red Sea vacation is likely to prove somewhat disappointing. Seaside resorts are few and far between and often rather dreary. The actual town of Hurghada is fairly uninteresting.
◆ The only possible excursion, to the Temple of Luxor, involves a day's bus journey which is extremely tiring.
◆ Sharm el-Sheikh is not much better in this respect, although it does have one advantage over its rival, Hurghada: the proximity of Mount Sinai and St Catherine's Monastery.
◆ Other than that there are the shores

Holiday resort
Beach Port
Windsurfing center
Diving center
Airport (regular services)
Surfaced roads
Ferries
Coral reefs

of the Red Sea, bordered by a range of mountains whose contrasting colors offer an unprecedented view of Egypt: a truly spectacular sight at sunset when the mountains are ablaze with color and the name of the Red Sea takes on its full significance. An unforgettable experience.

BEACHES

Clear, warm waters, permanent sunshine and a guaranteed suntan all the year round are the main – and sole – attractions of the Red Sea coast. There are several resorts spread along the coast: Hurghada and Sharm el-Sheikh, Dahab with its golden sands, Nuweiba – and the Gulf of Aqaba, the villages of El-Salam and Bassata, and Taba on the Egypt-Israeli border, with its many bays.
◆ N.B. Don't go into the water without putting on a barrier cream or a T-shirt as the sun is extremely strong and the water acts as a magnifying glass.

Foreign tourists do not tend to visit the Mediterranean coast of Egypt, which is still very much the Cairene vacation destination during the summer months. However, a late-spring and early-fall tourist season is beginning to develop and resorts are springing up along the 740-mile coastline. Although the beaches are generally clean they are still not equipped for water sports and are more suited to swimming or simply relaxing.

BEACHES

ALEXANDRIA
Leading resort with 25 miles of sandy beaches ▲ 195. Agami, to the west of Alexandria, is famed for its Bianchi Beach, the fashionable rendezvous for young Cairenes.
◆ Alexandria (map ◆ 522) has some magnificent, late 19th-century hotels and the largest hotel infrastructure on the Mediterranean coast.
◆ Good quality hotels and vacation villages have been built on the main vacation sites.
◆ Several options – with breakfast only, half or full board – are available. Reservations must be made well in advance for the summer. September is a better month. For further information contact:
Hotel reservations
8, Shari' el-Sad el-Ali
Doqqi
Tel: 361 42 84 / 85

SIDI KRER
Vacation village (22 miles west of Alexandria): 2 miles of beach, casino.
◆ About ⅔ mile away King Mariut has health and treatment facilities.

MARAKIA
Village consisting of chalets, villas and apartments (32 miles from Alexandria). Information and reservations:
Tel: 99 13 04 / 05

EL-ALAMEIN
Second largest tourist center on the Mediterranean coast (65 miles from Alexandria) ▲ 204. Large hotel development. Magnificent white sandy beach.
◆ About 30 miles away the beach of Sidi Abd el-Rahman stretches around a calm bay.

MERSA MATRUH
One of the most beautiful sites on the coast with its tiny port and 4 miles of fine, sandy beaches. Its calm, clear waters are protected by a chain of rocks which limit access to small craft (180 miles west of Alexandria).
◆ About 12 miles further west are the famous beaches of Obaye and Aguiba.

RAS EL-BARR
Vacation resort, bordered to the east by the eastern branch of the Nile and the Mediterranean to the north. Accommodation in thatched cabins.

BALTIM
Vacation village with thatched cabins and huts (132 miles from Cairo).

GAMASA
Recently built seaside resort (120 miles from Cairo). Its atmosphere contains high levels of iodine. 15 miles of beaches.

PORT SAID
At the northern end of the Suez Canal ▲ 234. Very flat beaches.
◆ El-Gamil, 7 miles away, is ideal for fishing.
Three coastal resorts lie to the east, between Port Said and El-Arish: En-Nagila, Bir-Masa'id and Romani.

Mersa Matruh (above)
Suez Canal (below)

GULF OF SUEZ

SUEZ
Egypt's second largest port. Attractive beaches as far as Port Tawfiq.

EL-AÏN EL-SUKHNA
The nearest resort to Cairo. Fine beaches. Underwater photography.

SUEZ CANAL
Navigation is controlled and ships pass through the canal in convoy: Port Said–Suez in the mornings and Suez–Port Said in the afternoons.
◆ Charges (in $) for use of the canal are high.
◆ Only motorized vessels can pass.

ISMAÏLIYA
Ismaïliya ▲ 250 is popular with yachting enthusiasts. It lies midway between Port Said and Suez on the western shores of Lake Timsah, which is ideal for sailing.

YACHTING HARBORS
There are two harbors – in Alexandria and Port Said – where a yacht club controls access to the Suez Canal (canal charges, hire of moorings, visa for a straight passage or longer stay, etc.).

COMMON
◆ EXPRESSIONS ◆

YES: naam, aywa
NO: la
PERHAPS: yemken
POSSIBLY: mumken
IMPOSSIBLE: mesh mumken
NECESSARY: daruri
PLEASE: men fadlak (m.) men fadlik (f.)
THANK YOU: shukran
SORRY/EXCUSE ME: afuan
GOOD MORNING: sabah el-kheir; marhaba
GOOD EVENING: masa el-kheir
GOODBYE: saïda
MY NAME IS: esmi
WHAT IS YOUR NAME?: shu esmak?
HOW ARE YOU?: ez zayyak? (masc) ez zayyek? (fem)
TODAY: en-nahar da
TOMORROW: bukra
YESTERDAY: imbarih
I SPEAK ENGLISH: ana batkallam englizi
I DON'T SPEAK ARABIC?: ma-batkallamsh 'arabi
I DON'T UNDERSTAND. ana mish fahem
DO YOU SPEAK ENGLISH?. batkallam englizi?
CAN YOU HELP ME?: mumken tsaadni?
INFORMATION: istiilamat
WHAT TIME IS IT?: el-saa kam?

DAYS
◆ OF THE WEEK ◆

MONDAY: el-etnein
TUESDAY: el-talata
WEDNESDAY: el-arbaa
THURSDAY: el-khamis
FRIDAY: el-gumaa
SATURDAY: el-sabt
SUNDAY: el-had

MONTHS
◆ OF THE YEAR ◆

JANUARY: yanayer
FEBRUARY: febrayer
MARCH: mars
APRIL: abril
MAY: mayu
JUNE: yunyu
JULY: yulyu
AUGUST: aghustus
SEPTEMBER: september
OCTOBER: oktober
NOVEMBER: nofanber
DECEMBER: dissanber

◆ SEASONS ◆

WINTER: sheta
FALL: kharif
SPRING: rabla
SUMMER: seif

◆ NUMBERS ◆

ONE: wahad
TWO: tnein
THREE: talata
FOUR: arbaa
FIVE: khamsa
SIX: sitta
SEVEN: sabaa
EIGHT: tamania
NINE: tesaa
TEN: ashara
FIFTY: khamsin
ONE HUNDRED: mia
FIVE HUNDRED: khams mia
ONE THOUSAND: alf

◆ TRAVEL ◆

AIRPLANE: tayara
AIRPORT: matar
TICKET: tazkara
CHANGE: sarf
CUSTOMS: gumruk
STATION: mahatta
PORTER: hammal
TRAIN: trein
SUITCASE: shanta
DEPARTURE: dahab
ARRIVAL: wussul
DELAY: taakhkhor
TRAVEL AGENT: wikalat safar
BUS STATION: mahattet el-otobus
WHEN DOES THE ... ARRIVE?: emta wussul?
WHEN DOES THE ... LEAVE?: emta qiyam ...?
I WANT TO GO TO ...: Ayez aruh a ....
STOP HERE, PLEASE: waeff hena men fadlak
CAN YOU WAIT FOR ME?: mumkin tantazirni?
WAIT: intazir

FINDING YOUR
◆ WAY AROUND ◆

WHERE IS ....?: fein ....?
IS IT NEAR?: qarib?
IS IT FAR?: baïd?
(ON THE) LEFT: shmal
(ON THE) RIGHT: yamin
ABOVE: fuq
BELOW: taht
IN FRONT OF/OUTSIDE: uddam
BEHIND: uara
HERE: hena
OVER THERE: henak
BEFORE: abl
AFTER: baad
SOUTH: janub
NORTH: shamal
EAST: sharq
WEST: gharb
STREET: sharia/shari'
VILLAGE: qaria
TOWN: medina
SEA: bahr

GETTING
◆ AROUND ◆

CAR: sayara
DRIVER: sawaa
PETROL/GAS STATION: mahattet benzine
PETROL/GAS: benzine
PUMP UP: nafkh
OIL: zeit
HIRE: ajar
BRIDGE: kubri
GATE: bab
WHEEL: dulab

ROAD: tariq
TAXI: taxi

◆ AT THE HOTEL ◆

HOTEL: fundoq
ROOM: ghorfa
KEY: meftah
BATHROOM: hammam
TOWEL: futa, manchafa
SHEET: sharshaf
BLANKET: hiram
I WOULD LIKE A ROOM: mumken oda
I HAVE RESERVED A ROOM: hagazt oda
HOW MUCH DOES A ROOM COST?: bi kam el-oda?

AT THE
◆ RESTAURANT ◆

RESTAURANT: mataam
BREAKFAST: ftur
LUNCH: ghada
DINNER: asha
WATER: mayya
MINERAL WATER: mayya maadania
WINE: nebid
JUICE: assir
GLASS: kas
PLATE: sahn
BREAD: aïsh
BUTTER: zebda
OLIVES: zeitun
CHEESE: jibna
SALAD: salata
VEGETABLES: khodra
MEAT: lahma
CHICKEN: dajaj
FISH: samak
DESSERT: helu
FRUIT: fakiha
ICE-CREAM: buza
COFFEE: ahua
COFFEE WITHOUT SUGAR: ahua sada
FAIRLY SWEET: mazbut
VERY SWEET: ziada
TEA: shay
SUGAR: sokkar
MILK: halib
HOT: sokhn
COLD: bared
MAY I HAVE THE TAB, PLEASE?: mumken lehsab men fadlak?

◆ VISITS ◆

VISIT: ziara
OPEN: maftuh
CLOSED: msakkar
TICKET OFFICE: shubbak
TICKET: tazkara
TOWN: medina
QUARTER: hay
HOUSE: beit
GARDEN: hadiqa
THEATER: masrah
CINEMA: cinama
MUSEUM: mathaf
MOSQUE: gamea
MAY I VISIT THE MOSQUE?: mumken azur el-gamea?

◆ THE POST OFFICE ◆

WHERE CAN I TELEPHONE?: fein mumken atalfein?

POST OFFICE: el-barid
POSTAGE STAMP: tabea baridi
TELEPHONE: talifon
TELEGRAM: barqiya

◆ EMERGENCIES ◆

POLICE: shurta
FIRE BRIGADE: atfaïya
INFIRMARY: mashfa
HOSPITAL: mustashfa
PHARMACY: saydaliya
DOCTOR: tabib; hakim
PLEASE CALL THE DOCTOR: tlob el-tabib men fadlak

◆ SHOPPING ◆

BUREAU DE CHANGE: maktab es-sarf
MONEY: fuluss
I WOULD LIKE TO CHANGE SOME MONEY: ayez asarref fuluss
CHANGE (COINS): fakka
HAVE YOU ANY CHANGE?: andokom fakka?
PRICE: el-taman
WHERE CAN I BUY...?: fein mumken ashtari ...?
HOW MUCH?: kam?
HOW MUCH IS THIS?: bi kam da?
IT'S TOO EXPENSIVE: ghali awi
A LITTLE: shuaya
A LOT: ktir
THAT'S FINE/PERFECT: tamam
BAKER: khabbaz
GROCER: baqqal
BUTCHER'S: majzara
SHOP: mahal
PHOTOGRAPHER'S: mahal suar
BOOKSHOP: maktaba
NEWSPAPER: jarida
BOOK: kitab
ANTIQUE DEALER: tajir athariyat
JEWELER: sayegh

◆ MATERIALS ◆

GOLD: dahab
SILVER: fodda
IRON: hadid
BRONZE: bronz
COPPER: nhas
TERRACOTTA: fokhar
SILK: harir
COTTON: qotn
SYNTHETIC: tarkibi
WOOL: suf
GLASS: ezaz
IMITATION: taqlid
ORIGINAL: assli
PAPER: waraq

◆ COLORS ◆

WHITE: abiad
BLACK: asuad
RED: ahmar
GREEN: akhdar
BLUE: azrak
YELLOW: asfar
ORANGE: burtuqali
PINK: wardi
PURPLE: banafsagi

◆ GUIDED TOURS

Egypt is famed for the unique wealth of its remarkably well-preserved ancient sites. For lovers of art and history, pyramids, tombs and temples, Pharaonic and Graeco-Roman remains line the route. As the land of the early hermits, Egypt also conceals many Christian treasures. Finally, a visit to Islamic Cairo offers a glimpse of the splendor of the Fatimid and Mameluke periods.

GUIDES

There are any number of English-speaking guides and interpreters attached to the Egyptian Department of Antiquities. Guides are allocated to organized tour groups by a local tourist agency acting on behalf of the foreign tour-operator. These guides have the necessary permits (renewed for each group) for visiting Upper and Lower Egypt. Only official guides are entitled to give the relevant explanations on the sites visited. Unless special authorization has been obtained, non-Egyptians who give commentaries to organized groups are liable to be fined or even expelled from the country.

◆ Apart from one or two disastrous and rare exceptions, tour guides know their subject well and speak English fluently. They provide information on all periods of Egyptian history as well as everyday life in modern Egypt.

◆ There are no local guides attached to a particular site or museum. Individual tourists who want to hire a guide must go to a local agency.

NECROPOLISES AND TOMBS

These sites are often extensive. Visitors are directed to the

Temple of Esna.

tombs by site attendants. A board outside each tomb gives a résumé in English and French. Don't forget to take a torch. Opening hours are between 9am and 5pm (ticket sales end at 4pm).

◆ The main necropolises are located at Saqqara (Old Kingdom) and Luxor (New Kingdom), on the west bank of the Nile. Tickets are on sale at the entrance to the necropolises and entitle the holder to visit several tombs (specified when you buy the ticket). If you want to visit all the tombs on a particular site, you have to buy a ticket for each group of tombs.

◆ "Photo" tickets for the necropolises can be bought at the same time as the entrance tickets.

Temple of Edfu.

Taghri Bardi Mosque.

◆ In the Valley of the Kings a separate ticket (which can be bought on the site) is required to visit Tutankhamun's tomb.

◆ Photographs may be taken without a flash. The charge is £E 5 a tomb.

◆ There is a charge of between £E 10 and £E 25 per tomb for movie cameras. These may not be used in the Valley of the Kings.

TEMPLES

A ticket is bought at the entrance which is valid for the entire complex.
At Karnak a separate ticket (which can be bought with the entrance ticket) is required for the open-air museum situated within the temple complex.

◆ Temples are open daily between 8am

and 5pm. There is no charge for cameras and movie cameras. Flashes are not permitted at Abydos or Abu Simbel. Torches are useful.

COPTIC CHURCHES

There is no entrance charge for Coptic monasteries and churches which are still active (Wadi Natrun, St Catherine's). Visitors must be suitably dressed (no shorts, arms should be covered). You can make a contribution (around £E 5) as you leave. Ask the monks for permission to take photographs.

◆ There are no monks at the Monastery of St Simeon in Aswan where there is a charge of £E 8 per visitor.

◆ Churches are open between 9am and 4pm.

MOSQUES

The most beautiful mosques, although still used for prayer, are considered as monuments. There is therefore an entrance charge but none for cameras and movie cameras.

◆ Dress should be the same as for churches and shoes are removed at the entrance. Allow a tip for the shoe attendant (£E 0.50).

◆ Mosques are open daily between 8.30am and 4pm (sometimes 5pm).

Graeco-Roman terracotta vase (left).

Graeco-Roman amphitheater, Alexandria.

Temple of Luxor.

MUSEUMS

The museums of Cairo, Alexandria and Luxor cover the four main periods of Egyptian history: Pharaonic, Graeco-Roman, Christian and Islamic.

♦ A special ticket is required – in addition to your entrance ticket – if you want to take photographs: £E 10 (camera); £E 100 (movie camera).

♦ Flashes are not permitted. Take care with automatic flashes since, even if they go off unintentionally, you will be fined and your film will be confiscated.

♦ In some museums an additional ticket is required to visit a particular room, such

as the "Mummy" room in the Cairo Museum and the Luxor Museum.

♦ Lighting can be poor, so buy in a light-sensitive film before you leave.

♦ Each exhibit is explained in English.

♦ The Cairo Museum is old and although its apparent disorder can be confusing it also adds to its charm.

♦ Museums are open daily between 9am and 4pm (5pm for the Cairo Egyptian Museum). They are closed on Fridays between 11.15am and 1.30pm. Luxor opening hours are: 10am–noon and 4–9pm (10pm in summer).

"SOUND AND LIGHT"

There are Sound and Light Shows – at the Pyramids, Karnak and Philae – with three shows per day on each site. See table below.

♦ The Sound and Light Show at the Pyramids (which lasts for an hour) is outside, so wear warm clothing in winter. Blankets can be hired at the entrance for £E 2.

♦ At Karnak (1¼hours) and Philae

(1 hour), you walk in the temple during the first part of the show and sit down during the second.

♦ At the Pyramids the ticket office is behind the cafeteria. At Karnak and Philae tickets are sold in the same place as the entrance tickets. Price: £E 34. There is there is a charge of £E 30 for movie cameras. For further information: Tel. 385 28 80 or 385 73 60

SHOWS IN ENGLISH

	Pyramids		Karnak		Philae	
	Winter	Sum.	Winter	Sum.	Winter	Sum.
Mon.	6.30pm	7.30 pm	6pm	8pm	6pm	8pm
Tue.	–	–	8pm	10pm	7.30pm	9.30pm
Wed.	6.30 pm	7.3 pm	6pm	8pm	6pm	8pm
Thur.	7.30pm	8.30pm	8pm	10pm	–	–
Fri.	6.30pm	8.30pm	8pm	10pm	6pm	8pm
Sat.	6.30pm	7.30pm	6pm	8pm	6pm	8pm
Sun.	–	–	–	–	–	–

NB: Please check times of shows as they may be subject to changes.

> **WARNING**
> To avoid the intense summer heat, visit sites early in the morning.

URBAN ARCHITECTURE

♦ In Cairo a few old houses have been restored (there is an entrance fee).

♦ A walk through any town or city shows the architectural legacy of the

various civilizations that have lived in Egypt.

♦ Ismaïiya's old town, for example, is a veritable open-air museum of the colonial period.

REDUCTIONS

These apply on all sites. There is a 50 percent reduction for children under 10 (no charge for the under-3's) and those who have an international student's card.

EXCURSIONS . . .

. . . ON HORSEBACK

Horses can be hired at the foot of the Pyramids (opposite the Mena House Hotel)

for visits to the Pyramid site or Saqqara via the desert route. This is a delightful excursion early in the morning. Bargain on the basis of between £E 20 and £E25 per hour (plus a £E 10 tip).

♦ Not advisable for young women on their own (for reasons of safety) or for non-riders, as the 7-hour ride is exhausting.

. . . BY CAMEL

The same excursion for the same price, but it takes longer!

♦ There are any number of excursions by camel (Saqqara, Sinai, Aswan). Always bargain on the basis of £E 20 to £E 25 per hour.

◆ ALTERNATIVE SITES

Pharaonic period

Saqqara ▲ 344
Open daily: 8am–5pm
£E 10 for a choice of three visits
Buy several tickets if you want to see everything:
pyramids of Djoser, Unis, Teti; mastabas of Idut,
Mehu, Kagemni, Mereruka, Ptahhotep, Ti;
Serapeum
The largest necropolis in Egypt.

Giza ▲ 334
Open daily: 8am–5pm (Solar Boat Museum:
8am–4pm). £E 10: Menkaure (Mycerinus)
+ the Sphinx
£E 10: Pyramid of Khufu (Cheops)
£E 10: Solar Boat Museum.

Cairo Museum ▲ 276
Shari' Mariette, Midan at-Tahrir
Open daily: 8am–5pm
Closed Fridays: 11.15am–13.30pm
£E 10 + £E 30 for the "Mummy" room
*Egypt's largest museum. Remarkable quality of
exhibits which are stored rather than classified.*

Beni Hassan ▲ 374
Open daily: 8am–4pm
£E 8
Photos (no flashes) free of charge
*Middle-Kingdom, rock-cut tombs. Splendid view of
the Nile Valley.*

Tell el-Amarna ▲ 378
Open daily: 8am–4pm.
£E 6
*Amarnian tombs in an advanced state of disrepair.
A truly amazing site.*

Abydos ▲ 386
£E 6
Photography without flash permitted
*Magnificent temple of Sety I (some of the finest
bas-reliefs in Egypt).
Behind the temple, the small temple of Ramesses II.*

Karnak ▲ 404
Open daily: 6am–6pm (5.30pm for the museum)
£E 10 + £E 10 for the open-air museum with the
delightful kiosk of Senwosret.
Vast complex of temples, chapels and obelisks.

Temple of Luxor ▲ 398
Open during the day and evening (closes at 9pm in
winter and 10pm in summer)
£E 10
The illuminations enhance its beauty.

Luxor Museum ▲ 403
Open daily: 10am–noon and 4–9pm (5–10pm in
summer)
£E 15 for the entire collection
*Remarkable collection of exhibits, magnificently
presented.*

*Tickets for all sites on the Necropolis of Thebes are
on sale at the landing stage. There is a ferry
service from the Hotel Etap every 10 min (£E 2).*

Valley of the Kings ▲ 417
£E 10 for three of the twelve or so tombs open.
£E 20 for the Tomb of Tutankhamun (ticket office
on site). "Photo" tickets from the office beyond
the colossi of Memnon. Movie cameras not
permitted.

Valley of the Queens ▲ 440
£E 6 for two princes' tombs (Amenhikopeshef and
Khaemwese).
£E 100 for the tomb of Nefertari
*Buy tickets as early as possible (from 6am) at the
ticket and photo booth close to the Colossus of
Memnon: only 150 tickets available each day*

Sheikh Abd el-Qurna ▲ 430
£E 6 per group of two dignitaries' tombs:
Ramose/Userhet, Rekhmire/Sennefer,
Nakht/Menna.
*Necropolis of Qurna. The very best of Egyptian
bas-relief -truly magnificent.*

Deir el-Medina (Valley of the Artists) ▲ 438
£E 6 for two tombs: Sennedjem and Inkerhau.

Temple of Deir el-Bahri ▲ 426
£E 6
*Rock-cut temple in the Mountain of Thebes.
Surprisingly modern.*

Temple of Medinet Habu ▲ 434
£E 6
*Magnificent funerary temple of Ramesses III.
Some of the colors can still be seen.*

Ramesseum ▲ 432
£E 6
*Funerary temple of Ramesses II. In an advanced
state of disrepair, but still some remains of black
granite colossi.*

Temples of Abu Simbel ▲ 464
£E 15 + £E 6 (additional charges) to visit the
temples of Ramesses II and Nerfertari.
Photography (without flashes) permitted. Direct
Egyptair bus service between the airport and the
site.

Ptolemaic and Roman periods

Alexandria Museum ▲ 186
Shari' Gamal-Abdel-Nasser: £E 8
*Some extremely fine exhibits (including the Faiyum
portraits) and a large collection of coins.*

Amphitheater of Kom el-Dikka ▲ 185
£E 3
*A gem (more of an odeum than a theater) in the
heart of Alexandria. The only one of its kind in
Egypt.*

Kom es-Shogafa Catacombs ▲ 192
£E 6 – Cameras £E 5 – Movie cameras £E 25
*Enchanting. The last room is a fine example of how
Roman art was adapted to Egyptian criteria.*

Pompey's Pillar ▲ 194
Shari' el-Awud as-Sawari: £E 3 – Movie cameras
£E 25
*This huge, pink granite pillar dating from the reign
of Diocletian is one of the symbols of Alexandria. It
stands in a garden surrounded by several older
sphinxes.*

Tuna el-Jebel ▲ 377
£E 6
Cameras without flashes are permitted.
*Ancient Hermopolis. Tomb of Petosiris (its décor
an amazing combination of Greek and Egyptian
styles) and the necropolis of the sacred ibis: a
veritable underground maze.*

Ashmunein ● 72

The ancient town of Hermopolis. The *agora* (currently being restored) is a fine example of the Greek period. Same ticket as for Tune el-Jebel

Dendera ▲ 388

£E 6
The first of the Pharaonic-style temples built during the Graeco-Roman period.

Esna ▲ 446

£E 4
All that remains of this temple is a small room with richly decorated ceilings.

Edfu ▲ 448

£E 10
Complete temple, from the entrance pylon to the inner sanctuary. A fine example of this architectural period.

Kom Ombo ▲ 452

£E 4
The only double temple in Egypt. Famed for its "surgical instruments" wall. A beautiful site.

Philae ▲ 462

£E 10
A masterpiece of grace and harmony. One of the temples reconstructed by UNESCO. Reached by boat (£E 0.75).

Kalabsha ▲ 460

£E 6
Temple overlooking Lake Nasser. A truly remarkable site. Reached by fishing boat in winter and on foot in summer.

Christian period

Monasteries of Wadi Natrun ▲ 208

Between Alexandria and Cairo: reached via the new Desert Road. Free admission
The most beautiful are the Monastery of the Syrians, Deir Amba Bishoi and the Monastery of St Makarios.

Coptic Museum, Cairo ▲ 322

Open daily: 9am–4pm. Closed Fridays: 11am–1pm – £E 8 – Cameras £E 5 – Movie cameras £E 100.
Opposite the Mari Girgis underground station
One of Cairo's three main museums. Collections of early Christian and Coptic art (cloth, stelae, icons).

Churches in the Coptic quarter ▲ 318

Near the museum (same opening hours)
Free admission for the Hanging Church, £E 10 for the rest of the churches
The most beautiful is El-Muallaqa – the "Hanging Church" – an architectural masterpiece in stone and wood.

St Catherine's Monastery ▲ 244

Open daily: 9.30am–noon. Closed Fri, Sat, Sun. Free admission
The main interest is the site – the church is fairly unremarkable and the library is closed to the public.

Monastery of St Simeon ▲ 459

£E 8
Spectacular site in the desert west of Aswan. Reached by crossing the Nile in a felucca and continuing on foot or by camel (£E 20–25 roundtrip).

Islamic Cairo

1 Citadel and Ibn Tulun district

Citadel ▲ 304

Overlooks Cairo. Open daily: 8am–5pm
£E 10 for the Mohammed Ali Mosque (Ottoman style). £E 3 for the Mosque of Nasser ibn Qala'un
Citadel dates from the reign of Salah ad-Din, the mosques are more recent.

Sultan Hassan Medersa ▲ 308

Shari' el-Qal'a (Mohammed Ali): £E 6
Masterpiece of Mameluke architectural art.

Ibn Tulun Mosque ▲ 312

£E 3
One of the oldest and most beautiful mosques in Cairo.

2 El-Azhar district and Shari' el-Muizz

El-Azhar Mosque ▲ 294

Shari' el-Azhar – Ghuriya: £E 6
Cairo's seat of learning dates from the Fatimid period. The richness of the materials used and the columns of the prayer hall are truly impressive.

El-Hakim Mosque ▲ 291

Shari' el-Muizz li-Din-Allah: £E3

Qala'un Mausoleum ▲ 289

Shari' el-Muizz li-Din-Allah: £E3
A beautiful complex (Mameluke period). Openwork stone façade, stained-glass windows and some magnificent interior marble.

Barquq Medersa ▲ 289

Shari' el-Muizz li-Din-Allah: £E3
Remarkable mosaic entrance and finely worked façade (Mameluke Koranic school).

El-Mu'ayyad Mosque ▲ 298

Shari' el-Muizz li-Din-Allah: £E3
Famed for its two minarets which dominate the Bab Zuwaila: a masterpiece of Mameluke architecture.

3 City of the Dead

Barquq Mausoleum ▲ 328

Shari' el-Sultan Ahmed – City of the Dead: £E 3
Perfection and harmony. The Mameluke minarets offer a splendid view of the City of the Dead, an ancient necropolis which is today inhabited by the living.

Qaitbay Mausoleum ▲ 328

Shari' Bab el Wazir – City of the Dead: £E 3
Another masterpiece of Mameluke architecture. Possibly the finest minaret in Cairo.

Imam as-Shafi'i Mausoleum ▲ 330

Imam as-Shafi'i Avenue: £E 3
The resting place of the founder of one of the four orthodox schools of Sunni jurisprudence. Beautiful interior wood paneling. Place of pilgrimage.

4 Museum of Islamic art ▲ 316

£E 8. Shari' Port Said – el-Muski
Open daily: 9am–4pm
Closed Fridays 11am–1pm
At the end of the Shari' el-Azhar. Very well presented with a wide variety of exhibits.

Markets are found everywhere in Egypt. They are the expression of the country's rich diversity of traditional crafts and agricultural produce. The centrally located *suqs* are often masterpieces of medieval architecture which play an important part in modern everyday life. Markets are less structured and located on the outskirts of towns and cities. They also tend to be more specialized and are only held on certain days of the week. If you like to wander, take your time and satisfy your curiosity; markets are ideal places for making extraordinary discoveries and friendly contacts.

CAMELS

Cairo is the home of Egypt's largest camel market, the so-called Suq el-Gamal. It is held beyond Shari' el-Sudan, near Imbaba Airport (on the left bank). The animals are brought from western Sudan along the Darb el-Arbaïn ("the Road of Forty Days") – which brings them to Aswan across the Nubian Desert. From there they are transported by lorry to Cairo where they are sold. To buy a camel costs between £970/ $1540 and £2430/ $3855.The market is held every Friday and Monday morning. There is an entrance charge for tourists. But as it is also an Islamic stronghold, the district has been closed by the police for an indefinite period.

MARKETS

Markets sell vegetables or livestock. They are well worth a visit for the sheer visual impression and the very special atmosphere that is generated, with *fellaheen* selling their produce and animals tied or hobbled according to type in different sectors.
◆ Tourists – easily identified and obviously not buying – may feel somewhat disorientated. Avoid taking photographs without the permission of the person(s) involved.

ALEXANDRIA
◆ Sunday morning fruit, vegetable and fish market in the streets near Pompey's Pillar.
◆ Late-morning fish markets in the port area when the boats return.

CAIRO
◆ Permanent poultry and vegetable market behind the El-Azhar Mosque.
◆ Meat market every morning in the Midan el-Ataba (Ataba Square).

LUXOR
◆ Luxor's famous – and very busy – livestock market is held every Tuesday morning on the edge of the town in the direction of the airport.
◆ Other – lesser known – markets are held periodically in other towns: Edfu, Kom Ombo.

HORSES

Arab thoroughbreds are bred in Egypt. It is possible to attend sales two or three times per year. For information contact Saqqara Country Club, Saqqara Road. Tel: 385 22 82 or 385 05 71

AGRICULTURAL PRODUCE

Agricultural produce varies according to season and location. With the exception of dates (which are grown everywhere) fruit comes mainly from the Delta region, while the spices sold in the south come mainly from the Sudan.
◆ Winter is the season for oranges, mandarins, grapefruit and small bananas.
◆ Summer is the time for melons, water melons, figs, mangos (the best come from Ismaïliya), guavas, dates (a great many varieties) and grapes.
◆ Vegetables are grown all the year round but summer is the season for *mulukhiya* and *bamia* (okra).

TRADITIONAL CRAFTS AND SOUVENIRS

ANTIQUES
Antiques (which have in fact become extremely rare) may not be taken out of Egypt. Amidst the mass of crude reproductions you occasionally come across a carefully executed piece in limestone or granite. Luxor is the main center for this type of object.
◆ There are some good artists in the Valley of the Kings or the Temple of Hatshepsut.

PAPYRUS
Papyrus is the Egyptian souvenir *par excellence*. The most beautiful papyri, sold in the "papyrus institutes" on the Avenue of the Pyramids (Ani, New Pharao, Sobek), are decorated with paintings copied from tombs or ancient papyri.
◆ Street sellers offer papyri of average quality at unbeatable prices.

COPPER- AND BRASSWARE
The Cairo *suqs* offer the widest selection of copper and brass trays, dishes, boxes and other objects.
◆ Avoid the tasteless Pharaonic motifs in favor of the classic arabesque designs (sometimes decorated with silver).

GLASS BLOWING
This is one of Cairo's specialties.
Glass blowers are found behind the Khan el-Khalili ▲ 286, 512, near Bab el-Futuh.
◆ There are some really beautiful pieces (vases, glasses, ewers) in blue, green and brown glass.

ALABASTER
Alabaster is found in the Qurna region, near Luxor, and also in Cairo.
◆ There are several types, ranging from milky white to dark brown.
Handmade objects have a more "rustic" appearance, whereas those made by machine are much smoother. Some of the vases are true masterpieces of restrained elegance.

CARPETS
Carpets are found particularly in the area around Saqqara. There are increasing numbers of carpet and weaving schools where the work done by children, as well as the famous "naive" carpets, whose motifs are inspired by scenes of country life, are on display.
◆ The schools also produce the classic wool and silk carpets which,

although their reputation does not equal that of Turkish or Persian carpets, are nevertheless beautifully made.

JEWELRY
◆ The silver used to make all kinds of objects (jewelry, boxes, mirrors, key rings) is inexpensive.
◆ The gold is renowned: 18 carats in quality jewelry stores.
◆ There is no shortage of copies of Western and Pharaonic jewelry. The most famous is the cartouche: a

pendant with the wearer's name inscribed in hieroglyphs.
◆ There is some very beautiful turquoise and lapis lazuli.
◆ Stores in Cairo:
Sabry (opposite the Manyal Palace)
Tel: 84 80 27
El-Refaey
27, Shari' el-Refaey
Citadel
Tel: 91 66 78
Galal
Khan el-Khalili
Tel: 92 26 28
◆ Stores in Luxor
Philippe Jewels (Hotel Philippe)
Tel: 58 00 60 / 50
Hadwan (opposite the Hotel Isis)
Tel: 38 16 55
or 37 46 43

PERFUMES
The village of Nazlet el-Semman, near the Pyramids, sells most types of perfume (jasmine, musk, amber). Every known perfume is made up to order.
◆ There is a wide range of bottles of all shapes and sizes.

COTTON GOODS
There are any number of stores selling high-quality cotton clothing in both Eastern and Western styles (T-shirts, shirts). The printed and damask table cloths are also very good quality. In fact you could re-stock an entire wardrobe at very reasonable prices.

Cairo's Khan el-Khalili is one of the largest *suqs* in the Middle East: trade has been carried on here since 1382. Today every kind of traditional craft and all kinds of produce compete for space in its brightly colored, perfumed bustling streets with their animated and constantly moving crowds. It is as much a place for visiting, making discoveries and meeting people as it is a place to do your shopping.

CAIRO "SUQ"

The Khan el-Khalili, near the El-Hussein Mosque, is the most famous *suq* in Egypt both in terms of its size and its history. It has some masterpieces of Mameluke and Ottoman architecture.

◆ Although jewelry, silver plate and copper- and brassware predominate, all types of traditional Egyptian crafts are found here.

◆ The *suq* is divided into sectors according to trade, although they are not as clearly defined as in other Oriental *suqs*, with shops selling copper- and brassware next to goldsmiths and carpet sellers. There is a wider choice of spices, seeds and perfumes in the Shari' el-Muizz and Shari' Gowhara el-Qa'id, near the Shari el-Azhar.

It is easy to find your way around, as the *suq* lies between the Shari' el-Azhar, the Shari' el-Muizz and the Midan el-Hussein.

◆ The *suq's* attraction lies as much in the amazingly animated atmosphere that predominates, especially in the evening. The shops stay open late, the cafés – including the famous El-Fishawi (the *Café of Mirrors*), the oldest and most charming café in Cairo – remain full, and crowds throng the streets late into the night.

◆ During Ramadan the evenings in the Khan el-Khalili are unforgettable. The shops stay open until 11pm, and the cafés until midnight.

◆ It is pleasant to wander along the maze of narrow streets, watching the craftsmen at work and observing the commercial life of the *suq*.

Shari' el-Muizz

El-Ashraf Barsbey

El-Mutahar complex

Shari' el-Azhar

Khan Abu el-Takam

Mamarr an-Nasr

Zuqaq el-Midaqq

Shari' el-Muski, (el-) Sikka, el-Gadida

Charia el-Sanadqiya

Wakala el-Gallaba

Shari' el-Azhar

Wakala (Raba el-Silahe

Haret el-Bosta
Suq el-Fatimi

Haret el-Wakala

SUQS

A street in the suq (top left), a shop (bottom left), glass blower (top right) and "foot" ironer (bottom right).

◆ Bargaining is the rule (although if you don't, the vendor will be delighted).

◆ Take your cue from the vendor(s). Accepting coffee or tea doesn't mean you have to buy. But don't negotiate a price until you have an idea of the true value of the item.

◆ Never offer a price that you are not prepared to pay.

◆ N.B. There are tourist traps. For some shops this is their *raison d'être*. It's up to you to get the "feel" of a situation and distinguish between the true and the false. Everything in Egypt is a matter of tact and diplomacy.

SPICE "SUQ"

The spice *suq* is near the Khan el-Khalili, in the area of the Shari' el-Muizz. Its narrow streets harbor an impressive number of herbalists. It is one of the most picturesque parts of medieval Cairo.

Map labels:
Shari' El-Sagha
Shari' Bein el-Qasrein
Suq el-Nahassin
Wakala el-Firakh
Harit el-Suramatiya
Harit el-Salihiya
'akala Badawiya Shahin
Wakala el-Makwa
Haret el-Salihiya
Bab el-Badistan
Harel Khan el-Khalili
Shari' Sikka el-Badistan
ka Khan Khalili
Wikala el-Qotn
Wakala Waqf el-Haramein
'Imarat Shuikar
Khan Gaafar
Ahmed Pasha Sabil-Kuttab
Shari' el-Mashhad el-Husseini

◆ < £E 100
◆◆ £E 100 to £E 300
◆◆◆ £E 300 to £E 600
◆◆◆◆ > £E 600

	PAGE	PRICE	CITY CENTER	PLEASANT SURROUNDINGS	RESTAURANT	SWIMMING POOL	GARDEN	QUIET	SPORTS / BEACH	NO. OF ROOMS
ALEXANDRIA AND THE COAST										
ALEXANDRIA										
HELNAN PALESTINE HOTEL ***** ★	522	◆◆◆		●		●		●	●	208
MERCURE ROMANCE****	522	◆◆◆	●		●	●			●	64
METROPOLE HOTEL *** ★	522	◆	●	●	●					82
MUNTAZA SHERATON HOTEL *****	522	◆◆◆			●	●			●	305
RAMADA RENAISSANCE *****	522	◆◆◆	●		●	●			●	171
SOFITEL CECIL HOTEL**** ★	523	◆◆◆	●	●	●					86
WINDSOR HOTEL ****	523	◆◆	●	●	●					54
EL-ALAMEIN										
AIDA BEACH *****	523	◆◆			●	●		●	●	120
BEAU SITE HOTEL ***	523	◆◆◆			●	●		●	●	103
HÔTEL EL-ALAMEIN **** ★	524	◆◆◆		●	●			●	●	209
DELTA REGION AND THE SUEZ CANAL										
ISMAÏLIYA										
MERCURE HOTEL ETAP FORSAN IS.****	524	◆◆◆			●	●	●	●	●	152
PORT SAID										
HELNAN PORT SAID HOTEL*****	524	◆◆	●		●					81
NEW REGENT HOTEL***	524	◆◆	●		●	●				36
SUEZ										
RED SEA HOTEL***	524	◆◆			●			●		81
SUMMER PALACE HOTEL***	524	◆◆			●			●		77
TANTA										
ARAFA HOTEL***	524	◆◆	●		●					43
SINAI										
SHARM EL-SHEIKH										
CLIFF TOP HOTEL ***	525	◆◆			●			●		30
GAFI LAND TOURIST VILLAGE ***	525	◆◆	●		●			●	●	45
GHAZALA HOTEL ****	525	◆◆◆			●	●		●	●	
HILTON AL-FAIROUZ *****	525	◆◆◆◆	●	●	●	●	●	●	●	
MARRIOTT ***** ★	525	◆◆◆◆	●	●	●	●		●	●	
MÖVENPICK SHARM EL-SHEIKH *****	525	◆◆◆◆		●	●	●		●	●	210
NOVOTEL AQUAMARINE HOTEL **** ★	525	◆◆◆		●	●	●		●	●	152
TIRAN VILLAGE ***	525	◆◆			●	●		●	●	75
EL-ARISH										
EL-ARISH OBEROI HOTEL*****	525	◆◆◆			●	●		●	●	
HURGHADA										
CORAL BEACH VILLAGE****	525	◆◆◆		●	●	●		●	●	174
EL-GIFTUN TOURIST VILLAGE*** ★	525	◆◆			●	●		●	●	282
HURGHADA SHERATON HOTEL****	525	◆◆◆			●	●		●	●	125
JASMINE HOLIDAY VILLAGE***	525	◆◆			●	●		●	●	434
MAGAWISH TOURIST VILLAGE**** ★	525	◆◆		●	●	●		●	●	314
SONESTA BEACH RESORT ****	526	◆◆◆		●	●	●	●	●	●	132
NUWEIBA										
EL-SAYADEEN TOURISTIC VILLAGE*** ★	526	◆◆		●	●	●		●	●	66
EL-WAHA TOURISTIC VILLAGE**	526	◆			●			●	●	38
HILTON CORAL HOTEL****	526	◆◆◆			●	●	●	●	●	
NUWEIBA HOLIDAY VILLAGE***	526	◆◆◆			●	●		●	●	172
PORT SAFAGA										
MENAVILLE VILLAGE****	526	◆◆◆			●	●		●	●	152
SAFAGA PARADISE VILLAGE****	526	◆◆				●		●	●	244
ST CATHERINE										
ST CATHERINE TOURIST VILLAGE****	526	◆◆◆		●	●			●		100
TABA										
HOTEL HILTON TABA*****	526	◆◆◆◆			●	●		●	●	326

Thereterences given in brackets after some of the Cairo hotels and restaurants indicate their position on the map ◆ 518.

	PAGE	PRICE	CITY CENTER	PLEASANT SURROUNDINGS	RESTAURANT	SWIMMING POOL	GARDEN	QUIET	SPORTS / BEACH	NO. OF ROOMS
CAIRO										
CAIRO HELIOPOLIS MÖVENPICK***	534	◆◆◆◆		●	●	●			●	412
CAIRO JOLIE-VILLE MÖVENPICK***	534	◆◆◆◆		●	●	●	●	●	●	240
CAIRO MARRIOTT HOTEL*** ★ (C2)	534	◆◆◆◆	●	●	●	●	●		●	1147
CAIRO RAMSES HILTON HOT. *** (D3)	534	◆◆◆◆	●	●	●	●			●	849
CAIRO SHERATON HOTEL*** (B5)	534	◆◆◆◆	●	●	●	●			●	660
COSMOPOLITAN HOTEL* ★ (E3)	534	◆◆	●	●	●					84
EL-GEZIRA SHERATON HOTEL*** (C5)	534	◆◆◆◆	●	●	●	●			●	520
FORTE GRAND PYRAMIDS HOTEL*** ★	534	◆◆◆		●	●	●	●		●	523
HELNAN SHEPHEARD HOT.*** ★ (D4)	534	◆◆◆◆	●	●	●				●	281
LE MÉRIDIEN CAIRO HOTEL*** (C6)	535	◆◆◆◆		●	●	●			●	275
LE MÉRIDIEN HELIOPOLIS HOTEL***	535	◆◆◆◆	●	●	●	●			●	302
LONGCHAMPS HOTEL* (C2)	535	◆◆	●	●	●			●		30
LOTUS HOTEL (E4)	535	◆	●	●	●					50
MENA HOUSE OBEROI HOTEL*** ★	535	◆◆◆◆		●	●	●	●	●	●	520
NILE HILTON HOTEL*** (D4)	535	◆◆◆◆	●	●	●	●			●	434
**NITOCRISSE HOTEL* (F3)	535	◆	●	●	●					43
OASIS HOTEL**	535	◆◆◆		●	●	●	●	●	●	253
**PENSION ROMA CAIRO (F3)	535	◆	●							
PRESIDENT HOTEL* (C2)	535	◆◆	●	●	●			●		119
PYRAMIDS PARK *** ★	535	◆◆◆◆		●	●	●	●	●	●	481
SEMIRAMIS INTER-CONT.*** (D4)	535	◆◆◆◆	●	●	●	●			●	840
SIAG PYRAMIDS HOTEL CAIRO***	535	◆◆◆		●	●	●		●	●	352
SOFITEL MAADI TOWERS HOTEL ***	536	◆◆◆		●	●	●			●	176
SWISSHOTEL CAIRO*** ★	536	◆◆◆◆		●	●	●	●	●	●	323
THE FAIYUM										
AUBERGE DU LAC FAYOUM **	537	◆◆◆		●	●	●	●	●		77
PANORAMA SHAKSHUK HOTEL *	537	◆◆		●	●	●	●			30
EL-MINYA										
P.L.M. AZUR NEFERTITI**	537	◆◆◆		●	●	●	●	●		
THEBES										
LUXOR										
AKHETATON VILLAGE BELLADONNA**	538	◆◆◆		●	●	●	●	●		144
HORUS HOTEL	538	◆		●						25
ISIS HOTEL LUXOR*** ★	538	◆◆◆		●	●	●	●	●	●	500
LUXOR HILTON***	538	◆◆◆		●	●	●	●	●	●	261
LUXOR SHERATON H. & RESORT*** ★	538	◆◆◆		●	●	●	●	●	●	298
MERCURE HOTEL**		◆◆◆	●	●	●	●	●	●		306
MÖVENPICK JOLIE-VILLE LUXOR*** ★	539	◆◆◆		●	●	●	●	●	●	320
NOVOTEL EVASION LUXOR HOTEL**	539	◆◆◆◆		●	●	●				145
PHARAON HOTEL*	539	◆◆◆		●	●	●	●			61
SOFITEL WINTER PALACE** ★	539	◆◆		●	●	●	●			370
ASWAN AND NUBIA										
ABU SIMBEL										
NEFERTARI ABU SIMBEL**	539	◆◆◆		●	●	●	●			110
ASWAN										
AMUN HOTEL* ★	540	◆◆		●	●	●	●			56
AMUN TOURIST VILLAGE***	540	◆◆◆		●	●	●	●		●	252
ASWAN OBEROI HOTEL*** ★	540	◆◆◆◆		●	●	●	●		●	244
ISIS HOTEL ASWAN**	540	◆◆	●	●	●	●			●	100
KALABSHA HOTEL **		◆◆◆◆			●		●			
P.L.M. AZUR NEW CATARACT***	540	◆◆◆		●	●	●	●		●	144
SOFITEL CATARACT HOTEL*** ★	540	◆◆◆		●	●	●	●	●	●	136

Prices between:
♦ £E 30 and 80
♦♦ £E 50 and 100
♦♦♦ £E 80 and 140

	PAGE	PRICE	TERRACE / GARDEN	ORIENTAL SPECIALTIES	SPECIALTIES	VIEW	OPEN FOR LUNCH AND DINNER	CITY CENTER	PLEASANT SURROUNDINGS	ENTERTAINMENT
ALEXANDRIA										
ADHURA ★	521	♦	●		FS		●	●		
DYNASTY	521	♦			C			●		
GRILLADE	521	♦			I	●	●			
L'ENTRECÔTE	521	♦♦			F					
LE CLOVIS	521	♦			F		●			
LE PLAT D'OR	522	♦		●	I			●		
RANG MAHAL	522	♦			IN			●	●	
SAN GIOVANNI ★	522	♦♦		●	I / FS	●	●	●	●	
SANTA LUCIA	522	♦♦			I		●	●	●	
SEA GULL	522	♦♦♦			FS	●	●	●		
TIKKA GRILL ★	522	♦			FS	●	●	●		
CAIRO										
AIDA RESTAURANT ★	530	♦♦			F			●		
ALADIN (B5)	530	♦♦	●				●			●
ANDREA	530	♦	●	●			●			
ANGUS (C2)	530	♦			I					
ARABESQUE ★ (E4)	529	♦		●			●	●	●	
ASIA HOUSE ★ (D4)	529	♦			IN / C		●	●	●	
CHIN CHIN (FOUR CORNERS) (C2)	529	♦			C		●	●		
CHRISTO	530	♦	●		FS	●	●			
CITADEL GRILL (D3)	530	♦♦			I		●			
DON QUICHOTTE ★ (C2)	530	♦♦			I / FS		●			
DRAGON ★ (C5)	530	♦♦			C	●				
EL-EZBA ★	530	♦	●	●			●	●	●	
EL-FANUS (OMAM RESTAURANTS)	530	♦	●					●	●	
EL-MASHRABIYA	530	♦♦	●				●	●		
EL-SARRAYA	531	♦♦			FS			●		
EL-WALIMA ★	531	♦		●	FS			●		
EL-YOTTI (A5)	531	♦		●	I		●			
FALAFEL (D3)	531	♦♦		●				●		●
FELFELA ★ (D4)	531	♦		●			●	●	●	
GRILL GEZIRA (C2)	531	♦♦♦			I					
IBIS CAFÉ (D4)	531	♦			I		●			
IL CAMINO (OMAM RESTAURANTS) ★	531	♦			IT		●			
IL GIARDINO ★	531	♦	●		IT		●			
JUSTINE'S (FOUR CORNERS) ★ (C2)	531	♦♦			F	●				
KAN ZAMAN ★	531	♦	●	●			●			●
KEBABGY ★ (C5)	531	♦	●	●		●			●	
KHAN EL-KHALILI (H3)	531	♦♦		●			●	●	●	
KHAN EL-KHALILI (MENA HOUSE)	531	♦		●	I		●	●		
LA BRASSERIE (C6)	531	♦			I	●	●	●		
LA CHARMERIE (C2)	531	♦♦			I		●			
LA FARNESINA ★	532	♦			IT		●			
LA MAMMA (B5)	532	♦♦			IT	●	●			●
LA PIAZZA (FOUR CORNERS) (C2)	532	♦			IT		●		●	●
LE CHALET (SWISSAIR RESTS.)	532	♦♦			I	●			●	
LE CHAMPOLLION (C6)	532	♦♦♦			F	●	●	●		
LE CHÂTEAU (SWISSAIR RESTS.)	532	♦♦♦			F	●			●	
LE CLOVIS	532	♦♦♦			F					
LE MARCO POLO	532	♦♦			F		●			
LES AMBASSADEURS GRILL ★ (C5)	532	♦♦♦			F	●		●	●	●
MARQUIS	532	♦			I		●			
MOGHUL ROOM ★	532	♦♦♦			IN				●	●

Key to specialties

A: Austrian	IT: Italian
C: Chinese	J: Japanese
F: French	FS: Fish and
I: International	seafood
IN: Indian	S: Swiss

	PAGE	PRICE	TERRACE / GARDEN	ORIENTAL	SPECIALTIES	VIEW	OPEN FOR LUNCH AND DINNER	CITY CENTER	PLEASANT SURROUNDINGS	ENTERTAINMENT
MÖVENPICK RESTAURANT	532	◆◆			S / I					
NILE P. & GOL. P. BOATS & REST. ★ (B5)	532	◆◆		●	I	●	●		●	●
NUBIAN VILLAGE (C6)	532	◆	●	●		●				●
OMAR'S CAFÉ (C2)	532	◆◆			I		●			
ONYX & TOPAZ BOATS & REST. ★	532	◆◆		●	I	●	●		●	●
PAPRIKA ★ (D3)	533	◆	●	●	I			●		
PEACE	533	◆			FS	●				
RÉGENCE (D4)	533	◆◆◆			F		●	●		
RUBAYYAT	533	◆◆◆			I		●	●		
SAKKURA (OMAM RESTAURANTS)	533	◆◆◆			J		●	●		
SEAHORSE ★	533	◆			FS	●	●			
SHANDANI (OMAM RESTAURANTS)	533	◆			IN		●	●		
SILVER FISH ★ (B5)	533	◆			FS	●				
STARLIGHT	533	◆◆			I	●		●		
TAJ MAHAL (B5)	533	◆◆			IN					
TANDOORI (A3)	533	◆◆			IN		●			
TAVERNE DU CHAMP-DE-MARS (D4)	533	◆			I		●	●		
THE CARAVAN (D4)	533	◆◆			I		●			
THE CELLAR (C2)	533	◆		●	I		●			
THE GRILL (D4)	533	◆◆			F	●		●		
THE TERRACE ★ (C2)	533	◆◆		●					●	●
TIROL (A3)	533	◆	●		A		●			
WINDOWS ON THE WORLD (D3)	533	◆			I	●		●		●
YAMATO (D3)	533	◆◆					●			
THEBES										
LUXOR										
BELLA DONNA	537	◆◆			I		●			
CLASS	537	◆	●	●	I		●			
DAKKA ★	537	◆			I		●	●	●	
EL-DAWAR ★	538	◆	●	●		●			●	
EL-KARNAK	538	◆	●		I / FS	●	●			
EL-MADIRIYA ★	538	◆		●						
EL-SAKKIA	538	◆◆	●	●				●	●	
FELLAH'S TENT	538	◆◆				●			●	●
FELUCCA LUNCHES ★	538	◆	●		I	●	●			
HATY	538	◆	●	●				●		
LA MAMMA ★	538	◆◆			IT		●		●	●
LE FLAMBOYANT	538	◆◆	●		F		●			
LE MARHABA	538	◆◆		●	I	●		●		
SHEHERAZADE TERRACE ★	538	◆◆	●	●	I	●		●		
ASWAN AND NUBIA										
ASWAN										
CLUB 1902 ★	539	◆◆			I				●	●
EL-MASRY ★	540	◆		●			●	●		
LA TRATTORIA	540	◆			IT	●	●	●		
NEFERTARI ★	540	◆		●	I	●	●			
ORANGERIE	540	◆◆		●	I / IN	●	●		●	
PANORAMA	540	◆	●	●		●	●	●		

Map legend:

1 Cairo Heliopolis Mövenpick
1 El-Sarraya
1 Il Giardino
1 Le Méridien Heliopolis
1 Le Marco Polo
1 Swisshotel Cairo El-Salam
1 Aida Restaurant
1 Marquis
1 Starlight
2 Sofitel Maadi Towers
2 Le Clovis
2 Onyx & Topaz Boat

3 El-Mashrabiya
3 Il Camino Omam Rest.
3 Kan Zaman
3 Le Chalet Swissair Rest.
3 Le Château Swissair Rest.
3 Mövenpick Restaurant
3 Peace
3 Sakkura Omam Rest.
4 Paprika
5 Arabesque
6 Nile P. & Golden P. Boats
7 El-Yotti
8 Felfela
9 Silver Fish
9 Taj Mahal
10 Tajndoori
10 Tirol

2 SEAHORSE
3 CAIRO JOLIE-VILLE MÖVENPICK
3 FORTE GRAND PYRAMIDS
3 EL-WALIMA,
3 LA FARNESINA
3 MENA HOUSE OBEROI HOTEL
3 KHAN EL-KHALILI
3 MOGHUL KOOM
3 RUBAYYAT
3 OASIS HOTEL
3 PYRAMIDS PARK SOFITEL
3 SIAG PYRAMIDS HOTEL CAIRO
3 ANDREA
3 CHANDANI OMAM REST.
3 CHRISTO
3 EL-EZBA
3 EL-FANOUS OMAM REST.

11 KHAN EL-KHALILI
12 ANGUS
12 GRILL GEZIRA
12 OMAR'S CAFE
12 THE TERRACE
12 CHIN CHIN FOUR CORNERS REST.
12 DON QUICHOTTE
12 JUSTINE'S FOUR CORNERS REST.
12 LA CHARMERIE
12 LA PIAZZA FOUR CORNERS REST.
12 PRESIDENT HOTEL
12 LA TERRASSE
12 THE CELLAR
13 CAIRO RAMSES HILTON HOTEL

13 CITADEL GRILL
13 FALAFEL
13 YAMATO
13 WINDOWS ON THE WORLD
14 CAIRO SHERATON HOTEL
14 ALADIN
14 LA MAMMA
15 COSMOPOLITAN HOTEL
16 GEZIRA SHERATON HOTEL
16 DRAGON
16 KEBABGY
16 LES AMBASSADEURS GRILL
17 HELNAN SHEPHEARD HOTEL
17 ASIA HOUSE
17 RÉGENCE
17 THE CARAVAN
18 LE MÉRIDIEN CAIRO HOTEL
18 LA BRASSERIE
18 LE CHAMPOLLION
18 NUBIAN VILLAGE
19 LOTUS HOTEL
20 NILE HILTON HOTEL
20 IBIS CAFÉ
20 TAVERNE DU CHAMP-DE-MARS
21 NITOCRISSE HOTEL
21 PENSION ROMA CAIRO
22 SEMIRAMIS INTER CONTINENTAL
22 THE GRILL

KEY
Restaurants are shown in bold and hotels in plain type.

◆ Towns are shown on the map of Egypt on the front endpaper of the guide.
◆ Key addresses in Cairo are shown on the back endpaper of the guide. For hotels and restaurants see page 518–9.

GENERAL INFORMATION

INTERNATIONAL DIALING CODE
20

PRACTICAL INFORMATION

EGYPTIAN CONSULATES
◆ UK
2 Lowndes Street
London SW1X 9ET
Tel. 0171 235 9777

◆ US
1110 Second Avenue
New York, NY 10022
Tel. (212) 759 7120

◆ CANADA
454 Laurier Avenue
E. Ottawa, Ontario
K1N 6R3

◆ AUSTRALIA
125 Monaco Crescent
Red Hill
Canberra ACT 2603
Tel. 062 950 394

EGYPTIAN TOURIST OFFICES
◆ UK
EGYPTIAN STATE TOURIST OFFICE
Egyptian House
170 Piccadilly
London W1V
Tel. 0171 493 5282

◆ US
EGYPTIAN TOURIST AUTHORITY
– 630 Fifth Avenue
Suite 1706
New York, NY 10111
Tel. (212) 332 2570
– 645 Madison Avenue
Suite 829
Chicago, IL 60611
Tel. (312) 280 4666
– 83-83 Wilshire Blvd
Suite 215, Beverly Hills,
California CA 90211
Tel. (213) 653 8815

◆ CANADA
EGYPTIAN TOURIST AUTHORITY
1253 McGill College Ave
Bureau 8250, Montreal
Quebec H3B 2Y5
Tel. (514) 861 44 20
Fax (514) 861 80 71
Open Mon.–Fri.
9am–6pm

EGYPTIAN YOUTH HOSTEL ASSOCIATION (EGYPT)
1, Shari' el' Ibrahim
Cairo
Tel. 354 0527

INTERNATIONAL STUDENT HOUSE
229 Great Portland St
London W1

TRANSPORT

◆ UK
BRITISH AIRWAYS
156 Regent Street
London W1
Tel. 0181 759 2525

EGYPTAIR
29 Piccadilly
London W1V 9PF
Tel. 0171 437 6309
or 0171 580 4239

◆ US
EGYPTAIR
(New York)
Tel. (800) 334 6787
or (212) 315 0900

TWA
(New York)
Tel. (800) 221 2000

◆ EGYPT
AIR SINAI
Tel. 760948 or 770948

TOUR OPERATORS

◆ UK
DIVERS LODGE
Turney Crook Mews
11 Ivegate, Colne
Lancashire BB8 9BP
Tel. 0282 871309

THE IMAGINATIVE TRAVELLER
14 Barley Mow Passage
Chiswick, London W4 4PH
Tel. 0181 742 8612
Fax 0181 742 3045

NOUVELLES FRONTIÈRES
11 Blenheim St,
London W1Y
Tel. 0171 629 7772

TOP DECK TRAVEL
131–5 Earl's Court Rd
London SW5
Tel. 0171 370 4555

WESTERN AND ORIENTAL TRAVEL
56 Ledbury Road
London W11 2AJ
Tel. 0171 221 8677
Fax 0171 221 7808

◆ US
ARCHEOLOGICAL TOURS
271 Madison Ave.,
Suite 904
New York, NY 10016
Tel. (212) 986 3054
Fax (212) 370 1561

EGYPT TOURS
1248 South Glendale Ave
Glendale, CA 91205
Tel. (818) 549 1149
Fax (818) 549 9071

EGYPT TOURS AND TRAVEL
4353 North Harding Ave
Chicago, IL 60618
Tel. (800) 343 4978
Fax (312) 463 4001

FREEGATE TOURISM, INC.
1156 Avenue of the Americas, Suite 720
New York, NY 10036
Tel. (212) 764 1818
or (800) 223 0304
Fax (212) 764 1722

GENESIS TOURS INTERNATIONAL
424 Madison Avenue
New York, NY 10017
Tel. (800) 888 8167
Fax (212) 644 3544

MISR TRAVEL
630 Fifth Avenue
Suite 555
New York, NY 10111
Tel. (212) 582 9210
or (800) 22 EGYPT
Fax (212) 247 8142

NABILA TOURS AND CRUISES
605 Market Street
Suite 1310
San Francisco
CA 94105
Tel. (800) 443 6453
Fax (415) 979 0163

NIKI TOURS
444 North Larchmont
Boulevard, #203
Los Angeles, CA 90004
Tel. (213) 464 8427
Fax (213) 466 5631

OVERSEAS ADVENTURE TRAVEL
625 Mount Auburn St
Cambridge MA 02138
Tel. (617) 876 0533
or (800) 221 0814
Fax (617) 876 0455

SPHINX TOURS
271 Route 46 West
Suite C201, Fairfield
NJ 07004
Tel. (201) 882 9300
or (800) 53 TOURS
Fax (201) 882 2822

N.B.
◆ Necropolises and tombs are generally open 9am–5pm. Temples are open 8am–5pm and sometimes earlier in summer when it is advisable to go early in the morning to avoid the heat.
◆ Churches are technically open from 9am to 4pm.
◆ Mosques are open 8.30am–4pm, sometimes 5pm.
◆ Most tourist restaurants are air conditioned.
◆ Three-star hotels and above are all air conditioned. One- and two-star hotels may not have air conditioning.
◆ Be careful as air conditioning may cause chills. Put on additional clothing.
◆ Only four- and five-star hotels have heating, which is an advantage on cold winter nights.

◆

ALEXANDRIA

DIALING CODE
(0) 3
Map of Egypt E2

USEFUL ADDRESSES

POST OFFICE
GENERAL POST OFFICE
Shari' el-Sahafa
Tel. 493 29 95
or 494 06 37
Open 8am–2.30pm
Closed Fri.
Behind the Midan Orabi.

HOSPITALS
COPTIC HOSPITAL
Shari' Muharram Bey
Tel. 48 35 87 06
Near the Midan Gumhurriya
MEDICAL CITY HOSPITAL
Shari' Mustafa Kamel
Tel. 85 21 50

TOURIST OFFICES
MAIN TOURIST OFFICE
Midan Saad Zaghlul
Open 9am–6pm
Although incomplete, maps of the city do list the main places of interest.

⌦ VIEW		⌂ STANDARD HOTEL	⌂ QUIET	⌓ OUTDOOR DINING		
⌖ CITY CENTER		⌂ ECONOMY-CLASS HOTEL	⌓ SWIMMING POOL	⬢ LUXURY RESTAURANT		
⌦ SECLUDED		P CAR PARK/PARKING	▭ CREDIT CARDS	◑ STANDARD RESTAURANT		
⌂ LUXURY HOTEL		⛟ SUPERVISED GARAGE	✿ GARDENS, GROUNDS	○ ECONOMY RESTAURANT		

ANNEX
Central station
Midan Gumhurriya
Tel. 492 59 85
Open 9am–6pm
TOURIST INFORMATION
Harbor station
Western Harbor
Tel. 492 59 86
Open 9am–6pm
TOURIST INFORMATION
Nuzha International
Airport – Alexandria
Tel. 420 20 20
Open 8am–4pm

TOURIST POLICE
Midan Saad Zaghlul
Tel. 547 33 95
or 86 38 04
City center

BANKS, BUREAUX DE CHANGE

AMERICAN EXPRESS
26, Midan el-Hurriya
Tel. 482 30 49
Open 9am–1pm
and 5–7pm
Open Fri. and Sat.
9am–1pm
Closed Sun.

MISR BANK
9–18, Midan Tal'at Harb
Tel. 482 38 72
or 482 21 15
Closed Fri. and Sat.
*Money can be changed
using Visa.*

TRANSPORT

ALEXANDRIA INTERNATIONAL AIRPORT
Tel. 420 20 21
or 420 10 36

EGYPTAIR
SHARI' EL-HURRIYA
MIDAN GLIM
Tel. 586 54 61 or 34
Fax 586 65 36
19, MIDAN SAAD
ZAGHLUL
Ramleh Station
Tel. 483 33 57
Fax 482 41 44

STATION
Midan el-Gumhurriya
Tel. 491 31 88
At the end of the Shari'
Nabi Daniel

BUS STATIONS
MIDAN EL-GUMHURRIYA
Next to the railway
station
*Bus and communal taxi
terminal.*
MIDAN SAAD ZAGHLUL
*Super Jet bus terminal
(service to Cairo).*

CAR RENTAL

ALEX LIMOUSINE
5, MIDAN ALBERT
EL-AWAL
Tel. 422 29 99
Open 24 hours
City center
HELNAN PALESTINE
HOTEL
Muntaza Palace
Muntaza
Tel. 547 40 33
(ext. tel. Alex Lim.)
SOFITEL CECIL HOTEL
16, Midan Saad Zaghlul
Tel. 483 71 73
or 483 14 67
MUNTAZA SHERATON
HOTEL
Corniche
Tel. 548 05 50
(ext. tel. Alex Lim.)
RAMADA RENAISSANCE
HOTEL
544, Midan el-Geish
Tel. 548 39 77
or 549 09 35
(ext. tel. Alex Lim.)

AVIS
SOFITEL CECIL HOTEL
16, Midan Saad Zaghlul
Tel. 483 71 73
Open 24 hours

TOUR OPERATORS

NACOTOURS
63, Midan Nabi Daniel
Tel. 483 00 50
Fax 482 72 03
Open 9am–4pm
Near the Midan Saad
Zaghlul
*Specializing in
Mediterranean
cruises. Also offers trips
to Cairo from
Alexandria.*

CULTURE

ANFUSHI CATACOMBS
Shari' Ras el-Tin

KOM EL-SHOGAFA CATACOMBS
Shari' Abu Mansur

FRENCH CULTURAL CENTER
30, Shari' Nabi Daniel
Tel. 492 08 04
Open 9am–1pm
and 4.30–7.30pm
Library: 10am–1pm
(except Tue. am)
and 5–7pm
Closed Fri. and Sat.
*Situated in the street
running between the
Midan Gumhurriya
and the Sofitel
Cecil Hotel.*

POMPEY'S PILLAR
Shari' Awud as-Sawari

GRAECO-ROMAN MUSEUM
Shari' Gamal Abd el-
Nasser
Open daily, 9am–4pm
Closed Fri.
11.30am–1.30pm

ROMAN AMPHITHEATER
Shari' el-Emir Abd el-
Kader
Kom el-Dikka

FOR THE GOURMET

★ PASTROUDIS
39, Shari' Gamal Abd
el-Nasser
Tel. 492 96 09
In the street running
past the Graeco-Roman
Museum
*Worth a visit for its
excellent Oriental and
Western patisserie and
its unique atmosphere.*
⌂ ⌖

★ PÂTISSERIE DÉLICES
Midan Saad Zaghlul
Tel. 482 14 32
*One of Egypt's most
famous patisseries and
tearooms. Pre-1940's
atmosphere. Very good
Western and Oriental
patisserie.*
⌂ ⌖

RESTAURANTS

★ ADHURA
In a narrow street
running between the
Western Harbor and the
Abu el-Abbas mosque.
Open noon–midnight
*The tables are set out at
the end of a narrow
street which is scattered
with sawdust. This fish
store-cum-restaurant,
where customers
choose their own fish
and seafood, is an
example of the basic
"eating-house" in its
simplest form. The food
is delicious, helpings
are generous and the
prices reasonable. One
of the best restaurants
in Alexandria.
No alcohol.*
⌖ ⌓

DYNASTY
Ramada
Renaissance Hotel
544, Shari' el-Geish
Sidi Bishr
Tel. 548 39 77
Open 7–11pm
Between the city center
and El-Muntaza
*Alexandria's only
Chinese restaurant.
Pleasant, muted
atmosphere.*
⌂ ⌖ ▭

ENGLISH BRASSERIE
Plaza Hotel
394, Shari' el-Geish
Zizinia
Tel. 587 87 14
or 587 87 15
*À la carte menu and
theme buffets – fish-
seafood, Italian and
international cuisine –
in a fairly ordinary
setting.*
⌂ ⌖ ▭ P

GRILLADE
Muntaza Sheraton Hotel
Corniche, Muntaza
Tel. 548 05 50
Open 1–4pm
and 7–11pm
At the end of the
Corniche, before
El-Muntaza Park
*A terrace restaurant
on the 15th floor of
the hotel (magnificent
view). Buffet and
menu: mainly grills.*
⌦ ▭ ⌓ P

L'ENTRECÔTE
Muntaza Sheraton
Hotel
Corniche, Muntaza
Tel. 548 05 50
Open 7–11pm
*Sophisticated French
restaurant, renowned
for its excellent meat
dishes.*
⌂ ▭ P

LE CLOVIS
Mercure Romance
303, Shari' el-Geish
Saba Pasha
Tel. 587 64 29
or 587 65 08
Open noon–3pm
and 7.30–11pm
Good French restaurant.
⌂ ▭

1 YOUTH HOSTEL
2 HELNAN PALESTINE HOTEL
3 MUNTAZA SHERATON HOTEL
3 GRILLADE
3 L'ENTRECÔTE
4 SOFITEL ROMANCE EGOTEL
4 LE CLOVIS
5 RAMADA RENAISSANCE
5 DYNASTY
6 SAN GIOVANNI

1. Shatby Casino
2. El-Muaskar Beach
3. Ibrahimiya Beach
4. Cleopatra's Beach
5. Sidi Gaber Beach
6. Stanley Beach
7. Côte d'Azur
8. Glym Beach
9. Sidi Bishr Beach
10. Miami Beach
11. El-Muntaza Palace

0   3 miles

Main roads
Gardens
Main monuments
Railway station

MEDITERRANEAN

West Port   East Port

ALEXANDRIA   Shari' El-Geish   El-Nasser College   (Corniche)   El-Muntaza Park   Road to Abukir

Central Station   Shari' el-Hurriya BACOS   Sidi Bishr   MANDARA

MOHARRAM BEY   Sidi Gabir   EL-ZAHIRIYA

Mahmudiya   EL-HADRA   Zoo   Antoniadis Gardens   Airport

Lake Mariut

LE PLAT D'OR
Sofitel Cecil Hotel
16, Midan Saad Zaghlul
Ramleh Station
Tel. 483 71 73
On the Corniche
International and
Egyptian cuisine in
the fine setting of
the Sofitel Cecil
Hotel.

RANG MAHAL
Sofitel Cecil Hotel
16, Midan Saad Zaghlul
Tel. 80 70 55
Classic Indian cuisine.

RAS EL-TEEN
Landmark Hotel
163, Shari' Abd el-
Salam Aref
San Stefano
Tel. 586 78 50
or 587 78 50
Road to the right
from the Corniche
Classic fish and
seafood restaurant.

★ SAN GIOVANNI
San Giovanni Hotel
205, Shari' el-Geish
Stanley
Tel. 546 77 74 or 75
Open noon–4pm
and 8.30pm–midnight
On the Corniche after
Stanley Beach
Possibly Alexandria's
best hotel-restaurant,
offering a wide variety
of Middle-Eastern
and European dishes,
fish and seafood.
Pleasant
surroundings.

SANTA LUCIA
40, Shari' Safiya Zaghlul
Tel. 596 78 30
Open noon–3pm
and 7.30–11pm

Street leading onto the
Midan Saad Zaghlul
Good European
restaurant (a few
Egyptian dishes),
rather antiquated but
charming. Reasonable
prices.

SEA GULL
On the Agami road
Tel. 445 55 75
Open noon–4pm
and 7pm–midnight
A fish and seafood
restaurant which
looks rather like a
fortress, situated
near the sea.
Reasonable but not
exceptional.

★ TIKKA GRILL
26, Shari' el-Geish
Tel. 480 51 19
or 480 51 14
Open noon–4pm
and 8–11pm
At the end of the
Corniche before
Fort Qaitbay
An elegant restaurant in
wonderful position: huge
bay windows overlook
the harbor and Fort
Qaitbay. Fish and
seafood specialties.
Other dishes on
request. Good value.

ACCOMMODATION

EL-HARAM HOTEL ***
162, Shari' el-Geish
Tel. 546 40 59
or 39 84
Fax 546 45 78
Corniche
Very well-kept hotel
near the public
beaches. Facilities
rather limited.

★ HELNAN PALESTINE
HOTEL *****
Muntaza Palace
Muntaza
Tel. 547 35 00
Tel. and fax 547 35 00
At the end of the
Corniche
Near the beach and
surrounded by the
El-Muntaza park.
Spacious rooms with
balcony and sea view.

LANDMARK
HOTEL ****
163, Shari' Abd
el-Salam Aref
San Stefano
Tel. 588 05 00
or 586 78 50
Fax 586 05 15
Small street to the right
of the Corniche, before
the San Stefano beach
Near the city center
and the sea. Very
good service. No
private beach. Busy
in summer.

MAAMOURA
PALACE HOTEL ****
El-Maamoura
Tel. 547 31 08
or 547 33 83
On the Corniche beyond
Alexandria and El-
Muntaza in the direction
of Abukir
A little too far out and
lacking the comfort of
a large hotel (doesn't
really warrant four
stars).

MERCURE
ROMANCE ****
303, Shari' el-Geish
Saba Pasha
Tel. 587 65 08
or 587 68 04
Fax 587 05 26

Good, centrally located
hotel with nearby sports
club. All rooms are
suites (i.e. vast rooms)

★ METROPOLE
HOTEL ***
52, Shari' Saad Zaghlul
Tel. 482 14 67 or 66
Fax 482 20 40
Midan Saad Zaghlul
Charming, early 20th-
century hotel. Ideally
located for visiting the
city center. Excellent
value for money. Ask for
rooms with sea view.

MUNTAZA SHERATON
HOTEL *****
Corniche
Muntaza
Tel. 548 05 50
or 548 12 20
Fax 540 13 31
12½ miles from the
center, at the end of the
Corniche, just before
El-Muntaza Park.
Friendly atmosphere
and efficient service, but
the rooms are small and
the hotel is noisy in
summer (outside
nightclub). The beach is
across the road.

PLAZA HOTEL ****
394, Shari' el-Geish
Zizinia
Tel. 578 87 14
or 587 87 15
Fax 587 53 99
Near the city center and
the sea.

RAMADA
RENAISSANCE *****
544, Shari' el-Geish
Sidi Bishr
Tel. 548 39 77
Fax 549 76 90

1 METROPOLE HOTEL
2 SOFITEL CECIL HOTEL
2 LE PLAT D'OR
2 RANG MAHAL
3 WINDSOR HOTEL
4 ADHOURA
6 PASTROUDIS
7 PÂTISSERIE DÉLICES
8 SANTA LUCIA
9 TIKKA GRILL

On the Corniche, in the direction of Muntaza
Large, centrally located hotel (rather noisy). Good service, but the rooms are rather small. Near the beaches.
🏨 C ⌂ 🏊 P

REGENCY HOTEL ★★★
696, Corniche
Miami
Tel. 87 15 47
or 87 05 92
Fax 87 15 08
Small, very reasonably priced hotel close to the public beaches. Good value for money.
C ⌂ P

SAN GIOVANNI HOTEL ★★★
205, Shari' el-Geish
Stanley
Tel. 546 77 75
or 546 77 74
Fax 546 44 08
Corniche
Ideally located on Stanley Beach (but no private beach) and near the city center. Very popular in the evenings with the local Egyptians (good restaurant).
C 🏊 ⌂ P

SEMIRAMIS HOTEL ★★★
80, Shari' el-Geish
Tel. 483 08 24
or 482 78 37
Fax 482 68 37
Corniche

Reasonable, near the public beaches and Alexandria's main places of interest.
C 🏊

★ SOFITEL CECIL HOTEL ★★★★
16, Midan Saad Zaghlul
Tel. 483 71 73
or 483 14 67
Fax 483 64 01
Alexandria's most famous early 20th-century hotel has retained all its original charm. The rooms have been renovated and the central location is ideal.
C 🏊 ⌂

WINDSOR HOTEL ★★★★
17, Shari' el-Shohada
Tel. 480 87 00
or 480 81 23
Fax 480 90 90
Street overlooking the sea, behind the Pullman Cecil Hotel and the Midan Saad Zaghlul
All the comfort and charm of a traditional hotel, vast rooms and a friendly atmosphere.
C 🏊 ⌂

YOUTH HOSTEL
32, Shari' Port Said
Shatby
Tel. 597 54 59
In the street running parallel to the Shari' el-Geish, in the direction of El-Muntaza

SPORTS

YACHT CLUB
Shari' Sittawa Ashrin Yulyu
Tel. 80 23 66
Situated at the end of the street, near Fort Qaitbay

EL-ALAMEIN

DIALING CODE
(0) 3
Map of Egypt D3

ACCOMMODATION

AIDA BEACH ★★★★★
13½ miles west of Alexandria
Tel. (Cairo) 360 38 88
Extremely comfortable, luxury hotel overlooking the sea. Half board only.
🏨 🏠 🚪 🏊 ⌂ 🏊 P

ALAMEIN RESTHOUSE
65½ miles from Alexandria on the road to Mersa Matruh
P.O. Box 852
Tel. 430 27 85
Near the El-Alamein beaches
Typical Egyptian resthouse offering very basic but comfortable facilities.

MERSA MATRUH

DIALING CODE
(0) 3
Map of Egypt C2

USEFUL ADDRESSES

TOURIST OFFICES
Governorate Building
Tel. 94 31 92
Open summer 9am–3pm and 6–8pm
Open winter 9am–3pm

ACCOMMODATION

BEACH HOUSE HOTEL ★★★
Shari' el-Shatee
Tel. 90 20 66
or 93 59 66
Fax 93 33 19
Corniche,
Mersa Matruh
Good, but rather expensive hotel. Only has suites (large rooms). Full board.
🏠 🏊 ⌂ 🏊 P

BEAU SITE HOTEL ★★★
Shari' el-Shatti
Tel. 90 20 66
or 93 59 66
Fax 93 33 19
Via the Corniche
Ideal for a vacation. Friendly atmosphere. Rooms overlooking private beach. Often fully booked throughout the summer.
🏊 ⌂ 🏊 P

MIAMI HOTEL ★★★
Corniche
Tel. 93 58 91
Good hotel overlooking the

523

beaches, but no
private beach.
⌂ ☼ P

NEGRESCO HOTEL ★★★
Corniche
Tel. 93 44 92
or 93 44 91
*Ideal for a vacation.
Breakfast only.*
☼ ▭ ▵ P

RADI HOTEL ★★★
Corniche
Tel. 93 48 28
*Full board only.
Good value for
money.*
▱ ☼ ▭ ▵ P

REEM HOTEL ★★
Corniche
Tel. 93 36 05
Fax 93 36 08
*Clean and
reasonably priced hotel.
Full board only.*
▱ ☼ P

ROMMEL HOUSE HOTEL ★★★
Corniche
Tel. 93 54 66
*Comfortable hotel.
Good value for
money.*
⌂ ☼ P

YOUTH HOSTEL
4, Midan el-Galaa
P.O. Box 51512
Tel. 93 23 31
Sallum road.

SIDI ABD ER-RAHMAN

DIALING CODE
(0) 3
Map of Egypt D3

ACCOMMODATION

★ HOTEL EL-ALAMEIN ★★★★
Tel. 492 12 31 or 30
On the outskirts of Sidi
Abd er-Rahman in the
direction of El-Alamein
*The only hotel in Sidi
Abd er-Rahman.
Beautiful location with
chalets overlooking the
beach. Sports facilities
still rather limited.
Usually fully booked
throughout the
summer.*
⌂ ▱ ☼ P

DAMIETTA

DIALING CODE
(0) 57
Map of Egypt F2

ACCOMMODATION

HOTEL EL-MANSHY ★
5, Shari' el-Nokrashy
Tel. 32 33 08
City center
*Basic comfort. This is
the only hotel in a
town of little touristic
interest.*
C P

ISMAÏLIYA

DIALING CODE
(0) 64
Map of Egypt F3

CULTURE

ISMAÏLIYA MUSEUM
Mohammed Ali Quay
Open daily, 9am–4pm

ACCOMMODATION

MERCURE HOTEL ETAP FORSAN ISLAND ★★★★
P.O. Box 77
Tel. 33 80 40
or 33 80 41
Fax 33 80 43
On the Corniche,
in the direction of the
Suez Canal
*The only good hotel
in Ismaïliya.
Overlooking the canal.
Good restaurants,
especially L'Eugénie.
Small rooms.*
⌂ ☼ ▭ ▵ P ♨

PORT SAID

DIALING CODE
(0) 66
Map of Egypt F2

USEFUL ADDRESSES

TOURIST OFFICES
Shari' Palestine
Tel. 22 16 87
or 23 52 89

ACCOMMODATION

HELNAN PORT SAID HOTEL ★★★★★
Corniche
P.O. Box 1110
Tel. 32 08 90
or 39 08 98
Fax 32 37 62
*Port Said's only large
hotel.*
⌂ C ☼ ▭ ▵

HOLIDAY HOTEL ★★★
Shari' Gumhurriya
P.O. Box 204
Tel. 22 07 11
Near the port
*Very comfortable.
Reductions if you stay
more than 3 days.*
C ▭ P

NEW CONCORDE HOTEL ★★★
Shari' Salah Salem &
Mustafa Kamel
Tel. 23 53 42
*Good hotel. Reductions
if you stay more than 3
days.*
C P

NEW REGENT HOTEL ★★★
Shari' Gumhurriya
Tel. 22 38 02
Near the port
*Very comfortable hotel,
one of the few in Port
Said with a swimming
pool.*
C ▵ P

YOUTH HOSTEL
Shari' el-Amin –
Corniche
Tel. 22 87 02
Fax 22 64 33
Opposite the stadium.

SPORTS

YACHT CLUB
Tel. 40 05 87
Near the entrance to the
port

SUEZ

DIALING CODE
(0) 62
Map of Egypt G3

USEFUL ADDRESSES

TOURIST OFFICE
Shari' Canal
Tel. 22 35 89

CULTURE

NATIONAL MUSEUM
Shari' Palestine
Open daily,
9am–3.30pm

ACCOMMODATION

BEL AIR HOTEL ★★
1, Shari' Saad Zaghlul
Tel. 22 32 11
*Reasonably
comfortable, but clean
and moderately priced.*
C P

GREEN HOUSE HOTEL ★★★
Shari' Port Said
Tel. 22 33 30
Near the Suez Canal
*Comfortable hotel. Way
station on the Sinai
route.*
C ▭ ▵ P

RED SEA HOTEL ★★★
13, Shari' Riad
Port Tawfiq
Tel. 22 33 34 or 22 77
61
Fax 22 77 61
On the port of Suez
⌂ ▭ P

SUMMER PALACE HOTEL ★★★
Port Tawfiq
Tel. 32 19 44
*Good hotel, well
positioned on the port.*
⌂ P

YOUTH HOSTEL
Shari' el-Hurriya
P.O. 171
Tel. 22 19 45
Opposite the stadium.

TANTA

DIALING CODE
(0) 40
Map of Egypt F3

ACCOMMODATION

ARAFA HOTEL ★★★
Midan el-Mahatta
(Station Square)
First Tanta

Tel. 33 69 52
Very reasonable.
C ⊟ P

GREEN HOUSE HOTEL ★★★
Shari' el-Borsa
Midan Gumhurriya
Tel. 33 07 61
or 33 07 62
Fax 33 03 20
Very reasonable.
C ⊟ P

YOUTH HOSTEL
2, Shari' Ahmed Ali
Tel. 33 79 78

◆

SHARM EL-SHEIKH

DIALING CODE
(0) 62
Map of Egypt H5

USEFUL ADDRESSES

TOURIST OFFICE
Airport
Tel. 60 04 15

TRANSPORT

SHARM EL-SHEIKH AIRPORT
Tel. 60 04 15

EGYPTAIR
Mövenpick Hotel
Na'ama Bay
Tel. in the city 60 10 56
or 60 10 57
Fax 60 06 64

CAR RENTAL
MAX RENT-A-CAR
Main street
Tel. 60 01 40
Open 24 hours
HERTZ
Mövenpick Hotel
Tel. 60 04 59
or 60 01 00
Open 24 hours

ACCOMMODATION

CLIFF TOP HOTEL ★★★
Tel. 60 02 51
Fax 60 02 53
Tel. (Cairo):
393 03 01 (res.)
Near the hotel district

Very good value for money. No private beach.
⌂ ⊻ ⊟ P

GAFI LAND TOURIST VILLAGE ★★★
Na'ama Bay
Tel. 60 02 11 or 12
Tel. and fax 60 02 10
Hotel district, 15
minutes from the airport.
Charming hotel, lovely rooms. Very reasonably priced.
⌂ ⊻ ⊟ P

GHAZALA HOTEL ★★★★
Na'ama Bay
Tel. 60 01 50 or 56
Fax 60 01 55
Hotel district
All mod cons and sporting facilities on the Red Sea.
⌂ ⌂ ⊻ ⊟ ⊿ P

HILTON AL-FAIROUZ ★★★★★
Na'ama Bay
Tel. 60 01 40
or 60 01 37
Fax 60 10 40
or 60 10 43
Luxury hotel situated in a busy hotel area. Offers all types of watersports.

★ MARRIOTT ★★★★★
Tel. 60 01 90
Fax 60 18 57
Originally the Mövenpick, this hotel has now changed hands and recently re-opened. Magnificent hotel offering a range of watersports. Attractive rooms and reception areas. Exquisite.

MÖVENPICK SHARM EL-SHEIKH ★★★★★
Na'ama Bay
Tel. 60 01 00 or 01
Fax 60 01 11
Hotel district
The most attractive hotel in Sharm el-Sheikh and indeed on the Red Sea coast. Luxurious rooms, entertainment and a full range of sporting facilities.
⌂ ⌂ ⊻ ⊟ ⊿ P

★ NOVOTEL AQUAMARINE HOTEL ★★★★
Tel. 60 01 79
or 60 01 75
Fax 60 01 93
Hotel district
Series of chalets.

Well-situated, terrace restaurants, evening entertainment and a full range of watersports.
⌂ ⌂ ⊻ ⊟ ⊿ P ☂

TIRAN VILLAGE ★★★
Na'ama Bay
Tel. 60 02 21
Fax 60 02 20
Hotel district
Very comfortable and reasonably priced. watersports facilities. Half board only.
⌂ ⊻ ⊟ ⊿ P

YOUTH HOSTEL
B.P. 46619
Tel. 60 03 17

SPORTS

MÖVENPICK MARINA
Na'ama Bay
Tel. 60 01 00

SPORTING AND NAUTIC CLUB
Tel. 60 04 50

EL-ARISH

DIALING CODE
(0) 68
Map of Egypt H2

USEFUL ADDRESSES

TOURIST OFFICE
Shari' Fuad Zikry
Tel. 34 10 16

ACCOMMODATION

EL-ARISH OBEROI HOTEL ★★★★★
Tel. 35 13 21 or 35 13 22
Fax 35 23 52
The best hotel in El-Arish. Sports facilities. Reservations essential in summer.
⌂ ⌂ ⊻ ⊟ ⊿ P

HURGHADA

DIALING CODE
(0) 65
Map of Egypt H5

USEFUL ADDRESSES

TOURIST OFFICE
Shari' Banque-Misr
Tel. 44 05 13
Open 9am–2pm
10 mins from city center

TRANSPORT

HURGHADA AIRPORT
Tel. 44 28 31

EGYPTAIR
Tel. 44 35 94
Tel and fax 44 35 91

CAR RENTAL
HERTZ
Airport
Road to Safaga
Tel. 44 28 84 or 85
Open 24 hours

ACCOMMODATION

CORAL BEACH VILLAGE ★★★★
13½ miles along the road to Safaga
Tel. 44 21 60 or 61
Fax 44 35 77
Ideal for a vacation on the Red Sea. Full range of sports facilities.
⌂ ⌂ ⊻ ⊟ ⊿ P

★ EL-GIFTUN TOURIST VILLAGE ★★★
Tel. 44 26 67
Tel. and fax 44 26 66
Near Magawish, via the Corniche
Well-kept chalets on the beach. Full range of watersports facilities.
⌂ ⌂ ⊻ ⊟ ⊿ P

HURGHADA SHERATON HOTEL ★★★★
Tel. 44 20 00/1
Fax 44 20 33
On the Corniche
Excellent hotel, although architecturally disappointing (looks rather like a blockhouse).
⌂ ⌂ ⊻ ⊟ ⊿ P

JASMINE HOLIDAY VILLAGE ★★★
About 4 miles from Hurghada Airport
Tel. 44 24 42
or 44 24 40
Fax 44 24 41
Tel. (Cairo): 578 68 32
Good hotel near the sea with all standard Red Sea sports facilities. Half board only. Reasonably priced.
⌂ ⊻ ⊟ ⊿ P

★ MAGAWISH TOURIST VILLAGE ★★★★
Magawish
Tel. 44 26 20
or 44 26 21
Fax 44 27 59
Very comfortable chalets, dotted along the desert. Ideal vacation venue with full watersports facilities.
⌂ ⊻ ⊟ ⊿ P

MASHRABIYA VILLAGE ★★★★
Tel. 44 33 30/1
Fax 44 33 44
Ideal for a relaxing or sporting (including fishing) vacation. Children supervised.
🏠 ⛴ ☐ 🅿

MOON VALLEY HOTEL★★
On the road to the Sheraton
Tel. 44 28 11
Fax 44 38 30
Small hotel with watersports facilities. Very reasonable rooms. Half board only.
🏠 ⛴ ☐ 🅿

SONESTA BEACH RESORT HURGHADA ★★★★
P.O. Box 18
Tel. 44 36 60
or 44 36 62
Fax 44 36 61
Hurghada's top luxury hotel. Magnificent rooms and a full range of watersports (fishing, diving, windsurfing) activities. Half board.
🏠 ⛴ ☐ 🅿

SPORTS

YACHT CLUB
Tel. 44 29 74

NUWEIBA

DIALING CODE
(0) 62
Map of Egypt H4

ACCOMMODATION

BAWAKI BEACH HOTEL ★★★
11¼ miles from Nuweiba
Tel. 50 04 70
Fax 50 04 71
On the road to Taba Excellent hotel. Well-equipped for water sports and good value for money. Half board.
🏠 ⛴ ☐ 🅿

EL-SALAM VILLAGE ★★
Hotel district
Tel. 50 04 41
Pleasant vacation village. Well equipped and reasonably priced.
🏠 ⛴ ☐ 🅿

★ EL-SAYADEEN TOURISTIC VILLAGE ★★★
Hotel district
Tel. 52 03 18
Lovely vacation village. Recently built, comfortable and a full range of sports facilities.
🏠 ⛴ ☐ 🅿

EL-WAHA TOURISTIC VILLAGE ★★
Hotel district
Tel. 50 04 20
Fax to Cairo:
385 59 86
Well-equipped vacation village. Excellent value for money.
🏠 ⛴

HILTON CORAL HOTEL ★★★★
Tel. 52 03 20
Hotel district
The best hotel in Nuweiba (and the most expensive). Recently built, extremely comfortable and a full range of watersports facilities.
🏠 ⛴ ☐ 🅿 ⚑

NUWEIBA HOLIDAY VILLAGE ★★★
Hotel district
Tel. 50 04 02
Fax 392 22 28
Comfortable chalets. Full watersports facilities.
🏠 ⛴ ☐ 🅿

SALLY LAND TOURIST VILLAGE ★★
Tel. 53 03 80
Between Nuweiba and Taba
Small, clean and fairly comfortable chalets. watersports facilities.
🏠 ☐– ⛴ 🅿

SPORTS

HARBOR AUTHORITIES
Tel. 52 00 05
No yacht club. To berth, apply to the harbor authorities.

PORT SAFAGA

DIALING CODE
(0) 65
Map of Egypt H6

ACCOMMODATION

MENAVILLE VILLAGE ★★★★
Tel. 45 17 61
fax 45 17 64
Hotel district
Luxury vacation village in a relatively undeveloped region. A full range of sports facilities and marina. Half board.
🏠 ⛴ ☐ 🅿

SAFAGA PARADISE VILLAGE ★★★★
Tel. 45 16 33/4
Fax 45 16 30
Hotel district
Very comfortable hotel, ideal for a vacation in a relatively undeveloped tourist region. Half board compulsory.

SHAMS SAFAGA VILLAGE ★★★★
Tel. 45 17 83 or 45 17 82
Fax 45 17 80
Hotel district
Ideal for family vacations. General comfort and standard Red Sea activities.
🏠 ⛴ ☐ 🅿

SPORTS

YACHT CLUB
Menaville Village
Tel. 45 17 61
Berths available in the Menaville Village marina.

ST CATHERINE

DIALING CODE
(0) 62
Map of Egypt H4

ACCOMMODATION

DANIELA VILLAGE ★★★
Tel. 47 03 79 or
(Cairo): 348 26 71 (res.)
The second of

St Catherine's hotels. Lacks comfort but clean and reasonable. Half board only.
🏠 ☐

ST CATHERINE TOURIST VILLAGE ★★★★
Wadi el-Raha
Tel. 47 03 33
Fax 47 03 23
Tel. (Cairo) 356 45 65
Fax 356 40 05
Attractive, comfortable chalets scattered over a wide area. Dominated by the hillside restaurant. No alcohol.
🏠 ☐– ☐ 🅿

TABA

DIALING CODE
(0) 62
Map of Egypt H4

ACCOMMODATION

HOTEL HILTON TABA ★★★★★
Taba Beach
Tel. 53 01 40
Tel. (Cairo) 578 03 22
Extremely comfortable, luxury hotel offering watersports facilities. Near the Israeli border.
🏠 ☐– ⛴ ☐ 🅿

DAKHLA

DIALING CODE
(0) 88
Map of Egypt D7

USEFUL ADDRESSES

TOURIST OFFICES
Tel. 94 04 07

KHARGA

DIALING CODE
(0) 88
Map of Egypt E7

USEFUL ADDRESSES

POLICE STATION
ADMINISTRATION
El-Wadi el-Guedid
Tel. 90 08 33 or
90 04 50

Tourist service.
TOURIST POLICE
Kharga Airport
New Valley
Tel. 90 15 02

TOURIST OFFICE
Governorate Building
New Valley
Tel. 90 12 05 or 06
(Difficult to obtain
connection.)

TRANSPORT

KHARGA AIRPORT
New Valley
Tel. 90 04 57

ACCOMMODATION

BARIS RESTHOUSE
Tel. 90 19 11
*One of the few
resthouses in Egypt.
Difficult to obtain
telephone link from
Cairo.*

**BULAQ TOURIST
RESTHOUSE**
Bir Bulaq
Tel. 90 16 11
See Baris Resthouse.

**EL-WADI EL-GUEDID
TOURIST RESTHOUSES**
Kharga Oasis
Tel. 90 07 28
*"Head-quarters" of
the Libyan Desert
resthouses. The
telephone number
(information and
reservations) is difficult
to obtain. Telephone
links in the region are
poor.*

CAIRO

DIALING CODE
(0) 2
Map of Egypt F3

USEFUL ADDRESSES

POST OFFICE
GENERAL POST OFFICE
Midan Ataba (G3)
Tel. 391 01 06
Open 8am–7pm
Closed Fri.
Behind the Midan Opera

POLICE STATION
MUGAMAA
Midan at-Tahrir (E4)
Tel. 354 37 61
Open daily,
7.30am–1pm
*Visitors should register
their passport within
seven days of their
arrival (if not they will be
fined £E 30 as they
leave the country). For
visitors not staying in a
hotel, this can be done
at the Mugamaa. Hotels
are required to
complete these
formalities for tourists
(in theory the service is
free although some
hotels make a modest
charge of £E 1). Should
you lose your passport
contact either your
consulate or the
Mugamaa, which also
deals with visa
extensions.*

TOURIST OFFICES
Main tourist office
Misr Travel Tower
(tall blue and white
tower)
Midan Abbassiya
Tel. 82 35 10
Fax 23 08 22
Open 9am–3pm
*Provides the same
information as other
Egyptian tourist offices.*
TOURIST INFORMATION
5, Midan Adli (F3)
Tel. 391 34 54
or 394 34 54
Open 9am–2pm
Closed Fri.
Near the Midan Opera.
*A few maps of Cairo
and tourist brochures
on various Egyptian
regions.*
RAMESSES STATION
Midan Ramesses
Tel. 76 42 14
Open 9am–6pm
CAIRO INTERNATIONAL
AIRPORT
Terminal 1
Tel. 66 74 75
or 291 42 55
Open 8am–4pm
Terminal 2
Tel. 291 42 77
(ext. tel. 2223)
or 291 42 88
(ext. tel. 2224)
Open 8am–4pm

TOURIST POLICE
EGYPTIAN MUSEUM
Midan at-Tahrir (E4)
Tel. 354 43 19
RAMESSES STATION
Midan Ramesses
Tel. 575 35 55

CAIRO INTERNATIONAL
AIRPORT
Tel. 96 20 28
5, MIDAN ADLI
Next to the Tourist office
Tel. 126

BANKS, BUREAUX
DE CHANGE

**AMERICAN
EXPRESS**
15, Shari' Qasr el-Nil
Tel. 574 79 91
or 574 79 92
Closed Fri.–Sat.
Between the Midan at-
Tahrir and Tal'at Harb
(E4)
*Money can be changed
using American
Express. Also possible
to withdraw dollars
using the same card
and travelers' checks.*

B.N.P.
4, Shari' Amrika el-
Latiniya
Garden City (D5)
Tel. 354 15 34
Closed Fri.–Sat.
Behind the
Semiramis
Intercontinental.

MISR BANK
Annex of the Nile Hilton
Midan at-Tahrir (D4)
Closed Fri.–Sat.
*Money can be changed
using Visa. Lengthy
procedure – allow at
least 1 hour.*

HOSPITALS

**ANGLO-AMERICAN
HOSPITAL**
Cairo Tower – Gezira
Tel. 340 61 62
Kubri at-Tahrir (C4)

**EL-SALAM
HOSPITAL**
3, Shari' el-Suriya
Mohandissine
Tel. 302 90 91
Street leading onto the
Gamaat el-Doual el-
Arabiya (Mohandissine)

HELIOPOLIS HOSPITAL
Shari' Hegaz
Heliopolis
Tel. 243 31 85
Between the airport and
the Swisshotel Cairo
el-Salam Hotel

**MISR INTERNATIONAL
HOSPITAL**
Midan Fini
Doqqi (D4)
Tel. 349 40 05
or 371 65 55
At the end of the Shari'
Fini, on the right after
the Midan Galaa.

NILE BADRAWI
Tel. 363 86 88
or 363 81 68
(ambulance)
Corniche, just before
you get to Maadi.

**QASR EL-AINI
HOSPITAL**
Roda Island (C6)
Tel. 362 93 90

At the north end of the
island, on the Corniche,
heading south toward
the Kubri Manyal

TRANSPORT

**CAIRO INTERNATIONAL
AIRPORT**
Heliopolis
Tel. 291 42 55
or 243 69 59
Fax 291 42 88
Lost luggage:
Tel. 291 42 89

**EAST DELTA BUS
COMPANY**
Midan Abbassiya
Tel. 76 22 93
Terminal for Sinai.

**EGYPTIAN COMPANY
FOR NAVIGATION**
20, Midan Tal'at Harb
Tel. 574 68 36 or 57 55

RAMESSES STATION
Midan Ramesses
Tel. 147 or 575 35 55
(information)

BUS STATIONS
MIDAN AHMED HELMI
Behind Ramesses
Station
*Bus and communal
taxi terminal
(northbound).*
MIDAN GIZA
Under the Kubri Giza
*Bus and communal
taxi terminal
(southbound).*

SUPER JET
Midan at-Tahrir
Tel. 77 26 63
*Buses for Alexandria
and Port Said.*

**UPPER EGYPT BUS
COMPANY**
MIDAN AHMED HELMI
Tel. 574 66 58
Behind Ramesses
Station
MIDAN AL-TAHRIR
Tel. 76 02 61
*For Upper Egypt and
the oases.*

**WEST DELTA BUS
COMPANY**
MIDAN AHMED HELMI
Tel. 76 55 82
*For Alexandria and
the Delta towns.*

AIRLINE COMPANIES

AIR FRANCE
2, MIDAN TAL'AT HARB
Tel. 574 33 00
or 574 34 79
CAIRO INTERNATIONAL
AIRPORT
Tel. 417 53 06
or 417 53 07

AIR SINAI
ANNEX OF THE NILE
HILTON HOTEL
Corniche
Midan at-Tahrir
Tel. 578 03 22
or 578 03 23
*Operates the only flights
between Cairo and
Tel Aviv.*

EGYPTAIR
ANNEX OF THE NILE
HILTON HOTEL
Corniche
Midan at-Tahrir
Tel. 77 24 10
or 77 27 89
CAIRO AIRPORT
Tel. 291 18 30
12, SHARI' TAL'AT HARB
Tel. 392 28 35
Fax 76 27 44

SWISSAIR
CAIRO INTERNATIONAL
AIRPORT
Tel. 291 02 83
22, SHARI' QASR EL-NIL
Tel. 393 79 55

TOUR OPERATORS

*All tour operators listed
have representatives in
the main tourist towns.*

ABERCROMBY & KENT
5, Shari' Bustan
Midan at-Tahrir
Tel. 393 62 55
Fax 391 51 79
Open 9am–3pm
Closed Fri.
*Excellent organization.
Luxury boats.*

BENU TRAVEL
6a, Shari' Liban
El-Egez Tower
Mohandissine
Tel. 346 34 49
*Agent for the Israeli bus
company Galilee Tours.*

EASTMAR
13, Shari' Qasr el-Nil
Tel. 574 50 34 or 24
Fax 76 93 60/574 34 82
Open 9am–3pm
Closed Fri.
Near the Midan Tal'at
Harb
*One of the oldest
agencies in Egypt.
Excellent service.*

EMECO TRAVEL
2, Shari' Tal'at Harb
Tel. 390 70 45
Fax 574 42 12
Open 9am–4pm
Closed Fri.
At the end of the Shari'
Tal'at Harb, in the
direction of Midan at-
Tahrir
*A very good agency.
Ask for M. Georges
Faouzi (renowned for
his efficiency).*

ETAMS TRAVEL
13, Shari' Qasr el-Nil
Tel. 575 47 21
Fax 574 14 91
Open 9am–3pm
Closed Fri.
*Specializes in vacations
for the physically
handicapped.*

HAPI TRAVEL
17, Shari' Qasr el-Nil
Tel. 393 35 62
Fax 393 93 62
Open 9am–3pm
Closed Fri.
Near the Midan
at-Tahrir

JET ARROW TRAVEL
12, Shari' Mahmud
Bassiwni
Tel. 575 80 70
Fax 76 03 05
Open 9am–3pm
Closed Fri.
Street leading onto the
Midan at-Tahrir and the
Midan Tal'at Harb
*This agency deals
mainly with bus travel,
offering bus rental to
large groups.*

MEMNON TOURS
10, Shari' Hoda
Shaarawi
Tel. 393 01 95
Fax 391 74 10
Open 9am–3pm
Closed Fri.

**MISR SINAI/
YOUSSEF EL GUINDY
TOURIST CO**
Bab el Louk
Tel. 356 40 11
Tel. & fax 356 40 05
Open 9am–3pm
*Subsidiary of Misr
Travel, specializing in
travel and vacations in
Sinai.*

MISR TRAVEL
1, Shari' Tal'at Harb
Tel. 393 00 10
Fax 390 31 77
Open 9am–4pm
Closed Fri.
Near the Midan Tal'at
Harb
*Government agency
with branches
throughout Egypt
(often combined with
Egyptair).*

MISR TRAVEL TOWER
Midan Abbassiya
Tel. 283 20 85
Fax 284 35 25
Open 9am–3pm
Tall tower dominating
the Midan Abbassiya
*Misr Travel's second
main office in Cairo.
Also houses the tourist
office.*

P.N.C. TRAVEL
13, Shari' Maraashli
Zamalek
Tel. 341 19 60 or 28 40
Fax 340 67 80
Open 9am–3pm
Closed Fri.

PAN ARAB TOURS
55, Shari' Gumhurriya
Tel. 590 21 33
Fax 362 09 71
Open 9am–3pm
Closed Fri.
Near the Midan Opera

*This company
specializes in adventure
tours (oases and
deserts).*

PYRAMIDS TOURS
56, Gaamiat el-Doual
el-Arabiya
Mohandissine
Tel. 360 01 46
Fax 360 43 99
Open 9am–3pm
Closed Fri.

SIAG TRAVEL
Road to Saqqara
P.O. Box 107
Arham – Giza
Tel. 383 14 44
Fax 384 08 74
Open 9am–3pm
Closed Fri.
At the Cairo end of the
road to Saqqara, near
the Siag Pyramids Hotel
Cairo
*Specializes in adventure
tours in the Western
Oases, Sinai and the
Arabian Desert.
Organizers of the
Pharaoh's Rally.*

**THOMAS COOK
TRAVEL**
17, Shari' Mahoud
Bassiouny
Tel. 574 39 55
or 574 37 76
Fax 76 27 50
*Good quality service.
Branches throughout
Egypt. One of the best
tour operators in the
country.*

TRAVCO
112, Shari' Sittawa
Ashrin Yulyu (26 July)
Tel. and fax 342 04 88
Open 9am–3pm
Closed Fri.
Center of Gezira
Island
*Extremely efficient
agency. Excellent
buses, boats and
services.*

WAGONLIT TRAVEL
2, Shari' Ibrahim el-
Lakani Roxy
Tel. 257 42 97 or 98
Fax 258 74 90
Open 9am–3pm
Closed Fri.
Old town of Heliopolis
*Excellent agency.
Customers can be
sure of a first-class
"after-sales service"
throughout their stay
in Egypt. M. Mohamed
Leheta is permanently
at the service of his
"guests".*

CAR RENTAL

AVIS

CAIRO INTERNATIONAL
AIRPORT
Tel : 291 42 66
LE MÉRIDIEN CAIRO
HOTEL
Tel. 98 94 00
or 362 17 17
NILE HILTON HOTEL
Tel. 578 04 44
(ext. tel. Avis)

BUDGET

CAIRO INTERNATIONAL
AIRPORT
Tel. 291 42 55 or 66
(ext. tel. Budget)
CAIRO RAMSES
HILTON HOTEL
Tel. 575 49 99
(ext. tel. Budget)
NILE HILTON HOTEL
Tel. 578 04 44
(ext. tel. Budget)
SEMIRAMIS
INTERCONTINENTAL
Tel. 355 71 71
(ext. tel. Budget)

EUROPCAR

CAIRO INTERNATIONAL
AIRPORT
Tel. 291 42 55 or 66
(ext. tel. Europcar)
27, SHARI' LIBAN-
HOHANDISSIMEI
Tel. 347 47 12
Open 24 hours
Between the
Midan at-Tahrir and
the Midan Tal'at
Harb

HERTZ

CAIRO INTERNATIONAL
AIRPORT
Tel. 291 42 55 or 66
(ext. tel. Hertz)
CAIRO RAMSES
HILTON HOTEL
Tel. 575 49 99
(ext. tel. Hertz)
FORTE GRAND
PYRAMIDS HOTEL
Tel. 383 03 83
(ext. tel. Hertz)
SEMIRAMIS
INTERCONTONENTAL
Tel. 355 71 71
(ext. tel. Hertz)
SONESTA HOTEL
Tel. 262 81 11
or 262 82 61
(ext. tel. Hertz)

LIMOUSINE MISR

CAIRO INTERNATIONAL
AIRPORT
Tel. 418 96 75
or 418 96 76
CAIRO RAMSES
HILTON HOTEL
Tel. 575 80 00
(ext. tel. 29 33)

SÉMIRAMIS INTERCONTINENTAL

Tel. 355 71 71
(ext. tel. 89 89)
Open 24 hours
*Luxury Car rental.
Large chauffeur-driven
vehicles only.
Chauffeurs speak
English and
occasionally French.
Expensive.*

MAX RENT-A-CAR EUROPCAR

CAIRO INTERNATIONAL
AIRPORT
Tel. 265 22 12
(ext. tel. 2212)
27, SHARI' LIBAN
Mohandissine
Tel. 347 47 12
Open 24 hours
*One of the few four-
wheel drive agencies.*

RAWAS LIMOUSINE

EL-GEZIRA
SHERATON HOTEL
Tel. 341 13 33 or 15 55
(ext. tel. Rawas)
CAIRO SHERATON HOTEL
Tel. 336 98 00
or 336 97 00
(ext. tel. Rawas)

CULTURE

BARQUQ MAUSOLEUM

Shari' el-Sultan Ahmed
City of the Dead (I2)

BARQUQ MEDERSA

Shari' el-Muizz li-Din-
Allah

BEIT AS-SUHAYMI

19, Shari' Darb el-Asfar

BESHTAK PALACE

Shari' el-Muizz li-Din-
Allah

CAIRO (EGYPTIAN) MUSEUM

Shari' Mariette
Midan at-Tahrir (D3)
Open daily, 9am–5pm
Closed Fri. 11.15am–
1.30pm

CAIRO OPERA HOUSE

Shari' Tahrir (C4)
Shari' Mahmud Moukhtar
Tel. 341 29 26
Gezira Island, after the
Kubri at-Tahrir
*Dancing, singing and
music from all over the
world. Reservations
essential.*

CITADEL

Shari' Sikkat el-Maghar
and Shari' Tariq Salah
Salem (H6)

Open daily, 9am–5pm
Museums close at 4pm

COPTIC MUSEUM

Shari' Mari Girgis
Old Cairo
Open daily, 9am–4pm
Closed Fri. 11am–1pm

EL-AZHAR MOSQUE

Shari' el-Azhar (I4)
Ghuriya
Open daily, 9am–7pm
Closed Fri. 11am–1pm

EL-HAKIM MOSQUE

Shari' el-Muizz li-Din-
Allah

EL-MARIDANI MOSQUE

Shari' Tabbana

EL-MU'AYYAD MOSQUE

Shari' el-Muizz li-Din-
Allah

GAYER-ANDERSON MUSEUM

Shari' Tulan (G7)
Open daily, 8am–4pm
Closed Fri. noon–1pm

IBN TULUN MOSQUE

Shari' el-Khudayri (G7)

IMAM AS-SHAFI'I MAUSOLEUM

Shari' Imam as-Shafi'i
(H10)

MANYAL PALACE

Roda Island (north) (D7)
Open daily, 9am–4pm

MOVIE THEATERS

LIDO
Shari' Emad el-Din
Tel. 93 42 84
Near Midan Orabi
METRO
Shari' Tal'at Harb (E3)
Qasr el-Nil district
Tel. 393 75 66
MIAMI
Shari' Tal'at Harb (E3)
Qasr el-Nil district
Tel. 74 56 56
PIGALLE
Shari' Emad el-Din
Tel. 93 85 94
Near Midan Orabi
QASR EL-NIL
Shari' Qasr el-Nil (E3)
Tel. 575 07 61
Before Midan at-Tahrir
RADIO
Shari' Tal'at Harb (E3)
Qasr el-Nil district
Tel. 574 60 99
RIVOLI
Shari' Sittawa Ashrin
Yulyu (26 July) (E2)
Tel. 578 50 95
Near Midan Orabi
TAHRIR
Shari' Tahrir (D4)

Tel. 335 47 26
Near Midan at-Tahrir
EL-NIL MOVIE STUDIO
Arts Center
Avenue of the Pyramids
Tel. 85 32 20
Street on the left at the
end of the Avenue of
the Pyramids
*Most famous studio in
Cairo. No guided tours.*

MUKHTAR MUSEUM

Shari' Tahrir (B5)
Open 10am–1pm
and 5–9pm
Closed Mon.

MUSEUM OF ISLAMIC ART

Shari' Port Said
Muski (G4)
Open daily, 9am–4pm
Closed Fri. 11am–1pm

QAITBAY MAUSOLEUM

Shari' Bab el-Wazir
City of the Dead (H5)

QALA'UN MAUSOLEUM

Shari' el-Muizz li-Din-
Allah
Open daily, 9am–6pm

QIJMAS EL-ISHAQI MOSQUE

Shari' Darb el-Ahmar
Ghuriya

SULTAN HASSAN MOSQUE

Shari' el-Qalaa
(Mohammed Ali) (H6)
Open daily, 8am–5pm
(6pm in summer)
Closed on Fridays for
midday prayer

FOR THE GOURMET

★ GROPPI

Midan Tal'at Harb (E3)
Open 9am–10pm
*Before the Revolution,
Groppi's was a famous
meeting place for
Cairene intellectuals.
Today it is rather old
fashioned but has
retained its original
charm. A haven of
peace in the city center.
Specialty: dates stuffed
with chocolate.
Excellent croissants.*
⌂ ▣

KOUEDER

42, Shari' Tal'at Harb
(E3)
Open 10am–9pm
*Famous city-center
patisserie offering a
wide selection of
Western and Oriental
confectionery:*

basbussa, konafa, bakhlava, lukums (Turkish delight). Customers eat standing up.
🅲

PATISSERIE EL'ABD
Shari' Tal'at Harb
Next to the French Consulate
Excellent Egyptian specialties at reasonable prices. Take away or eat at the counter.

RESTAURANTS

★ AIDA RESTAURANT
Swisshotel Cairo el-Salam Hotel
Shari' Abd el-Hamid Badawi
Heliopolis
Tel. 297 40 00
Open 7.30–11.30pm
In the superb setting of this classic hotel, French haute-cuisine and excellent value for money.
🏠 🍴 🖵 🍲 🅿

ALADIN
Cairo Sheraton Hotel
Midan Galaa
Doqqi – Giza (B5)
Tel. 336 98 00
or 336 97 00
Open 12.30–4pm and 8pm–1am
Good quality Lebanese and Middle-Eastern cuisine. Evening entertainment (music, dancing).
🅲 🖵

ANDREA
On the Suez Canal road
The Pyramids
Tel. 383 11 33
Open 11am–11pm
Opposite the road to Saqqara, at the end of Avenue of the Pyramids. Egyptian food. Excellent chicken grilled with herbs. Simple and inexpensive.
🏠 🖵 🅿 🍶 ♠

ANGUS
34, Shari' Yehia Ibrahim
Zamalek (C2)
Tel. 341 13 21
Open 7–11pm
*Via the Kubri Sittawa Ashrin Yulyu (26 July Bridge)
Friendly atmosphere. "English drawing room" setting with equestrian prints and paintings. Very small (reservations*

essential). Mainly charcoal grills. Good desserts (whisky icecream).
🏠 🖵

★ ARABESQUE
6, Shari' Qasr el-Nil (E4)
Tel. 578 88 96
or 575 98 96
Open noon–3pm and 7–11pm
*At the end of the street before you get to the Midan at-Tahrir.
One of Cairo's best Egyptian restaurants. Delightful Oriental décor (mashrabiya work, copper and brass).*
🏠 🅲 🖵

★ ASIA HOUSE
Helnan Shepheard Hotel
Corniche
Garden City (D4)
Tel. 355 38 00
or 355 39 00
Open noon–3.30pm and 7–11pm
Excellent Indian and Chinese cuisine in a superb setting (interior fountain, Mogul-style décor).
🏠 🅲 🖵

BAALBAK
Sonesta Hotel
4, Shari' el-Tayaran
Medinet Nasr
Tel. 262 81 11
Open 7–11pm
Lebanese restaurant with evening entertainment.
🖵 🅿

**CHIN CHIN
(FOUR CORNERS RESTAURANTS)**
4, Shari' Hassan Sabri
Zamalek (C2)
Tel. 341 29 61
or 340 75 10
Open 7–11pm
*Zamalek Island
Delicious Chinese food in very pleasant surroundings.*
🏠 🅲 🖵

CHRISTO
Avenue of the Pyramids
Tel. 387 35 82
Open noon–midnight
*On the corner of the Avenue of the Pyramids, (far end) and the desert road to Alexandria.
Very simple setting with a terrace overlooking the Pyramid of Khufu. Grilled fish and*

seafood restaurant. Excellent value for money.
☀ 🖵 🅿

CIAO ITALIA
Gezira Sheraton Hotel
Gezira Island (C5)
P.O. Box 264
Orman–Giza
Tel. 341 13 33
or 341 15 55
Open 7pm–midnight
*Southern tip of Gezira Island
Tiny, traditional Italian restaurant (reservations essential) overlooking the Nile. Extremely good but service tends to be slow.*
🏠 ☀ 🖵 🍲 🅿

CITADEL GRILL
Cairo Ramses Hilton Hotel
1115, Corniche
Maspero (D3)
Tel. 575 49 99
Open 7–11.30pm
Meat a specialty. Enormous (imported) steaks but also offers a few seafood dishes.
🏠 🅲 🖵 🍲

**DA MARIO
NILE HILTON**
Corniche
Midan at-Tahrir
Tel. 578 04 44
or 578 06 66
Open noon–2am
Small Italian restaurant. Good, traditional cuisine. Quick service. Evening entertainment after 8pm.
🅲 🖵 🍲

DARNA
Sofitel Maadi
Towers Hotel
29, Corniche Maadi
Tel. 350 60 92
or 350 60 93
Open 7–11.30pm
Good Oriental restaurant.
🏠 🖵 🅿

★ DON QUICHOTTE
9, Shari' Ahmed Heshmet Zamalek (C2)
Tel. 340 65 15
Open 7–11pm
*Behind the Algerian Embassy
Small, friendly restaurant. Very good international cuisine. Particularly delicious fish dishes (reservations essential).*
🏠 🖵

★ DRAGON
Gezira Sheraton Hotel
Gezira Island (C5) .
P.O. Box 264
Orman–Giza
Tel. 341 13 33
or 341 15 55
Open 7pm–midnight
Small, basic restaurant overlooking the Nile. Excellent Chinese cuisne, including a particularly delicious grilled Mediterranean prawn dish.
🏠 ☀ 🖵 🍲 🅿

EL-EZBA
On the main Saqqara road
Tel. 384 03 08
Open noon–3.30pm and 7.30–11pm
Generous helpings of inexpensive Egyptian food in a delightful setting: typical interior of an Upper-Egyptian house. Large garden with animals. This country restaurant is a popular lunchtime venue with groups.
🏠 🍴 ☀ 🅿 🍶 ♠

**EL-FANUS
(OMAM RESTAURANTS)**
5, Wissa Wassef
Omam Tower
Giza
Tel. 570 12 26
Open 7pm–midnight
For those who like couscous. Cairo's best Moroccan restaurant in a magnificent setting. No alcohol.
🏠 🅲 🖵 🅿

★ EL-MASHRABIYA
4, Shari' Ahmed Nessim
Giza
Tel. 348 35 01 or 28 01
Open noon–3pm and 7.30–11pm
*Small street on the right, just before the Saudi Embassy
Excellent Egyptian restaurant in a simple setting. Good value for money.*
🏠 🅲 🖵

EL-NILE RÔTISSERIE
Nile Hilton Hotel
Corniche
Midan at-Tahrir
Tel. 578 04 44 or 06 66
Open 12.30–3.30pm and 7–11.30pm
Luxury restaurant overlooking the Nile, but an unfriendly (verging on unpleasant)

atmosphere. Special
business lunches.
🅲 ⤳ 🖵 ⤳

EL-SARRAYA
Cairo Heliopolis
Mövenpick
Airport road
Heliopolis
Tel. 247 00 77
or 291 94 00
Open 6pm–midnight
*Specialties: fish and
seafood. Luxurious
décor.*
🖻 🖵 ⤳ 🅿

★ **EL-WALIMA**
Forte Grand
Pyramids Hotel
P.O. Box 25
The Pyramids
Tel. 383 03 83
or 383 07 72
Open 7.30pm–midnight
Desert road to
Alexandria
*Excellent Lebanese
restaurant, still relatively
unknown. Beautiful
décor and very friendly
service.*
🖻 🖵 🅿

EL-YOTTI
44, Mohy el-Din Abu
el-Ezz
Mohandissine (A5)
Tel. 349 49 44
Open 12.30–3pm
and 7–11.30pm
At the end of the Shari'
Tahrir, on the right
before the Shari' Sudan
*Popular restaurant in
a pleasant setting.
Good Egyptian and
international cuisine.*
🖵

★ **FALAFEL**
Cairo Ramses Hilton
Hotel
1115, Corniche
Maspero (D3)
Tel. 575 49 99
Open 8pm–midnight
*An excellent setting in
which to enjoy Egyptian
food. Two cabarets
every evening
(Egyptian dancing,
belly dancing) at 8pm
and midnight.
Very pleasant
atmosphere.*
🅲 🖵 🅿

★ **FELFELA**
15, Midan Huda
Shaarawi (D4)
Tel. 392 27 51
Open 11am–1am
Near the Midan Tal'at
Harb, opposite Air
France
*One of the most
famous restaurants in
Cairo. Inexpensive
Egyptian cuisine (good
mezzeh and pigeons)
served in an amazing
setting: an Aladdin's
cave of wood paneling,
ceiling fans, naive
paintings. Busy.*
🅲

GRILL GEZIRA
Cairo Marriott Hotel
Shari' Saraya el-Gezira
Zamalek (C2)
Tel. 340 88 88
Open 7–11pm
*Luxury restaurant
serving excellent meat
dishes.*
🖵 🅿

IBIS CAFÉ
Nile Hilton Hotel
Corniche
Midan at-Tahrir (D4)
Tel. 578 04 44 or 06 66
Open 24 hours
*Modest menu and
international buffets at
reasonable prices. Near
the museum – ideal for
a late lunch after a long
visit.*
🅲 🖵 ⤳

★ **IL CAMINO
(OMAM RESTAURANTS)**
5, Shari' Wissa Wassef
Giza
Tel. 570 12 26
Open 7pm–midnight
Omam Tower
*Italian atmosphere, very
good cuisine. No
alcohol,*
🖻 🅲 🖵 🅿

★ **IL GIARDINO**
Cairo Heliopolis
Mövenpick
Tel. 247 00 77
or 291 94 00
Open 9am–1am
*Italian restaurant
(amazing
icecreams)*

on the edge of the
Mövenpick swimming
pool. Barbecues Thur.,
Fri. and Sun.
🖻 🖵 🅿 ⤳ 🍴

IL GIARDINO
Cairo Jolie-Ville
Mövenpick Hotel
P.O. Box 1
Giza
Tel. 385 25 55
or 385 26 66
Open 9am–midnight
Desert road to
Alexandria
*Italian restaurant on the
edge of the swimming
pool. Menu not very
imaginative. Good
bar.*
🖻 🖵 ⤳ 🅿 🍴

ITALIANO
Helnan
Shepheard Hotel
Corniche
Garden City (D4)
Tel. 355 38 00
or 355 39 00
Open noon–midnight
*Small, unpretentious
Italian restaurant. Very
reasonable.*
🖻 🅲 🖵

★ **JUSTINE'S
(FOUR CORNERS
RESTAURANTS)**
Le Méridien Hotel
4, Shari' Hassan Sabri
Zamalek (C2)
Tel. 341 29 61
or 340 75 10
Open 7pm–midnight
On the right after the
Kubri Sitta Uktubir
(6 October Bridge)
*Luxury French
restaurant – one of the
best in Cairo. Setting on
a par with the cuisine.*
🖻 ⤳ 🖵 🅿

★ **KAN ZAMAN**
Main Saqqara road
Tel. 385 06 44
Open noon–3pm
and 8–11pm
*The restaurant is next
to a famous art gallery
and was decorated by
various Cairene artists.
Good Egyptian cuisine
with evening
entertainment.*
🖻 🖵· 🅿 🎵

★ **KEBABGY**
Gezira
Sheraton Hotel (C5)
P.O. Box 264
Gezira Island
Orman-Giza
Tel. 341 13 33
or 341 15 55

Open noon 3.30pm
and 7pm–midnight
*Ideally located on the
Nile, with a delightful
Egyptian décor. One of
the best restaurants in
Cairo for Egyptian
cuisine.*
🖻 ⤳ 🖵 ⤳ 🅿 🍴

★ **KHAN EL-KHALILI**
5, Shari' ol Badistan
Lane, Khan el-Khalili
Bazaar (H3)
Open noon–3pm
and 7–11pm
*This magnificent,
almost palatial
restaurant comes as
quite a surprise in the
suq of Khan el-Khalili.
Delicious Egyptian
cuisine. No alcohol.
Rather expensive.*
🅲 🖵

KHAN EL-KHALILI
Mena House
Oberoi Hotel
Road to the Pyramids
El-Ahram
Tel. 383 32 22
or 383 34 44
Open 24 hours
At the foot of the
Pyramids
*Fairly ordinary
Oriental and
Western cuisine, but the
restaurant has a
magnificent view of the
Pyramid of Khufu.*
🖻 ⤳ 🖵 ⤳ 🅿

LA BRASSERIE
Corniche
Garden City (C6)
Tel. 362 17 17
Open noon–3pm
and 8–11pm
Brunch Fri. 11am–4pm.
*International buffet
lunch. Different theme
buffet each evening:
Lebanese, Italian,
Egyptian, fish . . .
View of the Nile.
Often busy.*
🅲 ⤳ 🖵 🅿

LA CHARMERIE
157, Shari' Sittawa
Ashrin Yulyu (26 July
Street) (C2)
Tel. 340 96 40
Open 7–11pm
*Very pleasant setting
and carefully prepared
cuisine (international
and seafood).*
🖻 🅲 🖵

LA CHESA
21, Shari' Adli
Tel. 393 93 60
Open noon–10pm

531

Just before the Miami movie theater
Swiss and international restaurant (sandwichs, snacks, menu). Its main recommendation is that it is located in the heart of Cairo's shopping center.
C

★ LA FARNESINA
Forte Grand Pyramids Hotel
P.O. Box 25
The Pyramids
Tel. 383 03 83
or 383 07 72
Open 12.30–3pm and 7–11pm
Desert road to Alexandria
Top luxury restaurant (on a par with this superb hotel) serving excellent Italian cuisine.
⌂ ▭ ⊇ P

LA MAMMA
Cairo Sheraton Hotel
Midan Galaa (B5)
Doqqi-Giza
Tel. 336 98 00
or 336 97 00
Open 12.30–3.30pm and 8pm–1am
Very good Italian restaurant with evening entertainment. Quite expensive.
⌂ ⊻ ▭ P

LA PIAZZA (FOUR CORNERS RESTAURANTS)
4, Shari' Hassan Sabri
Zamalek (C2)
Gezira Island
Tel. 341 29 61
or 340 75 10
Open noon–4pm and 9am–11.30pm
Popular Italian restaurant. Extremely good menu and pleasant surroundings. Regular evening entertainment.
▭ P

LA TERRASSE
President Hotel
22, Shari' Taha Hussein (C2)
Zamalek
Tel. 340 07 18
or 340 06 52
Open 1–4pm and 7pm–1am
Fairly ordinary lunch menu (cold buffet), but à la carte menu with very good meat dishes and theme buffets (Chinese,

grills, fondue bourguignonne) in the evening. Very reasonably priced.*
⌂ ▭ P

LE CHALET (SWISSAIR RESTAURANTS)
El-Nasr Building
Shari' el-Nil
Giza
Tel. 348 53 21 or 62 70
Rural Swiss cuisine served in a luxurious, authentic setting – you could easily be in Switzerland. Disorientation guaranteed.
⊻ ▭ P

LE CHAMPOLLION
Le Méridien Cairo Hotel
Corniche(C6)
Garden City
Tel. 362 17 17
Open 12.30–3.30pm and 7–11.30pm
This is one of the best-known French restaurants in Cairo. Excellent cuisine, muted atmosphere. View of the Nile. Special business lunches.
⌂ C ⊻ ▭ P

LE CHÂTEAU (SWISSAIR RESTAURANTS)
El-Nasr Building
Shari' el-Nil, Giza
Tel. 348 53 21 or 62 70
Above Le Chalet restaurant
Excellent French restaurant. Beautiful décor and delightful setting. Very expensive French wines.
⌂ ⊻ ▭ P

LE CLOVIS
Sofitel Maadi Towers Hotel
29, Corniche, Maadi
Tel. 350 60 92 or 93
Open 7–11.30pm
High-status French restaurant in a residential district. Some distance from the center.
⌂ ▭ P

LE MARCO POLO
Le Méridien Heliopolis Hotel
51, Shari' Oruba
Heliopolis
Tel. 290 50 55
or 290 18 19
Open 1pm–1am
Luxury French restaurant. Impeccable

service and gourmet cuisine. Popular. Dinner reservations particularly advisable.*
⌂ ▭ P

★ LES AMBASSADEURS GRILL
Gezira Sheraton Hotel
Gezira Island (C5)
P.O. Box 264
Orman – Giza
Tel. 341 13 33
or 341 15 55
Open 7pm–1am
Magnificent restaurant overlooking the Nile. Remarkable French cuisine served with piano and string accompaniment. Extremely sophisticated.
C ⊻ ▭ P

MARQUIS
Swisshotel Cairo
el-Salam Hotel
Shari' Abd el-Hamid
Badawi
Heliopolis
Tel. 297 40 00
Open 10am–1am
Lunch and dinner buffets, extensive menu. Carefully prepared cuisine and very pleasant setting.
⌂ ▭ ⊇ P

★ MOGHUL ROOM
Mena House
Oberoi Hotel
Road to the Pyramids
El-Ahram
Tel. 383 32 22
or 383 34 44
Open noon–3pm and 7–11pm
Open Fri. noon–3pm
At the foot of the Pyramids
A wonderful little restaurant – reservations here are essential. Indian statues to greet you at the entrance, warm and friendly atmosphere, Indian music in the evening and excellent cuisine: quite spicy and truly delicious.
▭ ⊇ P

MÖVENPICK RESTAURANT
P.O. Box 1
Giza
Tel. 385 25 55
or 385 26 66
Open 6pm–midnight
Desert road to Alexandria
Unremarkable Swiss

and international cuisine. Luxurious setting.*
⌂ ▭ P

★ NILE PHARAO & GOLDEN PHARAO BOATS & RESTAURANTS
Midan Galaa (B5)
Doqqi–Giza
Tel. 570 10 00
Open 2.30–8.15pm or 10.45pm (times change according to the season. Ask for details.)
Near the Cairo Sheraton Hotel
Two boats run by Oberoi offer short buffet-cruises. Magnificent evening buffets with entertainment (Eastern dancing). Reservations essential.
⊻ ▭

NUBIAN VILLAGE
Le Méridien
Cairo Hotel
Corniche (C6)
Garden City
Tel. 362 17 17
Open 8pm–midnight
Closed Dec.–Feb.
Terrace restaurant overlooking the Nile. Egyptian and Middle-Eastern cuisine. Entertainment and Eastern music every evening.
⊻ ▭

OMAR'S CAFÉ
Cairo Marriott Hotel
Shari' Saraya el-Gezira
Zamalek (C2)
Tel. 340 88 88
Fax 318 77 54
Open 24 hours
Gezira Island
Rather noisy and usually very crowded. Delicious international theme buffets.
▭ ⊇ P

★ ONYX & TOPAZ BOATS & RESTAURANTS
Corniche
Maadi
Tel. 319 00 90
Fax 318 77 54
Lunch 2.30pm
Dinner 8.30pm and 9.30pm
Two boats run by Misr Travel. Mini-cruises with good buffets and evening entertainment (Eastern dancing). Based on the same

principle as Golden &
Nile Pharao.
Reservations
essential.
🍴 ▱

★ **PAPRIKA**
Corniche (D3)
Tel. 578 78 87
or 578 94 47
*Small Egyptian
restaurant. Simple and
inexpensive. Some
international dishes.*
🅒 ▱ 🅟

PEACE
Tel. 383 36 86
or 383 36 87
Open noon–midnight
Desert road to
Alexandria
*Extremely, possibly too
popular fish restaurant
(a lot of groups). Simple
décor but very good
grilled fish and
seafood at competitive
prices.*
▱ 🅟

PRESTIGE
43, Shari' Gezirct el-
Arab Mohandissine
Tel. 347 03 83
Open 7–11pm
Reached via the Kubri
Sitta Uktubir (6 October
Bridge). On the Shari'
el-Doual el-Arabiya
*Once a top restaurant
but standards have
declined a little in recent
years. Renowned for its
meat dishes.
International cuisine.*
🅐 ▱

RÉGENCE
Helnan Shepheard
Hotel
Corniche (D4)
Garden City
Tel. 355 38 00
or 355 39 00
Open 7–11pm
*Luxury restaurant.
Muted atmosphere.
Very good French
cuisine.*
🅐 🅒 ▱

RUBAYYAT
Mena House
Oberoi Hotel
Road to the Pyramids
El-Ahram
Tel. 383 32 22
or 383 34 44
Open noon–3pm
and 8pm–midnight
At the foot of the
Pyramids
*A vast, magnificent
dining room. Lunch
buffets are not*

exceptional but a good
evening menu with
traditional Egyptian
entertainment (9.30pm).
▱ 🥢 🅟

**SAKKURA (OMAM
RESTAURANTS)**
Omam Tower
5, Wissa Wassef
Giza
Tel. 570 12 26
*Friendly atmosphere.
Reproduction of a
Japanese interior where
the cooking is done in
front of the customers.
Very good cuisine. No
alcohol.*
🅐 🅒 ▱ 🅟

★ **SEAHORSE**
Corniche
Maadi
Tel. 363 88 30
Open noon–11pm
Opposite the El-Salam
Hospital
*Excellent fish and
seafood restaurant at
competitive prices. On
the shores of the Nile.
Generous helpings.
Simple décor.*
🅐 ▱ 🍴 🅟

**SHANDANI
(OMAM RESTAURANTS)**
5, Shari' Wissa Wassef
Omam Tower
Giza
Tel. 570 12 26
*One of the four Omam
tower restaurants.
Luxurious Indian décor.
Good quality cuisine.
Quite expensive. No
alchohol.*
🅐 🅒 🅟

★ **SILVER FISH**
39, Mohy el-Din
Shari' Abu el-Ezz
Doqqi (B5)
Tel. 349 22 72
Open noon–3pm
and 7.30–11pm
*The best fish restaurant
in the city center. An
extremely varied menu
and pleasant
surroundings.*
🅐 🅒 ▱

STARLIGHT
Baron Hotel
Shari' Off Orouba
P.O. Box 2531
Heliopolis
Tel. 291 57 57
Airport road
*Luxury international
restaurant offering a
panoramic view of the
city. Stylish setting.*
🍴 ▱ 🅟

TAJ MAHAL
15, Shari' Ibn Affan
Doqqi (B5)
Tel. 348 48 81
Open 7.30pm–midnight
*Popular Indian
restaurant. Mild dishes
on request.*
🅐 🅒 ▱

TANDOORI
11, Shari' Shehab
Mohandissine (A3)
Tel. 348 63 01
Open 7–11.30pm
*Good Indian
restaurant which
competes with the
nearby Taj Mahal. Good
menu and pleasant
setting.*
🅐 🅒 ▱

**TAVERNE DU CHAMP-
DE-MARS**
Nile Hilton Hotel
Corniche (D4)
Midan at-Tahrir
Tel. 578 04 44
or 578 06 66
Open 11am–1am
*Fairly unoriginal
international lunch
buffets. In the evening,
the meeting place for
Cairo's (well-to-do)
younger set: piano-bar
and à la carte menu.
Very crowded.*
🅒 ▱ 🥢

THE CARAVAN
Helnan Shepheard
Hotel
Corniche (D4)
Garden City
Tel. 355 38 00
or 355 39 00
Open 24 hours
*Good international
buffets and à la carte
menu.*
🅒 ▱

THE CELLAR
President Hotel
22, Shari' Taha-Hussein
(C2)
Zamalek
Tel. 340 07 18
or 340 06 52
Open noon–3am
*A lively restaurant
popular with the
Cairene and foreign
younger set. Very
reasonable cuisine,
including some good
meat dishes.*
▱ 🅟

THE GRILL
Semiramis
Intercontinental
Corniche
Garden City (D4)

Tel. 355 71 71
(ext. tel. 80 32)
Open 7pm–midnight
*Excellent French cuisine
with a magnificent view
of the Nile.*
🅐 🅒 🍴 ▱ 🅟

★ **THE TERRACE**
Cairo Marriott Hotel
Shari' el-Saraya el-
Gezira Zamalek (C2)
Tel. 340 88 88
Open 7pm–midnight
Closed Dec.–Apr.
Gezira Island
*In the magnificent
gardens of the Marriott
Hotel (former palace of
the khedive Ismaïl).
Good Egyptian food
(grills). Entertainment.*
▱ 🅟 🍴 🎻

TIROL
38, Geziret el-Arab
Mohandissine (A3)
Tel. 344 97 25
*Very good value for
money and a warm and
friendly atmosphere.
Tyrolean cuisine and
some international
dishes.*
🅒 ▱

**WINDOWS
ON THE WORLD**
Cairo Ramses
Hilton Hotel
1115, Corniche
Maspero (D3)
Tel. 575 49 99
Open 4pm–2am
*Very ordinary food
(snacks) but a
wonderful view and
good entertainment
(dancing) from
9.30pm*
🅒 🍴 ▱ 🅟

YAMATO
Annex to the Cairo
Ramses Hilton Hotel
Corniche el-Nil (D3)
Shari' Tahrir
Tel. 575 49 99
*Traditional Japanese
cuisine in a cool setting.
Popular with Japanese
visitors.*
🅐 🅒 🅟

ACCOMMODATION

**ARC EN CIEL –
EL-BORG HOTEL** ★★★
Shari' Saray el-Gezira
Gezira
Tel. 34 11 68 27
or 34 11 34 01
Fax 34 11 76 55
At the far end of the
Kubri at-Tahrir, near the
Cairo Tower

Not particularly prepossessing and service mediocre, but rooms very acceptable. Near the Cairo Tower gardens.
C ⚴ ▱

BARON HOTEL HELIOPOLIS ★★★★
Shari' Off Orouba
P.O. Box 2531
Heliopolis
Tel. 291 24 68
or 291 57 57
Fax 290 70 77
Only just warrants its four stars. No swimming pool or activities but restaurants are extremely good.
🏨 ⌂ ▱ P

BELAIR CAIRO HOTEL ★★★★
Moqattam Hill
P.O. Box 996
Tel. 506 09 11 or 17
Fax 506 28 16
On Jebel Moqattamm, reached direct from the airport via the Shari' Salah Salim
Comfortable. Overlooks the city of Cairo but close to the city center and the El-Azhar and suq districts.
⌖ ⚴ ▱ ⌿ P

CAIRO HELIOPOLIS MÖVENPICK ★★★★★
Road to Cairo International Airport Heliopolis
Tel. 291 94 00
or 247 00 77
Fax 667 73 74
Luxury hotel with good restaurants and a pleasant garden. Ideal for short stays (between connections).
🏨 ▱ ⌿ P ♠

CAIRO JOLIE-VILLE MÖVENPICK ★★★★★
Desert road to Alexandria
P.O. Box 1
Giza
Tel. 385 26 66
or 383 50 06
Beautiful hotel. Comfortable and quiet. Ideal for a longer visit to the Pyramids of Giza and Saqqara.
🏨 ⌂ ⌖ ▱ ⌿ P ♠

★ CAIRO MARRIOTT HOTEL ★★★★★
Shari' Saraya
el-Gezira Zamalek (C2)
Tel. 348 86 00
or 340 88 88

Fax 340 66 67
Gezira Island via the Kubri at-Tahrir
Former palace of the khedive Ismaïl with a beautiful garden, bars and magnificent restaurants (huge 19th-century paintings). The very spacious rooms are located in two huge modern towers at either end of the palace. Excellent service and the height of luxury. Avoid the far end of the garden as it overlooks the street.
🏨 C ⚴ ▱ ⌿ P ♠

CAIRO RAMSES HILTON HOTEL ★★★★★
1115, Corniche
Maspero (D3)
Tel. 575 49 99
Fax 575 71 52
A top category hotel, overlooking the Nile, with a full range of facilities. Next to the hotel is a famous shopping mall. Several restaurants and a bar with a magnificent view.
🏨 C ⚴ ▱ ⌿

CAIRO SHERATON HOTEL ★★★★★
Midan Galaa
Doqqi-Giza (B5)
Tel. 336 98 00
or 336 97 00
Fax 336 46 01
At the far end of the Kubri Galaa, at the intersection leading to the Avenue of the Pyramids.
Large, luxury hotel with a modern wing added to the "old" wing. Spacious rooms with all mod cons. Bars, restaurants.
🏨 C ⚴ ▱ ⌿

CARLTON HOTEL ★★★
21, Shari' Sittawa Ashrin
Yulyu (26 July) Ezbekiya
Tel. 575 51 81 or 50 22
Comfortable hotel but situated in a rather noisy district. Rooms and hotel well kept.
C ▱ P

CLEOPATRA PALACE HOTEL ★★★
1, Shari' Bustan
Midan at-Tahrir
Tel. 575 99 00 or 23
Fax 346 67 85
Centrally located (rather

noisy) near the museum and the Midan Tal'at Harb. More in keeping with a two-star hotel.
C ▱

CONCORDE HOTEL ★★★
146, Shari' at-Tahrir
Doqqi
Tel. 336 11 93
or 336 11 94
Fax 336 11 89
Comfortable hotel near the city center, but not many facilities. Good value for money.
C ▱

★ COSMOPOLITAN HOTEL ★★★
1, Shari' Ibn Tahlab (E3)
Tel. 392 38 45
or 392 75 22
Midan Tal'at Harb, and Shari' Qasr el-Nil, second on the right
Well-situated in the city center. Comfortable hotel with a great deal of early 20th-century charm. Very good value for money.
C ▱

EL-GEZIRA SHERATON HOTEL CAIRO ★★★★★
Gezira Island
P.O. Box 264
Orman Giza (C5)
Tel. 341 13 33
or 341 15 55
Fax 340 50 56
Southern tip of Gezira Island, near the Kubri at-Tahrir
A fine piece of architecture in a splendid position. All the rooms overlook the Nile. Several restaurants. Ask for an upper-story room.
🏨 C ⚴ ▱ ⌿ P 🚗

FLAMENCO HOTEL ★★★★
2, Shari' el-Gezira
el-Wosta
Zamalek
Tel. 340 08 15
Fax 340 08 19
Conveniently situated, but at best only warrants three stars. Atmosphere often leaves something to be desired.
C ▱

★ FORTE GRAND PYRAMIDS HOTEL ★★★★★
P.O. Box 25
The Pyramids
Tel. 383 03 83

Fax 383 17 30
Desert road to Alexandria
Excellent hotel. Remarkable service. Several restaurants (including a renowned Lebanese restaurant). Spacious, well-decorated rooms.
🏨 ⚴ ▱ ▱ P ♠

GRAND HOTEL ★★★
17, Shari' Sittawa Ashrin
Yulyu (26 July)
Ezbekiya
Tel. 575 77 00
or 575 75 09
Fax 575 75 93
Large, centrally located hotel, but rather noisy. Large rooms and very friendly atmosphere. Competitively priced.
C P

★ HELNAN SHEPHEARD HOTEL ★★★★★
Corniche
Garden City (D4)
Tel. 355 39 00
or 355 38 00
Fax 355 72 84
On the Nile, behind the Mugamaa and near the Kubri at-Tahrir
Probably only warrants four stars, but has a great deal of charm with its traditional architecture and huge, Moorish-style rooms. Top-quality restaurants. Rather noisy, so ask for a room overlooking the Nile.
🏨 C ⚴ ▱

HORUS HOUSE HOTEL ★★★
21, Shari' Ismaïl
Mohammed
Zamalek
Tel. 340 39 77
or 340 36 34
Fax 340 31 82
Very comfortable, competitively priced hotel in a residential district. Good Egyptian restaurant.
⌂ ▱

HÔTEL LES TROIS PYRAMIDES ★★★★
229, Avenue of the Pyramids, Giza
Tel. 582 22 23
or 582 16 30
Fax 582 37 00
Midway between the city center and the Pyramids
Very noisy, as it is situated on the avenue, but comfortable rooms

and good service. Rather expensive.

LE MÉRIDIEN CAIRO HOTEL ***
Corniche
Garden City (C6)
Tel. 362 17 17
Fax 362 19 27
Beyond the Midan at-Tahrir in the direction of Maadi
Luxury hotel with a number of restaurants, indoor and outdoor bars and huge, comfortable rooms. Excellent position on the northern tip of Roda Island. Ask for a room overlooking the Nile.

LE MÉRIDIEN HELIOPOLIS HOTEL ***
51, Shari' Orouba
Heliopolis
Tel. 290 18 19
Fax 291 85 91
Main airport road, opposite "old" Heliopolis
Very luxurious, French-style hotel. Conveniently situated for visiting Heliopolis and the City of the Dead . . 20 mins drive from the city center.

LONGCHAMPS HOTEL *
21, Shari' Ismaïl Mohammed
Zamalek (C2)
Tel. 340 23 11
Shares the building – as well as conditions and prices – with the Horus House Hotel. Meals are slightly less expensive.

LOTUS HOTEL **
12, Shari' Tal'at Harb (E4)
Tel. 575 09 66
or 575 06 27
Fax 575 47 20
Conveniently situated but, like all two-star Egyptian hotels, devoid of luxury. Inexpensive and clean.

MAADI HOTEL ***
P.O. Box 196
Maadi
Tel. 350 50 50
or 350 65 55
Fax 351 87 10
Reached via the Corniche road.

First entrance on the left as you come into Maadi
Some distance from the center. Comfortable with a good French restaurant.

★ MENA HOUSE OBEROI HOTEL ***
Road to the Pyramids El-Ahram
Tel. 383 32 22
or 383 34 44
Fax 383 77 77
At the intersection with the desert road to Alexandria
Former palace of the khedive Ismaïl. All the crowned heads of Europe have stayed here (including the French Empress Eugénie for the opening of the Suez Canal). Charlie Chaplin and T.E. Lawrence were among its many regular guests. One of the finest hotels in the world.

NILE HILTON HOTEL ***
Corniche
Midan at-Tahrir (D4)
Tel. 578 04 44
or 578 06 66
Fax 76 08 74
The most famous of Cairo's city-center hotels, next to the Egyptian Museum. Beautiful rooms, excellent restaurants and bars but unfortunately very noisy. Large Egyptair office. The rooms overlooking the garden are quieter.

NITOCRISSE HOTEL *
171, Shari' Mohammed Farid (F3)
Tel. 391 51 66 or 57 38
Near the Shari' Adli, one of the main streets in the city center
Ideal for lower budget vacations. Basic comfort but clean and conveniently situated. One of the reasonable one-star hotels.

NOVOTEL CAIRO AIRPORT HOTEL ***
Cairo Airport
P.O. Box 8
Heliopolis
Tel. 291 85 77

or 679 10 80
Fax 291 47 94
Uprepossessing and rather "poky" but ideal for a stop-over between flights.

OASIS HOTEL **
P.O. Box 44
The Pyramids
Tel. 383 17 77/383 27 77
Fax 383 09 16
On the outskirts of Giza on the desert road to Alexandria
Some distance from the center but quiet, comfortable and close to the Pyramids of Giza.

★ PENSION ROMA CAIRO
169, Shari' Mohammed Farid (F3)
Tel. 391 10 88
or 391 13 40
City center
Not luxurious but a very well-kept boarding house. Extremely pleasant atmosphere. Ideally located for visiting the center of Cairo and very reasonably priced.

PRESIDENT HOTEL *
22, Shari' Taha-Hussein
Zamalek (C2)
Tel. 341 67 51
or 341 31 95
Fax 341 17 52
Via the Kubri Sittawa Ashrin Yulyu (26 July Bridge)
Very reasonable, good value for money and relatively quiet for the city center. Good French restaurant and popular night club.

★ PYRAMIDS PARK ***
Tel. 383 66 66
Fax 383 90 00
On the outskirts of Cairo, on the desert road to Alexandria
Pleasant place for a vacation. The extensive park has a number of chalets in a large garden and the finest swimming pool in the Middle East. The rooms are spacious, but the small and badly positioned "cabanas" should be avoided.

SAFIR CAIRO HOTEL ***
Shari' el-Missaha
P.O. Box 138
Doqqi
Tel. 348 24 24
or 348 28 28
Near Gezira Island, across the Kubri Galaa
This hotel is more in keeping with a good three-star hotel. Situated in a fairly uninteresting district but within easy reach of the city center.

SAFIR ZAMALEK HOTEL **
21, Shari' Mohammed Mazhar
Zamalek
Tel. 342 00 55
or 342 11 80
Fax 342 12 02
Via the Kubri Sittawa Ashrin Yulyu (26 July Bridge)
A large building situated in a fairly quiet residential district. Suites only. Very expensive for the facilities available (no swimming pool).

SEMIRAMIS INTER-CONTINENTAL ***
Corniche
Garden City (D4)
Tel. 355 71 71
Fax 356 30 20
At the end of the Kubri at-Tahrir, behind the Mugamaa
Extremely comfortable, but a very unfriendly atmosphere. The building is of station-like proportions. Ideal for conferences. Ask for an upper-floor room overlooking the Nile.

SIAG PYRAMIDS HOTEL CAIRO ***
Road to Saqqara
P.O. Box 107, Arham
Tel. 385 60 22
or 38 50 05
Fax 385 74 13
At the Cairo end of the road to Saqqara, as you leave the Avenue of the Pyramids
Became famous as the starting point for the Pharaoh's Rally. Ideally located for visiting Saqqara and Giza. Very comfortable but doesn't really warrant five stars.

SOFITEL MAADI TOWERS HOTEL *****
29, Corniche Maadi
Tel. 350 60 92
or 350 60 93
Fax 350 62 09
Very comfortable hotel, some distance from the center near the residential district of Maadi. Swimming pool on the terrace. Very pleasant in summer. Excellent French restaurant. Ask for a room overlooking the Nile.
🏠 ⚒ ⌂ ⌐ P

SONESTA HOTEL *****
4, Shari' el-Tayaran-Medinet Nasr
Tel. 262 81 11
or 261 71 00
Fax 245 57 55
Road from the airport to the city center. Turn left after the Air Force barracks.
In an unattractive district but comfortable and near the airport. Expensive for the area.
🏠 ⌐ ⌂ P

★ SWISSHOTEL CAIRO EL-SALAM HOTEL *****
Shari' Abd el-Hamid Badawi
Heliopolis
Tel. 297 40 00
or 297 60 37
Fax 245 57 55
Road from the airport to the city center, then right toward Ismaïliya
Extremely well-kept hotel with an early 20th-century charm (featured in Jacobs' film "Mystery of the Great Pyramid"). Beautiful rooms and excellent restaurants. Quite possibly the finest airport hotel in Egypt.
🏠 🏠 ⌐ ⌂ P ♯

YOUTH HOSTEL
135, Shari' Abd el-Aziz el-Seoud-el Manyal
Roda Island
Tel. 364 07 29
Near the Kubri Gamaa

NIGHTLIFE

NIGHTCLUBS
AFTER 8
Shari' Qasr el-Nil
Near the Qasr el-Nil movie theater
Tel. 574 08 55

LE CELLARS
President Hotel
Zamalek
Tel. 341 67 51
LE HARRIS PUB
Cairo Marriott Hotel
Zamalek
Tel. 340 88 88
LE JACKY'S
Nile Hilton Hotel
Tel. 578 06 66
PIANO PIANO
World Trade Center
Bulaq
Tel. 76 28 10
PUB 28
Zamalek
Tel. 340 92 00
REGINA
Gezira Sheraton Hotel
Tel. 341 13 33
SULTANA
Semiramis Intercontinental
Tel. 355 71 71

CABARETS (BELLY DANCING)
CASINO EL-LEL
Avenue of the Pyramids
Tel. 585 42 52
LA CAVE DES ROIS
10, Shari' Mohamed Sakeb
Zamalek
Tel. 340 70 89
LE PARISIANA
Avenue of the Pyramids
Tel. 383 39 11
LE TIVOLI
Midan Almaza
Heliopolis
Tel. 290 64 96
SALT AND PEPPER
Shari' Abul Fedda
Zamalek
Tel. 342 05 29

EL-FISHAWI CAFÉ
Shari' Gawhara el-Saïd
Khan el-Khalili
Oriental café.

PIANO BAR
CLUB 36
Cairo Ramses Hilton Hotel
Tel. 575 49 99
Very fashionable. Magnificent view of the city.

SHOPPING

AKHENATON CARPETS
Tel. 20 14 88 or 15 02
Road to Saqqara, just before the Pyramids
Carpets, naive tapestry. Good quality. Haggling.

ANI PAPYRUS
Avenue of the Pyramids
Giza
Open 9am–9pm
Before you get to the

Pyramids, on the left of the street.
Good quality papyri. Beautiful designs. Set prices.

CANADA DRY
Road to Saqqara, just before the Pyramids
Good quality carpets and naive tapestry. Bargaining.

CARPET SCHOOL OF EGYPT
Road to Saqqara, just before the Pyramids
Carpets and naive tapestry. Bargaining.

DR RAGAB PAPYRUS
3, Shari' el-Nil
Giza
Open 9am–9pm
Near the Cairo Sheraton Hotel
Set prices.

EL-REFAEY
27, Shari' el-Refaey
Citadel
Tel. 511 22 73
Near the Sultan Hassan Mosque
Good quality jewelry. 18 carats guaranteed.

GALAL
Shari' el-Muski
Tel. 588 26 66
or 588 27 77
Khan el-Khalili
Main street of the suq district
Luxury jewelry.

KARNAK BAZAAR PYRAMIDS
16, Avenue of the Pyramids
Tel. 383 00 47 or 43 45
An Aladdin's cave. All types of Egyptian souvenirs of varying quality. Bargaining.

KING RAMSES CARPET SCHOOL
Road to Saqqara, just before the Pyramids
Carpets and tapestry. Bargaining.

L'ORIENTALISTE
15, Near the Midan Tal'at Harb
Tel. 575 34 18
Reputable bookshop: old editions in French and English, prints and old postcards of Egypt.

MAAT PAPYRUS
Avenue of the Pyramids
Giza
Open 9am–9pm

On the left, before the Pyramids
Set prices.

MOBACO
18, SHARI' TAL'AT HARB
Tel. 347 37 91
CAIRO RAMSES HILTON HOTEL
1115, Corniche Maspero
Tel. 575 49 99
NILE HILTON HOTEL
Corniche
Midan at-Tahrir
Tel. 578 04 44
SEMIRAMIS INTER CONTINENTAL
Corniche
Garden City
Tel. 355 71 71
Very good quality, Western-style, cotton clothing at competitive (set) prices which do, however, increase from one month to the next.

NEW PHARAO PAPYRUS
Avenue of the Pyramids
Giza
On the left, before the Pyramids
Open 9am–9pm
Good papyrus institute. Set prices.

NUT PAPYRUS
Avenue of the Pyramids
Giza
Open 9am–9pm
On the left, before the Pyramids
Good papyrus institute. Set prices.

OCTOPUS
15, SHARI' BAGDAD
Heliopolis
Tel. 664 33 78
Western-style cotton clothing at set prices.

SAFARI
20, SHARI' EL-SHERIFA DINA
Maadi
Tel. 375 91 94
10, SHARI' LUTFALLAH
Zamalek
Tel. 340 19 09
Western-style cotton clothing. Excellent quality. Set prices.

SOBEK PAPYRUS
Avenue of the Pyramids
Giza
Open 9am–9pm
On the right, before the Pyramids
Good quality papyri at set prices.

SPHINX CARPET SCHOOL
Road to Saqqara, before the Pyramids
Carpets and tapestry. Bargaining.

THE OLD SHOP
Shari' Sikkit el-Badestan
Main street in the Khan el-Khalili
*Well-known antique dealer. Mostly bric-a-brac rather than genuine antiques. Bargaining.
N.B. It is forbidden to export pre-Revolutionary items.*

SPORTS

YACHT CLUB
Giza
Tel. 348 94 15
Near the Cairo Sheraton Hotel

THE FAIYUM

DIALING CODE
(0) 84
Map of Egypt F4

ACCOMMODATION

AUBERGE DU LAC FAYOUM ★★★★
Tel. 70 00 02 or 70 07 30
On Lake Qarun, via the road to Medinet el-Faiyum
Luxury hotel with splendid English lounges. Ideal for a relaxing vacation.
⌂ ⌂ ⌂• ⠠⠇ ⊡ ⌴ P ♨

PANORAMA SHAKSHUK HOTEL ★★★
Shakshuk
Tel. 70 17 46 or 70 13 14
Fax 70 17 57
Road to Shakshuk via Medinet el-Faiyum
Extremely pleasant hotel with comfortable, spacious rooms. Friendly atmosphere.

YOUTH HOSTEL
Building no. 7
El-Hadeka
Tel. 32 36 82 or 32 00 05
Near the main square.

ASSIUT

DIALING CODE
(0) 88
Map of Egypt F6

ACCOMMODATION

BADR TOURISTIC HOTEL ★★★
Shari' el-Thallaga
Tel. 32 98 11 or 98 12
The best hotel in a town of little touristic interest.
C P

YOUTH HOSTEL
El-Walideh Building 503
Tel. 32 48 46
Next to the station.

EL-MINYA

DIALING CODE
(0) 86
Map of Egypt E5

USEFUL ADDRESSES

POLICE STATION
TOURIST POLICE
Tel. 32 45 27
Corniche

TOURIST OFFICE
Corniche
Tel. 32 01 50
Open 9am–2pm
Little information. A few maps and brochures on Middle Egypt.

ACCOMMODATION

P.L.M. AZUR NEFERTITI ★★★★
Corniche
Tel. 34 15 15
Fax 32 64 67
The best hotel in Middle Egypt. Opposite the main building, chalets overlooking the Nile. Good restaurants and pleasant bar.

Departure point for visits to Beni Hassan.
⌂ ⠠⠇ ⊡ ⌴ ♨
◆

LUXOR

DIALING CODE
(0) 95
Map of Egypt G7

USEFUL ADDRESSES

AMERICAN EXPRESS
Corniche
Tel. 37 28 62 or 58 13 01
Closed Fri.
Next to the Winter Palace Hotel

POST OFFICE
Tel. 37 20 37
Shari' el-Mahatta (behind the temple)
Open 8am–2.30pm
Closed Fri.

HOSPITAL
Corniche
Tel. 37 20 25
After the museum in the direction of Karnak

MISR BANK
Etap Luxor Hotel
Open daily

TOURIST OFFICE
Corniche
Tel. 37 32 94
Open 9am–3pm and 6–9pm
Between the temple and the Winter Palace Hotel
Little information.

TOURIST POLICE
Luxor International Airport
Tel. 38 21 20

TRANSPORT

LUXOR INTERNATIONAL AIRPORT
Tel. 37 46 55

EGYPTAIR
Shari' el-Nil
Tel. 38 05 80 or 38 05 82
Fax 38 05 85

STATION
Midan el-Mahatta (Station Square)
Tel. 37 20 18

BUS STATIONS
SHARI' EL-KARNAK
Heading north out of Luxor, toward the Horus Hotel
Bus terminal.
SHARI' TELEVISION
Heading north out of Luxor
Communal taxi terminal.

CULTURE

LUXOR MUSEUM
Corniche

RESTAURANTS

BELLA DONNA
Shari' Khaled Ibn el-Walid
Tel. 38 08 50
Open 12.30–2pm and 8–9.30pm
Situated in an inner courtyard, at the Club Méditerranée. Very good international buffets. À la carte dinner menu.
⌂ ⊡ ⌴ ₸

CLASS
Shari' Khaled Ibn el-Walid
Open noon–3pm and 7–11pm
At the end of the Corniche, just before the Isis Hotel Luxor
Now restaurant on the second floor of a bazaar. A selection of European and Egyptian dishes. Good value for money.
⌂ ⊡ P

★ DAKKA
Mercure Hotel
Tel. 37 49 44 or 38 09 44
Open 9am–11pm
Small restaurant on the edge of the swimming pool.

537

An ideal place to relax after visiting the sites. Small international menu.
🏠 🅲 ⬚ ⟲ ♨

★ EL-DAWAR
Isis Hotel Luxor
Shari' Khaled Ibn el-Walid
Tel. 37 27 50 or 33 66
Open noon–4pm
At the end of the Corniche, in the direction of Esna
Delightful reconstruction of a Nubian village on the shores of the Nile. Very good Egyptian cuisine.
🏠 ⚒ ⬚ ⟲ ♨

EL-KARNAK
Luxor Sheraton Hotel and Resort
Road to El-Awamiya
P.O. Box 43
Tel. 37 40 13 or 37 45 44
Open 24 hours
At the end of the Corniche, before the main Esna road
Amazing theme buffets: Latin-American, Russian, Swiss, fish & seafood. Reservations essential.
⚒ ⬚ ⟲ 🅿

★ EL-MADIRIYA
Shari' Khaled Ibn el-Walid
Open 7pm–midnight
Narrow street at right angles to the Shari' Khalid, before the Isis Hotel Luxor
Excellent Egyptian restaurant with a varied menu and friendly service. Simple setting and modestly comfortable. Inexpensive.
🏠 ⬚• 🅿 ⟟ ♨

EL-SAKKIA
Luxor Etap Hotel
Corniche
Tel. 37 49 44 or 38 09 44

Open 6.30–10.30pm
Good Oriental cuisine in a (reconstructed) Bedouin tent. Delightful atmosphere.
🏠 🅲 ⬚ ⟲

FELLAH'S TENT
Mövenpick Jolie-Ville Luxor
Crocodile Island
Tel. 37 49 37 or 37 48 55
Open Thur. and Fri. 5–9pm
As you leave Luxor in the direction of Esna
The tent offers an Egyptian buffet and a dance cabaret. The island – near the hotel – is reached by "felucca".
🏠 ⚒ ⬚ ⟲ 🅿 ⟟

★ FELUCCA LUNCHES
Luxor Hilton Hotel
Tel. 37 49 33 or 37 49 46
Open 1–3pm and 7–9pm
On the Corniche, after the Temple of Karnak
Lunch- or dinner-trips aboard a "felucca". Order before you leave.
🏠 ⬚• ⚒ ⬚ ⟟

HATY
Shari' el-Mahatta
Open noon–11pm
Small, simple and inexpensive restaurant serving a wide variety of Egyptian dishes.
🅲

KHAN EL-KHALILI
Isis Hotel Luxor
Shari' Khaled Ibn el-Walid
Open 12.30–3pm and 6.30–10.30pm
At the end of the Corniche, in the direction of Esna
Unoriginal international menu in an ordinary setting.
🏠 ⬚ ⟲

★ LA MAMMA
Luxor Sheraton Hotel and Resort
Road to El-Awamiya
P. O. Box 43
Open noon–11.30pm
The most delightful Italian restaurant in Egypt. Situated in a park where peacocks, geese and pelicans preen themselves near a pond. Excellent seafood risotto.
🏠 ⬚ ⟲ 🅿 ⟟ ♨

LE FLAMBOYANT
Etap Luxor Hotel
Corniche
Open 7.30–10.30pm
French restaurant. Good menu at reasonable prices in an ordinary setting.
🅲 ⬚ ⟲

LE MARHABA
Nile Corniche
Open 11am–11pm
Between the Temple of Luxor and the New Winter Palace Hotel
Its main attraction is its central location, near the temple and suqs. Unimaginative European cuisine and basic Egyptian dishes (broad beans). View of the Nile.
🏠 🅲 ⚒ ⟟

★ SHEHERAZADE TERRACE
Mövenpick Jolie-Ville Luxor
Crocodile Island
Tel. 37 49 37 or 37 48 55
Open 7.30–11pm
As you leave Luxor in the direction of Esna
Grills and theme buffets (Italian, Egyptian, Indian, Swiss) in the splendid "Jolie-Ville" gardens. Magnificent setting with a view of the Nile.
🏠 ⚒ ⬚ 🅿 ⟟

ACCOMMODATION

AKHETATON VILLAGE BELLADONNA ★★★★
Shari' Khaled Ibn el-Walid
Tel. 38 08 50 or 38 09 14
Fax 38 08 79
In the direction of Esna
Club Méditérranée village in a beautifully lush setting. Magnificent swimming pool, lovely rooms and a popular discothèque. Remarkable view of the Nile.
🏠 🏠 ⚒ ⬚ ⟲ ♨

EMILIO HOTEL
Shari' Yussef Hassan
Tel. 37 35 70
Fax 37 00 00
Coming from the direction of Karnak, turn left before the former Etap Luxor Hotel and then right before the Franciscan school
Not particularly

luxurious but conveniently situated near the suqs and Temple of Luxor.
🅲 ⬚ ⟲

HORUS HOTEL ★★
Road to the Temple of Karnak
Tel. 37 21 65 /38 21 65
Small, well-kept and inexpensive hotel.
⬚

★ ISIS HOTEL LUXOR ★★★★★
Shari' Khaled Ibn el-Walid
Tel. 37 33 66 or 01 00
Fax 37 29 23
On the Corniche, in the direction of Esna
Well situated on the Nile with spacious rooms and various restaurants and bars. Splendid swimming pool and basement night club. Ask for a room overlooking the Nile.
🏠 🏠 ⚒ ⬚ ⟲ 🅿 ♨

LUXOR HILTON ★★★★★
Corniche
New Karnak
Tel. 37 49 33
Fax 38 65 71
Beautiful rooms and excellent atmosphere. Delightful setting with a magnificent view of the Nile.
🏠 🏠 ⬚• ⚒ ⬚ ⟲ 🅿 ♨

★ LUXOR SHERATON HOTEL & RESORT ★★★★★
Road to El-Awamiya
Tel. 37 45 44 or 37 40 13
Fax 37 49 41
At the end of the Corniche
Stands in an attractive, lawned park on the banks of the Nile. The rooms are large and pleasant, especially in the restaurants and outdoor bar, theme buffets and nightclub.
🏠 🏠 ⬚• ⚒ ⬚ ⟲ 🅿 ♨

MERCURE HOTEL ★★★★
Corniche el-Nil
Tel. 38 09 44 or 37 49 44
Fax 37 49 12
Haven of peace in an attractive setting. Several restaurants and bars. Small, comfortable rooms and a fine swimming pool.
🏠 🏠 🅲 ⚒ ⬚ ⟲ ♨

MINA PALACE HOTEL**
Corniche
Tel. 37 20 74
Just before the
Temple of Luxor
Small, simple and clean hotel. Well situated on the Nile.
◙ ⥾

★ **MÖVENPICK JOLIE-VILLE LUXOR *******
Crocodile Island
Tel. 37 48 55
or 49 37
Fax 37 43 96
Reached via the
Corniche and the main
Esna road
Large, comfortable chalets surrounded by trees and flowers. Splendid swimming pool and children's play area with animals (monkeys, camels).
🏠 🏠 ⮞ ⥾ ▭ ⟶ 🅿

NEW WINDSOR HOTEL ***
Shari' Nefertiti
Tel. 37 55 47
Fax 37 34 47
Near the Etap
Luxor Hotel
Recently built with pleasant rooms. Conveniently situated for visiting the temples and suqs.
◙ ⟶

NOVOTEL EVASION LUXOR HOTEL ****
Shari' Khaled Ibn
el-Walid
Tel. 58 09 25
Fax 58 09 72
At the end of the
Corniche
Original architecture with a central light well. Pleasant rooms.
🏠 🏠 ⥾ ▭ ⟶ ⟶

PHARAON HOTEL ***
New Karnak
Tel. 37 49 24
or 38 10 77
Fax 38 64 77
To the north of the
town, on the Corniche,
after the Temple of
Karnak
Ideal for longer visits to the Temple of Karnak. Small pleasant garden with a view of the Nile. Rather small but clean rooms. Good value for money.
🏠 ⥾ ▭ ⟶ ⟶

PHILIPPE HOTEL LUXOR ★★★
Shari' Labib-Habashy
Tel. 37 22 84
or 37 36 04
Just before the Luxor
Etap Hotel
Small, clean hotel. Not luxurious but conveniently situated between the Nile and suqs. Famed for its jewelers.
◙ ⟶

★ **SOFITEL WINTER PALACE ******
Corniche
Tel. 38 04 22
Fax 37 40 87
Two hotels once owned by the Pullman group. The Old Winter Palace has a traditional "English" charm with exposed beams in the bars and huge rooms. The New Winter Palace is more modern. It has less charm but is more comfortable. They currently share the same reception facilities.
🏠 ⥾ ▭ ⟶ ⟶

YOUTH HOSTEL
16, Shari' Mohammed
Farid
Tel. 37 21 39
Between the Corniche
and the airport road.

SHOPPING

PHILIPPE JEWELS
Philippe Hotel Luxor
Tel. 37 22 84
A very good jeweler's with a wide selection of gold, silver, turquoise and lapis lazuli. Bank inside the store.

RADWAN
Shari' Khaled Ibn
el-Walid
Tel. 38 16 55
or 37 46 43
Opposite the Isis
Hotel Luxor
The second best jeweler's in Luxor. Excellent quality and a wide selection.

Cotton goods are on sale below the store (very good T-shirts). Bank inside the store.
◆

ABU SIMBEL

DIALING CODE
(0) 97
Map of Egypt F9

ACCOMMODATION

NEFERTARI ABU SIMBEL ****
Tel. 40 05 08
or 40 05 09
Fax 40 05 10
5 minutes from the
airport in the direction
of the temples
Divided into a main wing and a series of chalets. Magnificently situated on Lake Nasser. Possibly only warrants three stars as the rooms are rather dreary and often shared by agamas, small (harmless) mosquito-eating gray lizards. But this seems unimportant when you are only 5 minutes' walk from the temples and can see them floodlit at night from the hotel.
🏠 ⮞ ⥾ ▭ ⟶ 🅿 ⟶

NOBALEH RAMSES HOTEL ***
Tourist City
Tel. 31 16 61
Tel. and fax 31 16 60
5 mins from the airport,
in the direction of the
temples
Clean hotel, within easy reach of the temples.
🏠 ⮞ 🅿

ASWAN

DIALING CODE
(0) 97
Map of Egypt G8

USEFUL ADDRESSES

AMERICAN EXPRESS
Pullman Cataract Hotel
Tel. 30 29 09
Open 8.30am–5pm
Closed Fri.

POST OFFICE
Corniche
Tel. 32 35 33
Open 8am–2.30pm
Closed Fri.
Open daily for telephone
only: 5–9pm

GERMAN HOSPITAL ASWAN
Corniche
Tel. 32 21 76

MISR BANK
Corniche
Open 9am–1pm
and 6–8pm
Closed Fri.
Money can be changed using Visa but it can take rather a long time.

TOURIST OFFICE
Tourist Suq
Tel. 32 32 97

TOURIST POLICE
Tel. 32 31 63
At the end of the
Corniche, before the
post office
Also an office at the airport.

REGISTRY OFFICE
Corniche
Next to the post office
Deals with the same formalities as the Mugamaa.

TRANSPORT

ASWAN AIRPORT
Tel. 48 03 07

EGYPTAIR
Shari' Abtal at-Tahrir
Tel. 31 50 01
or 31 05 00
Fax 31 50 05

STATION
Tel. 38 20 18
At the end of the main
suq street.

BUS STATION
MIDAN EL-MAHATTA
(STATION SQUARE)
Taxi rank.
SHARI' ABTAL AT-TAHRIR
Near the station and
Governorate building
Bus terminal.

RESTAURANTS

★ **CLUB 1902**
Pullman Cataract Hotel
Shari' Abtal at-Tahrir
Tel. 31 60 00
This British colonial-style restaurant – the best in Aswan – provided the setting

for a scene from "Death on the Nile" (1978).
Very luxurious, excellent service, orchestra, good dance cabaret. European cuisine.
🍴 P

★ EL-MASRY
Shari' Abd el-Magid Abu Zid
Open noon–midnight
Street leading into the suq, in the direction of the station
A well-known, well-kept and extremely popular restaurant. Good Egyptian cuisine (generous helpings and inexpensive). The El-Masry "Whisky" – a cold, spiced vegetable soup – is highly recommended.
🍴

LA TRATTORIA
Isis Hotel Aswan
Corniche
Tel.31 51 00
or 31 52 00
Open noon–midnight
Basic Italian restaurant. Not much atmosphere but near the suqs and has an extremely good view of the Nile.
🍴 ☂ 🍷

★ NEFERTARI
P.L.M. Azur
New Cataract Hotel
Shari' Abtal at-Tahrir
Tel. 32 34 34
or 32 32 22
Open noon–3pm
and 6.30–10.30pm
Huge, 1960's dining room. Rather old-fashioned but charming. Magnificent view of the Nile and Elephantine Island. Extensive, good-quality (international and Egyptian) buffets.
☂ 🍷 🥂 P

ORANGERIE
Aswan Oberoi Hotel
P.O. Box 62
Tel. 32 34 55
Open noon–3pm
and 7–9.30pm
Elephantine Island
(free ferry service)
Luxury restaurant, offering European, Egyptian and Indian cuisine. Not particularly original but a beautiful setting.
🏠 ☞ 🥂 🍷 🥂 ♨

PANORAMA
Corniche
Open 10am–midnight
South end of the Corniche, just before the Eastmar jetty
Small, unpretentious restaurant, well situated on the Nile. Friendly atmosphere. Rather ordinary Egyptian cuisine.
🍴 🥂

ACCOMMODATION

★ AMUN HOTEL ★★★
Amun Island
Tel. 32 25 55 or 32 28 16
Fax 32 25 55
Boat-cum-ferry from the end of the Corniche
Remarkable location on an island beyond the Elephantine. Very comfortable hotel with a magnificent garden and which really warrants an additional star. Run by the Club Méditerranée.
🏠 ☞ 🥂 🍷 🥂 ♨

AMUN TOURIST VILLAGE ★★★★★
Sahara City
P.O. Box 118
Tel. 48 04 45 or 39
Fax 48 04 40
10 mins from the airport and 20 mins from the city center
Chalets overlooking Lake Nasser. Near the main tourist sites (Temple of Kalabsha, Aswan High Dam) and a pleasant place in which to relax.
🏠 🏠 🥂 🍷 🥂 P

★ ASWAN OBEROI HOTEL ★★★★★
Elephantine Island
P.O. Box 62
Tel. 30 34 55
Fax 31 35 38
Free ferry service every 10 mins from the Corniche
Hotel with huge, comfortable rooms and a large swimming pool. Situated in a magnificent garden on Elephantine Island.
🏠 🏠 ☞ 🥂 🍷 🥂 ♨

BASMA HOTEL ASWAN ★★★
Shari' el-Fanadek
Tel. 31 09 01 or 02
Fax 31 09 07
In the direction of the airport

Recently built, comfortable hotel but some distance from the center. Reductions if you stay more than 3 days.
🏠 ☞ 🥂 🍷 🥂 P ♨

EL-SALAM HOTEL ★
Corniche
Tel. 32 36 49
Ideal for lower budget vacations. The classic one-star Egyptian hotel. Lacking in comfort but clean and well situated (suqs in the next street).
🍴 🥂

HATHOR HOTEL ★
Corniche
Tel. 31 45 80
Small and lacking in comfort but clean and well situated. Inexpensive. Ask for a room overlooking the Nile.
🍴 🥂

HORUS HOTEL ★★
Corniche
Tel. 31 33 13
Small, lacking in comfort but inexpensive and well situated.
🍴 🥂

ISIS HOTEL ASWAN ★★★★
Corniche
Tel. 31 51 00 or 52 00
Fax 31 55 00
Chalets on the shores of the Nile with small but comfortable rooms. Near the suq.
🏠 🍴 🥂 🍷 🥂 ♨

KALABSHA HOTEL ★★★★
Shari' Abtal at-Tahrir
Tel. 31 66 64
or 30 26 66
Fax 30 59 74
At the end of the Corniche, on the right before the airport road
Good hotel but set back and does not enjoy the panoramic view of the nearby Pullman Cataract

Hotel. Service sometimes slow.
🏠 ☞ P ♨

P.L.M. AZUR NEW CATARACT ★★★★★
Shari' Abtal at-Tahrir
Tel. 31 60 00
Fax 31 60 11
At the end of the Corniche, near the Kalabshat
Rather "heavy" 1960's architecture but the rooms are huge and comfortable. Very good buffets in the vast restaurant.
🥂 🏠 🥂 🍷 🥂 P ♨

★ SOFITEL CATARACT HOTEL ★★★★★
Shari' Abtal at-Tahrir
Tel. 31 60 00
Fax 31 60 02
Near the New Cataract Hotel
Former colonial hotel. Absolutely charming with a magnificent view of the Nile and Elephantine Island. Truly wonderful. It is a privilege to stay there: an unforgettable experience.
🏠 🏠 🥂 🍷 🥂 P ♨

YOUTH HOSTEL
96, Shari' Abtal at-Tahrir
Tel. 32 23 13
Near the station in the direction of the Corniche

ESSENTIAL ◆ READING ◆

◆ ALDRED (C.): *Egyptian Art in the Days of the Pharaohs*, London and New York, 1980
◆ IDRIS (B.H.): *Egypt from Alexander the Great to the Arab Conquest*, Oxford, 1948
◆ MURNANE (W.J.): *Penguin Guide to Ancient Egypt*, London and New York, 1983

ANCIENT ◆ EGYPT ◆

◆ ALDRED (C.): *The Egyptians*, London, 1984
◆ ALDRED (C.): *Akhenaten and Nefertiti*, London, 1973
◆ BAIKIE (J.): *Egyptian Antiquities in the Nile Valley*, Methuen, 1932
◆ BAINES (J.) and MALEK (J.): *Atlas of Ancient Egypt*, Oxford, 1980
◆ BEVAN (E.): *A History of Egypt under the Ptolemaic Dynasty*, London, 1927
◆ BREASTED (J.H.): *History of Egypt*, London and New York, 1905
◆ BUNSON (M.): *The Encyclopaedia of Ancient Egypt*, New York and Oxford, 1991
◆ DAVIES (W.V.): *Egyptian Hieroglyphics*, London, 1987
◆ DESROCHES-NOBLECOURT (C.): *Tutankhamen*, English trans., 1963
◆ EDWARDS (I.E.S.): *Tutankhamen, his Tomb and its Treasures*, New York, 1977
◆ ERMAN (A.): *The Ancient Egyptians, A Sourcebook of their Writings*, English trans., New York, 1966
◆ GARDINER (A.H.): *Egypt of the Pharaohs*, Oxford, 1961
◆ GRIMAL (N.): *A History of Ancient Egypt*, Oxford, 1992
◆ HARRIS (J.R.): *The Legacy of Egypt*, Oxford, 1971
◆ HOBSON (C.): *The World of the Pharaohs: A Complete Guide to Ancient Egypt*, New York and London, 1987
◆ JAMES (T.G.H.): *An Introduction to Ancient Egypt*, London, 1964
◆ MONTEL (P.): *Lives of the Pharaohs*, English trans., London, 1968
◆ SIMPSON (W.K.): *The Literature of Ancient Egypt*, New Haven, 1972
◆ WILKINSON (J.G.): *Manners and Customs of the Ancient Egyptians*, London, 1855 (later editions)

HISTORY OF THE ◆ DISCOVERIES ◆

◆ BELZONI (G.): *Narrative of the Operations and Recent Discoveries*, London, 1820
◆ CARTER (H.): *The Tomb of Tutankhamun*, London, 1923–33
◆ CLAYTON (P.): *The Rediscovery of Ancient Egypt*, London, 1982
◆ FAGAN (B.M.): *The Rape of the Nile*, London, 1977
◆ GREENER (L.): *The Discovery of Egypt*, London, 1966
◆ JAMES (T.G.H.): *Excavating in Egypt, the Egypt Exploration Society 1882–1982*, London, 1982
◆ JAMES (T.G.H.): *Howard Carter, the Path to Tutankhamun*, London and New York, 1992
◆ LEPSIUS (R.): *Discoveries in Egypt, Ethiopia and the Peninsula of Sinai*, London, 1853
◆ MAYES (S.): *The Great Belzoni*, London, 1959

ART AND ◆ARCHITECTURE◆

◆ EDWARDS (I.E.S.): *The Pyramids of Egypt*, 3rd ed., London, 1972
◆ KISCHKEWITZ (H.): *Egyptian Drawings*, London, 1972
◆ OTTO (E.): *Egyptian Art and the Cult of Osiris and Amon*, London, 1968
◆ SCHÄFER (H.): *Principles of Egyptian Art*, English trans. Oxford, 1974
◆ Smith (W.S.): *The Art and Architecture of Ancient Egypt*, Harmondsworth, 2nd ed. 1981
◆ TERRACE (F.L.B.) and FISCHER (H.G.): *Treasures of the Cairo Museum*, London, 1970
◆ Wilkinson (R.H.): *Reading Egyptian Art*, London, 1992

EGYPTIAN ◆ RELIGION ◆

◆ CERNY (J.): *Ancient Egyptian Religion*, London, 1952
◆ MORENZ (S.): *Egyptian Religion*, English trans., London, 1973
◆ RUNDLE-CLARK (R.T.): *Myth and Symbol in Ancient Egypt*, London, 1978
◆ SAUNERON (S.): *The Priests of Ancient Egypt*, London, 1960
◆ SHORTER (A.W.): *The Egyptian Gods*, London, 1937
◆ WAINWRIGHT (G.A.): *The Sky Religion in Egypt*, Cambridge, 1938

LATER ◆ HISTORY ◆

◆ BAKER (R.W.): *Egypt's Uncertain Revolution under Nasser and Sadat*, Harvard, 1978
◆ BLUNT (W.S.): *The Secret History of the English Occupation of Egypt*, London, 1923
◆ BUTLER (A.J.): *The Arab Conquest of Egypt*, Oxford, 1902
◆ CAMERON (D.A.): *Egypt in the 19th Century*, London, 1898
◆ COOPER (A.): *Cairo in the War 1939–1945*, Hamish Hamilton, 1989
◆ DODWELL (H.H.): *The Founder of Modern Egypt, Mohammed Ali*, Cambridge, 1931
◆ ELGOOD (P.G.): *The Transit of Egypt*, London, 1928
◆ HEROLD (J.C.): *Bonaparte in Egypt*, London, 1963
◆ HOLT (P.M.): *Egypt and the Fertile Crescent, 1516–1922*, London, 1966
◆ ISSAWI (C.): *Egypt in Revolution*, Oxford, 1963
◆ KYLE (K.): *Suez*, London, 1992
◆ LACOUTURE (J.): *Nasser, A Biography*, London, 1973
◆ LANE (E.W.): *Manners and Customs of the Modern Egyptians*, London, 1836
◆ LANE-POOLE (S.): *History of Egypt in the Middle Ages*, London, 1925
◆ LLOYD (C.): *The Nile Campaign: Nelson and Napoleon in Egypt*, Newton Abbot, 1973
◆ RUSSELL (D.): *Medieval Cairo*, London, 1962
◆ SANDERSON (G.N.): *England, Europe and the Upper Nile, 1822–1899*, Edinburgh, 1965
◆ VATIKIOTIS (P.J.): *The History of Egypt from Mohammed Ali to Sadat*, London, 1980
◆ WATERFIELD (G.): *Egypt (New Nations and Peoples)*, London, 1967
◆ WOODWARD (P.): *Nasser*, London, 1992

TRAVEL WRITING ◆ AND FICTION ◆

◆ BURKHARDT (J.L.): *Travels in Nubia*, London, 1819
◆ CHRISTIE (A.): *Death on the Nile*, London, 1937
◆ DURRELL (L.): *The Alexandria Quartet*, London, 1985
◆ EDWARDS (A.): *A Thousand Miles up the Nile*, London, 1877
◆ FLAUBERT (G.): *Flaubert in Egypt*, English trans. by Francis Steegmuller, London, 1972
◆ FORSTER (E.M.): *Alexandria, a History and a Guide*, Alexandria, 1922 (many later editions)
◆ GAUTIER (T.): *L'Orient*, Paris, 1877
◆ GORDON (Lady D.): *Letters from Egypt, 1862–1869*, London, 1969
◆ KINGLAKE (A.W.): *Eothen*, London, 1844 (and later editions)
◆ MAILER (N.): *Ancient Evenings*, London and New York, 1983
◆ NIGHTINGALE (F.): *Letters from Egypt*, London, 1987
◆ PRESCOTT (H.F.M.): *Once to Sinai: the Further Pilgrimage of Friar Fabri*, London, 1957
◆ WALTARI (M.): *Sinuhe the Egyptian*, English trans., London, 1949

◆ GUIDES ◆

◆ HART (G.): *Pharaohs and Pyramids, a Guide through Old Kingdom Egypt*, London and New York, 1991
◆ MARTINENGO (L.): *Egypt (Odyssey Guides)*, Hong Kong, 1994
◆ ROCHESTER (D.) and O'BRIEN (K.): *Egypt (Rough Guides)*, London, 1993
◆ SETON-WILLIAMS (V.) and STOCKS (P.): *Egypt (Blue Guides)*, London and New York, 1990

545

idem. Pectoral of Ramesses. Louvre. © Scala. Statue of a dignitary, bronze. Louvre. © RMN, Paris. *Seated scribe*, painted limestone . *idem*.

478 Statue of a bearded man, Nagada period. Musée de Lyon. © Bulloz. Augustus in Egyptian dress, bas-relief. Musée Champollion, Figeac. © Dagli-Orti.

479 Boat with figures, wooden model from a tomb. Kunsthistorisches Museum, Vienna. © E. Lessing/Magnum. Heads of Semite prisoners, glazed clay. *idem. Dark-skinned woman*, Faiyum portrait, painting on wood. Pushkin Museum, Moscow. © Cercle D'art/Édimédia. Make-up dish. Barbier-Mueller Museum, Geneva. Ph. Guillemot/CdA. © Édimédia. Egyptian funerary statuette, wood polychrome. Gulbenkian Museum, Lisbon. Ph. Hinous/CdA. © Édimédia.

482 *The Ten Commandments*, Cecil B. De Mille, 1923. © BFI, London. *Cleopatra*, *idem*, 1934. © *idem*. El-Kit-Kat, *Proud Beggars*, cinema posters. Coll. Paul Geday. *The Land*, directed by Yussef Shahin © Cristophe L.

483 *Alexandria – Why?*, poster for the film directed by Yussef Shahin. Karl Freund's *The Mummy*, 1932. *The Son of the Sheikh*, directed by George Fitzmaurice. *Ali Baba and the Forty Thieves*, directed by Jacques Becker. Pasolini's *The Arabian Nights*. © Cristophe L. Cecil B. De Mille during shooting of *The Ten Commandments*. © BFI, London.

Practical information:
485 Tell el-Amarna, bas-relief. © J. Livet. path to the summit of Mount Sinai. © Sénéchal/Diaf.

486 Kubri At-Tahrir in Cairo and the Pyramids. Ph. Y. Travert/Gallimard.

490 Cruise boats between Luxor and Aswan. Ph. *idem*.

491 Hotel Cataract, Aswan. © I. Morath/Magnum. Felucca boatmen. Ph. Y. Travert/Gallimard.

492 Cairo, Midan At-Tahrir. Ph. *idem*.

493 Insignia of the city of Cairo. Ph. Gallimard. Sohag, taxi. © P. Chapuis.

Subway sign, letter boxes, signs. Ph. Gallimard.

495 Egyptian products. Ph. *idem*. Pharmacy and telephone signs, bottle of Baraka mineral water. Ph. J.-L. Berger.

497 Suq. Ph. Y Travert/Gallimard. Dervish. © Hicham Labib, Cairo.

498 White Desert and El-Areg Oasis. © N. Levallois.

499 Palm trees, camping in Wadi Rayan, Cleopatra's Pool. © *idem*.

500 Abandoned village of Aghurmi, fortress of Aïn Umm Labakha. © *idem*.

501 St Catherine's Monastery. © *idem*.

502 Shores of the Red Sea. © N. Levallois. Windsurfing regatta. © Karasic/Rapho.

503 Diving in the Red Sea © S. Grandadam. Windsurfing. © P. Dannic/Diaf.

504 Mersa Matruh, Cleopatra's Bath. © Serapis, Alexandria. Suez Canal. © N. Levallois.

506 Temple of Esna, bas-relief. Ph. Y. Travert/Gallimard. Mosque, Cairo. Ph. P. Godeau/ Gallimard. Temple of Edfu. Ph. Y. Travert/Gallimard.

507 Graeco-roman Theater. Ph. Gallimard. Luxor, Avenue of the Sphinxes. Ph. Y. Travert/Gallimard. Horse near the Pyramids. © S. Grandadam.

510 Market. © S. Grandadam.

511 Bazaar. Ph. Y. Travert/Gallimard. Carpet seller. Ph. W. Mehanna/Gallimard. Jewelry. Ph. Gallimard.

513 Khan el-Khalili. © N. Levallois. Glass blower. © W. Louvet. Cairo, Fatimed district. Ph. Y. Travert/Gallimard. "Foot" ironer. © W. Mehanna.

List of illustrators: Nature:
16–23: François Desbordes
20–23: Gilbert Houbre
26–27: Gilbert Houbre François Desbordes, Claire Felloni, Jean Chevali
28–29: François Desbordes
30–31 Bruce Pearson François Desbordes, Claire Felloni, Jean Chevali
32–33: François Desbordes, Claire Felloni
34–35: Anne Bodin
36: François Desbordes, Jean Chevali

Architecture:
82–83: Jean-Claude Sené
84–85: Jean-Claude Sené
86–87: Jean-Claude Sené, François Brosse

88–89: Jean-Claude Sené, François Brosse
90–91: François Brosse
92–93: Jean-Claude Sené
102: Jean-Pirre Lange
104: Jean-Pire Lange
106–107: François Brosse
108–109: Philippe Biard,
110–111: Philippe Candé
112–113: Claude Quiec
114–115: Jean-Claude Sené
116–117: Jean-Claude Sené
118: Jean-Claude Sené

Art and Tradition:
60–61: Nathalie Fonteneau
120–121: Philippe Biard
122–123: Maurice Pommi

Itineraries:
218: Jean-Pire Lange
348: Philippe Biard
418: Gilbert Houbre.
418: Jean-Claude Sené

Practical information:
Maurice Pommi

Acknowledgments:
We would like to thank the following for permission to use the literary excerpts from pages 150 to 164:

◆ CURTIS BROWN: Excerpt from *Passenger to Teheran*, by Vita Sackville-West, copyright © 1926 by Vita Sackville-West (The Hogarth Press, London, 1926). Reprinted by permission of Curtis Brown London, on behalf of the author's estate.

◆ JONATHAN CAPE LTD and TWEEDIE & PRIDEAUX: Excerpt from letter of January 23, 1912 from T.E. Lawrence to Mrs Rieder from *The Letters of T. E. Lawrence*, edited by David Garnett (Jonathan Cape Ltd, 1938). Reprinted by permission of Jonathan Cape Ltd, and Tweedie & Prideaux for the Trustees of the Seven Pilgrims of Wisdom Trust.

◆ DOUBLEDAY: Excerpt from *Palace Walk*, by Naguib Mahfouz, translated by William Maynard Hutchins and Olive E. Kerry (1991). Reprinted by permission of Doubleday, a division of Bantam Doubleday Dell Publishing Group, Inc.

◆ DUTTON SIGNET and FABER AND FABER LIMITED: Excerpt from *Clea*, by Lawrence Durrell, copyright © 1960 (renewed 1988) by Lawrence George Durrell. Rights in Canada administered by Faber and Faber Limited, London. Reprinted by permission of Dutton Signet, a division of Penguin Books U.S.A. Inc., and Faber and Faber Ltd.

◆ FABER AND FABER INC. and FABER AND FABER LTD:

Excerpt from *An Egyptian Journal*, by William Golding, copyright © 1985 by William Golding. Rights outside the United States administered by Faber and Faber Ltd, London. Reprinted by permission.

◆ HARPERCOLLINS PUBLISHERS LTD: Excerpt from *On the Shores of the Mediterranean* by Eric Newby (Harvill, 1984). Reprinted by permission of Harvill, an imprint of HarperCollins Publishers Ltd.

◆ HARVARD UNIVERSITY PRESS: Excerpt from *The Letters of Gustave Flaubert*, edited by Francis Steegmuller, Cambridge, Mass.: The Belknap Press of Harvard University Press, copyright © 1979, 1980 by Francis Steegmuller. Reprinted by permission.

◆ JOHN MURRAY (PUBLISHERS) LTD: Excerpt from *East Is West* by Freya Stark (1946). Reprinted by permission.

◆ PENGUIN BOOKS LTD: Excerpt from *The Histories* by Herodotus, translated by Aubrey de Sélincourt, copyright © 1954 the Estate of Aubrey de Sélincourt. Reprinted by permission.

◆ PETERS FRASER & DUNLOP GROUP LTD: Excerpt from *Labels - A Mediterranean Journey*, by Evelyn Waugh (Duckworth 1930). Reprinted by permission.

◆ PRINCETON UNIVERSITY PRESS: Excerpt from two journal entries of Dec., 1856, and Jan., 1857, from *Journal of a Visit to Egypt and the Levant*, by Herman Melville, edited by Howard C. Horsford (1955). Reprinted by permission.

◆ RANDOM HOUSE, INC.: Excerpt from "Nasser's Egypt" from *United States: The Complete Essays* by Gore Vidal, copyright © 1993 by Gore Vidal. Reprinted by permission.

◆ WATSON LITTLE LTD: Excerpt from letter from Edward Lear to his wife on "The Knack of Riding Camels" from *Edward Lear Selected Letters*, edited by Vivien Noakes (The Clarendon Press, 1988). Reprinted by permission.

◆ WEIDENFELD AND NICOLSON: Excerpt from Rudyard Kipling letter of Feb. 1913, to his children from *O Beloved Kids – Rudyard Kipling's Letters to His Children*, edited by Elliot L. Gilbert (1983). Reprinted by permission.

INDEX

◆ INDEX

Page numbers in bold refer to the Practical information section.

◆ INDEX